Science and Golf III

PROCEEDINGS OF THE 1998 WORLD SCIENTIFIC CONGRESS OF GOLF

M.R. Farrally
University of St. Andrews, UK

A.J. Cochran
Royal and Ancient Golf Club
St. Andrews, UK

Editors

Human Kinetics

ISBN: 0-7360-0020-8

ISSN: 1520-2658

Developmental Editor: Laura Hambly; **Assistant Editors:** Leigh LaHood, Cynthia McEntire; **Copyeditor:** Joyce Sexton; **Graphic Designer:** Robert Reuther; **Graphic Artist:** Denise Lowry; **Photo Editor:** Boyd LaFoon; **Printer:** Creative Print and Design Group

Printed in the United Kingdom   10   9   8   7   6   5   4   3   2   1

Human Kinetics
Web site: http://www.humankinetics.com/

United States: Human Kinetics, P.O. Box 5076, Champaign, IL 61825-5076
1-800-747-4457
e-mail: humank@hkusa.com

Canada: Human Kinetics, 475 Devonshire Road Unit 100, Windsor, ON N8Y 2L5
1-800-465-7301 (in Canada only)
e-mail: humank@hkcanada.com

Europe: Human Kinetics, P.O. Box IW14, Leeds LS16 6TR, United Kingdom
(44) 1132 781708
e-mail: humank@hkeurope.com

Australia: Human Kinetics, 57A Price Avenue, Lower Mitcham, South Australia 5062
(088) 277 1555
e-mail: humank@hkaustralia.com

New Zealand: Human Kinetics, P.O. Box 105-231, Auckland 1
(09) 523 3462
e-mail: humank@hknewz.com

WORLD SCIENTIFIC CONGRESS OF GOLF
ST. ANDREWS, SCOTLAND
20-24TH JULY 1998

Held at the University of St. Andrews and approved and grant-aided by the Royal and Ancient Golf Club of St. Andrews and the United States Golf Association

Administration Committee

A.J. Cochran

M.R. Farrally

D. Kemp

R. Price

D. Richens

J.I.C. Scott

A. Wright

Scientific Committee

P.M. Canaway

A.J. Cochran

D.J. Crews

D. DiPonziano

M.R. Farrally

L. Hardy

B.B. Lieberman

M. McNicholas

R. Price

B. Stoddart

F.W. Thomas

E. Wallace

G. Wiren

Steering Committee

A.J. Cochran

D.J. Crews

M.R. Farrally

F.W. Thomas

P.R. Thomas

Congress Director

M.R. Farrally

University of St. Andrews

Congress Administrator

A. McFetridge-Kemp

Contents

Part II   Equipment

Sponsors and Patrons

The third World Scientific Congress of Golf would not have been possible without the help of a wide range of organisations who gave us patronage, publicity, or financial support. We would like to express our thanks to all of them who include:

British Association of Sports and Exercise Sciences
British Association of Sports Medicine
Golf Digest
International Council of Sports Science & Physical Education
Professional Golfers' Association
Professional Golfers' Association of America
PGA European Tour
PGA of Europe
PGA Tour
Royal and Ancient Golf Club of St. Andrews
Scottish Golf Union
Scottish Sports Council
United States Golf Association
University of St. Andrews
World Commission for Sports Biomechanics

Authors' Names and Addresses

The names and addresses in this list are those of the contact authors of the papers in this book, who are not always the first-named authors.

Aitken, V.J.
47 Woodside Road
Mt. Eden
Auckland 3 New Zealand
Tel: 649 6315 186
e-mail: aitken.fam@xtra.co.nz

Anthony, N.
1384 Burgundy Drive
Ft. Myers, FL 33919
USA
Tel: 941-482-6058

Aoki, K.
Tokai University
Shonan Campus
1117 Kitakaname
Hiratsuka-shi
Kanagawa 259-12, Japan
Tel: 81 463 58 1211
Fax: 81 463 35 2456

Aoyama, S.
Titleist and Foot-Joy Worldwide
P.O. Box 965
Fairhaven, MA 02719-0965
USA
Tel: 508-979-3576
Fax: 508-979-3903

Baker, S.W.
Sports Turf Research Institute
Bingley
West Yorkshire BD16 1AU
UK
Tel: 01274 565131
Fax: 01274 561891

Beard, J.B.
International Sports Turf Institute
1812 Shadowood Drive
College Station, TX 77840
USA
Tel: 409-693-4066
Fax: 409-693-4878

Beasley, D.E.
Department of Mechanical Engineering
Clemson University
102 Fluor Daniel Engineering
    Innovation Bldg.
Clemson, SC 29634-0921
USA
Tel: 864-656-3470
Fax: 864-656-4435
e-mail: don.beasley@ces.clemson.edu

Beauchamp, P.
SPVS Corp.
Westmount Station
P.O. Box 223
Westmount, Quebec H3Z 2T2
Canada
Tel: 514-486-6468
Fax: 514-486-5540
e-mail: sportdoc@videotron.ca

Bosworth, R.J.B.
University of Western Australia
Department of History
Nedlands, Western Australia 6907
Tel: 61 8 9380 2131
Fax: 61 8 9390 1069
e-mail: rjbb@arts.uwa.edu.au

Bruneau, A.H.
Department of Crop Science
North Carolina State University
College of Agriculture and Life
   Science
Campus Box 7620
Raleigh, NC 27695-7620
USA
Tel: 919-515-2547
Fax: 919-515-7959
e-mail: Art_Bruneau@ncsu.edu

Cochran, A.J.
65 Heath Croft Road
Four Oaks
Sutton Coldfield, West Midlands,
   B75 6RN
UK
Tel: 0121 241 5588
Fax: 0121 241 6688

Cook, A.
Sports Turf Research Institute
Bingley, West Yorkshire BD16 1AU
UK
Tel: 01276 565131
Fax: 01276 561891

Coop, R.
University of North Carolina
Peabody Hall
Chapel Hill, NC 27599-3500
USA
Tel: 919-966-5266
Fax: 919-962-1533

Crews, D.J.
Dept. of Exercise Science and Physical
   Education
Tempe, AZ 85287-0404
USA
Tel: 602-965-4676
e-mail: Crews@espe1.la.asu.edu

Dalton, J.
Titleist and Foot-Joy Worldwide
333 Bridge Street
Fairhaven, MA 02719-0965
USA
Tel: 508-979-2000
e-mail: Jeff_Dalton@tfjww.com

Donnelly, P.M.
48 Wells Hill Road
Weston, CT 06883
USA
Tel/Fax: 203-221-7944
e-mail: pmdonnelly@aol.com

Ekstrom, E.A.
Mechanical Engineering & Mechanics
   Department
Lehigh University
Bethlehem, PA 18015
USA
Tel: 717-474-6761 (ext. 4898)
Fax: 717-474-3229
e-mail: eae3@lehigh.edu

Ellis, W.H.
McGill University (Retired)
Montreal, Quebec
Canada
Fax: 001 519 744 7621
e-mail: 44wellis@mach1.wlu.ca

Finch, C.
School of Human Movement
Deakin University
221 Burwood Highway
Victoria 3125, Australia
Tel: 61 3 9521 7084
Fax: 61 3 9244 6950
e-mail: cfinch@deakin.edu.au

Gange, A.C.
School of Biological Sciences
Royal Holloway
University of London
Egham, Surrey TW20 0EX
UK
Tel: 01784 443773/6
Fax: 01784 470756
e-mail: a.gange@rhbnc.ac.uk

Gatt, C.J.
University Orthopaedic Associates
215 Easton Avenue
New Brunswick, NJ 08901
USA
Tel: 732-545-0400
Fax: 818-246-7673
e-mail: cjgatt@pol.net

Guadagnoli, M.A.
Department of Kinesiology
University of Nevada
4505 Maryland Parkway
Las Vegas, NV 89154-3034
USA
Tel: 702-895-0966
Fax: 702-895-1500

Haig-Muir, M.
SAIS/Arts
Deakin University
Geelong, Australia 3217
Tel: 61 3 5227 2820
Fax: 61 3 5227 2018
e-mail: marnie@deakin.edu.au

Hale, T.
Centre for Sport Science and Medicine
Chichester Institute
College Lane
Chichester P.O.19 4PE
UK
Tel: 01243 816000
Fax: 01243 816080

Haller, N.
Clinical Psychology
1450 Frazie Road
Suite 300
San Diego, CA 92108
USA
Tel: 619-297-5400

Hamilton, G.
Department of Agronomy
The Pennsylvania State University
221 Agricultural Sciences and Indus-
    tries Building
University Park, PA 16802-3504
USA
Tel: 814-865-3007
Fax: 814-863-7043

Hansen, J.R.
History Department
310 Thatch Hall
Auburn University
Auburn, AL 36849-5207
USA
Tel: 334-844-6628
Fax: 334-844-6673

Hubbard, M.
Sports Biomechanics Laboratory
Department of Mechanical and
    Aeronautical Engineering
University of California
Davis, CA 95616
USA
Tel: 916-752-6450
Fax: 916-752-4158
e-mail: mhubbard@ucdavis.edu

Hurdzan, M.J.
Hurdzan Fry Golf Course Design, Inc.
1270 Old Henderson Road
Columbus, OH 43220
USA
Tel: 614-457-9955
Fax: 614-457-2250
e-mail: Mjh@hurdzan.com

Jackson, R.
University of Glamorgan
Department of Psychology
Wales CF37 1DL
UK
Tel: 01443 482679
Fax: 01443 482138
e-mail: rcjackson@glam.ac.uk

Johnson, S.
Mechanical Engineering and
    Mechanics
Packard Laboratory
Lehigh University
19 Memorial Drive West
Bethlehem, PA 18015-3085
USA
Tel: 610-758-4100
Fax: 610-758-6224

Johnston, W.J.
Department of Crop and Soil
    Sciences
Washington State University
Pullman, WA 99164-6420
USA
Tel: 509-335-3620
Fax: 509-335-8674
e-mail: wjohnston@wsu.edu

Jones, D.
9 John Glenn Road
Morristown, NJ 07960
USA
Tel: 973-267-5163
Fax: 973-984-0238

Jones, R.
Department of Manufacturing
    Engineering
Loughborough University
Loughborough
Leicestershire, LE11 3TU
UK
Tel: 01509 222903
e-mail: r.jones@lboro.ac.uk

Judge, M.
Golf Research Group
P.O. Box 1203
London, WA4 4ZG
UK
Fax: 0181 995 1573

Kawashima, K.
Biomechanics Laboratory
College of Bioresource Sciences
Nihon University
Fujisawa, Kanagawa-ken, Japan
Tel/Fax: 81 466 84 3737
e-mail: kkawashima@brs.nihon-u.ac.jp

Kenna, M.
United States Golf Association
Green Section Research
Stillwater, OK 74076-2227
USA
Tel: 405-743-3900
Fax: 405-743-3910
e-mail: mkenna@usga.org

Kingston, K.
School of Sport Health & Physical
    Education Sciences
University of Wales
Ffriddoedd Building
Bangor, LL57 2EN
UK
Tel: 01248 382756
Fax: 01248 371053

Kirsch, G.B.
Manhattan College Parkway
History Department
Riverdale, NY 10471-4098
USA
Tel: 718-862-7127
Fax: 718-862-8044
e-mail: Gkirsch@manhattan.edu

Krahenbuhl, G.S.
Arizona State University
Tempe, AZ
USA

Landsberger, L.M.
SPVS Corp.
Westmount Station
P.O. Box 223
Westmount, Quebec H3Z 2T2
Canada
Tel: 514-931-3147
Fax: 514-938-1705
e-mail: leslie@ece.concordia.ca

Larkey, P.D.
H. John Heinz III
School of Public Policy and
    Management
Carnegie Mellon University
Pittsburgh, PA 15213-3890
USA
Tel: 412-268-3034
Fax: 412-268-1267
e-mail: p115@andrew.cmu.edu

Lawther, S.
Scottish Tourist Board
23 Ravelston Terrace
Edinburgh, EH4 3EU
UK
Tel: 0131 332 2433
Fax: 0131 343 2023

Lee, B.Y.B.
910 Hillcrest Street, #1
Tallahassee, FL 32308
USA
Tel/Fax: 850 224 8492
e-mail: bll6108@garnet.acns.fsu.edu

Leigh, R.J.
Chichester Institute of Higher
    Education
College Lane
Chichester, P.O.19 4PE
UK
Fax: 01243 816080

Lemons, L.D.
Maxfli Golf
100 Maxfli Drive
Westminister, SC 29693
USA
Tel: 864-647-4144
Fax: 864-647-4040
e-mail: lemons@ww-interlink.net

Lennon, H.M.
MacGregor Golf Academy
City West Golf & Country Club
Saggart
Dublin, Ireland
Tel: 35 331 458 7011

Linder, D.E.
Liberal Arts and Science
Arizona State University
Main Campus
Tempe, AZ 85287-1104
USA
Tel: 602-965-3326
Fax: 602-965-8108

Lockwood, J.
2 Holly Bush
Makeney
Derbyshire, DE56 0RX
UK
Tel: 01332 841928

Lutz, R.
Department of ESPE, PEBE-107B
Arizona State University
Tempe, AZ 85281
USA
Tel: 602-965-4676
e-mail: lutz@espe1.la.asu.edu

Magnusson, G.
Box 5626
114 86
Stockholm, Sweden
Tel: 468 402 22 00
Fax: 468 402 22 80

McNicholas, M.J.
University of Dundee
Department of Orthopaedic & Trauma
    Surgery
Dundee, DD1
UK
Tel: 01382 660111

Melvin, T.
Spalding Sports Worldwide
Chicopee, MA 01021-0901
USA
Fax: 413-536-4831

Melvin, V.C.
16 Kirk Crescent
Old Kilpatrick
Glasgow G60 5NL
UK
Tel: 01389 872379

Miao, T.
Research and Development Division
Nippon Shaft Co. Ltd.
2-1-15 Sachiura
Kanazawa-ku
Yokohama, Kanagawa 236
Japan
Tel: 81 45 782 2861
Fax: 81 45 786 4951
e-mail: tjmiao@zzz.or.jp

Morgan, D.
Good Samaritan Medical Center
P.O. Box 3166
West Palm Beach, FL 33402
USA
Tel: 561-650-6159
Fax: 561-650-6314
e-mail: david_morgan@bellsouth.net

Miura, K.
3-9-7 Tsurukawa
Machida
Tokyo 195, Japan
Fax: 81 427 35 6946
e-mail: koryo@po.iijnet.or.jp

Nesbitt, R.D.
Spalding Sports Worldwide
425 Meadow Street
Chicopee, MA 01021-0901
USA
Tel: 413-536-1200

Otto, D.K.
31-A North Winchester
Olathe, KS 66062
USA
Tel: 913-780-6725
Fax: 913-780-6759
e-mail: dkotto@turfdiag.com

Price, R.J.
16 Northbank Road
Kirkintilloch
Glasgow G66 1EU
UK
Tel: 0141 776 4282
Fax: 0141 776 5402
e-mail: price@cableinet.co.uk

Reyes, M.G.
3413 Summerhill Drive
Woodridge, IL 60517
USA
e-mail: mgreyes@uic.edu

Rooney, J.F.
Oklahoma State University
Department of Geography
Stillwater, OK 74078-4073
USA
Tel: 405-744-6250
Fax: 405-744-5620

Scheid, F.
135 Elm Street
Kingston, MA 02364
USA
Tel: 781-585-6866
Fax: 781-585-8201

Schempp, P.G.
University of Georgia
School of Health and Human
    Performance
300 River Road
Athens, GA 30602-6551
USA
Tel: 702-895-0966
Fax: 702-895-1500

Senyard, J.E.
History Department
University of Melbourne
3rd Floor John Medley Building
Parkville 3052, Australia
Tel: 61 3 9344 4658
Fax: 61 3 9344 7894
e-mail: j.senyard@history.unimelb.edu.au

Smith, J.A.
c/o The Scottish Greenbelt Foundation
375 West George Street
Glasgow G2 4NT
UK
Tel: 0141 221 3444
Fax: 0141 221 3110

Staz, R.J.
Dupont
Experimental Station Bldg. 269-234
Wilmington, DE 19880-0269
USA
Tel: 302-695-4067
Fax: 302-695-2772

Stewart, R.
Trends and Traditions
11 Cotton Court
P.O. Box 74
Diamond Point, NY 12824
USA
Tel: 518-792-3682
Fax: 518-668-4980

Stoddart, B.
RMIT College at Penang
Jalan Krian Kedah
14200 Jawi
Seberang Perai Selatan
Penang, Malaysia
Tel: 61 3 9660 5153

Stubbs, D.
EGA Ecology Unit
51 South Street
Dorking, RH5 4EG
UK
Fax: 01306 742496

Sugaya, H.
Orthopaedic Surgery & Sports
    Medicine
Kawatetsu Hospital
Minami-cho
Chiba 260 0842, Japan
Tel: 81 43 261 5111
Fax: 81 43 261 2305
e-mail: hsugaya@mb.infoweb.or.jp

Takeshita, S.
College of Physical Education
National Institute of Fitness and Sports
#1 Shiromizu
Kanoya
Kagoshima 891-23, Japan
Tel/Fax: 81 994 46 4921

Tavares, G.
Spalding Sports Worldwide
425 Meadow Street
Chicopee, MA 01021-0901
USA
Tel: 413-536-1200
Fax: 412-536-4831
e-mail: gtavares@ix.netcom.com

Thomas, J.R.
Department of Exercise Science and
    Physical Education
Tempe, AZ 85287-0404
USA
Tel: 602-965-8469
Fax: 602-965-8108
e-mail: jthomas@asu.edu

Thomas, K.T.
Exercise & Sport Research Institute
Arizona State University
Tempe, AZ 85287-0404
USA
Tel: 602-965-3913
e-mail: Thomask@imap2.asu.edu

Thomas, P.R.
Centre for Movement Education and
    Research
Griffith University
Brisbane 4111, Australia
Tel: 61 7 3875 5634
Fax: 61 7 3875 5910
e-mail: P.Thomas@edn.gu.edu.ac

Tierney, D.
Richards & Tierney, Inc.
Chicago, IL
USA
Tel: 312-461-1100
Fax: 312-461-0001

Turner, A.B.
School of Engineering
University of Sussex
Brighton BN1 9QT
UK
Tel: 01273 678488
Fax: 01273 678486

Watanabe, K.
System Control Engineering
    Department
School of Engineering Hosei
    University
3-7-2 Kajinocho Koganei
Tokyo 184, Japan
Fax: 81 423 87 6123
e-mail: bob@wtng.sc.hosei.ac.jp

Williams, K.R.
Department of Exercise Science
University of California
Davis, CA 95616
USA
Tel: 916-752-3337
Fax: 916-752-6681
e-mail: krwilliams@ucdavis.edu

Williamson, M.G.
MW Associates
P.O. Box 6677
Edinburgh EH14 3YB
UK
Tel/Fax: 0131 476 6677
e-mail: mw.assoc@virgin.net

Winfield, D.C.
Titleist and Foot-Joy Worldwide
333 Bridge Street
Fairhaven, MA 02719-0865
USA
Tel: 508-979-3409
Fax: 508-979-3903
e-mail: Doug_Winfield@tfjww.com

Yamaguchi, T.
Sports Goods Research Department
Sumitomo Rubber Industries, Ltd.
1-1, 2 chome
Tsutsui-cho
Chuo-ku
Kobe 651, Japan
Tel: 81 78 265 5673
Fax: 81 78 265 5685
e-mail: 118635@sri.dunlop.co.jp

Young, E.P.
Department of Sport and Leisure
   Studies
Shore Road
Newtownabbey
Co. Antrim BT37 0QB
UK
Tel: 01232 366416
Fax: 01232 368255
e-mail: e.young@ulst-ac.uk

Zakus, D.H.
School of Marketing & Management
Gold Coast Campus
Griffith University
PMB 50 Gold Coast Mail Center
Queensland 9726, Australia
Tel: 61 7 5594 8053
Fax: 61 7 5594 8085
e-mail: D.Zakus@bhm.gu.edu.au

Preface

The World Scientific Congress of Golf is organised by the World Scientific Congress of Golf Trust, a non-profit body founded on 19th December, 1996, to promote and disseminate golf-related research. The Trustees are representatives of the Royal and Ancient Golf Club of St. Andrew, the United States Golf Association, and the University of St. Andrews.

The primary purpose of the Trust is to ensure the continued staging of the Congress every four years in St. Andrews. It will also encourage and support other conferences and meetings elsewhere in the world, and develop a resource and information centre for golf science information which is accessible to all.

This book contains the papers presented orally to the 1998 Congress. More than 130 papers were submitted for consideration and we would like to thank all authors who sent us papers for consideration. Also, we are indebted to the many reviewers whose professional advice was invaluable in selecting papers for inclusion and recommending improvements to authors.

In producing this book we have followed the same structure as for the 1990 and 1994 Congresses. The papers are grouped in three themes entitled The Golfer, Equipment, and The Golf Course. Inevitably, some papers bridge topics so we have tried to provide a logical order where similar topics are located as near to each other as possible.

The 1998 Congress was more than a collection of scientific papers. Important issues also arose in discussion of papers, and in the three cross-theme workshops on ageing, injuries, and supply and demand. Reports of these discussions, as well as some of the poster presentations at the Congress, appear in subsequent editions of the Trust newsletter.

We are gradually seeing a change in golf science research. Much of the work presented in 1990, and to a lesser extent in 1994, was done primarily for interest's sake. Although the Congress will always welcome work from the curious scientist, this volume contains a significant amount of material produced from funded research and reflects the increased commercial interest in golf. The World Scientific Congress of Golf Trust has an important role to play in bringing this information to the attention of everyone with an interest in and love for the game of golf.

Martin Farrally
Alastair Cochran

PART I

The Golfer

CHAPTER 1

A Three-Link Mathematical Model
of the Golf Swing

A.B. Turner and N.J. Hills
Thermo-Fluid Mechanics Research Centre, University of Sussex

A numerical procedure is described that models the golf swing as three connected links: the hub axis to the shoulder joint, the left arm, and the golf club, all swinging in a single plane at any specified angle to the vertical. Torques applied to the hub, the arm, and the club produce the golf swing motion, and these can be specified as sets of constants or polynomials with switch points between succeeding sets. The complete golf swing can thus be simulated, backswing, downswing and follow-through, although the follow-through is largely academic. Some results are presented which show that representative clubhead speeds and clubhead paths can be reproduced by two sets of three constant torques: one set for the backswing and one set for the downswing. The six torques are surprisingly closely linked, and any change to one requires careful changes to the others if a well-timed swing is to be produced.

Keywords: Biomechanics, three-link model, golf swing.

INTRODUCTION

The principal objective of this work was to model the golf swing as a three-link mechanism, rather than the usual two-link one (figure 1.1) in the hope that new insights could be provided into the relationship between the torques and forces exerted by the human golfer. For the analytically minded golfer, the one not afraid of "paralysis through analysis," a more complete understanding of the close linkage between the shoulder, arm, and hand torques may perhaps help him or her to prioritise the different aspects of the swing.

Several authors have studied the golf swing taking the two-link flail, or double pendulum (Williams 1967, Cochran and Stobbs 1968, Jorgensen 1993, Lampsa 1975, Budney and Bellow 1982, Milne and Davis 1992, among others) either as the basis for a system analysis or for the reduction of photographic data sets. Cochran

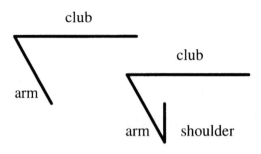

Figure 1.1   Two-link vs. three-link model of the golf swing.

and Stobbs presented a thorough analysis of the action of the whole body during the golf swing and one that remains unrivaled as a first reader for the analytical golfer. A recent review of the many biomechanical studies of the golf swing was presented by Dillman and Lange (1994). The development of a golfing android was described in the same publication by Nesbit et al. (1994), who also presented a brief snippet of the results. A full three-dimensional android swinging a golf club is mathematically extremely complex, not only in terms of the initial formulation but also with the interaction of the many, largely unknown, torque functions.

The two-link model—club and arm only—has the advantage of simplicity, but its ability to reproduce the typical human golf swing is quite limited. The shoulder-arm interaction is not present, and whereas the effective radius of the hand motion in the real swing almost doubles during the downswing, the hand radius in the two-link model is fixed. This shortcoming prevents the two-link model from being used for comparisons with stroboscopic photographs of real golfers. The most successful use of the two-link model has probably been that of Milne and Davis, who used it to show that shaft bending stiffness per se played a minor dynamic role in the golf swing.

THE NUMERICAL METHOD

If any mass, such as one of the links in the diagram shown in figure 1.2, is subjected to an unbalanced system of forces and torques, then the centre of mass will accelerate both linearly and angularly—Newton's second law. If at any time we know the position and velocity, for a small increment in time we can calculate a new position and velocity and so step forward, "time-march," through the problem. Difficulties can occur if too large a time step is taken, but for smooth functions of applied torques with modern PCs the time step can be reduced until a step-independent solution is obtained.

With n links a system of algebraic equations has to be solved at each time step, and with reference to the force diagram (figure 1.2), in which the conventional symbols are self-explanatory, the equations are:

Constraint equations:

$$x_1 - r_1\cos\theta_1 = 0 \qquad y_1 - r_1\sin\theta_1 = 0$$

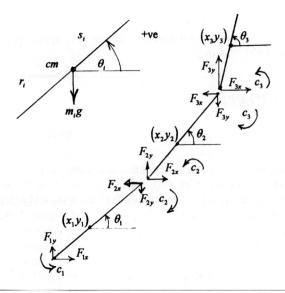

Figure 1.2   Force diagram.

$$x_i - r_i\cos\theta_i = x_{i-1} + s_{i-1}\cos\theta_{i-1} \qquad n \geq i \geq 2$$
$$y_i - r_i\sin\theta_i = y_{i-1} + s_{i-1}\sin\theta_{i-1} \qquad n \geq i \geq 2$$

x:
$$m_i\ddot{x}_i = -F_{i+1x} + F_{ix} \qquad (1)\ n-1 \geq i \geq 1$$
$$m_n\ddot{x}_n = F_{nx}$$

y:
$$m_i\ddot{y}_i = -F_{i+1y} + F_{iy} - m_ig \qquad (2)\ n-1 \geq i \geq 1$$
$$m_n\ddot{y}_n = -F_{ny} - m_ng$$

Angular:

$$I_i\ddot{\theta}_i = C_i - C_{i+1} + F_{ix}r_i\sin\theta_i - F_{iy}r_i\cos\theta_i \qquad (3)\ n-1 \geq i \geq 1$$
$$+ F_{i+1x}s_i\sin\theta_i - F_{i+1y}r_i\cos\theta_i$$

$$I_n\ddot{\theta}_n = C_n + F_{nx}r_n\sin\theta_n - F_{ny}r_n\cos\theta_n$$

Differentiate constraints twice:

$$\dot{x}_i + r_i\dot{\theta}_i\sin\theta_i = \dot{x}_{i-1} - s_{i-1}\dot{\theta}_{i-1}\sin\theta_{i-1}$$
$$\ddot{x}_i + r_i\ddot{\theta}_i\sin\theta_i + r_i\dot{\theta}_i^2\cos\theta_i = \ddot{x}_{i-1} - s_{i-1}\ddot{\theta}_{i-1}\sin\theta_{i-1} - s_{i-1}\dot{\theta}_{i-1}^2\cos\theta_{i-1} \qquad (4)$$

$$\dot{y}_i - r_i\dot{\theta}_i\cos\theta_i = \dot{y}_{i-1} + s_{i-1}\dot{\theta}_{i-1}\cos\theta_{i-1}$$
$$\ddot{y}_i - r_i\ddot{\theta}_i\cos\theta_i + r_i\dot{\theta}_i^2\sin\theta_i = \ddot{y}_{i-1} + s_{i-1}\ddot{\theta}_{i-1}\cos\theta_{i-1} - s_{i-1}\dot{\theta}_{i-1}^2\sin\theta_{i-1} \qquad (5)$$

Hence, from the positions and velocities, equations (1) to (5) were solved to give the accelerations, $\ddot{x}_i, \ddot{y}_i, \ddot{\theta}_i$. A first-order forward time-stepping scheme was then used to calculate the new positions and velocities for the next time step. A time step of 0.5 ms was found to be adequate.

CODE VALIDATION

No complete validation of the code is possible, but several dynamic and static checks have been successfully made. The motions of the simple pendulum, the single rod falling from the vertical, and the angular acceleration of a simple rod under a constant torque were all successfully predicted for each link in turn (achieved by setting the other two rod lengths to zero). A static check with the three links held in a straight line confirmed the correct torque interaction between the links—equivalent to the golfer holding a club out at arm's length.

INPUT PARAMETERS

The mass and inertia assumed for the arm (6 kg, 0.72 kgm^2 about the c.m.) are typical of an adult male, and those for the club (0.34 kg, 0.057 kgm^2 about the c.m.) are representative of a driver. The mass and inertia that should be assumed for the shoulders are less easily defined. While the shoulders themselves move through a large angle (-90° to +90°), the back and hips have less movement but not directly coupled to the arm. Nevertheless, the inertia of the shoulders (0.3 kgm^2) is very important since it carries the arm-shoulder joint, and any torque exerted on the arm has an opposite reaction on the shoulders and so affects the angular velocity of the hub. The hub velocity and shoulder joint position have a crucial effect on the arm and club.

To start with, a constant set of torque values for the backswing and another (larger) set of constant values for the downswing were assumed for the club, the arm, and the shoulder. The motions of the shoulders, arm and club are assumed to be "in plane" and at an angle of 35° to the vertical. This gives an effective acceleration due to gravity "g" acting on the arm and club of 8.0 m/s^2. Although the shoulders generally rotate on a flatter plane during the backswing, photographs show that the shoulder plane is much steeper during the downswing and more in line with the left arm.

Experimental measurements of strong male players in static positions show that the hub torque is of the order of 100 Nm and is fairly constant over the usual range of hub movement. The left arm is braced by the right hand and arm, and for most of the downswing lies across, and is driven by, the upper chest. Maximum arm torque values are therefore only slightly lower in magnitude than the hub torque at 75 Nm—until the left arm moves out and away from the body. The value then drops to about 50 Nm. The torque on the club from the hands (both of them) is rather easier to measure and is about 20 Nm over most of the range of the downswing, from the top of the backswing position (0°) and through the horizontal position (180°); it then falls to about 15 Nm as the impact position is approached (270°) and the right hand is less able to exert a torque.

The numerical procedure is capable of taking sets of any type of function for the hub, arm, and club torques, such as would result from curve-fitting experimental data; the problem is that there are very few reliable data available, except for those of Milne and Davis for the hands torque.

RESULTS AND DISCUSSION

The program is capable of simulating the whole swing from the start of the backswing through to the end of the follow-through (figure 1.3). For this the hub, arm, and hand torques were set to the constant values −14, −26.8, and −7.3 Nm respectively for the backswing and 105, 75, and 20 Nm for the downswing. The switch from backswing to downswing torques had to occur 0.65 s into the backswing to just allow the club, arm, and hub (shoulder line) to reach the representative positions shown in figure 1.3; that is, the club just about horizontal, the arm at about 125°, and the shoulder (hub) line about 270°—making the golfer's back face the target. The detailed numerical output reveals that, for the standard swing, the maximum backswing position for the shoulders is reached 0.73 s after the start with the arm decelerating to rest 0.02 s later and the club coming to rest 0.02 s after the arm. The shoulders thus start the downswing while the club is continuing the backswing (and with the real golfer the hips would start back well before the shoulders). This phase difference has been measured and is discussed by Grimshaw et al. (1997). The deceleration-acceleration and apparent dip of the club at the top

Figure 1.3   The predicted 'constant torques' driver swing viewed from plane axis. Clubhead impact speed 45.6 m/s.

of the backswing reproduce the effect of a powerful golf swing when viewed on the computer screen.

Although it has been known for a long time that the torques applied by the human golfer are far from constant, it may be of value to the human golfer in his or her preparation to simply think of applying, smoothly, three torques for the backswing (shoulders, arm(s), and club) and similarly three torques for the downswing. The overall standard swing shown in figure 1.3 produced a clubhead speed at impact of 45.6 m/s or slightly more than 100 mph, which is typical of a reasonably good amateur golfer. This figure also shows that as the arms and club proceed into the follow-through, still accelerating in this case, they move up and away from the body, bringing the shoulders to rest and then even reversing the motion of the hub. Allowing the upper arms too much freedom to move away from the body has for many years been known to produce poor golf—one of the reasons is probably that "flailing arms" prevent a full shoulder rotation through the ball.

Figure 1.4 shows a swing, viewed as it would appear to the observer, that is, at an angle of 35° to the plane axis, with backswing torques of −14, −28 and −7.3 Nm specified for the hub, arm and hands and downswing torques of 84, 73, and $C_3 = 15.0 + 14.73\theta_3 - 5.806\theta_3^2 + 0.2762\theta_3^3$. This cubic hands-club torque distribution is similar to that reported by Milne and Davis. After impact for this plot, the three torques were taken to be 84, −5 and 0 Nm for the hub, arm(s), and club, respectively. However, after impact the club positions are of little importance in a numerical simulation (but not to the human golfer of course), since from about 400 mm after impact the right arm-shoulder link controls the swing radius and the human golfer is beginning to straighten up and move the axis of rotation anyway. Nevertheless, such a swing, controlled by the right arm after impact, is shown in figure 1.5. This is shown for the downswing only and is viewed along the plane axis.

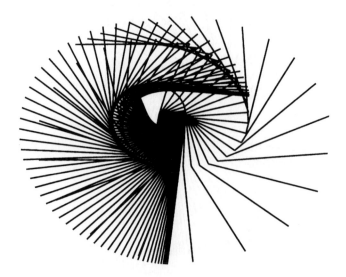

Figure 1.4   Resulting swing with a cubic hand-club torque distribution for the forward swing. Viewed at 35° to the plane axis.

Figure 1.5   A 'constant torques' swing with the right arm controlling the swing radius after impact. Viewed along the plane axis.

The clubhead path predicted by figure 1.4 is quite realistic as can be seen from figure 1.6, which shows that of Billy Casper taken with a light on the end of the club—a technique dating back to the 1930s (Adwick 1970). These figures confirm the old dictum for the path of the clubhead—"longest way up, shortest way down." The average player usually has a clubhead path very different from this, often with the backswing and downswing traces crossing over.

SOME USES OF THE CODE

The program runs faster than real time on a Pentium 233 MHz PC, and, by varying the various torque functions and switch points, the interaction of the various parameters can be investigated on the screen directly. The golf swing as simulated is very sensitive to the relative values of the torques applied; and any change to one must be accompanied by changes to all the others to produce a good swing.

For example, what is the effect of increasing the right hand torque, by say 10%, with all other parameters held constant? For the 'constant torques' swing with a driver, the result of such a change is illustrated in figure 1.7, for the downswing only: it can be seen that the hands are well behind the clubhead at impact. With a human golfer such an action would tend to pull the ball to the left. If now the hub and arm torques are increased (by about 10%), a well-timed golf swing is restored. This would seem to confirm the sound operational advice often given to golfers: "If the basic swing is correct and you begin to pull the ball to the

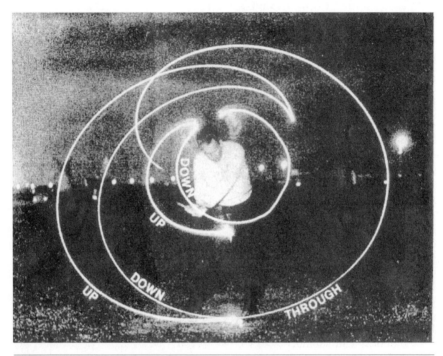

Figure 1.6   The clubhead path of Billy Casper.
Reprinted, by permission, from Ken Adwick, 1971, *X-ray Way to Master Golf*, (London: Pelham Books).

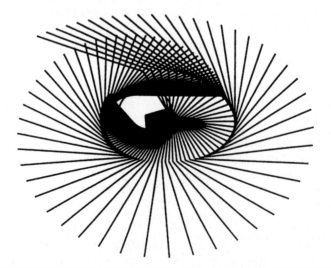

Figure 1.7   The predicted swing with a 10% increase in the downswing hand torque above that in the standard swing of figure 1.3, all other values unaltered. Clubhead arrives at impact ahead of the hands. Viewed at 35° to plane axis with image interval 5 ms.

left, turn the shoulders faster; if you hit it straight out to the right, hit harder with the hands."

It is possible for the code to be used in an interactive way by comparing the predictions with stroboscopic pictures of actual golfers and changing the torque functions specified until the two sets of positions agree. The characteristic appearance of different professional golfers' swings could thus be described mathematically. Comparison of an individual golfer's torque functions could provide information on the relative importance of each part of the swing. The torque functions could then be adjusted to predict numerically the consequences of any changes he or she might wish to make.

CONCLUSIONS

Preliminary work with the code has shown that the complete golf swing can be simulated reasonably well with two sets of three constants, one set representing the torques on the shoulders, the arm, and the club for the backswing and another set for the downswing. However, the two sets of torques are surprisingly closely related, and the well-timed golf-swing, as simulated, is very sensitive to their relative values. The shoulder-hub torque is perhaps the most sensitive since it is the one that has most effect in bringing the arm, hand, and thus the club into the correct positions. With the code, if the shoulder motion is incorrect it is almost impossible to simulate a "good" golf swing.

The predictions using a more representative nonlinear ramp function for the downswing hands-club torque do not appear at first sight to be very different from the constant torques solution. However, a ramp function for the downswing hands torque starting from a low value at the top of the backswing produces a 'lower' downswing with a wider spacing between the backswing and downswing clubhead paths together with a more acute angle between the club and the left arm initially. This is characteristic of long hitters. Commensurate changes have to be made to the backswing torques and to the ramp peak values to produce a well-timed swing.

The predictions of the code when viewed on the computer screen are surprisingly representative and show that any over- or underspecification of hand torque can be corrected by changing the arm and shoulder torques in proportion. Very specifically, if the hand torque is too high, the club arrives too early at impact—a common fault and one that can be cured by turning the shoulders faster. Any attempt to decelerate the arm or hub motions near impact produces weak, badly timed swings.

Operation of the code shows clearly that any movement of the arms away from the body markedly slows the hub/shoulder rotation by unnecessarily absorbing energy and forcing the club to move out too soon. Thus any hitting with the arms without simultaneously applying a strong torque to the hub will throw the club and the arms out, increase the moment of inertia of the system, slow the hub, and wreck the timing. This effect is very apparent on the screen whenever changes to the code are being made. The preliminary results indicate that a simple powerful golf swing would result from keeping the upper arms close to the body. This would make the swing more consistent, by reducing the number of degrees of freedom of the system, and more powerful by allowing the right arm, assisted by the body, to supply the large torque needed by the left arm.

References

Adwick K (1970), *X-Ray Way to Master Golf*, Pelham Books, London.

Budney DR and Bellow DG (1982), *On the Swing Mechanics of Matched Set of Golf Clubs*, Research Quarterly for Exercise and Sport, Vol 53, No 3.

Cochran AJ and Stobbs J (1968), *The Search for the Perfect Swing*, Heinemann, London.

Dillman CJ and Lange GW (1994), *How Has Biomechanics Contributed to the Understanding of the Golf Swing?*, Science and Golf II, Proc World Scientific Congress of Golf, Ed A J Cochran and MR Farrally, E & FN Spon, London.

Grimshaw PN, Burden AM, and Wallace E (1997), *Hip and Shoulder Rotations during the Golf Swing of Sub 10 Handicap Players*, Journal of Sports Sciences.

Jorgensen T (1993), *Physics of Golf*, American Institute of Physics, USA.

Lampsa MA (1975), *Maximizing Distance of the Golf Drive: An Optimal Control Study*, J Dyn Systems, Measurement and Control, ASME, Dec 1975.

Milne RD and Davis JP (1992), *The Role of the Shaft in the Golf Swing*, Biomechanics, Vol 25, No 9, pp 975-983.

Nesbit SM, Cole JS, Hartzell TA, Oglesby KA, and Radich AF (1994), *Dynamic Model and Computer Simulation of a Golf Swing*, Science and Golf II, Proc World Scientific Congress of Golf, Ed AJ Cochran and MR Farrally, E and FN Spon, London.

CHAPTER 2

A Mathematical Swing Model
for a Long-Driving Champion

M.G. Reyes
Department of Pathology, University of Illinois, Chicago
A. Mittendorf
Wigwam Country Club, Litchfield Park, Arizona

We describe the use of a two-dimensional mathematical model of the golf swing by a long-driving champion. Our model's predictions corroborated his observations and ideas and provided a systematic plan for increasing the distance of his drives.

The plan included lengthening his swing by increasing his backswing angle or wrist cock angle or both, using longer drivers with lighter heads, and increasing his torque through muscle strengthening. He readily hit longer drives with his longer swings and with the longer and lighter drivers but was unable to attain during the off-season the consistency needed for competition. He prepared for competition using his usual 51-inch driver with 191 gm head and his usual swing and placed third in the senior division of this year's National Long Drive Competition in Las Vegas, Nevada, with a drive of 359 yards in the final round. He plans to continue with the program again in the off-season and to work on muscle strengthening until he gets the consistency needed for competition.

Keywords: Swing model, long-driving champion.

INTRODUCTION

We have derived the equations for a two-dimensional model of the golf swing and coded them to allow easy input of club and swing parameters in a program that runs with Visual Basic (Mittendorf and Reyes 1997). Since our model applies primarily to the drive, we approached a long-driving champion to compare our model's predictions with his own observations and to explore the possibility of developing a plan that might help him gain longer driving distance.

Our driving champion is a Professional Golfers Association of America (PGA) professional who has been competing in regional, sectional, and national long-driving championships for over 30 years. In the past, he adopted or rejected ideas on how to increase his driving distance almost exclusively through trial and error. For example, to find out if a longer driver would give him longer drives he would have to first assemble the club and then try the club to see how far he could hit the ball with it. The same was true for different head weights, shaft weights, and so on, at considerable cost of time and money. He has kept notes of some of his finding but generally relies on his memory for the characteristics of the clubs and their performance. For the past several years, he has used a 51-inch driver with 191 gm head in competition and occasionally a 47-inch driver with 191 gm head. After he gets what he considers a competitive drive with his 51-inch club, he may try the other clubs that have given him longer distances in practice. He has made no changes with his swing but this year has begun toying with the idea of increasing the length of his backswing as a possible way to get around the demands of physical conditioning, which he is finding more difficult to maintain. He was thrilled to find out that the theoretical predictions of our model agree with his intuition and observations of his swing, equipment, and physical conditioning.

This report details how we used our swing model to provide our champion with a plan to increase his driving distance and presents the initial results of the program.

MATERIALS AND METHODS

Swing Model

The model is two-dimensional and consists of three inelastic members representing the upper and lower arms and the golf club. Shift force, gravity, and torque are applied to the shoulder, and two torques are applied at the elbow and wrist, although one or both of the latter may be zero. The equations were written using Lagrange's modifications of Newton's laws of motion. The diagram (figure 2.1) and equations with the torque of the elbow set at zero are shown as a two-rod model.

(1) $(M_a + M_c)\ddot{X}_0 - [(J_a + M_c l_a)Cos\theta + J_c Cos(\theta + ß)]\ddot{\theta} +$
$[J_c Sin(\theta + ß)](\dot{\theta} + \dot{ß})^2 - [J_c Cos(\theta + ß)]\ddot{ß} + [(J_a + M_c l_a)Sin\theta)\dot{\theta}^2 = F_l$

(2) $-[(J_a + M_c l_a)Cos\theta + J_c Cos(\theta + ß)]\ddot{X}_0 + [I_a + I_c + M_c l_a^2 + 2l_a J_c Cosß]\ddot{\theta} +$
$[I_c + l_a J_c Cosß]\ddot{ß} - [2l_a J_c Sinß]\dot{\theta}\dot{ß} - [l_a J_c Sinß]\dot{ß}^2 = T_l - g(J_a + M_c l_a)Sin\theta$
$-gJ_c Sin(\theta + ß)$

(3) $-[J_c Cos(\theta + ß)]\ddot{X}_0 + [I_c + l_a J_c Cosß]\ddot{\theta} I_c\ddot{ß} + [l_a J_c Sinß]\dot{\theta}^2 = T_2 - gJ_c Sin(\theta + ß)$

Our model matched the speed curves of the clubheads of the drives of two professional golfers that were measured by Jorgensen (1994) with stroboscopic photography. We set our model swing to match the following parameters of Jorgensen's golfers: (1) golfer's arm length, 2.2 ft; weight, 6.8 lb; (2) arm, 1st

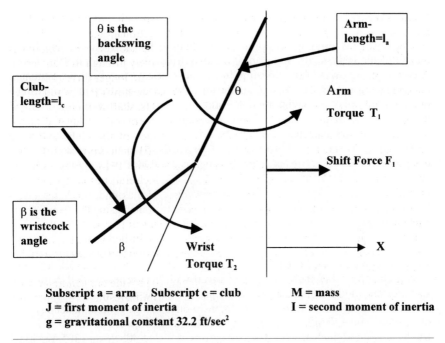

Figure 2.1   Two-rod model.

moment, 0.4418 slug-ft; arm, 2nd moment, 0.5402 slug-ft; (3) club length, 43.5 inches; shaft length, 41 inches; total club weight, 392 gm; head weight, 202 gm; shaft weight, 130 gm; (4) club, 1st moment, 0.0586 slug-ft; club, 2nd moment, 0.1623 slug-ft; club mass 0.0268 slugs; (5) backswing angle, 166 degrees; wrist cock angle, 124 degrees at the top of the backswing; release angle, 110 degrees. Using these parameters, we adjusted the torques and shift force of our model to match the average clubhead speeds of Jorgensen's golfers and obtained the best match of the clubhead speed curves with an initial torque of 60 lb-ft, final torque of 60 lb-ft, added wrist torque of 0.0 lb-ft, and a shift force of 9 lb. We designated these parameters as the default parameters of our model swing. In swings with the default parameters, the initial and final torques showed a linear relationship to clubhead speed at impact: 30 lb-ft initial torques gave 88 mph while 82 lb-ft gave 125 mph. In addition, we incorporated the ball velocity and ball carry in our model, which we determined with standard collision equations of physics on data presented by the golf manufacturers (Cashera 1995); ball velocities and carries of a 10.5-degree lofted driver with a 202 gm, 17-4 ph stainless steel head swung at 80, 90, and 100 mph by a hitting machine. Analysis of the data showed: (1) a linear relationship between ball velocity and ball carry; and (2) a constant coefficient of restitution for the given clubhead speeds was determined from the masses of the clubhead and the ball and the velocities of the clubhead and the ball. Using the coefficient of restitution, the ball velocities and carries were readily determined in our model.

Long-Driving Champion

We measured our driving champion's arm length and weight and the length and weight of the head, shaft, and grip of the two drivers he used in the 1966 North American Long Drive Championship; from videotapes of his swings, we estimated his backswing and wrist cock angles at the top of his swing and then input the values into the program of our swing model. Using the input parameters, we determined the initial and final torque and shift force of the model swing that matched the head speeds and, although probably not strictly comparable, the ball carry measured by a radar device, Distance Caddy (Gebhart 1996). We then used the program to predict head speeds and ball carries of other drivers, his usual and longer swings, and his swings with greater torque.

RESULTS

Table 2.1 compares the head speeds measured by the Distance Caddy of our long-driving champion's 47-inch and 51-inch drivers with 191 gm head with the clubhead speed of our model using the same club and swing parameters. With a constant torque of 70 lb-ft and shift force of 20 lb, the model swings generated head speeds of 127 mph and 130 mph, similar to the measured head speeds of 127 to 131 mph for the 47- and 51-inch drivers. The ball carries of 292 to 305 yd and 305 to 340 yd measured by the Distance Caddy, however, were greater than the 296 yd and 302 yd predicted by the model for the 47-inch and 51-inch drivers. We do not have an explanation for the difference in carries between the actual swings and the model swings of our golfer's 51-inch driver, which fall outside the average error ± standard deviation of $3.93 \pm 3.3\%$ of the Distance Caddy (Gebhart 1998).

Next, we used the swing model to predict head speeds and ball carries for longer swings, longer clubs with lighter heads, and greater torques and compared them with the predicted values of what we have designated as our champion's standard competition model swing: a 51-inch, 191 gm head driver swung with a backswing

Table 2.1   Measured vs Model Head Speeds and Carry

	Torque/shift force	Head speed	Ball carry
47-inch driver			
Actual swing	Not known	125-127 mph	292-305 yd
Model swing	70 lb-ft/20 lb	127 mph	296 yd
51-inch driver			
Actual swing	Not known	127-131 mph	305-340 yd
Model swing	70 lb-ft/20 lb	130 mph	302 yd

angle of 180 degrees and wrist cock angle of 90 degrees at an estimated initial and final torque of 70 lb-ft and shift force of 20 lb. This standard competition swing model gives a head velocity of 130 mph and ball carry of 302 yd. Adding 10 degrees to the wrist cock angle alone and 10 degrees to the backswing angle alone increases the head speed by 1.5% and 3.1%, respectively. Ten degrees added to both the wrist cock and backswing angles gives a 5.4% increase of head speed over that of the competition model swing. A lighter head weight of 170 gm or an increase of torque to 90 lb-ft will each increase the head speed by 8.5%, but as expected, the lighter head gets less carry. A 55-inch driver and a 60-inch driver increase head speeds by 1.5% and 3.1%, respectively. By contrast, a 60-inch driver with a lighter 170 gm head weight gives an increase of head speed of 6.1%. Lastly, a 60-inch, 170 gm driver, a longer swing, and 90 lb-ft of torque increase the head speed by 12.3%. The results are shown in Table 2.2.

Table 2.2 Comparison of Swing Models With Competition Swing Model

Torque	backswing/Wrist cock angles	Head speed	Ball carry
*Competition swing model: 51-inch driver [333 gm overall weight, **191** gm head weight]*			
70 lb-ft	180/90 deg	130 mph	302 yd
Longer swing			
70 lb-ft	180/100 deg	132 mph (1.5%)	309 yd
70 lb-ft	190/90 deg	134 mph (3.1%)	315 yd
70 lb-ft	190/100 deg	137 mph (5.4%)	322 yd
*Lighter head weight [**170** gm]*			
70 lb-ft	180/90 deg	141 mph (8.5%)	324 yd
Greater torque			
80 lb-ft	180/90 deg	135 mph (3.8%)	318 yd
90 lb-ft	180/90 deg	141 mph (8.5%)	333 yd
*Longer club: 55-inch driver [333 gm overall weight, **191** gm head weight]*			
70 lb-ft	180/90 deg	132 mph (1.5%)	307 yd
*Longer club: 60-inch driver [333 gm overall weight, **191** gm head weight]*			
70 lb-ft	180/90 deg	134 mph (3.1%)	315 yd
*Longer and lighter club: 60-inch driver [312 gm overall weight, **170** gm head weight]*			
70 lb-ft	180/90 deg	138 mph (6.1%)	317 yd
90 lb-ft	190/100 deg	146 mph (12.3%)	335 yd

COMMENTS

We presented our findings to our long-drive champion and pointed out to him that the predicted values are not necessarily absolute values but can be useful for comparison of not only the direction but also the magnitude of changes resulting from the modifications of the swing or club. As an example, our model predicts that a 29% increase of torque from 70 to 90 lb-ft only gives a 8.5% increase in head speed over his competition swing model. This increase is comparable to the 8.5% increase of head speed with a 51-inch, 170 gm head driver. It would appear at first glance that it would be a lot easier for him to put a lighter head on his competition driver, swing with his usual swing, and get a head speed equal to what he would get if he could increase his torque by 29% by increasing his muscle strength. Similarly, it would seem to be easier to work on a longer swing by increasing his backswing angle, wrist cock angle, or both than to increase his torque. In the final analysis, however, it will be up to him to determine which avenues will give him the longest drives most consistently. He understands that our model shows what is possible but not how to attain the possible. Similarly, he is aware that our swing model does not address the bending of the shaft in the golf swing as a possible source of longer drives (Cochran and Stobbs 1968 and Jorgensen 1994).

Our models predict that a lighter head weight gives faster head speeds. This agrees with our champion's observations, but he has not seriously pursued the use of lighter head weights because some of the heads that he has modified to weigh less than 180 gm have collapsed on impact and, importantly, because he feels that he does not get a corresponding increase in distance even with the lighter heads that appear structurally sound. His observations are probably correct, because it is true that for the same speed, a heavier head will carry the ball farther than a lighter head. This was clearly shown in table 2.2: the same head speed of 141 mph gave a carry of 324 yd for the 51-inch, 170 gm head driver compared with a 333 yd carry of the 51-inch, 191 gm head driver. However, it is probably true that the lighter heads were not structurally sound, which results in a lower coefficient of restitution and lower ball velocity. Therefore, he will continue to try lighter heads and has already built 51-inch and 60-inch drivers with 170 gm titanium heads that were given to him by a major club manufacturer.

He worked on the program in the off-season, but after six months he did not feel that his new swing or drivers were ready for competition. While he was hitting them longer, most of his drives did not hit the fairways. He put the improvement program on hold and began preparing for the 1997 season with his 51-inch, 191 gm head driver and his usual swing. In October 1997 at the North American Long Drive Championship in Las Vegas, Nevada, he placed third in the newly created senior division with a drive of 359 yd in the finals and a drive of 391 yd in the semifinal round. This was a better showing than in the 1996 North American Long Driving Competition in Las Vegas, where he failed to make the finals in spite of a 356 yd drive in the semifinal round. He plans to continue with the program this year and hopes that he will be able to approximate some of the model's predictions and use them in competition.

References

Cashera LG. Jr. (1995). *Strictly golf balls: The golf ball handbook.* Progressive Publications, Auburn Hills, MI.

Cochran A & Stobbs J. (1968). *Search for the perfect swing.* Triumph Books, Chicago.

Gebhart W. (1996). *Distance Caddy.* Internet site. **http: // Distancecaddy.com.**

Gebhart W. (1998). *Personal Communication on report of Golf Laboratories comparing distances of actual golf ball and Distance Caddy carries.*

Jorgensen TP. (1994). *The physics of golf.* American Institute of Physics Press, New York.

Mittendorf A & Reyes MG. (1997). *Golf Physics Presents a Swing Model.* Internet site. **http: // www.Golfphysics.com.**

CHAPTER 3

A Kinetic Analysis of the Knees During a Golf Swing

Charles J. Gatt Jr., MD; Michael J. Pavol, MS; Richard D. Parker, MD; and Mark D. Grabiner, PhD
The Cleveland Clinic Foundation, Cleveland, Ohio, USA

The purposes of this study were to (1) determine the external forces and moments about the knees during a golf swing, (2) determine whether type of shoe worn affects knee joint kinetics, (3) determine whether golf skill level is a determinant of knee joint kinetics.

Thirteen golfers of varying skill levels, determined as a function of their reported USGA handicap, were studied. Each subject, using a five iron, hit a standard golf ball into a safety net with the instructions to use his "typical" golf swing. The subjects stood with each foot on a strain gauge force plate covered with a firmly attached rubber mat. Reflective markers were placed over lower extremity anatomical landmarks to represent the lower extremities and pelvis as a biomechanical link model. The motion of these markers was measured using six high-speed video cameras and synchronized with the ground reaction force data from the two force plates. Each subject performed 10 trials in two types of footwear: (1) golf shoes with spikes and (2) golf shoes with spikeless rubber outsoles. A mathematical model of the lower extremity that requires input of anthropometric, position, acceleration, and force plate data calculated the forces and moments about the knee.

The average peak knee compressive force for the front knee was 756N (100% of body weight [BW]) and 540N (72%BW) for the rear knee. Anteriorly directed shear force was generated only in the rear knee and was quite low; the average peak value was 75N (10%BW). The average peak posterior shear force was 296N (39%BW) for the front leg and 149N (20%BW) for the rear leg. The average peak internal rotation moment was 27.7Nm (normalized to body weight times height, this becomes 2%BW $\times$ BH) for the front knee and 19.1Nm (1.4%BW $\times$ BH) for the rear knee. For external rotation moments, the average peak value was 16.1Nm (1.2%BW $\times$ BH) for the front knee and 38.8Nm (2.8%BW $\times$ BH) for the rear knee. Average peak varus moments for the front and back knees were 63.7Nm (4.7%BW $\times$ BH) and 19.6Nm (2.9%BW $\times$ BH), respectively. Average peak valgus moments for the front and back knees were 24.4Nm (1.8%BW $\times$ BH) and 52.6Nm (3.9%BW $\times$ BH), respectively. There were no statistically significant differences between average peak forces or moments with respect to shoe type. There was no significant correlation between USGA handicap and average peak knee joint forces and moments. The magnitude of forces and moments generated in the knee during a golf swing equal or exceed the forces generated in several activities, such as running and performing a side-cut maneuver, that are incorporated into standard knee rehabilitation protocols.

Although golf is not conventionally considered to be a strenuous sport, significant knee joint forces and moments can be generated during the swing that may create undesirable stresses on repaired or reconstructed tissues. The type of shoes worn during the activity does not significantly influence the magnitude of the forces and moments, and clinically, one can not predict the magnitude of the forces and moments to which a particular patient will be subjected based on handicap. Return to golf after knee surgery should be allowed at the same time as rehabilitation activities that generate similar forces and moments in the knee.

Keywords: Kinetics, golf, knee, biomechanics.

INTRODUCTION

Knee injuries account for approximately 9% of musculoskeletal injuries sustained by golfers (McCarroll et al., 1990). Since the golfing population consists of men and women in all age ranges, there are many different injuries and pathologic conditions involving the knee that may affect the ability to participate in golf. These golfers may not have enough disability to warrant surgery, but will complain of pain and disability during or after golf. In addition, it is common for patients to inquire when they can return to golf after orthopaedic procedures such as partial meniscectomy, anterior cruciate ligament (ACL) reconstruction, and total knee arthroplasty.

The role of footwear on lower extremity forces during a golf swing has yet to be determined. The most commonly worn shoe consists of a leather upper and a firm sole with 8 to 12 spikes. Recently, the cleatless shoe has become more popular among golfers. This shoe is similar to the turf shoe used in football. Although traction and stability play a role in the golfer's choice of shoe, comfort seems to be the most important factor.

The purpose of this study was to determine the forces and moments generated in the lead and trail knees during a golf swing. In addition, the effect of footwear and golf skill level on the knee joint kinetics was analyzed. Finally, using this data, recommendations are made regarding golf participation during rehabilitation from knee injuries and surgery.

MATERIALS AND METHODS

Subjects

Thirteen male golfers (mean [std. dev.] age: 35 [14.2] yrs; height: 1.79 [0.12] m; mass: 76.8 [9.0] kg) participated in this study after giving their informed consent.

Skill level was determined by the subject's self-reported USGA handicap. Subject handicaps ranged from 4 to 18 with a mean of 11.2.

Data Collection

Kinematic and kinetic data were collected over two sets of 10 golf shots for each subject, one set with each of two types of footwear: spiked golf shoes (FootJoy DryJoys, Brockton, MA) and spikeless, rubber-soled golf shoes (FootJoy SoftJoys, Brockton, MA).

Subjects stood in their normal golf stance with each foot on an individual force plate (AMTI Inc., Newton, MA). Force plates were mounted flush with the laboratory floor, with a securely attached 4mm-thick rubber mat providing traction. Each foot contacted only the mat of its force plate throughout each swing. All subjects used the identical five iron to hit a standard golf ball, resting on the synthetic grass mat of a commercial club speed-measuring device and placed at the preferred location of each individual. The target was a safety net positioned approximately 2m away. Subjects were instructed to hit the ball into the net as they would in executing a perfect, straight, five-iron fairway shot of average length and to give a verbal indication of the start of backswing for each shot. The order of shoe-type testing was randomized.

During each golf shot, three-plane ground reaction forces and moments were collected from the force plates. Simultaneously, golf swing kinematics were recorded by a six-camera stereophotometric data acquisition system (Motion Analysis Corp., Santa Rosa, CA). Sixteen hemispherical reflective markers were employed on appropriate body landmarks.

Knee Force, Moment, and Angle Decomposition

To aid in their interpretation, resultant knee joint forces and moments were decomposed into the components acting in each of the clinically used directions. The knee proximal-distal (PD) axis was taken as the line joining the ankle and knee joint centers. The medial-lateral (ML) axis was assumed to intersect the knee joint in a direction perpendicular to the line between the hip and knee joint centers and to lie in the plane of the greater trochanter. The anterior-posterior axis was the perpendicular at the knee to the PD and ML axes. Curves were constructed for the components of the knee orientations, forces, and moments for each leg and shoe type for each subject. Results of different swings were aligned at the time of lowest filtered hand-marker height for averaging, and only the sample points common to all swings were included. The knee orientation of each subject at the time of the peak force or moment in each direction was determined from the ensemble average curves for each leg and shoe type.

Statistics

The effects of handicap, leg (lead vs. trail), and shoe type (spikes vs. spikeless) on the raw and normalized average peak knee forces and moments in each direction were determined through repeated measures multiple regression analysis (Cohen and Cohen, 1983).

RESULTS

The average peak forces and moments on the lead and trail knees are displayed in table 3.1 and table 3.2. Surprisingly, the effect of shoe type on the forces and moments generated was not statistically significant. Thus, the values in tables 3.1 and 3.2 are the combined results from trials with golf spikes and spikeless shoes.

Table 3.1   Peak Forces Along Each Axis Acting on Each Knee

Direction	Lead knee (N)	Lead knee (% BW)	Trail knee (N)	Trail knee (% BW)
Distal	756 (185)	99.9 (18.7)	540 (100)	71.5 (8.7)
Anterior	296 (92)	39.0 (10.7)	149 (40)	19.9 (5.1)
Posterior	−2.8 (19.3)	−0.3 (2.6)	75.3 (26.7)	10.1 (3.5)
Medial	73.3 (24.9)	9.9 (3.4)	70.9 (20.0)	9.5 (2.8)
Lateral	133 (80)	17.0 (8.6)	87.7 (38.0)	11.4 (4.2)

Values are in Newtons with standard deviation in parentheses. Values are also normalized to body weight. n = 26 in each case.

Table 3.2   Peak Moments About Each Axis Acting on Each Knee

Direction	Lead knee (Nm)	Lead knee (% BW × BH)	Trail knee (Nm)	Trail knee (% BW × BH)
Flexion	20.8 (23.0)	1.62 (1.86)	68.4 (13.9)	5.15 (1.16)
Extension	96.9 (28.7)	7.17 (1.93)	58.6 (14.6)	4.40 (1.18)
Internal	16.1 (4.8)	1.20 (0.34)	19.6 (8.0)	1.46 (0.53)
External	27.7 (9.4)	2.05 (0.65)	19.1 (5.4)	1.41 (0.36)
Abduction	63.7 (24.6)	4.73 (1.74)	38.8 (17.1)	2.85 (1.16)
Adduction	24.4 (11.0)	1.78 (0.66)	52.6 (15.9)	3.89 (0.95)

Values are in Nm with standard deviation in parentheses. Values are normalized to body weight times height. n = 26 in each case.

An example (subject TC) of the hand height, knee flexion angles, and average forces and moments on both knees as a function of time is displayed in figure 3.1. In general, there was significant variability in swing patterns between subjects. Consequently, the force and moment versus time curves differed significantly from

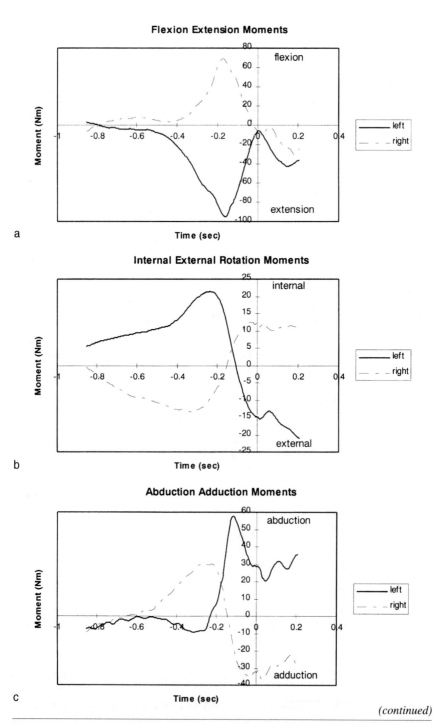

Figure 3.1   A sample of lead and trail knee kinetics as function of time. Time zero is the time of club-ball impact.

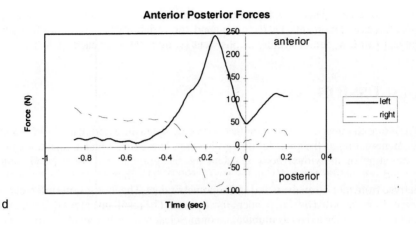

Anterior Posterior Forces

d

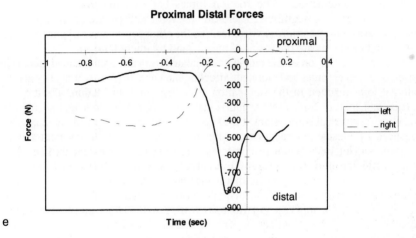

Proximal Distal Forces

e

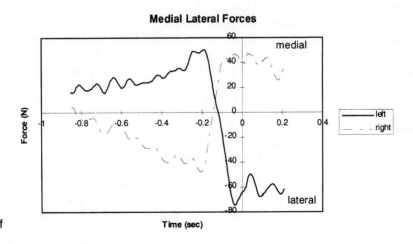

Medial Lateral Forces

f

Figure 3.1   *(continued)*

subject to subject. This is evidenced by the large standard deviations for the average peak forces and moments. On the other hand, the variability between trials for each subject was low, demonstrating a consistent swing pattern for each subject.

DISCUSSION

The biomechanical model used for this study calculated the external joint forces and moments acting on the knee during a golf swing. These forces and moments are the summation of individual body segment inertia, gravitational forces, and foot-ground interaction forces (Vaughn et al., 1992). The inertial components were derived from motion analysis and anthropometric data. The foot-ground interaction forces were recorded by independent force plates. The resultant external forces and moments are balanced by a combination of muscle tensions, ligament tensions, and joint surface interactions. The friction forces between the tibial and femoral articular surfaces are negligible. Therefore, the joint surface interaction forces are interpreted as purely compressive forces, and the other components of joint reaction forces and moments are the result of muscle and ligament tension.

The average peak forces and moments calculated from the mathematical model are based on external forces and moments affecting the knee. In other words, they are the internal joint reaction to the summation of foot-ground interaction, gravitational forces, and inertial forces of the individual body segments (foot and shank). To maintain mechanical equilibrium at the knee, these external forces and moments are balanced by muscle contractions and ligament tension. Thus, a resultant flexion moment is an internal reaction to an external moment tending to extend the knee. This resultant flexion moment is generated by a net contraction of the hamstrings. In reality, this may be a net flexion moment that is the sum of hamstrings flexion torque and quadriceps extension torque. A resultant posterior force will be generated by tension in the ACL (the ACL applies a posterior force to the proximal tibia) and posterior shear force from hamstrings contraction. This would be in response to external forces tending to displace the tibia in an anterior direction relative to the femur.

The forces and moments generated in the knees during the golf swing are certainly not of a magnitude that makes golf a high-risk sport for traumatic knee injury. This is confirmed in the literature by reviews citing knee injuries as relatively uncommon in the golfing population (Batt, 1993; McCarroll, 1996). Those that do occur are primarily overuse-type injuries. However, many patients who sustain knee injuries or develop pathologic conditions of the knee enjoy golf as a primary form of recreation. Yet no estimates of the forces and moments on the knee during the golf swing have been published. Therefore, judgment regarding return to golf after an injury or surgical procedure has often been based on a physician's personal experience as a golfer or from treating golfers.

Activities that produce excessive anterior shear forces, varus moments, or internal rotation moments on the knee are thought to endanger the ACL graft as it heals (Arms et al., 1984). This is especially true if the activities are performed with the knee flexed from zero to 30 degrees. Several studies have used motion analysis to estimate the forces and torques on the knee during rehabilitation activities. Open chain knee extension exercises have been estimated to produce 285N of anterior shear force on the knee (Lutz et al., 1993). Motion analysis studies have estimated that external anterior shear forces (stress on the ACL) equivalent to 10% of body weight, posterior shear forces equivalent to 100% body weight, and internal rotation moments equivalent to 2% of body weight times height are generated in the knee during side-cutting maneuvers (Andriacchi et al., 1985).

In our study, footwear did not have a significant effect on the forces and moments generated in the knees during the golf swing. Inherently, one might suspect that the spikes of standard golf shoes would increase foot-ground interaction forces, leading to increased forces and moments at the knee. The fact that very little linear displacement of the foot occurs during the golf swing and that most of the energy is created by weight transfers may account for the lack of differences between the trials with cleats and the trials with cleatless shoes. When the subjects in this study were asked if they noticed a difference in the trials with and without cleats, they all responded that no difference was detectable.

The forces and moments generated in the knee during the golf swing did not correlate with golf skill level as determined by USGA handicap. However, USGA handicap is determined as a function of a player's average golf scores. Since 50% of the allowable strokes in golf are dedicated to putting, the USGA handicap is probably not a reliable method of evaluating the golf swing apart from all other aspects of the game. In addition, although the number of subjects did not allow for a statistical analysis, the overall technique of the golf swing was highly variable among our subjects. For example, some subjects used very little lower extremity motion while others had large amounts of pelvic and lower extremity rotation. This is further evidenced by the high standard deviations for average peak forces and moments.

CONCLUSION

This study provides an estimate of the forces and moments on both the front and back knees during a golf swing. Since many patients recovering from surgical procedures or having acute knee injuries or underlying pathologic conditions of the knee desire to return to golf, this information is useful to the clinician in these decision-making processes. During the golf swing, the forces and moments in the knee approximate those of many commonly used rehabilitation techniques. Therefore, when deciding when a return to golf is safe, the clinician should compare our kinetic data to the data published for other activities and make a scientifically educated determination in conjunction with his or her own personal biases regarding rehabilitation.

References

Andriacchi TP, Kramer GM, and Landon GC (1985) The biomechanics of running and knee injuries. In *The American Academy of Orthopaedic Surgeons, Symposium on Sports Medicine. The Knee*, 23-32. Edited by Gerald Finerman. St. Louis: Mosby.

Arms SW, Pope MH, Johnson RJ, Fischer RA, Arvidsson I, and Eriksson E (1984) The biomechanics of anterior cruciate ligament rehabilitation and reconstruction. *Am J Sports Med* 12(1): 8-18.

Batt, ME (1993) Golfing injuries. An overview. *Sports Med* 16(1): 64-71.

Cohen J and Cohen P (1983) *Applied Multiple Regression/Correlation Analysis for the Behavioral Sciences* (2nd ed.). Hillsdale, NJ: Erlbaum.

Lutz GE, Palmitier RA, and Chao EYS (1993) Comparison of tibiofemoral joint forces during open kinetic-chain and closed kinetic-chain exercises. *J Bone and Joint Surg* 65A: 732-739.

McCarroll J, Rettig A, and Shelbourne KD (1990) Injuries in the amateur golfer. *Phys and Sports Med* 18(3): 122-126.

McCarroll JR (1996) The frequency of golf injuries. *Clin Sports Med* 15(1): 1-8.

Vaughn CL, Davis BL, and O'Connor JC (1992) *Dynamics of Human Gait*. Champaign, IL: Human Kinetics.

CHAPTER 4

Golf Swing and Skill

K. Watanabe, S. Kuroki, M. Hokari, and S. Nishizawa
System Control Engineering Department, School of Engineering Hosei University

Golfers always want to score well. Here we investigate the factors in golf club swing motions that are most related to improving the score. In experimental studies, we found that the average score of a golfer is accurately estimated from the linear equation of the conventional factors and the factors involved in body-twist motion. From a sensitivity analysis of the linear function, we found that the factors most related to improving the score are (1) faster driver head velocity, (2) higher ball angle, (3) less standard deviation of ball velocity, (4) faster body-twist angular velocity, and (5) later timing of maximum body-twist acceleration in relation to impact time.

Keywords: Golf driver swing, body-twist motion, score improvement.

INTRODUCTION

Golf is one of the most popular sports, and the golf population is gradually increasing. Most golfers practice hard and/or pay for good clubs to improve their average score, but their scores stabilize unless they can improve their skill level. To improve their scores, two basic strategies are considered: (1) the employment of scientific training by measuring and analyzing the golf swing motion and (2) employment of training that adjusts the golf club swing motions that are effective in improving the score and/or sensitive in relation to the score.

For the first strategy, we found many studies of biomechanics that treat the golf swing as a mechanical motion.[1,3,6-13] Image processing is also among the most powerful technologies to be applied to sports measurement.[2,4-5,14]

In the golf swing, the body-twist motion or the rotation around the body axis is considered an important motion. However, only a few experimental investigations that treat this motion can be found.

This paper describes a new body-twist motion and rotation sensing system that uses a small gyro. By using the system sensing body-twist motion as well as the conventional image-processing system, we measure the various motion variables in the golf club swing and estimate accurate linear equations that relate the average score to some of the variables. Sensitivity of these variables to the average score identifies the most effective variables (or motion in the golf swing) for improving the score.

GOLF DRIVER SWING AND ASSUMPTIONS AND PROBLEM DESCRIPTION

Golf Driver Swing

Figure 4.1, a and b, show the driver movement, ball flight, and body-twist motion in a driver swing. In the figure, we define the variables as V_h: head velocity; V_b: initial ball velocity; ω_u: ball flight angular velocity of backspin; ω_s: ball flight angular velocity of side spin; θ_u: upper angle; θ_s: side angle; c: estimated carry; θ: twist angle; ω_{max}: maximum body-twist angular velocity; α_{max}: maximum body-twist angular acceleration; $t_{\omega max}$: time when the body-twist angular velocity is maximum; $t_{\omega max}$: time when the body-twist angular acceleration is maximum; $\omega(t_i)$: twist angular velocity at impact time; $\alpha(t_i)$: twist angular velocity at impact time; S: the average score of the golfer.

Assumptions and Problem Description

Assume for golfers and the average scores declared by them:

   (A1)   Advanced golfers swing a driver in an advanced manner.

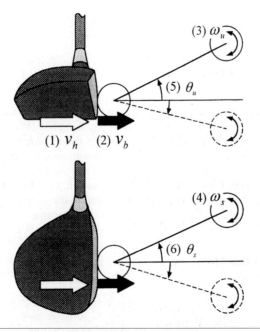

Figure 4.1a   Driver movement and ball flight.

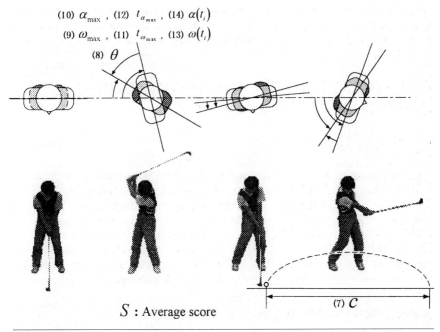

(10) α_{max} , (12) $t_{\alpha_{max}}$, (14) $\alpha(t_i)$

(9) ω_{max} , (11) $t_{\omega_{max}}$, (13) $\omega(t_i)$

(8) θ

S : Average score

(7) C

Figure 4.1b   Body-twist motion.

(A2)   The declared average score is reliable.

(A3)   The average score is given by a linear equation of some of the variables that have been defined.

Under these assumptions, we will consider the relation between the score (skill) and the variables associated with the driver swing motions. The problems are to

(P1)   find the equations that relate the score S and the variables listed in Table 4.1 in the driver swing motion shown in figure 4.1, a and b, and

(P2)   determine the most effective factors for improving the score.

RELATION BETWEEN THE SCORE AND THE DRIVER SWING VARIABLES; SENSITIVITY OF THE VARIABLES TO THE SCORE

Estimation of the Relation Between the Score and the Driver Swing Variables

The movement of a driver swung by a human golfer always includes fluctuation. Thus the variables must be treated as stochastic variables (average, standard deviation) by repeated measurements.

Table 4.1   Reference Variable

No.	Variable	Unit	Average	Standard deviation	To improve the score
—	Score	—	$\hat{S}$	—	—
(1)	Head speed	[m/s]	$\hat{V}_h$	σ_{V_h}	Up Down
(2)	Ball speed	[m/s]	$\hat{V}_b$	σ_{V_b}	Up Down
(3)	Back spin	[rpm]	$\hat{\omega}_u$	σ_{ω_u}	— Down
(4)	Side spin	[rpm]	$\hat{\omega}_s$	σ_{ω_s}	— Down
(5)	Upper angle	[deg]	$\hat{\theta}_u$	σ_{θ_u}	Up Down
(6)	Side angle	[deg]	$\hat{\theta}_s$	σ_{θ_s}	Up Down
(7)	Carry	[y]	$\hat{c}$	σ_c	Up Down
(8)	Twist angle	[deg]	$\hat{\theta}$	σ_{θ}	Up Down
(9)	Maximum twist velocity	[deg/s]	$\hat{\omega}_{max}$	$\sigma_{\omega_{max}}$	— Down
(10)	Maximum twist acceleration	[deg/s²]	$\hat{\alpha}_{max}$	$\sigma_{\alpha_{max}}$	— Down
(11)	Time at maximum twist velocity	[s]	$\hat{t}_{\omega_{max}}$	$\sigma_{t_{\omega_{max}}}$	— Down
(12)	Time at maximum twist acceleration	[s]	$\hat{t}_{\alpha_{max}}$	$\sigma_{t_{\alpha_{max}}}$	— Down
(13)	Twist velocity at impact	[deg/s]	$\hat{\omega}(t_i)$	$\sigma_{\omega(t_i)}$	Up Down
(14)	Twist acceleration at impact	[deg/s²]	$\hat{\alpha}(t_i)$	$\sigma_{\alpha(t_i)}$	Up Down

$\hat{}$: average, σ : standard deviation

Table 4.1 shows the averages and standard deviations of the variables associated with the driver swing shown in figure 4.1, a and b. The relation between the score and all 29 variables in table 4.1 is meaningless. We would like to know the relation that explains the score with fewer variables.

First, we select the proper variables $x_i (i = 1, 2, \ldots, n)$ from table 4.1. Under assumption (A1), we estimate the score from the selected variables. Further, from assumption (A2), the declared score is accurate and the equation that relates the score and the variables is linear. Thus the score S can be described as follows:

$$S = b_0 + b_1 x_1 + b_2 x_2 + \ldots + b_n x_n \tag{1}$$

The coefficients $b_0, b_1, b_2, \ldots, b_n$ in eq. (1) are estimated by substituting the player's data $\{S, x_i\,(i = 1, 2, \ldots, n)\}$ into eq. (1) and by applying the multi-regression method. Let R^2 be the contribution ratio and let R^{*2} be the adjusted contribution ratio. Assumption (A3) is recognized to be reasonable. The variables are selected by a procedure so that their number is minimum.

Sensitivity of the Variables to the Score

Supposing the estimated model of eq. (1) to be reasonable, the sensitivity of the variable to the score S can be calculated.

$$\frac{\frac{\partial S}{S}}{\frac{\partial x_i}{x_i}} = \frac{\partial S}{\partial x_i} \cdot \frac{b_i x_i}{S} \tag{2}$$

We calculate the sensitivity of score for all the variables in eq. (1). The variable with the maximum sensitivity most strongly influences the score.

EXPERIMENTS

An arbitrary group of 22 amateur golfers whose average score ranges from 80(T21) to 150(T1) were selected as the subjects of our experiments.

Measurement System

Figure 4.2 shows the measurement system, which is composed of three elements: (1) impact timing-detecting optical sensor, (2) camera set to measure the driver movement and ball flight, (3) body-twist motion-detecting jacket-type sensor.

Measurements of Variables of the Ball Flight, Driver Movement, and Body-Twist Motion

Table 4.2 shows the variables measured for the subject T1 (the worst golfer, with average score of 150) and T21 (one of the best golfers with average score of 82). The

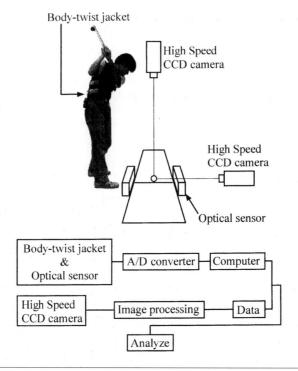

Figure 4.2   Measurement system.

variables correspond to those in table 4.1. Figure 4.3 shows the body-twist angle, angular velocity, and acceleration for these subjects. The variables for the other 90 players were similarly measured.

RELATION BETWEEN THE SCORE AND DRIVER SWING VARIABLES

Score and Driver Movement, Ball Flight, and Body-Twist Motion

We estimate the score by the variables of driver movement, ball flight, and body-twist motion. The score is estimated by the following nine variables:

$$\hat{V}_h, \sigma_{v_b}, \hat{\omega}_u, \hat{\omega}_s, \hat{\theta}_u, \hat{\alpha}_{max}, \hat{t}_{\omega_{max}}, \sigma_{t_{\omega_{max}}}, \hat{\alpha}(t_i).$$

The score is given by

$$S = 198 - 1.5\hat{v}_h + 3.62\sigma_{v_b} + 0.00422\,\hat{\omega}_u - 0.0108\hat{\omega}_s$$
$$-3.55\hat{\theta}_u - 0.00247\hat{\alpha}_{max} + 195\hat{t}_{\omega_{max}} - 208\sigma_{t_{\omega_{max}}} + 0.000871\hat{\alpha}(t_i) \tag{3}$$

Table 4.2   Reference Variables for T1 and T21

No.	Variable	Unit	T1 Average	T1 Standard deviation	T21 Average	T21 Standard deviation
—	Score	—	150	—	82	—
(1)	Head speed	[m/s]	40.17	1.347	43.61	0.563
(2)	Ball speed	[m/s]	53.30	9.291	60.78	1.483
(3)	Back spin	[rpm]	2946	1149	3475	670.0
(4)	Side spin	[rpm]	−30.90	325.1	134.4	264.0
(5)	Upper angle	[deg]	15.31	13.26	16.22	3.964
(6)	Side angle	[deg]	1.370	10.22	−0.140	1.802
(7)	Carry	[y]	160.9	39.96	212.5	5.416
(8)	Twist angle	[deg]	49.88	4.495	75.14	4.774
(9)	Maximum twist velocity	[deg/s]	295.8	33.94	630.6	23.88
(10)	Maximum twist acceleration	[deg/s^2]	4184	1384	10457	875.2
(11)	Time at maximum twist velocity	[s]	0.110	0.020	0.061	0.003
(12)	Time at maximum twist acceleration	[s]	0.039	0.085	0.032	0.002
(13)	Twist velocity at impact	[deg/s]	121.1	17.78	225.3	32.36
(14)	Twist acceleration at impact	[deg/s^2]	1078	631.0	3095	913.1

The adjusted contribution ratio was $R^{*2} = 0.91$. The real average scores and those predicted are shown in figure 4.4. The maximum error is less than 10% and the average error is 4% by the model. The regression model unbelievably accurately predicts the average score. Once the nine listed variables are measured, we can predict the individual's average golf score.

Influence of the Variables on the Score

Here we investigate how each variable influences the score by the sensitivity in eq. (2). Figure 4.5 shows the sensitivity of variables to the score.

From figure 4.5, that is from the model of body-twist motion, the score can be improved by changing the following motions:

1. Driver head velocity (up)
2. Angle of ball flight (up)

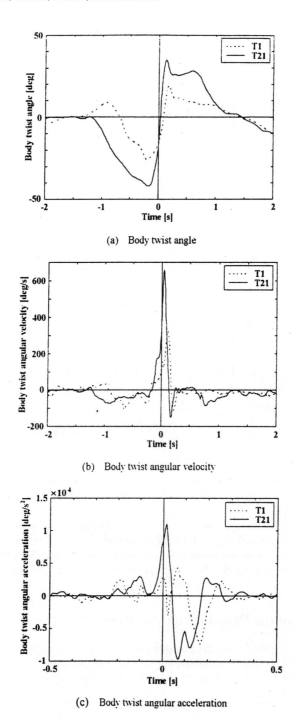

(a)   Body twist angle

(b)   Body twist angular velocity

(c)   Body twist angular acceleration

Figure 4.3   Measured body-twist motion.

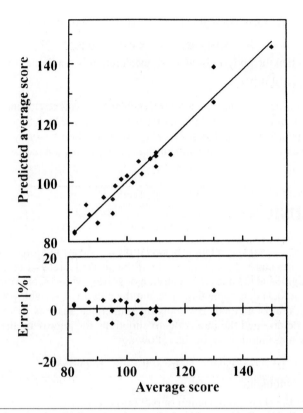

Figure 4.4   Result of multiple regression analysis (driver and ball and body-twist motion).

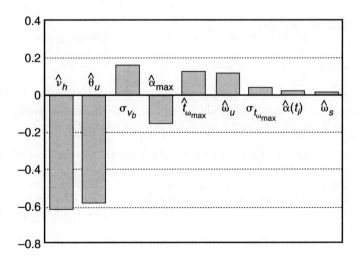

Figure 4.5   Sensitivity of partial regression coefficient.

3. Standard deviation of ball velocity (down)

4. Maximum of body-twist angular acceleration (up)

5. Time when the body-twist angular acceleration is maximum (delay)

6. Backspin (down)

That is, in order to improve the score, increase the velocity of the driver head keeping the driver movement stable (from 1, 3), hit the ball high (from 2), increase the body-twist acceleration (from 4), delay the time when the body-twist angular velocity is maximal in reaction to the impact time (from 5), and reduce the backspin (from 6).

CONCLUSIONS

Here we investigated the relation between driver swing motions and golf skill (score) experimentally. First, we measured the variables related to driver movement, ball flight, and the body-twist motion of golfers whose scores range from 80 to 150. The models that relate the score and the measured variables are estimated by multi-regression method. By applying sensitivity analysis to the estimated models, we determined the most effective motions for improving the score. Our results show these motions to be the following:

1. Increase the driver head velocity at the time of impact.

2. Hit the ball high.

3. Reduce the standard deviation of ball initial velocity.

4. Increase the maximum body-twist acceleration.

5. Delay the time when the body-twist angular velocity is maximum in relation to impact time.

6. Reduce the backspin.

References

H. Aoyama, K. Nishida, N. Okawa, M. Ogura, T. Hatori, S. Noro, Y. Abe, T. Yamamoto, "A Study of the Torque at the Gripping in Golf-club Swing—in the case of Women Golf Player," *Tokyo Journal of Physical Education,* pp. 87-92, 1989.

T. Arakawa, Y. Sakino, "Motion Analysis in Golf Swing," *Annual Support Report of Shiga,* vol. 1, pp. 27-30.

T. Ikushima, A. Tenma, T. Yamaguchi, T. Matsumoto, Y. Kaneyoshi, "Investigations on Technical Similarities between Baseball-Batting and Golf-Swing," *Osaka Gakuin University, Natural Science Research Reports,* vol. 19, pp. 21-25, 1989.

K. Kaneko, "Coiling on Golf Swing," *Japan Journal of Golf Science,* vol. 3, no. 2, pp. 1-4, 1990.

K. Kawashima, "Bio-mechanics on Golf—Research on Hints to Improve Golf Swing from the Human Body Apsects, *Japan Journal of Sports Science,* vol. 10, no. 12, 10-12, pp. 777-783, 1991.

K. Kawashima, "Gripping Forces and Hand Acceleration Waves During the Golf Swing," *Japan Journal of Golf Science,* vol. 2, no. 2, pp. 28-32, 1989.

K. Kawashima, "The Bio-mechanics of the Golf Swing—A Partial Application to Golf Swing by Weight Transfer Loci," vol. 10, no. 12, 10-12, pp. 777-783, 1991.

K. Nishida, H. Aoyama, M. Ogura, Y. Abe, T. Yamamoto, "A Study of the Torque at Golf-Club Swing—Measurement of torque on the driver," *Tokyo Journal of Physical Education,* vol. 15, pp. 45-49, 1988.

H. Sato, "Study on Golf Swing—Characteristics of Shift of Center of Gravity of Body at the Impact Timing," *Research Report of Faculty of Economics at Nihhon University,* vol. 14, pp. 31-57, 1991.

H. Sato, "Study on Golf Swing—Shift of Center of Gravity of Body during the Take Back," *Research Report of Faculty of Economics at Nihhon University,* vol. 15, pp. 55-67, 1990.

N. Shimizu, M. Nakamura, "An Analysis Study of Golf Swing with Computer," *Toyko Institute of Technology, Research Reports on Human Science,* vol. 11, pp. 1-28, 1985.

N. Shimizu, M. Nakamura, "An Analysis Study of Golf Swing with Computer," *Toyko Institute of Technology, Research Reports on Human Science,* vol. 12, pp. 61-69, 1986.

M. Taguchi, H. Kajiyama, S. Kitahara, M. Kawakami, H. Nakahara, T. Katamine, "Biomechanical Analysis of Acquisition of Golf Swing Proficiency," *Japan Journal of Golf Science,* vol. 3, no. 2, pp. 82-93, 1990.

N. Tanaka, et al., "Motion of Scapulothoracic Joint in a Golf Swing," *Japanese Journal of Orthopedic Sports Medicine,* vol. 14, no. 1, pp. 79-87.

CHAPTER 5

A Kinematic Analysis of Foot Force Exerted on the Soles During the Golf Swing Among Skilled and Unskilled Golfers

Kazuaki Kawashima
Biomechanics Lab., College of Bioresources Sciences, Nihon University, Fujisawa, Japan

Tetsuo Meshizuka
Japan Society of Golf Sciences, Tokyo, Japan

Shunichi Takeshita
Sports Management Lab., Kanoya Institute of Physical Education, Kanoya, Japan

Small load-cells were placed on the soles of the right and left feet of seven skilled and seven unskilled golfers, and each individual's force exertion patterns in his backswing (BS), downswing (DS), impact (IM), and follow-through (FT) phases were recorded and analyzed. Skilled golfers tended to exert force on the central area of the right foot sole in BS, then transfer it onto the inner edge of the left foot sole in DS, at IM on the left toe and calcaneous area, and by transferring weight onto the left foot in the FT. Unskilled golfers tended to meet IM with force on their right foot, and there was a tendency for the weight to remain there during the FT.

Keywords: Foot force, golf swing, skilled and unskilled golfers.

INTRODUCTION

The golf swing must be executed from power originating from muscular-skeletal energy exerted on the soles, which is utilized there as reactional forces back to the head speed of the club. It is obvious, therefore, that a stable and firm base for both feet is indispensable for a good golf swing, as recommended by many U.S. professional golfers. Wallace et al. (1994) compared sole pressures with and without spiked shoes during the swing to observe the transition of weight transfer. Likewise,

Kawashima (1987) found that skilled golfers always kept their weight within the stance, while the unskilled moved it out of the stance during the swing; in addition, the force volume (against the force plate) exerted onto the stance base in the swing reached 1.6 times body weight in men and 1.4 times body weight in women. Richards et al. (1985) recorded measurements taken from six different plantar areas of the soles. Using a similar technique, we attempted to evaluate the forces exerted on the soles so that the results might be useful in improving the golf swing.

METHODOLOGY

The subjects of the study were seven skilled (handicap = 5.5 ± 1.8) and seven unskilled (handicap = 28.0 ± 4.0) males aged between 19 and 21 years. Foot sizes were measured prior to the experiment, and individuals were selected as subjects who had shoe sizes of 25.0-25.5 cm so that the sole surface remained similar among subjects. Subjects were asked to use only a 5 iron to hit straight balls, and the sole pressures exerted on six different plantar areas were recorded: right and left digitus minimus areas (RDM, LDM), right and left hallux areas (RHA, LHA), and right and left foot calcaneous areas (RCA, LCA). (See figures 5.1 and 5.2.)

The forces on these six areas were measured by six small sensors (diameter 12 mm) placed onto the soles, with calibration up to 100 N made individually for each sensor. A video camera was utilized to record the phases of the swing as described earlier, and IM phase was recorded by means of a laser sensor (1 ms).

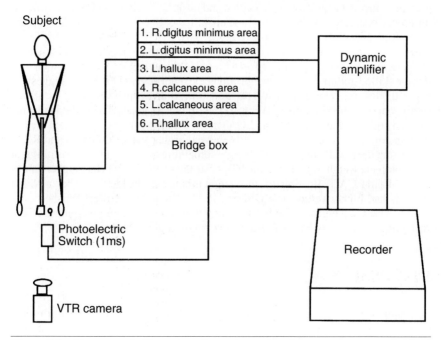

Figure 5.1   Diagrammatic illustration of experimental environment.

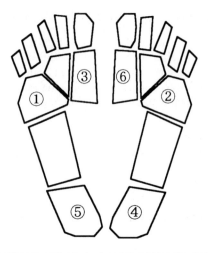

Figure 5.2   Measured foot force areas: (1) LDM, (2) RDM, (3) LHA, (4) RCA, (5) LCA, (6) RHA.

RESULTS

Tables 5.1 to 5.3 and figure 5.3 show the results of the analysis of plantar foot pressures during the golf swing in skilled and unskilled golfers. In BS, a significant difference occurred between skilled and unskilled golfers in LCA and RDM. In the other four areas of the foot soles (LDM, LHA, RHA, RCA), no significant differences were found between the two groups with their weight loaded less than 30 N. In DS, the skilled put more force onto RDM and RHA. This result indicates that the skilled golfers put more weight along the inner edges of both feet, suggesting a greater leg movement and weight transfer. At IM, the two groups differed significantly in the amounts of force exerted in the six areas. The skilled subjects showed higher values on LHA and LCA, and at IM they put more weight on the left foot. In contrast, the unskilled subjects showed higher values on RDM and RCA, suggesting they make impact with weight remaining on the right foot, resulting in an incomplete weight transfer. In the FT phase, the skilled golfers had higher values on LDM and LCA, indicating that the weight is borne on the left foot. The unskilled subjects had higher values on RDM and RCA. The skilled golfers finished their swings with the weight on the left foot, and they also kept more weight on RHA, sustaining their steady FT by putting force on the right toes.

DISCUSSION

Few studies have been conducted on the forces exerted onto the soles during the swing, despite belief in the importance of forces and weight placed and transferred

Table 5.1   The Maximal Force Values (N) of Foot Force Pressure During the Golf Swing (Skilled)

Skilled	(n = 7)					(N)	
		LDM	RDM	LHA	RHA	LCA	RCA
BS	M	4.86	17.71	14.71	16.18	24.29	17.71
	SD	2.80	4.50	2.71	3.56	7.42	2.31
DS	M	12.29	51.71	16.43	38.57	18.57	21.29
	SD	3.92	19.50	2.38	3.25	1.68	2.96
IM	M	8.71	16.00	37.29	19.00	45.00	16.29
	SD	1.58	3.21	4.74	3.46	4.87	3.41
FT	M	33.43	25.71	21.86	22.71	62.43	15.29
	SD	3.92	7.25	3.18	3.24	5.80	1.39

Left digitus minimus area = LDM, Right digitus minimus area = RDM, Left hallux area = LHA, Right hallux area = RHA, Left calcaneous area = LCA, Right calcaneous area = RCA
Back swing = BS, Down swing = DS, Impact = IM, Follow through = FT
M = Mean, SD = Standard deviation

Table 5.2   The Maximal Force Values (N) of Foot Force Pressure During the Golf Swing (Unskilled)

Unskilled	(n = 7)					(N)	
		LDM	RDM	LHA	RHA	LCA	RCA
BS	M	4.86	11.14	13.57	13.14	10.43	16.86
	SD	2.36	3.76	3.02	3.98	1.29	2.03
DS	M	24.71	14.86	14.29	12.29	21.71	21.71
	SD	3.45	4.10	3.06	3.24	3.49	2.71
IM	M	20.14	39.43	23.14	12.14	31.86	34.43
	SD	4.36	11.16	4.64	2.03	4.26	4.72
FT	M	16.71	39.43	17.71	7.71	40.43	33.86
	SD	6.13	11.16	1.39	1.39	4.27	3.27

Table 5.3   Significant Differences (t Test) Between the Groups

t Test	(Skilled = 7, Unskilled = 7)					
	LDM	RDM	LHA	RHA	LCA	RCA
BS	0.00 N.S	2.90 *	0.60 N.S	1.70 N.S	4.59 ***	0.68 N.S
DS	5.83 ***	4.89 ***	1.35 N.S	14.00 ***	1.98 N.S	0.26 N.S
IM	6.00 ***	5.38 ***	5.22 ***	4.18 ***	5.37 ***	7.63 ***
FT	5.62 ***	2.72 *	2.92 *	10.43 ***	7.47 ***	12.80 ***

p < .05 = *, p < .001 = ***, N.S = Non significant

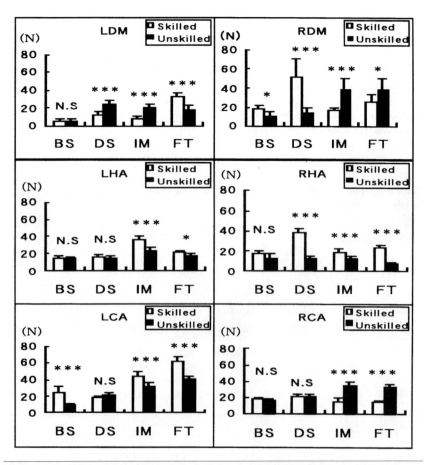

Figure 5.3   Maximal foot force of phases BS, DS, IM, and FT during the golf swing: LDM, RDM, LHA, RCA, LCA, RHA.

p < .05; = *; p < .001 = ***; N.S: nonsignificant.

during the golf swing. Generally speaking, sole movements are carried out involuntarily, but they are affected by environmental conditions and the mental status of the golfer. We assumed, for instance, that the fit and size of golf shoes affect the swing; consequently all the subjects of this study wore their fitted shoes. The four phases of the golf swing were recorded and analyzed with regard to the force exerted on the plantar surface of the foot soles. Statistically valid differences were found between skilled and unskilled golfers in BS, DS, IM, and FT. We suggest that unskilled golfers try to keep their weight within a central area of the right foot sole (RDM to RHA) and a central area of the left foot sole (LHA to LCA). The unskilled golfers failed to transfer body weight between the right and left foot during the swing.

The stability of the lower body seems to be quite important for a smooth transfer of weight in a good golf swing; it is also important for execution of the most effective swing with a higher clubhead velocity. A firm and steady stance, with sole pressure kept within the inner edges of the feet, helps keep the golfer from losing uncoiling power generated by the trunk rotary motion to be conveyed from the hip, back, shoulders, arms, ankles, and shaft to the clubhead.

ACKNOWLEDGMENTS

Our gratitude goes to Mr. Yozo Hasegawa (Mizuno Sport Co. Ltd.), who generously provided golf shoes for our study, and also Nihon University students of the College of Bioresources, who faithfully cooperated with us in our data analyses: Messrs. H. Tozaki, T. Kitagawa, Y. Nonaka, T. Fujikawa, S. Fukuda, and Miss T. Aramaki.

References

Kawashima, K. (1987) The biomechanics of golf swing: A practical application to golf swing by weight transfer loci. *Japanese Journal of Golf Science* 1(1): 34-40.

Richards, J., Farrell, M., Kent, J., and Kraft, R. (1985) Weight transfer patterns during the golf swing. *Research Quarterly for Exercise and Sports* 56(4): 361-365.

Wallence, E.S., Grimsaw, P.N., and Ashford, R.L. (1994) Discrete pressure profiles of the feet and weight transfer patterns during the golf swing. *Science and Golf II. Proceedings of the World Scientific Congress of Golf,* 26-32.

CHAPTER 6

The Effects of Proprioceptive Neuromuscular Facilitation Flexibility Training on the Clubhead Speed of Recreational Golfers

D. Jones
Montclair State University, USA

Sixteen recreational golfers participated in an eight-week training study designed to examine the effect of proprioceptive neuromuscular facilitation (PNF) flexibility on clubhead speed during simulated golf swings. Pre- and posttraining measurements were recorded for hip, shoulder, and trunk joint ranges of motion and clubhead speed. The PNF flexibility treatment induced a significant increase in joint flexibility and clubhead speed. These results imply that performance enhancement measured consequent to the flexibility training was a direct result of the enhanced muscle and tendon elasticity contribution to the effectiveness and efficiency of performance.

Keywords: Proprioceptive neuromuscular facilitation (PNF), golf, clubhead speed.

INTRODUCTION

Speed is defined as the distance covered divided by the time it takes to cover that distance. Each golf drive has two requirements: distance and direction. In order to hit a tee shot of maximum distance, the clubhead must attain maximum speed upon impact of the club to the ball. Numerous studies have been conducted to help determine what factors affect clubhead speed, for example, Jorgensen in 1970 and Milburn in 1982. However, there seems to be no agreement on exactly what factors create this maximum speed.

In 1982, Milburn classified the factors that affect clubhead speed into three categories:

1. Greater muscular force applied through the limb segments
2. An increased distance over which the force acts

3. The number of segments that are brought into action and the sequence in which they contribute to the final velocity

Greater muscular force can be produced when a concentric contraction is preceded by a stretching eccentric phase. The force, power, and work produced are greater than for a contraction without prestretch (Cavagna, Dusman, and Margaria 1968). An increased distance over which the forces act can be achieved by increasing range of motion, thereby enabling the golfer to potentially create more torque in the upper body. The number of segments that are brought into action during a golf swing was not the focus of this study.

The purpose of the present study was to examine the effect of flexibility training on the clubhead speed of recreational golfers. Prior research by numerous investigators (Sady, Wortman, and Blanke 1982; Prentice 1983) showed that proprioceptive neuromuscular facilitation (PNF) techniques produced the largest gains in flexibility as compared with other forms of stretching. The experimental hypothesis was that the PNF flexibility training would increase joint range of motion, creating greater muscular force in the stretching eccentric phase, increasing distance over which the forces act, thereby increasing clubhead speed.

METHODS

Subjects

Sixteen right-handed recreational golfers participated in the study; ages ranged from 47 through 82, with a mean age of 58 ± 9. Club handicaps ranged from 8 to 34, with a mean of 18 ± 7. Each subject was screened prior to participation in the study by answering a medical health history profile.

Protocol

Using Norkin and White's (1985) standards for joint range of motion measurements, sequential measures of each subject's dominant side were determined utilizing a goniometer. Specifically, shoulder abduction, shoulder external rotation, hip flexion, and hip extension were measured. Right and left trunk rotation were also recorded pre- and posttraining.

The subject's clubhead speed was measured utilizing a SwingMate by Beltronics. The validity of the SwingMate was tested against the Titleist Flight Analyzer (T.F.A.), the present industry standard, at the United States Golf Association's Research and Testing Center. Thirty trials were recorded. Between the two instruments' measures there was a mean absolute difference of 3.3 miles per hour, ± 1.91, indicating the acceptable accuracy of the SwingMate. There was a five-minute warm-up period. Then, using their own drivers, subjects performed five golf swings, swinging over the SwingMate. The mean of these last five swings was then recorded. These swings were performed indoors on a prepared tee-box area without the use of a tee or golf ball. However, there was a visual reference in the form of a marker that was placed on the surface where the tee would have been.

Flexibility Treatment

Subjects participated in an eight-week experimental study conducted pre-golf season (February and March, 1997). The group met three times per week for 45 minutes each session. The PNF method of flexibility was taught to the subjects. Specifically, each subject stretched in a three-step sequence. Step one involved a six-second maximal contraction of a specified muscle group. During this contraction, resistance to movement was facilitated by an opposing force, either a towel or the subject's arm. Next, each subject moved the limb passively, through as large a range of motion as possible to the point where limitation of movement was felt. During step three, the subject remained in this static position for 15 seconds. The process was repeated three times for each muscle group. Joints targeted were the shoulders and hips bilaterally and the spine. Muscles targeted were the rotator cuff muscles, pectorals, triceps, hamstring group, hip adductors, hip abductors, and the internal and external abdominal oblique muscles (Evjenth and Hamberg 1989; McAtee 1993).

RESULTS

The statistical analysis used in this study was a t-test for dependent measures with a criterion p-value set at .001. Pre- and posttraining goniometer measures of hip flexion and extension, shoulder abduction and external rotation, and trunk rotation right and left were taken for all subjects. Table 6.1 contains the pre- and posttraining mean values and standard deviations and the percentage change for each joint angle measure and for clubhead speed. The results of the PNF flexibility training demonstrated a significant change ($p < .001$) (see table 6.1). Pre- and posttraining measures for clubhead speed were also recorded for each subject using the SwingMate. A mean increase of 5.56 miles per hour was measured. This represents an increase of 7.2%, p-value of .0004.

Table 6.1   Mean (±SD) Values, (n = 16) for Joint ROMs and Club Head Speed

Variable	Pre ±	Post ±	% Change
Hip flexion	80.31 ± 6.73	86.00 ± 9.06	7.1
Hip extension	18.56 ± 3.67	25.13 ± 6.42	35.3
Shoulder abduct.	146.25 ± 17.16	158.88 ± 13.51	8.6
Shoulder ext. rot.	84.44 ± 6.77	91.94 ± 10.64	8.9
Trunk rot. right	33.50 ± 8.66	41.38 ± 6.76	23.5
Trunk rot. left	26.13 ± 5.29	32.69 ± 5.85	25.1
Clubhead speed+	77.31 ± 12.46	82.88 ± 9.91	7.2

+mph   Significant $p \leq 0.001$

DISCUSSION

Flexibility is a component of athletic performance that is usually associated with an increase in range of motion and injury prevention. Prior research has supported the belief that the more flexible an athlete is, the better the athletic performance (Beaulieu 1981). For the golfer, an increase in performance can be equated, in part, to an increase in clubhead speed.

Range of motion of a joint can be increased through flexibility training (Hartley-O'Brien 1980). However, PNF flexibility has not been widely used as a technique for increasing flexibility. This may be due to the belief that PNF technique can be performed only with a partner. In this study, PNF technique was taught without the assistance of a partner. Significant increases were measured in all joint ranges of motion treated with PNF flexibility.

The possibility that mechanical energy may be temporarily stored in the series elastic components of active muscles for reuse in a following contraction was investigated by Asmussen and Bonde-Peterson (1974). The ability to preload or store energy elastically within contractile and viscoelastic musculotendinous components becomes the cornerstone of sport performance. Therefore, stretching a muscle-tendon system allows for more elastic energy to be stored and more recovery of energy to occur. The results of the present study support this statement. The increases measured in the specific joint ranges of motion of the subjects had a positive effect on their athletic performance as seen in the increases in clubhead speed.

One question arises from this study: Did the increase in any one joint's range of motion contribute more than that in any other to the gains measured in clubhead speed? The answer cannot be determined from this investigation. Additional research needs to be done. Another possible concern regarding flexibility training may be whether there can be too much flexibility of a joint as it pertains to athletic performance. This is also an area that needs further investigation.

In conclusion, muscle and tendon elasticity contribute to the effectiveness and efficiency of human performance through the mechanisms of force enhancement and elastic energy storage. The influence of elasticity is most valuable in activities that include the eccentric stretch of an active muscle group prior to a concentric contraction. Results of this study demonstrated that increases in joint range of motion could be obtained through PNF flexibility training, which subsequently increased clubhead speed. Therefore, the use of PNF flexibility training may be a positive step in maximizing the individual potential of recreational golfers.

References

Asmussen, E., and F. Bonde-Peterson. 1974. Apparent efficiency and storage of elastic energy in human muscles during exercise. *Acta Physiol. Scand.* 92: 537-545.

Beaulieu, J. 1981. Developing a stretching program. *The Physician and Sports Medicine* 9: 59-69.

Cavagna, G., B. Dusman, and R. Margaria. 1968. Positive work done by a previously stretched muscle. *Journal of Applied Physiology* 24(1): 21-32.

Evjenth, O., and J. Hamberg. 1989. *Auto stretching*. Milan, Italy: New Interlitho Spa.

Hartley-O'Brien, S. 1980. Six mobilization exercises for active range of hip flexion. *Research Quarterly for Exercise and Sport* 51(4): 625-635.

Jorgensen, T. 1970. On the dynamics of the swing of a golf club. *American Journal of Physics* 38(5): 644-651.

McAtee, R. 1993. *Facilitated stretching.* Champaign, IL: Human Kinetics.

Milburn, P.D. 1980. Summation of segmental velocities in the golf swing. *Medicine and Science in Sports and Exercise* 14(1): 60-64.

Norkin, C.C., and D.J. White. 1985. *Measurement of joint motion. A guide to goniometry.* Philadelphia: Davis.

Prentice, W. 1983. A comparison of static stretching and PNF stretching for improving hip joint flexibility. *Athletic Training* 56-59.

Sady, S., M. Wortman, and D. Blanke. 1982. Flexibility training: ballistic, static of PNF? *Archives of Physical Medicine Rehabilitation* 63: 261-263.

CHAPTER 7

Golf: Exercise for Fitness and Health

G. Magnusson
Department of Physiology and Pharmacology, Karolinska Institute, and Department of Human Biology, College of Physical Education, Stockholm, Sweden

This study examined the physiological responses in middle-aged golfers during the game of golf. The issue to be resolved was whether golf may be classified as aerobic training for fitness for middle-aged individuals.

In 19 middle-aged golfers, heart rate, blood pressure, and oxygen uptake responses were assessed during golf play. Three golf holes with differing degrees of incline in the terrain represented the work to be performed on a golf course.

The mean relative work intensity for the golfers varied between 43% and 55% of maximal oxygen uptake. The main source of energy was derived from fat. The heart rate and systolic blood pressure varied continuously. The female golfers had higher heart rates and lower systolic blood pressure than the male golfers.

Golf is low- to moderate-intensity exercise, with interval character and long duration, which will maintain or increase the aerobic power in middle-aged individuals, indirectly contributing to health and longevity.

Keywords: Middle-aged golfer, oxygen uptake, heart rate, blood pressure, workload, fitness.

INTRODUCTION

Golf has not directly been associated with exercise for aerobic fitness. It is obvious that golf is a low-intensity type of exercise. It is, however, performed over a fairly long period of time (4 hours/round) compared to other normal exercise activities such as walking, working out, or jogging. Even though all golfers know how strenuous a round of golf may be, it remains to be shown how middle-aged male and female golfers physiologically respond during the game of golf and what health effects might result from playing golf (walking) on a regular basis.

METHOD

Nineteen middle-aged golfers (10 male—age 48.9 [4.9] years, weight 8.24 [14.8] kg; 9 female—age 46.9 [3.4] years, weight 66.9 [7.2] kg) played three specially selected golf holes. Heart rate was measured with a Holter monitor. Blood pressure was obtained by sphygmomanometry. Oxygen uptake was determined by using the Douglas bag technique. Air was collected in each bag for at least 90 s during the walking on the golf course. Gas volumes were measured in a Tissot spirometer. The fractions of oxygen and carbon dioxide were measured with an oxygen analyzer (AMTEC) and a carbon dioxide analyzer (Beckman LB2), respectively. On a separate occasion, maximal oxygen uptake was determined on a treadmill, in the laboratory, using an incremental protocol.

Three golf holes were selected in order to demonstrate responses on different slopes of the terrain. The first hole was flat, sloping downhill toward the green. The second hole was flat, sloping a little uphill toward the green. The last hole was slightly uphill with a steeper incline toward the green. Heart rate was monitored continuously, blood pressure was taken during both rest and exercise, and oxygen uptake was taken when the subjects walked the characteristic part of each hole. There was no pressure on the subjects to perform golf at a high level.

Statistics: Values in the text are mean with standard deviation (SD). Analysis of variance was used to test intra- and intergroup differences. Paired t-tests were applied to analyse intragroup differences. The level of significance was set at $p < 0.05$.

RESULTS

During the golf game, the heart rate varied continuously for both men and women (figure 7.1). The heart rates never reached resting values during stops or when subjects were performing a shot. Rather the heart rates tended to rise when the golfer tried to hit the golf ball.

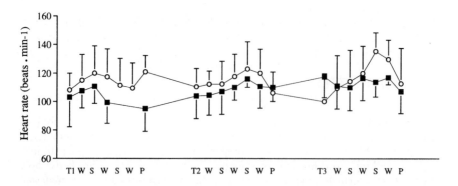

Figure 7.1   Variations in mean heart rate on three golf holes. Open circles (O) represent women, and filled squares (■) represent men. T, tee; W, walk; S, shot; P, putt. Values are means (SD).

Table 7.1   Heart Rate at Rest and Maximal Exercise, Resting Blood Pressure, and Maximal Oxygen Uptake

	n	Heart rate (Beats · min⁻¹) Rest	Heart rate (Beats · min⁻¹) Max	Blood pressure (mm Hg) Systolic/Diastolic	$\dot{V}O_2$ $1 \cdot min^{-1}$ Max	$\dot{V}O_2$ $(ml \cdot kg \cdot min^{-1})$ Max
Men	10	68 (7)	176 (13)	123 (19)/77 (9)	3.14 (0.49)	38.5 (5.0)
Women	9	73 (9)	182 (9)	111 (14)/70 (8)	2.21 (0.39)	33.2 (3.4)

Values are given as means (SD).

When the mean maximal heart rate (table 7.2) during walking was related to the maximal heart rate, the male golfers reached 68% and 66% of their maximal heart rate on the first and second golf holes. The women walked at 74% and 72% of maximal heart rate on those holes. At the third hole, the male and female golfers walked at 73% and 80% of maximal heart rate, respectively.

The absolute oxygen uptake for all golfers was lowest at the first hole, 10% ($p < 0.05$) higher at the second hole, and 26% ($p < 0.05$) higher at the third hole (figure 7.2A). The rise in aerobic power from hole 1 to hole 3 describes an increase of average workload. The oxygen uptake for the male golfers was about 30% ($p < 0.05$) higher than that of the female golfers at each of the three golf holes.

The relative oxygen uptake showed a similar pattern for men and women (figure 7.2B). The lowest power output was recorded at the first hole; output was somewhat higher at the second hole and was highest at the third hole. The mean relative intensity of work (the relative oxygen uptake divided by the maximal oxygen uptake) varied between 43% and 55% of maximal oxygen uptake with no difference between men and women. There was no difference in this value between the three golf holes. However, five of the women reached work intensities of between 59% and 71% of their maximal oxygen uptake.

The mean respiratory exchange ratios (RER; determines the mixture of food being utilized as fuel in the process of producing energy) were between 0.74 and 0.78 for both male and female golfers (figure 7.3A). The RER values were similarly

Table 7.2   Mean Maximal Heart Rates During Walking on Three Different Fairways

Group	n	Hole 1	Hole 2	Hole 3
Men	10	120 (104-137)	117 (101-131)	128 (102-150)*
Women	9	135 (120-164)	131 (112-154)	146 (131-161)*

Values are given as means (min - max values).

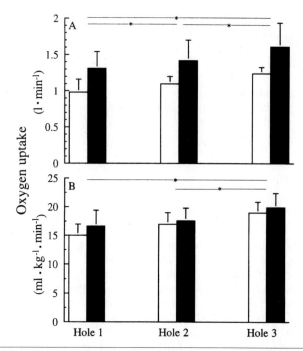

Figure 7.2   Absolute oxygen uptake (A) and relative oxygen uptake (B) on three golf holes for women (unfilled bars) and men (filled bars). Values are means (SD).

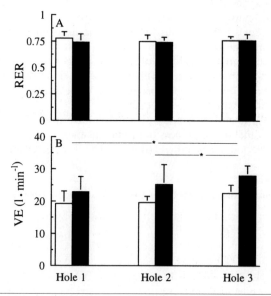

Figure 7.3   Respiratory exchange ratio (RER) and pulmonary ventilation (VE) during walking on three different golf holes. Women are represented by unfilled bars and men by filled bars. Values are means (SD).

independent of the type of golf hole being played. This implies that about 80% of the energy was derived from fat and 20% from carbohydrates.

On hole 1, the golfers had the lowest recorded pulmonary ventilation (figure 7.3B). The pulmonary ventilation was not altered at hole 2, whereas it was raised by 21% ($p < 0.05$) on the third hole. This indicates an increased demand for oxygen. The pulmonary ventilation for the male golfers was between 17% and 26% higher than that of the female golfers on the three golf holes.

The systolic blood pressures for the golfers were close to resting values at the three tees (figure 7.4). During the walking on the first and second fairway, the systolic blood pressure rose by 7% ($p < 0.05$); it rose by 13% ($p < 0.05$) on the third fairway. The male golfers had an approximate 30% ($p < 0.05$) higher systolic blood pressure than the females at the tees as well as during walking. The diastolic blood pressures were unchanged throughout the test. None of the golfers reached any extremely high blood pressure values.

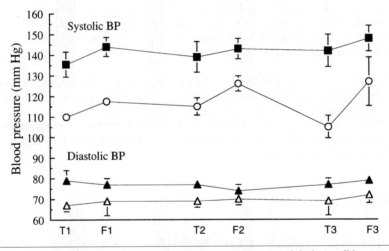

Figure 7.4   Mean systolic and diastolic blood pressure at tee and during walking on fairway. Open circles (O) represent women and filled squares (■) men. T, tee; F, fairway. Values are means (SD).

DISCUSSION

Playing golf was low- to moderate-intensity aerobic exercise for the presently investigated middle-aged female and male golfers.

The present golfers walked at an intensity of about 50% (individual variations between 35% and 70%) of their maximal aerobic power, primarily reflecting the variations of the terrain, since these golfers could not be defined as sedentary. Thus, they pursued exercise at an intensity that is classified at light to moderate (American College of Sports Medicine 1990). An aerobic training effect can be expected, but is dependent on the duration of exercise at a certain intensity. Furthermore, the exercise intensity will be determined by the terrain: a hilly golf course will put a higher strain on the aerobic capacity than a flat golf course. In addition, the length of the walking intervals will depend on skill level, age, and sex. A skilled golfer, who hits the ball far, will get long and few intervals of walking. In contrast, the majority of females and elderly men hit the ball fairly short, which will result in several short walking intervals.

The fluctuations in heart rate and blood pressure in the present golfers were within normal range for exercise. Even though these factors may be affected by mental stress, causing a rise in both heart rate and blood pressure, such changes are highly individual and will probably come most into play during competitive golf.

The present golfers derived about 80% of the energy from fat during the play. In contrast, in activities with a higher intensity of aerobic exercise, the major portion of energy will be derived from carbohydrates (80%) (McArdle, Katch, and Katch 1986). The total amount of energy used by the present golfers is estimated to be 700 kcal/round for the females and 900 kcal/round for the males. Interestingly, according to Paffenbarger et al. (1986), individuals whose weekly energy output during exercise was 2000 or more kcal were found to live approximately two years longer than less active individuals (energy expenditure < 500 kcal/week). Therefore, it may be speculated that if a middle-aged golfer plays three 18-hole rounds per week, he/ she will reach that criterion of caloric expenditure, potentially leading to a longer life.

Since regular walking has been found to increase aerobic fitness, improve blood lipid profile, decrease body weight, and lower blood pressure, causing a low number of orthopaedic problems (Porcari et al. 1989; Davison and Grant 1993), and since few individuals but golfers walk 12 to 16 hours per week on a regular basis, it may be proposed that golf indirectly may contribute to physical health and reduce the risk for coronary heart disease.

CONCLUSION

Golf (walking) for middle-aged individuals is exercise at low to moderate intensity and long duration, which may increase or maintain aerobic fitness and promote health.

ACKNOWLEDGMENTS

The guidance by Professor Bengt Saltin and the technical assistance by Anne-Britt Olrog are greatly appreciated. This study was supported by grants from the Swedish Golf Association.

References

American College of Sports Medicine. Position Stand. 1990. The recommended quantity and quality of exercise for developing and maintaining cardiorespiratory and muscular fitness in healthy adults. *Medicine and Science in Sport and Exercise* 22: 265-274.

Davison, R.C.R., and S. Grant. 1993. Is walking sufficient exercise for health? *Sports Medicine* 16(6): 369-373.

McArdle, W.D., F.I Katch, and V.L. Katch, eds. 1986. *Exercise Physiology.* 2d ed. Philadelphia: Lea & Febiger.

Paffenbarger, R.S., et al. 1986. Physical activity, all-cause mortality, longevity of college alumni. *New England Journal of Medicine* 314: 605-613.

Porcari, J.P., et al. 1989. Walking for exercise testing and training. *Sports Medicine* 8: 189-200.

CHAPTER 8

Physiological Profiling and Physical Conditioning for Elite Golfers

H.M. Lennon
MacGregor Golf Academy, Golfing Union of Ireland Training Centre, Dublin, Ireland

Golf is a highly individual sport with no two golfers having the same physique or golf swing. The underlying problem on which the following studies are based is that little is known about the physiological development or physical characteristics of elite golfers. The objectives were to assess physiological components considered important for high-level performance, decrease the incidence of golf injuries among national players, and raise the level of performance in Irish golf. Descriptive data gained from the studies suggest that there are specific anthropometric and physiological differences between golfers at various levels. The findings indicate significant changes in body mass, grip strength, leg strength, shoulder and trunk flexibility, aerobic endurance, and the skill level and performance of golfers on physical conditioning programs. The programs developed from the studies place emphasis on particular areas of physical development, movement and proprioceptor training, and new, more holistic approaches to golf practice and training.

Keywords: Physiological profiling, physical conditioning, performance, proprioceptor training.

INTRODUCTION

Physical fitness is a key parameter for almost every sport. In golf, attention has traditionally focused on the technical, tactical, and mental aspects of the game to the relative neglect of physiological factors. Today, however, many players appreciate the physical demands of the sport and recognise that a good fitness level is paramount to good performance. Elite golfers require strength and flexibility in key body areas. Differences exist between tour players and amateurs. Tour players are able to rotate much faster in the swing (McTeigue et al. 1994). The golf swing produces tremendous forces with intense loading of the lumbar spine (Hosea et al. 1990). Professional golfers are subjected to these forces for a shorter time and they can accelerate mainly in the last stages of the downswing, creating more power with less effort. Amateurs are less efficient in their loading patterns due probably to a combination of inferior swing mechanics and physique.

Numerous factors go into creating optimal performance; some of these are coordination, strength, flexibility, technique, muscular endurance, cardiovascular fitness, proprioception, and mental toughness. In the golf swing, a crucial factor in the skilled movement of elite golfers is the importance of flexibility as a biomechanical parameter. The difference between good skill and excellent skill is simply a matter of degree. Flexibility can provide the crucial difference between good and outstanding performance (Lennon 1996). Somatotype, weight, skin-fold thickness, and body surface area have all been investigated in terms of their relationships to flexibility. Correlations between flexibility and somatotype are generally found to be insignificant (McCue 1963), perhaps providing one explanation why elite golfers range in somatotype. While elite golfers do vary in body type, total muscular balance is ideal. The physical conditioning programs used in the studies targeted trunk rotators, legs (quadriceps, gastrocnemius, hamstrings), lower back, left forearm flexor, upper back, abdominals, abductors and adductors, triceps, and rotator cuff.

Elite players, like the normal population, also tend to favour a dominant side and may possess greater strength, coordination, and proprioceptor awareness on one side. Professionals may become overdeveloped on one side, resulting occasionally in injury (Delacave 1997). Studies have provided evidence of the effect of dominant laterality on the normal musculoskeletal system. Hand grips are stronger and bone density is reportedly greater on the dominant side (Haywood 1980). Conditioning programs must be designed to address the fact that the golf swing is a balanced movement with equal muscular output on each side. Centinela research has shown that in the golf swing, the right side is at least as active as the left.

RESEARCH

When great players build a golf swing, they do not try to do things with their body that it is not capable of doing. Their repeatable swings are in compliance with the natural laws of force and motion, showing body control, club control, and swing control (Hebron 1993). Effort-free swings are based on a transfer of momentum from proximal-end links to distal-end links. In many golf swings, too much effort is made, precipitating injuries. Golf swing analysis of the subjects revealed that this was so. Statistical injury reports from the European Tour highlight the necessity for physical conditioning for elite golfers. Research has shown that torso-conditioning exercises can increase rotational power output (Larkin et al. 1990).

Two studies were performed with subjects from the Irish National squads: Study A, an investigation into a golf-specific strength and flexibility program, and Study B, physiological profiling and physical conditioning for elite golfers.

Study A: An Investigation Into a Golf-Specific Strength and Flexibility Program

The primary aim of this study was to investigate the effects of a golf-specific conditioning program on junior golfers to determine whether they could increase the distance a golf ball could be struck with a 5 iron. Fourteen junior golfers (mean age ± SD = 16 ± 0.4 yrs) were randomly assigned to either a control or an experimental group. Anthropometric measures were taken; the subjects performed a number of physical performance tests, and each completed a 5-iron test that measured both distance and accuracy. The experimental group were given a conditioning program to be performed four times weekly, and all subjects were retested after eight weeks.

The research hypothesis suggests that by applying positive changes to the body a golfer will acquire greater control of the club and an improvement in distance. On completion of the conditioning program, the experimental group improved in a number of the physical fitness tests; more significantly, they improved in skill performance. Compliance was high, with only one golfer unable to complete the conditioning program.

Statistically significant changes ($p < 0.05$) in body mass, grip strength, leg strength, and aerobic endurance and in the 5-iron skill test occurred. In shoulder rotation, which is a very important flexibility characteristic for golf, the experimental group again improved significantly (Scheffe F-test = 3.59, $p < 0.05$). The control group was similar between pretest and posttest, but it should be noted that this group was slightly less flexible at the onset (table 8.1).

Table 8.1   Means and Standard Deviations for Flexibility Tests

Test	Pretest	Posttest
Sit & reach (cm)		
Experimental (n = 7)	8.0 ± 2.3	11.1 ± 2.7
Control (n = 7)	11.0 ± 3.6	10.4 ± 1.5
Shoulder rotation (cm)		
Experimental (n = 7)	49.0 ± 16.9	22.7 ± 17.7*
Control (n = 7)	51.5 ± 14.2	56.4 ± 11.1

Note: A lower numerical reading in shoulder rotation denotes a higher flexibility.

*Significant differences ($p < 0.05$)

Discussion

The golfers in the experimental group improved in both strength and flexibility and were better able to fully rotate the club on an inside plane and straight to target. They acquired more power following the conditioning program, enabling them to send the ball farther while still remaining balanced. This may be attributed to the significant improvement in shoulder rotation, as more power can be generated when the angles are increased. However, it may also be that an overall improvement in physical condition results in an improvement in skill level.

Improvement in strength, particularly grip strength, occurred in the experimental group. The hands must be stronger than neutral to prevent manipulation of the club. This is important if the club is to be delivered squarely onto the ball, the ultimate objective of the golf swing. Hand and arm strength is crucial for elite golfers. Every good swing should go down and out to follow through, and both arms are stretched down plane by a centrifugal reaction. This is the only time when both arms are straight. A golf swing will never function without a good arm swing (Jacobs and Bowden 1972).

Leg power ability also improved. Leg strength is necessary to pivot correctly and to hold the resistance. Strength in the legs enables the golfer to maintain stability and remain balanced throughout the swing. Although the strength characteristics of the golfers in the experimental group improved, this was not at the expense of flexibility. They achieved flexibility gains in the shoulders, wrists, hamstrings, and lower back. The improvement in hamstring and lower back flexibility did not reach significant levels; a longer period of time would be necessary to effect significant changes in these areas.

In the 5-iron skill test, the experimental group improved significantly, hitting the ball consistently farther than the control group. They were able to achieve greater distance with less effort and still retain their accuracy.

Sound golf swings use the large muscles of the body to generate the momentum in the swing. The arms, hands, and wrists must not work independently. Obviously the more correlated they are to the centre or body pivot, the more consistent the golf swing becomes in terms of direction, angle, and power. Good flexibility is required to achieve a well-connected, compact golf swing.

The study shows correlations between physical fitness and the ability to strike a golf ball for distance and accuracy. The information gained assists in prescribing physical conditioning programs to improve fitness and skill levels.

Study B: Physiological Profiling and Physical Conditioning for Elite Golfers

Twenty-eight males took part in this study; two were European Tour players, while the remainder were members of the Irish National panels. The aim of the study was to investigate player profiling, the physiological changes arising from physical conditioning, and the effects of the training on the golf swing and performance. Physical performance tests were both static and dynamic. A high-speed video computer system (V.Com) with 3-D cameras and a computer graphic measuring facility was used to measure dynamic flexibility during the swing. Appropriate physical conditioning and practice programs were given to each golfer. Golfers with dominant laterality were given exercises to strengthen the weaker side. The training programs encouraged a balance between strength and flexibility; they included specific exercises for flexibility, muscular strength, muscular endurance, movement speed, cardiovascular endurance, and proprioceptor training to be performed four times weekly.

The conditioning programs focused on specific performance variables at different times in the year. All golfers were retested one year later. Significant improvements occurred in their physical condition; a statistically significant improvement in dynamic flexibility ($p < 0.05$) also occurred (see figure 8.1). Golfers in each category achieved their best-ever performances. The Irish Boys Team won the R & A Home International title for the first time; and the Tour players recorded their highest earnings, with both finishing in the top five of the British Open. Ireland (inclusive of one of these above players) also won the World Cup at Kiawah Island. Research on this project is continuing; however, the major findings so far indicate the following:

- Physical conditioning is important for high-level performance; there is a strong relationship between a golfer's physical condition and the ability to produce power in the swing.

- Profiling players to highlight weaknesses in range of motion, and addressing these through flexibility programs, improve performance and reduce injury.

- Strength and flexibility gains improved rotational power; they also enable the player to hold the club on the target line for longer.

- Golfers who were in relatively poor physical condition were in one year able to achieve good muscular balance.

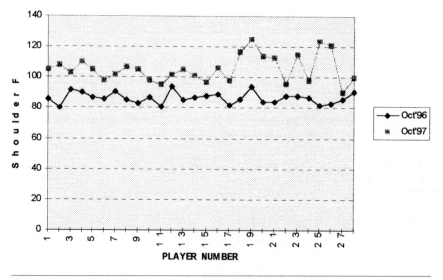

Figure 8.1   V.COM. FLEX Analysis Pre/Post Exercise Programme.

CONDITIONING PROGRAMS

Each conditioning session began with a warm-up. It was composed of a selection of the following: aerobic work (cross-training), strength exercises, pivot exercises, golf drills, flexibility exercises, and proprioceptor training (see table 8.2). The year

Table 8.2   Conditioning Program Schedule

Period 1 Oct.–Jan.	Period 2 Feb.–May	Period 3 June–Sept.
Aerobic training—cycling, jogging, fitness walking	Aerobic training—cycling, jogging, fitness walking	Pivot exercises
Resistance training	Resistance Training	Flexibility exercises
Muscular endurance	Muscular endurance	Golf drills
Pivot exercises	Pivot exercises	Proprioceptor training
Flexibility exercises	Flexibility exercises	
	Golf drills	
	Proprioceptor training	

was split into three four-month periods for training purposes, each focused on specific training performance variables. Golfers were continually assessed and their programs adjusted accordingly. Compliance was high (90%), with players being regularly interviewed and assessed.

CONCLUSION

Improving the distance a golfer can strike a ball while still maintaining accuracy greatly improves the chances of making birdies, vital for success in today's game. The concomitant improvement in shoulder rotation allowed the golfers to increase the angle of backswing without disturbing their ability to remain balanced. More power can be generated when the angles can be increased (Hebron 1993). Improvements in the wrist flexibility of many of the subjects allowed the wrist cock to function correctly as an integral part of the backswing and not as an independent action. The wrists must be flexible to enable the wrist cock to occur as a natural reflex action in response to the swinging weight of the clubhead so as to cock the club correctly in plane. One of the most important features of a good golf swing is the ability to keep the spine angle constant (McTeigue et al. 1994); improving trunk flexibility enhanced the golfers' ability to maintain their spine angle.

The quality of training in golf has suffered from an overriding concentration by coaches and players on parts of the golf swing without sufficient attention being given to the process of integrating physical development, swing mechanics, and mental skills into one picture. The implications from these studies are that at a fundamental level there should be an ongoing stage of profiling and golf-related physical conditioning, a physiological equivalent to the practice and mental parts of golf. The neuromuscular qualities built up through physical conditioning act during the golf swing, allowing the golfer to create an appearance of ease, smoothness of movement, and freedom in the swing. Golf training is vital for elite players; good physique allows good technique. Along with performance-improving factors, physical conditioning, in particular flexibility, can help protect the body from injury, allowing golfers to reach and sustain optimum performance.

ACKNOWLEDGMENTS

The studies conducted for the Golfing Union of Ireland were sponsored by MacGregor Golf.

References

Delacave, G. 1997. Physiotherapy on the European Tour. *First Congress of Medicine in Golf.* In press.

Ekman, B., Ljungquist, K.G., and Stein, U. 1970. Roentgenologic-photometric method for bone mineral determinations. *Acta Radiologica* 10(July): 305-325.

Haywood, K.M. 1980. Strength and flexibility in gymnasts before and after menarche. *British Journal of Sports Medicine* 14(4): 189-192.

Hebron, M. 1993. *Golf Mind, Golf Body, Golf Swing.* Smithtown, NY: Rost Assoc., 173-175.

Hosea, T.M., Gatt, C.J., Galli, K.M., Langrama, W.A., and Zamwssky, J.P. 1990. Biomechanical analysis of the golfer's back. In A.J. Cochran, ed., *Science and Golf. Proceedings of the First World Scientific Congress of Golf,* University of St. Andrews, Scotland. London: Spon, 43-48.

Jacobs, J., and Bowden, K. 1972. *Practical Golf.* London: Stanley Paul, 43-44.

Larkin, A.F., Larkin II, W.F., Larkin, W.F., and Larkin, S.L. 1990. Annual torso specific conditioning program for golfers. In A.J. Cochran, ed., *Science and Golf. Proceedings of the First World Scientific Congress of Golf,* University of St. Andrews, Scotland. London: Spon, 43-48.

Lennon, H.M. 1996. An investigation into a golf specific strength and flexibility physical fitness program. Master's thesis, University of Ulster.

McCue, B.F. 1963. Flexibility measurements of college students. *Research Quarterly* 24(3): 316-324.

McTeigue, M., Lamb, S.R., Mottram, R., and Pirozzolo, F. 1994. Spine and hip motion analysis during the golf swing. In A.J. Cochran, ed., *Science and Golf. Proceedings of the First World Scientific Congress of Golf,* University of St. Andrews, Scotland. London: Spon, 50-58.

CHAPTER 9

Golf Injuries in Scotland

M.J. McNicholas
University of Dundee Orthopaedic Dept., Dundee, Scotland

A. Nielsen and R.P. Knill-Jones
University of Glasgow, Dept. of Public Health, Glasgow, Scotland

We report the experience of 18 sports medicine clinics across Scotland in the treatment of golf-related sports injuries from 1990 to 1995. There were 286 injuries in 280 individuals. There appears to be a seasonal variation in the time of injury, with peak incidence in the first two months of the year. The anatomical areas most commonly affected were the upper limb and torso. Mechanical back pain, enthesopathy (pathology at the insertion of ligament into bone), and ligament sprain were the most common diagnoses. About a third of patients visited the clinic on one occasion only; of these, 51 patients required only advice on technique modification. Of the remaining two-thirds, 22 were referred back to their general practitioner, 19 for further treatment elsewhere, and 5 for an orthopaedic opinion. Sixty-seven of the patients reported a similar injury in the past; of these, 25 had been forced to take time off sport, and 5 even time off work. Delay in seeking treatment for such problems seems to be associated with a less satisfactory outcome. Earlier attendance for assessment of the need for treatment after golfing injury is encouraged.

Keywords: Golf injury, sports medicine, sports injury, Scotland.

INTRODUCTION

Golf is one of the United Kingdom's most popular sports, particularly in Scotland, the country credited with its invention.

The very existence of a golf-related sports injury is denied by some, but there is no doubt that it does exist. There are a small number of studies in the literature that outline the pattern of injury. One review from the United States indicated that amateur golfers' most common injuries are to the back and elbow and that more studies of prevention were needed (McCarroll, 1996). Serious head injuries to golfers in Scotland are included in a review of 52 sport-related admissions for cranial trauma (Lindsay, McLatchie, and Jennett, 1980). Muscular-skeletal injuries are surveyed in two reports related to sports clinic attendance in Scotland (Nielsen and Knill-Jones, 1996; Nielsen, 1996). A case control study of disk herniations found no evidence that golf was a risk factor (Mundt et al., 1993). Neurological problems related to sporting activity in Germany include some in golfers (Kross and Barolin, 1983).

In Scotland there are 38 sports medicine clinics that received setup funds from the Scottish Sports Council. They are staffed by doctors and physiotherapists interested in the treatment of sport-related injuries. Patients pay to be seen at these clinics and may be referred by their doctors or coaches or may self-refer (Knill-Jones, 1997). Eighteen of these clinics use a common data collection proforma (Nielsen and Knill-Jones, 1996; Nielsen, 1996).

We set out to define their experience of the treatment of golf-related injury.

It is important to appreciate that this is a descriptive study of injury. The total number of golfers playing during the time of the study is not known; it is therefore very difficult to generate any quantitative analyses of the risks of injury associated with playing golf. However, it is estimated that each year between 5.7% and 6.6% of the Scottish adult population participate in golf (1989-1993), the peak month being July (Campbell and O'Driscoll, 1995).

METHODS

Injury is defined as a problem causing the patient to seek advice and/or treatment from these clinics.

Data were collected prospectively at the time of attendance at the clinic using a standard proforma completed by the patient, outlining demographic details describing the circumstances of the injury. Information on diagnoses, therapeutic interventions (up to three per visit to the clinic), and outcomes was recorded by clinical staff. These data were then collated centrally at the University of Glasgow's Department of Public Health onto a computer database. The database was searched for any patient contact episode in which golf was the primary sport to which the cause of the injury was attributed by the patient and staff.

RESULTS

There were 280 golfers seen with 286 injuries in 18 clinics over a five-year period from 1990. These injuries form 4.2% of injuries in the database of 9,487 records—a proportion similar to that for badminton (4.4%) and weights and aerobics (3.2%). Most of the injuries seen in the clinics are related to football (30%) and jogging/running (18%). Only 38 (12%) of the golfing injuries were seen in a clinic based in the "home of golf"—St. Andrews in Fife.

The age and sex distribution of the patients is shown in figure 9.1; 25% were female, 27% were under 40, and 18% were aged 60 or more. Over one-third had professional or managerial jobs.

The level of expertise is shown in figure 9.2. Nearly 90% were recreational golfers, of whom about half were club members.

The month in which the patients were injured is shown in figure 9.3. Injuries happened least frequently in the later part of the year, with a marked rise in the new year.

The anatomical distribution of the injuries is shown in figure 9.4. Shoulder/arm injuries dominate (45%), followed by trunk/torso injuries (21%).

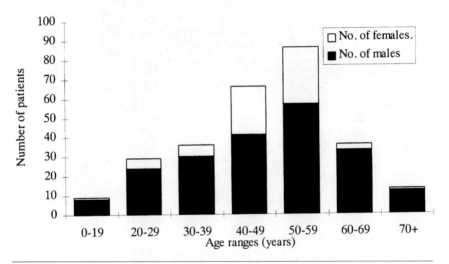

Figure 9.1   Age-sex distribution of patients with golf injuries.

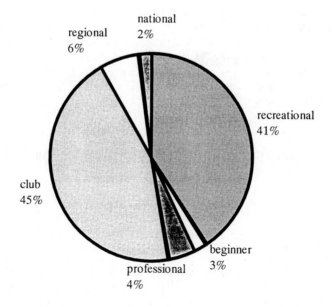

Figure 9.2   Level of experience (%).

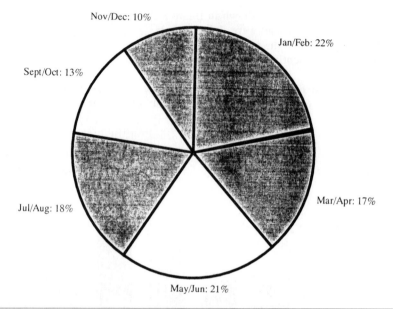

Figure 9.3   Month of injury (% of known).

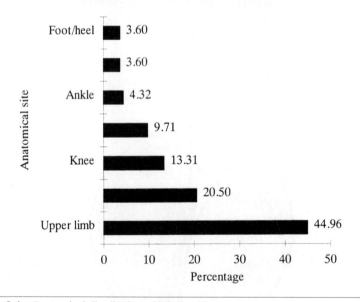

Figure 9.4   Anatomical distribution of injuries (%).

The two anatomical areas most commonly injured were upper limb and torso. The age and sex distributions of patients with these injuries are shown in figures 9.5 and 9.6, respectively.

Upper limb problems included tennis elbow (lateral epicondylitis), diagnosed in 30 patients, compared to golfer's elbow in only 12; shoulder impingement occurred in 19.

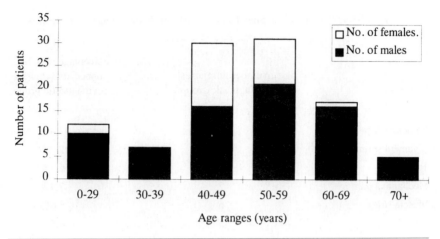

Figure 9.5   Age and sex distribution of upper limb injuries.

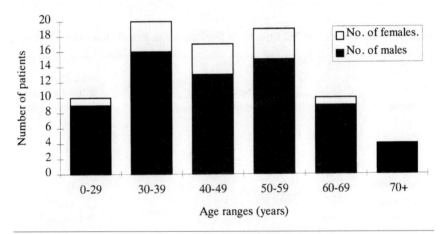

Figure 9.6   Age and sex distribution of patients with torso problems.

Diagnoses were recorded for 99% of injuries. The distribution by broad grouping of diagnosis is shown in table 9.2.

Enthesopathies composed the single largest diagnostic group, with 50 patients. Of these, 12 required further referrals: 2 for orthopaedic opinion, 5 to their general practitioner, 3 for National Health Service physiotherapy, and 2 for acupuncture.

Male golfers under the age of 40 accounted for many of the muscle strains (35.7%), whereas older age groups (40-59 years) had most of the enthesopathies (54.8%), ligament sprains (41.7%), and tendinitis (43.5%). For the age group 60+, the distribution is as follows: 32.3% of the enthesopathies, 27.8% of the ligament sprains, and 34.8% of the tendinitis.

Golfers under 40 accounted for nearly half of the 37 individuals with back pain. Only four cases of back pain occurred in the 60+ age group, all in males. Back pain had occurred as a previous injury in 16 individuals; 8 had taken time off sport and 3 off work.

Table 9.1   Distribution of 102 Upper Limb Injuries in Broad Diagnostic Groups

Diagnosis	Number of injuries in diagnostic group	Percentage of defined upper limb injuries in diagnostic group
Enthesopathy	42	44.4%
Ligament sprain	24	22.2%
Tendinitis	17	15.7%
Mechanical pain	2	7.4%
Muscle strain	6	5.6%
Miscellaneous	5	4.6%
Total	102	100%

Table 9.2   Distribution of 282 Injuries in 280 Patients in Broad Diagnostic Groups

Diagnosis	Number of injuries in diagnostic group	Percentage of all defined injuries in diagnostic group
Mechanical pain	88	31.2%
Ligament sprain	51	18.1%
Enthesopathy	50	17.8%
Muscle strain	33	11.7%
Tendinitis	30	10.6%
Miscellaneous	30	10.6%
Total	282	100%

The treatment of the injuries is outlined in table 9.3. A total of 1,032 treatments were recorded for 255 individuals (4.05 each). Ultrasound constituted 38% of all treatments recorded, with advice and active physiotherapy (frictions, mobilisations, stretching) accounting for about 23% each. There was a trend for older patients to have more treatments—on average 3.8 for those under 40, 4.1 for 40-59-year-olds, and 4.4 for those 60 and over.

A single visit to the clinic was made by 107 patients; these have been excluded from figure 9.7, as there are in effect no follow-up data on them. For the 173 patients seen more than once, the median follow-up period was 28 days. The bar chart shows the outcome at discharge versus the median length of time from injury to presentation for injuries to the upper limb and torso.

Table 9.3   Types of Treatment Administered to 255 Patients

Treatment	Number of treatments administered	Porportion of all treatments administered
Ultrasound	417	42%
Active physiotherapy	279	28%
Advice/patient action	173	17%
Other electrical	91	9%
Miscellaneous	41	4%
Total	1001	100%

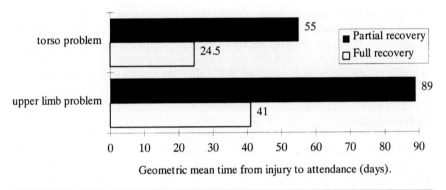

Geometric mean time from injury to attendance (days).

Figure 9.7   Completeness of recovery compared to time from injury to presentation.

No relationship was found between the time from original injury and the number of treatments recorded. However, patients with a good outcome had more recent injuries than those with a partial response to treatment.

DISCUSSION

January and February were the months the patients most commonly reported as the time of injury. This does not reflect larger numbers participating at that time. Therefore it may be due to environmental factors such as weather or ground conditions, or may reflect a real chance of an increased risk of injury after the Christmas break, a trend seen in other sports (Nielsen and Knill-Jones, 1996).

Referral for orthopaedic consultation was required for 9 patients: 6 with knee problems, 2 for arm/shoulder problems, and 1 with an Achilles tendonopathy. Interestingly, of the 37 patients with back pain (the second largest single diagnostic group), none required referral elsewhere. This may support the conclusions of several well-controlled studies in the recent literature showing that patients suffering with mechanical low back pain are best treated by physical therapy (Waddell, 1996).

From these data it is clear that while it may be relatively uncommon, there is a problem of sports injury related to golf. This affects the young and old, the recreational as well as the professional golfer. Golfing associations, club participants, and other players have a responsibility to encourage practices that reduce the chances of injury.

Chronic, recurrent, or old injuries respond least well to treatment. Golfers need to be advised to seek appropriate professional help. The availability of these sports medicine clinics must be made known, and prompt attendance in the early acute phase after injury should be encouraged.

ACKNOWLEDGMENTS

The study was made possible by the enthusiasm and support of the staff of the sports injury clinics who faithfully and regularly submitted the data collection forms. We would like to thank the Scottish Sports Council for their funding of the clinics and the research project. We would also like to express our gratitude to the Department of Public Health, University of Glasgow, for allowing us access to the database and for their statistical support of this project.

References

Campbell, H., and O'Driscoll, S. 1995. The epidemiology of leisure accidents in Scotland. *Health Bulletin* 53(5): 380-293.

Knill-Jones, R.P. 1997. Leader. *British Journal of Sports Medicine* 31: 95-96.

Kross, R., and Barolin, G.S. 1983. "Typical" and "less typical" sports injuries in the field of neurology. *Weiner Medizinsche Wochenschrift* 133: 345-353.

Lindsay, K.W., McLatchie, G., and Jennett, R. 1980. Serious head injury in sport. *BMJ* 281: 789-791.

McCarroll, J.R. 1996. The frequency of golf injuries. *Clinics in Sports Medicine* 15: 1-7.

Mundt, D.J., et al. 1993. An epidemiologic study of sports and weight lifting as possible risk factors for herniated lumbar and cervical discs. The Northeast Collaborative Group on Low Back Pain. *American Journal of Sports Medicine* 21: 854-860.

Nielsen, A. 1996. Disseminating information on injuries to sports associations to help develop guidelines for injury prevention. MPH dissertation. Dept. of Public Health, University of Glasgow.

Nielsen, A., and Knill-Jones, R.P. 1996. Usage of sports medicine clinics in Scotland. *Final Report to the Scottish Sports Council.*

Waddell, G. 1996. Clinical guidelines for the management of acute low back pain. *Royal College of General Practitioners HMSO Publication,* GP62 9.96.

CHAPTER 10

The Epidemiology of Golf Injuries in Victoria, Australia: Evidence From Sports Medicine Clinics and Emergency Department Presentations

Caroline Finch and Cheyne Sherman
School of Human Movement, Deakin University, Melbourne, Australia

Trefor James
Sports Medicine Centres of Victoria, Melbourne, Australia

Little has been previously published about the incidence and types of golf injuries that occur to Australian golfers. Furthermore, there have been no published reports of the types of golf injuries treated at sports medicine clinics. This paper describes golf injuries treated at general sports medicine clinics and hospital emergency departments in Victoria, Australia. Typically, the sports medicine clinics treated overuse-type problems, and emergency departments treated more serious, acute traumatic injuries due to strikes from a ball or club. Combining data about injury cases that present to these two treatment settings provides a comprehensive picture of golf injuries requiring medical treatment.

Keywords: Golf injury, epidemiology, sports medicine clinics, emergency departments, Victoria.

INTRODUCTION

As in other parts of the world, golf is a popular competitive and recreational sport in Australia, particularly in the state of Victoria. There are 365 golf clubs in Victoria with approximately 100,000 registered male members (Victorian Golf Association 1996). In addition, there are 374 ladies' golf clubs with approximately 30,000 registered players.

In recent statistics obtained from a population-based household survey describing the numbers of Victorian sport participants, golf is ranked as the third highest participant sport (behind "aerobics" and "tennis") among all Victorians aged over 15 years (Australian Bureau of Statistics 1997b). In males, golf was ranked as the highest participant sport, being undertaken by 4.4% of all Victorian males aged over 15 years. Additional population data about participation in leisure activities rank golf as the third most popular leisure activity in Victoria (behind "walking for exercise" and "swimming") (Australian Bureau of Statistics 1997a). For males, golf as a leisure activity ranked as the second most popular leisure pursuit, with over 15% of Victorian males having played golf in the 12 months prior to the survey.

To date, there have been few published data about the incidence and types of golf injuries that are sustained by Australian golfers. The main available sources of golf injury data are from studies outside Australia (McCarroll et al. 1990; Batt 1992; Batt 1993; Mallon 1993). Apart from a paper describing hospital emergency department visits in Queensland (Wilks and Jones 1996), there have been no other studies specifically describing the incidence and types of golf-related injuries in Australia.

Wilks and Jones (1996) described golf-related injuries among 300 patients who attended emergency departments of Queensland hospitals over a six and a half-year period. They identified common mechanisms of golf-related injury to be mainly hits from golf clubs (37%) or golf balls (28%), sprains and strains (10%), and slips/falls (7%). These collision-type injuries were often severe, for example, fractures, and required significant treatment.

A recent Australian study ranked all sports and active recreational activities leading to Australia-wide emergency department presentations in terms of the frequency of injuries and their severity (Finch et al. 1995). Golf did not rank in the top 20 sports or active recreational activities leading to presentation at an emergency department in either adults or children (Finch et al. 1998). However, 45% of all children (aged less than 15 years) who presented to an Australian emergency department with a golf-related injury were subsequently admitted to hospital for further treatment (Finch et al. 1995). This ranked golf as the top sport and active recreational activity leading to the highest proportion of hospital admissions in Australia following an emergency department presentation (Finch et al. 1995). Injuries in this group typically occurred during unsupervised play with golf clubs while a child was standing too close when observing others' golf swings; they were generally severe head injuries caused by hits from a club or ball. Among adults, golf was ranked as the 20th highest sport and active recreational activity leading to the highest proportion of hospital admissions in Australia, following an emergency department presentation, with 8% of all initial presentations requiring admission.

With most golf injuries being overuse in nature, it is likely that the majority of cases would seek treatment at a sports medicine clinic, physiotherapy practice, or general practice clinic. Nevertheless, a number of golf injuries are so severe that they require treatment in a hospital emergency department. This paper presents information about golf injuries receiving medical treatment at general sports medicine clinics and hospital emergency departments in the Australian state of Victoria. This is also the first detailed report of golf injuries presenting to sports medicine clinics.

METHODS

The data for this study were obtained from two sources: sports medicine clinics and emergency departments.

In August 1996, a sports medicine injury surveillance (SMIS) system was implemented in five large multidisciplinary sports medicine clinics in metropolitan Melbourne (Finch and Gabbe 1997). The SMIS system collected full details about every new sports injury case treated by the full range of professionals practicing at these sports medicine clinics. Information about the injured person, circumstances of the injury, and the nature of injury was collected from patients and practitioners using a standardised data collection form. A full auditing process was undertaken to ensure that a full 100% capture rate of eligible cases was achieved. Currently, full information about all new sports injury cases reported during the six-month period 12/8/96 to 11/2/97 is available. This paper therefore describes the new golf injury cases that presented to one of the participating sports medicine clinics during this period.

The second source of data explored in this paper is the Victorian Emergency Minimum Dataset maintained by the Victorian Injury Surveillance System (VISS), which contains details of injuries treated at the emergency departments of 24 Victorian hospitals. These hospitals provide (incomplete) coverage of both urban and rural areas in Victoria. Golf injury data from the emergency department database for the period October 1995 to March 1997 were obtained and analysed. Because of the sampling frame for the collection of emergency department data, the data are presented separately for adults and children. Cases are also classified as occurring during formal (i.e., competitive) or informal (i.e., noncompetitive or social) golf activity.

RESULTS

Sports Medicine Clinic Visits

Over the period 12/8/96 to 11/2/97, a total of 2498 new sporting injuries were treated at the participating sports medicine clinics. Of these, 34 cases (or 1.4%) occurred during golf. This ranked golf as the 13th highest sport or active recreation activity leading to presentation with a new sports injury at these clinics.

The injured golfers were all aged between 24 and 65 years (median 40.5 years). Only six injured players were females, with males composing 83% of the total sample. More than half (56%, n = 19) of the cases were employed as managers, administrators, or other professionals; six people were retired.

On average, the injured golf players participated in golf for 6.3 hours per week (range: < 1 hour to 20 hours per week). The majority of players (61%, n = 21) had been playing golf for at least five years. Five injured players had been playing golf for less than one year. At the time of injury, two-thirds of players were participating in golf for recreation or social reasons. Eight players (24%) reported that they were playing for competition at the time of injury, and a further three (9%) patients stated that they were self-training. Of the players participating in some form of competition (formal or social), 58% were playing in social competition and 27% in club competition, and 9% were playing pennant golf.

A large proportion of injuries (59%, n = 20) occurred while the player was on a golf course, but a significant number (32%, n = 11) occurred on a general playing field or oval. One case occurred while the golfer was at a driving range, and a further player noticed the injury while resting after a game.

Table 10.1 summarizes the major causes of the golf injuries treated at the sports medicine centres. Not surprisingly, overuse was the major mechanism of injury, accounting for more than one-third of all cases. Poor swing mechanics contributed to 29% of injuries, where there was a large twisting or rotational component in the injury mechanism. Forceful impacts were also a significant cause of injury and resulted from miss-hits of the golf ball. In one instance, a player hit a tree trunk with his club while trying to hit a ball out from a bad lie. Other causes of injury included overstretching while playing golf.

Table 10.1   Major Causes of Golf Injuries Treated at Sports Medicine Clinics (n = 34)

Cause of injury	Proportion of all cases
Overuse	35%
Twisting/rotational component	29%
Aggravation of previous injury	15%
Forceful impact (miss-hits)	12%
Fall at ground level	6%
Forward flexion	6%

Table 10.2 summarizes the body regions injured and the nature of injury sustained by the golfers treated at sports medicine clinics. As would be expected, the lower back was the most commonly injured body region (25% of all cases). Injuries to the elbow (18% of cases), knee (18%), and neck/cervical spine (15%) were also common. The category "other" includes injuries to the foot, hip, ankle, and wrist.

Injuries to the lower back/lumbar spine were classified by the treating practitioner as either a disk or facet joint injury in all cases. These injuries were typically overuse injuries, with symptoms becoming apparent in the action of swinging or after playing or practicing.

Injuries to the elbow were all classified as extensor carpi radialis brevis (ECRB) tendinosis ("tennis elbow") and occurred in the nondominant elbow in all cases. Although overuse was a frequent cause (67%), miss-hits also accounted for a significant number (33%) of elbow injuries. Knee injuries generally represented an acute presentation of a degenerative condition (chondropathology or a degenerative meniscal tear). Neck/cervical spine injuries were all due to disk and facet joint injuries. The shoulder injuries (n = 2) both represented rotator cuff pathology (1 tear,

Table 10.2   Body Regions Injured in Golfers Treated at Sports Medicine Clinics (n = 34)

Body region	Proportion of all cases
Lumbar spine/lower back	24%
Elbow	18%
Knee	18%
Neck/cervical spine	15%
Shoulder	6%
Hand/finger	6%
Other	13%

1 impingement). The hand/finger injuries (n = 2) consisted of a metacarpal fracture and an MCP joint RCL sprain and both occurred as a result of miss-hits.

Injury Severity

The majority of players (88%) did not stop playing golf when they first noticed their injury. Only three players (9%) stopped playing immediately, and one player noticed the injury after cooling down.

Almost equal numbers of patients saw a doctor or a physiotherapist for their first point of treatment in the sports medicine centre. One patient required no further treatment, and four patients were classified as requiring significant further treatment. Almost half of all patients (47%) required minimal further treatment, and 38% required a moderate amount of further treatment.

On average, the injured golfers were expected to miss 4.3 weeks of full participation from golf because of their injury, and this ranged from requiring no time off golf to requiring up to 24 weeks. This demonstrates that golf injuries can limit the performance and participation of golfers in their chosen sport.

Adult Golf Injury Emergency Department Presentations

Over the period October 1995 to March 1997, a total of 61 persons aged at least 15 years presented at one of the VISS emergency departments for treatment of a golf injury. Of these injuries, 44% (n = 27) occurred during formal golf. Males outnumbered females 8:1, and about half of all formal golf-injured cases (48%) were more than 40 years of age. While the age distribution was similar for people injured during informal golf, the male-to-female ratio for the informal situation was 2.7:1.

The injuries during formal golf typically occurred in an area for formal sport (59% of cases) or in a place for recreation (26%). The reverse was true for the informal-golf injuries; 50% of these occurred in a place for recreation and 21% in an area for formal sport. The home was also a common setting for informal-golf injuries, accounting for 15% of all cases.

Table 10.3 summarizes the major causes of golf injuries in adults presenting to emergency departments. Unlike the sports medicine clinic cases, these cases are most commonly associated with being hit by a golf ball or with falls. This is not surprising, since impacts from a golf ball can be very severe, and only the most severe cases of golf injury would present to an emergency department for treatment. The fact that hits from a golf club are more common among informal players than among formal golfers suggests that the former do not appreciate the need to stand well clear of someone swinging a club. The category "other" includes assaults (on a golf course while playing golf, by someone with a golf club) and foreign bodies (e.g., dirt and grass) entering eyes.

Table 10.3   Major Causes of Golf Injuries Treated at Victorian Emergency Departments

Cause of injury	Proportion of all formal golf injury cases		Proportion of all informal golf injury cases	
	Adults n = 27	Children n = 8	Adults n = 34	Children n = 41
Hit by golf ball	52%	75%	44%	20%
Fall, slip, trip (includes ankle inversions)	15%	–	18%	7%
Overuse	11%	–	12%	–
Hit by golf club	4%	25%	18%	71%
Other	18%	–	8%	2%

The nature of the main injury sustained by the injured golfers is shown in table 10.4. Sprains/strains were common in both groups of adult golfers. Superficial injuries and open wounds were also relatively common, accounting for 37% of all formal-golf injuries and 24% of all informal-golf injury cases. Injuries to the head and facial region (including eyes) were the most common (table 10.5), accounting for 41% of all formal-golf injury cases and 30% of all informal-golf injury cases. All of these injuries were due to being hit by a golf ball or club, and the majority (78%) were superficial or open wounds. Among formal golfers, fractures were to the face (n = 1), wrist (n = 1), and lower leg (n = 1). Fractures in informal golfers were to the face (n = 1), forearm/wrist (n = 2), and foot (n = 1). All foreign body injuries were to the eye.

All cases of formal-golf injury in adults were treated at the emergency department and discharged to home. Four (12%) of the informal-golf injury cases were so severe that they had to be admitted to hospital or transferred to another hospital.

Child Golf Injury Emergency Department Presentations

Over the same period, a total of 47 children (aged less than 15 years) presented at a VISS emergency department for treatment of a golf injury. Among these, 17% (n

Table 10.4   Nature of the Main Golf Injury Treated at Victorian Emergency Departments

Cause of injury	Proportion of all formal golf injury cases		Proportion of all informal golf injury cases	
	Adults n = 27	Children n = 8	Adults n = 34	Children n = 41
Sprain or strain	19%	–	24%	–
Fracture	11%	–	15%	5%
Superficial (excluding eye)	22%	25%	12%	10%
Open wound	15%	13%	12%	54%
Intracranial injury	7%	–	12%	–
Injury to muscle or tendon	7%	–	9%	–
Eye injury	7%	13%	6%	5%
Foreign body	7%	13%	6%	2%
Other/unknown	5%	36%	4%	24%

Table 10.5   Most Commonly Injured Body Regions Treated at Emergency Departments

Injured body region	Proportion of all formal golf injury cases		Proportion of all informal golf injury cases	
	Adults n = 27	Children n = 8	Adults n = 34	Children n = 41
Head, excluding face, eye	19%	13%	9%	24%
Face, excluding eye	15%	13%	15%	44%
Eye	7%	25%	6%	5%
Lower leg (including ankle)	15%	–	6%	–
Knee	7%	–	9%	–
Forearm	4%	–	12%	–
Other/unknown	33%	49%	43%	27%

= 8) sustained the injuries during formal golf. There were about three times as many boys as girls; the majority of cases (47%) were aged between 5 and 9 years, and a significant proportion (16%) were aged 0 to 4 years.

All children sustaining formal-golf injuries were 10-14 years of age. Formal-golf injuries typically occurred in an area for formal sport (63%) or in a place for recreation (13%). One-quarter of the cases classified as formal golf occurred in the home setting. The home setting accounted for the majority of informal-golf injuries in children, 61% of cases.

As with the situation in adults, child emergency department cases are most commonly associated with being hit by a golf ball or club (table 10.3). Among formal child golfers, hits from a golf ball are the most common type of injury. This is in contrast to informal-golf injuries; the majority of these occur from strikes (usually to the head/face) by a golf club. This supports other studies indicating that strikes to the head from a swinging club are the most common cause of child golf injury. Proper storage of all golf equipment is also essential, as demonstrated by the "other" informal-golf injury case due to a young child sticking a golf marker up his/her nose.

The nature of the main golf injury sustained by the injured children is shown in table 10.4. Superficial injuries and open wounds were common, accounting for 38% of all formal-golf injuries and 64% of all informal-golf injury cases. Injuries to the head and facial region (including eyes) were the most common (table 10.5), accounting for 51% of all formal-golf injury cases and 63% of all informal-golf injury cases. All of these injuries were due to being hit by a golf ball or club. The majority (78%) of these injuries were superficial or open wounds, though one child involved in informal golf sustained a fracture to the face.

All but one case of formal-golf injury in a child was treated at the emergency department and discharged to home. The remaining case was transferred to another hospital. Eight (or 15%) of the informal-golf injury cases were so severe that they had to be admitted to hospital for further treatment.

CONCLUSIONS

Golf is a popular sport and recreational pursuit that has no gender or age limits, and it is relatively safe. Although it is a relatively low-intensity sport with a low overall injury risk compared to contact and collision sports, short periods of high-intensity play, such as during practice, can lead to muscle imbalances in high-level players. The major motor skill required to play the game is the basic golf swing, and the specific equipment used to hit the ball requires a golfer to have at least some level of physical conditioning. Like other bat-and-ball sports, this equipment introduces a certain degree of injury risk, particularly among younger players and with those who have poor technique, and there is a chance of miss-hitting. Furthermore, the very nature of the technique and mechanics of the swing may entail some risk of injury, especially with an accumulation of swings at training. Predisposing factors such as the golfer's age, health, strength, flexibility, and amount of practice can all play a role in the occurrence of injuries (Batt 1993).

The pattern of injuries seen in sports medicine clinics in Victoria is similar to that reported by McCarroll et al. (1990) in an amateur golfing population. Improved and ongoing collection of golf injury data, across all levels of play, is required to monitor golf injuries over time, identify potential prevention strategies, and monitor the success of implemented injury prevention measures.

These data have highlighted the problem of serious head injuries to children. These injuries mainly occur at home and are usually a result of unsupervised experimentation with golf clubs or of strikes from a golf ball. Attention should be given to community awareness regarding the safe storage and handling of golf equipment. Education of children and adult players about the dangers of standing too close to someone swinging a club or hitting a ball should also be undertaken as a priority.

Comparison in this paper of the emergency department injury data with those from sports medicine clinics clearly highlights the inherent biases involved in considering data from one source only. Typically, sports medicine clinics treat overuse-type problems, whereas emergency departments treat the more serious, acute traumatic injuries due to strikes from a ball or club. Through joint consideration of data on injury cases that present to these two types of treatment place, a more comprehensive picture of golf injuries can be obtained.

ACKNOWLEDGMENTS

Collection of the sports medicine clinic data was funded by the National Sports Research Centre (Australian Sports Commission). All staff and patients of the Sports Medicine Centres of Victoria are gratefully thanked for participating in the SMIS project. The emergency department data were provided to the authors by the Victorian Injury Surveillance System, a project of the Monash University Accident Research Centre. Some additional support for this research was provided by Sport and Recreation Victoria.

References

Australian Bureau of Statistics. 1997a. *Leisure participation, Victoria, October 1996*. Catalogue No. 4176.2. Melbourne: Australian Bureau of Statistics.
Australian Bureau of Statistics. 1997b. *Participation in sporting and physical recreational activities, Victoria, 1995-96*. Catalogue No. 4177.0. Melbourne: Australian Bureau of Statistics.
Batt, M.E. 1992. A survey of golf injuries in amateur golfers. *British Journal of Sports Medicine* 26: 63-65.
Batt, M.E. 1993. Golfing injuries: An overview. *Sports Medicine* 16: 64-71.
Finch, C., and Gabbe, B. 1997. The sports medicine injury surveillance (SMIS) project. Part I—Project design and methodology. Abstract presented at the 1997 Australian Conference of Science and Medicine in Sport.
Finch, C., Ozanne-Smith, J., and Williams, F. 1995. *The feasibility of improved data collection methodologies for sports injuries*. Monash University Accident Research Centre. Report No. 69.
Finch, C., Valuri, J., and Ozanne-Smith, J. 1998. Sports injuries in Australia—evidence from emergency department presentations. *British Journal of Sports Medicine*. In press.

Mallon, W.J. 1993. Epidemiology of golf injuries. In *Medical aspects of golf,* ed. W.J. Mallon, J.R. McCarroll, and C.S. Stover. Philadelphia: Davis.

McCarroll, J.R., Rettig, A.C., and Shelbourne, K.D. 1990. Injuries in the amateur golfer. *Physician and Sports Medicine* 18: 122-126.

Victorian Golf Association. 1996. Annual Report.

Wilks, J., and Jones, D. 1996. Golf-related injuries seen at hospital emergency departments. *The Australian Journal of Science and Medicine in Sport* 2: 43-45.

CHAPTER 11

Low Back Injury in Elite and Professional Golfers: An Epidemiologic and Radiographic Study

H. Sugaya and A. Tsuchiya
Department of Orthopaedic Surgery and Sports Medicine, Kawatetsu Hospital, Chiba, Japan

H. Moriya
Department of Orthopaedic Surgery, Chiba University, Chiba, Japan

D.A. Morgan and S.A. Banks
Orthopaedic Research Laboratory, West Palm Beach, FL, USA

The purpose of this study was to determine the prevalence of low back pain and the characteristics of the symptoms in elite golfers and their relationship to golf swing mechanics. A study by self-reported questionnaire was performed at four Japanese professional golf tournaments. In total 154 (55%) professional golfers reported a history of low back pain of sufficient intensity to miss at least one tour event, or to play at an unsatisfactory level as a direct result. The symptoms were predominantly right-sided and were aggravated during the impact through the follow-through phase with statistical significance. We also analyzed radiographic changes in the lumbar spine in 26 right-handed elite golfers with low back symptoms. Controls were 105 randomly selected age-matched, nongolfing patients with low back symptoms. When golfers were compared to controls, golfers exhibited a higher rate of right-side osteophyte formation on x-ray (p < 0.01) as well as facet joint degenerative changes on CT (p < 0.01). The present study demonstrated a high prevalence of the history of low back pain with significant laterality as well as the close association to swing phase, and significant degenerative changes on the right side of the lumbar spine in elite golfers. These findings suggest a mechanical etiology closely related to the motions occurring during the golf swing. We believe that this and future studies will greatly help us in understanding the etiology of the low back injuries in golfers.

Keywords: Golf, low back pain, epidemiology, lumbar spine, radiography.

INTRODUCTION

Many golfers suffer from various injuries related to the golf swing. Among them, low back injuries are among the most frequent and occasionally disabling problems in amateurs and professionals (Batt 1990; Jobe and Schwab 1991; McCarroll and Gioe 1982; McCarroll et al. 1990). However, to the best of our knowledge, only one report has described the frequency of low back pain in professional golfers (McCarroll and Gioe 1982), and no report has focused on the detailed symptomatology or radiographic findings in the lumbar spine. In recreational golfers, poor swing mechanics, excessive practice, and poor physical conditioning are reported to be the main cause of low back injuries (Batt 1990; Hosea et al. 1990; Hosea and Gatt 1996; McCarroll et al. 1990). In professionals whose swing techniques are established, overuse is believed to be the most frequent cause of injury (McCarroll and Gioe 1982). We hypothesized that the asymmetric nature of the golf swing is potentially harmful to the lower back (Sugaya et al. 1996; Sugaya, Moriya et al. 1997; Sugaya, Morgan et al. 1997). Therefore, we surveyed three highly skilled groups of professional golfers to establish the characteristics of the low back symptoms and determine whether those symptoms have any association with the phase of the swing. Further, we analyzed radiographic changes in the lumbar spine in elite golfers with low back symptoms, seeking their relationship to golf swing mechanics.

EPIDEMIOLOGIC STUDY

Materials and Methods

We distributed a questionnaire to each golfer in the following three Japanese major golf tournaments and one ladies' qualifying test: 1993 Japan Professional Golf Championship (JPGA Championship), 1993 Japan Professional Golf Senior Championship (JPGA Senior Championship), 1993 Japan Ladies Professional Golf Championship (JLPGA Championship), and the final qualifying test for the 1994 JLPGA Tour. The questionnaire was divided into two parts. The first part included demographic information such as age, weight, height, and golf experience. The second part contained questions about incidence, location of symptoms, and symptom-related phase of the swing. The golfers were requested to indicate their injury location on body figures on the questionnaire sheets, permitting easy detection of the location and laterality of injuries and symptoms. In these questionnaires we divided the golf swing into seven segments, including three events, three phases, and the approaching/putting position, in order to allow golfers to easily differentiate swing segments:

1. Address
2. Take-away: from ball address to the top of backswing
3. Top of backswing
4. Forward swing: from the top of backswing to ball impact

5. Impact through follow-through: from the impact to the follow-through

6. Finish

7. Approaching/putting

We received responses from 283 professional golfers, including 115 regular male tour golfers, 55 men's senior tour golfers, and 113 female tour golfers. The overall response rate was 57% (65% PGA, 80% Senior PGA, and 45% LPGA). Among respondents, 10 were Caucasian golfers and the others were Asian. All golfers except one male regular tour golfer were right-handed.

The 283 golfers were grouped by tour participation to assess the frequency of injuries to body part. One left-handed golfer was excluded to simplify consideration of symptom laterality. Golfers reporting a history of low back pain were divided into three subgroups according to the laterality of the symptoms: right-sided, central and/or no laterality, and left-sided. The swing segments in which the symptoms were aggravated were described in each symptom group. The chi-square test was used for statistical analysis.

Results

The mean ages of men's regular and senior and ladies' tour golfers were 35 years (range, 21-54 years), 53 years (50-63 years), and 31 years (20-48 years), respectively. The average golf career was 20, 34, and 14 years, respectively. The average length of tour experience was 11, 27, and 8 years, respectively.

Table 11.1   Frequency of Injuries to Body Part by Number

	Overall (%) n = 281	Regular PGA n = 113	Senior PGA n = 55	LPGA n = 113
Lower back	154 (55)	63	28	63
Neck/high back	93 (33)	37	17	39
Elbow	45 (16)	21	17	7
Shoulder	44 (16)	26	13	5
Wrist	42 (15)	20	9	13
Knee	26 (9)	9	8	9
Ankle	20 (7)	10	3	7
Fingers	7 (2)	4	2	1
Toes	7 (2)	1	1	5
Foot	6 (2)	3	0	3
Others	14 (5)	9	4	1

PGA, Professional Golfers Association of Japan; LPGA, Japan Ladies Professional Golfers Association

Two hundred and four golfers (72%) experienced injuries that caused them to miss at least one tournament or to play at an unsatisfactory level as a direct result. Most of the injuries occurred in the back and upper extremities. Lower back pain showed the highest prevalence. Of responding golfers, 154 of 283 (55%) had a history of low back pain; in prevalence this was followed by neck and high back (33%), elbow (16%), shoulder (16%), wrist (15%), and knee (9%) symptoms (table 11.1).

Among 154 golfers with low back pain, 137 identified the location of the symptoms: 70 of the 137 golfers (51%) reported right-side low back symptoms, 38 (28%) left-side, and 29 (21%) central or no laterality. The right-side location predominated with statistical significance ($p < 0.05$) (figure 11.1). The laterality of other symptoms—high back, shoulder, elbow, and wrist—was mainly left-sided, but there was no statistical difference. Figure 11.2 shows the relationship between

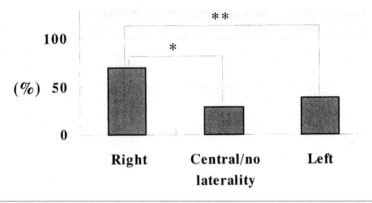

Figure 11.1   Laterality of low back symptoms. The prevalence of right-sided low back symptoms was significantly higher than those of others (*$p < 0.01$, **$p < 0.05$).

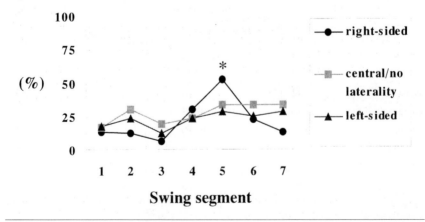

Figure 11.2   Association between swing segments and low back symptoms. Of 70 golfers who had a history of right-sided low back symptoms, 37 (53%) reported that those symptoms were aggravated at the phase of impact through follow-through (segment 5) (*$p < 0.05$).

low back symptoms and swing phase. Golfers reporting right-side low back pain experienced aggravation of symptoms during the impact through follow-through phase ($p < 0.05$). There was no association between swing phase and symptoms in golfers reporting central or no laterality or left-side low back pain.

RADIOGRAPHIC STUDY

Materials and Methods

X-ray and CT changes on the lumbar spine in 10 male elite amateur and 16 professional golfers (14 male, 2 female) with low back symptoms were studied. All subjects were right-handed, with an average age, golf career, and handicap of 42 years, 21 years, and 4.3, respectively. We randomly selected 105 age-matched, nongolfing patients (71 male, 34 female) with low back symptoms as a control group. Vertebral osteophyte formations on plain x-rays were graded into five groups according to Nathan's classification (Nathan 1962), using anteroposterior, bilateral oblique, and profile views: Grade 0—no osteophyte formations; Grade I—mild osteophyte formation; Grade II—moderate osteophyte formation; Grade III—severe osteophyte formation; Grade IV—kissing or fusion of osteophyte. We also classified facet joint changes on the CT into four groups: Grade 0—normal; Grade I—mild joint space narrowing; Grade II—moderate joint space narrowing or presence of osteoarthritis; Grade III—severe osteoarthritis. The chi-square test was used for statistical analysis.

Results

In golfers, vertebral osteophyte formations were observed most frequently at the L2/3, L3/4, and L4/5 levels, while severe degenerative changes higher than Grade I predominated at L4/5. In the control group, the incidence of degenerative changes (all grades) was the highest at L4/5. When golfers were compared with controls, golfers exhibited a higher rate of right-side L3/4 changes ($p < 0.01$) and total right-side changes ($p < 0.01$) (figure 11.3).

In both groups, the overall incidence of facet joint osteoarthritis (all grades) was highest at the L4/5 level. When golfers were compared with controls, golfers exhibited a higher rate of right-side L3/4 ($p < 0.05$), L4/5 ($p < 0.01$), and total right-side facet joint changes ($p < 0.01$) (figure 11.4).

DISCUSSION

The only previous report of injuries in professional golfers revealed that the wrist was the most frequently injured body part, followed by the lower back, with 106 (47%) and 93 (41%) of 226 golfers, respectively (McCarroll and Gioe 1982). Our results suggest that back injuries now significantly surpass wrist injuries in frequency (55% vs. 15%). Differences in the race, gender, and age makeup of the study populations could account for the injury rate differences, but we believe a

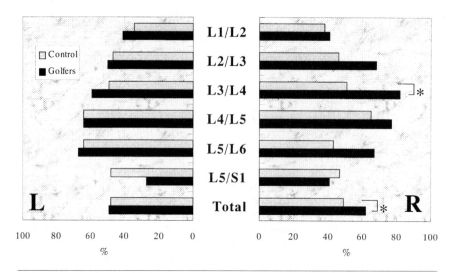

Figure 11.3   Incidence (without grading) of vertebral osteophyte formation both in golfers and in the control group. When golfers were compared to controls, golfers exhibited a higher rate of right-side L3/L4 changes (*p < 0.01) and total right-side changes (*p < 0.01).

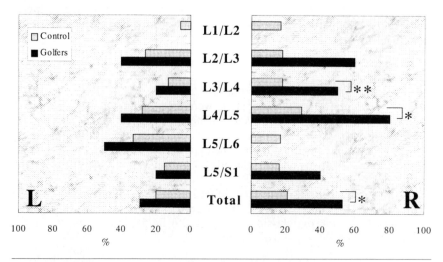

Figure 11.4   Incidence (without grading) of facet joint changes both in golfers and in the control group. When golfers were compared to controls, golfers exhibited a higher rate of right-side L3/L4 (**p < 0.05), L4/L5 (*p < 0.01), and total right-side facet joint changes (*p < 0.01).

fundamental change in the style of golf swing may be responsible. Materials of the clubhead, shaft, and ball are improving each year, as is the physical conditioning of the golfers. The available clubs and prominent golfers influence the "ideal" golf swing at any given time. For instance, the "modern" swing requires a greater shoulder turn relative to the hips to improve distance and accuracy, clearly increasing the potential for increased stresses on the lower back.

In the present study, we found that right-sided low back symptoms occurred at a significantly higher rate and that there was close association to a particular swing phase; the symptoms were aggravated from impact through follow-through. We also found that the golfers exhibited a significantly higher rate of right-side osteophyte formation, as well as right-sided degenerative changes at the facet joints, than controls. This laterality of low back symptoms and radiographic asymmetry appear to be characteristic of low back injuries in elite and professional golfers. Our interpretation is that the radiographic findings result directly from the asymmetric motion of the golf swing.

We also analyzed trunk kinematics during the golf swing in Japanese collegiate golfers using a three-dimensional motion analysis system (Sugaya, Moriya et al. 1996). We found that trunk motion during the swing is a combination of counter-clockwise axial rotation and right lateral bending, a distinctly asymmetric motion. Both axial rotation velocity and right lateral bending angle increase during the forward swing through the follow-through, with both parameters reaching peak values almost simultaneously just after impact.

Hosea and colleagues used a combination of kinematic measurements and a computed model of the spine to estimate the forces and torque at the L3/4 level during the golf swing (Hosea et al. 1990; Hosea and Gatt 1996). They found a complex loading pattern with large components of A/P shear and compressive loads, and lateral bending and axial torque, that peaked during the forward swing and follow-through. They stated that the peak loads occurred during the forward swing through acceleration phase before impact. The timing of the peak load to the L3/4 level of the lumbar spine, just before the impact, is consistent with the results of electromyography studies (Bechler et al. 1995; Pink et al. 1993; Watkins et al. 1996), in which the trunk and thigh muscles were most active during the forward swing through acceleration phase (before the impact). During this phase, trunk and thigh muscles are thought to accelerate spine rotation as well as lateral bending. Following impact, maximum lumbar rotation velocity and lumbar lateral bending occur almost simultaneously, possibly contributing to asymmetric forces and degeneration of the lumbar spine.

McTeigue et al. (1994), using an instrumented spatial linkage, reported on the average hip and trunk rotations, lumbar axial rotations, lumbar lateral bending, and swing timing in groups of PGA Tour players and amateur golfers. In comparing spine kinematics between professional and amateur golfers, they found that amateurs had a significantly higher degree of lumbar lateral bending at peak backswing, but a significantly lower degree of lumbar lateral bending at ball impact. In recreational golfers, swing techniques are not refined and may place greater stress upon the musculoskeletal system (Batt 1990; Hosea et al. 1990; Hosea and Gatt 1996; McCarroll et al. 1990). We think the causes of low back injuries of such golfers may be somewhat different from those for professional golfers, who have good swing mechanics. Professional golfers' swings are very consistent from the forward swing through the follow-through, while the amateurs' are characterized by highly variability, poor mechanics, and less physical fitness (Batt 1990; Hosea et al. 1990; Hosea and Gatt 1996; McCarroll et al. 1990). Therefore, low back injuries in elite and professional golfers, characterized by the laterality of the symptoms and asymmetric degeneration in the lumbar spine, may have different pathology and etiology from general low back injuries. We believe that the repetitive asymmetric motion of the golf swing and overuse jointly contribute to cause low back injuries in elite golfers.

In our ongoing biomechanical study, we hypothesize that lateral bending angle and axial rotation velocity jointly contribute to lumbar degeneration and injuries. We also proposed a new parameter, the "crunch factor," which is defined as the product of these two parameters, in an attempt to objectively quantify lumbar spine mechanics that may result in injury and serve as the basis of comparison between "healthy" and "pathological" golf swings (Sugaya, Morgan et al. 1997). We hope this and future studies help us to realize better-targeted strategies for swing modification, rehabilitation, and prevention.

CONCLUSION

The present study demonstrated the high prevalence of low back pain in professional golfers. Many golfers reported right-side pain that was aggravated from impact through follow-through. Moreover, elite golfers with low back pain exhibited asymmetric degenerative changes on the lumbar spine in comparison to a nongolfing control group. We concluded that laterality of symptoms and asymmetry of radiographic findings characterized low back injuries in elite golfers, suggesting that these injuries were closely related to the asymmetric motion of the golf swing.

References

Batt, M.E. (1990). A survey of golf injuries in amateur golfers. *Br J Sports Med,* 26(1), 63-65.

Bechler, J.R., Jobe, F.W., Pink, M., Perry, J., and Ruwe, P.A. (1995). Electromyographic analysis of the hip and knee during the golf swing. *Clin J Sports Med,* 5, 162-166.

Hosea, T.M., and Gatt, C.J. (1996). Back pain in golf. *Clin Sports Med,* 15(1), 37-53.

Hosea, T.M., Gatt, C.J., Galli, K.M., Langrana, N.A., and Zawadsky, J.P. (1990). Biomechanical analysis of the golfer's back. In: A.J. Cochran (ed.), *Science and Golf. Proceedings of the First World Scientific Congress of Golf.* University of St. Andrews. London: Spon, 43-48.

Jobe, F.W., and Schwab, D.M. (1991). Golf for the mature athlete. *Clin Sports Med,* 10(2), 269-282.

McCarroll, J.R., and Gioe, T.J. (1982). Professional golfers and the price they pay. *Physician SportsMed,* 10(7), 64-70.

McCarroll, J.R., Retting, A., and Shelbourne, K. (1990). Injuries in the amateur golfer. *Physician SportsMed,* 18(3), 122-126.

McTeigue, M., Lamb, S.R., Mottram, R., and Pirrozzolo, F. (1994). Spine and hip motion analysis during the golf swing. In: A.J. Cochran and M.R. Farrally (ed.), *Science and Golf II. Proceedings of the 2nd World Scientific Congress of Golf.* London: Spon, 50-58.

Nathan, H. (1962). Osteophytes of the vertebral column. *J Bone Joint Surg,* 44A(2), 243-268.

Pink, M., Perry, J., and Jobe, F.W. (1993). Electromyographic analysis of the trunk in golfers. *Am J Sports Med,* 21(3), 385-388.

Sugaya, H., Morgan, D.A., Banks, S.A., Cook, F.F., and Moriya, H. (1997). Golf and low back injury: Defining the crunch factor. Presented at 22nd annual meeting of AOSSM, June, Sun Valley, ID.

Sugaya, H., Moriya, H., Takahashi, K., Yamagata, M., and Tsuchiya, A. (1996). Motion analysis of the trunk during the golf swing. *Jpn J Orthop Sports Med,* 16(4), 330-337.

Sugaya, H., Moriya, H., Takahashi, K., Yamagata, M., and Tsuchiya, A. (1997). Asymmetric degenerative changes on the lumbar spine in the elite and professional golfers. *Orthop Trans,* 21(1).

Watkins, R.G., Uppal, G.S., Perry, J., Pink, M., and Dinsay, J.M. (1996). Dynamic electromyographic analysis of trunk musculature in professional golfers. *Am J Sports Med,* 24(4), 535-538.

CHAPTER 12

Back Pain Among Junior Golfers

R.J. Leigh
Chichester Institute of Higher Education, Chichester, England

D.B. Young
Farnham Chiropractic Clinic, Farnham, England

The purpose of this study was to determine whether the incidence of back pain among junior golfers was any greater than among the general adolescent population. Fifty-one junior golfers replied to a questionnaire; 41.2% of subjects reported pain following play or practice. This falls within the parameters of previously reported research for similarly aged children.

Keywords: Back pain, adolescents, junior, golfers.

INTRODUCTION

Back pain has a lifetime incidence of about 80% among the general population (Frymoyer et al. 1983). Among children there is a reported (via a variety of studies cited in Troussier et al. 1994) prevalence of back pain of between 7% and 51.2%. A number of studies (McCarroll and Gioe 1982; Jobe and Yocum 1988; Hosea et al. 1990; Van Der Steenhoven et al. 1994) have shown adult golfers to exhibit common incidences of back pain resulting from practice, but very little research has taken place to identify any possible problems among juniors.

It is generally recognised that the golf swing places intense strain upon the back, particularly the lumbar spine (Hosea et al. 1990). Yet there is perhaps a reluctance to appreciate that resulting damage may be as likely to occur among younger golfers as among their more adult counterparts.

This study, the first part of a longitudinal piece, set out to identify whether, among younger golfers, a significant proportion suffer back problems.

SUBJECTS AND METHODS

The subjects consisted of a number (n = 51) of junior members of golf clubs in the south-east of England. Their ages ranged from 10 to 18 years with a mean of 13.49 ± 1.95. The vast majority were boys, but a small percentage of girls (n = 5) responded. The greater proportion were also right-handed (n = 48).

They were all requested to reply, with the assistance of their parents if necessary, to a questionnaire containing 15 items requiring information relating to their play and practice habits: that is, the frequency of play and practice and the duration of an individual practice session, the length of time they had been playing in years, whether they had back problems requiring medical attention from either a doctor or other medical practitioner and whether and for how long those problems may have persisted, whether they had suffered pain after play or practice, the location of such (self-identified on a diagram), and whether they were involved in any other physical activity on a regular basis. The information was then subjected to a variety of forms of statistical enquiry. Descriptive statistics were used in accordance with the level of measurement, and chi-square analysis and its derivatives were used to analyse the data. Where appropriate, Kendall Tau and Cramer's V were used as measures of association.

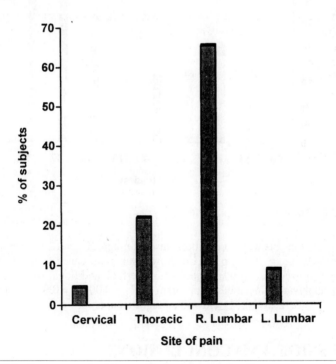

Figure 12.1   Percentage of subjects suffering from pain by site.

RESULTS

Results showed that 13.7% of subjects suffered problems that had required medical attention; 41.2% of the group identified pain following play or practice. Modal scores indicated that subjects played once per week and practiced additionally at the same time. The duration of practice was about 1 hour per practice session.

The location of the problems is indicated on figure 12.1, which shows that the lumbar region was the most common site.

Looking at pain in the right lumbar region, it is interesting to note that 93.3% of reported cases were among right-handed golfers. However, pain in the left lumbar region was not reported by any of the left-handed golfers.

The numbers of subjects encountering pain increased with both age and experience of the game. Figures 12.2 and 12.3, although showing some fluctuations, do indicate a general upward trend.

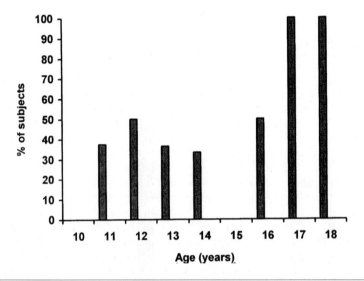

Figure 12.2   The incidence of pain with age.

Chi-square analysis was used in both cases; for age, $X^2_{(8)} = 12.11$, $p = 0.15$, and for experience, $X^2_{(8)} = 10.37$, $p = 0.17$, showed no significance at the 5% level.

The data showed that 70.6% of subjects undertook additional sporting activity, but again, analysis against medical problems ($X^2_{(2)} = 0.002$, $p = 0.95$) and incidence of pain ($X^2_{(2)} = 0.12$, $p = 0.91$) showed no significance.

DISCUSSION AND CONCLUSIONS

The number of juniors requiring medical treatment (13.7%) is certainly not as great as the number of adult injuries reported among professional golfers by McCarroll

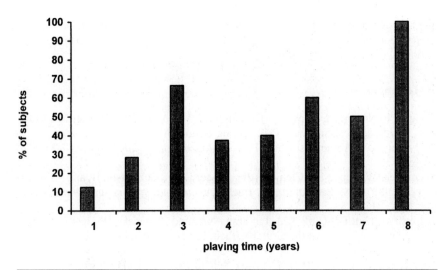

Figure 12.3   Incidence of pain against years of play.

and Gioe (1982) (23.7%), but this would not be unexpected, as professionals will have been playing considerably longer and would be spending far more time in play and practice. Also, general levels of flexibility at this stage, particularly at early adolescence, should be reasonably sound and would not necessarily have started the natural process of reduction by increased muscle development (McNaught-Davis 1991). The figures are similar to those provided by Troussier et al. (1994) (15.5%), among whose subjects only 2.3% did not participate in any form of sporting activity. The self-reporting of pain following play or practice at 41.2% does not fall outside the figures provided by others working in the area of children's back problems (Troussier et al. 1994; Balague et al. 1994). It would not appear therefore that involvement in golf is any more likely to cause back problems than any other form of activity in which children or adolescents are involved. The rise in the figures with experience of the game, associated as it is with a similar pattern according to age, is also consistent with figures provided by Troussier et al. (1994) and Balague et al. (1994) for the general adolescent population. Their research confirms that youngsters incur back pain for a variety of reasons, some of which are activity related and others of which are more a reflection of the modern trend toward a more sedentary life style.

The relationship between the high percentage of right-handed subjects and the reporting of pain in the right lumbar region may be explained by an analysis of the follow-through action that results in hyperextension of the lumbar spine (McCarroll and Gioe 1982) and right sacroiliac joint. Excessive rotation and extension in a person who has not sufficiently warmed up properly may cause damage to the joint capsule and ligaments around the lumbosacral facet joints and right sacroiliac joint, commonly causing a sacroiliac sprain or facet jamming syndrome.

Another possibility may be related to the tendency for the right-handed golfer to lead with the right foot and hand when performing many of the bending activities associated with both play and practice.

This possibility of damage may be further offset not only by sufficient prepractice preparation but also through a strengthening of the contralateral side to bring about a more symmetrical development.

References

Balague F, Nordin M, Skovron ML, Dutoit G, Yee A, and Waldburger M (1994). Non-Specific Low-Back Pain among Schoolchildren: A Field Survey with Analysis of Some Associated Factors. *Journal of Spinal Disorders* 7(5): 374-379.

Frymoyer JW, Pope MH, Clements JH, Wilder DG, MacPherson B, and Ashikaga T (1983). Risk Factors in Low Back Pain. *Journal of Bone and Joint Surgery* 65A: 213-218.

Hosea TM, Gatt CJ, Galli KM, Langrana NA, and Zawadsky JP (1990). Biomechanical Analysis of the Golfer's Back. In *Science and Golf,* ed. AJ Cochran, 43-48. London: Spon.

Jobe F, and Yocum L (1988). The Dark Side of Practice. *Golf* 30(3): 22.

McCarroll JR, and Gioe TJ (1982). Professional Golfers and the Price They Pay. *The Physician and Sportsmedicine* 10(7): 64-70.

McNaught-Davis P (1991). *Flexibility: How to Understand It. How to Achieve It.* London: Partridge.

Troussier B, Davioine P, de Gaudemaris R, Fauconnier J, and Phelip X (1994). Back Pain in Schoolchildren: A Study among 1178 Pupils. *Scandinavian Journal of Rehabilitative Medicine* 26: 143-146.

Van Der Steenhoven GA, Burdorf A, and Tromp-Klaren EGM (1994). Back Pain in Novice Golfers, a One Year Follow-up. In *Science and Golf II,* ed. AJ Cochran and MR Farrally, 20-26. London: Spon.

CHAPTER 13

A Multidisciplinary Approach to Performance Enhancement in the Aging Golfer: A Preliminary Study

N. Haller, PhD
San Diego Golf Academy, San Diego, California

D. Haller, Pharm.D.
Clinical Pharmacist, San Diego, California

D. Herbert, Professional Golf Instructor
San Diego, California

T. Whalen, MPH
San Diego Golf Academy, San Diego, California

Golf is viewed as one of the sports available to seniors (50 years and older). However, alterations in their physiology and psychology present athletic performance challenges for senior golfers. A multidisciplinary survey to determine the attitudes and behaviors related to performance enhancement was completed by 70 senior golfers. The findings focus on instruction, physical fitness, mental aspects, medications, and nutrition. They are presented along with archival data with the ultimate aim of providing recommendations for senior golfers and those working with them.

Keywords: Flexibility, nutrition, pharmacological, psychological.

INTRODUCTION

According to the National Golf Foundation (1996), there are over 6 million United States seniors who play golf. They account for 50% of the rounds played. They spend more per person on golf equipment, merchandise, and fees than other adult golfers. In essence, the senior golf market is thriving and will continue to grow as the population ages. Therefore it is imperative to determine the needs of this group and respond accordingly. Since one of the primary reasons for golfing is recreational, it is important to examine those issues that relate most closely to performance and enjoyment of play.

Research indicates that there are physical and psychological correlates to good sport performance. Teaching professionals have observed that range of motion greatly influences the ability to add distance to golf shots. Fitness experts emphasize the importance of strength training to reduce injuries. It is widely acknowledged that mental preparation and practice improve confidence and resiliency. Medical professionals agree that nutrition and pharmacologic agents impact golf performance.

This preliminary multidisciplinary survey was designed to provide a clearer understanding of the attitudes and behaviors of senior golfers as related to instruction, physical and psychological fitness, medications, and nutrition. This information will help senior golfers to enhance their performance, which will lead to greater enjoyment of the sport.

METHOD

A 27-item questionnaire was completed by a convenient sample of senior golfers throughout San Diego County, California, USA. It was distributed by the authors, with the largest channel being private and public golf course pro shops. Senior golfers were invited to fill out the brief questionnaire prior to or after playing golf. Inclusion criteria were age (50 years and older) and ability to report or estimate handicap/index.

Demographic information requested was age, gender, length of time playing golf, frequency of play, and handicap/index (6 questions). The content of the questionnaire was on instruction and exercise habits (12 questions), psychological practices (4 questions), and medication and nutritional habits (5 questions). A total of 71 surveys were collected. One incomplete questionnaire was eliminated, and the remaining 70 were analyzed.

RESULTS

Table 13.1 provides descriptive statistics for the respondents in the study.

Instruction and Physical Fitness

Studies have found that age-related impairment in older golfers can be compensated for by greater reliance on skills that remain stable or improve with age. For example, Over and Thomas (1995) found that older golfers (mean age 62.3 years) drove the ball a shorter distance than younger golfers (mean age 33.6 years) but reported fewer negative emotions and thoughts in relation to performance. In the present study, 58 golfers (83%) reported a desire to improve some aspect of their game. Twenty-one percent of those who responded to this question (n = 12) wanted to become more proficient in putting and/or short-game skills. A total of 19% (n = 11) wanted to

Table 13.1   Descriptive Statistics

	N	Mean	Std. deviation
Age*	70	61.49	9.43
# Years in golf	70	29.84	16.16
Handicap	70	16.69	9.13
# Lessons/yr	70	3.56	7.55
# Rounds/mo	69	9.62	6.21
# Rounds/wk	66	2.51	1.45

*Gender—12 females/58 males

increase distance, and the same number seek better psychological skills (i.e., visualization, goal setting, relaxation, etc.). Seventeen percent (n = 10) noted a desire to improve a mechanical part of their game, such as "smooth swing," "tempo," "timing," "weight shift," and the like. Other issues were divided among consistency (7%; n = 4); practice (5%; n = 3); frequency of play (4%; n = 2); long irons (4%; n = 2); and greens in regulation, partners, and lessons (each at 2%; n = 1).

When asked if practice improves their game, 98% (n = 68) of the respondents answered yes, and the same number reported that their game had improved over the years. They did not take many lessons (mean is only 3.56 lessons per year) despite the fact that 92% (n = 67) claimed that lessons improved their game. However, the majority of the respondents, 87% (n = 68), find golfing enjoyable even without improvement in their game. They play golf predominately for the sport itself (51%), and not for social reasons only (10%). Thirty-five percent reported golfing for a combination of the two reasons.

The survey revealed much about the exercise habits of this population. Forty-five percent of the respondents reported that they engaged in physical activity that was hard enough to increase breathing and heart rate in accordance with the minimum recommendation set by the American College of Sports Medicine (ACSM, 1991), that is, for at least 20 minutes per day three or more times per week. While the benefits of such exercise are numerous, their applicability to golf performance is unclear. It can be assumed that cardiovascular fitness is beneficial, but it has not been proven to have an effect on any specific golf performance outcome such as handicap.

One mode of exercise that has been studied in relation to golf is strength training. It has been shown to be effective in performance outcomes such as clubhead speed (McCarroll, Rettig, and Shelbourne, 1990). In a more recent study (Westcott, Dolan, and Caviacchi, 1996), subjects were able to improve clubhead speed by 5% after eight weeks of strength training. In the present survey, 21.1% (n = 4) of the respondents reported that they performed strength training, with the majority of these (78.6%) doing so two to three days per week. This frequency has been established as effective in increasing strength in this population (Nichols, Hitzelberger, and Sherman, 1995; Whalen, 1996) and is endorsed by the ACSM (1991) as the recommended frequency. In addition, as most golf injuries are musculoskeletal in origin, increasing strength in golf-specific muscle groups can work to prevent injuries.

Another area of concern for seniors is flexibility. Flexibility not only prevents injury but also allows the golfer to execute a more perfect swing by enhancing the body's ability to get into the required positions. In Westcott, Dolan, and Caviacchi's (1996) program, a flexibility component significantly increased participants' shoulder and hip flexibility. The authors noted that these results stand in sharp contrast to the beliefs held by golfers in their sample, who thought that strength training might reduce their flexibility and hinder their driving ability. In the present survey, 53.5% of respondents reported performing flexibility exercises. Among these, the mean frequency was 4.11 days per week, which exceeds the ACSM's recommended minimum.

Mental Aspects

Several studies have examined the psychological skills required for peak performance. In one study by Orlick (1980), there was disagreement from sport to sport about the physical attributes needed for excellence, but nearly total agreement across sports on psychological skills required for success. In the present survey, 53 golfers (76%) acknowledged the use or practice of at least one or more psychological techniques. In descending order these were setting goals for practice and play (66%; n = 35), visualization or imagery (62%; n = 33), reading books on the mental game (60%; n = 32), watching videos on the mental game (32%; n = 17), listening to audiotapes on the mental game (25%; n = 13), and relaxation or meditation exercises (25%; n = 13). It is noteworthy that the most frequently practiced skill was reported to be goal setting. In many studies, goal setting has been linked to increased commitment, a factor believed to be an essential factor for top performance (Orlick, 1980).

In addition to commitment, other distinguishing features of top performance have been studied in amateur and professional athletes. McCaffrey and Orlick (1989) interviewed professional touring golfers and discovered a psychological profile that is linked with winning. These are associated with confidence and remaining calm and composed under pressure. The majority of the respondents in the present survey (61.4% of the sample of 70; n = 43) reported that their ability to cope with pressure was above average or excellent. There were 22 golfers (31.4%) who reported moderate coping skills under pressure situations. When these groups are combined, there is a total of 92.8% of respondents who believe they have at least average or better-than-average coping abilities. Only 7.2% (n = 5) of the golfers reported getting upset or very upset under pressure.

With such favorable findings, it was expected that confidence levels would be equally high. Collegiate golfers and touring and teaching professionals acknowledged in Cohn's (1991) study that feeling highly self-confident was associated with peak performance. However, the majority of the survey respondents reported lacking such a level of confidence (61.5%, n = 43). Only 38.6% (n = 27) felt sufficiently confident about their game.

Medication and Nutrition

In the general population, older people have more health problems and are prescribed more medications than younger people. Therefore it would stand to reason that medication usage in senior golfers also would be significant. In this survey, prescribed medication usage was reported in 50.7% (n = 36) of the respondents. Some of the medications used were not necessarily related to golf, i.e. cardiovascular disorders. However, the respondents reported using some medication that may be directly related to golf or golf injuries, that is, arthritis/pain medications. It is widely acknowledged that the majority of golfing injuries are soft tissue musculoskeletal injuries (Batt, 1992, 1993). A total of 47% (n = 17) of these respondents used medications to treat hypertension, 39% (n = 14) to treat arthritis or pain, 11% (n = 4) to treat eye disorders, and 8% (n = 3) to control diabetes. It should be noted that 39% (n = 14) of the golfers used two or more pharmaceutical agents. In this survey, other disorders treated with medications included hypothyroidism, cardiac arrhythmia, hypercholesteremia, allergies, hormonal replacement, and temporal arthritis.

While many pharmaceutical agents may be detrimental to athletic performance, including that in golf, some may be advantageous due to their pharmacologic properties. This situation has caused the banning of many agents by the United States Olympic Committee (USOC) (Fuentes, Rosenberg, and Davis, 1994). The antihypertensive agents used by the participants in the present study included beta blockers, calcium channel blockers, diuretics, and ACE inhibitors. The arthritic/pain medications included the nonsteroidal anti-inflammatory agents, skeletal muscle relaxers, and acetaminophen. Various glaucoma agents and oral hypoglycemic agents and insulin were used for the reported eye disorders and diabetes, respectively.

Although some of the medications used by survey respondents may have advantageous effects on sport performance, only 3% (n = 1) of respondents reported medications to have a positive effect. Only 8% (n = 3) of the golfers reported that their medications affected their game negatively. The negative side effects included tiredness and decreased concentration. The positive effect was pain relief during play. Only 6% (n = 2) of the golfers reported changing their medication administration time in relation to their golfing schedules. Both of these golfers reported improvement in their game after the change.

It is estimated that the total energy expenditure during 18 holes of golf is more than 960 Kcal with a decrease in blood glucose (Murase, Kamir, and Hoskikawa, 1989). Results on the nutritional habits of our golf respondents revealed that 57% of the golfers eat high-carbohydrate meals before golfing and 35.2% (n = 25) eat high-protein meals before golfing. Interestingly, 45.1% (n = 32) of the respondents drink coffee before playing. Fruit and juices are consumed by 28.2% (n = 20) and 25.4% (n = 18), respectively, before golfing.

It was reported that during the golf round, 28.2% (n = 20) consume "sports" drinks, 26.8% (n = 19) eat snacks, 19.7% (n = 14) have nutritional supplements, 18.3% (n = 13) eat fruit, 9.9% (n = 7) drink juice, 8.5% (n = 6) drink alcohol, and 4.2% (n = 3) drink coffee. Surprisingly, 59.2% (n = 42) of the respondents did not feel their eating habits affected their game.

DISCUSSION

This survey reflects that this population of senior golfers is utilizing some of the necessary components for enhanced golf performance. Half of the respondents reported performing flexibility exercises. A vast majority believe that lessons have helped or could help improve their game. They report engaging in mental skills training, and they understand that improvements in putting and the short game are key factors to lowering their scores. Although the number is small, some golfers have modified their medication regime with good results. Many golfers appear to have good nutritional habits.

Despite these favorable indications, however, the survey results underscore the importance of educating senior golfers about essential practices and behaviors that are widely known to improve performance. For example, this sample of senior golfers wants to pursue added yardage as one of their priority goals, yet many variables could be attributed to their lack of satisfactory distance. These include decreased motor coordination, decreased stamina, fatigue from medications, and the like. While strength training and flexibility training are two activities for improving such conditions, nutritional, physiological, and psychological education also are warranted.

It is interesting to note that essentially the same numbers of participants in the study reported desiring better short-game skills and wanting to add distance. Yet the participants' lack of response on consistency, practice, and hitting greens in regulation reflects incongruent beliefs about how to improve their game. This corroborates the aforementioned importance of communication of basic information about performance enhancement.

There also is an apparent contradiction in two survey findings related to psychological factors. This is striking because the respondents as a whole appear to be rather sophisticated about the mental side of golf (76% engage in mental training). Although the vast majority of respondents (92%) believe that lessons have helped or could help their game, they did not behave in accordance with such a belief (the mean number of lessons was only 3.56 per year). Secondly, the majority of the respondents rated themselves as above average to excellent in their ability to cope with pressure, but they reported a confidence level that was incongruent with this. Although 83% of the surveyed sample reported a desire to improve their game, the results may reflect the overall lack of confidence that senior golfers have about their ability to do so, a common problem seen by teaching professionals. Such low levels of confidence undoubtedly trigger feelings of inadequacy causing many senior golfers to abandon a recreational activity that otherwise holds so much positive benefit.

Medical and nutritional behaviors reported in this sample also support the need for educating senior golfers. Although one-half of the golfers in the survey used medications, few acknowledged the impact medications could have on their athletic performance, either positively or negatively. In fact, some of the medications used by these golfers are banned by the USOC for their presumed positive effects. Accordingly, some of the participants used agents that could have a deleterious effect on their performance. Presumably some of these medications could be changed to less problematic agents and/or their times of administration could be adjusted so that peak blood levels would not occur during playing time, which would lessen the negative effect.

Most of the participants eat high-carbohydrate meals before golfing. This could be appropriate if they continued with carbohydrates throughout their game. Otherwise energy levels fall, with a decrease in performance most likely following. Interestingly, almost half of our population drink coffee before playing. This would cause an increase in their caffeine blood level during the first few hours and a decreased level through the last few hours. Depending on the golfer, this could result in erratic nervous system stimulation, with lower consistency. Clearly, the medication and nutritional habits of those surveyed support the need for communicating information. What is not apparent is whether golfers' lack of awareness about these practices is due to a lack of knowledge and/or an unwillingness by seniors to change habits. In either case, education is crucial.

It is through training in these areas that senior golfers are most likely to improve their performance as well as their enjoyment of golf. This includes strength training, instruction and quality practice, sound psychological and nutritional habits, and improved medication regimens. However, the communication channels for disseminating such information to seniors have not been established clearly. In the past, teaching professionals were the point of contact, but with so few senior golfers taking lessons, other avenues of education must be developed.

Country club and golf course personnel and representatives should explore the possibilities of offering educational seminars along with exhibits on equipment. While advances in technology for "hard" merchandise can improve distance and accuracy for seniors, it is equally important to include training on the "soft" but essential foundations of good performance. In assisting the growing population of senior golfers, the entire golf industry will benefit, especially those within it who play the game.

References

American College of Sports Medicine. (1991). *Guidelines for Exercise Testing and Prescription.* 4th ed.

Batt, M.E. (1992). A survey of golf injuries in amateur golfers. *British Journal of Sports Medicine* 26: 63-65.

Batt, M.E. (1993). Golfing injuries: An overview. *Sports Med (New England)* 16: 64-67.

Cohn, P.J. (1991). An exploratory study on peak performance. *The Sport Psychologist* 8: 227-238.

Fuentes, R.J., Rosenberg, J.M., and Davis, A. (eds.). (1994). *Athletic Drug Reference '94.*, NC: Clean Data, Inc.

McCaffrey, N., and Orlick, T. (1989). Mental factors related to excellence among top professional golfers. *International Journal of Sport Psychology* 20: 256-278.

McCarroll, J., Rettig, A., and Shelbourne, K.D. (1990). Injuries in the amateur golfer. *Physician and Sports Medicine* 18: 122-126.

Murase, Y., Kamir, S., and Hoskikawa, T. (1989). Heart rate and metabolic response to participation in golf. *Journal of Sports Medicine and Physical Fitness* 29: 269-272.

National Golf Foundation. (1996). *Senior Golfer Profile.* Jupiter, FL.

Nichols, J.F., Hitzelberger, L.M., and Sherman, J.G. (1995). The effects of resistance training on muscular strength and functional abilities of older adults. *Journal of Aging & Physical Activity* 3: 238-250.

Orlick, T. (1980). *In Pursuit of Excellence.* Champaign, IL: Human Kinetics.

Over, R., and Thomas, P. (1995). Age and skilled psychomotor performance: A comparison of younger and older golfers. *International Journal of Aging & Human Development* 41: 1-12.

Westcott, W., Dolan, F., and Caviacchi, T. (1996). Golf and strength training are compatible activities. *Journal of Strength and Conditioning* 18: 54-56.

Whalen, T. (1996). Project Independence: A Falls Prevention Program Analysis. Master's thesis. San Diego State University.

CHAPTER 14

Psychomotor Disability in the Golf Swing: Case Study of an Aging Golfer

P.R. Thomas
Centre for Movement Education and Research, Griffith University, Brisbane 4111, Australia

This is a case study of a male amateur golfer who, at the age of 58 years, developed a psychomotor disability that severely affected his golf swing. The paper describes the disability, the effects of various factors, the psychological interventions that have been conducted over 6 years, and their effectiveness. The challenges faced by this individual highlight the importance of automaticity in skilled performance.

Keywords: Psychological skills, swing disability, yips, automaticity, golf performance.

INTRODUCTION

Much of the research on the theme of The Golfer at the 2nd World Scientific Congress of Golf was directed at producing maximum distance, accuracy, control, and consistency in each golf shot (Cochran & Farrally, 1994). Many of the studies reported significant differences between elite golfers and other players in the biomechanics of the swing, respiratory and psychophysiological patterns, and psychological and psychomotor skills, strategies, and states associated with optimal performance during competition. In contrast, relatively few studies focused on golfers' errors or problems or on issues of remediation or rehabilitation.

Previous research by McDaniel, Cummings, and Shain (1989) suggested that between 12% and 28% of golfers experience the "yips," an involuntary motor disturbance occurring during the execution of focused, finely controlled, skilled motor behaviour. Involuntary movements, frequently described as "jerks," "tremors," "spasms," and "twitches," are much more likely to be experienced during putting (54%) than when chipping (5%) or driving (2%). However, "freezing" is also frequently described, especially prior to the forward stroke into the ball. Data from the McDaniel et al. (1989) sample indicated that on average, golfers who experienced the yips were first affected at 35.9 years, some 20.9 years after they began playing. Those affected had been playing longer (mean 35.6 years) than those who were unaffected (mean 31.0 years), and were correspondingly older (mean 50.5 years) than their counterparts (mean 47.5 years). Golfers affected by the yips scored higher on an item designed to assess obsessional thinking, "It's hard to concentrate because of unwanted thoughts or images that come into my mind and won't go away." Approximately three-quarters of those affected reported that the yips intensified with anxiety: 46% experienced the yips during practice, whereas 99% were affected during competition.

The purpose of this study was to examine the deterioration in the golf swing of an experienced amateur player, to describe the psychological interventions that have been conducted over several years, and to report on their effectiveness.

METHOD

Case History

Jim was initially referred by a general practitioner in 1992. He had recently retired from work at the age of 58 years, and after 40 years of golf was looking forward to playing more than twice a week. At 184cm and 95kg, Jim's physical strength was impressive. In 1982 his handicap was 15, and his estimated average driving distance was 200 metres.

At the time of the initial consultation in 1992, Jim played two competition rounds a week but did not practice or play any social golf. His practice swing in competitions seemed reasonably sound in technique. When playing the shot, however, Jim would often "freeze" after the backswing and be unable to bring the club down to make contact with the ball. Several times during a round he would take 10 or more full backswings before being able to strike the ball. Not surprisingly, Jim reported a loss of some 30 metres in his average driving distance (170 metres) and marked inaccuracy in his shot-making, and his handicap was out to 20. This disability did not affect approach shots less than 100 metres, his chipping, or his putting.

Prior to the initial consultation, Jim completed the Golf Performance Survey (Thomas & Over, 1994). His profile revealed high ratings on the seeking improvement, putting skill, conservative approach, and striving for maximum distance subscales and low ratings on automaticity, concentration, mental preparation, and commitment. Despite his difficulties, Jim's profile showed that his emotions and cognitions on the course were no more negative than those of the average golfer.

After verifying the profile, Jim visited the practice range, initially hitting plastic training balls. His smooth execution of the golf swing in this setting suggested that factors associated with the pressure of performing in competition were contributing to Jim's disability. The initial consultation session was therefore aimed at training relaxation techniques that enabled him to recognise and reduce unwanted muscle tension during a round. A progressive muscle relaxation script was taped for Jim to use repeatedly before the next session, and instructional materials on beating tension were also provided (Leadbetter, 1989).

The second consultation, a week later, further developed his relaxation skills and included training in centering techniques (Nideffer, 1985). This session also focused on developing an appropriate preshot routine that would permit Jim to execute the swing automatically without consciously trying to control his skilled movements. To improve his tempo, Jim used a swing cue, "Edelweiss," suggested by Tom Watson (1992). Starting his take-away with the first syllable, he would reach the top of his backswing by the second and swing through to impact by the third. Use of such a cue in this way is consistent with the "back-hit" exercise recommended by Gallwey (1979).

Less than 3 months after the second consultation, Jim amassed 47 points in a single Stableford competition to win by a margin of 10 points. Three days later he scored 40 points in a 15-hole midweek event to win a major club competition by 4 points. For the next 2 years, Jim swung the club smoothly and participated regularly in competitions. During the following year, however, his swing gradually deteriorated to the point that he requested a third consultation in October 1995. This session included revising some earlier techniques, examining their use in the preshot routine by an expert (Nick Faldo's second shot to the 15th green in the final round of the 1992 Open at Muirfield), and recommending the exercises for developing concentration and promoting automatic execution of the swing demonstrated by Fine (1993).

Jim requested further help in September 1996 after his swing disability began to affect practice on the driving range. Increased tension was attributed to stress following the poor health of a family member, and he reported that he was not enjoying golf as much as previously. In addition to addressing these issues, Jim agreed to work on initiating the downswing with his hips rather than his arms. Two months later, Jim's score for nine holes was four shots better than his handicap. In the next 2 weeks he won his social club's B Grade championship, and for the first time in years won the main Saturday competition at his club. Despite these successes, Jim advised, "I am still having some trouble getting the club down within 6 attempts—but improving."

Instruments and Procedure

In early 1997, Jim agreed to participate in this study of his swing disability and gave permission for the results to be published. The research design involved the collection of baseline data prior to any further interventions. A card was designed, similar in format to the club's scorecard, on which his partner would record Jim's swings per shot, his result, and any pertinent comments (trees, water, bunker trouble). Jim was also asked to complete a golf performance diary after each competition round. This provided a record of the competition and his result, his precompetition preparation (extent of practice, arrival time, health and fitness, thoughts and feelings), experiences during the competition (course/weather conditions, playing partners, health and fitness, preshot routine, thoughts and feelings), and his reflections on the day. The researcher also videotaped Jim's practice warm-up and play on three or four holes during several competitions.

After baseline data were collected for 3 weeks (five rounds), Jim was given a videotape of his swing at practice and in competition, together with the Sybervision golf videotape featuring Al Geiberger. He was instructed to view the videotape of his own swing, study the Sybervision manual, and then watch the Sybervision videotape after using his progressive relaxation technique.

A psychological skills training intervention commenced 3 weeks later. Using the performance profiling approach advocated by Butler and Hardy (1992), Jim identified the technical, psychological, and psychomotor skills he needed to play effectively. He rated his current level on a 10-point scale and set realistic target ratings for each skill. Jim also completed the Test of Performance Strategies (Thomas, Hardy, & Murphy, 1996) during this session. Feedback on these profiles was provided 3 weeks later during a session when active progressive muscle relaxation was coupled with imagery training.

RESULTS

In his initial diary entry, Jim commented that the shorter the shot was, the fewer swings he required. In order to test this claim, the number of swings taken for first and second shots on Par 3, Par 4, and Par 5 holes played during the five rounds prior to any interventions was analysed in a 2 (Shots) × 3 (Par) ANOVA. Preliminary analyses revealed no serial dependency in the data, the first-order autocorrelation coefficient of .02 having a Box-Ljung value of .09, $p > .05$. Significantly more swings were taken on tee shots than on second shots, $F (1,186) = 45.25$, $p < .001$, and on longer holes than on shorter holes, $F (2,186) = 13.18$, $p < .001$. The Shot × Par interaction was also significant, $F (2, 186) = 4.62$, $p < .05$. Figure 14.1 shows that substantially fewer swings were taken on the second shot to Par 3 holes.

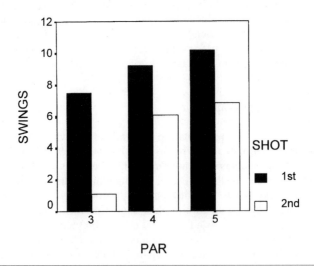

Figure 14.1   Mean number of swings taken on first and second shots to different par holes.

Four more cards were returned after Jim had repeatedly studied videotape of his own swing and the Sybervision golf videotape. Three of these cards reported the number of swings for tee shots only, as it was difficult for his markers to monitor subsequent shots. The numbers of swings for tee shots before and after viewing the videotapes were therefore compared in a 2 (Stage) × 3 (Par) ANOVA. No significant effects were revealed. Jim's diary entries indicated he was unable to relate to the Geiberger swing because of differences in physical build. He also commented, "I could not seem to get the Sybervision image into my mind."

Jim commented several times that he felt good and took fewer swings on the early holes during his rounds, but then lost touch and rhythm and couldn't get them back. The numbers of swings taken for tee shots in the early, middle, and late segments of his rounds were therefore compared in a 3 (Segment) × 3 (Par) ANOVA. Although the data suggested he was taking more swings on Par 3 and Par 4 tee shots late in his rounds, the effects were not significant.

On the day the psychological skills training (PST) commenced, Jim requested that he no longer submit a card showing the number of swings for each shot. He had originally been content to have someone else count his swings. When playing with unfamiliar partners, however, he had decided to count the swings himself. Subsequently, even when a regular partner completed his card, Jim continued to count his swings and felt pressured to hit after five or six swings even if he didn't feel ready. His request was granted even though this prevented statistical analysis of PST effects on the number of swings.

In compiling his performance profile, Jim identified his need to work on several technical skills (weight transfer, shoulder turn, completing the backswing), his need for a practice swing and consistent preshot routine, and his need to develop psychological and psychomotor skills (relaxation, positive self-talk, imagery, confidence, belief, trust, automaticity) that would enable him to swing effectively. He also identified strategies that he would implement, such as listening to preferred music when driving to the course and recalling past successes.

Various aspects of Jim's performance profile were confirmed by his low scores on most subscales of the Test of Performance Strategies, particularly automaticity, activation, imagery, and goal setting for practice and competition. He also had difficulty relaxing in competitions where his thinking tended to be negative. Generally his psychological and psychomotor skills and strategies differed little between practice and competition.

Jim scored 34 single Stableford points in his first game after the profiling consultation, reporting a positive approach after hitting the ball well in the practice nets the day before, staying relaxed, and "not thinking about the swing just letting it happen." He reported generally taking four or five swings for shots on the first 14 holes, with more swings on the last 4 holes though never more than 10. After a good start in the following round, his swing again deteriorated as he became frustrated when his group fell behind the field and were unable to catch up. In the next three rounds he focused on completing his backswing, but no improvement was evident from his diary entries.

After a relaxation and visualisation training session, Jim returned diary entries for two more rounds. In the first he tried to focus on hitting the ball off the "sweet spot" but gained no benefit from this performance cue. In the second, played after a 3-week break, he reported feeling relaxed in his shoulders, thinking "how good this feels again," and playing the best he had for months to score 18 Stableford points on the first nine holes. His swing deteriorated on the second nine, he could not relax, and he scored very poorly. In the next week, one of Jim's regular partners advised that he would no longer play in the same group, which prompted Jim to withdraw from Saturday competitions until he had solved his swing problems.

There was one further session in which Jim played nine practice holes. He took more than 30 swings on his first tee shot, much to the consternation of the next group. Later, when he was well ahead of those players, some experimentation was possible. Stopping after three swing attempts and beginning again did not help, nor did playing a short (9) iron for a long second shot. Jim then agreed to hit some shots with his eyes closed, initially hitting a long second shot to a Par 4 hole on his first swing. He dropped a second ball and again hit it on his first swing with his eyes closed. The following tee shot took five swings with his eyes open, but he needed just one swing to hit another ball with his eyes closed. Similarly, he needed four swings to hit his second shot to this Par 4 hole with his eyes open, but just one swing to hit a second ball with eyes closed. This pattern was repeated on the next two holes, both tee shots over water hit the first time with his eyes closed. There was very little difference in accuracy or length between the shots hit with eyes open and closed. He played all shots on the last Par 5 hole with eyes open, needing three swings on the first and second shots, two swings on the third shot, and one swing for his approach to the green.

After this session, Jim agreed to hit balls on the practice fairway or in a park to determine whether swinging the club with his eyes closed was a viable option and to examine whether it helped him to swing the club with his eyes open. Following such practice he would decide if this tactic could be used in competition. Soon afterward, however, the club's newsletter advised members that Jim was "having a break from golf taking up bowls." Although he had started to play lawn bowls, he had not authorised the notice and had not intended taking such a break. He has not played in a competition in the 2 months since, but has retained his membership and remains hopeful of finding a solution to his problem.

DISCUSSION

Jim has always been able to execute a technically sound practice swing on his first attempt, suggesting that his physical and physiological systems were functioning normally and that the motor programs governing the golf swing were intact. No neurological or electromyographic assessments have been conducted to support these assumptions. Clearly Jim's physical and physiological systems were unable to function normally when it came to hitting the ball, and the evidence presented suggests that psychological factors were contributing to the progressive deterioration in his golf swing. That deterioration is such that whereas he originally experienced the disability only in competition, it is now also affecting his practice.

The data collected in this study confirmed that the disability was more pronounced for longer shots. Jim also felt that his disability was more pronounced later in his rounds. This is consistent with previous research showing that such problems are related to fatigue, effort, and the duration of activity (McDaniel et al., 1989). Although such trends were apparent in the data, the effects were not statistically significant.

The benefits derived from PST in relaxation, imagery, and self-talk were more evident after initial consultations than they have been recently. Whereas previously Jim was able to apply these skills in dealing directly with his problem, they are now also needed to cope with various psychosocial processes, including the response of others to his disability.

This study has highlighted the importance of automaticity in skilled performance. Previous research on aging golfers has not shown a general decline in psychomotor automaticity (Over & Thomas, 1995). In this case, Jim dealt with his problem by carefully analysing aspects of his technique and found it difficult to refrain from consciously monitoring and controlling his skilled movements. Implicit knowledge has thus been made explicit, leading to further breakdown in performance under stress (Hardy, Mullen, & Jones, 1996; Masters, 1992). Regaining the trust that Moore and Stevenson (1994) argued is needed to execute the golf swing automatically has been a major challenge.

References

Butler, R.J., & Hardy, L. (1992) The performance profile: Theory and application. *The Sport Psychologist,* 6, 253-264.

Cochran, A.J., & Farrally, M.R. (Eds.) (1994) *Science and golf II. Proceedings of the World Scientific Congress of Golf.* London: Spon.

Fine, A. (1993) *Mind over golf* [Videotape]. London: BBC.

Gallwey, W.T. (1979) *The inner game of golf.* London: Pan Books.

Hardy, L., Mullen, R., & Jones, G. (1996) Knowledge and conscious control of motor actions under stress. *British Journal of Psychology,* 87, 621-636.

Leadbetter, D. (1989, December) Beating tension. *Australian Golf Digest,* 22-28.

Masters, R.S.W. (1992) Knowledge, knerves and know-how: The role of explicit versus implicit knowledge in the breakdown of a complex motor skill under pressure. *British Journal of Psychology,* 83, 343-358.

McDaniel, K.D., Cummings, J.L., & Shain, S. (1989) The "yips": A focal dystonia of golfers. *Neurology,* 39, 192-195.

Moore, W.E., & Stevenson, J.R. (1994) Training for trust in sport skills. *The Sport Psychologist,* 8, 1-12.

Nideffer, R.M. (1985) *Athletes' guide to mental training.* Champaign, IL: Human Kinetics.

Over, R., & Thomas, P.R. (1995) Age and skilled psychomotor performance: A comparison of younger and older golfers. *International Journal of Aging and Human Development,* 41, 1-12.

Thomas, P.R., Hardy, L., & Murphy, S. (1996) Development of a comprehensive test of psychological skills for practice and performance. *Journal of Applied Sport Psychology,* 8 (Supplement), S119-S120.

Thomas, P.R., & Over, R. (1994) Psychological and psychomotor skills associated with performance in golf. *The Sport Psychologist,* 8, 73-86.

Watson, T. (1992, March) Tempo. *Australian Golf Digest,* 64-67.

CHAPTER 15

A Small-Scale Local Survey
of Age-Related Male Golfing Ability

J. Lockwood
Derby, England

A cross-sectional analysis of the handicaps of 1342 amateur male golfers was performed with the primary objective of finding the rate at which the golfing ability of aging senior golfers may be expected to decline.

The through-life characteristics obtained from the survey data are as expected, but the indicated rate of decline is surprising. Supplementary data are used to support the interpretation of the survey data. A transformation of the handicap trends to a more general representative measure of golfing ability is effected.

The findings are discussed and inferences are made.

Keywords: Golf handicaps, aging, statistics.

INTRODUCTION

The primary objective of this study was to explore available data to obtain an estimate of the rate at which the ability of older golfers may be expected to decline.

The performance of golfers can be analysed by comparing particular shot-making abilities so as to determine how the differences in scoring arise or, as in this study, by comparing an overall measure of the golfers' ability. The most common method of defining players' overall ability is by reference to an awarded golf handicap, which relates to the ability to achieve a particular 18-hole score on the golf course being played.

The large variations in the 18-hole scores achieved by golfers of similar ability make handicapping a complex subject, and several different systems are in use. The handicap values for the players surveyed were those given by the Council of National Golf Unions (*Standard Scratch Score and Handicapping Scheme,* 1983) system of handicapping, which is in general use throughout Britain and Ireland. This system limits handicaps to a maximum of 28.

Age-related studies are inherently difficult to perform if confident conclusions are required. In "longitudinal" studies, the problems of time scale may not be manageable, and the maintenance of objective measures and control of the selected sample individuals and social environment may not be possible. In "cross-sectional" studies (such as this), the validity of using different individuals of different ages results in an unquantifiable uncertainty in the enumerated rates of change. To supplement the cross-sectional analysis, a few individual histories of handicap variations over a relatively small time scale are included for comparison with the trends indicated by the main survey.

Scope of Survey

The 1342 players in the main survey are all the male playing members of three golf clubs in Derbyshire, England, whose birth dates were included in the members' records.

The Council of National Golf Unions (CONGU) system gives players an "exact" handicap that discriminates to a level of 1/10 of a stroke, but this cannot be taken as the true accuracy of this measure. The "exact" handicap values in the survey were those recorded by their respective clubs on a particular date during the "off-season" period between the end of 1996 and the start of the 1997 season. The age of the individual is the age on the date of the recorded handicap value. The available club records of annual handicap changes were also examined for individual histories of selected main survey golfers.

An additional set of handicap/age data was extracted from the English Golf Union (EGU) records of 1996 for players who had participated in their National Senior competitions during that year. Their handicaps ranged from +1 to 10, and their ages ranged between 50 and 75.

Age Distribution

Although the primary interest was in the older golfers, the whole age range of the players in the main survey was included in the analysis. This provided further information to assist interpretation and comparison with the data for the older golfers. The age distribution of the survey subjects is given in figure 15.1 and compared with the 1991 (UK) Census of Population data for Derbyshire males grouped into the same age ranges, with the survey distribution normalised to the 50-59 age group. The level of golf participation varies considerably throughout the full age range. Age groups 10-19 and 20-29 are similar in participation level, but low. The 50-59 and 60-69 age groups have the same, highest level, which then falls dramatically for the 70-79 group and again for the 80-89 group. When commenting on the rates of change of golfing ability indicated by this study, it will be assumed that the reductions in participation levels for these oldest golfers are attributable to age rather than being the consequence of societal changes in leisure activities at some earlier period of time.

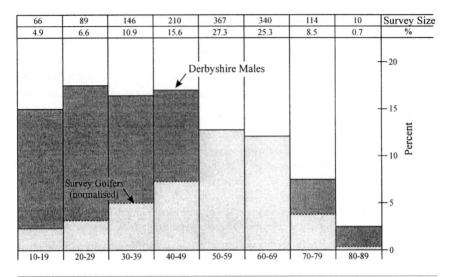

| 66 | 89 | 146 | 210 | 367 | 340 | 114 | 10 | Survey Size |
| 4.9 | 6.6 | 10.9 | 15.6 | 27.3 | 25.3 | 8.5 | 0.7 | % |

Figure 15.1   Age distributions.

METHODOLOGY AND PRESENTATION

Handicap Distributions

The main survey data were grouped into either 10-year or 5-year age intervals. The distribution of handicaps within each of the age groupings chosen was examined by grouping handicaps into 4-stroke intervals to cover the full handicap range. The results of this exercise can be summarised as follows:

- The 10-19 age group has a single-sided distribution with the highest frequency at high handicaps.
- Within the age range 20-39, the distributions are fairly close to a normal distribution. Tentatively, this is believed to be indicative of a mature golfing population.
- The distributions in the four age groups covering the range 55-79 years are more peaked than a normal distribution.
- The distribution in the 40-49 age group shows a possible bimodality.
- The distribution in the 50-54 group is more peaked than a normal distribution, but not as markedly as in the 55-79 age range.

Means and Standard Deviations of Handicaps Within the Age Groups

Table 15.1 shows the means and standard deviations of handicaps as calculated within the age groups. It should be noted that the values of the means and standard

Table 15.1   Means and Standard Deviations of Handicaps Within the Age Groups

Age group	10-19	20-29	30-39	40-49	50-54	55-59	60-64	65-69	70-79	80+
No. in group	66	89	146	210	193	174	188	152	114	10
Mean	18.5	13.4	13.1	15.5	15.6	16.0	17.0	18.2	18.9	19.6
S.D.	6.7	6.4	6.1	5.7	5.6	5.0	5.2	5.3	4.9	4.7

deviations of the lowest group and the higher age groups are affected by the restriction on maximum handicap value allowed.

Main Survey Presentation

These preliminary investigations led to the decision that the most appropriate analysis was simply to evaluate the medians and upper and lower quartiles and deciles of the chosen age groups. The results are shown in figure 15.2. Clear trends

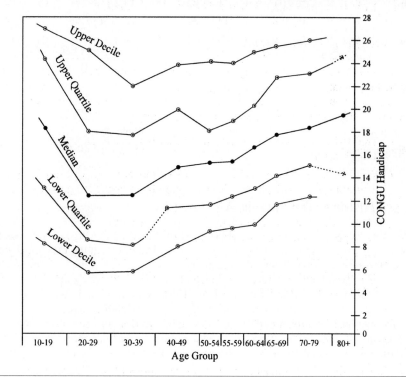

Figure 15.2   Main survey analysis.

are evident over the complete age range of the data. The expected lifetime characteristics curve is consistently followed; that is, young golfers improve at a relatively rapid rate, and peak abilities occur in the 20-39 age range and are followed by a general decline into old age.

Supplementary Survey Data

The EGU data, being of much more limited scope (although of direct relevance to the primary objective), have been treated differently. The recorded handicaps of 221 players were the integer "playing" values, not the "exact" values as in the main survey, and the group sizes for the selected age groups are shown in table 15.2.

Choosing only the arithmetic mean as worthy for comparison with the main survey data gives the results shown in table 15.3.

Table 15.2   Playing Handicap Distributions

Age (years)	+1	0	1	2	3	4	5	6	7	8	9	10	Totals
50-59	1	2	6	2	4	11	22	18	10	4	1	0	82
60-69	0	0	0	0	3	13	34	25	22	18	3	2	124
70-75	0	0	0	0	0	0	1	5	4	4	1	0	15

Table 15.3   Main Survey Data: Age Group, Mean

Age group	50-59	60-69	70-75
Mean handicap	4.8	5.9	6.9

Case Histories for Various Age Groups

Personal recollection and anecdotal evidence of the rates of change of both young and aging golfers' abilities are likely to be very different from the rates emerging from the survey. Some recorded data, albeit of very limited scope and time scale, have been examined to effect some factual historical comparisons. Table 15.4 shows, for six selected individuals, their (1997) age group and their (CONGU) handicaps at the start of each summer season in the available records.

The available records for all the golfers aged 75 and older were also examined to obtain an estimate of the average rate of decline for this final period in a golfer's lifetime. This special grouping comprised 44 golfers with handicaps ranging from 11.0 to 28.0 (median 20.4, s.d. 4.70).

Table 15.4   Age Group and Handicaps for Six Selected Individuals

Case	1	2	3	4	5	6
(Age group)	10-19	30-39	50-54	60-64	65-69	70-79
1990	—	10.3	18.3	20.9	8.9	14.0
1993	18.8	11.0	12.0	20.6	9.9	15.9
1994	10.3	10.8	13.9	20.3	10.0	16.4
1995	6.0	10.7	14.5	18.3	10.5	17.2
1996	4.5	9.9	14.9	16.1	10.7	18.2
1997	2.8	9.6	14.5	16.3	10.2	18.8
1998	1.2	9.9	14.9	15.2	10.1	19.6

The investigation showed that only 16 of the 44 had played two or more rounds that qualified for handicap adjustment during the 1997 season. This subgroup of 16 players had handicaps ranging from 12.2 to 28.0 (median 20.6, s.d. 4.75), and its oldest individual was aged 82. Within the subgroup, annual handicap adjustments after the players had reached the age of 75 were available for only 4 players. For the remaining 12, handicap adjustments were available only for the 1997 season. The yearly changes in handicap for the individuals in the subgroup varied between +1.5 and –0.9. Combining all the available data for the subgroup resulted in an average rate of increase in handicap of 0.33 strokes per year.

Transposition of the Handicap Data

The CONGU handicap added to the Standard Scratch Score for the course does not equate to a central measure of the player's scoring ability. From an ongoing investigation being conducted by the author, a first-order approximation to the expected median gross score of a golfer playing on his home course when the Competition Scratch Score is 71 can be derived from the relationship

Median Gross Score = 73.4 + 1.19 (CONGU handicap).

This will be used to convert the main trend rates of the handicap survey to rates of change of golfing ability based on a central measure, rather than the deliberately noncentral measures of the prevailing handicapping systems—one that has an absolute, rather than a differential scale.

INDICATED ABILITY TREND RATES

The presentation of the main survey data (figure 15.2) indicates the major trend rates to be of the order of a 1 stroke per year decrease in CONGU handicap for the youngest golfers and an average increase of 0.13 strokes per year for golfers in the 40-79 age range.

The supplementary data for EGU Seniors competitors indicate an average rate of increase of 0.12 strokes per year for low-handicap players in the 50-75 age range, which supports the main survey evaluation.

From the short-term histories, Case 1 illustrates the rates at which gifted players *can* develop in their teenage years. Cases 2 and 4 illustrate how individuals can develop against the trend. For the older individuals (Cases 3-6), the year-by-year changes range between +1.9 and –2.2, with an average value near zero for this particular sampling.

Transposition, as defined above, of the main survey trend rates gives rates of change of golfing ability of, typically, a 1.2% per year improvement for teenage golfers and a 0.2% per year decline for golfers aged 40-79.

FURTHER OBSERVATIONS

Two additional features are noticeable in the main survey results. The first is an apparent upward discontinuity in the data at the 40-year class limit, particularly evident in the middle 50% range of handicaps. The second is an apparent reduction or even reversal in the rate of change in the 50-64 age range percentiles.

The variations in the handicap frequency distributions noted previously (q.v.), and the evidence of a large influx of new golfers into the golfing population (figure 15.1), support the conjecture that both these features are a consequence of newer golfers developing their skills over a period of many years until a relatively stable level of ability is reached.

In gerontological terms, Schaie and Willis (1991) have proposed that "old age" should be split into three different periods with the following age ranges:

The "young old": 65 to 75/80

The "old old": 75/80 to around 90

The "very old": older than about 90

The golfers surveyed do not include any in the "very old" category. Neither the main nor the supplementary survey data indicate any increase in the average rate of decline for players in the "young old" category. The limited historical data for golfers aged 75 and older do indicate a significant increase in the average rate of decline during the "old old" phase of aging.

CONCLUSIONS

In conclusion, despite the inherent uncertainties of a cross-sectional study, and the small size and limited geographical scope of this particular study, the analysis has yielded surprisingly consistent trends over the age and handicap range of the data.

The indicated average rate of decline in golfing ability for players aged 40+ is so low that it seems reasonable to conclude that almost all amateur golfers should be capable of improving their current playing ability. For "single figure" handicap players over the age of 50, a target rate of no more than a 1 stroke increase in handicap every 8 years should be achievable until they reach their mid-70s, provided they remain in normal health and mobility.

Beyond the age of 75, the average rate of decline for the golfers surveyed showed a significant increase.

Individual case histories support these conclusions.

References

1991 Census of Population. 1994. *Population Profile: Derbyshire.* Published by Research and Intelligence Unit, Derbyshire County Council.

Schaie, KW, and Willis, SL. 1991. *Adult Development and Aging,* 3rd ed., 86. New York: Harper Collins.

The Standard Scratch Score and Handicapping Scheme 1983, The. 1997, January. Published by the Council of National Golf Unions.

CHAPTER 16

The Influence of Age on Lumbar Mechanics During the Golf Swing

D. Morgan, F. Cook, and S. Banks
Orthopaedic Research Lab., Good Samaritan Medical Center, W. Palm Beach, FL 33401

H. Sugaya
Department of Orthopaedic Surgery & Sports Medicine, Kawatetsu Hospital, Chiba 260, Japan

H. Moriya
Department of Orthopaedic Surgery, School of Medicine, Chiba University, Chiba 260, Japan

Low back injuries are not uncommon in golfers, with reported incidence as high as 40-50% in amateur and professional golfers. Very few studies have focused on the mechanics of the lumbar spine during the golf swing, and none have investigated the influence of age on lumbar spine motions in golfers. In this study we investigated how lumbar spine kinematics vary with age in healthy golfers and determined which parameters might provide an indication of risk for low back injury or long-term degenerative changes. We tested 43 male golfers, ages 18 to 84, and grouped them into three age categories: college (18-21), adult (22-49), and seniors (50+). All subjects had handicaps under 20. Six 200-Hz cameras were used to record 29 reflective markers on the subject, ball, and club. Two force plates were used to record ground reaction forces during the swing. College golfers exhibited significantly greater lumbar lateral bending and axial rotation velocity than the senior golfers. We also investigated two derived parameters: "crunch factor," which is the instantaneous product of lumbar lateral bend and axial rotation velocity, and "lag time," which is the time between peak lumbar lateral bend and axial rotation velocity. The timing of peak crunch factor correlates well with data from previous reports of back pain during the swing and exhibits a consistent (and significant) decrease with increasing age. By understanding the factors that contribute to low back pain, we hope to help golfers at all ages and skill levels continue to play safely.

Keywords: Golf, kinematics, axial rotation, age difference, biomechanics, lumbar spine, low back injury.

INTRODUCTION

Golf is one of the most popular sports in the world for people of all ages and skill levels. Unfortunately, low back injuries are not uncommon in golfers, with reported incidence as high as 40-50% in amateur and professional golfers (Sugaya et al. 1994). Very few studies have focused on the mechanics of the lumbar spine during the golf swing (Hosea and Gatt 1990; McTeigue et al. 1994; Sugaya et al. 1996; Morgan et al. 1997), and none have investigated the influence of age on lumbar spine motions in golfers.

Peak forces and torques at the L3/L4 level of the lumbar spine have been reported to occur during the forward swing and follow-through (Hosea and Gatt 1990). This is in agreement with many golfers' subjective reports of pain just after impact (Sugaya et al. 1994). Further, it is generally accepted that golfers who exhibit an exaggerated lateral bend with back extension (reverse "C") during follow-through will experience higher stress and a greater incidence of injury in the low back. Radiographic findings have shown distinctly asymmetric arthritic changes in golfers with back injuries, demonstrating greater right-side degeneration at the facet joints and vertebrae in right-handed golfers (Sugaya et al. 1996).

The purpose of this study was to investigate how lumbar spine kinematics vary with age in healthy golfers and determine which parameters might provide an indication of risk for injury or long-term degenerative changes. Intuitively, bending to the side (or lateral bending) will produce increased pressure on the compressed side of the vertebrae, and high twisting velocities will increase shear forces on the viscoelastic tissue between facets and vertebrae. In order to explore the possibility that lumbar lateral bending angle (LBA) and lumbar axial rotation velocity (ARV) jointly influence low back injury or degeneration, we define the "crunch factor" as the instantaneous product of LBA and ARV, and "lag time" as the time between peak LBA and ARV.

METHODS

Forty-three male, right-handed, experienced golfers between the ages of 18 and 84 participated in this study. No current injuries prevented these men from golfing. Eight golfers, age 18 to 21, competed on a collegiate level, with a mean age of 19 $\pm$ 1 years and a mean handicap of 3 $\pm$ 3. Recreational golfers composed two groups: 21 adults, age 24 to 48 (36$\pm$ 6) with a handicap of 9 $\pm$ 7, and 14 seniors, over 50 years old (65 $\pm$ 10) with a handicap of 17 $\pm$ 7. After the subjects went through their normal stretching and warm-up routine (including shots with irons and/or woods), the subject swung with the driver, or longest club used during normal play. Three shots were recorded and processed. Only shots that were assessed by the subject as "good" were saved for analysis.

A total of 26 reflective spherical markers were placed on the subject, including 20 over the following landmarks: the head and back of the neck at the C7 level (1 marker each) and the shoulders, elbows, wrists, thighs, knees, shanks, ankles, toes, and heels (bilateral markers). Since our objective was to define lumbar mechanics, 3 markers were used to define the upper portion of the lumbar spine: right and left ribs and the lowest point on the rib cage and at the T12/L1 level of the spine. The lower boundary of the lumbar spine was marked at the L5/S1 level of the back and the right and left anterior superior iliac spine. Reflective tape was applied directly to the golf ball, and 2 markers were placed on the club. A six-camera (200 Hz) motion system was used to capture marker motion and compute three-dimensional kinematics (Motion Analysis Corp., Santa Rosa, CA). A fourth-order, zero phase shift Butterworth filter was used to smooth the marker displacement data. All body marker displacements were filtered using a resultant cutoff frequency of 6 Hz, and the ball and club marker displacements were filtered at 12 Hz. Angular position and velocity data were calculated from the filtered marker data. Two six-component force plates were used to record ground reaction forces at 1000 Hz (model LG-6, AMTI, Watertown, MA). A computer animation program was developed and used to give three-dimensional video feedback to the subject and to verify that all markers were identified correctly.

We report results on two measured parameters (LBA and ARV, both defined in the body reference frame) and two derived parameters (lag time, crunch factor). The LBA is defined by the frontal plane rotation between the rib segment and the pelvis segment; ARV is the first time derivative of the transverse plane angle between the rib and pelvis segments. Lag time is defined as the time difference between peak LBA and peak ARV during a swing. The crunch factor is defined as the product of the LBA and ARV for each instant in time (Morgan et al. 1977).

One-way analysis of variance and pairwise multiple comparison procedures (Dunn's method or Student-Newman-Keuls) were used to assess the significance of differences in the mean LBA, ARV, crunch factor, and lag times between the age groups. Spearman rank order correlation was used to determine which variables most influenced the crunch factor for each age group. The significant alpha value for all tests was 0.05.

RESULTS

The college golfers exhibited significantly greater peak LBA than either the adult or the senior golfers (table 16.1). The timing of peak LBA was approximately 100 ms after impact in all three groups. Average LBA increased monotonically from 250 ms before impact to 100 ms after impact (figure 16.1 shows a graphical average of all golfers' data). As would be expected, maximum ARV decreased with age, college golfers having significantly higher rotational velocities than the senior golfers. Timing to peak ARV was variable in all groups, and no significant differences were found. All three groups of golfers exhibited two ARV peaks: one smaller peak preceding impact by approximately 100 ms, and a larger peak just after impact (figure 16.2 shows a graphical average of all golfers' data).

The college golfers had significantly higher maximum crunch factors than the senior golfers (table 16.2; figure 16.3 shows a graphical average). Maximum crunch

Table 16.1   LBA and ARV as a Function of Age

	LBA$_{max}$ (deg)	LBA$_{max}$ time (ms)	ARV$_{max}$ (deg/s)	ARV$_{max}$ time (ms)	Crunch$_{max}$ (deg^2/sec)	Crunch$_{max}$ time (ms)	Lag time (ms)
No. in College	16 ± 3	117 ± 16	202 ± 19	63 ± 44	2586 ± 1245	78 ± 35	60 ± 25
Adults	$11 \pm 4^*$	95 ± 34	143 ± 44	26 ± 78	1519 ± 986	56 ± 63	82 ± 75
Seniors	$12 \pm 5^*$	104 ± 20	$115 \pm 50^*$	3.5 ± 88	$1270 \pm 935^*$	15 ± 125	101 ± 87

* Significant difference from college.

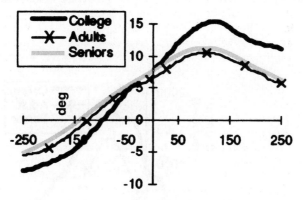

Figure 16.1   Lumbar lateral bend during the golf swing.

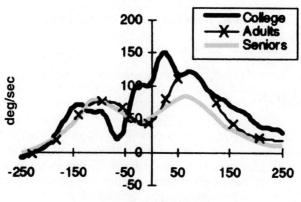

Figure 16.2   Lumbar axial rotation velocity during the golf swing.

followed impact in all three groups, but timing was not statistically different. Lag time, the time between peak LBA and peak ARV, increased with age but was not statistically different for the three groups. Crunch was significantly influenced by LBA and ARV in all groups, while lag time was not a significant factor for the college group (table 16.2). Interestingly, there were consistent (although not statistically significant) trends for both crunch and lag time with age (figure 16.4).

Table 16.2   Crunch Factor Influences

	LBA	ARV	Lag time
College	*	*	no
Adults	*	*	*
Seniors	*	*	*

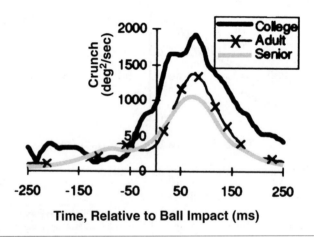

Figure 16.3   Crunch factor during the golf swing.

DISCUSSION

Golf is increasingly popular among seniors, and with the expected "boom" in seniors, golf-related injuries are expected to significantly increase. The purpose of this study was to examine the influence of age on the kinematics of the lower back during the golf swing and to explore parameters that might be useful for understanding low back injury. The subjects' ages spanned 66 years, and all golfers had handicaps below 20 strokes. Although skill levels were different for each age group, there were no significant differences in weight shift during the swing, and each individual would be considered a very good player for his age range.

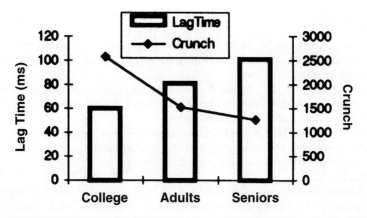

Figure 16.4   Crunch factor and lag time as a function of age.

An important factor that cannot be addressed by this study is the influence of "swing style" practiced by each group. It is well known that the "ideal" swing has changed quite dramatically over the past century, and it is almost certain that this will have influenced golfers in the present study. The senior golfers exhibited lower ranges of lumbar lateral bending, axial rotation, and ARV. Although these might be expected sequelae of age and lost flexibility, it is equally plausible that these differences reflect a swing style with less emphasis on trunk coil. The important aspect of the results presented here is that normative data for different age ranges are established. Thus, it will be unnecessary to compare "young healthy" swings with those of seniors with back pain in future studies. Indeed, it will be possible to compare individuals with "healthy" swings and those experiencing pain or injury at any age.

We introduced two derived parameters to quantify the temporal relationship between LBA and ARV. Lag time was smallest in the collegiate golfers, in whom peak LBA and ARV occurred almost simultaneously, whereas older golfers exhibited larger lag times. The crunch factor magnitude appears to change with age and/or swing style, and the timing of peak crunch factor coincides with subjective reports of pain during the swing (Sugaya et al. 1994). However, the utility of these parameters cannot be assessed until additional studies characterize lumbar kinematics in a range of golfers with low back pain or injury. In addition, further studies will be required to relate the motion parameters to structural and physiological factors like passive/active range of lumbar motion and trunk muscle activity (EMG).

We have shown that lumbar lateral bending and rotation velocity decrease with age and that a combination of these two parameters, the crunch factor, correlates well with previous findings of back pain. By understanding the factors that contribute to low back pain, we hope to help golfers at all age and skill levels play safely and avoid injury.

References

Hosea, T.M. and Gatt, C.J. Jr. (1990). Biomechanical analysis of the golfer's back. In: A.J. Cochran (ed.), *Science and Golf,* 43-48. London: Spon.

Hosea, T.M. and Gatt, C.J. Jr. (1996). Back pain in golf. *Clinics in Sports Medicine* 15(1): 37-53.

McTeigue, M., Lamb, S., Mottram, R., and Pirozzolo, F. (1994). Spine and hip motion analysis during the golf swing. In: A.J. Cochran (ed.), *Science and Golf II,* 50-58. London: Spon.

Morgan, D., Sugaya, H., Banks, S., and Cook, F. (1997). A new twist on golf kinematics and low back injuries. *Proceedings of the 21st Annual Meeting of the American Society of Biomechanics.*

Sugaya, H., Moriya, H., Takahashi, K., Yamagata, M., and Tsuchiya, A. (1994). Low back injuries in professional golfers: An epidemiologic study in Japan. *Japan Journal of Orthopaedic Sports Medicine* 16.

Sugaya, H., Moriya, H., Takahashi, K., Yamagata, M., and Tsuchiya, A. (1996). Asymmetric degenerative changes of the lumbar spine in golfers. Presented at the American Orthopaedic Society for Sports Medicine, 22nd Annual Meeting.

CHAPTER 17

The Effects of Age on the Performance of Professional Golfers

S.M. Berry
Texas A&M University, College Station, TX, USA

P.D. Larkey
Carnegie Mellon University, Pittsburgh, PA, USA

How does aging affect the scoring performance of professional golfers in Major tournaments? If great past players at the peak of their careers had played in the 1997 Majors, what would their stroke average have been? This paper summarizes an exploratory study on these questions. Most players peak between 30 and 35 years of age in their ability to score in Majors, but there are important differences among players in terms of how quickly they reach their peak and fall away from it. Jack Nicklaus, Ben Hogan, Tom Watson, Arnold Palmer, and Gary Player would have had, according to this statistical analysis, the best scoring average for the 1997 Majors had they all been able to play them in their prime.

Keywords: Golf, performance, aging, Major championships.

INTRODUCTION

Age affects the playing ability of professional golfers. Conventional wisdom about the career performance profiles of the touring professionals is that they go through essentially three phases. In the first phase, maturation, they learn a variety of things from improved swing mechanics to course management and emotional control, particularly patience, in playing a fickle game against ferocious competition. At some point they become tournament "hardened" and enter the second phase, prime. In their prime they reach their apex in terms of scoring ability given their innate talent and work ethic. The more gifted and hard-working become "ready" to compete effectively in, if not win, Major championships. In the third phase, decline, players lose their ability to score and compete because of physical problems or mental changes—for example, the eyesight and flexibility go, or "off-course distractions" such as family or business interfere with their focus.

Conventional wisdom admits exceptions. Sam Snead and Don January, for example, seemed impervious to age, remaining competitive well into their 50s. Other players such as Seve Ballesteros and Johnny Miller had brilliant but short competitive peaks.

There is much more conventional wisdom than analysis of the relationship between aging and performance. There is only one identifiable study, by Riccio (1994), addressing the relationship between aging and performance. Riccio's work, based on shot-by-shot data for one player, Tom Watson, in one event, the U.S. Open, over a post-1980 period concluded that the conventional wisdom about putting as the source of deterioration in Watson's play was wrong.

This paper explores the relationship between aging and performance statistically. The following questions are posed:

1. At what age do professional golfers on average peak in their ability to post low scores in Major tournaments?

2. How do players differ from the average in terms of the amplitude and duration of their peak performing ability?

3. If great past players at the peak of their careers had played in the 1997 Majors, what would their stroke average have been?

The analysis is based on the performances of 489 players in 13,792 rounds of golf in the four Majors: 1935 to 1997 for the Masters and U.S. Open (not held during the war years), 1958 (advent of stroke play) to 1997 for the PGA, and 1960 (when Arnold Palmer led a resurgence in the strength of Open fields) to 1997 for the Open Championship. The analysis includes most (over 90%) of the players participating in at least 10 Majors over the long study period. The only exclusions were players for whom we could not find a birth date—primarily amateurs, or players who participated in the Open but did not play in many, if any, of the U.S. Majors, or non-U.S. professionals from the earlier era. None of the legitimate contenders for "one of the best of all time" on any grounds was excluded so long as a significant part of his career occurred after 1935; a few of the greatest players such as Gene Sarazen are disadvantaged by this sample of years because it does not capture their prime.

Sadly for comparisons, the greatest golfers tend to appear seriatim; head-to-head confrontations among the greatest golfers with all at the peak of their skill, in their "prime," are the exception rather than the rule. Figure 17.1 shows the annual average score posted in Majors by Ben Hogan, Arnold Palmer, Jack Nicklaus, Tom Watson, and Tiger Woods. (The performances of Hogan, Nicklaus, and Palmer are truncated in the year they turned 50. The breaks in Hogan's performances reflect his service in World War II and his recuperation from the near-fatal collision with the bus.) For this set, there are only two instances in which two players are competing in their primes (or near-primes): Nicklaus and Palmer in the early 1960s and Nicklaus and Watson in the late 1970s. The other possible comparisons of players in direct competition are problematic because at least one of the players is far from his prime.

Fortunately, with 489 players and thousands of rounds, there are many overlaps of good and nearly great players in their primes in each year. These many contests provide a sort of statistical bridge among players over the years, a basis for estimating the skill of each player and of the population as a function of age.

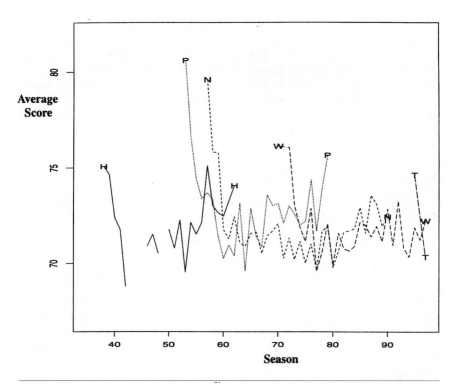

Figure 17.1   The average score in the Majors for each year for Hogan (H), Palmer (P), Nicklaus (N), Watson (W), and Woods (T). Older players' performances are truncated at age 50.

Any comparison of players from different eras is necessarily complicated because of changes in players, equipment, levels of competition, courses, course conditioning, and purses. The only cross-era player career comparison statistics that the U.S. PGA Tour provides are tournament victories and career earnings, neither of which is at all useful. Tournament victories is not useful because the number of quality players participating has steadily increased over the past six decades and the difficulty of winning a tournament has increased commensurately. Career earnings is not a useful measure because of the steadily increasing amounts of money available to win and the less-than-offsetting decreases in the value of the dollar. Only 244 players over the past 30 years have career earnings greater than $720,000, David Duval's payday at the Tour Championship in 1997. Sam Snead, one of the greatest all-time players, has nominal dollar career earnings of $620,126. Snead won 81 times officially on tour; Duval now has three victories. Duval may turn out to be as good as Snead, but we won't know for a long time and then we will only know statistically; changes in the levels of competition and purse sizes assure that Duval will win fewer tournaments and more money than Snead.

There is no perfect variable for comparing players. This study uses scoring average in Major tournaments. The best players, or course, strive to shoot low scores and care most about Major tournaments. Unfortunately, scoring average is imperfectly correlated with tournament victories and money earnings because scoring variance also matters; four consecutive low rounds at the right time may lead to a Major victory and a large payday, while the contribution of those rounds to scoring average based on 60 to 100 rounds is, at best, modest. Table 17.1 shows the performances of the top 10 stroke average players in all Majors in 1997 with respect to money won. The ordering of players clearly changes as a result of the performance criterion used. Lehman had the fourth best scoring average, but was only eighth in terms of winning the most money. Maggert, Tolles, and Westwood each played 16 rounds, and each had 1145 strokes, yet Maggert and Tolles won almost $200,000 more than Westwood.

Table 17.1   Results of 1997 Majors

Player	Stroke average	Earnings ($)
1. Leonard	70.06	790,928 (1)
2. Love III	70.13	629,371 (2)
3. Woods	70.38	548,902 (4)
4. Lehman	70.75	310,110 (8)
5. Furyk	70.94	335,240 (7)
6. Els	71.00	550,145 (3)
7. Montgomerie	71.19	344,607 (6)
8. Kite	71.38	443,057 (5)
9. Parnevik	71.44	297,436 (11)
T-10. Maggert	71.56	305,769 (9)
T-10. Tolles	71.56	299,024 (10)
T-10. Westwood	71.56	111,095 (20)

Round score is a random variable that is a complex function of player ability, equipment, course difficulty (length, speed of greens, difficulty of pin placements, hazards, etc.), scoring conditions (wind speed and direction, temperature, humidity, etc.), and psychological context (the hype and pressure of Majors make scoring more difficult than usual for most players).

There have been dramatic changes in players, equipment, courses, and rules between 1935 and 1997. Most of these changes contribute to generally lower scoring. Players are better conditioned and have survived an increasingly competitive selection process in earning their right to play. Modern equipment enables greater length and consistency. There are fewer scruffy-to-unplayable fairway lies, and greens and bunkers are much more consistent. There are no longer stymies. On the other hand, the better modern players enjoying exemptions, large purses, and lucrative endorsements may not be, many have argued, as "hungry" as players of the earlier era who often had to cash in the current event to go on to the next event rather than returning to a club professional job. While the course conditioning is much better, the greens are much faster, the courses are longer, and watering systems enable high, punitive rough even in the driest climates and years.

THE MODEL

The following linear model is used for scoring:

$$X_{ij} = \theta_i + \gamma_{\text{year, round}} + f(\text{age}) + \epsilon_{ij}$$

where X_{ij} is the score for player i in round j. The score is modeled as a function of the player (θ_i), the year and round within the year ($\gamma_{\text{year, round}}$), and the age of the player ($f(\text{age})$). The error term, ϵ_{ij}, is assumed to be normally distributed with mean 0 and standard deviation σ.

A nonparametric function, $g(\text{age})$, is used to model the average effects of aging. The innate ability of each player is measured by θ, which is separate from the era played in and the age of the player. The γ parameters capture the difficulty of the era and round. This may include the equipment effects, course conditions, and weather effect. The aging function captures the effects of aging on each player's ability to score. Assuming there are not interactions, each of these effects is isolated from the other effects and measured. To account for individual aging differences, each player i has two parameters: M_i is a "maturing" parameter and D_i is a "declining" parameter. The age function for each individual is

$$f(\text{age}) = \begin{cases} M_i g(\text{age}) & \text{if age} < 30 \\ g(\text{age}) & \text{if } 30 \leq \text{age} \leq 35 \\ M_i g(\text{age}) & \text{if age} < 30 \end{cases}$$

Therefore, when $D_i = 1$, the player declines at the same rate as the average player. If $D_i > 1$, player i declines more slowly than the average player, playing nearer to peak performance for a longer period. Likewise for the maturing parameter, if $M_i = 1$, the player reaches his peak at the same rate as the average player. If $M_i < 1$, player i plays closer to a peak level at an earlier age; and if $M_i > 1$, player i approaches his peak at a later age. A Bayesian philosophy is used in the modeling approach, and the calculation is done using Markov chain Monte Carlo ideas (see Gilks et al. 1996 for details on the Bayesian approach and calculation methods).

RESULTS

Figure 17.2 summarizes the average effects of age on performance ($g(\text{age})$). The best professional golfers, on average, reach their peak ability to score in Majors at 32 years of age with a "peak range" of 30-35. The height of the curve for each age is the additional strokes for a player of that age. A 20-year-old is, on average, 2.47 strokes worse than at his peak. Likewise, a 50-year-old is 2.87 strokes worse than his peak value. The curve is, however, steeper for ages less than 30 than for ages greater than 35; players reach their peaks faster than they decline. The estimate for the standard deviation of the error term, σ, is 2.90. That is, if the conditions were held

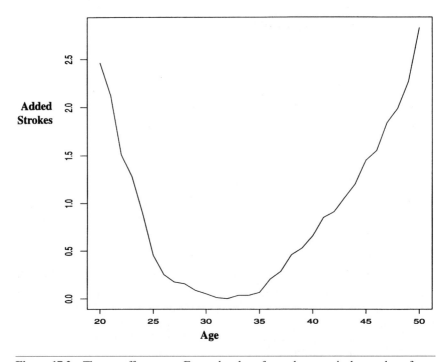

Figure 17.2   The age effect curve. For each value of age, the curve is the number of strokes worse than peak performance for the player.

identical for two rounds, the standard deviation in scores (for the same individual) is 2.90. The distribution of golfers in this study is estimated to be approximately normal with a mean of 7.26 and a standard deviation of .88.

Table 17.2 ranks the top 100 players in terms of an estimate of what their scoring average would have been in the 1997 Majors had they participated at their peak ability. There are few surprises. Nicklaus's record in the Majors has been astonishing. Hogan was widely considered to be the best player in the history of the Majors in an earlier era. Hogan's θ of 70.45 is an estimate of how he would have performed using modern equipment on 1997 courses. Nicklaus is estimated to have been .51 shots per round (more than 2 shots per tournament) better than Hogan and more than a stroke per round better than all but four other players. Nicklaus's success in Major championships was against stiffer competition than faced by any prior player, including Hogan.

Justin Leonard, Tiger Woods, and Ernie Els are traveling in very fast company at a relatively young age. The model estimates that they are closer to their peaks than other players at the same ages; their Ms are less than 1. The model does not know where their peaks will be, and few players have ever scored as well; consequently, the estimates of their θs are regressed toward the mean, giving each a result higher in the simulation than their actual scoring averages in 1997. If a player has not reached his declining age yet, or if he never played during the maturing state, then our estimate is 1, the mean value for all players.

Table 17.2   Top 100 All-Time Best Players

Rank	Player	θ	M	D	Rank	Player	θ	M	D
1	Jack Nicklaus	69.96	0.74	0.95	33	Jimmy Demaret	71.64	1.08	0.52
2	Ben Hogan	70.45	1.26	0.39	34	Gil Morgan	71.65	1.00	0.68
3	Tom Watson	70.55	1.15	0.95	35	Jerry Pate	71.67	0.16	1.17
4	Arnold Palmer	70.72	1.45	0.89	36	Hubert Green	71.67	1.10	1.59
5	Gary Player	70.94	0.68	0.66	37	Peter Jacobsen	71.68	0.83	1.20
6	Billy Casper	70.98	1.06	1.40	38	Payne Stewart	71.68	1.21	1.21
7	Nick Faldo	71.03	0.75	1.37	39	Jerry Barber	71.68	1.00	1.18
8	Byron Nelson	71.13	1.19	0.92	40	Johnny Miller	71.69	0.36	1.48
9	Sam Snead	71.15	1.24	0.11	41	Jim Ferrier	71.69	1.13	0.81
10	Justin Leonard	71.16	0.86	1.00	42	Doug Sanders	71.71	0.91	1.09
11	Greg Norman	71.17	1.16	0.64	43	Al Geiberger	71.72	0.85	1.38
12	Lee Trevino	71.22	0.99	0.64	44	Dan Pohl	71.74	0.90	1.00
13	Lloyd Mangrum	71.24	1.06	0.82	45	Don January	71.74	1.33	0.00
14	Tiger Woods	71.27	0.79	1.00	46	Jay Hebert	71.74	1.00	1.22
15	Ernie Els	71.31	0.90	1.00	47	Tom Lehman	71.74	1.05	0.61
16	Fred Couples	71.34	0.82	0.96	48	Dick Metz	71.74	1.00	0.25
17	Hale Irwin	71.34	1.07	0.48	49	Craig Stadler	71.75	1.47	1.09
18	Julius Boros	71.35	0.99	0.21	50	Roberto Devicenzo	71.75	1.03	0.16
19	Calvin Peete	71.36	1.00	0.53	51	Curtis Strange	71.78	1.02	1.20
20	Ben Crenshaw	71.36	0.34	1.48	52	Nick Price	71.78	0.91	0.69
21	Tom Weiskopf	71.38	1.45	1.20	53	Mike Souchak	71.79	1.00	1.62
22	Ray Floyd	71.43	0.75	0.23	54	Dan Sikes	71.82	1.00	0.64
23	Cary Middlecoff	71.45	1.09	1.88	55	David Graham	71.82	1.36	1.16
24	Tom Kite	71.47	1.00	0.59	56	Jose-Maria Olazabal	71.82	0.39	1.00
25	Lanny Wadkins	71.51	0.57	0.92	57	Bruce Lietzke	71.83	1.24	0.84
26	Stan Leonard	71.53	1.00	0.77	58	Kel Nagle	71.84	1.00	0.37
27	Bobby Locke	71.54	1.00	1.00	59	Fuzzy Zoeller	71.85	1.20	0.67
28	Gene Littler	71.57	0.73	0.45	60	Scott Hoch	71.87	1.40	0.51
29	Seve Ballesteros	71.58	0.31	1.78	61	Jack Burke	71.87	1.07	1.14
30	Doug Ford	71.60	1.06	1.48	62	Scott Simpson	71.87	0.92	1.04
31	Tommy Bolt	71.62	1.00	0.71	63	Bert Yancey	71.88	1.08	1.01
32	Tony Lema	71.62	1.25	1.00	64	Bob Rosburg	71.88	0.91	1.19

(continued)

Table 17.2   *(continued)*

Rank	Player	θ	*M*	*D*	Rank	Player	θ	*M*	*D*
65	Peter Thomson	71.89	1.00	0.64	83	Bernhard Langer	71.99	1.32	0.85
66	Bruce Crampton	71.89	0.80	0.74	84	Paul Harney	71.99	1.02	0.77
67	Bruce Devlin	71.91	1.02	0.82	85	Jeff Sluman	72.00	1.31	0.80
68	Ted Kroll	71.92	1.00	0.67	86	Larry Nelson	72.00	0.98	0.77
69	Jay Haas	71.92	0.73	0.42	87	Andy Bean	72.00	0.95	1.37
70	Ed Oliver	71.93	1.00	0.79	88	John Cook	72.01	1.10	0.95
71	Miller Barber	71.94	1.00	0.51	89	Loren Roberts	72.01	1.00	0.71
72	Henry Picard	71.94	0.96	0.89	90	Dave Hill	72.01	1.16	0.92
73	Phil Mickelson	71.94	0.51	1.00	91	Ralph Guldahl	72.02	0.65	1.13
74	Steve Elkington	71.96	0.99	1.00	92	Gene Sarazen	72.02	1.00	0.54
75	Ken Venturi	71.96	0.63	1.85	93	Graham Marsh	72.02	1.09	0.50
76	Billy Maxwell	71.96	1.19	0.89	94	Bob Lunn	72.03	0.57	1.16
77	Rod Funseth	71.97	1.00	0.56	95	Bobby Cruickshank	72.03	1.00	0.74
78	Dave Stockton	71.97	0.84	1.11	96	Dow Finsterwald	72.04	1.42	1.97
79	Keith Fergus	71.98	0.95	1.00	97	Corey Pavin	72.05	1.25	0.95
80	Colin Montgomerie	71.98	1.00	1.00	98	Chip Beck	72.05	1.13	1.11
81	J.C. Snead	71.98	1.00	1.11	99	Frank Beard	72.06	0.80	1.13
82	John Mahaffey	71.98	0.89	1.39	100	Jodie Mudd	72.06	1.33	1.00

Clearly, different players age differently. Some players are closer to their peak when they are 25 than other players. Nicklaus, Crenshaw, and Lanny Wadkins were very good before they reached age 32. Some players aged less well than others. After the age of 35 the abilities of Crenshaw, Casper, and Middlecoff declined faster than those of the average player, while Sam Snead, Hale Irwin, and Julius Boros played at near peak levels beyond the age of 35. Ben Crenshaw's $M = 0.34$ implies that when he was 24 years old he was only 0.30 (0.34 × 0.89) strokes worse than his peak value, while the average player would be .89 strokes worse than his respective peak value. On the other hand, Arnold Palmer has an M parameter of 1.45, which means that he was 1.29 strokes worse than his peak value when he was 24. Referring back to figure 17.1, Palmer at 30 (1959) was just beginning to play at a high level.

The parameter D_i represents how a player ages after reaching 35. Seve Ballesteros (1.78), Billy Casper (1.4), and Cary Middlecoff (1.88) were great players whose performance deteriorated quickly after their prime. "Ageless" Sam Snead's D value of 0.11 shows his astounding durability in scoring proficiency in the Majors.

Figures 17.3 and 17.4 show the estimate of the mean score for various players from age 20 to 50. At their peak levels, Snead and Nelson were very similar; Nelson aged like an average player—more time on the ranch than on the course—while Snead sustained his peak play until after he turned 50. At his peak, Jack Nicklaus was the best ever. But, interestingly, a 43-year-old Hogan is estimated to have been better than a 43-year-old Nicklaus. Dow Finsterwald and Johnny Miller were good at a young age and then declined rapidly after their peaks. Gary Player and Ray Floyd were models of consistency, good at a young age and still scoring well in their 40s. Don January matured slowly—he didn't get to near peak performance until his late 20s, but he then played at peak performance until after age 50.

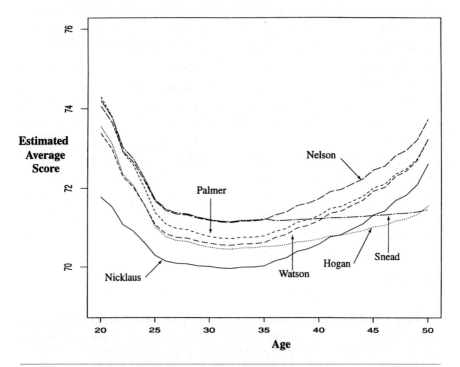

Figure 17.3   The relative abilities of some of the best players of all time. The graph shows the estimated number of strokes that player would have averaged in the 1997 Majors had he been the specified ages.

The "early bloomers" (low M) from the top 100 were Jerry Pate (.16), Steve Ballesteros (.31), Ben Crenshaw (.34), Johnny Miller (.36) and Jose-Maria Olazabal (.39). The "late bloomers" (high M) were Craig Stadler (1.47), Arnold Palmer and Tom Weiskopf (1.45), and Dow Finsterwald (1.42). The most durable performers (low D_i) were Don January (0.00), Sam Snead (.11), Roberto Devicenzo (.16), Julius Boros (.21), and Raymond Floyd (.23). The least durable performers (high D_i) were Dow Finsterwald (1.97), Cary Middlecoff (1.88), Ken Venturi (1.85), and Seve Ballesteros (1.78).

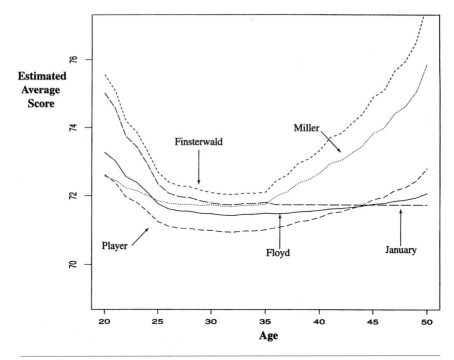

Figure 17.4   Different age curves for selected individuals. The graph shows the estimated number of strokes that player would have averaged in the 1997 Majors had he been the specified ages.

CONCLUSION

This paper has summarized an exploratory study on the effects of aging on the scoring performance of professional golfers. We found clear effects with average peak performance in the 30 to 35 age range. We find clear individual differences in the rates at which players get to their peak scoring ability and in their rates of performance deterioration. The "face validity" of these results is very high: the model clearly finds Jack Nicklaus and Ben Hogan where the conventional statistics on career accomplishment do not.

The model described here has also been used to study other issues. Other findings (details available from the authors) include the following:

1. The competition in Major championships is getting stiffer. The very best players are getting only slightly better as they approach nearly impenetrable limits on scoring potential. The midlevel players have improved somewhat more, closing the gap with the best players. The greatest improvement is found in the "bottom of the field" players who are increasingly competitive and can legitimately contend for championships.

2. Controlling for player quality, the scoring has become easier in each of the Majors over the period studied, but not monotonically. The conditions of today are worth approximately 2 shots a round over those of 1950 in the Masters and U.S. Open; the PGA has gotten about 2 shots easier since the late 1980s, and the Open since the late 1970s. Our data do not permit detailed analysis of the "conditions" contributing to better scoring—for example, is it clubs, balls, or course conditions?

There are many possible refinements and extensions to this work. The analysis presented here for all Majors in each year can be done for each Major championship individually. The work can be extended to other measures of player accomplishment such as Quality Points (see Larkey 1994) and to non-Major events. The assumptions in this particular model and estimation procedures should be altered for an understanding of the sensitivity of the results to particular assumptions.

The relationship between age and performance is an understudied area in golf. More research is needed on both professionals and amateurs.

ACKNOWLEDGMENTS

We are indebted to Marino Parascenzo for assistance with player birth dates. Marino has enjoyed a long prime as a golf writer; the world awaits his prime as a player.

References

Gilks, W.R., Richardson, S., and Spiegelhalter, D.J. (eds.). (1996). *Markov Chain Monte Carlo in Practice*. London: Chapman & Hall.

Larkey, P.D. (1994). Comparing Players in Professional Golf. In A.J. Cochran and M.R. Farrally (eds.), *Science and Golf II*. London: Spon.

Riccio, L.J. (1994). The Aging of a Great Player; Tom Watson's Play. In A.J. Cochran and M.R. Farrally (eds.), *Science and Golf II*. London: Spon.

CHAPTER 18

An Overview of Psychological Techniques Used for Performance Enhancement in Golf

Benedict Y.B. Lee
Florida State University

The purpose of this paper is to review the main psychological techniques and interventions aimed at enhancing the golfer's performance level. Techniques will be discussed from a sport psychology perspective. Specifically, goal setting, positive self-talk, relaxation, imagery, and the preshot routine are addressed. The utilization of these psychological skills has been shown to increase the golfer's performance level. With the aid of a sport psychologist, golfers of all ages and abilities can develop these psychological skills and improve their golf game.

Keywords: Performance enhancement, psychological techniques, preshot routine.

INTRODUCTION

As the millennium approaches, the number of people that play the game of golf will continue to increase. Advances in technology have produced golf equipment that can greatly assist golfers in improving their performance, whether it be for fun or in the quest to become the next Tiger Woods, Annika Sorenstam, or Hale Irwin. However, to reach the very top of the game and achieve optimal performance, one must pay serious attention to the psychological aspects of the sport. Cohn (1991) found that professional golfers obtained peak performances when they were highly focused and immersed in the task at hand and when they felt physically relaxed and mentally calm.

There are a number of psychological tools and techniques that either a sport psychologist or a performance enhancement consultant can teach to a golfer. These tools can help to improve both practice and competitive performances. This paper briefly introduces and reviews the main mental preparation strategies a sport psychologist can apply to help the golfer in achieving an optimal level of performance. Techniques that will be discussed include goal setting, positive self-talk, relaxation, imagery, and the importance of a preshot routine.

GOAL SETTING

Goals are the aims or purposes of an action. Goal setting is a method of identifying what one is attempting to accomplish or achieve. The positive effect of goal setting on performance is one of the strongest and most replicable findings in psychological literature and research (Burton, 1992; Locke, Shaw, Saari, and Latham, 1981). McCaffrey and Orlick (1989) found that the top touring professionals in golf are all very goal-oriented people and that they played better when they set goals. Also, top tour professionals were much more proficient in setting goals than regular club professionals (McCaffrey and Orlick, 1989).

Goals are effective because they help improve performance by directing one's attention to what is important and relevant. Properly set goals also help to motivate the individual to perform better. Lastly, goal setting can help to improve the quality of practice by increasing the use of relevant learning strategies, as well as relieving boredom by making practices more challenging.

Goals have traditionally been placed into two general categories. First, outcome goals focus on the end result or outcome of a competitive performance (i.e., winning or losing). The main drawback of setting outcome goals is that they rely on the ability of the opponents (e.g., a golfer shoots a personal best of 66, but loses because another player manages to shoot 65). The second category of goals consists of performance goals. Performance goals focus on improvements relative to one's own standard of excellence (i.e., improving consistency or putting average). Performance goals have nothing to do with the opposition, but are dependent upon the end products of one's own performance. In the field of sport psychology, recent studies (Burton, 1989; Gould, 1993; Martens, 1987) suggest that performance goals are more effective than outcome goals.

However, the most current body of goal-setting research has looked at a third category of goals, namely process goals. Process goals specify behaviours (e.g., correct body alignment before each shot) in which the golfer will engage during performance (Kingston and Hardy, 1997). Complex behaviours can be broken down into discrete behaviours (processes), and focusing on and adhering to these processes will increase the likelihood of successful execution of the target behaviour (Kingston and Hardy, 1994). Kingston and Hardy (1994, 1997) investigated the effect of process goals on golf performance and contended that process goals may be more effective than performance goals. Thus, to reap the maximum benefits of goal setting, the golfer may have to set a combination of performance, process, and even outcome goals. For a full understanding of the effectiveness of the different types of goals, further research is needed.

When setting goals, one should also make sure that they are specific, measurable, appropriate, realistic, and time bound. The goals set should identify minimum performance and never limit performance. For goals to be really effective, the golfer should set both short- and long-term goals. Short-term goals should be set daily, weekly, and monthly; they are stepping-stones to the long-term goals. Long-term goals may encompass anywhere from one to five years, or even longer. To help the golfer set effective goals, the sport psychologist can use a number of different tools and techniques. These include a mission statement, the "staircase approach," or a goal achievement card. Proper goal setting, along with a strong commitment to reaching these goals and overcoming obstacles along the way, will assist a golfer in reaching improved performance levels.

POSITIVE SELF-TALK

Most golfers recognize that controlling their golf swing, as well as the flight of the golf ball, is very difficult. However, the golfer's thought process is one of the hardest things to control on the golf course or the driving range. If left unchecked, negative thoughts can be distracting. Subsequently this distraction may affect the physical aspects of the game and possibly damage the golfer's self-confidence. For example, if the golfer thinks about missing those "knee-trembling" short putts, his or her putting may be adversely affected. Self-talk becomes especially destructive when individuals attach negative labels (e.g., "choke artist") to themselves and then perform in ways that confirm these labels (Bunker, Williams, and Zinsser, 1993).

When golfers think about something on the course, they are in a sense talking to themselves through words and pictures. Good performances on the golf course are usually accompanied by self-talk that is positive and instructional. This positive self-talk helps the golfer to stay in the present and prevents him or her from dwelling on past mistakes or projecting too far into the future. In contrast, poor performances are usually accompanied by negative self-talk that hinders performance because it is irrational, counterproductive, and anxiety producing. Skilled golfers (those with lower handicaps) have been found to have fewer negative emotions and thoughts than golfers with higher handicaps (Thomas and Over, 1994). Also, Thomas and Fogarty (1997) found that golfers' performances improved after they engaged in a programme that improved their self-talk and imagery techniques.

The sport psychologist can help a golfer become aware of self-talk through self-monitoring, retrospection, or imagery techniques. Once the golfer has identified situations in which negative self-talk is likely to occur, the sport psychologist can teach the golfer to utilize positive self-talk. Techniques that can be used for controlling and changing self-talk include thought stopping, rational thinking, countering, and reframing. Eliminating negative self-talk and introducing positive thoughts and self-talk will enhance self-confidence, attentional focus, and performance. Lastly, with the guidance of a sport psychologist, a tool such as positive self-talk can further be used in acquiring skills, breaking bad habits, initiating action, and sustaining effort when fatigue or boredom occurs.

RELAXATION

Relaxation is a powerful psychological tool that can be used to help the golfer's performance in tense situations. Used in conjunction with imagery, relaxation techniques will allow the golfer to regulate different areas of muscular tension and arousal in the body. This assists the golfer in dealing with his or her golf game actively and effectively. Relaxation can also be used to promote the onset of sleep, aid in the recovery from fatigue and injury, and help prepare the body for self-suggestion and imagery. In preparation for relaxation, a sport psychologist can teach the athlete a number of different breathing exercises (e.g., circle breathing).

There are two main categories of relaxation, "muscle to mind" techniques and "mind to muscle" techniques. Jacobson's progressive relaxation is an example of a muscle-to-mind technique and involves contracting specific muscle groups followed by relaxation of these muscle groups. The mind-to-muscle techniques incorporate imagery and include procedures such as self-hypnosis and centering. Centering focuses attention on one's centre of gravity as a means of maintaining control over tension and concentration under pressure. (Centering may also be used in situations of underarousal to energize the golfer.)

There is no right way to relax, so the golfer and sport psychologist should work together and discover the best method to achieve a state of optimal arousal. Regardless of the method, an effective relaxation technique should elicit both a physiological response (e.g., a decrease in cardiovascular and respiratory rates) and a psychological response (such as a calm focusing upon relevant stimuli). Relaxation skills must be practised on a regular basis to reap the maximum benefits of this tool. Some individuals may take longer to develop relaxation skills, but improvements should be noticeable after several weeks of regular practice. Using relaxation to reduce overarousal will assist in increasing concentration, precision, and confidence, which in turn will increase the likelihood of performing optimally.

IMAGERY

Imagery is a mental technique through which the golfer is able to create and recreate experiences in the mind. One of the most famous proponents of imagery is Jack Nicklaus, who said that his strongest weapon in golf was his "mind." Nicklaus (1974) said, "I never hit a shot, even in practice, without having a very sharp in-focus picture of it in my head. It's like a colour movie."

By mastering the technique of imagery, the golfer can see and feel the golf swing, the ideal flight path of the ball, and the end result. This is because imagery is not just visual; it should involve all of the senses if possible (i.e., auditory, olfactory, gustatory, tactile, and kinaesthetic). Also, emotions associated with certain situations should be an integral part of imagery (e.g., satisfaction, pride, high self-confidence). The images should be vivid, controlled, and in real time, so that the brain interprets the images as identical to the real-life situation. Finally, it would probably be beneficial for a golfer to use an internal imagery perspective (seeing the image from one's own eyes) rather than an external imagery perspective (seeing the image from an outsider's perspective).

Imagery can be used to improve physical, perceptual, and psychological skills. The acquisition of physical skills can be enhanced by developing mental blueprints. These new skills can then be practised through imagery rehearsal. Perceptual skills such as rehearsing ideal golf strategies can also be improved with the utilization of imagery. Lastly, imagery can be used in conjunction with other psychological skills to reduce stress and improve athletic performance. Martin and Hall (1995) found that subjects who used mental imagery spent more time practising a golf putting task, set higher goals for themselves, had more realistic self-expectations, and adhered more to their training programmes. Thus, with practice, golfers can use imagery effectively and efficiently to elevate their performance to optimal levels.

PRESHOT ROUTINE

An important but often neglected aspect of golf is the preshot routine, which precedes one's shot and putt. Golf is a game of consistency, and having a preshot routine will help the golfer to achieve consistently lower scores. The main purpose of a preshot routine in golf is to prepare the golfer mentally and physically for the shot or putt. Using a preshot routine, the golfer will be able to align the body correctly, concentrate properly, reduce and eliminate distracting thoughts or stimuli, and direct behaviour to relevant actions that will enable him or her to carry out the intended shot or putt. The preshot routine can also help to control anxiety or other negative emotions.

The benefits of preshot routines are maximized when both behavioural strategies (e.g., taking practice swings or waggling the golf club) and cognitive strategies (using psychological tools such as imagery, relaxation, and positive self-talk) are combined. Boutcher and Zinsser (1990) and Crews and Boutcher (1986) have shown that the top elite golfers use more consistent preshot routines for full shots and putting than beginning- and amateur-level golfers. Other studies in sport psychology have shown that the performance levels of beginning-level and highly skilled golfers improved after they participated in a preshot routine training programme (Beauchamp, Halliwell, Koestner, and Fournier, 1996; Cohn, Rotella, and Lloyd, 1990; Crews and Boutcher, 1986a).

With a sport psychologist, golfers can develop a comfortable routine so that it can be used consistently before each shot. Effective practice may lead to the routine's being automated, enabling the golfer to play each shot in a ritualistic manner. Even though the preshot routine for different types of shots might vary, the goal always remains the same. The routine will enable the golfer to get into some state of automatic functioning prior to shot execution. If attention lapses or distractions occur during a round of golf, the preshot routine can assist the golfer in refocusing on the relevant and important aspects of the golf game.

DISCUSSION

Psychological skills training in golf that utilizes mental strategies such as goal setting, self-talk, relaxation, imagery, and the development of a preshot routine has been shown to increase the golfer's performance level (Beauchamp et al., 1996; Cohn et al., 1990; Kirschenbaum and Bale, 1980; Thomas and Fogarty, 1997). These skills can be developed with the aid of a sport psychologist or performance enhancement consultant. Beauchamp, Halliwell, and Fournier (1995), as well as

McCaffrey and Orlick (1989), have found that PGA Tour professionals utilize superior mental preparation skills in tournaments and practice as compared to other golfers.

Many beginners and advanced-level golfers employ a coach to help improve their game. A coach can help with the physical aspects of the game but cannot instruct the golfer adequately on psychological issues. PGA Tour professionals have started to realize this, and many have begun employing a sport psychologist. Additionally, a sport psychologist can benefit golfers of all ages and abilities. For example, Cohn (1990) found that the most frequently cited source of competitive stress for youth golfers was playing a difficult shot or playing up to personal standards. A sport psychologist can help address these issues using relevant mental preparation strategies. Thus, no matter what the golfer's level and handicap, a sport psychologist can use psychological techniques to help each individual player reach his or her peak performance.

References

Beauchamp, P.H., W.R. Halliwell, and J.F. Fournier. 1995. Mental preparation strategies of PGA Tour golfers: An exploratory study of putting performance. Paper presented at the annual meeting of the Association of the Advancement of Applied Sport Psychology, September, New Orleans, LA.

Beauchamp, P.H., W.R. Halliwell, R.K. Koestner, and J.F. Fournier. 1996. Effects of cognitive-behavioral psychological skills training on the motivation and putting performance of novice golfers. *The Sport Psychologist* 10 (2): 157-170.

Boutcher, S.H., and N.W. Zinsser. 1990. Cardiac deceleration of elite and beginning golfers during putting. *Journal of Sport & Exercise Psychology* 12: 37-47.

Bunker, L., J.M. Williams, and N. Zinsser. 1993. Cognitive techniques for improving performance and building confidence. In *Applied sport psychology: Personal growth to peak performance,* ed. J.M. Williams, 225-242. Mountain View, CA: Mayfield.

Burton, D. 1989. Winning isn't everything: Examining the impact of performance goals on collegiate swimmers' cognitions and performance. *The Sport Psychologist* 3 (2): 105-132.

Burton, D. 1992. The Jekyll/Hyde nature of goals: Reconceptualizing goal setting in sport. In *Advances in sport psychology,* ed. T.S. Horn, 267-297. Champaign, IL: Human Kinetics.

Cohn, P.J. 1990. An exploratory study on sources of stress and athlete burnout in youth golf. *The Sport Psychologist* 4: 95-106.

Cohn, P.J. 1991. An exploratory study on peak performance in golf. *The Sport Psychologist* 5: 1-14.

Cohn, P.J., R.J. Rotella, and J.W. Lloyd. 1990. Effects of cognitive-behavioral intervention on the preshot routine and performance in golf. *The Sport Psychologist* 4: 33-47.

Crews, D.J., and S.H. Boutcher. 1986a. Effects of structured preshot behaviors on beginning golf performance. *Perceptual and Motor Skills* 62: 291-294.

Crews, D.J., and S.H. Boutcher. 1986b. An exploratory observational behavior analysis of professional golfers during competition. *Journal of Sport Behavior* 9 (2): 51-58.

Gould, D. 1993. Goal setting for peak performance. In *Applied sport psychology: Personal growth to peak performance,* ed. J.M. Williams, 158-169. Mountain View, CA: Mayfield.

Kingston, K.M., and L. Hardy. 1994. Factors affecting the salience of outcome, performance, and process goals in golf. In *Science and golf 2,* ed. A. Cochran and M. Farrally, 144-149. London: Chapman-Hill.

Kingston, K.M., and L. Hardy. 1997. Effects of different types of goals on processes that support performance. *The Sport Psychologist* 11 (3): 277-293.

Kirschenbaum, D., and R. Bale. 1980. Cognitive-behavioral skills in golf: Brain power golf. In *Psychology in sports: Methods and applications,* ed. R. Suinn, 334-343. New York: Burgess.

Locke, E.A., K.N. Shaw, L.M. Saari, and G.P. Latham. 1981. Goal setting and task performance. *Psychological Bulletin* 90: 125-152.

Martens, R. 1987. *Coaches' guide to sport psychology.* Champaign, IL: Human Kinetics.

Martin, K.A., and C.R. Hall. 1995. Using mental imagery to enhance intrinsic motivation. *Journal of Sport & Exercise Psychology* 17: 54-69.

McCaffrey, N., and T. Orlick. 1989. Mental factors related to excellence among top professional golfers. *International Journal of Sport Psychology* 20: 256-278.

Nicklaus, J. 1974. *Golf my way.* New York: Simon & Schuster.

Thomas, P.R., and G.J. Fogarty. 1997. Psychological skills training in golf: The role of individual differences in cognitive preferences. *The Sport Psychologist* 11: 86-106.

Thomas, P.R., and R. Over. 1994. Psychological and psychomotor skills associated with performance in golf. *The Sport Psychologist* 8: 73-86.

CHAPTER 19

Stress Responses and Performance in Intercollegiate Golfers

G.S. Krahenbuhl, J. Harris, J. Stern, and D.J. Crews
Arizona State University

N. Hubalik
University of Alaska at Fairbanks

The nervous system activation that occurs in stressful states is known to affect shot-making in golf. The purpose of the investigation was to examine the relationship between golf performance and neurotransmitters that modulate nervous system activation. Four neurotransmitters (all biogenic amines) were monitored: epinephrine (EPI), norepinephrine (NE), dopamine (DA), and serotonin (5HT). Subjects (n = 12) were members of nationally ranked golf teams. Performance and excretion data were gathered on multiple occasions under conditions of play, qualifying, and competition. The excretion rates for EPI averaged 7.96, 17.60, and 15.28 ng $\cdot$ min^{-1} for these conditions, respectively. The excretion rates (ng $\cdot$ min^{-1}) for NE were 39.68, 50.05 and 47.64; for DA were 198.02, 196.63, and 184.93; and for 5HT were 64.37, 62.61, and 61.75, respectively. These excretion rates reflected significant deviation from basal states, thereby indicating a significant stress response. When individual scatterplots of stress and performance were examined collectively using standardized scores, two distinct response profiles were detected. Three of the lesser skilled golfers exhibited one pattern of response; the more accomplished subjects exhibited a coherent, but different pattern. These results suggested that biogenic amine response patterns may differentiate ability levels of skilled performers in golf.

Keywords: Biogenic amines, competition, dopamine, epinephrine, golf, norepinephrine, serotonin, shot-making, stress, strokes.

INTRODUCTION

Golf is a sport requiring steadiness, precision, and control for effective shot-making. From beginners to professionals, every golfer who cares about his/her score has been in a state of heightened nervous system activation due to stress and experienced its effect on performance. Very few studies have simultaneously assessed indicators of nervous system activation and shot-making in golf; however, there are many related studies that have examined activation states and other performance criteria.

The purpose of the present investigation was to examine the relationship between golf performance and accompanying responses of neurotransmitters that modulate nervous system activation. Subjects (n = 12; 5 males and 7 females) were members of a nationally ranked golf team. The group included a United States amateur champion and three first-team All-Americans. Four of the eleven (2 male, 2 female) subjects went on to the PGA and LPGA tours. Performance and excretion data were gathered on multiple occasions under conditions of play, qualification, and competition. Four neurotransmitters (all biogenic amines) were monitored: epinephrine (EPI), norepinephrine (NE), dopamine (DA), and serotonin (5HT).

METHODS

The experimental design employed in this investigation featured data collection under four conditions: a basal condition and three performance conditions that experienced coaches believed would result in three levels of stress. Each subject was monitored under basal conditions on two occasions. In each instance the subject sat quietly in a private room for 120 minutes. The subjects were monitored during play conditions on two to four occasions. On these days, subjects chose whom they would play with, and the round took place in a recreational atmosphere, independent of coaching interventions.

The qualifying condition consisted of intersquad competition aimed at selecting team representatives in upcoming tournaments. The subjects were monitored on three to eight qualifying conditions. Competition measures were gathered for three days of tournament play. Performances were monitored under each corresponding play, qualifying, and competition condition. Golfers' scores relative to the course rating served as the general performance criterion. Data were also gathered on putts, the number of fairways hit, and greens hit in regulation.

Timed urine samples were obtained from the subjects during each experimental condition. Fifteen minutes prior to teeing off, subjects emptied their bladders and the time was noted. Urine voided during the round was collected, and all subjects emptied their bladders 15 minutes after the end of each round, thereby providing full collection of all urine excreted. The time and total volume were noted. Aliquots of these samples were stabilized and frozen at $-90°C$ for later analysis.

Levels of EPI, NE, and DA were analyzed according to the method of Riggin and Kissinger (1977). The analysis for 5HT was carried out using the modified procedure of Koch and Kissinger (1979). The substances were quantified by comparing areas of the constituent amine with its respective internal standard and to external standards. Excretion rates were calculated by multiplying sample concentrations of the biogenic amines by volume divided by time. Statistical tests were made using ANOVA with planned contrasts.

RESULTS AND DISCUSSION

The excretion rates for the biogenic amines are displayed in table 19.1. The excretion rates for EPI and NE during all of the experimental conditions were significantly elevated over basal levels. The excretion rates for DA and 5HT were significantly lower than those typically observed in normal basal conditions. The increased excretion of EPI and NE and the decreased excretion of DA and 5HT are the typical deflections from normal that occur during the human stress response (Harris et al., 1984) and provided physiological verification that the experimental conditions were stressful.

Table 19.1   Execretion Rates* of the Biogenic Amines (ng/min)

	Basal condition	Experimental conditions			Significant** contrasts
		Play	Qualification	Competition	
Number of observations per subject	2	4	8	3	
EPI	6.4 ± 3.3	8.0 ± 7.4	17.6 ± 9.8	15.3 ± 10.3	B, P < Q, C
NE	22.4 ± 10.3	39.7 ± 23.3	50.1 ± 16.7	47.6 ± 18.7	B < P, Q, C
DA	145.4 ± 74.8	198.0 ± 79.5	196.6 ± 58.8	184.9 ± 46.0	B < Q
5HT	84.6 ± 55.4	64.4 ± 33.6	62.6 ± 28.9	61.8 ± 16.1	

*All values are expressed as the mean ± standard deviation.
**($p \leq 0.05$)

Table 19.2 displays the performance results. The only significant difference detected was for overall relative score, where the mean number of strokes over the course rating was higher in the qualification condition than during the play condition.

The relationship between stress responses and performance results was accomplished by converting within-subject raw data on each stress indicator to z-scores ($z = (z - \dot{x}) \div SD$) and plotting the results for each subject on a common standardized two-dimensional graph (figure 19.1). Arithmetic signs were set so that the positive (+) values reflected better performance (fewer strokes) and greater stress. The negative values indicated lower-than-normal stress and poorer-than-normal performance (more strokes). The resulting plots connected three z-values for each subject's deviation around his/her own mean for all observations on that variable under each of the three stress conditions, thereby revealing individual patterns of

Table 19.2   Golf Performance Indicators

	Experimental conditions			Significant* contrasts
	Play	Qualification	Competition	
Number of observations per subject	4	8	3	
Score: Strokes above course rating	5.0 ± 3.4	7.7 ± 5.2	7.2 ± 5.1	P < Q
Tee-shots in fairway	9.5 ± 1.7	8.6 ± 1.7	9.5 ± 1.4	
Green hits in regulation	9.5 ± 2.5	9.3 ± 2.1	9.3 ± 2.6	
Putts	31.4 ± 1.5	32.3 ± 1.5	31.8 ± 1.8	

*($p \leq 0.05$)

response for all subjects. Primary interest was given to stress levels, not to the condition that created the state; therefore, the lines connecting a subject's x,y points always moved from the least stressful to the most stressful state, regardless of whether it occurred under conditions of play, qualifications, or competition.

A visual examination of figure 19.1 reveals two distinct patterns of response. Three subjects responded in what might be described roughly as an inverted "V"; for the balance (and a majority) of the subjects, the pattern is an upright or modestly tilted "V."

For the former (inverted V) subjects, low and high levels of stress were associated with poor performance, while a moderate level of stress was associated with highest performance levels. In the case of the latter subjects (upright V), the outcome was reversed. For most of these subjects, the best performances accompanied the lowest stress levels; the poorest performances occurred at moderate levels of stress; and the highest levels of stress occurred with performances in the intermediate range. Interestingly, the three subjects who exhibited responses consistent with what would be predicted by the inverted-V hypothesis were the poorest performers in the group. Conversely, all the better performers were in the group that exhibited the upright-V response.

These results suggest that nervous system activation (as indicated by the excretion rates of biogenic amines) and performance in golf exhibit two patterns of response that differentiate levels of ability in collegiate golfers.

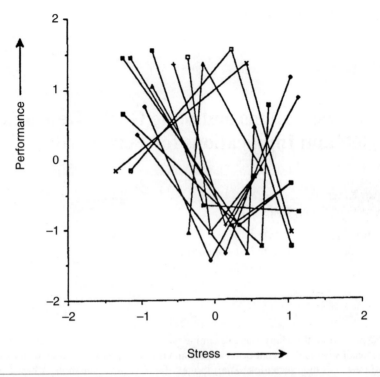

Figure 19.1   The relationship between stress and performance in golfers. Each set of three *x,y* data points connected by a solid line represents a subject's response under three experimental conditions, committed to a common standardized scale for all subjects. Each subject's line progresses from the least to the most stressful state (left to right), regardless of the condition that produced that state.

References

Koch, D.D. and Kissinger, P.T. (1979). Determination of tryptophan and several of its metabolites in physiological samples by reverse-phase liquid chromatography with electrochemical detection. *Journal of Chromatography,* 164, 441-455.

Riggin, R.M. and Kissinger, P.T. (1977). Determination of catecholamines in urine by reverse-phase liquid chromatography with electrochemical detection. *Analytical Chemistry,* 49, 2109-2111.

CHAPTER 20

Goal Orientations and State Goals: Research in Golf and Implications for Performance

Kieran Kingston
University of Wales, Bangor, UK

Austin Swain
Lane 4 Management Group Ltd., Maidenhead, UK

The purpose of this study was to examine the relationship between certain transient personality variables (goal orientations) and the state goals that individuals set for different sporting scenarios. The rationale for this amalgamation is based upon congruence that exists across what may at first seem to be diverse research paradigms, and the aim is to address the "apparent" paradoxical nature of the goal orientations that elite performers hold. The conclusions that can be drawn from both empirical and anecdotal accounts are that (a) all performers should be encouraged to prioritise state goals according to their appropriateness for a given situation, and (b) it is not necessarily inappropriate to focus on beating opponents providing that this does not prevent one from maintaining a focus on the task at hand.

Keywords: Goal orientation profiles, state goals, competition performance.

INTRODUCTION

The role of personality variables such as goal orientations is important; these variables determine how performers think, feel, and act in achievement situations such as sport. It has been accepted for a number of years that individual goal orientations interact with the situation to determine the "state" involvement that one holds and that in turn is reflected in the specific goals that one sets (Burton, 1992; Dweck and Leggett, 1988; Swain and Harwood, 1996). Within the goal-setting literature, it has been demonstrated that the specific state goals that performers set impact upon performance and associated cognitions (Burton, 1989; Kingston and Hardy, 1994, 1997). Furthermore, some of the most recent goal-setting research suggests that it is the prioritisation of state goals that is important (e.g., Kingston and Hardy, 1995), as different types of discrete goals (outcome, performance, or process) may have different benefits according to the *specific* demands of the situation.

Consequently, to achieve some congruence within the literature, it is important to understand more clearly the nature of this goal orientations-state goals relationship. Furthermore, given that our aim is to provide guidelines for best practice, this congruence is meaningful only if it enables performers to more readily achieve optimal levels of performance. The purpose of this paper is to demonstrate that the similarities that exist across the two research paradigms enable us to outline procedures for best practice that support (rather than challenge) the goal orientations held by highly competitive and elite performers (in particular).

PROCESS-ORIENTED GOALS

Although studies attesting to the effectiveness of process goals have been thin on the ground for many years, a growing body of literature now appears to be providing some compelling evidence of the value of such goals to performance-related variables. Process goals specify behaviours in which the performer will engage during performance (e.g., ensuring the appropriate alignment prior to playing a shot) and can provide the performer with a primary focus that, if adhered to, can increase the likelihood of successful execution of the target behaviour (Kingston and Hardy, 1994). Additionally, process goals can form part of the strategy and technique development that leads to the eventual automation of performance (Hardy, Jones, and Gould, 1996). Preliminary research into the efficacy of process goals has indicated that they may reduce the performer's susceptibility to somatic anxiety and enhance performance in otherwise stressful competitive situations (Kingston, Hardy, and Markland, 1992). This followed suggestions of Hardy and Nelson (1988), who argued that the task focus of process-based goals might facilitate concentration. Hardy and Nelson stated that such goals may exert their influence on performance through effective allocation of attentional resources. Furthermore, it has also been argued that process goals enhance self-efficacy through increases in perception of control. Burton (1989) and Hall and Byrne (1988) have argued that performance goals enable performers to exert greater control over the performance outcome than do normatively referenced outcome goals. Although correct, this does not mean that performance goals are entirely independent of external factors. For example, environmental conditions and the nature of opponents/playing partners can impact on the potential for goal achievement. Process goals enable the individual to exert almost total control because they are those behaviours in which the performer engages in pursuit of the performance objectives.

The most comprehensive study in this area is the recent investigation by Kingston and Hardy (1997b). A year-long goal-setting intervention programme involving 37 golfers revealed significant improvements in self-efficacy, cognitive anxiety control, and concentration for a process-goal group, whereas no changes emerged for either the control or the performance-goal group. Of most salience to performers and practitioners were the improvements in skill level for the process-goal group (through the recognised measure of golf handicap) over a relatively short period of time (5 months). Furthermore, by the conclusion of the study, *both* goal-setting training groups had realised significant levels of improvement, indicating that self-referent goal setting *per se* has beneficial effects on performance. It is important to consider the positive impact of process goals on the psychological skills mentioned previously. The results of the Kingston and Hardy study suggest that training players to set goals having strategy development as a primary focus may serve as a mechanism for improved performance. Burton (1988) has argued that, for complex tasks, strategies may need to be defined and acquired in order for goal setting to have an effect. Clearly, however, process goals are often, by their very nature, *the* strategy for reducing the complexity of a given task and hence may have double the value.

GOAL ORIENTATION PROFILES

Originating as a social cognitive approach to achievement motivation, goal perspectives theory (Dweck, 1986; Maehr and Nicholls, 1980) proposes that performers may pursue two predominant goals of action. According to the theory, these "goal perspectives" reflect how competencies are judged and how personal success is defined. An individual's goal orientation is the predisposing tendency to hold these goal perspectives in achievement-related contexts.

A task orientation stems from a self-referenced conception of ability, where the performer places importance on personal progress, improvement, and the development of new skills. In essence, this conception reflects a goal of achieving subjective success with the performer utilising past and present performance and effort levels to construe "current" levels of ability. In contrast, an ego orientation feeds off a normative conception of ability whereby personal success is measured and evaluated by social comparison processes and by the amount of ability that the performer holds relative to other performers. This conception reflects the need to outperform others in competition to allow the individual to construe a higher capacity than others.

An important underpinning of this research is that the two goal orientations are orthogonal (independent), implying that performers may be high (or low) on both task and ego orientation simultaneously (Hardy, Jones, and Gould, 1996). In light of the independence of these orientations, a recent development in goal perspectives research has been to combine performers' self-reported task and ego levels to form a goal orientation "profile." Utilising this research paradigm (for example with golfers), Kingston and Hardy (1997a) reported that players demonstrating a high level of ego orientation and a low task orientation performed significantly ($p < .05$) worse than those holding profiles involving high levels of task orientation (irrespective of the level of ego orientation). See table 20.1.

These authors also report a highly significant main effect for task orientation ($p < .01$), indicating that generally a high rather than a low level of task orientation is desirable. It should be noted that this contention was not fully substantiated because those with a profile combining low levels of task *and* low levels of ego orientation did not perform at a significantly lower level than those with high levels of task

Table 20.1   Means and Standard Deviations of Competition Performance Scores

Group	N	M (SD)
1. high ego/high task	35	1.20 (2.81)
2. high ego/low task	54	4.17 (3.68)
3. low ego/high task	55	1.96 (2.98)
4. low ego/low task	29	2.45 (5.48)

*Mean scores represent the number of strokes *over par* (net scores). These scores can be positive or negative. Consequently standard deviations may appear inflated relative to the mean scores.

orientation. It could be argued that the combination of high ego/low task has the most damaging effect upon performance because there are insufficient levels of task orientation (and the inherent process goal setting that results) to moderate the potentially debilitating social comparison focus that highly ego-oriented individuals hold. These findings corroborate Brunel and Avanzini's (1997) suggestion that being highly ego oriented in an elite sport should lead to better performance on the proviso that performers also exhibit a high task orientation.

The finding that the high task/high ego group in Kingston and Hardy's (1997a) study did not suffer in terms of performance suggests that for some individuals, the potentially ego-involving nature of golf competitions may be insufficiently powerful to override a resilient task orientation. It is plausible that a high level of task orientation retains a high degree of robustness because it supports an internal locus of causality (Dweck and Leggett, 1988). Similarly, it may be that in a competitive situation, those holding a high task/high ego profile might consciously focus their attention on task performance. Such performers avoid focusing on social evaluation issues because they perceive this as being the most effective strategy for optimising their chances of winning (Kingston and Hardy, 1994). The benefit of using a golf competition in which to measure/assess performance is that the environment can support the performer's need for competition and provides opportunities for mastery/learning. While winning undoubtedly exists as a criterion for success, the scoring system in golf enables all individuals to self-monitor their performance relative to a self-referenced norm, should they prefer that as their criterion for success. Moreover, as a self-paced sport, it allows individuals to consistently monitor and regulate their performance and thus gain information in relation to the acquisition and mastery of skills. It also encourages the establishment of preperformance routines that invariably contain a process emphasis.

GOAL ORIENTATION AND STATE GOALS

Burton's (1992) competitive goal-setting model proposes that goal orientations form the basis of the discrete goals that we set (notwithstanding the influence of the situation). He argues for greater synergy in the literature because, in his view, performance goals essentially stem from a task orientation while outcome goals emanate from an ego orientation (orientations in this context relate to a tendency or inclination to behave in a particular way). According to these distinctions and the orthogonality of the goal orientations, a number of predictions can be made regarding the state goals that individuals with specific profile patterns would favour. Those performers with profiles consisting of a high ego orientation *and* high task orientation (or a low ego and low task orientation) would be expected to favour equally outcome-, performance-, and process-based goals. A performer high in task orientation and low in ego orientation would be predicted to favour performance- and process-based goals as opposed to outcome goals. Conversely, a performer high in ego orientation and low in task orientation would have a bias toward setting outcome goals. One criticism of Burton's model, however, is that it fails to differentiate between process and performance goals when describing self-referent discrete goals.

SITUATIONAL INFLUENCES

Research examining the effects of goal orientations has consistently supported the proposal that the situation plays an important role in determining the predictive validity of goal orientations to state goals (see, for example, Burton, 1992; Dweck and Leggett, 1988; Swain and Harwood, 1996). Most recently, Kingston and Hardy (1997c) attempted to shed some alternative light on this issue, and their results highlight the need for researchers to seek clearer understanding of the nature of goal orientations. Goal orientations have long been regarded as relatively stable personality constructs (see Duda, 1992). They are predominantly measured using Duda and Nicholls's (1992) Task and Ego Orientation in Sport Questionnaire (TEOSQ), a sport-specific version of an inventory developed by Nicholls and his colleagues to assess goal orientations in academic settings. Furthermore, this instrument has been validated primarily using children in physical education settings.

Kingston and Hardy's study supported *their* contention that goal orientations (measured using TEOSQ) are situationally sensitive, and further suggested that ability has a moderating effect on the proneness of an individual to such variations. Their most interesting finding highlighted the differences between high-handicap golfers and a group of golf professionals. They observed that as a competition approached, both groups experienced a significant increase in ego orientation levels ($p < .05$); however, for the low-ability group, this was accompanied by a significant ($p < .05$) reduction in task orientation (see table 20.2).

These results draw attention to Harwood and Swain's (in press) argument that the issue of task orientation in competitive sport requires delicate attention. One might venture to state that the golfers in the Kingston and Hardy (1997c) study are not

Table 20.2   Means and Standard Deviations for Goal Orientation Levels Across Situations

	Task orientation			Ego orientation		
Group	pre-season	pre-practice	pre-competition	pre-season	pre-practice	pre-competition
Professionals						
M	3.98	3.71	3.55	3.63	3.36	4.30
SD	(.47)	(.32)	(.42)	(.74)	(.31)	(.28)
20-28 Handicap						
M	3.43	3.42	2.84	2.93	2.75	3.95
SD	(.41)	(.49)	(.81)	(.67)	(.69)	(.52)

necessarily truly task involved nor do they recognise the true meaning of personal performance from an intrinsic viewpoint. In valued matches, task involvement may remain high, yet function purely as a protection mechanism against a high level of ego orientation. In other words, for a highly ego-oriented person, the task involvement may be acting as a secondary satisfaction guarantor or "escape hatch" should the player not "win." Truly task-involved performers would pursue task goals and recognise the role of performance processes, regardless of the situational constraints, with perceptions of ability being less pertinent, due to their high levels of internal control. What would be interesting to observe is whether the players in Kingston and Hardy's study actually modified their behaviour in competition and, if so, how. For example, did their preshot focus change in any way? It seems clear that the literature would benefit from observational studies that also access within-performance thoughts and feelings.

CONCLUSIONS

There is reasonable empirical evidence to support the use of self-referenced process-based goals in competitive situations. However, there is *also* anecdotal and empirical evidence to suggest that outcome goals (those based on performance relative to others) and performance goals have an important cognitive role for performers across a variety of situations (see, for example, Burton, 1989; Hardy, Jones, and Gould, 1996; Orlick and Partington, 1988). Additionally, it is clear from the evidence provided that individual goal orientation profiles cannot be readily classified as being adaptive or maladaptive—a proposition that is contrary to much of the earlier research into goal perspectives.

IMPLICATIONS FOR BEST PRACTICE

An important implication of the goal-setting research is that performers should be encouraged to prioritise state goals according to the specific situation in which they find themselves. It is acknowledged that different types of state goals might have very specific benefits across situations, and thus it is fruitless to suggest avoiding certain goal types. For example, a goal of "wanting to rub your opponent's nose in the mud" might be highly appropriate if it acts as a trigger to focus on the task. Equally, a goal of "winning the next Open Championship" might be acceptable if it motivates the professional to spend that extra hour working on his chipping. While accepting the multiple benefits of different goals, there remains compelling evidence that process-based goals (those that focus on aspects of the to-be-performed task, for example the grip, the stance, the preshot routine) may alleviate some of the anxiety and attention problems that may arise during competition.

A second implication that arises from the research into goal orientation profiles is that it is not necessarily inappropriate to have a high level of ego orientation, and indeed it may even help one perform to one's optimum. Most importantly, performers should be encouraged to possess a high level of task orientation (focus on setting performance and process state goals) and should not be discouraged from maintaining a high level of ego orientation (focus on setting outcome goals). This supports the views of many coaches and performers, and is certainly more palatable (and realistic) for those involved in the upper echelons of competitive sport. The key for those individuals with a high level of task and ego orientation (in particular) is to prioritise their state goals appropriately according to the specific situation, or the varying circumstances within that situation.

References

Brunel, P.C., and Avanzini, G. (1997). Achievement orientation and intrinsic motivation at the Olympic Games. *Journal of Sport and Exercise Psychology, 19*, S36.

Burton, D. (1988). Do anxious swimmers swim slower? Re-examining the elusive anxiety-performance relationship. *Journal of Sport and Exercise Psychology, 10*, 45-61.

Burton, D. (1989). Winning isn't everything: Examining the impact of performance goals on collegiate swimmers' cognitions and performance. *The Sport Psychologist, 3*, 105-132.

Burton, D. (1992). The Jekyll/Hyde nature of goals: Re-conceptualizing goal setting in sport. In T.S. Horn (Ed.), *Advances in sport psychology,* 267-297. Champaign, IL: Human Kinetics.

Duda, J.L. (1992). Motivation in sport settings: A goal perspective approach. In G.C. Roberts (Ed.), *Motivation in sport and exercise,* 57-92. Champaign, IL: Human Kinetics.

Duda, J.L., and Nicholls, J.G. (1992). Dimensions of achievement motivation in schoolwork and sport. *Journal of Educational Psychology, 84*, 290-299.

Dweck, C.S. (1986). Motivational processes affecting learning. *American Psychologist, 41*, 1040-1048.

Dweck, C.S., and Leggett, E.L. (1988). A social-cognitive approach to motivation and personality. *Psychological Review,* 95, 256-273.

Hall, H.K., and Byrne, T.J. (1988). Goal setting in sport: Clarifying recent anomalies. *Journal of Sport and Exercise Psychology,* 10, 184-198.

Hardy, L., Jones, J.G., and Gould, D. (1996). *Understanding psychological preparation for sport: Theory and practice of elite sports performers.* Chichester: Wiley.

Hardy, L., and Nelson, D. (1988). Self regulation training in sport and work. *Ergonomics,* 31, 1673-1683.

Kingston, K., and Hardy, L. (1994). Factors affecting the salience of outcome, performance and process goals in golf. In A. Cochran and M. Farrally (Eds.), *Science and golf 2,* 144-149. London: Chapman-Hill.

Kingston, K., and Hardy, L. (1995). Directives for goal setting in applied situations. Paper presented at the annual meeting of the Association for the Advancement of Applied Sport Psychology, September, New Orleans, LA.

Kingston, K., and Hardy, L. (1997a). Can goal orientation profiles impact upon competition performance? *Journal of Applied Sport Psychology,* 9, S116.

Kingston, K., and Hardy, L. (1997b). Effects of different goals on processes that support performance. *The Sport Psychologist,* 11, 277-293.

Kingston, K., and Hardy, L. (1997c). Situational influences on goal orientations amongst golfers of different ability levels. Manuscript submitted for publication.

Kingston, K., Hardy, L., and Markland, D. (1992). Study to compare the effect of two different goal orientations on a number of situationally relevant performance sub-components. *Journal of Sports Sciences,* 10, 610-611.

Maehr, M.L., and Nicholls, J.G. (1980). Culture and achievement motivation: A second look. In N. Warren (Ed.), *Studies in Cross Cultural Psychology,* 221-267. New York: Academic Press.

Orlick, T., and Partington, J. (1988). Mental links to excellence. *The Sport Psychologist,* 2, 105-131.

Swain, A.B.M., and Harwood, C.G. (1996). Antecedents of state goals in age-group swimmers: An interactionist perspective. *Journal of Sports Sciences,* 14, 111-124.

CHAPTER 21

Psychophysiological Indicators of Confidence and Habituation During Golf Putting

D. Crews, R. Lutz, P. Nilsson, and L. Marriott
Arizona State University, Tempe, AZ, USA

Confidence is a state that all golfers strive to achieve. Golfers who attain "automatic" performance levels enhance their ability to achieve this state. That is, when the skill is well learned, consistent successful performance will increase one's confidence level. The best measure of this state is electroencephalography (EEG), since it can be recorded during preparation of the performance without interrupting the golfer. The purpose of the present investigation was to determine the psychophysiological indicators of confidence. Secondly, it was of interest to determine the relationship of confidence to a state of habituation when a new stimulus is presented. A very different putter was used to study habituation effects while EEG and performance were recorded and analyzed. Swedish European female tour players (N = 10) volunteered to participate in this study. They completed twenty 13 ft putts in both a baseline condition and in the habituation condition. Players defined which putts they knew were going in the hole before they stroked the ball. They informed the researcher after the putt, and these were marked as confident putts. These trials were compared with successful putts that were not indicated as confident putts. Results indicated that confident putts were characterized by lower activity in the brain, particularly in the parietal area. The habituation condition produced elevated levels of EEG activity, particularly at P3. It was concluded that lower activity represents less cortical involvement needed in the final second before the putt. Furthermore, new stimuli may provide opportunities to recreate low levels of balanced activity in the two hemi-spheres of the brain for optimal performance in golf putting.

Keywords: Golf putting, EEG, confidence, habituation.

INTRODUCTION

Golfers of all ages and skill levels strive to obtain a state of confidence to achieve consistent and successful performance. Anecdotal reports suggest that successful performance often feels effortless. Effortless performance also has been used to describe the state of "automaticity" in sport. Fitts and Posner (1967) suggest that automatic performance, the final stage of learning a motor skill, is effortless and also requires low attentional demands. Electroencephalographic (EEG) measures of automatic, successful performance confirm that low levels of activity exist in various areas of the brain immediately prior to initiating the stroke during the golf putt (Crews & Landers, 1993). Since EEG measures electrical activity at the cortex where conscious thought occurs, this suggests that conscious thought is reduced. Therefore, it is likely that subcortical areas of the brain are responsible for automatic performance. If this is the case, then what is the role of the cortex, or conscious thought during preparation for performance? How is confidence achieved and maintained throughout the preparation and performance of the task? Furthermore, how is this state altered when a novel influence is introduced to an action that is considered to be performed automatically? In golf, new stimuli are often introduced (i.e., new equipment, new attentional cue, new golf course) to the automatic performer. It would be of interest to determine the effects on EEG and performance to understand one's adaptation to new stimuli.

The state of confidence is defined in *Webster's* (1966) as a "consciousness of feeling sure" and is typically measured using a pencil and paper questionnaire that assesses a general state prior to performance. Situationally specific self-confidence, or self-efficacy, is often assessed closer to performance by asking a few questions with rating scale responses. However, having to rate self-efficacy too close to the initiation of the putt can interfere with one's attentional focus and in fact may change in the final seconds of preparation. Advanced-level players often report putts that, in the final second before initiating the stroke, they know are going in the hole. Indicating this state to an observer may alter the state of confidence. In the present study it was possible to measure EEG patterns of successful putts that golfers reported they knew were going in the hole before they putted the ball.

Habituation refers to the "process of making habitual or accustomed," possibly resulting in a state of tolerance to a given stimuli (*Webster's,* 1966). This is very similar to the concept of automatic performance. The question remains whether this state is optimal for performance. If attention can be directed to important sources of information (i.e., the target) rather than detailed mechanics, performance may be optimized. However, the question remains: Can the movement become too automatic? Perhaps as one habituates to clubs, cues, and so on, less intensity is used to prepare for the action, resulting in poorer performance. This question was addressed by introducing novel stimuli (i.e., a new putter) to the automatic performance of putting among highly skilled golfers. Thus, the purpose of the investigation was to determine the psychophysiological indicators of confidence and to determine the relationship of confidence to the psychophysiological indicators of habituation during golf putting.

METHOD

Participants

Swedish European female tour players (N = 10) volunteered to participate in this study. All players were right-handed. The average age of the players was 24.8 years, and the average handicap was +1.3. The golfers had been playing for an average of 15.4 years with an average of 10.3 years of competitive experience.

Performance Measures

Each putt was measured as cm error from the hole, and the maximum error was 140 cm due to the size limitations of the indoor putting surface. Total putts made was also recorded as a measure of performance.

EEG Measures

A Grass Instruments amplifier was used to record EEG from eight areas of the brain: F4, F3, C4, C3, T4, T3, P4, and P3. These sites were in accord with the International 10-20 system (Jasper, 1958), and an electrode cap was used to secure the position of each electrode. The sampling rate for all data was 250 samples. The high- and low-frequency filters were set at 0.01 and 100 Hz, and the signals were amplified by a factor of 50,000. Linked mastoids were used as the reference electrode, and the ground was located anterior to FZ in the electrode cap. The resistance for all EEG electrodes was below 5K ohms.

Electrooculogram was recorded to control for eye blinks. Electrodes were placed on the lateral canthus and the superior orbital ridge of the right eye to avoid interference with the putt. Impedance was below 10K ohms for this measure. Electrooculogram was used as a marker to filter EEG values above 50 uV. Eye blinks that remained after filtering and that occurred during the final 3 s before the putt were marked, and this portion of the EEG was removed from the analyses.

A photoelectronic device (Telemecanique XUG-J04313) was used to send a marker to one channel in the Neuroscan data acquisition system indicating the initiation of the putting stroke. The device positioned a beam of light that passed perpendicular to the putting line, directly behind the putter head. As the putter began its motion backward, the shaft of the putter broke the beam of light and sent a marker to one channel of the data acquisition system. All data were analyzed in 1 s increments backward from this mark.

Procedures

Informed consents and descriptive information were obtained from all subjects while the electrodes were being attached. Participants then completed a minimum of 10 practice putts followed by twenty 13 ft putts in a baseline condition and another twenty putts with a new and very different putter (habituation condition). The head of the new putter was centered at the bottom of the shaft and extended 3 in. forward of the shaft instead of backward as seen in traditional putters. Golfers were instructed to inform the researcher, after each putt, of those putts they knew were going in the hole before being stroked. One limitation of the study was that the indication of the confident putts had to be reported retrospectively to avoid influencing the state of confidence. Consequently, the outcome of the putt could have influenced the consideration of the putt as confident or nonconfident. To control for the influence of the outcome of the putt, the comparison of interest was confident versus nonconfident putts that went in the hole.

Statistical Analysis

Because of the low number of highly skilled, professional golfers that participated in this study, the number of statistical analyses were limited in an attempt to control for Type I errors. In addition, the Bonferronit technique was applied to each analysis of variance (ANOVA); however, all results equal to or below an alpha level of .05 were reported. Furthermore, only the final second prior to initiating the stroke was analyzed. Previous research (Crews & Landers, 1993) has shown that it is only the final second that is related to golf putting performance. The power spectrum analysis (Neuroscan Inc.) was grouped into four ranges that consisted of theta (5-7 Hz), alpha (8-12 Hz), beta (13-20 Hz), and beta II (21-30 Hz).

   One set of ANOVAs was used to compare the EEG measures from confident and nonconfident successful putts. A second set of ANOVAs compared the EEG measures from baseline putting and the habituation condition. Because of the small number of subjects it was not possible to examine the interaction effect of these two conditions. Pearson product-moment correlation examined the relationship of the EEG measures with performance in the baseline and habituation conditions. Effect sizes (ES) were included to indicate the meaningfulness of the results. Hedges and Olkin's (1985) formula was used to compute ES.

RESULTS

Performance results are presented in table 21.1. Interestingly, the tour players made 43% and 42% of the 13 ft putts in the baseline and habituation conditions, respectively. Across both the baseline and habituation conditions, 21% of the trials were confident trials that went in the hole. These trials were compared with nonconfident trials that went in the hole (20%). Another 9% of the putts were confident trials that didn't go in the hole. Lastly, 50% of the putts were nonconfident putts that didn't go in the hole.

   During the final second prior to initiating the golf putt, there was lower EEG activity at every site and every frequency band (32 comparisons) for confident putts compared to nonconfident putts with baseline and habituation conditions combined. In addition, during baseline there was lower EEG activity in almost every site and every frequency band compared to the habituation condition (26 of 32 comparisons). Table 21.2 illustrates the power frequency of the EEG bands that showed significant differences between confident and nonconfident successful putts across baseline and habituation conditions combined.

Table 21.1   Average Error (in cm) and Putts Made During Baseline and Habituation Conditions

Measure	Confident		Nonconfident		Baseline	Habituation
	Makes	Misses	Makes	Misses		
Error (in cm)	0	26.67	0	32.21	17.88	16.58
Putts made	85	37	78	200	86	84

Table 21.2   Significant Differences in EEG Power Spectrum for Theta, Alpha, Beta, and Beta II During Confident and Nonconfident Successful Putts

Frequency band	Confident (uV)	Nonconfident (uV)	F	p	ES
Theta					
C4	1.59	3.18	12.36	.01	.95
F4	2.04	4.59	7.66	.03	.68
F3	2.13	4.49	6.22	.05	.70
P4	1.84	3.51	33.60	.001*	1.41
P3	2.00	4.00	12.76	.01	1.12
T3	1.02	2.46	14.06	.01	1.12
Alpha					
P4	1.51	3.63	30.86	.001*	2.80
P3	1.70	3.61	52.45	.001*	1.79
T4	1.21	2.86	12.27	.01	1.08
T3	1.53	3.38	11.17	.02	1.00
Beta					
C4	.79	1.36	7.31	.04	.77
P4	1.51	2.37	37.05	.001*	1.93
P3	1.13	2.07	21.02	.004	1.31
T4	.93	1.98	16.28	.007	1.76
T3	1.26	2.13	8.86	.03	.79
Beta II					
C4	.58	1.16	8.87	.03	1.16
P4	.88	1.84	12.16	.02	1.58

*Significance with Bonferroni correction (.05/32 = .0016)

Comparing the EEG activity between baseline and habituation conditions produced only one marginally significant difference in beta activity at P3, $F(1,9) = 2.27$, $p = .05$. Beta was lower (1.37 uV) during baseline putting than during habituation (1.62 uV), and the ES = .26. However, of the 32 possible comparisons, 26 sites showed lower activity during baseline than during habituation. Furthermore, the 6 sites that showed higher baseline values were all in the right hemisphere: three at P4, two at F4, and one at T4.

Lastly, it was of interest to examine the relationship of the EEG measures to performance (cm error) during baseline and habituation conditions. Table 21.3 illustrates the marginally significant results suggesting that less theta, more alpha, and more beta II were associated with reduced error. However, none of these correlations were below the .0016 alpha level, and thus these results must be considered with caution.

Table 21.3   Correlations of EEG Activity With Performance (cm Error) for Baseline and Habituation Conditions

Frequency Bands		Baseline		Habituation	
		r	p	r	p
Theta	F4			.68	.03
Alpha	T3	−.66	.04		
Beta II	F4	−.63	.05		
	T4	−.69	.03	−.71	.03
	T3	−.73	.02	−.75	.02
	P3	−.69	.03		

DISCUSSION

The primary purpose of this investigation was to determine the psychophysiological state associated with self-reported "confidence." The pattern of EEG activity showed lower activity at every site for confident trials during the final second prior to initiating the putting stroke. These differences were significant at P4 and P3 for theta, alpha, and beta activity. The parietal area of the brain is known to be active to process information. Thus, the present data suggest that it is imperative to quiet this area of the brain for confident, successful performance.

The meaningfulness of comparisons between groups is indicated by the ES measure. Cohen (1988) has suggested that an ES = .2 is considered low, an ES = .5 is considered moderate, and an ES = .8 is large. The results comparing the confident and nonconfident putts produced 13 large ESs and 4 moderate ESs for the significant and marginally significant comparisons. While the sample size was small, and thus did not produce many significant results when Type I error was controlled for, the ES results suggest that the differences were meaningful. It is likely that a larger sample size would confirm these results.

It was also of interest to determine the psychophysiological changes that occur during automatic performance when a novel stimuli is introduced. In this case, the introduction of a new and very different putter produced a general increase in activity across most areas of the brain. However, there was only one marginally significant difference (P3) that occurred between baseline and the new putter condition. Left hemisphere, parietal activity was higher during the habituation condition, perhaps to help adjust to the new stimuli. This suggests that the parietal site was instrumental both in distinguishing confident from nonconfident putts and in adapting to the introduction of a new stimuli to an automatic task, golf putting.

Similar to findings from past research (Crews & Landers, 1993; Hatfield, Landers, & Ray, 1984) increased alpha activity was related to reduced error, and quieting the left hemisphere appears to be important for successful performance. However, these results must be considered with caution, since none of the correlations were significant when corrected for alpha inflation.

As was the trend in previous research, more right frontal theta was detrimental to performance (Crews & Landers, 1993). Theta being a measure of pleasure/displeasure and the frontal area of the brain expressing emotion, may indicate that higher activity in this location (right frontal) represents excessive displeasure, such as anxiety (Harman & Ray, 1977).

Lastly, increased beta II activity in the right and left hemispheres was related to more putts made and to less error. This is contradictory to earlier research with archers showing that more beta II was associated with poor performance (Salazar et al., 1990). It is unclear at this time how beta II activity relates to sport performance, and future research is needed to clarify these findings.

Biofeedback training could be used to define the relationship of beta II activity with golf putting performance (Landers et al., 1991). In fact, biofeedback is a technique that can be used to facilitate all of the described EEG patterns that lead to enhanced performance among highly skilled golfers.

In summary, confident performance is displayed as low activity in the brain, and the introduction of novelty increases this level of activity. The parietal areas of the brain appear to be important for distinguishing patterns of successful performance. It appears that it may be necessary to increase activity in the brain to maintain optimal performance in novel situations. Conversely, new situations may facilitate the process of achieving optimal states by challenging the brain to recreate low levels of balance in the two hemispheres of the brain.

ACKNOWLEDGMENTS

This project was supported by a grant from Titleist and Foot-Joy Worldwide.

References

Cohen, J. (1988). *Statistical Power Analysis for the Behavioral Sciences*. Hillsdale, NJ: Erlbaum.

Crews, D.J., & Landers, D.M. (1993). Electroencephalographic measures of attentional patterns prior to the golf putt. *Medicine and Science in Sports and Exercise* 25(1): 116-126.

Fitts, P.M., & Posner, M.I. (1967). *Human Performance.* Belmont, CA: Brooks/ Cole.

Harmon, M.W., & Ray, W.J. (1977). Hemispheric activity during affective verbal stimuli: An EEG study. *Neurophysiology* 15: 457-460.

Hedges, L.D., & Olkin, I. (1985). *Statistical Methods for Meta-analysis.* New York: Academic Press.

Jasper, H.H. (1958). Report of the committee on methods of clinical examination in electroencephalography. *EEG Clinical Neurophysiology* 10: 370-375.

Landers, D.M., Petruzzello, S.J., Salazar, W., Crews, D.J., Kubitz, K.A., Gannon, T.L., & Han, M. (1991). The influence of electrocortical biofeedback on performance in pre-elite archers. *Medicine and Science in Sports and Exercise* 23(1): 123-129.

Salazar, W., Landers, D.M., Petruzzello, S.J., Crews, D.J., & Kubitz, K.A. (1990). The effects of physical/cognitive load on electrocortical patterns preceding response execution in archery. *Research Quarterly in Exercise and Sport* 61: 351-359.

Webster's Seventh New Collegiate Dictionary. (1966). Springfield, MA: 174, 373.

CHAPTER 22

Using "Swing Thoughts" to Prevent Paradoxical Performance Effects in Golf Putting

Robin C. Jackson and Robert J. Willson
University of St. Andrews, Scotland, UK

Being able to perform well-learned skills under the intense pressure of competition is believed to be a crucial factor that separates top performers from "also-rans." It has recently been suggested that one of the reasons for "choking" in these situations is that golfers reinvest rules concerning how to perform the task. The present paper describes three experiments addressing the possibility that using "swing thoughts" can help golfers to maintain a high level of performance under pressure by preventing reinvestment of explicit rules. The results provide support for this position while also suggesting that additional factors might determine the effectiveness of such a strategy.

Keywords: Choking, reinvestment, paradoxical performance.

INTRODUCTION

Paradoxical performance effects have been defined as "the occurrence of inferior performance despite striving and incentives for superior performance" (Baumeister and Showers, 1986, p. 361). Such performance is colloquially referred to as "choking," and typical examples include, firstly, an athlete who performs flawlessly in practice but then poorly in a competitive situation and, secondly, an athlete who performs well for most of a competitive event but then very poorly at critical moments, or "clutch situations" (Leith, 1988).

Recently, Masters (1992) proposed that choking in skills such as golf putting may be caused by "reinvesting" control by explicit rules of performance that were present during the early stages of learning. This theory has its roots in the principles of motor skill learning and, in particular, the observation that skilled motor performance is characterised by a high level of automaticity and/or lack of conscious control of the precise mechanics of performance (Kimble and Perlmuter, 1970). For example, when first learning to play golf an individual may be given many instructions regarding how to grip the club, the correct set-up position to adopt, and how to actually swing the club. After much practice, however, these aspects of performance become automatic in that they are not subject to verbal control.

Masters (1992) predicted that learning a skill implicitly would prevent choking because the performer would have no explicit knowledge to reinvest when under pressure. To test this hypothesis, a study was conducted in which novice golfers learned to putt either with instructions (explicit learning: EL), without instructions (stressed control: SC), or without instructions while also carrying out a backward-counting task to suppress rule formulation (implicit learning: IL). The task involved putting a golf ball up a 1:4 incline into a standard-size golf cup from a distance of 1.5m with the dependent variable being the number of putts holed out of 100 attempts on five consecutive sessions. In the final session, subjects putted under a pressure manipulation in which they were led to believe that their performance was being evaluated by a "professional golfer" who could either increase or decrease the payment for participation in the experiment.

In accordance with the hypothesis, Masters found that the group of subjects who acquired the skill implicitly continued to improve in the final session, whereas subjects who acquired the skill with the aid of explicit instructions performed slightly worse. On the strength of these results and a replication of this experiment, Masters (1992) and Hardy, Mullen, and Jones (1996) have suggested that coaching practices that employ a great deal of explicit instruction might increase the likelihood of choking. A problem with this interpretation is that the SC group, who were given no instruction, showed a pattern of performance similar to that of the EL group in the final stage of the experiment. The SC group reported a mean of approximately three explicit rules after the experiment, which suggests that simply withholding explicit instruction during motor skill learning does not prevent self-rule formation. In addition, if the reinvestment theory of choking is correct, then attempting to consciously control just three aspects of technique appears to be sufficient to disrupt performance.

An alternative to trying to prevent individuals from developing explicit knowledge about how to perform a skill is to try to prevent them from reinvesting that knowledge in pressure situations. One way in which this might be achieved is by the use of a "swing thought" in the moments prior to the initiation of the putting action (Boutcher and Rotella, 1987). Thus, focusing attention on a single aspect of technique, or attending to a visual stimulus, could help to prevent the performer from trying to consciously control too many aspects of performance.

EXPERIMENT 1

Golfers use many different concentration techniques. The aim of this experiment was to test the hypothesis that attending to three different types of swing thought would prevent reinvestment and hence choking under pressure in golf putting.

Previous research has shown that focusing on a specific cue leads to superior performance of self-paced skills in beginners. For example, Singer, Lidor, and Cauraugh (1993) recommended the use of a 5-step strategy for performing all self-paced skills. These steps include readying, imaging, focusing, executing, and evaluating. In a throwing task, the authors found that subjects using the 5-step strategy, or a "non-awareness" strategy (consisting of the focusing and executing steps), had significantly less radial error than subjects in the control group. However, such experiments have not typically used a pressure manipulation.

Method

Forty male golfers (mean age = 19.7 years, mean handicap = 9.6) were assigned to one of four groups: Verbal Cue (subjects verbalise a phrase relating to one or two aspects of putting techniques), Visual Cue (subjects attend to either the dimple pattern on the ball or the texture of the putting surface), R-G-Y-B (subjects verbalise the task-irrelevant words "red-green-yellow-blue"), and Control (no strategy).

The golf putting task required the subject to putt the ball so that it came to rest as near as possible to the centre of five concentric circles. The centre of the target was located 3m away, and each putt was scored according to how far it finished from this point. Scores ranged from 5 points for a ball ending up less than 0.1m from the centre point to 0 points for a ball finishing more than 0.5m from the centre point.

The experiment consisted of four stages: Warm-up, Baseline, Intervention, and Competition. Prior to the intervention, subjects had at least 20 putts in the "warm-up" stage followed by 20 putts to determine baseline performance. Subjects were then given the appropriate instructions for their particular group and had 20 further putts in order to become used to putting using the assigned attention strategy. Up to 20 additional putts were allowed in this stage if the subject requested them or if the experimenter was not satisfied that performance had returned to the level achieved in the baseline stage. Before the 20 putts in the competition stage, subjects were shown scores reported to be from five other individuals in "the same handicap bracket" as the subject (0 to 5, 6 to 10, 11 to 15, or 16 to 20). In fact, the scores that were shown were yoked to each subject's baseline score so that this score was always below the 3rd-place score but was no worse than equal to the 4th of the 5 scores posted. The subject was then told that he could win a monetary price of £6, £4, £2, or £1 for beating the 1st-, 2nd-, 3rd-, or 4th-place score in this stage of the experiment.

Results

The mean scores for each group in the baseline and competition stages of the experiment are illustrated in figure 22.1. The data were examined by a one-factor analysis of covariance with competition score the dependent variable and baseline score the covariate. This analysis revealed a significant effect for group ($F(3,35) = 4.47, p < 0.1$). A Tukey HSD post hoc test indicated that the Verbal Cue and Visual Cue groups scored significantly more points than the Control group during the competition stage while the scores of the R-G-Y-B group were not significantly different from those of any of the other three groups.

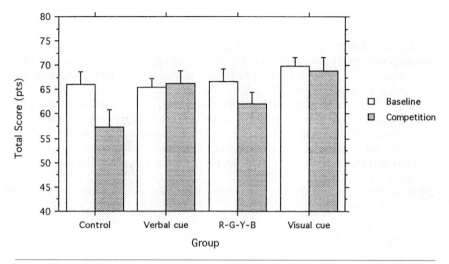

Figure 22.1   Mean point scores (maximum = 100 points) for each group in the baseline and competition stages of Experiment 1.

Discussion

The results indicate, firstly, that the pressure manipulation was successful in disrupting the performance of the Control group. Secondly, attending to a verbal (task relevant) or visual cue in the moments before initiation of the putting stroke was effective in preventing choking. Finally, the results of the group verbalising a task-irrelevant stimulus were inconclusive. Thus, the competition performance of the R-G-Y-B group was not significantly different from those of either the Control group, which choked, or the other two groups, which did not choke.

EXPERIMENT 2

The purpose of Experiment 2 was, firstly, to test the assumption that thinking about several aspects of putting technique in the few seconds *before* initiation of the swing will disrupt performance. Secondly, an assumption implicit in the reinvestment theory of choking is that the individual will reinvest rules concerning the putting action and not other aspects of putting. One possibility not previously addressed is that reinvestment of rules concerning the set-up will also disrupt performance. Support for this possibility comes from psychophysiological studies using tasks such as archery, a skill in which the focus of most explicit instructions is on the correct set-up position to adopt. For example, Hatfield, Landers, and Ray (1984) found that expert archers showed an increase in left hemisphere alpha activity in the few seconds prior to release and suggested that this might indicate a reduction in "excessive self-instruction and covert verbalisations" (p. 56). It was hypothesised that both attending to four rules concerning the correct set-up and attending to four rules concerning the putting stroke would be disruptive to performance.

Method

Twenty male golfers (mean age = 20.3 years, mean handicap = 7.5) putted under five instructional conditions. Two "Set-up" conditions required subjects to verbalise shortened versions (either 8 or 16 syllables) of four instructions relating to the correct set-up to adopt for putting. Two "Swing" conditions required subjects to verbalise shortened versions (either 8 or 16 syllables) of four instructions relating to the putting stroke. The 8- and 16-syllable conditions were used to explore the possibility that the amount of disruption might simply be related to the length of the stimulus, independent of the content. The "Baseline" condition did not require subjects to attend to any aspects of either the set-up or the swing. The putting task was the same one used in Experiment 1. After the warm-up putts, the subject putted 20 balls under each of the five conditions, the order of which was completely counterbalanced.

Results

A one-way repeated measures ANOVA revealed a significant effect for condition ($F(4,76) = 8.09$, $p < .001$). Planned contrasts indicated, firstly, no significant difference between the 8- and 16-syllable conditions. Secondly, a significant difference was found between the mean scores in the Swing and Baseline conditions, but not between the Set-up and Baseline conditions. These results are illustrated in figure 22.2, which shows the mean number of points scored in each of the five conditions.

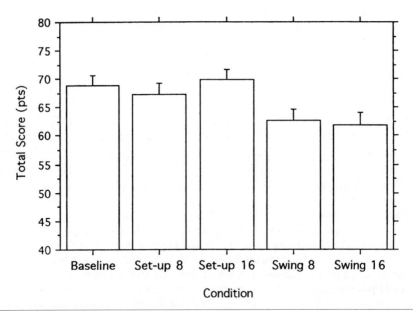

Figure 22.2   Mean total point scores (maximum = 100 points) for the five conditions in Experiment 2, with standard error bars.

Discussion

Contrary to the hypothesis, only the instructions relating to the putting stroke were disruptive to performance. This extends previous research by Backman and Molander (1991), who found that attending to a variety of technical aspects concerning both the set-up and putting stroke led to decreased accuracy. With respect to the reinvestment theory of choking, the present results suggest that performance disruption will only occur if golfers reinvest rules concerning the putting action. A question that follows from this is whether swing thoughts focusing on the set-up will also prevent choking.

EXPERIMENT 3

There were three main aims of Experiment 3. The first was to replicate the finding from Experiment 1 that using a verbal (task relevant) cue is effective in preventing choking. The second aim was to test the hypothesis that attending to a verbal swing thought relating to the set-up would also be effective in preventing choking. Thirdly, the source of the swing thought was manipulated so that it was either self-formulated or given to the subject by the experimenter.

Method

Fifty male golfers (mean age = 21.5 years, mean handicap = 7.0) were assigned to one of five groups: Set-up (self), Set-up (given), Swing (self), Swing (given), and Control. The task and procedure for Experiment 3 mirrored those of Experiment 1.

Results

Analysis of covariance revealed a significant effect for group ($F(4,44) = 4.58$, $p < .01$). A Tukey HSD post hoc test indicated that the Swing (self) group scored significantly more points than the Swing (given) and Control groups. No other differences reached significance. The baseline and competition performance of each group is illustrated in figure 22.3.

Discussion

The main finding of Experiment 3 was that the Swing (given) group performed worse in the competition stage than the Swing (self) group. This result was unexpected and suggests that other factors might influence the effectiveness of a swing thought in pressure situations. An interpretation in terms of the origin of the verbal cue does not account for the fact that both the Set-up (self) and Set-up (given) groups showed no signs of choking, scoring an almost identical number of points in the baseline and competition stages.

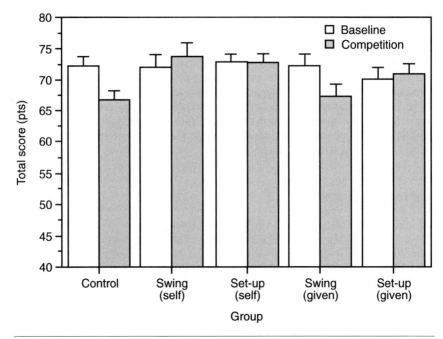

Figure 22.3   Mean total point scores for each group in the baseline and competition stages of Experiment 3, with standard error bars.

SUMMARY

Overall, the experiments outlined provide support for reinvestment theory (Masters, 1992) and the hypothesis that using swing thoughts can help to prevent paradoxical performance effects in golf putting. It should be noted, however, that the putting task and the pressure manipulation lack the ecological validity of pressure situations in actual tournament play. Research into the reinvestment theory of choking is in its infancy; and there is a need to see, firstly, whether the results prove to be robust, and secondly, whether they generalise to more ecologically valid situations. In addition, the results of Experiment 3 suggest that there may be other factors that determine the effectiveness of any particular concentration strategy. Investigating the nature of these factors is a logical next step.

References

Backman, L., and Molander, B. (1991). Cognitive processes among skilled miniature golf players: Effects of instructions on motor performance, concentration time, and perceived difficulty. *Scandanavian Journal of Psychology, 32,* 344-351.

Baumeister, R.F., and Showers, C.J. (1986). A review of paradoxical performance effects: Choking under pressure in sports and mental tests. *European Journal of Social Psychology,* 16, 361-383.

Boutcher, S.H., and Rotella, R.J. (1987). A psychological skills educational program for closed-skill performance enhancement. *The Sport Psychologist,* 1, 127-137.

Hardy, L., Mullen, R., and Jones, G. (1996). Knowledge and conscious control of motor actions under stress. *British Journal of Psychology,* 87, 621-636.

Hatfield, B.D., Landers, D.M., and Ray, W.J. (1984). Cognitive processes during self-paced motor performance: An electroencephalographic profile of skilled marksmen. *Journal of Sport Psychology,* 6, 42-59.

Kimble, G.A., and Perlmuter, L.C. (1970). The problem of volition. *Psychological Review,* 77, 361-384.

Leith, L.M. (1988). Choking in sports: Are we our own worst enemies? *International Journal of Sport Psychology,* 19, 59-64.

Masters, R.S.W. (1992). Knowledge, knerves and know-how: The role of explicit versus implicit knowledge in the breakdown of a complex motor skill under pressure. *British Journal of Psychology,* 83, 343-358.

Singer, R.N., Lidor, R., and Cauraugh, J.H. (1993). To be aware or not aware? What to think about while learning and performing a motor skill. *The Sport Psychologist,* 7, 19-30.

CHAPTER 23

Attentional Interference as Motor Program Retrieval or as Available Resources and the Effects on Putting Performance

N. Anthony
Arizona State University, Tempe, Arizona, USA

Skilled golfers typically have relatively consistent swing mechanics, and ideally they perform automatically. The question remains, If attentional capacity is not being used to perform the skills, where is attention directed to achieve optimal performance? Unfortunately, many golfers focus their attention on distracting thoughts, which results in poor performance. It would be interesting to determine whether distraction that interferes with the retrieval of the motor program from memory, or distraction that competes for available resources, is more disruptive to performance. Results could influence practice programs to optimize performance.

Twenty highly skilled (USGA handicap 0-8) male golfers completed a dual-task paradigm that included a variable-distance putting task while executing a choice reaction time (RT) and digit recall task. The choice RT condition was designed to disrupt the golfers' putting performance by interfering with the available attentional resources. The digit recall condition was designed to disrupt the immediate retrieval of the motor program from memory. Both conditions produced a decrement in performance. Statistical analyses comparing the putting task performances showed that the choice RT condition was the more disruptive to putting performance and accounted for the most performance variance during the golf putt. Therefore, the present investigation suggests that golfers need consistent preparation routines to appropriately focus attention. Finally, the use of distracting conditions during practice may facilitate the development of effective coaching strategies for optimal performance.

Keywords: Golf putting, attention, distraction.

INTRODUCTION

Hardy and Nelson (1988) identified the ability to control attention as a key component benefiting motor performance. Also, many preperformance routines (e.g., relaxation, meditation, preshot routines) designed to enhance sport performance are based on influencing an athlete's attentional focus. Golf-specific (Crews & Boutcher, 1986; Crews & Landers, 1993) and other sport-specific studies (Barabasz, Barabasz, & Bauman, 1993) have supported the notion that attentional focus strategies may improve sport performance.

In the present investigation, a self-paced putting paradigm was utilized to examine the role of attention in golf putting performance. In the first condition, a choice RT task was simultaneously completed during the putting task to interfere with the available resources needed to produce the golf putt (following Wickens's [1984] multiple-resource attentional theory). Putting performance would suffer when completed with the choice RT task because both tasks demand the anticipation of manual output processes (i.e., moving fingers to depress RT buttons on the putter grip and moving the arms to execute a putt). Catch trials were also used in which no RT tones were given in order to determine whether the intention to move or the actual RT response movement interfered with golf putting performance.

In a second condition, a digit recall task was simultaneously completed during the putting task. The digit recall condition was designed to disrupt the retrieval of the putting motor program from memory (Logan, 1988). The digit recall condition required subjects to memorize a series of numbers while preparing to putt and to recite those same numbers after completing the putt. This condition has been shown to disrupt putting performance because memorizing a series of digits while preparing to putt was designed to interfere with the golfers' distance calculations (Piparo, 1992).

Therefore, the purpose of this investigation was to examine whether distraction that interferes with the retrieval of the motor program from memory or distraction that interferes with the intention to produce the motion is more disruptive to performance.

EXPERIMENTAL METHODS

Twenty male golfers between the ages of 18 and 45 years participated in the investigation. All golfers had USGA handicaps between 0 and 8 and were screened for putting proficiency.

Pilot data was collected to establish the reliability of the golf putt as an experimental task. After 20 practice putts, golfers were screened for putting ability, and only golfers equal to and less than 37 cm mean error from the painted target qualified for the experiment. Subjects acquainted themselves with the experimental putting surface and began when they felt ready. The subjects completed the putting baseline, which consisted of 20 balls at randomly ordered distances of 24, 20, 16, and 12 feet, with five putts from each distance. With a motion similar to that for a lag putt, the golfers were to place the ball as close to the hole as possible. Performance was measured for each trial as cm error from the target painted on the putting surface.

After the putting baseline was completed, all subjects received a 4-minute rest. Then half of the subjects completed the choice RT condition, and half completed the digit recall condition. Subjects then completed the opposite experimental condition. These conditions were completed with RT microswitches attached to the putter grip. Both conditions were conducted over the same course of 20 putts hit from randomly ordered distances of 24, 20, 16, and 12 feet, with five putts from each distance. Thus, conditions were randomly assigned to each individual and counterbalanced across participants to preclude any possible order effects.

Each baseline secondary task condition consisted of 20 trials and was conducted to compare these results with those for the dual-task condition. Subjects completed the RT task and the digit recall task without putting. The subject's baseline digit recall performance consisted of the average number of seven-digit numbers the subject correctly recalled for each of the 20 trials. For the choice RT task, the microswitches were attached to the subjects' putter in the same manner as in the experimental condition. Subjects then listened for tones, depressing the corresponding microswitch as quickly as they were able. The baseline measurement was the average of the RT for each trial. For both baseline measurements, the golfers did not putt; however, they were instructed to assume their normal putting stance on the putting surface to make the baseline conditions as similar to the dual-task conditions as possible. Baseline digit recall and choice RT measurements were randomly assigned and counterbalanced among subjects as in the experimental conditions to control for order effects. The secondary task baseline conditions were completed after the dual-task conditions to control for learning effects (Landers, Wang, & Courtet, 1985).

RESULTS

Primary Task

Paired-samples t-tests were used to compare different orders on primary task performance. A paired-samples t-test was used to compare the order of the putting task during the baseline condition, during the choice RT condition, and during the digit recall task. All paired-samples t-tests failed to reach statistical significance, $t_{(9)} = -1.673, p > .05, t_{(9)} = .651, p > .05,$ and $t_{(9)} = -1.364, p > .05,$ respectively. All further statistical analyses were collapsed across order.

A repeated measures ANOVA was computed to compare putting performance during the baseline condition (M = 33.63 cm, SD = 1.65 cm), choice RT condition (M = 54.96 cm, SD = 7.36 cm), and the digit recall condition (M = 44.62 cm, SD = 7.73 cm). (See table 23.1 for putting performance means.) The difference among the means was statistically significant, $F_{(2,38)} = 65.83, p < .05$ (Huynh-Feldt Epsilon = .876). Tests of within-subjects contrasts yielded significant values among the experimental conditions, $F_{(1,19)}$ = 153.62 (baseline and choice RT condition, M difference = 21.33 cm), $F_{(1,19)}$ = 44.8 (baseline and digit recall condition, M difference = 10.99), $F_{(1,19)}$ = 19.38 (choice RT and digit recall condition, M difference = 10.34).

Using the pooled standard deviation formula, ESs for primary task performance indicated that subjects' putting performance suffered a greater decrease during the choice RT condition (ES = 3.99) than during the digit recall (ES = 1.85). The significant difference between the conditions also yielded a large ES (1.84).

A paired-samples t-test was used to compare putting performance during catch and non-catch trials during the choice RT condition. This test failed to reach statistical significance, $t_{(79)}$ = .429, p > .05. Pearson product-moment correlation coefficients were used to determine the strength of association between putting performance and digit recall and choice RT task performance. The correlation coefficient for choice RT task performance and putting performance yielded a value of –.13. The correlation coefficient for digit recall task performance and putting performance yielded a value of .35. Because the correlation coefficients failed to reach significance, no relationship could be drawn regarding subjects' primary and secondary task performance. While these correlations were not significant, the direction suggests that as the secondary task performance improved, the primary task performance was inhibited.

To estimate the amount of primary task performance variance that may be due to the experimental treatments, an omega-squared test was conducted comparing baseline and dual-task conditions. Results of the omega-squared test showed that more putting task variance could be accounted for by the choice RT condition (.81) than by the digit recall condition (.52). (See table 23.1 for effect sizes, mean difference, and omega-squared scores).

Table 23.1   Effect Sizes, Mean Difference and Omega Squared Scores for Putting Performances

	ES	Mean diff.	Ω^2
Baseline to choice reaction-time	3.99	21.33 cm	.81
Baseline to memory perturbation	1.85	10.99 cm	.52
Memory perturbation to choice reaction-time	1.84	10.34 cm	—

Secondary Task

Paired-samples t-tests were used to compare the order of the secondary task performance: (a) digit recall, $t_{(9)}$ = .325, p > .05; (b) choice RT, $t_{(9)}$ = –1.15, p > .05. These failed to show significant differences and therefore all analyses were collapsed across order.

Subjects' performance of secondary tasks during baseline and experimental conditions was compared by paired-samples t-tests. Results indicated that subjects' baseline performance of the choice RT task (M = 532.99 ms, SD = 140 ms) was significantly better than their experimental condition performance (M = 624.88 ms, SD = 93 ms), $t_{(19)}$ = –4.652, p < .05 (see table 23.2). Subjects also performed significantly better on the digit recall task during the baseline condition (5.2 missed trials/20 trials) as compared to the experimental condition (10.25 missed trials/20 trials), $t_{(19)}$ = 8.603, p < .05 (see table 23.2). Percentage of change scores showed that the digit recall task (91% increase in error) suffered a greater decrease during the dual-task condition than the choice RT task (24% increase in error). Using the pooled standard deviation formula, *ES*s computed on the significant differences in secondary task performance indicated that subjects' digit recall scores (*ES* = 1.92) suffered a greater decrease than choice RT scores (*ES* = 1.2) when baseline and experimental conditions were compared.

Table 23.2   Effect Sizes, Mean and Standard Deviations for Secondary Task Performances

	ES	Baseline Mean	SD	Experimental Mean	SD
Choice reaction-time	1.2	523.99 ms	140 ms	624.88 ms	93 ms
Memory perturbation	1.92	5.2/20	2.46/20	10.25/20	2.79/20

DISCUSSION

Results of statistical analyses examining primary task performance showed choice RT as the condition most disruptive to putting performance and explained more performance variance than the digit recall condition. The choice RT condition was designed to disrupt the available resources needed to produce the motor program of putting. Significant decrements in primary task performance during the choice RT condition lend support for disruption in the intention to produce the putt as explaining more performance variance. Statistical analyses examining the differences between catch and non-catch trial putting performances failed to reach statistical significance. Both catch and non-catch trials were detrimental to putting performance as compared to baseline performance. This result may support the notion that the movement of depressing the RT buttons on the putter grip was not the distracting element; rather, the intention to press the buttons provided enough attentional distraction to impair performance. This paradigm significantly decreased putting performance because both the putting and the RT task demand the anticipation of manual output processes. It is possible that the relative difficulties of the two tasks were not equivalent. The results suggest that the choice RT task may be more difficult than the digit recall task (i.e., moving fingers to depress RT buttons and moving arms to execute the putt). However, if this were the case, RT non-catch trials, a more difficult task, would show a reduction in putting performance as compared to that with the RT catch trials. Since this was not the case, attentional resource, either voluntary or involuntary, may better explain putting performance than the difficulty of the secondary task.

Conversely, the digit recall condition was designed to disrupt the retrieval of the putting motor program from memory by requiring subjects to memorize a series of numbers while preparing to putt and to recite those same numbers after completing the putt (Piparo, 1992). Performing under this condition will cause decrements in putting performance because memorizing a series of digits while preparing to putt was designed to interfere with the golfer's distance calculations. The digit recall task also significantly decreased subjects' putting performance. While the digit recall condition did not explain as much variance as the choice RT condition, it still accounted for some variance and therefore cannot be rejected as an explanation for performance variance in the golf putt.

Both distraction conditions were shown to cause significant decrements in subjects' putting performance. However, it appears that attentional distractions that directly interfere with the intention to move are more debilitating than attentional distractions that attempt to interfere with distance calculations. While athletes may not become desensitized by practicing with distractions, they may develop effective strategies for coping in difficult situations. Lastly, distractions that interfere with the intention to move may be the most important to practice in order to optimize performance under a variety of conditions.

References

Abernethy, B. (1993). Attention. In R. Singer, M. Murphey, & L.K. Tennant (eds.), *Handbook of research on sport psychology* (pp. 127-170). New York: Macmillan.

Barabasz, A., Barabasz, M., & Bauman, J. (1993). Restricted environmental stimulation techniques improve human performance: Rifle marksmanship. *Perceptual and Motor Skills,* 76(3), 867-873.

Crews, D.J., & Boutcher, S.H. (1986). An exploratory observational behavior analysis of professional golfers during competition. *Journal of Sport Behavior,* 9(2), 51-58.

Crews, D.J., & Landers, D.M. (1993). Electroencephalographic measures of attentional patterns prior to the golf putt. *Medicine and Science in Sports and Exercise,* 25(1), 116-126.

Hatfield, B.D., Landers, D.M., & Ray, W.J. (1984). Cognitive processes during self-paced motor performance: An electroencephalographic profile of skilled marksmen. *Journal of Sport Psychology,* 6, 42-59.

Kahneman, D. (1973). *Attention and effort.* Englewood Cliffs, NJ: Prentice Hall.

Kahneman, D., & Chajczyk, D. (1983). Tests of the automaticity of reading: Dilution of Stroop effects by color-irrelevant stimuli. *Journal of Experimental Psychology: Human Perception and Performance,* 9(4), 497-509.

Landers, D.M., Wang, M.Q., & Courtet, P. (1985). Peripheral narrowing among experienced and inexperienced rifle shooters under low- and high-stress conditions. *Research Quarterly for Exercise and Sport,* 56, 122-130.

Loehr, J.E. (1982). *Athletic excellence: Mental toughness training for sports.* Denver: Forum.

Logan, G.D. (1985). Skill and automaticity: Relations, implications, and future directions. *Canadian Journal of Psychology,* 39, 367-386.

Logan, G.D. (1988). Automaticity, resources, and memory: Theoretical controversies and practical implications. *Human Factors,* 30(5), 583-598.

Nideffer, R.M. (1986). Concentration and attention control training. In J.M. Williams (ed.), *Applied sport psychology* (pp. 257-269). Palo Alto, CA: Mayfield.

Pilsbury, W.B. (1908). *Attention.* New York: Macmillan.

Piparo, A.J. (1992). Chronic effects of fitness on the golf putt. Doctoral dissertation.

Posner, M.I. (1978). *Chronometric exploration of the mind.* Hillsdale, NJ: Erlbaum.

Singer, R.N. (1988). Strategies and metastrategies in learning and performing self-paced athletic skills. *The Sport Psychologist,* 2, 49-68.

Singer, R.M., Cauraugh, J.H., Tennant, L.K., Murphey, M., Chen, D., & Lidor, R. (1991). Attention and distractors: Considerations for enhancing sport performances. *International Journal of Sport Psychology,* 22, 95-110.

Titchener, E.B. (1908). *Lectures on the elementary psychology of feeling and attention.* New York: Macmillan. As cited in Abernethy, 1993.

Welford, A.T. (1952). The psychological refractory period and the timing of high speed performance—A review and a theory. *British Journal of Psychology,* 43, 2-19.

Wickens, C.D. (1980). The structure of attentional resources. In R. Nickerson (ed.), *Attention and performance VIII.* Hillsdale, NJ: Erlbaum.

Wickens, C.D. (1984). *Engineering psychology and human performance.* Columbus, OH: Merrill.

Wickens, C.D. (1984). Processing Resources in Attention. In R. Parasuraman & D.R. Davies (eds.), *Varieties in attention* (pp. 63-98). Orlando, FL: Academic Press.

Wundt, W. (1905). *Grundiss der psychologie.* Leipzig: Engelmann. As cited in Abernethy, 1993.

CHAPTER 24

Peak Putting Performance: Psychological Skills and Strategies Utilized by PGA Tour Golfers

P.H. Beauchamp
Sports Performance Value Systems (SPVS), Montreal, Canada

This qualitative study explores the psychological skills associated with peak putting performance that are used by PGA Tour golfers. To assess peak putting performance, five PGA Tour golfers were asked to describe their all-time best putting performances. The results of the inductive analysis indicate that, for these five PGA Tour professionals, the psychological skills of mental imagery, confidence, and task focus play an important role in their competitive putting success. These three psychological factors are not static, but are dynamically interrelated. They were also found to either facilitate or disrupt putting performance. The results further indicate that all five PGA Tour golfers utilize psychological strategies embodied in pre-putt routines, which contributed to facilitating peak putting performances.

Keywords: Putting, peak performance, psychological skills, psychological strategies.

INTRODUCTION

Researchers in sport psychology have identified several common psychological factors characteristic of peak performance in sport:

a. Clearly focused attention

b. Positive mental attitude

c. Physical and mental readiness

d. Positive competitive affect

e. Effortless performance
f. Perception of time slowing
g. Feelings of supreme confidence
h. Immersion in the present moment
i. A sense of fun and enjoyment (Williams, 1993)

These characteristics and other popular terms in golf such as "in the groove" and "in the zone" are generally used in sport by athletes and coaches, but what they really mean to the athlete is not clearly known. At present, research related to psychological skills and strategies within a sport, such as putting in golf, is virtually nonexistent. This study utilized an idiographic approach in a naturalistic setting (Gould, Jackson, & Eklund, 1992) to provide a better understanding of PGA Tour golfers' subjective psychological skills and strategies.

PEAK PERFORMANCE IN SPORT

Jackson and Roberts (1992) characterize peak performance as a state of superior functioning resulting in personal bests and outstanding achievements. Several common psychological approaches are characteristic of several lines of research. Maslow (1968) introduced the concept of peak performance to explain those moments when an individual experiences feelings of "total unity, inner strength and wholeness of being." The "flow experience" describes an optimal psychological state, one involving total absorption in the task or activity (Csikszentmihalyi, 1990). Ravizza (1977) reported on the subjective peak experiences of top athletes, and Garfield and Bennett (1984) identified the characteristics associated with peak performance in sport. Researchers (Cohn, 1991; Mahoney, Gabriel, & Perkins, 1987) have also identified that top athletes and golfers dealt more readily with their competitive mistakes, possessed higher levels of self-confidence, engaged in positive self-talk, and were able to employ mental imagery to their advantage. In general, when athletes' energies are totally focused (e.g., utilizing a disciplined concentration on their pre-putt routine), they may begin to experience peak concentration that can lead to a state of flow. It is in this state that lifetime peak performances in sport often occur.

PSYCHOLOGICAL SKILLS

Psychological skills for sport can be described as either basic or advanced (Hardy, Jones, & Gould, 1996). The four basic psychological skills are goal setting, relaxation, imagery and mental rehearsal, and self-talk. Advanced psychological skills include confidence, motivation, arousal, concentration, and attentional control. These skills are seldom utilized in isolation. Rather, elite golfers combine them in response to the situational demands they face on the golf course.

Psychological Skills: Task Focus—Utilization of Process Goals

The goal-setting literature has identified three different types of goals (Hardy, Jones, & Gould, 1996): (a) outcome, (b) performance, and (c) process goals. Some athletes/coaches utilize *outcome goals,* which refer to outcomes of games or competition where comparison to others is predominant, in an effort to win the contest. Burton (1992) and other researchers have demonstrated that outcome goals are often accompanied by pressure and tension, which often disrupt optimal functioning. Utilizing a *performance goal* (e.g., a personal goal of shooting 69 today) means utilizing a self-referenced standard as a performance goal for a competition or round. The use of *process goals* involves selection of behaviors/ cognitions on which the golfer will focus during a competition. For example, focusing (e.g., in the pre-putt routine) on an individualized task-relevant cue (e.g., task focus), such as "put a good roll on the ball," can help the golfer cope with pressure situations and can contribute to the automaticity of pre-putt behaviors (Hardy, Jones, & Gould, 1996). Recent research has demonstrated that adherence to such a process-oriented approach may contribute to reduction of the golfer's susceptibility to somatic anxiety in pressure situations (Kingston, Hardy, & Markland, 1992), increased confidence (Krane, Williams, & Feltz, 1992), and improved concentration (Boutcher, 1992).

PSYCHOLOGICAL STRATEGIES FOR PEAK PERFORMANCE: PRE-PUTT ROUTINES

Psychological strategies consist of the application of several psychological skills in a specific mental preparation routine (Boutcher, 1995). One strategy particularly salient to the study of peak putting performance has been the use of *preperformance routines* (Crews & Boutcher, 1986a, 1986b; Kirschenbaum & Bale, 1980). For example, a golfer may utilize several psychological skills (e.g., imagery, confidence, and process goals), combined within a particular psychological strategy (e.g., pre-putt routine) for optimal execution of the putt. Recent research shows that collegiate golfers learn to develop consistent, highly systematic preparatory routines utilizing a preplanned sequence of imagery, arousal cues, and other cognitive and behavioral strategies as part of their complete routine (Boutcher & Crews, 1987; Cohn, 1990). Moreover, Kingston and Hardy (1997) have demonstrated the importance of focusing on process or performance cues during the preshot routine, as opposed to focusing on outcome goals during competition.

   The study of preperformance routines in sport psychology is a relatively new area of research. Athletes competing in self-paced sports such as golf are especially susceptible to the effects of stress during competition. Specifically, distractions, the opportunities for worry, and the demands of performing at a high level after a rest or stoppage are particularly challenging. Boutcher and Rotella (1987) suggest that a systematic, routinized pattern of behaviors and thoughts can improve athletic performance. A typical preperformance routine is made up of covert and overt activities. Professional golfers may have a cognitive-behavioral routine whereby they waggle the club a particular number of times during their setup routine (i.e., overt) and go through a preplanned sequence of imagery, arousal cues, and other cognitive strategies (i.e., covert) as part of their complete routine (Cohn, 1990). Such strategies, perhaps involving several psychological skills (e.g., visualizing the shot, utilizing a task focus, confident self-talk), may be employed as part of the preperformance routine to mentally and physically ready the golfer for his/her golf performance (Boutcher, 1995; Cohn, 1990).

METHODOLOGY

An in-depth qualitative study was chosen in order to gain a better understanding of the salient psychological factors that contribute to optimal putting results as experienced by PGA Tour golfers. The methodology was similar to that of other recent idiographic studies (Gould, Jackson, & Ecklund, 1992; McCaffrey & Orlick, 1989). The subjects for the study were five veteran PGA Tour golfers (m = 39 years), with a combined total of 28 PGA Tour victories.

A semi-structured guided interview protocol was used, and inductive analysis was conducted on the verbatim interview transcriptions. Recurrent higher-order themes were coded for each golfer and were then summarized into general dimensions. For example, the general dimension of "task focus" emerged from the coded categories of disciplined concentration, flow concentration, in the present, task-relevant cues, and key thoughts. Full descriptions of the method and detailed results would be beyond the scope of this paper and are described elsewhere (Beauchamp, 1995). Thus, relevant quotations are selected in order to highlight individual golfers' reflections on their best putting performances.

RESULTS

The results of the inductive analysis indicate that, for these five PGA Tour golfers, three general dimensions (psychological skills) played the most important roles in their best competitive putting performances: positive imagery, task focus, and confidence. Several revealing samples of interview text describing psychological skills and strategies are presented and discussed next.

One golfer implies that he adopts a *task focus* as part of his pre-putt routine: "When I played here, I shot 62. I made three putts that were just 30-40 footers. But when I hit them, after they rolled 10 feet, you knew they were going in the hole. You can see the ball rolling on a particular line over a particular undulation, into the hole. It's like you pick out a spot that you want to stroke the ball over, then it is all a matter of getting the right speed. But you've got to tie everything in. Once it rolls over that spot and the right speed, and if you're a pretty good reader of greens. You know if the ball has a chance to go in or not. When I shot 62 up here, I made quite a few putts, but the funny thing about it was, I lipped out six or seven putts that could have gone in" (G3). In his best putting performances, this PGA Tour golfer uses disciplined mental concentration combined with imagery such that he is able to "see the ball rolling on a particular line" and then get "the right speed" and "tie everything in."

Another golfer describes his high *confidence*, recounting his self-efficacy beliefs concerning his putting game: "I stood on that tee and all I knew that I had to do was hit it on the green. In my mind, I made eight birdies in a row on that hole. Each putt that I hit after that rolled with a look like it was going in. You make just about everything. You feel a high degree of certainty that you will be successful. Just get me on the green" (G1). This quotation highlights the person factors (i.e., high state and dispositional confidence) and situational factors (i.e., confidence in stroke and imagery to see and feel the line) this golfer possesses in his putting stroke and his overall game.

Golfers' descriptions of their *positive imagery* also provided evidence of this as a psychological skill linked to their best putting performances. One golfer says, "There was probably little excess thinking. Life was very simple. Basically, you saw, and you felt, and from that, the positive imagery was so strong and you just had the feel right that day. You make just about everything" (G2). This golfer's positive imagery is strong, involving both kinesthetic and visual impressions. Also, the golfer's concentration was task focused, eliminating "excess thinking."

Psychological skills were also found to be dynamically interrelated to facilitate putting performance, such that confidence was linked to positive imagery, and task focus was linked to confidence and imagery. For example, PGA Tour golfers made reference to their imagery and its link to their confidence in reading greens (i.e., visualization). One golfer commented, "I think you have to feel good about yourself, about your stroke, your overall ability to read greens" (G1). Thus, this golfer's confidence in himself as a golfer (i.e., state confidence), and in his putting stroke (i.e., technique), was linked to his ability to read greens. Another golfer described his ability to control his imagery (i.e., see and feel imagery), which was related to his confidence to putt aggressively: "The way you feel and the way you see. Learning the speed of the green on fast greens allows you to be aggressive. Controlled aggressive would be the word" (G2). This golfer's see-and-feel imagery allowed him to putt confidently or "controlled aggressive." These examples demonstrate that for these PGA Tour golfers, the psychological skills of task focus, confidence, and imagery can also be dynamically interrelated to facilitate putting performance.

In contrast, golfers also described their imagery, confidence, and task focus on the greens as critical factors that disrupted their putting performances. For example, one golfer commented on how his ability to control his imagery (i.e., controllability of imagery) affected his confidence: "One way or another, my imagery affects me more than anything . . . if I am seeing putts in the hole really well, I can really putt well . . . I think whenever I am having difficulty seeing putts, that's when I get into second-guessing. Anytime you start second-guessing yourself, it affects the physical part of your putting stroke" (G2). This golfer's inability to visualize the line was linked to self-doubts about his putts and ultimately his confidence in his putting stroke.

Another golfer described how his confidence and feel were linked to putting results (i.e., an outcome focus), which affected his putting success: "Confidence is very important in my ability to putt. I think you get confidence based on feel and results. If it feels good, and you get good results, you're going to be confident. If it feels good and you get bad results, you're still going to be fairly confident. But, you're going to say, why is the result bad—I've got to adjust somewhere else, because the feel is good. But if the results are bad and if it feels lousy, you've got no confidence" (G1). This quotation demonstrates how the golfer's confidence and feel imagery were linked to his putting results (i.e., outcome goals), over which he has little control. This example demonstrates the importance of focusing on *process goals* as opposed to outcome goals. Process goals are more flexible and are under the person's control, allowing the golfer to feel competent, focused, and confident under competitive pressure (Kingston & Hardy, 1994).

Furthermore, PGA Tour golfers' descriptions suggest that the perceived level of challenge (e.g., outcome focus of long vs. short putts) plays an important person-situation role in facilitating or disrupting disciplined concentration during their putting preperformance routine. "On long putts you have a tendency to feel like you're not supposed to make them, so you free it up a little more, whereas, in the short ones, you feel like you're supposed to make them and all of a sudden you put a little more pressure on yourself to make it" (G5). This quotation demonstrates how the perceived level of challenge (i.e., outcome focus vs. task focus) faced by golfers on the greens may be a situational factor that disrupts putting performance. In summary, the person and situational variables may work in combination to disrupt putting performance.

The psychological strategy of using a pre-putt routine integrated with psychological skills was common to all golfers. For example, one golfer described how he begins his pre-putt routine with a task focus: "Basically, what I did is stuck to my routine and freed it up. I went on my first instincts. There was little excess thinking. It was simple" (G4). His use of a disciplined-concentrated routine (i.e., task focus) was an effective psychological strategy that allowed this golfer to move toward a flow-concentration state. This unconscious-processing state (i.e., focusing on process goals) encourages the automaticity of behaviors and cognitions during the pre-putt routine for optimal putting performance (Kingston & Hardy, 1997).

Task focus, positive imagery, and confidence have emerged from the data as general dimensions highlighting the psychological skills associated with peak putting performances by PGA Tour golfers. In addition, these psychological skills appear to be dynamically interrelated to factors facilitating or disrupting putting performance. Moreover, adopting a task focus also allows the golfer to "free it up" (G4) and move from a disciplined-concentration pre-putt routine toward a flow-concentration mode for superior putting performance. This psychological strategy is illustrated by this golfer's description: "I start with my routine first until my focus becomes sharper and flow will come naturally" (G2). This golfer begins with his routine utilizing disciplined concentration. He understands that flow concentration will follow. The psychological strategy embodied in the pre-putt routine facilitates the use of psychological skills for optimal putting performance.

DISCUSSION

The psychological construct of confidence has received considerable support in the sport psychology literature related to peak performance. Csikszentmihalyi (1990) describes confidence as the paradox of control. He indicates that it is not being in control as such, but the possibility of control, that is enjoyable when golfers experience flow. This sense of control leads one into a feeling of total confidence.

As seen in G1's experience: "I stood on the tee and all I knew that I had to do was to hit it on the greens. In my mind, I made eight birdies in a row on that hole."

In the sport psychology literature, task or process orientation refers to the complete focusing of attention on the task. Task or process orientation has been associated with how hard one persists, with the level of competitive stress experienced while performing, and with the ability to direct one's attentional focus in competition. Moreover, research in sport suggests that a task or process orientation is also related to peak performance (Cohn, 1991; Jackson & Roberts, 1992) and flow in sport (Csikszentmihalyi, 1990). Jackson and Roberts (1992) found that athletes who utilized a task focus experienced peak performances and flow more often than athletes who were low in task orientation. From an educational or consulting perspective, teaching golfers to focus on process goals over which they have control would encourage stable expectations for success and thus would be more likely to positively affect confidence and putting performance.

The results demonstrate how, in addition to adopting a task process, PGA Tour golfers often set clear goals in advance that were associated with their best golf performances. In putting, these golfers perceive their task clearly and know exactly what goal they are trying to achieve. Moreover, the inductive analysis indicated that the setting of clear goals was interrelated with positive imagery and confidence. In particular, many of their descriptions demonstrate that their goal was a singular task focus: "I try to hit one putt at a time," "I go for feel, anytime." The setting of clear goals aids these PGA Tour golfers in adopting a task focus and also directing their focus of attention.

Automaticity or subconscious control characterizes how PGA Tour golfers felt when they experienced their best putting performances. For example, they did not have to think about their pre-putt routine; "things just happened automatically." They felt very comfortable and relaxed in their environment. Moreover, in this state they don't see or hear anyone; they described themselves as "totally absorbed in my stroke." Peak performances of highly skilled athletes are often described as effortless and without need for controlled attention. Thus, in order to achieve mastery over their putting stroke, the goal for these PGA Tour golfers is to attain automaticity during their preperformance routine.

This study has highlighted the dynamic interrelationship of positive imagery, task focus, and confidence with peak putting performances. Previous research has indicated that task focus and confidence are associated with peak sport performance (Cohn, 1991; Garfield & Bennett, 1984; Jackson & Roberts, 1992; McCaffrey & Orlick, 1989). In this study, PGA Tour golfers' descriptions of their best putting performances suggest the salience of these three factors as critical psychological skills necessary for peak performance. Moreover, these skills could either facilitate and/or disrupt putting performance. The consistency of these findings warrants further investigation by golf coaches and sport psychologists.

CONCLUSION

In summary, this qualitative study suggests that (1) confidence in one's game and putting stroke, (2) the ability to feel and see the line (i.e., positive imagery) on the greens, and (3) the ability to utilize a task focus during one's pre-putt routine are critical psychological skills that contribute to peak putting performance. In addition, the utilization of the psychological strategy of a disciplined overt/covert pre-putt routine facilitates the use of psychological skills for peak putting performance. Finally, the results also suggest that there may be a dynamic interplay occurring between these three psychological skills and peak putting performance. Further research should consider a person-situation model of putting performance that further outlines the many person (e.g., dispositional and state) and situational (e.g., task focus, confidence, imagery) factors underlying peak putting performance.

References

Beauchamp, P.H. (1995). Psychological influences on golfers' putting performance. Doctoral dissertation, University of Montreal.

Boutcher, S.H. (1992). Attentional and athletic performance: An integrated approach. In T.S. Horn (Ed.), *Advances in sport psychology,* pp. 251-266. Champaign, IL: Human Kinetics.

Boutcher, S.H. (1995). The role of performance routines in sport. In G. Jones & L. Hardy (Eds.), *Stress and performance in sport.* Chichester, UK: Wiley.

Boutcher, S.H., & Crews, D.J. (1987). The effect of a preshot routine on a well-learned skill. *International Journal of Sport Psychology* 18: 30-39.

Boutcher, P.H., & Rotella, R.J. (1987). A psychological skills educational program for closed-skill performance enhancement. *The Sport Psychologist* 1: 127-137.

Burton, D. (1992). The Jekyll/Hyde nature of goals. In T.S. Horn (Ed.), *Advances in sport psychology,* pp. 267-297. Champaign, IL: Human Kinetics.

Cohn, P.J. (1990). Performance routines in sport: Theoretical support and practical applications. *The Sport Psychologist* 4: 301-312.

Cohn, P.J. (1991). An exploratory study on peak performance in golf. *The Sport Psychologist* 5: 1-14.

Crews, D.J., & Boutcher, S.H. (1986a). The effects of structured preshot behaviors on beginning golf performance. *Perceptual and Motor Skills* 62: 291-294.

Crews, D.J., & Boutcher, S.H. (1986b). An exploratory observational analysis of professional golfers during competition. *Journal of Sport Behavior* 9(2): 51-58.

Csikszentmihalyi, M. (1990). *Flow: The psychology of optimal experience.* New York: Harper.

Garfield, C.A., & Bennett, H.Z. (1984). *Peak performance: Mental training techniques of the world's greatest athletes.* Los Angeles: Tarcher.

Gould, D., Jackson, S.A., & Eklund, R.C. (1992). 1988 U.S. Olympic wrestling excellence: I. Mental preparation, precompetitive cognition, and affect. *The Sport Psychologist* 6: 358-382.

Hardy, L., Jones, G., & Gould, D. (1996). *Understanding psychological preparation for sport: Theory and practice of elite performers.* New York: Wiley.

Jackson, S.A., & Roberts, G.C. (1992). Positive performance states of athletes: Toward a conceptual understanding of peak performance. *The Sport Psychologist* 6(2): 56-171.

Kingston, K.M., & Hardy, L. (1994). Factors affecting the salience of outcome performance and process goals in golf. In A.J. Cochran & M.R. Farally (Eds.), *Science and golf II,* pp. 144-149. London: Chapman & Hall.

Kingston, K.M., & Hardy, L. (1997). Effects of different types of goals on processes that support performance. *The Sport Psychologist* 11: 277-293.

Kingston, K.M., Hardy, L., & Markland, D. (1992). Study to compare the effect of two different goal orientations and stress levels on a number of situationally performance subcomponents. *Journal of Sport Sciences* 10: 610-611.

Kirschenbaum, D.S., & Bale, R.M. (1980). Cognitive behavioral skills in golf: Brain power golf. In R.M. Suinn (Ed.), *Psychology in sports: Methods and applications,* pp. 334-343. Minneapolis: Burgess.

Krane, V., Williams, J., & Feltz, D. (1992). Path analysis examining relationships among cognitive anxiety, somatic anxiety, state confidence, performance expectations, and golf performance. *Journal of Sport Behavior* 15(4): 279.

Mahoney, M.J., Gabriel, T.J., & Perkins, S.T. (1987). Psychological skills and exceptional athletic performance. *The Sport Psychologist* 1: 181-199.

Maslow, A. (1968). *Toward a psychology of being.* Princeton, NJ: Van Nostrand.

McCaffrey, N., & Orlick, T. (1989). Mental factors related to excellence among top professional golfers. *International Journal of Sport Psychology* 20: 256-278.

Ravizza, K. (1977). Peak experiences in sport. *Journal of Humanistic Psychology* 17(4): 35-40.

Williams, J.M. (1993). Psychological characteristics of peak performance. In J.M. Williams (Ed.), *Applied sport psychology: Personal growth to peak performance,* 2nd ed., pp. 123-132. Mountain View, CA: Mayfield.

CHAPTER 25

Senior Women of Lower and Higher Golf Handicaps: Factors Predicting Golf Scores

K.T. Thomas
Exercise and Sport Research Institute, Arizona State University

Eighteen senior women golfers with higher (m = 29.5) and lower (m = 13.8) handicaps were evaluated for golf skill (qualitative and quantitative), golf knowledge (declarative, procedural, and execution), golf play (3 rounds), and implicit versus explicit knowledge (comparing what is known and what is done). The groups differed (discriminant analysis) on quantitative and qualitative skill chipping and on "do not know or do." The results indicated that chipping skill and the number of items that the golfer did not know or do influenced golf performance, suggesting that improving chipping would lower golf scores for the higher-handicap players.

Keywords: Aging, women golfers, skill, knowledge.

INTRODUCTION

The development of skill, and particularly the attainment of expertise, is of interest in research to practitioners and performers (Gallagher, French, Thomas, & Thomas, 1996; Thomas & Thomas, 1994). Several factors have been identified that may contribute to higher skill, including knowledge, talent, physical characteristics, and practice (Abernethy, Thomas, & Thomas, 1993; Thomas, Thomas, & Gallagher, 1993). Physical characteristics and talent may be more important for younger performers, while cognitive factors have been hypothesized to become increasingly important in more highly skilled performance in older subjects. Knowledge has been divided into three categories: declarative, which includes facts and rules; procedural, which consists of "how to's"; and a special case of declarative knowledge related to skill that is called execution knowledge (Thomas, 1994). Execution knowledge is composed of facts or rules for performing the skill, for example where a body part begins and ends a movement. Typically, years of experience, or practice, varies between skill levels; however, experience and practice do not guarantee that skill will develop (Abernethy et al., 1993). When experience is constant and skill varies, it may be possible to identify which variables—other than experience—influence skill level. This study was done to identify factors that influence skill for golf play in mature women. The women were of similar ages and playing experience, but the difference in skill level between the two groups was substantial. The findings will have implications for theory and practical application for golf instruction.

METHOD

Participants

Eighteen women were recruited from a senior residential community in Sun Lakes, Arizona. The women had to be 50 years of age and participate in the Women's Golf Association. Subjects were placed in one of two groups, lower (12-16 handicap) and higher (26-37) handicap, depending upon the handicap assigned by the USGA. (See table 25.1 for descriptive data.) No player in the higher-handicap group (HHG) had ever had a handicap low enough to place her in the low-handicap group (LHG).

Procedures

Data were collected at the golf facility near where the subjects resided. Two trained female investigators collected the data. Subjects were tested in a single session, and all data were collected during a 1-month period. Before testing began, all subjects read and signed an informed consent form that was approved by the Committee for the Use of Human Subjects. Subjects were videotaped during the skill test, which included 10 trials each of wood shots, iron shots, chipping, and long (30 feet) and short (5 feet) putts. Subjects selected from their own clubs within a skill test and for the wood and iron shot selected their own target/distance. All subjects used the same target and placement position for putting and chipping skills tests. Demographic, golf, and physical activity interviews were also conducted during this time. Subjects were asked to play three rounds of golf within a week of being tested, recording the score, the club used for each shot, penalties, and any special information (e.g., wind).

Instruments

Knowledge Test

The written test consisted of 42 multiple choice questions about golf rules and etiquette (declarative knowledge) as well as skill execution and procedural knowledge ("how to or if then"), and 45 true/false statements about golf skill. The multiple choice items were selected from the test bank in *Teaching Golf: Steps to Success* (Owens & Bunker, 1990). For inclusion, the skill items had to be consistent with the skill checklist items outlined in the next section.

Skill Test

Skill was evaluated qualitatively and quantitatively. The investigators used a qualitative checklist composed of 49 items each for woods and irons, 27 items for chipping, and 19 items for putting. The checklist was developed by compiling information from golf books and magazines; then the list was reviewed by PGA golf professionals. Items that all three professionals agreed were valid were retained on the checklist. The professionals were encouraged to add items that were not on the list; those items were presented to the other professionals and were included when deemed valid by all three professionals.

The qualitative analysis was conducted by two trained investigators who viewed the tapes separately, rating each item on the checklist. When there was a disagreement between the observers rating the videotapes for the scoring of a checklist item for any subject on any trial, the video was viewed by both investigators simultaneously and agreement was reached. Initial agreement exceeded 90%. A higher score indicated that the golfer had more points of correct form or more correct trials.

The quantitative portion of the skill test consisted of measuring error, which was distance from the target. For woods and irons, this was done in 20-yard increments, so that a ball landing within 20 yards of the target was recorded as 1, 20-40 yards as 2, and so forth. The lowest possible score for the woods and iron skills tests was 10, and the highest was 30. The chipping skill test was conducted in a similar way, with 1 representing a chip going into the hole, 2 representing a ball within 36 inches of the hole, 3 representing 37 inches to 10 feet, 4 representing the green but more than 10 feet away, and 5 representing a chip that did not come to rest on the putting surface. The best score for the chipping test was a 10, and the worst possible score was 50. For long and short putting, a ball going in the hole was scored as 1; 2 was given for those 1-18 inches; 3 for those 19 inches to 5 feet, 4 for putts from 5 to 10 feet, and 5 for putts missing the hole by more than 10 feet. The target hole(s) and the placement for chipping, long putts, and short putts were selected to be relatively flat.

Statistical Analysis

The descriptive data were plotted and visually inspected. Descriptive statistics for the 22 variables are presented in table 25.1 for the two handicap groups and overall. Eight variables were used for a discriminant analysis using a forward stepwise method with handicap group as the grouping variable and the others as predictors. In this case, discriminant analysis is the same as a one-way MANOVA and produces follow-up univariate tests. The number of subjects was small, and these analyses are primarily exploratory.

RESULTS AND DISCUSSION

The LHG (n = 9) was 8 years younger than the HHG (n = 8); however, the mean of the HHG was biased by one subject's being 10 years older (80 years of age) than the next-oldest subject. Further, within the groups, age and handicap did not seem to be related; the oldest subjects did not have the highest handicaps, nor did the youngest

Table 25.1   Descriptive Data for LHG (n = 9) and HHG (n = 8) for Age, Handicap, Experience, Knowledge, Qualitative and Quantitative Skill, Game Play

Variable	LHG	HHG	Overall	Minimum	Maximum
Age in years	58.6 ± 4.9	66.8 ± 5.5	62.5 ± 6.6	52.5	80.0
Handicap	13.8 ± 1.6	30.3 ± 3.6	22.5 ± 8.5	12	34
Lowest lifetime handicap	11.6 ± 2.0	25.0 ± 4.1	18.3 ± 7.6	9	33
Years played	21.8 ± 9.1	19.9 ± 8.9	20.9 ± 8.8	8.0	38.0
Declarative knowledge (of 11)	8.6 ± 1.8	8.2 ± 1.0	8.4 ± 1.4	6	11
Skill knowledge (of 12)	11.1 ± 2.1	10.9 ± .9	11.0 ± 1.6	8	14
Procedural knowledge (of 19)	10.6 ± 2.1	9.1 ± 2.4	10.1 ± 2.3	6	14
Quantitative wood*	16.2 ± 2.3	16.9 ± 3.4	16.5 ± 2.8	12	23
Quantitative iron*	15.3 ± 4.2	19.7 ± 5.5	17.2 ± 5.1	11	30
Quantitative chipping*	22.6 ± 1.3	26.0 ± 2.0	24.5 ± 2.4	21	29
Quantitative long putts*	23.1 ± 2.0	26.2 ± 7.2	24.8 ± 5.1	20	44
Quantitative short putts*	17.4 ± 2.9	17.8 ± 1.5	17.4 ± 2.4	13	21
Qualitative wood (of 10)	8.5 ± 1.1	8.9 ± 1.1	8.7 ± .9	6.6	9.9
Qualitative iron (of 10)	9.4 ± .6	8.7 ± .8	9.1 ± .7	7.3	10.0
Qualitative chipping (of 10)	9.6 ± .6	8.0 ± 1.3	8.8 ± 1.3	5.8	10.0
Qualitative putts (of 10)	8.7 ± 1.5	8.0 ± 2.2	8.6 ± 1.8	5.0	10.0
Know and execute**	29.3 ± 5.2	24.4 ± 2.1	27.0 ± 4.4	21	37
Execute without knowing**	9.1 ± 4.3	10.1 ± 3.3	9.9 ± 3.7	4	18
Know and do not execute**	3.1 ± 3.4	5.0 ± 3.0	4.1 ± 3.1	0	11
Do not know or execute**	0.3 ± 7	1.7 ± 1	1.0 ± 1.1	0	3
Average putts per round	33 ± 1.5	35 ± 2.9	34 ± 2.3	31	40
Average score	87 ± 2	103 ± 3	94 ± 9	81	116

*For the quantitative skill tests 10 is the best score and 50 is the worst possible score.
**A total of 42 items for these 4 variables

subjects have the lowest handicaps in their respective handicap groups. The two groups had similar years of playing (about 20 years), while their handicaps were clearly different (14 vs. 30). Descriptive information for the dependent variables is presented in table 25.1.

Knowledge Test

All subjects performed well on the skill-related multiple choice items, and all subjects missed more declarative items than skill items.

• An example of an easy declarative item: *Pete chipped his third shot onto the green; it hit the pin and went into the hole. What was his score on the hole?*

   A. 3

   B. 4

   C. 5

   D. 6

   (A is the correct answer.)

• A more difficult item: *Betty and John are playing the 5th hole, a par 5. John is unsure of what club to hit and asks Susie for assistance. What is the ruling?*

   A. No penalty

   B. 1 stroke penalty

   C. 2 stroke penalty

   D. Disqualification

   (C is correct.)

   Golf rules were neither constituent of nor prerequisite to golf play; even though these women played in weekly competition, there were some rules (about 22% and 25% for LHG and HHG, respectively) they did not know. While this variable does not contribute to skill differences, there is reason for concern when women who play golf and compete regularly do not know the rules of play.

   All of these players had similar amounts of skill knowledge, which may represent the knowledge that is prerequisite to play.

• An example of an easier skill execution item: *Where is the ball position for the full swing with woods?*

   A. Near the center

   B. Toward the left heel

   C. Toward the right heel

   D. Varies with the wood

   (B is the correct answer.)

• An example of a more difficult skill item: *What do golfers tend to do when their hands are especially tight or tense?*

A. Hook

B. Slice

C. Birdie

D. Pull

(B is the correct answer.)

A list of characteristics was presented for each skill component to be identified individually as true or false; those associated with the stance for wood shots, for example, were the following:

- Ground club head with club face square to target
- Trunk bends forward at hips
- Knees should bend 45° or greater angle
- Arms relaxed
- Weight forward midstep to balls of feet
- Toes parallel to target line
- Feet hip distance apart
- Stance open
- Center of swing over or in front of ball at address

LHG knew more procedures than HHG.

- An example of an easier procedural question: *Susie is 15 yards from the green with a trap between the ball and the green. The pin is 20 feet from the fringe. Which club is most appropriate for Susie's next shot?*

A. 7 iron

B. 5 iron

C. 9 iron

D. Pitching wedge

(D is the correct answer.)

- An example of a more difficult procedural item: *You hit a ball into the sand. What is your first consideration?*

A. Club selection

B. Trajectory needed

C. Distance to the pin

D. Lie of the ball

(D is the correct answer.)

Declarative knowledge is often viewed as a prerequisite for performance in sport, with procedural knowledge often discriminating between skill levels (Abernethy et al., 1993; Thomas, 1994). These data are consistent with that notion.

Qualitative Skill Test

The skill test scores were summed within component (e.g., grip, stance), and the components were summed, yielding a composite score for the woods, irons, chipping, and putting. For example, these were the components of the wood stance:

- Ground club head with club face square to target
- Knees slightly bent
- Trunk bends forward at hips
- Arms relaxed from shoulders
- Weight forward midstep to balls of feet
- Toes parallel to target line
- Center of swing over or in front of ball at address
- Feet hip distance apart
- Square stance

This allowed an examination of the influence of each component and of the total swing quality. Examining the composite scores indicated that LHG had better form as shots approached the green, so that the best form was observed in the chipping and the poorest with the woods. The opposite was observed in the HHG; for this group the woods had the best form and the chip shots the poorest form. The two groups had similar qualitative scores for the woods (table 25.1). Overall, LHG demonstrated more correct points of form and trials than HHG, but the differences were small. Among the individual components of each stroke, as can be seen in figure 25.1, the backswing was the weakest part of the swing for the

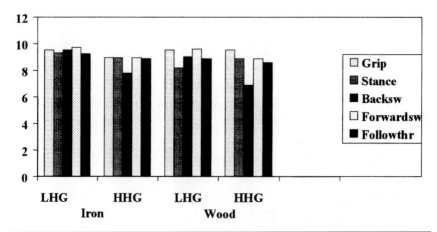

Figure 25.1   Qualitative scores for the components of the woods and irons, including backswing, grip, stance, forward swing, and follow-through, with possible score of 10 for each component.

HHG and the most different from its counterpart in LHG with both woods and irons. Putting form (e.g., stance, stroke, and follow-through) was generally good for both groups; only 3 of 19 points of form showed scores below 90% correct, and for those the LHG were superior. One final observation about the quality of the golf swings was that most of the missed points of form were attributed to individuals, not to random trials across individuals. In other words, these women, regardless of skill group, performed the same action on each swing—whether it was correct or incorrect, it was consistent. This would indicate that the women were not in the early stages of learning, during which inconsistency is the typical profile (Thomas et al., 1993).

Quantitative Skill Test

The LHG were more accurate for chipping and long putts (over 30 feet) than HHG. Short putting and woods were similar for accuracy (e.g., 50% of 5-foot putts were made; woods were typically 20-40 yards from target). The distance selected for the skill test by four of nine LHG and five of eight HHG was the same for the wood and iron skills tests; in other words, those women attempted to hit the wood and iron to the same target. A 50-yard or greater difference between targets was selected by five LHG and two HHG. LHG most frequently used the 7 iron (also using 5, 6, and 8) for an average distance of 121 yards; the HHG used the 5, 6, and 7 nearly equally for an average distance of 108 yards. Most (6 of 9 and 5 of 8) used the driver for the wood test; all but one of the rest used the 3 wood. The LHG used a 150-yard target, and the HHG used a 123-yard target. So the LHG hit their iron (typically a 7) about as far as the HHG hit the driver. The distance advantage for the LHG off the tee was small, as was the distance for the iron shots (20 yards). Two issues seem to contribute to the group differences. First, the same distance was selected for both the wood and iron by several LHG; further, the small differences in distances between the wood and iron were not due to selecting the "shortest" wood and the "longest" iron. Second, the place where LHG gained the most strokes was around the green, not in distance off the tee or on the fairway.

Knowing and Doing

A comparison of what the golfers did and what they knew was done by matching qualitative skill analysis to the knowledge test items. LHG correctly executed 38 of 42 skill items; interestingly, they could correctly answer 29 of those 42 items. This means the LHG had explicit knowledge of 29 (of 38 items executed correctly). Having explicit knowledge means that they answered the knowledge item correctly and did the item. Implicit knowledge is the ability to do or execute a skill without being able to verbalize the action. For the remaining 4 items, the LHG knew the item, but weren't able to execute the item. HHG executed 35 skill items (of 42), with explicit knowledge of 25 (knowing and executing). HHG knew 5 more items that they could not execute. HHG averaged 1 item that they did not know or execute. Once again, this is consistent with the cognitive expertise models suggesting that knowing precedes doing (Thomas, 1994). Clearly, there was implicit knowledge—10 items—that the golfers carried out but were not aware of consciously.

Discriminant Analysis

Quantitative iron, quantitative chipping, quantitative long putts, qualitative chipping, knowing and executing, knowing and not executing, do not know or execute, and average putts per round were entered into the discriminant analysis to predict group membership. Significant differences between the groups based on the associated univariate ANOVAs were found for quantitative skill chipping (F(1,15) = 15.7, p = .001), qualitative chipping (F(1,15) = 12.1, p = .003), and do not know or do (F(1,15) = 8.2, p = .012). Quantitative skill in chipping was entered on the first step. Qualitative skill in chipping was entered with quantitative skill in chipping on the second step. Don't know or do was close to entering at step 2 but did not meet the criteria after the two chipping variables were entered. The Wilks's Lambda was .3 with p = .0001. These variables predicted with 95% accuracy (one case was misclassified).

Golf Play

The LHG averaged 87 for three rounds and the HHG averaged 103; the average putts per round were 33 and 35, respectively.

SUMMARY AND CONCLUSIONS

The LHG were better around the green than HHG, while differences on the tee and fairway were small. This suggests that practice and instruction focusing on the short game would benefit HHG who desire to improve their games. The small differences in the power aspects of the game (woods and irons) also suggest that factors of physical characteristics (e.g., size and strength) are not important to these differential skill levels. Further, the weakest part of the game for the HHG could be remediable with instruction and practice. The data were consistent with the cognitive expertise literature (Abernethy et al., 1993; Thomas et al., 1993; Thomas, 1994; Thomas & Thomas, 1994), and identified both implicit and explicit knowledge. On the basis of this research, golf play could be improved by the following actions:

- Clinics and lessons should focus on chipping (and perhaps long putts), as the largest skill differences were observed around the green.
- Instruction should begin with explaining and developing an understanding of what is to be done, then practice to execute the skills.

ACKNOWLEDGMENTS

Sincere appreciation is extended to the women of Sun Lakes, Arizona, for participating as subjects and to the professional golf staff at Sun Lakes for assisting in recruiting subjects, reviewing testing materials, and making facilities available for the project. Further recognition and thanks are given to Cynde Lee for gathering the data and analyzing the videotapes of golf skills tests and to Stephanie Itsell for assisting with the video analysis and data organization.

References

Abernethy, B., Thomas, K.T., & Thomas, J.R. (1993). Strategies for improving understanding of motor expertise (or mistakes we have made and things we have learned). In J.L. Starkes & F. Allard (Eds.), *Cognitive issues in motor expertise.* Amsterdam: Elsevier.

Gallagher, J.D., French, K.E., Thomas, K.T., & Thomas, J.R. (1996). Expertise in Youth Sport: The relationship between knowledge and skill. In F. Smoll & R. Smith (Eds.), *Children and youth in sport: A biopsychological perspective.* Dubuque, IA: Brown and Benchmark.

Owen, & Bunker, L. (1990). *Teaching golf: Steps to success.* Champaign, IL: Human Kinetics.

Thomas, J.R., Thomas, K.T., & Gallagher, J.D. (1993). Developmental considerations in skill acquisition. In R.N. Singer, M. Murphey, & L.K. Tennant (Eds.), *Handbook on research in sport psychology.* New York: Macmillan.

Thomas, K.T. (1994). The development of expertise: From Leeds to legend. *Quest, 46,* 199-210.

Thomas, K.T., & Thomas, J.R. (1994). Development of expertise in children's sport. *International Journal of Sport Psychology, 25,* 295-312.

CHAPTER 26

Senior Women With Lower and Higher Golf Handicaps: How Psychological and Physical Characteristics Relate to Performance

J.R. Thomas and K.T. Thomas
Iowa State University, Ames, IA, USA

What motivates older women golfers to play for over 20 years? Women golfers completed a questionnaire about exercise and playing habits, played three 18-hole rounds, and were measured on physical fitness variables. Women golfers chose to play with other women of equal or better skill—a clear attempt to seek feedback about performance. Competition was an important motivator for the lower-handicap women but was never mentioned by the higher-handicap players. Two-thirds of the lower-handicap group practiced regularly outside of play, while only one-third of the higher-handicap players did. Most of the women (78%) believed that golf improves health and fitness (most walked when they played). Tennis players and golfers were more flexible and had greater grip strength than nonparticipants, but body mass index and skinfolds were similar.

Keywords: Aging, women golfers, motivation.

INTRODUCTION

Considerable research has addressed expert motor skill performance in young children (e.g., Thomas & Thomas, 1994) and adults (e.g., Starkes & Allard, 1993). However, little attention has been devoted to motor expertise in elderly performers. Yet the Senior Professional Golfers' Association tour regularly provides an example of how older players (even into the late 60s) maintain high-level performance.

A brief visit to retirement communities across the southern United States provides many examples of the interest and motivation of older women and men golfers of all skill levels. Often the golfers observed in retirement communities have been playing golf for many years regardless of the level of skill. What motivates these golfers with low and high handicaps to practice and play regularly for 20 years or more? While lower-handicap players may be motivated by improvement, achievement, and rewards to continue to play, what motivates high-handicap players to continue to practice and play? Health-related outcomes from golf that are associated with regular exercise may also be motivators, especially if most of the players walk when they play.

In this study we examined the motivation, skills, performances, and health-related outcomes reported by older women golfers from a retirement community outside Phoenix, Arizona. This community has several golf courses, but our research was conducted using players at just one course. We obtained a group of lower- and higher-handicap women players as well as comparison groups of women tennis players and nonsport participants. All women participants were of similar ages, and the women golfers had similar playing experience but substantially different levels in handicap. This allowed us to look at experience and expertise within the women golfers as well as to compare them to matched groups of novices who either participated in another sport or were nonparticipants; comparisons between participants of equal experience but varying skill level is often lacking in research in motor expertise (Abernethy, Thomas, & Thomas 1993).

METHOD

Participants

Thirty-five women were recruited from a senior residential community outside Phoenix, Arizona. All women were 50 years of age or older, and they were categorized into four groups: lower golf handicaps, $n = 9$ ($M_{age} = 58.6$ years, $SD_{age} = 4.9$); higher golf handicaps, $n = 8$ ($M_{age} = 65.5$ years, $SD_{age} = 2.4$); tennis players, $n = 8$ ($M_{age} = 61.4$ years, $SD_{age} = 6.4$); and nonsport participants, $n = 10$ ($M_{age} = 60.0$ years, $SD_{age} = 7.8$). The women golfers all participated in the local Women's Golf Association. The handicaps of the lower group of players ranged from 12 to 16 with a $M = 13.8$ and a $SD = 1.6$. The lowest handicap any woman in this group had ever had was 9. The handicaps of the higher group of players ranged from 26 to 37 with a $M = 30.3$ and a $SD = 3.8$. The lowest handicap any woman in this group had ever had was 21. Thus, there was no overlap between the groups' handicaps currently, nor had there ever been. In addition, the years of golf experience were similar between the lower ($M = 21.8$ years, $SD = 9.1$)- and higher ($M = 22.1$ years, $SD = 10.7$)-handicap players. None of the tennis players were regular golfers, and the nonparticipants did not play any sport regularly although most of them did exercise regularly (walking being the most common exercise).

Instruments

All golfers completed a questionnaire focusing on the following topics:

- Why do you play golf?
- How often do you play golf?

- With whom do you play golf?
- How does your skill compare to people you play with?
- When you have good and bad days, to what do you attribute your good days (e.g., luck, skill)?
- How did you learn to play?
- How do you practice?
- Do you regularly receive instructions?
- Do you play in competition?
- Do you sweat and breathe hard while playing golf (all golfers walked when they played)?
- Are you healthier than your golfing (nongolfing) friends?

This instrument is of course descriptive and has only face validity.

All participants (golfers, tennis players, and nonsport participants) completed a questionnaire about their exercise habits on the following topics:

- In what forms of exercise do you engage?
- Do you sweat and breathe hard during exercise?
- Are you healthier than your friends?
- Are you more active than your friends?
- What sports did you play as a child?

In addition, golf performance data (both skill and knowledge) were collected on all the women golfers (analyzed and reported in chapter 25 of this volume).

Field data on physical fitness were collected using standard procedures: flexibility (sit and reach) and grip strength (hand dynamometer) as described by Johnson and Nelson (1986); skinfolds (calf, subscapular, and triceps) and body mass index as described by Thomas, Keller, and Holbert (1997).

Procedures

Questionnaire and fitness data were collected individually on each woman by a trained experimenter during a two-month testing period. The experimenter had practiced the questionnaire and fitness procedures on numerous women until she achieved consistency in administering the questionnaire and a reliability above .9 on the fitness measures. Questionnaire data were coded by the experimenter who collected the data and were checked for accuracy by another experimenter. Procedures for the golf performance data are described in the other paper in this volume (chapter 25).

Statistical Analysis

The descriptive data were plotted and visually inspected, and they appeared to be normally distributed. Then frequencies or means and standard deviations were calculated as appropriate. Since the sample size was small, alpha was set at .05 but was not adjusted for multiple analysis on the same subjects (Thomas & Nelson, 1996). The analysis was primarily exploratory, using one-way ANOVAs with a Duncan's follow-up for any significant F-ratio.

RESULTS AND DISCUSSION

Motivational Factors

In table 26.1 we report descriptive data about the motivations of older women golfers with lower and higher handicaps. The desire to compete was reported as an important motivation by most of the lower-handicap players but was not listed by any of the higher-handicap players, even though all women golfers did compete each week in the local Women's Golf Association. Exercise and fitness benefits were listed as motivations by both lower- and higher-handicap players (we follow up on this in the next section of this paper). Finally, the social rewards from golf motivate most of the players, but particularly the lower-handicap ones. Interestingly, husbands were not generally listed as a motivational factor for playing. Indeed, the higher-handicap players reported that they never play golf with their husbands, while only four of the nine low-handicap women played golf with their husbands at least once per week. The higher-handicap women players indicated that they were uncomfortable playing with more highly skilled men.

The golfers were asked about practice characteristics. For the lower-handicap women, 67% (6/9) indicated that they practiced regularly, but none were taking lessons or participating in clinics as a form of practice. Only 25% (2/8) of the higher-

Table 26.1   Motivational and Playing Characteristics of Lower- and Higher-Handicap Women Golfers

Questions	Lower-handicap Players ($n = 9$)		Higher-handicap Players ($n = 8$)	
	#	%	#	%
Why do you play?				
Competition	5	56	0	0
Exercise	6	67	4	50
Health/Fitness	7	78	8	100
Husband	1	11	1	13
Social	8	89	4	50
Practice characteristics				
Taking lessons	0	0	4	50
Do you practice?	6	67	2	25

handicap players practiced regularly, but 50% (4/8) were taking lessons (all in golf clinics). Clearly, practice pattern discriminates between better and weaker players.

The women golfers were asked what caused them to have a good or bad day on the course. For the lower-handicap players, 78% (7/9) attributed playing well to mental attitude. In particular, they noted characteristics like mental state: just do it—don't think about it, positive frame of mind, and focus but not on mechanics. Only 50% (4/8) of the higher-handicap players suggested that mental factors were important in playing well. This tended to suggest that other factors like feeling good physically and luck were important in playing well. Thus, better players were more likely to attribute playing effectively to things they had some control over while poorer players attributed performance to factors they had little control over.

Exercise and Health-Related Fitness Factors

Since nearly all of the players (regardless of handicap) listed exercise and health-related fitness as important motivating factors in playing golf, table 26.2 provides some objective data on these variables. We also collected these data on the two comparison groups, women tennis players and nonsport participants. The average body mass index (BMI) for each group was in the desirable range (BMI = 20 to 25; Jequier, 1987), and the groups were not significantly different, $F(3,34) = 0.78$, $p = .51$. In fact, only one woman from the total sample of 35 had a BMI greater than 25, and it was only 27. Looking at body composition as estimated by skinfold measures, there were only small differences among the groups for sum of skinfolds, $F(3.34) = 0.16$, $p = .93$. However, the low-handicap women did tend to have larger calf skinfolds and smaller subscapular skinfolds than the other groups.

The groups were not significantly different on flexibility as estimated by the sit-and-reach test, $F(3,30) = 1.48$, $p = .24$. Compared to U.S. national norms for women over 50 years of age, all participants were in the excellent category for flexibility (Golding, Myer, & Sinning, 1989).

Table 26.2   Anthropometric Characteristics of Participants

Characteristics	Low-handicap Players ($n = 9$)		High-handicap Players ($n = 8$)		Tennis Players ($n = 8$)		Non-sport Players ($n = 10$)	
	M	SD	M	SD	M	SD	M	SD
Body mass index	20.3	1.6	21.4	3.5	20.1	1.3	21.4	1.6
Flexibility (cm)	26.2	5.7	21.9	7.1	24.6	6.0	19.8	7.7
Grip strength (kg)	32.7	6.5	28.2	5.7	32.4	4.1	25.3	7.0
Sum of skinfolds	48.4	8.0	49.2	8.8	49.6	8.5	51.2	12.9
Calf	18.1	4.6	15.6	4.6	16.4	2.1	13.3	5.0
Subscapular	13.0	4.5	17.2	6.0	17.3	4.0	20.2	5.2
Tricep	17.3	4.2	16.4	2.9	16.0	3.2	17.7	4.4

The only fitness category on which the groups differed significantly was grip strength of the dominant hand, $F(3.31) = 3.29$, $p = .03$. A Duncan's follow-up indicated that the nonparticipants had less grip strength than the low-handicap golfers and tennis players. The high-handicap players were not significantly different from any of the other groups, although they had higher mean grip strength scores than the nonparticipants but lower ones than the tennis and low-handicap players. Increased grip strength may have implications for upper body strength, which may be related to fewer health problems such as osteoporosis.

In table 26.3 we have provided the general exercise characteristics of the 35 participants in the study. These are just descriptive data and were not tested in a statistical model. For example, 46% (16/35) of the women reported that they either jogged, biked, or swam; 57% (20/35) reported that they walked at least 20 minutes three days per week, with the nonsport participants reporting slightly higher rates of exercising (of course exercising was in addition to golf for the women golfers). In fact, 43% (15/35) of the women indicated they exercised vigorously enough that they were breathing hard and sweating, a characteristic often associated with increased levels of physical fitness. Interestingly, 71% (25/35) of the women reported being more active than their friends while 74% (26/35) reported that they were healthier than their friends. Little difference existed among the groups for these two categories.

Finally, considering only the women golfers, 71% (12/17) reported that they were breathing hard and sweating at least some of the time while playing golf (note that all the women walked when they played). It is unclear why more of the women who were high-handicap players classed themselves as healthier than their friends while a lower number of the low-handicap players did so.

Table 26.3   Fitness Characteristics of Participants

Characteristics	Low-handicap Players ($n = 9$)		High-handicap Players ($n = 8$)		Tennis Players ($n = 8$)		Non-sport Players ($n = 10$)	
	#	%	#	%	#	%	#	%
Jog/bike/swim	3	33	3	37	4	50	6	60
Walk 20 min	3	33	5	63	6	75	6	60
Breathe hard/ sweat any exercise	4	44	1	13	6	75	4	40
More active than friends	7	78	6	75	7	86	5	50
Healthier than friends	7	78	6	75	6	75	7	70
Breathe hard/ sweat during golf	7	78	5	63				
Healthier than golf friends	2	22	5	68				

SUMMARY

While low-handicap women players reported competition as an important reason for playing golf, higher-handicap women players were not interested in competition (note that both groups of women competed each week in the local Women's Golf Association). Social factors were considered important motivators by both groups, but interestingly, this did not typically include playing golf with their spouses. As expected, low-handicap players practiced more than high-handicap players, but the high-handicap players were more likely to participate in golf clinics. Local golf professionals might encourage women golfers, particularly higher-handicap players, to practice regularly.

One of the prime motivational factors for women golfers regardless of handicap was exercise. When women golfers (low and high handicap) were compared to women tennis players and women nonsport participants, few differences were found in exercise or health-related variables. Generally, the women reported regular exercise patterns and considered themselves healthy, at least when compared to their friends.

References

Abernethy, B., Thomas, K.T., & Thomas, J.R. (1993). Strategies for improving understanding of motor expertise (or mistakes we have made and things we have learned). In Starkes, J.R., & Allard, F. (Eds.), *Cognitive factors in motor expertise* (pp. 317-356). Amsterdam: North-Holland.

Golding, L., Myer, C., & Sinning, W. (1989). *Y's way to physical fitness.* Champaign, IL: Human Kinetics.

Jequier, E. (1987). Energy, obesity, and body weight standards. *American Journal of Clinical Nutrition, 45,* 1035-1047.

Johnson, B.L., & Nelson, J.K. (1986). *Practical measurements for evaluation in physical education* (4th ed.). Edina, MN: Burgess.

Starkes, J.L., & Allard, F. (Eds.) (1993). *Cognitive factors in motor expertise.* Amsterdam: North-Holland.

Thomas, J.R., & Nelson, J.K. (1996). *Research methods in physical activity* (3rd ed.). Champaign, IL: Human Kinetics.

Thomas, K.T., Keller, C.S., & Holbert, K.E. (1997). Ethnic and age trends for body composition in women residing in the U.S. Southwest: I. Regional fat. *Medicine and Science in Sports and Exercise, 29,* 82-89.

Thomas, K.T., & Thomas, J.R. (1994). Developing expertise in sports: The relation of knowledge and performance. *International Journal of Sport Psychology, 25,* 295-312.

CHAPTER 27

Who Chokes and When? Situational and Dispositional Factors in Failure Under Pressure

Darwyn Linder, Rafer Lutz, Debra Crews, and Marc Lochbaum
Arizona State University, Tempe, AZ, USA

Participants first performed a baseline putting task in which they attempted twenty 5-ft putts on an indoor putting surface while being videotaped with hidden cameras. The performance score was number of putts made. Participants were then told that they now had to putt another twenty 5-ft putts while being videotaped for *NBC Dateline,* an international television show. In the final task, they were to putt, while again being videotaped for *NBC Dateline,* with an opportunity to earn $300 if they could match or exceed the number of putts made in the baseline condition but with the obligation to pay NBC $100 if they failed to meet this criterion. Results showed that five participants were successful and earned the $300, and five participants "choked" or failed to earn the money (although they did not have to pay NBC). Personality and experience variables were examined as predictors of choking.

Keywords: Choking, performance, anxiety.

INTRODUCTION

Lewis and Linder (1997) have shown that choking, suboptimal performance under pressure to perform well, is best explained as the result of self-focused attention. In their experiment, relatively inexperienced golfers putted to a target until they had reached a criterion of accuracy. Participants who were then challenged to perform even better in order to earn an extra reward (High Pressure treatment) putted less well than those who simply continued to putt without intervention (Low Pressure treatment). Participants who had practiced in the presence of a video camera (Pressure Adaptation treatment), which was then removed when the challenge was issued, performed better than High Pressure participants. Participants who were distracted by being required to count backward from 100 by twos while putting to meet the challenge (Distraction treatment) also putted better than High Pressure participants. These results were interpreted as reflecting the deleterious effects of self-focused attention on performance of a physical skill. The Pressure Adaptation treatment was effective because participants had experienced self-focused attention while acquiring skill at the task and had adapted to it. The distraction treatment was effective because it recruited cognitive capacity away from self-focused attention, reducing the impact of self-focused attention on performance of the primary task.

The present study was conducted to further examine the phenomenon of choking. In contrast to subjects in the Lewis and Linder (1997) experiment, the participants were experienced golfers. In addition, pressure to perform well was generated by their being videotaped for a national television audience and then by their having chance to win $300 for putting better than a baseline score or to lose $100 by putting worse than the baseline score. In addition, several personality and personal history measures were obtained in order to explore the correlates of choking.

METHOD

Participants

Volunteers, two females and eight males, were recruited from college classes at a large university in the southwestern United States. Mean age of participants was 24.5 years, ranging from 18 to 32 years. All participants had considerable golf experience, with a mean of 5.2 years of golf experience and mean estimated 18-hole score of 90.1 strokes.

Apparatus

Putting tasks were performed on a 16 ft long, 5 ft wide laboratory putting surface with a regulation hole in the center of the surface, 100 cm from one end. The surface was raised above the floor to allow placement of the cup and hidden video cameras, but was smooth and flat. The performance tests consisted of 20 putts from a 5 ft distance. Each of the 20 putts was completed from one of three slightly different angles (straight on, left side, and right side) in a predetermined order that was consistent for all participants.

Participants were asked to complete a questionnaire about their recreational and competitive experiences with golf and sport. The State-Trait Anxiety Inventory (STAI) (Spielberger et al., 1983) and anxiety ratings on a 10-point scale (1 = minimum anxiety, 10 = maximum anxiety) were used to assess participant state anxiety levels.

Procedure

Before testing, participants were allowed warm-up putts until they felt comfortably ready to begin (approximately 15 putts). There were three test conditions, baseline, NBC, and NBC+money. In the baseline test, subjects simply completed 20 putts, trying to make as many as possible. They were unaware of the later conditions or of the fact that they were being taped for a national television program. After completion of the baseline task, the NBC condition was introduced, that is, participants were told that they were putting on *NBC Dateline.* A television correspondent and camera crew appeared from a nearby room to film and document the participants' performances in a very obtrusive manner. Finally, in the NBC+money condition, participants were told they would earn $300 if they could match or better their baseline putting scores but would lose $100 if they did not. In effect, the television correspondent bet each of the participants, three-to-one, that they could not match their baseline efforts.

The STAI was completed before baseline putting to determine baseline state anxiety levels and again 1 day after the experiment to assess retrospectively the anxiety experienced during the NBC and NBC+money conditions. The 10-point anxiety ratings were given before the first putt in each of the three conditions.

RESULTS

Descriptive data are presented in table 27.1. Grouping the participants into chokers and nonchokers produced a significant interaction, $F(2, 16) = 6.30, p = .01$, for putts made across the three experimental conditions. Examination of the simple main effects indicated that nonchokers made significantly more putts, $F(1, 8) = 23.5, p = .001$, in the NBC+money condition compared to the chokers. The two groups did not differ in the NBC-alone condition, although the trend was similar. At baseline, the eventual chokers actually made more putts than the nonchokers, although the difference was not statistically significant. Interestingly, the main effect for the STAI was also significant, $F(1, 8) = 5.13, p = .05$, with state anxiety increasing from baseline to the NBC condition and increasing again in the NBC+money condition.

Table 27.1   Performance and Anxiety Scores

| | Putting performance | | STAI | | Anxiety | |
	M	SD	M	SD	M	SD
Baseline	10.6	3.24	30.2	7.58	2.05	.90
Chokers	12.2		33.4		2.3	
Nonchokers	9.0		27.0		1.8	
NBC	11.0	3.20	48.9	12.26	6.33	2.04
Chokers	10.2		55.8		6.9	
Nonchokers	11.8		42.0		5.8	
NBC+money	10.8	2.44	51.8	14.95	6.44	1.89
Chokers	8.8		58.4		7.4	
Nonchokers	12.8		45.2		5.5	

The difference in total putts made from baseline to the NBC+money condition was computed for each subject by subtracting the baseline score from the test score to obtain a measure of performance change. Correlations were computed between these scores, amount of competitive sport experience, STAI, and the 10-point anxiety scores (see table 27.2). Estimates of correlation parameters based on a small sample have a relatively large standard error. Tests of significance, however, take account of this fact and can be interpreted in the usual way, as estimates of the probability of Type I error.

Table 27.2   Correlations Between Performance, Anxiety, and Sport Experience

Performance variable	Baseline putts	NBC + money – baseline
Predictor variable		
STAI at baseline	.20	–.46
STAI change score	.00	.08
Anxiety at baseline	.08	–.31
Anxiety change score	.19	–.27
18-hole score	–.55	.70*
Competitive sports	–.74*	.59

*$P < .05$.

DISCUSSION

The situation created by the introduction of the NBC production crew and the $300 bet was a more naturalistic pressure situation than that employed by Lewis and Linder (1997), yet both settings produced performance decrements for some individuals and performance increments for others. In the present study, one participant made 8 fewer putts than at baseline when putting for $300, while another participant made 10 more putts when putting for $300. Performance under pressure was relatively consistent in that the change from baseline to the NBC condition was correlated with the change from baseline to the NBC+money condition ($r = .75$, $p < .05$).

The STAI at baseline was a nonsignificant predictor of performance at baseline. However, baseline STAI was related to performance change as might be expected; higher STAI scores were associated with poorer performance, although the correlation was not statistically significant. The STAI at baseline was unrelated to the retrospective STAI in the NBC and NBC+money conditions. The STAI change score, computed by subtracting the STAI baseline score from the retrospective STAI, was unrelated to either baseline performance or performance change. Of course "retrospective introspection" is a problematic methodology (Brewer et al., 1991). Anxiety at baseline, like baseline STAI, was unrelated to baseline putting and was a weak predictor of performance changes under pressure. Baseline anxiety was significantly related to the STAI at baseline ($r = .79$, $p < .01$), a relationship confirming the concurrent validity of the measure. That is, it has significant overlap with the STAI, as would be expected of a measure of state anxiety. The anxiety change score behaved very much like the baseline anxiety score. Both the simple measure of anxiety and the more sophisticated STAI show quite acceptable psychometric properties of reliability and concurrent validity. However, neither the anxiety measure nor the STAI shows a strong relationship to performance under pressure.

The strongest predictor of performance under pressure was the self-reported average golf score ($r = .70$, $p < .05$). The correlation between estimated score and performance under pressure is such that the lower the estimated score, the worse the person performed when putting for $300. It is interesting to note that all five participants who failed to putt as well under pressure as at baseline reported average scores below 90 (84, 84, 88, 83.5, 88), while all of those who succeeded reported average scores of 90 or above (95, 90, 95, 95, 98). It may be that reporting average scores below 90 is associated with a qualitatively different level of self-perceived ability than experienced by those who report scores above 90. In the minds of many golfers, "bogey golf," a qualitatively different descriptor than "duffer" or "hacker," applies to those who regularly break 90. That self-perception may have led those who reported scores in the 80s to monitor their performances more carefully in order to determine whether they were performing up to expectations. This is the process that Lewis and Linder (1997) hypothesize as the mechanism leading to choking. Those who reported scores above 90 were not burdened with a self-perception that demanded a high level of performance. Instead, they were free to focus on the task at hand rather than engaging in crippling self-evaluation, and they performed quite well. This account is, of course, very speculative, and based on a small-sample experiment that lacked some important methodological controls. Yet the interpretation is congruent with other research on the choking phenomenon; and the evidence that supports it, scanty as it is, is stronger than the evidence that dispositional measures of anxiety predicted performance under pressure in this setting.

One other finding of note is the correlation between experience in competitive sports and performance under pressure ($r = .59$). While not attaining a conventional level of significance, this was the second strongest predictive relationship in the NBC+money condition. This correlation indicates that the more experience participants had in competitive sports other than golf, the better they performed under pressure. This correlational finding is congruent with the experimental result obtained by Lewis and Linder (1997), demonstrating that adaptation to self-focused attention enabled better performance in a subsequent, high-pressure situation.

In summary, the results of this study indicate that successful performance under pressure is associated with reduced levels of self-focused attention and with more experience in demanding, competitive situations. There is little evidence that either simple or sophisticated measures of anxiety are useful predictors of putting performance under pressure for the intermediate-level golfers who participated in this study. It remains to be seen what factors are most important in determining performance for elite golfers in demanding competitive situations. A formidable challenge awaits future researchers attempting to create experimental situations, or to exploit naturally occurring competitions, that allow for incisive, experimental evaluation of the causes of choking.

References

Brewer, B.W., Van Raalte, J.L., Linder, D.E., & Van Raalte, N.S. (1991). Peak performance and the perils of retrospective introspection. *Journal of Sport and Exercise Psychology,* 13, 227-238.

Lewis, B.P., & Linder, D.E. (1997). Thinking about choking? Attentional processes and paradoxical performance. *Personality and Social Psychology Bulletin,* 23, 937-944.

Spielberger, C.D., Gorsuch, R.L., Luschene, R., Vagg, P.R., & Jacobs, G.A. (1983). *Manual for the State-Trait Anxiety Inventory.* Palo Alto, CA: Consulting Psychologists Press.

CHAPTER 28

Superstitious and Routine Behaviours in Male and Female Golfers of Varying Levels of Ability

V.C. Melvin and M.A. Grealy
Institute of Biomechanical and Life Sciences, University of Glasgow, Glasgow, Scotland

Routine and superstitious behaviours of 60 male and female golfers of three playing levels were examined. The playing levels were professional, low-handicap amateur, and club golfer. Subjects were required to complete a questionnaire that examined whether they engaged in routine and superstitious behaviours before, during, and after competitive golf. Analysis of variance indicated that level of involvement was important in terms of superstitious behaviour ($F(2, 54) = 5.52$, $p = 0.007$), with the low-handicap amateur group exhibiting the most superstitious behaviour. This study ultimately has implications for low-handicap amateur golfers and the type of subculture in which they are currently operating.

Keywords: Superstition, routine, level of ability.

INTRODUCTION

Golf is ripe with potentially superstitious behaviour, and examples of this range from lucky markers to the toilet used prior to play. Many golfers will use only a certain colour of tee or will leave their clubhead in a certain position on their bag in order to hit a good shot.

Pope and Gardner (1978) wrote an article on superstition in professional golfers and began it in the following way:

> Are you superstitious? Do you worry about Friday the 13th, about black cats crossing your path, about walking under ladders? Of course you're not superstitious. Neither are professional golfers. Ask any touring pro. He'll tell you, "Nobody out here

wants to admit they are superstitious." Then five minutes later he's laying it on you about lucky ball markers and unlucky chewing gum and charm clothes and even a hood from killing a water snake. (p. 53)

This indicates that superstition is very much in evidence in the golfing subculture, but the problem is that many individuals are reluctant to admit it. Instead they choose to say that they are engaging in routine behaviours. For example, Tom Weiskopf, winner of the British Open Golf Championship in 1973, claims that his behaviour is routine rather than superstition; but according to Pope and Gardner (1978), Weiskopf is quoted as saying:

It's all routine, but I never tee off without 3 cents on me. Plus 3 tees. Also I won't tee off on a part 3 hole except with a broken tee. (p. 55)

They also note that he will not carry a broken tee but will pick it up from the ground, the nature of such behaviour surely being indicative of superstition.

In the sport superstition literature, an important factor that determines superstitious behaviour is level of involvement. Buhrmann and Zaugg (1981) carried out a study on basketball players at high school, college, and university level. They found that the higher the level of involvement the more superstitions athletes held. This finding was supported by Neil et al. (1981), who also examined the role that level of involvement played in superstitious behaviours in competitive and recreational ice hockey players.

Superstition is related to the Latin word *superstes,* which means outliving or surviving. There is much evidence for the occurrence of superstition in times of anxiety or uncertainty: it is thought that superstition has a dual purpose in that it attracts favourable influences and wards off unfavourable ones. Jahoda (1969) said that superstition was the belief that

...one's fate is in the hands of unknown external powers governed by forces over which one has not control. (p. 156)

If you do not feel in control in any given situation you are bound to feel anxious, and this is why Jahoda's definition is particularly accurate. Therefore, it has been hypothesised that superstitious behaviours occur in times of high anxiety (Neil, 1982). Boutcher (1990) noted the importance of having a consistent and routine-like approach to performance, since this helps to focus attention by decreasing the negative effects that anxiety may have on attentional processes. This is similar to the effects that superstitions are hypothesised to have; they are developed to relieve anxiety. Superstitious behaviour is also seen as an attempt by the athlete to exert some form of control in an uncertain environment. Van Raalte et al. (1991) carried out a study with novice golfers that examined superstitious behaviour on the putting green. They found that those subjects with low chance orientation were more likely to engage in superstitious behaviour (which was selection of a "lucky" ball to putt with) than those with high chance orientation.

At present, little is known about the degree and extent to which golfers rely on superstition and how this is linked to routine behaviours. It may be that the sport psychologist could use the knowledge of such behaviours in assessing the extent to which an individual feels he or she is in control. The aim of this study was to investigate whether playing level affected the extent to which golfers reported engaging in superstitious and routine behaviours, as well as the extent to which superstitions were linked to their routine behaviours.

One potential problem for this area of research is that, as demonstrated by Tom Weiskopf, golfers may believe that they are engaging in routine behaviours when in fact the underlying motive for the behaviour is actually one of superstition. In an effort to quantify the prevalence of golfers' basing routines on superstition, this study incorporated questions aimed at identifying routine behaviours and then used a follow-up question to uncover whether the routine was in fact based upon superstition.

METHOD

Subjects

Subjects were male (n = 36) and female golfers (n = 24) of three levels of ability: professional, low-handicap amateurs, and club golfers. The professional golfers were either European or U.S. Tour players (n = 8) or golf club professionals who played in Scottish Tartan Tour events (n = 9). The low-handicap amateur golfers (n = 23) had all represented their county team, and 10 of them had played for Scotland. The maximum handicap in this group was 6, and the mean handicap was 1.56. The club golfers (n = 20) played regular recreational golf and weekend competitions. All had handicaps of over 6, and the mean handicap for this group was 15.8.

Design

The study was questionnaire based and involved comparing the scores of male and female golfers of three playing levels on routine behaviours, superstitious behaviours, and routine behaviours that were based on superstitions.

Questionnaire

The questionnaire was split into three areas: pregame, during-game, and postgame behaviours. The various components of these areas included activities undertaken the evening before a round and the morning of a game, equipment, teeing-area behaviour, green behaviour, and behaviour after play. A five-point Likert scale was the chosen response tool; but since three different aspects of behaviours were being examined, that is, routine, superstition, and routines based upon superstition, the questions were designed in different ways. Routine and superstition questions were designed in the same manner and asked directly. A typical example of a routine question is "Do you have a routine which you follow the evening before each tournament?" A typical example of a superstition question is "Do you have any lucky charms?" To determine the extent to which superstitions underlay routine behaviours, subjects were asked a routine question, and if they replied positively to engaging in this routine they were asked a further question such as "Do you believe this brings you luck?" or "Would it affect your luck if you did not engage in this routine?" The interpretation of a positive response to this further question was that superstition was the reason for the individual's engaging in the routine behaviour.

Procedure

After piloting of the questionnaire, subjects were approached and asked if they would like to participate in a study examining the routines and beliefs of golfers. Participation was voluntary, and those who were interested were provided with a questionnaire to complete together with a stamped addressed envelope to allow them to return the questionnaire. The response rate was 81%.

RESULTS

Means and standard deviations were calculated for the extent to which each of the groups of golfers reported engaging in routine, superstitious behaviours.

Superstitious Behaviours

A two-way ANOVA (3 × 2) was carried out to investigate whether level of ability or gender affected superstitious behaviour. This showed a significant effect for level of ability ($F(2, 54) = 5.52$, $p = 0.007$), and the post hoc Tukey HSD test confirmed the findings that are illustrated in figure 28.1, namely that the low-handicap amateurs were more superstitious than both the professional and club golfers. No significant difference existed between these latter two groups. Furthermore, no significant gender differences were found ($F(1, 54) = 2.66$, $p = 0.109$), and there was no significant interaction ($F(2, 54) = 0.64$, $p = 0.472$).

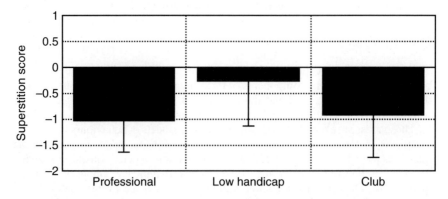

Figure 28.1   Graph showing the mean and standard deviations for reported superstitious behaviours for the three groups of golfers. Scores were obtained from responses on a five-point Likert scale where a score of +2 indicated that a player always engaged in a particular superstitious behaviour.

Routine Behaviours That Were Based on Superstitions

A two-way ANOVA (3×2) was carried out to investigate whether playing level or gender had an effect on the extent to which the routines golfers engaged in were based on superstitions. No significant differences for playing level ($F(2, 54) = 2.06$, $p = 0.137$) or gender ($F(1, 54) = 1.88$, $p = 0.176$) were found.

Did Playing Level Affect the Degree to Which Routine or Superstitious Behaviours Were Engaged In?

A two-way ANOVA was used to examine the degree to which golfers of different playing levels differed in the extent to which they reported participating in superstitious and routine behaviours. A significant main effect was found for the type of behaviour reported ($F(1, 57) = 8.28$, $p = 0.006$), with players engaging in more routine than superstitious behaviours. A significant interaction was also noted ($F(2, 57) = 7.56$, $p = 0.001$), and this reflected the previous finding that the low-handicap golfers engaged in more superstitious behaviours.

DISCUSSION

Superstitious Behaviour

The first aim of this study was to examine the extent to which superstitious behaviour was influenced by level of ability. A significant effect was observed, with the low-handicap amateur golfers reporting that they engaged in significantly more superstitious behaviours than the other groups. This finding contradicts previous literature in this area. Studies by Neil et al. (1981) and Buhrmann and Zaugg (1981) both supported the idea that the higher the level of involvement, the more likely athletes are to engage in superstitious behaviour—which would imply for the present study that professionals should have been the most superstitious, followed by low-handicap amateurs, then the club golfers. A possible reason for the differences in the findings between this study and those by Neil et al. (1981) and Buhrmann and Zaugg (1981) is the populations of athletes used. Both the other studies used top-class university athletes who could be equated with the low-handicap amateur group in the present study. The investigators were not examining professional athletes and therefore incorrectly assumed that the higher the level of involvement, the more athletes will engage in superstitious behaviours.

So why should such differences exist? First, the low-handicap amateurs were not full-time golfers, so most of them were restricted in the time they had to play golf. This time restriction could have left them feeling that more was left to chance, since they had not practised as much as they would have liked. Thus they may have been more anxious about their performance and consequently more likely to resort to superstitious behaviours in an attempt to get luck on their side. In addition, the marker for success in amateur golf is to play for your country, which creates a degree of uncertainty since teams are decided upon by selectors. In professional golf the marker for success is quite different; it is simply the amount of money you have won.

Team selection is not always so important; and in general, team selection is based on money earned, so this should give the professional a greater feeling of control. It is perhaps these differences that help to create the subculture of superstitious beliefs and behaviours that seem to exist for low-handicap amateurs.

Club golfers were less superstitious than the low-handicap amateur golfers, and this might reflect the recreational nature of their play. At the club level, investment in terms of time or emotion is often less; therefore success may not be exposed to the same subculture of superstition that seems to have developed in competitive golf, where the relationship between lucky objects or behaviours and success is reinforced on a regular basis.

Superstition Underlying Routine Behaviour

A further aim of the study was to examine the extent to which superstition underpinned the routines engaged in. No effect was found for this with regard to level of ability. This may be a result of the individual nature of routines as discussed by Albinson and Bull (1988), or alternatively it may be insensitivity of the measurement. Although nothing substantial was found as a result of this measurement, it has potential to be useful and should be developed, as it reveals the beliefs underlying the routine and identifies the individual who may be reluctant to admit to actual superstitions but willing to admit to engaging in certain routines to bring luck.

Were Routine Behaviours More Common Than Superstitious Behaviours?

An interesting finding from this study was that overall, golfers were more likely to engage in routine rather than superstitious behaviours. If this finding is a true reflection of actual behaviour, as opposed to reported behaviour, it is encouraging, since it indicates that golfers are more likely to engage in behaviours that could enhance their performance rather than basing their judgments on luck. However, these results might reflect a tendency for golfers to be more willing to admit to engaging in routine as opposed to superstitious behaviours. The analysis relating to the extent to which superstitions underlay routines did not provide any insights into this. However, the low-handicap amateur group were found to be more likely to engage in superstitious than routine behaviours, and this has considerable implications for this group. It was worrying to note that some of these golfers believed that wearing certain clothes would improve their game, while others felt the need to use the same colour of tee at certain holes or believed that a putt was more likely to be successful if they had used a particular marker. Their responses indicated that they lacked belief in their ability to control the outcome.

CONCLUSION

To conclude, superstitious behaviour in golfers does seem to be affected by the level at which the individual is performing. The extent to which superstitions underlie routines was not affected by either level of play or gender. Ultimately this paper has implications for low-handicap golfers and the subculture in which they are operating.

References

Albinson, J.G. and Bull, S.J. (1988). *A Mental Game Plan.* New York: Wiley.

Boutcher, S.H. (1990). The role of performance routines in sport. In Jones, G. and Hardy, L. (eds.), *Stress and Performance in Sport.* New York: Wiley.

Buhrmann, H.G. and Zaugg, M.K. (1981). Superstitions among basketball players: An investigation of various forms of superstitious beliefs and behaviour among competitive basketballers at the junior high school to university level. *Journal of Sport Behaviour,* 4, 163-174.

Jahoda, G. (1969). *The Psychology of Superstition.* London: Allen Lane, Penguin Press.

Neil, G.I. (1982). Demystifying sport superstition. *International Review of Sport Sociology,* 17, 99-124.

Neil, G.I., Anderson, B., and Sheppard, W. (1981). Superstitions among male and female athletes of various levels of involvement. *Journal of Sport Behaviour,* 4, 137-148.

Pope, E. and Gardner, F. (1978). What me, superstitious? *Golf World,* 17(9), Sept., 52-55, 57-58.

Van Raalte, J.L., Brewer, B.W., Nemeroff, C.J., and Linder, D.E. (1991). Chance orientation and superstitious behaviour on the putting green. *Journal of Sport Behaviour,* 14(1), 28-34.

CHAPTER 29

Match Play and Stroke Play Myths: Do Elite Amateur Golfers Play the Course or the Person?

Vicki J. Aitken
School of Physical Education, University of Otago, Dunedin, New Zealand

Match play and stroke play in golf served as unique "laboratories" for investigating task (where success is self-referenced; Nicholls 1984) and ego goal states (where success is defined relative to other people; Nicholls 1984). The goal climates of match play and stroke play, as well as the golfer's dispositional goal orientation, will determine whether he/she plays the course or the person. Qualitative case studies of four elite amateur golfers were compiled from their responses to the Task and Ego Orientation of Sport Questionnaire (TEOSQ) and from in-depth semi-structured interview data. The best male and female match players had predominant dispositional ego orientations but utilised both ego and task goal states during match play. In contrast, the best male and female stroke players had predominant task orientations and were predominantly involved in a task state during stroke play.

Keywords: Ego state goals, task state goals, match play, stroke play.

INTRODUCTION

Golfers use different goals to judge their success. Task and ego goal orientations are the key constructs in Nicholls's (1984) achievement motivation theory. Goal orientations are defined as a person's disposition toward a task or an ego goal, whereas a goal state refers to a person's involvement in a particular situation. When in a predominantly task orientation or state, people will self-reference their success or ability (e.g., they aim to better a personal best score or master the task in terms of learning), whereas predominantly ego-oriented or state-involved persons will regard their success or ability relative to others (e.g., they aim to beat others). However, a person can have multiple goal orientations. Fox et al. (1994) and Hodge and Petlichkoff (in press) have argued that one can be high (or low) in both task and ego at the same time, or high in one and low in the other.

A person's goal state in a particular situation may not always be the same as that individual's predominant goal orientation (Seifriz, Duda, and Chi 1992). Furthermore, Ames (1986) suggested that certain environments or goal climates may elicit a particular goal state. For example, a competitive climate, in which the most prominent performance information is that relative to other people (e.g., match play), may elicit an ego goal state (Ames 1986). In contrast, an individualistic climate, in which the most obvious performance information is that which is relative to past performances (e.g., stroke play), may elicit a task state (Ames 1986).

The purpose of the study was to determine which goal states were predominant in match play and stroke play and to find how the participants' state goal(s) compared to their predominant goal orientation.

METHODOLOGY

Four participants were recruited from New Zealand's national amateur golf squad using the method of purposeful critical sampling (Patton 1990). For each form of the game, one of New Zealand's best male and one of its best female players were selected as participants in the study.

The participants completed a Task and Ego Orientation of Sport Questionnaire (TEOSQ) at least one week prior to playing in the tournaments of interest. The TEOSQ measured the participant's goal orientation (Duda et al. 1995) in reference to his or her overall golf game. TEOSQ results were analysed in a profile format as used by Fox et al. (1994).

Participants were interviewed once after two rounds of tournament match play and once after two rounds of tournament stroke play. Semi-structured in-depth interviews were conducted in order to obtain information on the goal states used by each participant during match play and stroke play rounds. Interviews were transcribed and content was analysed (Coté et al. 1993; Patton 1990), and trustworthiness measures as outlined by Lincoln and Guba (1985) were employed.

RESULTS AND DISCUSSION

Matt was the best male match player (pseudonyms are used for all participants) and was predominantly ego oriented (see table 29.1). Matt's goals during both match and stroke play rounds were similar in that he aimed to keep his pace of play really consistent in stroke play and to be patient and calm during the match play. Both of these states are classified as task states. Matt's primary focus was his arousal level, and he felt that if he could control this his performance would be optimal. In stroke play he was predominantly task state involved, whereas in match play he was both task (i.e., focused on his goal) and ego state involved (e.g., "I just wanted to win but I wanted to do that by. . . achieving different goals"). Matt believed that match play differed from stroke play because players were forced to consider their opponent's performance. Matt perceived the pressure situations in match play to involve his opponent, but during pressure situations in stroke play he was more reliant on his own performance. Matt's results suggest that taking into consideration an opponent's game (i.e., adopting an ego goal state as well as a task state) will increase one's sense of control over the outcome, as he perceived he had a choice of options that in turn gave him a perception of having more control over the game's outcome.

Stan, the best male stroke player, was predominantly task oriented (see table 29.1). During stroke play, Stan aimed to "just let things happen" and to "try to take it shot by shot," which illustrated a task focus. Stan was effectively attempting to capture the characteristics of being in "flow" (Csikszentmihalyi 1974) or utilising Rotella and Cullen's (1995) trusting mentality. Stan believed that if he was confident in his ability, then he would perform well, so he also aimed to be confident in both match and stroke play rounds. In match play, Stan's typical aim was to make sure he won (an ego orientation), whereas his goal state involved both a task (e.g., he was thinking "just get off and make solid pars") and an ego focus (e.g., focus on making sure he won). Consequently Stan's strategies in match play were more "aggressive" (e.g., "I started going for the pin") than in stroke play, where he was more "conservative" (e.g., hit more percentage play). Stan's results suggest that utilising different goal states for the different games may result in a change of strategy. An ego goal state may encourage a match player to be more aggressive, while a task goal state may encourage a stroke player to be more conservative in strategy.

Table 29.1   Task and Ego Orientation of Sport Questionnaire (TEOSQ) Results for Each Participant (Measured on 1-5 Scale)

	Participants	Task	Ego
Best match-players	Matt	3.86	4.00
	Mary	2.71	3.33
Best stroke-players	Stan	3.86	3.67
	Steph	4.14	3.67

Mary, the best female match player, had a predominant ego orientation (see table 29.1). Her aims in both stroke and match play were to finish first. Mary's goal state during match play and stroke play alternated between task (e.g., thinking, "get the ball on the fairway and hit it close to the pin") and ego states. For example, when playing badly in her match she thought, "This is pathetic—there's no way that I'll lose to this person." This ego state was used as a motivator to try to play better. Mary's results suggest that to use both a task and ego state in match play may be advantageous, especially where the desire to win and the available relative performance information are used as a motivator. This could also help with refocusing on the task.

The best female stroke player (Steph) had a predominant task orientation (see table 29.1). In stroke play, Steph's overall aim was ego oriented, because she wanted a relative placing of seventh. However, her goal state during stroke play was mainly task involved, as she was concerned about the process of her game (e.g., on a putt she thought, "Just hit it at the hole and it will stay there"). Steph's strategy during stroke play was "aggressive" in that she would go right at the flag and "give the putts a bit of a go." In match play, Steph's overall goal was to win, but it was more important for her to play her best golf, thus indicating a predominant task orientation. Her goal state during match play was also task predominant as she focused on the process of playing. Steph's strategy in match play was "conservative" relative to her opponent, which indicated an ego goal state response (e.g., "If you've got two putts for the win take two putts—don't get aggressive"). Steph's results indicate that the reason she does not perform as well in match play may be that she changes her strategy or tactical approach. That is, she plays not to lose ("conservative") rather than playing to win ("aggressive"). In other words, the degree to which she can "play to not lose" is largely determined by her opponent's performance.

CONCLUSION

The adoption of both an ego goal state (i.e., playing the person) and a task goal state (i.e., playing the course) during match play was found to be beneficial for the best match players in the study, in terms of providing a perceived control over the outcome and a source of motivation to maintain maximum effort. The use of both types of goal states in golf is supported by Kingston and Hardy (1997). In contrast, the best stroke players tended to remain task focused (task goal state, i.e., play the course) throughout their stroke play rounds.

ACKNOWLEDGMENTS

I would like to thank Dr. Alex McKenzie for his significant help and guidance with this research and paper, and Dr. Ken Hodge for his comments.

References

Ames, C. (1986). Conceptions of motivation within competitive and noncompetitive goal structures. In *Self-Related Cognitions in Anxiety and Motivation,* ed. R. Schwarzer. Hillsdale, NJ: Erlbaum.

Coté, J., J.H. Salmela, A. Baria, and S.J. Russell. (1993). Organizing and interpreting unstructured qualitative data. *The Sport Psychologist* 7: 127-137.

Csikszentmihalyi, M. (1974). *Flow: Studies of Enjoyment.* Chicago: University of Chicago Press.

Duda, J.L., L. Chi, M.L. Newton, M.D. Walling, and D. Catley. (1995). Task and ego orientation and intrinsic motivation in sport. *International Journal of Sport Psychology* 26: 40-63.

Fox, K., M. Goudas, S. Biddle, J. Duda, and N. Armstrong. (1994). Children's task and ego goal profiles in sport. *British Journal of Educational Psychology* 64: 253-261.

Hodge, K., and L. Petlichkoff. (in press). Goal "profiles" in sport motivation: A cluster analysis.

Kingston, K., and L. Hardy. (1977). Can goal orientation profiles impact upon competition performance? *Journal of Applied Sport Psychology* 9: S116.

Lincoln, Y.S., and E.G. Guba. (1985). *Naturalistic Inquiry.* Beverly Hills, CA: Sage.

Nicholls, J.G. (1984). Achievement motivation: Conceptions of ability, subjective experience, task choice and performance. *Psychological Review* 91(3): 328-346.

Patton, M.Q. (1990). *Qualitative Evaluation and Research Methods.* 2nd ed. Beverly Hills, CA: Sage.

Rotella, R., and R. Cullen. (1995). *Golf Is Not a Game of Perfect.* New York: Simon & Schuster.

Seifriz, J.J., J.L. Duda, and L. Chi. (1992). The relationship of perceived motivational climate to intrinsic motivation and beliefs about success in basketball. *Journal of Sport and Exercise Psychology* 14: 375-391.

CHAPTER 30

The Effects of Traditional and Learning-Centered Golf Instruction on Skill Development and Attitudes Toward Golf

R. Lutz
Arizona State University, Tempe, AZ, USA

Two experiments were conducted to analyze the effects of learning-centered golf instruction in comparison to a traditional model. For Experiment 1, the learning-centered curriculum included modeling, reverse order of lesson progression (putting to short game to full swing), preshot routine, emphasis on preswing fundamentals and finish position, and a habituation technique for learning new swing mechanics. The traditional alternative emphasized swing kinematics, limited modeling, the traditional order of lesson progression (full swing to short game to putting), and equal emphasis on preswing and swing fundamentals. Learning-centered students improved putting performance and full-swing performances more from pre- to posttest than traditional students. Experiment 2 examined only full-swing instruction, comparing traditional instruction with a learning-centered alternative in which only preswing and finish fundamentals were taught. Effect sizes indicate that learning-centered students exhibited more positive attitudes than traditional students. It is concluded that incorporating techniques adapted from the findings of these two studies may provide more effective golf instruction.

Keywords: Golf, instruction, learning, teaching.

INTRODUCTION

Although 11 million individuals started playing golf in the United States between 1987 and 1992, only 71% were still playing one year later in 1993. Even more startling is the fact that of an estimated 48.3 million individuals over 18 years old who have played golf at some point in their lives, only about 48% were still playing in 1993. Among those who were no longer playing, some of the important reasons for not playing golf included the prohibitive costs of playing and instruction, unfavorable attitudes toward beginners by other golfers, the perception that golf is not interesting or enjoyable, and the perception that golf is too difficult or complicated. Among existing golfers, for example, 55% of occasional golfers, 63% of core golfers, and 55% of avid golfers stated that they would play more frequently if they could lower their average score (National Golf Foundation 1995). It may be possible to decrease attrition by improving golf instruction, and as a consequence, improve golfer performance and enjoyment.

Golf instruction has a well-established culture of coaching. A large number of books and articles have been dedicated to the game of golf and the golf swing in particular (e.g., Hogan 1957; Leadbetter 1990; Watson 1992). Anecdotal evidence suggests that the typical golf lesson consists of kinematic description of the student's golf swing, comparison of these kinematics to a "model" swing, and discussion or prescription of drills to help the student learn how to swing more like the "model." It is unclear at this point whether a more effective model of instruction can be implemented. Some areas in which we may start to examine different instruction techniques in golf include the order of skill presentation, understanding of performance compared to learning, implementation of preshot routine, use of modeling, and amount of kinematic description given to students.

The traditional method makes some use of modeling, but considering the positive results that can be elicited with the use of modeling (e.g., McCullagh 1993), perhaps it does not receive enough emphasis. It may be more effective to simply model for students a start- and end-point for their swing and allow the body to find the most efficient movement pattern. Preshot routines may allow more consistent aiming and facilitate learning. Interpretation of psychophysiological correlates of attentional patterns in golfers suggests that target awareness is associated with more effective performance (Crews and Landers 1993). Also, unfamiliarity with self-focus is associated with choking (Lewis and Linder 1997). Hardy, Mullen, and Jones (1996) present evidence that golf putting learned using explicit instructions deteriorated under a stress condition while putting learned using implicit techniques did not. From this perspective, traditional golf instruction may actually cause improper attentional focus and excessive self-instruction due to its emphasis on kinematic description of the golf swing.

The inconsistencies between research and practice with regard to golf instruction suggest a need for research that tests hypotheses in sport settings using theory-based approaches. Such studies should employ different teaching techniques implemented by the same instructor using systematic manipulation of curriculum while keeping the amount of practice equal. The dependent variables of interest include performance gains, attitudes, and enjoyment.

EXPERIMENT 1 METHOD

Participants

Golfers enrolled in beginning golf classes at a large university served as participants for this research (females $n = 24$; males $n = 65$; total $n = 89$). Participants were drawn from four beginning classes taught over two consecutive semesters. Two of the classes were taught a traditional curriculum ($n = 45$), and the other two classes were taught a learning-centered curriculum ($n = 44$). A total of 3% of participants estimated their average score to be less than 90, and 13% estimated their average 18-hole score as less than 100. A large portion (48%) of participants indicated that they had not played enough golf to estimate average 18-hole scores.

Apparatus

Traditional Instruction

Instruction began with full swing, progressing through the swing model advocated by a popular golf instructor (Leadbetter 1990). Students were taught proper setup, stance, alignment, and swing positions. Classes often emphasized kinematic description of the model swing. Participants were allowed to hit balls at their own pace between instructions, and the instructor would focus on individual teaching, emphasizing kinematic description, modeling, and positioning the student according to the model swing. After completion of the full-swing section (five classes) and video analysis (one class), participants were taught putting (two classes), chipping (two classes), and pitching (two classes), sequentially. Discussion of rules and etiquette (one class), sand (one class), on-course play (two classes), ball-flight laws (one class), and club-fitting (one class) followed. The last four classes consisted of open practice of mostly full swing.

Learning-Centered Instruction

Instruction began with putting (two classes) and then progressed through short game (chipping, two classes; pitching, two classes) to full swing (six classes). Discussion of rules and etiquette (one class), sand (one class), on-course play (two classes), ball-flight laws (one class), and club-fitting (one class) followed. The last four classes consisted of open practice of mostly full swing. Within these classes, participants were taught to distinguish between golf as a game and the mechanics of the game of golf, such as swing mechanics (Hogan 1993). Students were taught proper setup, stance, alignment, and swing positions. Classes emphasized preswing fundamentals, aiming procedures, preshot routine, and modeling. Participants were allowed to hit balls at their own pace between instructions, and the instructor would focus on individual teaching, emphasizing modeling, alignment, and start and finish positions. No emphasis was put on the top of the backswing position.

Full-Swing Test

Participants were given warm-up shots until they felt ready to begin testing (at least 5 but no more than 10 shots). Participants then hit eight shots that composed the test. The shots were hit to a 10 ft square net placed at approximately a 40° tilt toward the practice tee from 130 yd (males) and 100 yd (females). Three circles of traffic cones placed at successive 15 ft increments encircled the net. Participants were allowed to choose their own club based upon warm-up shots. Form and performance ratings were made by one of three raters who were blind to the experimental manipulations. The same rater assessed pre- and posttest scores for each subject. The form ratings were made based on form for the hold, aim, stance/posture, and the swing/finish according to a standard form showing points earned for each swing component that was exhibited over the eight test shots. A total of 15 points was possible. Ball flight was rated subjectively on the basis of contact, trajectory, and direction on a scale from 0 to 10 for each of the eight shots. Performance was rated objectively on the basis of where each of the eight golf balls landed (1 = outside all cones, 2 = inside first circle of cones, . . . 5 = hit the net itself).

Chipping Test

Participants were allowed warm-up chips (at least 5 but no more than 10 chips) before eight test chips. Chips were hit to a standard golf cup cut on a flat green at a distance of 45 ft. Three circles of string were placed at 3, 6, and 9 ft radii from the center of the cup. Similar to the procedure for the full-swing test, participants were rated and scored for performance by blind raters. Form ratings were obtained for hold, aim, stance/posture, and swing/finish with a maximum possible score of 15. Subjective performance ratings were made based on chip contact, trajectory, and direction on a scale from 0 to 10. Objective performance scores were recorded for the resting location of each of the eight chip shots (1 = outside all circles, 2 = inside first circle, . . . 5 = holed).

Putting Test

Participants were given warm-up putts (at least 5 but no more than 10 putts) before eight test putts. Putts were hit to a standard golf cup cut on a flat green at a distance of 15 ft. Three circles of string were placed at 1, 2, and 3 ft radii from the center of the cup. Participants were rated and scored for performance by blind raters. Form ratings were obtained for hold, aim, stance and posture, and putt stroke with a maximum possible score of 15. Objective performance scores were recorded for the resting location of each of the eight putts (1 = outside all circles, 2 = inside first circle, . . . 5 = holed).

Questionnaire

Participants were asked questions regarding golfing experience, frequency of practice per month, frequency of play per month, average 18-hole score, perception of golf difficulty, and attraction to the sport of golf. Responses for the latter two questions ranged on a Likert scale from 1 to 5 with larger numbers equaling more "favorable" responses.

Procedures

Students who enrolled in the classes received information about the experiment during the first week and signed a consent form approved by a Human Subjects Institutional Review Board. All students were told that participation was voluntary and that it would have no bearing either on their grade or on the content of the course itself. Skill testing was completed during the first two weeks of class before traditional or learning-centered instruction commenced. After completion of the respective curricula, students completed skill testing over the final two weeks of the semester. Traditional and learning-centered curricula both consisted of an 11-week training program during class. Classes met twice a week for 1.25 hours each.

EXPERIMENT 1 RESULTS

Sixteen students who were not beginning golfers (able to break 100 for 18 holes) were excluded from the analysis.

Four repeated measures MANOVAs were conducted in order to examine the results for putting, chipping, full swing, and attitudes. The instruction main effect reached significance for putting, $F(2, 70) = 3.95$, $p < 0.05$, but was not significant for any other subgroup, $Fs < 1.78$. There were significant time by instruction interactions for putting, $F(2, 70) = 3.42$, $p < 0.05$, and full swing, $F(3, 69) = 2.77$, $p < 0.05$, while no other subgroup showed a significant interaction, $Fs < 0.87$. There were significant time main effects for all subgroups (full swing, $F(3, 69) = 26.98$, $p < 0.01$; chipping, $F(3, 69) = 10.26$, $p < 0.001$; attitudes $F(5, 44) = 4.95$, $p < 0.01$) except putting, $F = 0.89$.

Univariate follow-up tests for the putting subgroup showed a significant time by instruction interaction for putting performance, $F(1, 71) = 5.34$, $p < .05$, but not for putting form, $F(1, 71) = 0.59$. Putting performance improved more from pre- to posttest in the learning-centered group than in the traditional group (see table 30.1). Follow-up tests for full swing showed a significant time by instruction interaction for full-swing subjective performance, $F(1, 71) = 5.94$, $p < 0.05$, and a marginally significant time by instruction interaction for full-swing form, $F(1, 71) = 3.20$, $p < 0.08$. Full-swing subjective performance and form both improved more from pre- to posttest in the learning-centered group than in the traditional group.

EXPERIMENT 2 METHOD

Participants

Sixty-three students enrolled in beginning golf classes at Arizona State University served as participants for this research (females $n = 15$; males $n = 48$; total $n = 63$). Participants were drawn from each of two beginning golf classes taught during the same semester (traditional $n = 33$; learning-centered $n = 30$). Participants had a mean age of 22 years and reported an average of 1.66 years of golf participation. Average estimated score for 18 holes equaled 108.99, ranging from 85 to 180.

Apparatus

Effect sizes from Experiment 1 indicated differences by teaching technique for full-swing form and performance. To further examine these variables and because golf instruction tends to focus on full swing, this component of golf was chosen as the dependent measure of interest for Experiment 2. Participants completed the full-swing test outlined for Experiment 1 during the first and seventh weeks of class. Participants also completed a questionnaire regarding golf attitudes. They were asked questions regarding estimated average 18-hole score, expected skill level, golf difficulty, affinity for golf, likelihood of continuation, instruction interest, instruction complexity, success in learning the material, and satisfaction with rate

Table 30.1   Experiment 1: Form, Performance, and Attitude Descriptive Statistics

| | Traditional | | | | | Learning-centered | | | | |
| | Pre | | Post | | | Pre | | Post | | |
	M	SD	M	SD	ES	M	SD	M	SD	ES
Putting (n = 73)										
Form rating	11.59	1.41	12.09	1.66	0.35	11.22	2.04	11.34	0.98	0.06
Objective performance	2.95	0.49	2.84	0.53	−0.22	2.91	0.61	3.12	0.43	0.34
Chipping (n = 73)										
Form rating	7.21	1.32	8.32	1.48	0.84	7.65	2.03	8.56	1.72	0.45
Objective performance	1.96	0.75	2.04	0.69	0.11	2.40	1.47	2.02	0.61	−0.26
Subjective performance	4.91	1.37	5.04	1.53	0.09	5.62	1.62	5.68	1.34	0.04
Full swing (n = 73)										
Form rating	8.50	1.80	10.20	2.27	0.94	8.48	1.88	11.25	2.00	1.47
Objective performance	1.17	0.32	1.44	0.59	0.84	1.26	0.52	1.56	0.79	0.58
Subjective performance	3.06	1.71	3.82	1.89	0.44	3.02	2.02	4.80	1.95	0.88
Attitudes (n = 50)										
Golf difficulty	3.64	0.70	3.80	1.00	0.23	3.59	0.76	3.40	1.04	−0.25
Golf affinity	4.00	0.76	4.48	0.71	0.63	4.24	0.78	4.28	0.79	0.05

ES represents Glass's delta ($M_1 - M_2$/Pretest *SD*) such that positive values indicate results in the predicted direction.

of progress. Except for the question about average 18-hole score, all questions ranged from 1 to 5 on a Likert scale with larger numbers equaling more "favorable" responses.

Traditional Instruction

Instruction followed the swing model advocated by a popular instructor (Leadbetter 1990). Students were taught grip, stance/posture, finish, aim/alignment, swing plane, and pivot with an emphasis on swing kinematics. Students also received video analysis and instruction during one class session. During each class, students practiced the concepts taught that day, and the instructor would check each individual for adherence to the principles taught. If students had questions regarding any component of the swing, they were answered.

Learning-Centered Instruction

Instruction was simplified to include only grip, stance/posture, aim/alignment, and finish. Similar to the procedure in the traditional class, students practiced the concepts taught each day and the instructor would check each individual for adherence to the principles taught. Students did not receive video analysis, nor were they given additional information regarding the swing even upon request.

Procedures

Students who enrolled in the classes were told of the experiment during the first week, and they signed a consent form approved by a Human Participants Institutional Review board. Skill testing was completed during the first week of class before traditional or learning-centered instruction commenced. After completion of the respective curricula, students completed skill testing during the seventh week of the semester. Traditional and learning-centered courses both consisted of a five-week training program during class. Classes met twice a week for 1.25 hours each.

EXPERIMENT 2 RESULTS

Six participants were excluded from the analyses since they were above beginning skill level (had scored below 100 for 18 holes). Repeated measures MANOVAs were used to examine the data for full swing and attitudes. For full swing, there were significant effects for instruction and time, $Fs(3, 53) = 3.28$ and 24.30, respectively, $ps < 0.05$, but the time by instruction interaction was not significant, $F(3, 53) = 0.93$. Pre- and posttest attitudes exhibited a significant effect for time, $F(5, 51) = 2.04$, $p < 0.09$, but did not exhibit a significant time by instruction interaction, $F(5, 51) = 0.93$.

A third MANOVA was used to examine postexperiment attitudes. There was no significant effect for instruction, $F(4, 52) = 1.91$. Descriptive data are listed in table 30.2.

DISCUSSION

The data indicate that both the traditional and learning-centered models of golf instruction improved performance considerably. Only 6 of 32 possible pre-post measures were not in the predicted direction. The data indicate that the learning-centered model may have a slight advantage over the traditional model of instruction in some respects. In the first experiment, the combined effect of reverse order of lesson progression, greater use of modeling, use of preshot routines, and use of a habituation technique led to more effective putting performance, full-swing subjective performance, and full-swing form. No other interactions reached or approached significance.

Table 30.2   Experiment 2: Form, Performance, and Attitude Descriptives

| | Traditional | | | | | Learning-centered | | | | |
| | Pre | | Post | | | Pre | | Post | | |
	M	SD	M	SD	ES	M	SD	M	SD	ES
Full swing (n = 57)										
Form rating	9.31	1.61	11.37	1.74	1.28	9.55	1.96	11.97	1.50	1.23
Objective performance	1.32	0.41	1.58	0.46	0.63	1.23	0.30	1.49	0.60	0.87
Subjective performance	4.48	1.37	5.32	1.32	0.61	3.25	1.89	4.77	1.90	0.80
Attitudes (n = 57)										
Golf difficulty	2.54	0.66	2.93	0.41	0.59	2.20	0.76	2.53	0.77	0.43
Golf affinity	3.76	0.73	4.17	0.71	0.56	3.77	0.85	4.16	0.50	0.46
Continue	4.60	0.54	4.54	0.76	−0.11	4.87	0.27	4.56	0.59	−1.15
18-hole score	108.43	11.44	111.23	18.17	−0.24	111.57	16.81	108.10	8.29	0.21
Expected skill	2.68	1.22	2.91	0.99	0.19	2.38	0.94	2.43	1.07	0.05
Post-experiment attitudes (n = 57)										
Satisfaction			3.44	0.48				3.77	0.65	*0.58
Success			3.87	0.48				3.87	0.70	*0.00
Complexity			3.52	0.53				3.40	0.57	*−0.22
Interest			3.83	0.65				4.22	0.58	*0.63

ES represents Glass's delta ($M_1 - M_2$/Pretest *SD* or *Pooled *SD*) such that positive values indicate results in the predicted direction.

Experiment 2 did not yield any statistically reliable findings. Effect sizes indicate that instruction type had little impact on full-swing form or performance, but that satisfaction with progress and instruction interest may be greater for learning-centered instruction. It should also be noted that the duration of Experiment 1 was 11 weeks as compared to 5 weeks in Experiment 2. Perhaps longer training periods are necessary to realize differences among the present instructional methods.

Results of these two studies, however, should be examined with caution. There was no true "no instruction" control group, and there were a variety of dependent measures analyzed with separate MANOVAs. Lastly, there is a lack of experimental control inherent in a field design such as that of the present investigation.

It is encouraging, however, that golfers in both instruction conditions showed large improvement over the course of their respective classes. Learning-centered instruction allowed at least equal, if not greater, improvements in performance despite the fact that these students received less direct knowledge concerning the golf swing, chipping, and putting mechanics. Therefore, golf instructors should feel comfortable giving their students smaller chunks of information about the golf swing and more of the instruction components used in the learning-centered classes. Instructors may feel obliged to give students swing information because "that is what they paid for." In reality, however, students desire lower scores instead of knowledge of swing mechanics. Overall, these results indicate that learning-centered instructional techniques hold promise for enhancing the performance and attitudinal response to golf instruction. Programmatic research is required to investigate systematically the effects of theory-based innovations in golf teaching methods.

References

Crews, D.J., and Landers, D.M. (1993). Electroencephalographic measures of attentional patterns prior to the golf putt. *Medicine and Science in Sports and Exercise,* 25, 116-126.

Hardy, L., Mullen, R., and Jones, G. (1996). Knowledge and conscious control of motor actions under stress. *British Journal of Psychology,* 87, 621-636.

Hogan, B. (1957). *Five Lessons: The Modern Fundamentals of Golf.* New York: Barnes.

Hogan, C. (1993). *Learning Golf.* Clifton, CO: Zediker.

Leadbetter, D. (1990). *The Golf Swing.* New York: Stephen Greene Press.

Lewis, B.P., and Linder, D.E. (1997). Thinking about choking? Attentional processes and paradoxical performance. *Personality and Social Psychology Bulletin,* 23, 937-944.

McCullagh, P. (1993). Modeling: Learning, developmental, and social psychological considerations. In R.N. Singer, M. Murphey, and L.K. Tennant (Eds.), *Handbook of Research on Sport Psychology* (pp. 106-126). New York: Macmillan.

National Golf Foundation. (1995). *Attrition/Retention: Test Study Results on Former Golfers, Recent Quitters, Beginning Golfers and Current Golfers.* Jupiter, FL: National Golf Foundation.

Watson, T. (1992). *Getting Back to Basics.* New York: Simon & Schuster.

Winstein, C.J., and Schmidt, R.A. (1990). Reduced frequency of knowledge of results enhances motor skill learning. *Journal of Experimental Psychology: Learning, Memory, and Cognition,* 16, 677-691.

CHAPTER 31

Mathemagenic Behaviours of Golfers: Historical and Contemporary Perspectives

R.H. Coop
University of North Carolina at Chapel Hill

Throughout history, each golfer has had to discover the most efficient and effective manner in which he/she could play the game. These attempts on the part of learners to engage in their own idiosyncratic learning activities are called mathemagenic behaviors by Rothkopf (1970). Educational psychologists have been interested in studying mathemagenic behaviors between students and teachers in the classroom or in tutorial sessions and have identified several variables that make up mathemagenic behaviors. They include learning set, attention, orienting reflex, information processing, cognition, and rehearsal. This paper is an examination of the historical and contemporary approaches utilized by golfers in their mathemagenic attempts to learn how to swing the club and play the game. Each type of learning has its own strengths and weaknesses from an educational psychology perspective, and these are discussed throughout the paper.

Keywords: Mathemagenic behaviors, golf learning, professional golfers.

INTRODUCTION

Golfers have attempted to improve their performance since the times when the Scottish shepherds hit pebbles with their staffs or the Dutch gentry played kolven—depending on your preference as to the historical origin of the game. This paper briefly explores the historical efforts of golfers to improve their skill level and then examines contemporary strategies based on scientific approaches to performance enhancement.

Educational psychologists have used the term "mathemagenic activities" to describe behaviors engaged in by learners that lead to successful learning outcomes. Rothkopf (1970), one of the leading researchers in mathemagenic activities, coined the term, which was derived from the Greek roots *mathemain,* that which is learned, and *gignesthai,* to be born. Rothkopf sees mathemagenic activities as behaviors that give birth to learning. He stresses the importance of the learner's systematic actions in leading to the achievement of learning outcomes. One of the most important aspects of the mathemagenic behavior of the learner is the learner's perception of the stimuli in the learning situation and the extent to which the learner transforms or elaborates on the stimuli. A number of variables studied by educational psychologists fall under the rubric of mathemagenic activities. According to Rothkopf, they include learning set, attention, orienting reflex, information processing, cognition, and rehearsal.

Throughout the history of golf, the mathemagenic behaviors of golfers have expanded and become more sophisticated, most recently with the advent of new scientific methodologies and the development of modern high-technology equipment and tools for studying the golf swing and the golfer's performance. In spite of this constant search for improvement, the relative performance level of the most elite professional golfers in the United States has not improved significantly over the past several years (table 31.1).

Table 31.1   Average Score of PGA Tour Players (1988-1997)

Year	Mean score
1988	71.02
1989	71.08
1990	71.18
1991	71.18
1992	71.23
1993	71.22
1994	71.15
1995	71.17
1996	71.18
1997	71.15

Additionally, Thomas (1994) reports that:

> over the last 25 years the average winning score is improving at 1 stroke per round per 21 years, the 5th place at 1 stroke per round at 17.5 years and the 25th place at 1 stroke per round per 14.5 years. If we compare this rate of improvement to most every other athletic activity over a similar period of time we may ask ourselves the question why is the rate of improvement not greater than it is?

However, before discussing this trend we should examine the history of mathemagenic behaviors of golfers from the beginnings of the game to contemporary times.

TYPES OF MATHEMAGENIC BEHAVIORS

The first learning activities of golfers were quite likely through what psychologists and learning theorists call experiential learning. This type of learning was also called trial-and-error learning (Thorndike 1932). The earliest golfers quite likely experimented with various ways of holding the club, turning their bodies, creating some type of swing plane, and so on, in order to hit the ball in a more efficient manner. Each golfer found what best worked for him or her by this trial-and-error method since there were no acknowledged expert players or teachers in the very earliest years. Even today we see some evidence of the experiential learning method exemplified by players such as Lee Trevino, Ben Hogan, and Moe Norman. Through experiential learning they found their own idiosyncratic method of playing without the aid of formal instruction.

As more and more skilled players began to develop and as competitions began to be held for the elite players, a type of observational learning evolved as an available mathemagenic behavior for golfers. The novice golfer could observe the swings and manner of playing of these expert performers. This learning through observation of other skilled performers is also called vicarious learning, imitative learning, or modeling. Even caddies learned to play the game from observing the best players for whom they caddied. One of the most important variables in modeling or observational learning is the perceived similarity between the model and the observer (Schunk 1987). Bandura (1986) believes that perceived similarity to a model particularly helps those persons who lack confidence in their ability to perform adequately on an unfamiliar task. Thus potential golfers who saw their peers develop a high level of skill at the game were more likely than others to engage in learning behaviors that enhanced their own golf performance. The four aspects that most determine whether an individual perceives similarity between him or herself and the model are age, gender, background, and status (Schunk 1987). Thus it is not surprising that pockets of skilled players grew up in specific geographical areas, particularly in Scotland and other areas of Britain. These potential golfers had the opportunity to learn from observing skilled performances from persons much like themselves with regard to age, gender, and background and were likely to learn through imitation or observational learning.

A second factor influencing modeling is the perceived competence of the model (Hohn 1995). Hohn says, "Models who demonstrate behaviors that successfully deal with the environment attract more attention than models who do not display such competence" (p. 163). Thus, golfers are more likely to model Jack Nicklaus, Tiger Woods, or Nick Faldo than to model less skilled players. Young Tom Morris was very fortunate to have had the opportunity to observe his father Old Tom as a model player throughout his all-too-brief life.

The development of professional teachers was a major advance for the mathemagenic behaviors of golfers. As club professionals added the task of teaching to their duties, the opportunity to learn golf in a more systematic manner became available to larger numbers of golfers. You didn't have to be fortunate enough to have Old Tom Morris as your father and model. Many of these early professional teachers were good players in their own right, but they also began to develop their own concepts of the golf swing and of how to play the game. It is quite likely that many of these early instructors taught their students the golf swing that best suited their own game. However, even with the state of the art instruction provided by the early professional teachers, learners still engaged in their own mathemagenic behaviors—just as two golfers today, receiving the same instruction from the same teacher, hear entirely different lessons based on their own unique learning styles and predispositions to learn.

The invention of photography provided golfers with still another opportunity to engage in their own mathemagenic behaviors. Now golfers could self-teach by observing closely the various positions of the swing in sequential photographs of the expert player. The highly motivated golfer who did not have the opportunity to receive hands-on instruction from the professional teachers could learn to mimic the photos of the best players of the day. Educational psychologists consider learning from photographs a special form of observational learning. This opportunity to learn from photographs is still used today, as witnessed by the many sequence photography sections in the golf magazines of the world.

It is also interesting to note that both Greg Norman and Ian Baker-Finch used Jack Nicklaus's book, *Golf My Way,* to learn their particular swings. Baker-Finch and his father cut out the sequence photography from the book and spread the pictures out on the practice ground, anchoring the pictures to the ground by sticking tees into them, and then modeled their swings on the pictures of Nicklaus (personal communication). The mathemagenic nature of the learning process is further demonstrated by the fact that the swings of Norman and Baker-Finch were quite different even though the same photos were used as the source of learning.

The invention of the flip-page books in the 1920s gave movement to the still photography, much as film and videotape do today, and allowed a further elaboration on mathemagenic behaviors by golfers. The sense of the swing moving as opposed to a sequence of still photographs was a special learning aid to many golfers.

With the advent of high-speed photography, newer and better video equipment, scientific studies of the golf swing such as *The Search for the Perfect Swing* (Cochran and Stobbs 1968), biomechanical analysis of the golf swing, computer simulations, development of high-tech equipment, sport psychologists who specialize in performance enhancement of golfers, and professional teachers who are as well known as most professional players, current-day golfers have a wide variety of choices on which to base their mathemagenic behaviors.

LIMITATIONS OF MATHEMAGENIC TECHNIQUES

As mentioned previously, today's golfers seem to be able to make better swings, at least on the practice grounds, than ever before. Yet their scores do not seem to be improving in any statistically significant fashion. The reasons for this disparity are numerous. One I think particularly germane for this congress is that golf science today has become much more commercialized than even in the days of the research studies described in *The Search for the Perfect Swing*. Currently, for-profit companies are doing much of the "scientific research" in golf. Unlike what occurs in the "true scientific community," the results of these studies, whether they be on space-age equipment or biomechanical analyses of the golf swing, are not freely disseminated to other scientists for further replication and verification. Rather they are used for financial gain for the companies that funded the research and are therefore specifically withheld from other researchers until the products can be marketed to the golf consumer. There are some exceptions to this principle, however. In the last two decades there has been a trend toward scientific and systematic research on golf performance primarily in the university settings. See, for example Hardy et al. (1996), Kingston and Hardy (1997), Smith et al. (1997), Miller et al. (1992), Asbell (1989), Meacci and Price (1985), Johnson et al. (1984), Masters (1992), and Crews and Landers (1993). However, the results of these studies often don't reach the teaching professional who is too busy on the lesson tee to find the time to read these academic journals.

Additionally, each type of mathemagenic behavior has its own difficulties or downsides. For example, in observational mathemagenic learning or modeling, the learner frequently tries to attend to several variables in the model's swing simultaneously and can become confused and frustrated without guided instruction. A second difficulty with the use of only observational learning is the lack of perceived similarity between the model and the learner. For example, the Sybervision program of instruction that has been so popular in the United States for the past decade used Al Geiberger as the model for the male golfer. Geiberger is 6 feet 3 inches and weighed approximately 165 pounds when the video of his swing was made. Very few golfers can relate to a body type that is this ectomorphic.

Experiential learning also has some practical limitations. Golfers who use this form of mathemagenic learning, which requires them to "dig it out of the dirt," as Hogan suggested, must be highly motivated individuals. Experiential learning is by its nature a trial-and-error process and therefore very inefficient. Without an instructor to guide and encourage their efforts, experiential learners frequently give up before the task is accomplished. Few learners have the tenacity of Hogan, Trevino, or Moe Norman.

The focus of this paper is on the educational psychologists' perspective of learning golf, and space limitations preclude a discussion of the important role played by motor learning theorists in mathemagenic behaviors. For an overview of generalized motor concept, dynamic systems theory, schema theory, and ecological theories of perception and action, the reader is referred to *A Multilevel Approach to the Study of Motor Control and Learning* by Rose (1997).

While I am generally very optimistic about computer-generated models of the golf swing based on biomechanical analyses, my experience in working with professional and amateur players who use them as a basis for their mathemagenic behaviors indicates that there are also some practical difficulties in this type of learning. The first difficulty lies in the fact that some teachers who use the "model" swings forget that the computer models and the biomechanical analyses are heuristics for teaching rather than a perfect algorithm. They focus on swing positions so much that the golfer becomes overly mechanical, to the extent that the proverbial paralysis by analysis sets in. This obviously is more a misuse of technology than a fault inherent in the technology per se. However, from my observations it is consistent enough to raise some concern. For example, a young PGA Tour player I recently worked with had just come from a lesson with a teacher who was using a model of the golf swing generated from a biomechanical analysis of the best tour players. This teacher had identified 12 major positions of the best swing with 6 subpositions for each of the 12 major positions. The tour player was trying to ingrain all 72 of these positions by standing in front of his mirror each evening and "hitting" each position as he made his full swings. He lost his tour card and has since abandoned this approach to learning.

The second difficulty with the computer models/biomechanical analyses is that they represent a compilation of the swings of many highly skilled golfers. The statistical techniques most often used to analyze these swings try to take as much variance out of the swings as it is reasonably feasible to do, both statistically and practically speaking. Therefore a "model swing" evolves that may not be exactly the swing of any one of the elite golfers but most closely represents the swing common-alities of all the golfers used in the study in a collective fashion. Since no one elite player swings exactly like the model, there may be no reason for any golfer to swing exactly in this manner. Yet in the golf schools and on teaching tees where the model swing is used, the major objective seems to be to get the student to swing as closely to the model as possible. Since most biomechanical analyses are done on highly skilled golfers, the sample is very skewed toward young, highly athletic, well-conditioned, and lithe individuals who have enough fast-twitch muscle fibers to generate tremendous clubhead speed. This model is then applied to older, weaker, less athletic, more endomorphic students who don't fit the model very well but who can afford to attend golf schools. Perhaps the saving grace in this instructional technique is the principle of getting the student's swing "as close to the model as possible."

Lastly, we examine the difficulties of the mathemagenic behavior of learners when taught by professional teachers. Many golfers put themselves into the hands of the instructor and assume a merely passive role in the learning process. Even some elite tour players fall into this mind-set. I once had a tour player come directly from a two-day session with his swing teacher. During these two days the instructor had identified and communicated to the player seven individual changes that needed to be made in his setup and swing. The player was committed to making all seven of these changes before his next tournament, which was six days away. I suggested to him rather firmly that it was going to be very difficult to process seven variables during each swing, but he was convinced that his teacher would not have told him all seven unless he really needed to change them. We negotiated this commitment for the two days we spent together and finally found three of the seven variables that could be handled in the player's setup to the ball at address. We found that two more variables could be handled with two separate practice or rehearsal swings before the shot, and the remaining two variables were handled with one backswing thought and one down-swing thought during the swing. The player was very pleased that he was still dealing with all seven variables but still had a relatively (for him) clear mind during the swing. He practiced this apportioning of attention to variables for four days and actually won his next tournament. I have always been curious as to how well he would have played had he gone straight from his swing teacher's lesson tee to his next competition.

Increasingly, professional players in America are taking a more active role in their instruction. Each year, more and more of the tour players are controlling which parts of their swings are off-limits to change when they enlist the services of a new swing teacher. They want to be a partner with the swing teacher in engaging in their mathemagenic activities. The extreme end of this control-of-learning continuum is coming from the newest members of the PGA Tour. Each year for the past eight years I have been invited by the PGA Tour to lecture to the new players who have qualified to receive their tour playing privileges for the coming year. I begin the lecture by asking them if they played collegiate golf, if they have a swing teacher with whom they work regularly, and if they have a mental game coach or sport psychologist with whom they work. The most surprising trend I have seen for the last four years is that fewer and fewer of the new tour players have a regular swing teacher; several players are adamant that they will not work with one because they fear they will become too mechanical or lose control over their own swing. Obviously, these observations are made on a rather small sample of elite players and may be only a four-year blip on the screen. However, if this is a true pattern, it may bring us right back to the shepherds hitting their pebbles and engaging in experiential learning with regard to their mathemagenic behaviors.

THE SEARCH FOR THE PERFECT PLAYER

So, where do we go from here with regard to helping golfers learn to play this game more efficiently and enjoy it to a greater extent? Can we develop teaching methods that will reduce the frustrations of beginning golfers and improve the performance of golfers at all levels of skill? I would propose that we use this World Scientific Congress of Golf as a springboard for developing *The Search for the Perfect Player.* In my view, this search can best be accomplished by cluster research. The research to develop the perfect player needs to be done by clusters of scientists working together and sharing their collective information regarding the maximum performance factors related to playing the game of golf, not just making perfect golf swings. I could envision a cluster of researchers, including a biomechanist, a sport psychologist, an expert teacher, an exercise physiologist, and a sport optometrist, working together on developing the playing skills of a sample of golfers at all ability levels. Actually, I have already taken part in a smaller-scale version of this cluster research paradigm, but it was with only one tour professional who financed the entire operation of a sport psychologist, an equipment expert, an exercise physiologist, a biomechanist, an expert teacher, and a nutritionist. In working with these experts, I learned a tremendous amount regarding the golfer as a total person and performer. Since the information was privately financed to help the performance of this golfer only, it became proprietary and thus not directly accessible to the public. Also, it was a cluster that worked well for this one particular elite player. Would this approach generalize to other golfers at differing skill levels? Could we bring this cluster approach to bear on improving the golf performance of special populations such as senior golfers, physically challenged golfers, women golfers, and junior golfers? Could we find a cost-effective way of transferring our findings to provide golf instruction to inner city youth who are economically disadvantaged? According to the National Golf Foundation, in the United States less than 2% of children ages 12-17 are exposed to golf each year and only 15% come from families earning less than $30,000 annually. Only 3% of American golfers are black and 2% are Hispanic. The average age of a United States beginner is nearly 30 years.

Could we do, on a much broader scale with a highly diverse population of golfers, what a few tour players have done in enhancing their own performance to the maximum? Much of the answer to this question lies in economics. It would not be inexpensive to fund the research and intercommunication of these clusters of researchers. However, there are some embryonic efforts by United States corporations and golf associations toward financing golf programs. Ford Motor Company and Shell Oil Company have supported youth golf programs financially. The PGA Tour, the PGA of America, the LPGA, and USGA, Augusta National Golf Club, and the Tiger Woods Foundation are supporting programs to get young people involved in golf. They have agreed to provide up to $6 million annually to this effort. Initial involvement alone, however, will not guarantee continued participation in golf by the young people or any other population group for that matter. We must find a way to do more systematic scientific research on learning and playing the game. We then must find ways of scientifically verifying and replicating this knowledge and systematically disseminating it to golfers across the world. The founding of the World Scientific Congress of Golf is a major and laudable first step in these endeavors, but we must continue to find ways in which scientists from diverse fields of expertise can work together and share knowledge that is not proprietary to the funding agency supporting the research. If we could achieve this objective, the mathemagenic behaviors of all golfers would be enhanced and the ultimate winner would be the game of golf.

References

Asbell, A. (1989). Golf Instruction: Application of Schmidt's Generalized Motor Program. *Journal of Physical Education, Recreation and Dance,* 60: 26-30.

Bandura, A. (1986). *Social Foundation of Thought and Action: A Social Cognitive Theory.* Englewood Cliffs, NJ: Prentice Hall.

Cochran, A., and Stobbs, J. (1968). *The Search for the Perfect Swing.* Philadelphia: Lippincott.

Crews, D.J., and Landers, D.M. (1993). Electroencephalographic Measures of Attentional Patterns Prior to the Golf Putt. *Medicine and Science in Sports and Exercise,* 25: 1, 116-126.

Hardy, L., Mullen, R., and Jones, G. (1996). Knowledge and Conscious Control of Motor Actions Under Stress. *British Journal of Psychology,* 87(4): 621-636.

Hohn, R.L. (1995). *Classroom Learning and Teaching,* p. 163. White Plains, NY: Longman.

Kingston, K., and Hardy, L. (1997). Effects of Different Types of Goals on Processes That Support Performance. *Sport Psychologist,* 11(3): 277-293.

Masters, R.S.W. (1992). Knowledge, Knerves and Know How: The Role of Explicit Versus Implicit Knowledge in the Breakdown of a Complex Motor Skill Under Pressure. *British Journal of Psychology,* 83: 343-358.

Meacci, W., and Price, E. (1985). Acquisition and Retention of Golf Putting Skill Through the Relaxation, Visualization and Body Rehearsal Intervention. *Research Quarterly for Exercise and Sport,* 56: 176-179.

Miller, G., Cross, T., and Barnhart, T. (1992). Golf Instruction: Learning From the Flight of the Golf Ball. *Journal of Physical Education, Recreation and Dance,* 63: 17-20.

Rose, D.J. (1997). *A Multilevel Approach to the Study of Motor Control and Learning.* Boston: Allyn and Bacon.

Rothkopf, E.Z. (1970). The Concept of Mathemagenic Activities. *Review of Educational Research,* 40(3): 325-336.

Schunk, D.H. (1987). Peer Models and Children's Behavioral Change. *Review of Educational Research,* 57(2): 149-174.

Smith, P., Peter, J.K., Taylor, S.J., and Withers, K. (1997). Applying Bandwidth Feedback Scheduling to a Golf Shot. *Research Quarterly for Exercise and Sport,* 68: 215-221.

Thomas, F.W. (1994). The State of the Game, Equipment and Science. In *Science and Golf II: Proceedings of the World Scientific Congress of Golf,* ed. A.J. Cochran and M.R. Farrally. London: Spon.

Thorndike, E.L. (1932). *The Fundamentals of Learning.* New York: Columbia University, Teachers College.

CHAPTER 32

Teaching and Sustaining the Child Player

Patricia M. Donnelly, PhD
Educational Sport Psychologist, Weston, Connecticut

Although Western society views childhood as a separate phase of development, in the game of golf, children are often treated as if they were adults. The success of Tiger Woods has exacerbated this phenomenon. To master golf one must master oneself, including one's self-esteem, self-discipline, and motivation. For a golf teacher to integrate this into his or her teaching, a knowledge of the psychological development of children is essential. The teacher can then capitalize on the child's stage of development and not run the risk of employing harmful or futile methods.

Keywords: Developmental psychology, learning, teaching, children.

INTRODUCTION

Contemporary Western society regards childhood as an independent and unique phase of development. Children are generally protected from the responsibilities of adulthood. In golf instruction, however, these distinctions are often absent. Due to the zealousness of the teacher, be it a parent, friend, or golf professional, children are often taught as if they were little adults. Especially since the meteoric rise of Tiger Woods, the teaching of golf to very young children has become exceedingly popular. The emphasis should not be upon teaching each child as an adult superstar. With all the hype and publicity about the superstars, it is easy to forget that out of 40 million golfers fewer than 300 earn more than $250,000 per year as tour professionals. Perhaps more important than the story of Tiger Woods is that of Beverly Klass. Like Tiger's, Beverly's father believed his very young child had physical talent, and when she was 3-1/2 he started teaching her golf (see figure 32.1). At age 8 she won the National Pee Wee Championship by 65 shots, and at age 10, in 1967, she was competing on the LPGA Tour (at that time the LPGA did not have a minimum age requirement). She then went through a troubled adolescence,

Courtesy of *Golf Digest*

Figure 32.1   Beverly Klass was encouraged to play golf at a tender age and met with disastrous results.

including being thrown out of her home and being placed for a period of time in a mental institution. At age 20 she returned briefly to the LPGA, but never achieved stardom (Netland 1977). The emphasis in teaching golf should not be to create a future superstar at all costs, but to teach so that the individual can grow in self-esteem and skill, and, most importantly, enjoy the game for a lifetime.

It was not until the Renaissance that children ceased being regarded as part of the adult world of work and play. John Locke's (1634-1704) words in *Some Thoughts Concerning Education* (1693) apply well to the teaching of golf to children today: "If the mind be curbed and humbled too much in children, if their spirits be abused and broken by too strict a hand over them, they will lose all vigour and industry and are in a worse state. . . ." Likewise, Jean-Jacques Rousseau (1712-1778) in *Emile* stated, "Make a preparation in advance for the exercise of his liberty and the use of his strength by allowing his body to have its natural habits, by putting him in a condition to be always master of himself." Rousseau continues, "Do not give your scholar any sort of verbal lesson, for he is to be taught only by experience." These notions have been theorized in modern psychology and can benefit the productive teaching of golf. It is this dynamic, developmental understanding that can be advantageously applied to the teaching of golf.

To master golf one must also master oneself. This includes achieving high levels of self-esteem, self-discipline, and motivation. For the golf teacher to facilitate this, he or she must be aware of the child's psychological development. The teacher can then capitalize on the child's stage of development and not run the risk of employing harmful or futile methods.

EARLY CHILDHOOD: 3 TO 6 YEARS OF AGE

Jean Piaget's stature in developmental psychology is probably unequaled. Although many critics debate the actual timing and content of his prescribed stages, it is important to remember that his theory presents an approximation explaining the evolution of one's cognitive capabilities and functions. He discovered the existence of a developmental sequence of learning in children. He claimed that a child must be intrinsically motivated. It is essential, he maintained, that the child achieve satisfaction from his or her own performance (Lefrancois 1988).

Children of approximately 3 to 6 years of age enjoy moving their bodies in ways that are fun. The developmentally appropriate teaching of golf at this age includes having children swing a golf club or other object in unconventional ways—horizontally around the body or straight up and down—or balancing it on a finger (see figures 32.2 and 32.3). This is similar to the Suzuki method of learning music, in which the young child first becomes acquainted with the instrument through activities such as moving a violin bow in various directions, touching different objects with the bow, and balancing the bow on a finger. Sometimes rudimentary instruments are made by the children (Suzuki 1983). Similarly, a golf teacher could encourage children to find or make their own golf clubs using sticks or broomsticks. This would add a multisensory component, which is important at this age. It would also add what Piaget referred to as animism, attributing lifelike qualities to inanimate objects, for example, pretending the club is a snake.

Teachers could encourage children to make up games using real or self-fashioned golf clubs. Touching five green objects with one's club, for example, would provide a multisensory, concrete game. Additionally, if the teacher or children incorporated fantasy play, this would add an element of imagination that is key to this stage of development (Miller 1985). Of particular note is that these early games do not include hitting or even using a golf ball (see figure 32.4). When a ball is introduced, it should be large, perhaps first a soccer ball and then a tennis ball. These types of balls will provide the child with more successes, enjoyment, and motivation (see figure 32.5). During this approximate bracket of 3 to 6 years of age the child's self-concept is physical and concrete. Inner qualities are not part of the child's self-concept (Damon and Hart 1982). Thinking is dominated by visual impressions.

Courtesy of *Golf Digest*

Figure 32.2   Young golfers need not, should not swing solely golf clubs.

Concrete explanations, through which children can see and imitate, are best. This points to the futility of attempting to teach complex rules of golf at this age and of explaining the mechanics or analysis of the golf swing.

The younger end of the 3- to 6-year stage is characterized by an extremely short attention span. Any activity should be stopped before the child's attention ends (Miller 1985).

The ages between 3 and 6 are egocentric. During this period, children are typically capable of understanding only their own point of view. If a child believes that he or she is entitled to another try at hitting the ball without counting a missed hit as a stroke, the child will not understand that others do not share this belief. Whatever children this age do they believe is right (Selman 1976). Their egocentricity allows them to believe that they are the "greatest." They are mostly oblivious to how they compare to their peers (Frey and Ruble 1985). The notion of being a good sport is not grasped at this stage (Allen and Marotz 1994).

Courtesy of *Golf Digest*

Figure 32.3   Unconventional equipment is one way to keep golf fun for children.

EARLY SCHOOL YEARS: 6 TO 8 YEARS OF AGE

This age group is characterized by a need to gain mastery. The desire for competence is fueled by a period of industriousness. It is particularly important to provide a child of this age with activities that can be mastered, for example, short putts and hitting an oversized ball with a high-lofted club (see figure 32.6). Because mastery is inherently related to self-esteem, it is critical that competition, which is not understood at this age, not be included (Miller 1985). It is important that the teacher emphasize personal goals and achievements as opposed to comparing one child to

Courtesy of Golf Digest

Figure 32.4   At the beginning stage, a ball is not necessary. Far better is a fantasy-packed object.

Courtesy of Golf Digest

Figure 32.5   When a ball is first introduced, large balls, such as soccer and tennis balls, will provide more success.

Courtesy of Golf Digest

Figure 32.6   It is critical to provide activities that can be mastered.

another (Allen and Marotz 1994). A positive way to incorporate mastery and self-esteem with the incipient sense of competition is through having children keep their own records, in essence competing with themselves.

This is an ideal stage at which to begin setting personal records and doing things by oneself. The emphasis should be on personal skill development (Miller 1985). Overall, individual play should be emphasized as compared to group or team play. Having children record how far they have hit various clubs is appropriate at this stage. Using a visual reference (the red flag on the practice range, etc.) would eliminate the inherent competition of recording in yards or meters.

Children now began to compare themselves with their peers. Children who come out on the short end of social comparisons suffer from deflated self-esteem (Dweck and Elliott 1983). One's ability in ball striking, for example, could be enhanced or diminished depending upon whom one was comparing oneself to. Constantly comparing one's abilities with those of an accomplished player will most likely be counterproductive. Grouping those with similar abilities is most effective. Rules should be kept to a minimum. Basic etiquette and fundamental scoring could be introduced.

At this stage, when a typical motor achievement is swinging a bat, it is essential for teachers to be aware that children are easily disappointed by self-perceived failure. They cannot accept their imperfections. Most cannot tolerate having their performance corrected (Allen and Marotz 1994). With these developmental checkpoints in mind, the successful teacher will reinforce what the child is doing right and model the correct way when something has been done wrong.

At any stage, and valuable throughout one's development, is observational learning. One learns by imitating. Learning does not require that one is reinforced for imitating. One does, however, learn whether the model's behavior has positive or negative consequences, and uses that information accordingly. These capacities mature throughout childhood (Bandura 1986).

During this stage children are moving constantly even when they attempt to be still. Vigorous physical activity is greatly enjoyed (Allen and Marotz 1994). Running the length of a par 3, for example, will keep children from getting bored and restless. These elements built into a golf lesson will provide a welcome relief from being talked at and concentrating.

Losing a game will most likely result in sulking, crying, or refusing to play. Instead of attempting the real game of golf, teachers could encourage children to make up games and rules of their own. This method fits well with the typical characteristics of this age group, which include a lack of tolerance for being told what to do but an eagerness to work with other children toward a specific goal (Allen and Marotz 1994).

LATE CHILDHOOD: 8 TO 10 YEARS OF AGE

This stage is referred to as concrete operational (Piaget 1952). Teaching and instruction should still use concrete examples. A greater understanding of cause and effect is mastered, and one begins to think logically. Abstract thinking begins, but should not be considered as mastered until the teenage years.

Children are now just beginning to understand another's point of view (Selman 1976). Children's sense of competition is not fully developed. They are more concerned with making friends through sport than with competing. Teams and leagues are therefore inappropriate at this age level.

At this point the child can start to predict others' reactions to his or her behaviors (Selman 1976). The teacher is looked up to at this stage. The teacher's praise and attention are extremely important. Overt and subtle messages need to be carefully given. Positive role models will enhance positive observational learning.

PRE-ADOLESCENCE: 10 TO 12 YEARS OF AGE

Much instruction at this age, not only in golf, is a repetition of what is taught to younger children or is a "watered-down version" of adult instruction. Yet this approximate age group responds to unique instruction.

The child is still thinking concretely at this stage, and teaching should not yet employ the abstract. This is a good time to use right-brain processes that stress the nonverbal and concrete (Quina 1989).

Peer interaction takes on new importance during this stage (Crockett, Losoff, and Peterson 1984). Self-esteem also looms with new magnitude. Learners need an accelerating sense of self-esteem and continual successes to stay motivated (Blyth and Traeger 1983). Yet the social-comparison evaluation of self is being replaced by more autonomous criteria. During this stage of high peer interaction, limited team play could be introduced. The goal should be to play for fun, however, not to engage in serious competition.

Children also respond well to opportunities to be autonomous and to accept responsibility. It is now appropriate for the child to come up with a practice routine and a practice schedule that could be fine-tuned by the golf professional. The child should also become more responsible for keeping to a practice schedule (Sigelman and Shaffer 1991).

If a high-achievement need exists coupled with a fear of failure, cheating is likely to occur. A study of sixth-grade boys (Hill and Kochendorfer 1969) who participated in a shooting gallery game showed that 57 percent of the boys who knew the others' scores cheated by changing their scores. Of the boys who did not know the others' scores, only 33 percent cheated. When the situation was manipulated such that the boys knew the others' scores and realized it was unlikely their cheating would be discovered, the level of cheating rose to 66 percent.

Golf, universally regarded as a game of honor, is a vehicle for teaching values and moral standards. Rules and rudimentary strategies are also appropriate at this age level.

ADOLESCENCE: 13 TO 17 YEARS OF AGE

Competition is now understood. Adultlike sport structures befit this age group. It is also the time when one begins to think abstractly and reflectively. (It is essential to remember that these thought processes are just beginning. Many individuals will feel more comfortable in the concrete as described above.) This is the stage Piaget referred to as the formal operational stage in which the learner's cognitive development embraces comprehension of concepts and is able to analyze to arrive at conclusions. It is now that the student's golf swing can be analyzed by the golf professional. Course strategy and mental approaches should now be taught.

A positive self-concept at this stage is critical (Dorman 1983). Adults need to make certain that the adolescent's sense of self-worth is not equated with winning. After a competition, for example, it is far better to ask "How did you play?" than to inquire "Did you win?" Personal performance goals need to be emphasized over the outcome goals of the individual and/or the team. Original and creative strategy on the course should be encouraged and lauded when attempted.

From about 13 to 17 years of age the individual is manifesting personal identity while appreciating views of the larger society (Sigelman and Shaffer 1991). Rules are now appropriate, and competitive play is developmentally apropos. Good sportsmanship needs to be taught and modeled and to be displayed by the young player.

SUSTAINING MOTIVATION

Assuming the developmental correctness of learning golf, the question then arises: how to sustain the junior player's motivation and enjoyment of the game?

Scanlon, Stein, and Ravizza (1989), building on previous studies of intrinsic and achievement-related sources, concluded that enjoyment of a sport is influenced by achievement and non-achievement factors, both of which can be either extrinsic or intrinsic. The intrinsic achievement factors include feelings of competence and mastery. The teacher must strive for every student to experience success. The extrinsic achievement sources include feedback from others, such as social status. Socializing with others involved in one's sport after practice or competition, sharing accomplishments, or commiserating over defeats are positive motivating factors. The non-achievement intrinsic factors inherent in performing the sport encompass movement sensations and the enjoyment of competition. The extrinsic non-achievement causes include sources not related to the performance of the sport, such as social interactions. These reveal the richness of participating in sport and stress that all sport performance is not about achievement. Clearly, enjoyment leads to maintaining motivation. Teachers need to include the motivating power of joy (Scanlon and Simons 1992).

A growing body of research suggests that motivation is more likely to occur when a mastery goal orientation exists. This in turn occurs where there is an emphasis on effort and learning. It is not merely stressing effort, however, that can lead to diminished self-esteem if success does not follow the effort. The mastery goal orientation (also referred to as learning goals, task involvement or accomplishment) views effort in a context of personal goals, personal bests, and personal pleasure (Ames and Archer 1988; Dweck 1986; Dweck and Leggett 1988).

The teachers of golf give children myriad messages that reveal their values. Once children enter the world of organized golf teams and associations, their outcomes are critical and are most valued by influential adults. Too often, mean-spirited competitiveness is stressed. The motivating purpose often becomes that of playing better than someone else. True self-esteem, however, does not result from winning competitions, but rather from playing to one's own satisfaction.

How the children are grouped reveals the coach's attitude and the values imparted. Grouping solely by ability, typical of high school golf teams, sets up a hierarchy in which the better players are considered more valuable. This leads to an enhanced self-image on the part of the lower-scoring players and a deleterious self-image on the part of the higher-scoring players, especially when the better players are given more privileges such as more playing time, more attention from the coach on and off the course, and more praise. The practice of "scrambling" the groups and whom the coach works with can offset this situation (Cicatelli and Gaddie 1992).

The method of recognition is critical. An off-hand comment can have as powerful an effect as a trophy. Praise only for winning has a harmful effect on those who have not won. Additionally, the child who has won is robbed of the all-important intrinsic reward of having played well. Likewise, the team that is playing primarily for an extrinsic reward of a coveted trophy or title is deprived of the intrinsic reward that will be a more lasting motivator (Csikszentmihalyi 1976; Deci 1975). Conversely, the positive comment for achieving one's personal goals will enhance a struggling player's self-esteem. An occasional statement, however, will not accomplish this.

The emphasis on personal goals must heavily outweigh that on outcome goals, that is, wins versus losses. The reaction to a loss or to not attaining one's personal performance goals is also critical. Berating children for not having done their best can antithetically affect their motivation. Additionally, an inherent sense of optimism that is essential to bring to competition is sabotaged. On the other hand, if after a loss the coach focuses on the things done well, and reframes the loss into a challenge toward which the individual's personal goals can be directed, motivation is far more likely to occur.

The importance of making golf fun cannot be overstated (Harter 1981). Many of the world's best players figured this out early on. Chi Chi Rodriquez, for example, as a 5-year-old growing up in Puerto Rico, made his own golf club out of the branch of a guava tree and attached a tin can to the end of it. He made his golf balls out of aluminum foil. Likewise, Sam Snead, growing up in the hills of Virginia, learned to whittle from his older brother Homer. He made golf clubs from hickory branches and even fixed them midround with rocks and nails. As a child, Seve Ballesteros hit balls up and down the beach in Pedrena, Spain, using a hand-me-down 3 iron. Lee Trevino added an element of fun to the competitive stage. He would bet golfers at a driving range in Texas that he could out-hit them. They could use their drivers but Trevino would use an oversized Dr. Pepper bottle. Interestingly, these four players are considered the best shot-makers in the game. All possess the ability to play by feel.

In this highly technological age of sophisticated equipment and complex analysis, it is critical to find the fun, the simplicity, the joy of golf. In this manner, young players will enjoy the game for a lifetime.

References

Allen, K.E., and Marotz, L.R. 1994. *Developmental profiles of pre-birth through eight,* 2nd ed. Albany, NY: Delmar.

Ames, C., and Archer, J. 1988. Achievement goals in the classroom: Students' learning strategies and motivation processes. *Journal of Educational Psychology,* 80: 260-267.

Bandura, A. 1986. *Social foundations of thought and action. A social cognitive theory.* Englewood Cliffs, NJ: Prentice Hall.

Blyth, D.A., and Traeger, C.M. 1983. The self-concept and self-esteem of early adolescents. *Theory into Practice,* 22: 91-97.

Cicatelli, P.A., and Gaddie, C. 1992. An intramural program that fits middle school. *Middle School Journal,* 24(2): 54-55.

Crockett, L., Losoff, M., and Peterson, A. 1984. Perceptions of the peer group and friendship in early adolescence. *Journal of Early Adolescence,* 4: 155-181.

Csikszentmihalyi, M. 1976. *Beyond boredom and anxiety.* San Francisco: Jossey-Bass.

Damon, W., and Hart, D. 1982. The development of self-understanding from infancy through adolescence. *Child Development,* 53: 841-864.

Deci, E.L. 1975. *Intrinsic motivation.* New York: Plenum Press.

Dorman, G. 1983. Making schools for young adolescents work. *Educational Horizons,* 61: 175-182.

Dweck, C.S. 1986. Motivational processes affecting learning. *American Psychologist,* 41: 1040-1048.

Dweck, C.S., and Elliott, E.S. 1983. Achievement motivation. In *Handbook of child psychology,* 4th ed., vol. 4, *Socialization, personality, and social development,* ed. E.M. Hetherington, 643-691. New York: Wiley.

Dweck, C.S., and Leggett, E.L. 1988. A social-cognitive approach to motivation and personality. *Psychological Review,* 95: 256-273.

Frey, K.S., and Ruble, D.N. 1985. What children say when the teacher is not around: Conflicting goals in social comparison and performance assessment in the classroom. *Journal of Personality and Social Psychology,* 48: 550-562.

Harter. 1981. The development of competence motivation in the mastery of cognitive and physical skills: Is there a place for joy? In *Psychology of motor behavior and sport-i*980, ed. G.C. Roberts and D.M. Landers, 3-29. Champaign, IL: Human Kinetics.

Hill, J.P., and Kochendorfer, R.A. 1969. Knowledge of peer success and risk of detection as determinants of cheating. *Developmental Psychology,* 1: 231-238.

Lefrancois, G.R. 1988. *Psychology for teaching,* 6th ed. Belmont, CA: Wadsworth.

Miller, K. 1985. *Ages and stages: Developmental descriptions and activities.* MA: Telshare.

Netland, D. 1977. The bizarre story of Beverly Klass. *Golf Digest,* July: 57-61.

Piaget, J. 1952. *The origins of intelligence in children.* New York: International Universities Press.

Quina, J. 1989. *Effective secondary teaching: Going beyond the bell curve.* New York: Harper & Row.

Scanlon, T.K., and Simons, J.P. 1992. The construct of sport enjoyment. In *Motivation in sport and exercise,* ed. G.C. Roberts, 199-216. Champaign, IL: Human Kinetics.

Scanlon, T.K., Stein, G.L., and Ravizza, K. 1989. An in-depth study of former elite figure skaters: 2. Sources of enjoyment. *Journal of Sport and Exercise Psychology,* 11: 65-83.

Selman, R.L. 1976. Social-cognitive understanding: A guide to educational and clinical experience. In *Moral development and behavior: Theory, research and social issues,* ed. T. Lickona. New York: Holt, Rinehart & Winston.

Sigelman, C.K., and Shaffer, D.R. 1991. *Life-span development.* Pacific Grove, CA: Brooks/Cole.

Suzuki, S. 1983. *Nurtured by love. The classic approach to talent education.* 2nd ed. Secaucus, NJ: Warner Bros.

CHAPTER 33

Psychological and Psychomotor Approach to the Development of Junior Golfers

W.H. Ellis
McGill University (retired), Montreal, Quebec, Canada

R. Filyer
Department of Psychology, Wilfrid Laurier University, Waterloo, Ontario, Canada

D. Wilson
Department of Psychology, Wilfrid Laurier University, Waterloo, Ontario, Canada

Perceptions of the importance of psychological and psychomotor skills are examined for a sample of junior golfers in Canada, with the view to using the findings for further development of their golfing skills. Although most emphasis is currently being placed on the mechanical aspects of the game, prior research indicates that psychological skills (such as mental preparation) and psychomotor skills (such as automaticity) are essential to the degree of proficiency of adult golfers. The current study provides a preliminary look at junior golfers' perceptions of the relative importance of these elements. The study also examines the relationship between these perceptions and golf prowess. The relevance of these findings in effecting the improved performance of junior golfers is discussed.

Keywords: Junior golfers, psychological skills, psychomotor skills, golf.

INTRODUCTION

There has been a tremendous amount of interest, growth, and development in the area of junior golf not only in North America but in many parts of the world. In Canada alone, the number of junior golfers, which by definition covers the ages up to 20, was estimated to be somewhat in excess of 356,000 in 1996 according to a study done by the Royal Canadian Golf Association. The number of facilities and junior golf camps has also grown at a rapid pace, offering excellent training. This training, however, mainly concentrates on the mechanical aspects and does not deal to any extent with the mental approach to the game of golf. While the "grip it and rip it" concept will appeal to many junior players, success at golf is correlated with processes such as mental preparation, concentration, automaticity, commitment, and control over thoughts and feelings (Cohn 1994; McCaffrey & Orlick 1989; Thomas & Over 1994). Thomas and Over found that more highly skilled players demonstrated significantly greater recognition of these processes than less-skilled players. In addition, the more highly skilled players were less prone to negative emotions and cognitions.

A survey of other research reveals similar findings. Rotella (1995) reported that golfers must blend work on mechanics with work on the mental approach to the game, and Orlick and Parkington (1988) also found that mental readiness is an extremely important factor influencing an athlete's performance. Young players learn more than they need to know about how to swing a club but rarely learn how to master and employ the one thing guiding all behavior—the mind (Cohn 1994). This is despite the fact that most athletes, including elite golfers such as Palmer and Nicklaus, believe that 60% to 90% of success in sport is due to mental and psychological factors (Garfield 1984; Scharff 1959).

Thomas and Over's (1994) Golf Performance Survey appeared to be the ideal vehicle for the current study. This self-report instrument was designed to assess psychological skills related to prowess in golf, psychomotor competencies, and commitment to the game. Previous research with this instrument (conducted in Australia) concentrated on adult golfers, but Thomas (personal communication) considered it equally suitable for younger players.

The aim of the present study was to obtain self-reports from junior golfers, using the Thomas Golf Performance Survey, to consider the applicability of these factors among junior players and also the differences that might exist between the various age categories. Finally, it was hoped that the findings would add a further dimension to the instruction and development of our junior players.

METHODOLOGY

Subjects

The 117 respondents to this exploratory study were participants in three junior golf club programs in Ontario, junior golfers affiliated with the Royal Canadian Golf Association at various locations across the country, and a number of individual junior golfers who either requested the opportunity to participate or were referred by individuals interested in the development of junior golf. Respondents ranged in age from 10 to 20 years ($M = 15.9$ years, $SD = 1.6$) and reported handicaps ranging from 35 down to 0 for a few juniors with long experience ($M = 10.9$, $SD = 9.9$).

The Questionnaire

The original Golf Performance Survey questionnaire contained 95 items assessing players' concentration, use of imagery, mental preparation, strategies and tactics, self-control, emotions and cognition, psychomotor skills, commitment, and competitiveness. Respondents rated each item on a 5-point scale ranging from "strongly disagree" to "strongly agree." On the basis of principal components analysis of the responses of their adult golfers, Thomas and Over (1994) developed a reduced set of 59 items measuring nine factors. Factors representing psychological approaches were labeled as

- negative emotions and cognitions,
- mental preparation,
- conservative approach,
- concentration, and
- striving for maximum distance.

Psychomotor factors were labeled as

- automaticity,
- putting skill, and
- seeking improvement.

A single factor measured commitment to golf. In addition, respondents in the current study were asked to rate the importance of 10 reasons or motivations for playing golf and to provide demographic data on age, years of playing, and handicap.

RESULTS

The initial question was whether the factor structure described by Thomas and Over (1994) was equally applicable to the Canadian junior golfers. Using a structural equations modeling approach, confirmatory factor analyses were performed on Thomas and Over's proposed factor structures. Their model for the psychological skills and tactics produced a covariance matrix that was not positive definite, indicating an extremely poor fit of the junior golfers' data to the model. Similarly, the psychomotor skills model did not fit the current junior sample, failing to converge after 100 iterations. In both of these cases, examination of the covariance matrices revealed many small or negative covariances between items that had been positively related in the adult sample. However, the commitment items did fit together as hypothesized (GFI = 0.99; adjusted GFI = 0.96; RMR = 0.03; RMSEA = 0.0; CFI = 1.00; IFI = 1.01; $X^2(5) = 3.97, p = .055$).

Given the poor fit of the adult models of psychological and psychomotor factors to this data set, we performed two exploratory principal components factor analyses. To facilitate comparisons between the adult and junior samples, the reduced set of items presented by Thomas and Over (1994) was entered into these analyses, assessing alternative solutions based on the criteria used by Thomas and Over (factor loadings of at least .35, internal consistency of at least .60, and item total correlations of at least .30). For both the psychological and psychomotor skill sets, the scree (discontinuity) principle indicated that fewer factors were necessary to explain the data structure for the junior sample than had been the case for the adult one. For the sake of completeness, descriptions have been included of additional factors where these had been presented for the adult sample, as long as current factor eigenvalues exceeded 1.0.

Psychological Skills and Tactics

Three factors accounted for 37.9% of the variance in the 30 psychological skill items. The first factor (9 items, Cronbach's alpha = .77) is similar to Thomas and Over's (1994) Negative Emotions and Cognitions, but was combined with the three items from their Concentration factor, which for the adults had been a related but distinct concept.

Two items, dealing with discrepancies in performance between practice rounds and competitions, no longer fit the Negative Emotions factor, having moved to a new factor discussed further on. One item ("Getting the yips in putting") was not of concern to the participants and was dropped from further analysis. Table 33.1 lists the items in order of factor loading (reading across the rows), with reverse-coded items marked (r).

The second factor, Mental Preparation (5 items, alpha = .77), again is similar in the two samples, juniors retaining six of the original nine items. The items dropped are "Mentally tough competitor," "Confident of playing to handicap," and "Consistent pre-shot routine." Nevertheless, for some junior golfers, these issues could still have a bearing on their mental preparations. A new third factor appeared, labeled Handling Competitive Stress (4 items, alpha = .72). It is composed of items formally placed either with Negative Emotions and Cognitions or on the adults' Concentration factor (a factor not present in this solution). These items describe people who perform well under the pressure of a competitive event, perhaps even better than during practice rounds.

The remaining factors, Striving for Maximum Distance (3 items, alpha = .79) and Conservative Approach (4 items, alpha = .64), would not be retained by the scree principle but are presented for comparison with the adult sample. Together they account for 10.7% of the variance in the sample, and are composed of the same items as in the adult sample except for the disappearance of the item "When driving off the tee, I go for accuracy more than distance" (this item's correlation with others in the factor was just 0.13, n.s.).

Psychomotor Skills

Principal components analysis of the 24 psychomotor skill items revealed one factor accounting for 15.7% of the variance in the set. This factor (4 items, alpha = .62) is quite different from any factor represented in the data of the older golfers. It seems to represent a "grip it and rip it" approach to the game rather than focusing on "automaticity" as had the adult sample (see table 33.2). Two further factors that had been relevant to Thomas and Over's (1994) analysis would not be retained according to the scree principle; these accounted for an additional 18.4% of the variance. The second factor listed in table 33.2, Practice (alpha = .61), was more narrow than Thomas and Over's Seeking Improvement factor, being composed of just two items.

Table 33.1   Factor Structure of Psychological Skill Items and Correlations of Factors With Handicap

---

Factor 1: negative emotions (.17)

Nervous when playing competitively	Negative self-talk during competition
Emotionally flat when playing poorly	Anxious before hitting off first tee
Thinking of past mistakes	Angry and frustrated by a poor start (.19*)
Upset with what others say or do (.19*)	Not easily distracted playing a shot (r) (−.20*)
Concentration is easily broken (.29**)	

Factor 2: mental preparation (−.19*)

Visualize where ball will finish	Visualize putting stroke and ball in hole
Thought how to best play each hole	Mentally rehearse each shot
Work out where to place shot	

Factor 3: handling stress of competition (−.36**)

Play best under pressure	Play better at practice than competition (r)
Concentration easily broken (r)	Choke under pressure in competitions (r)

Factor 4: striving for maximum distance (.42**)

Try to out-drive my opponent	Hit the ball as far as I can when driving
Satisfaction from longest drive in group	

Factor 5: conservative approach (−.11)

Lay up if unsure of clearing a hazard	Prefer safe shots rather than take risks
Play for heart of green	Stick to what I can do, nothing new

$* p < .05;\ ** p < .01$

The third factor, Putting Skill, was similar to Thomas and Over's second factor, but without the item "I am inconsistent in putting" (2 items, alpha = .66).

Commitment and Involvement

As in the adult sample, responses to the five items measuring commitment were highly correlated, and these items hold together as one factor (alpha = .68), shown in table 33.3.

Predicting Handicap

The correlation coefficients in parentheses beside the factor labels in tables 33.1 through 33.3 indicate which factors were statistically significant predictors of the

Table 33.2   Factor Structure of Psychomotor Skill Items and Correlations of Factors With Handicap

Factor 1: grip it and rip it (.40**)

Drives depend on luck and chance	Changing alignment, ball position
Practice putting before a round	Lose more than one ball a round

Factor 2: practice (–.21*)

Hit practice balls before a round	Lessons with a golf professional

Factor 3: putting skill (–.01)

Putting strength	Good at reading greens

* p < .05; ** p < .01

Table 33.3   Factor Structure of Commitment Items (Correlation of Factor With Handicap –.49*)

Playing golf is important in life	Competitive when playing golf
Think about golf when not playing	Always try to reduce handicap
Prefer social to competition golf (r)	

* p < .01

junior golfers' handicap levels. Where specific items were significantly related to handicap even though their factor as a whole was not, the significant correlations are included in parentheses beside the individual items. As with the adult golfers (Thomas and Over 1994), one psychological skill that predicts lower handicaps is mental preparation. On the other hand, negative emotions and cognitions appear to be unrelated, on average, to the juniors' handicaps. Certain individual emotions do, however, appear to be detrimental, specifically those involving frustration and loss of concentration. In addition, the respondents' perceived ability to cope with the stress of competition predicts good performance. Golfers who, on the other hand, placed emphasis on striving for maximum distance in their drives tended to have higher handicaps, as had also been true of the adult golfers.

Two of the psychomotor factors predicted the junior's performance. The "grip it and rip it" style of playing was associated with poor performance, whereas practice was associated with improved performance. As was true of Thomas and Over's (1994) adult samples, putting skills did not predict handicap. Similarly, strong commitment significantly predicted good performance in both samples.

Two of the motivation items predicted performance, "Beating other players," $r(115) = -.22, p < .05$ and "Fun and enjoyment," $r(115) = .19, p < .05$. It appears that these two items are associated with low handicaps. The remaining eight items, focusing on the physical, mental, and social benefits of the game, were unrelated to handicap scores.

Most of the items that predicted handicap were also related to age. In general, old juniors reported a significantly greater degree of commitment to the game and a greater degree of the various psychological skills that predicted improved performance than did the younger players in the sample.

DISCUSSION

These data showed that the junior golfers were less able than the adults to separate negative emotions and concentration. If they reported upset of any kind, they also reported damage to concentration, which is vital to success in the game of golf. Although practice did predict improved performance, the juniors who did best were those who had learned to handle the mental elements of the game.

One limitation of the current work is the sample size. The sample employed in this study was smaller than is recommended for the use of confirmatory factor analysis. Future work with the Golf Performance Survey would benefit from a larger group of respondents. Also, because a new factor structure has been proposed here for junior golfers, replication is needed in order to confirm the differences between adult and junior approaches to the game.

The Golf Performance Survey proved to be a useful tool for assessing junior golfers' understanding of the various aspects of the game as well as for pointing out the structural differences between junior and adult golfers. The findings indicated those attributes that can be emphasized in future training and development programs for young players.

References

Cohn, P.J. (1994). *The mental game of golf: A guide to peak performance.* South Bend, IN: Diamond Communications.

Garfield, C.A. (1984). *Peak performance: Mental training techniques of the world's greatest athletes.* Boston, MA: Houghton Mifflin.

McCaffrey, N., & Orlick, T. (1989). Mental factors related to excellence among top professional golfers. *International Journal of Sports Psychology, 20*: 256-278.

Orlick, T., & Parkington, J. (1988). Mental links to excellence. *The Sports Psychologist, 2*: 105-130.

Rotella, R.J. (1995). *Golf is not a game of perfect.* New York: Simon & Schuster.

Scharff, R. (1959). *Handbook of golf strategy.* New York: Harper & Row.

Thomas, P.R., & Over, R. (1994). Psychological and psychomotor skills associated with performance in golf. *The Sports Psychologist, 8*: 73-86.

CHAPTER 34

Variable and Constant Practice: Ideas for Successful Putting

Mark A. Guadagnoli
Department of Kinesiology, University of Nevada, Las Vegas

William R. Holcomb
Department of Health Science, University of North Florida

The goal of practice is generally to acquire skills for the purpose of recalling those skills at a later date. One of the common dilemmas in organizing practice for skill acquisition concerns the degree to which variability during practice benefits skill retention. In the present study, a variable practice protocol was compared to a constant practice protocol to assess the effectiveness of each protocol on learning the skill of putting. Additionally, practice protocol was crossed with performer experience to assess the nature of the relationship between the level of the performer and appropriate practice protocol. Participants performed a pretest, four practice putting sessions, and a posttest. Test scores were analyzed using a 2 (Practice Protocol) $\times$ 2 (Performer Experience) $\times$ 2 (Test) analysis of variance with repeated measures on the last factor. The results demonstrated that for novice performers, a consistent protocol yielded superior retention performance. However, for experienced performers, a variable protocol yielded superior retention performance.

Keywords: Variable practice, learning, putting.

INTRODUCTION

A common question among motor learning theorists and practitioners is the degree to which various practice protocols enhance learning (Guadagnoli, Dornier, & Tandy 1996). One such debate has existed with regard to constant and variable practice. Constant practice, for the purpose of this paper, is defined as practicing one version of a skill in a repetitive manner (Schmidt 1988). Constant practice contrasts with variable practice, which is typically defined as practicing several versions of a task in a repetitive manner. Since the 1975 publication of Dick Schmidt's Schema theory, a debate about the benefits of constant and variable practice has remained. Essentially, Schmidt (1975) suggested that variable practice was superior to constant practice because the practice variability provides a broader range of movement experiences on which to base the development of a set of rules for an action (i.e., schema). Others (e.g., Adams [1971]) argued that constant practice is superior to variable practice because the constant practice more efficiently develops a stable "perceptual trace" of a movement. Since these early works, much of the laboratory-based research on constant and variable practice has supported Schmidt's view that variable practice leads to superior skill retention (Shea & Kohl 1990; Catalano & Kleiner 1988; Shapiro & Schmidt 1982). However, in "real-life" settings, constant practice is often the preferred schedule.

The conflict between theory and application presents an interesting dilemma from both an applied and a theoretical perspective. From an applied perspective it is of interest whether or not the preferred schedule of practice (i.e., constant) is in fact best for efficient learning. From a theoretical perspective it is of interest whether the theoretically prescribed schedule of practice (i.e., variable) is better for efficient learning or whether there is something unique to putting that counters theory.

Several possible hypotheses could be forged to explain the discrepancy between theory-based findings that variable practice yields superior learning and the applied wisdom that constant practice yields superior learning. One hypothesis is that constant practice yields a temporary positive performance effect and does not positively affect learning of the criterion task. It has been demonstrated in a variety of laboratory settings, using manipulations of constant and variable practice, that practice performance is not necessarily indicative of learning. For example, Shea and Kohl (1990, 1991), using a constant/variable practice protocol, found that the performance of the group that practiced under a constant protocol was superior to that of the variable group during acquisition, but inferior to that of the variable group during retention. Therefore, it is possible that practitioners misinterpret the temporary performance benefits of constant practice as a learning effect. In a laboratory setting it is common to use some type of retention test to assess learning rather than using acquisition performance as an index of learning. This misinterpretation of acquisition and retention effects has been discussed in detail in a variety of motor learning publications (e.g., Adams 1971; Stelmach 1969; Swinnen et al. 1990).

A second hypothesis may be that there is a uniqueness to the skill of putting that creates an appropriate practice protocol that is counter to theory. It could be argued that putting is as much a skill of concentration and confidence as a skill of motor ability. As already mentioned, a consistent practice protocol has been shown to yield more successful practice performance than a variable protocol. Therefore, the success gained in practice by having a constant protocol may develop confidence, yielding successful performance at a later date. Thus, the positive benefits of a constant practice protocol may result more from a psychological effect than from a learning effect.

In addition to the uniqueness of the skill of putting with regard to concentration and confidence, putting fits into a category of skills that are performed in a stable environment and require a great deal of movement consistency. The environment is considered stable, or closed, because there is little or no movement in the environment, which includes the ball prior to being struck, the green, the hole placement while the ball is being struck, and so on. Although there are several environmental variables to be considered in calculating the putt, those variables remain constant at the time the ball is being struck. Another sport example within this category is a free throw in basketball. Gentile (1972) has suggested that skills that must be performed with a high level of movement consistency in a stable environment are poorly suited for practice in a variable fashion. Therefore, it could be argued that the uniqueness of putting precipitates a constant, rather than variable, practice protocol for efficient learning.

Finally, a third hypothesis is that both theory and application are correct. It has been established previously in studies of skill acquisition that the factors of task difficulty, level of the performer, and practice/feedback schedule interact with efficient learning (Guadagnoli et al. 1996; Shea, Kohl, & Indermill 1990). Del Ray, Wughalter, and Whitehurst (1982) found that experienced women who learned a task under variable practice were more accurate and had less variability during a test of the skill than did novice subjects. Additional insight into this third hypothesis can be gained by extending beyond literature on variability of practice. Shea et al. (1990), in a protocol similar to constant/variable practice, found that the benefits of a more consistent protocol (blocked) occurred for novice performers, while the benefits of a more variable protocol (random) were apparent for experienced performers. Guadagnoli et al. (1996), in a study of knowledge of results, stated that "the overall efficiency of processing information is based on relative task difficulty, which is based on the level of the performer and the complexity of the task" (p. 248). Further, relative task difficulty should be matched to the performer in order for efficient learning to take place. The relative task difficulty can be manipulated by altering the practice protocol, and under normal circumstances, it is believed that a variable practice protocol provides more relative task difficulty than a constant practice protocol (McCracken & Stelmach 1977). Therefore, it is possible that constant practice is well matched to novice performers, resulting in successful acquisition and retention performance. Variable practice, which provides a greater challenge, may be well matched to experienced participants; thus variable practice would be predicted to hinder acquisition performance but enhance retention performance, relative to constant practice.

Experimental Rationale

Most research and laboratory-controlled tests support a variable putting practice protocol as the preferred method for skill acquisition, especially with experienced participants. However, constant practice is generally more often used by practitioners as the most efficient means by which the skill of putting can be learned or improved. Therefore, the present study was designed to remedy this conflict by comparing application-based putting practice methods (constant) with theory based-practice methods (variable) to assess the degree to which these methods affect practice and retention performance. Additionally, the variable of practice technique was crossed with performer experience to assess the nature of the relationship between these variables. Finally, it is important to note that the task used in the current experiment is a putting task and does not include all aspects of putting.

Such aspects as reading the slope and line of the putt are not major components of the experimental design.

METHODS

Participants

Forty-eight college-aged students (mean age of 22.3 years) volunteered to participate in the present study. Participants were naive to the theoretical question of the study and signed an informed consent prior to participation.

Design

The study was a 2 [Practice Protocol (constant, variable)] × 2 [Experience (novice, experienced] × 2 [Test (pretest, posttest)] mixed design study. The independent variables practice protocol and experience were between-subjects factors. The independent variable test was a within-subject factor. The dependent variable of interest was score on a putting task.

Apparatus and Task

The apparatus for this study consisted of one artificial putting surface, 36 golf balls, and a putter. The putting surface was a 3.67 × 6.1 m (12 ft × 20 ft) carpet that approximated the stimp rating of an average putting green (figure 34.1). The 36 golf balls comprised 12 white, 12 yellow, and 12 orange balls. Each color of ball was assigned to one of the three target distances/locations. The three targets varied in distance and location. The target distances were 1.8 m (6 ft), 3.1 m (10 ft), and 4.9 m (16 ft). The white balls were assigned to the 1.8 m target, the yellow balls to the 3.1 m target, and the orange to the 4.9 m target.

The task in all occasions was to attempt to putt the golf ball from the home position to the target on the carpet. The target consisted of a 15 cm (6 in.) diameter circle (drawn in chalk) on the carpet. The target circle was surrounded by larger circles such that the pattern of the target circle and accompanying circles resembled that of a dartboard (figure 34.1).

Surrounding the target was a circle with a radius 15 cm (6 in.) greater than that of the target. This circle was surrounded by a circle with a radius another 15 cm (6 in.) greater. There were a total of five such circles. Each circle was assigned a score. The score for each putt was determined by closeness to the target circle. A putt stopping in the target hole received a score of 5, one ring out received a score of 4, the next ring 3, the next 2, and the last 1. Any putt stopping 50 cm (24 in.) or more away from the target hole received a score of 0. Higher scores were considered desirable because stopping the ball closer to the target yielded higher scores. The authors realize that typically it is not desirable to leave a putt short. However, in the current study, the target was equated to a distance hit. Likewise, most golfers attempt to hit a putt a particular distance. Again, a putting task was used to assess the learning of putting mechanics and not putting strategy.

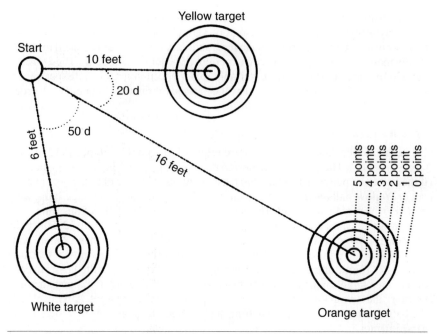

Figure 34.1   Schematic of a topical view of the artificial putting surface and target arrangement.

Procedures

Pretest (Session 1)

Prior to any data collection, participants completed a questionnaire designed to assess putting experience. The questions concerned experience with golf, and putting in general. Specifically, participants were asked if they considered themselves "experienced putters." Participants categorized themselves as "experienced putters" or "novice putters." After completing the questionnaire, participants completed a pretest. The pretest consisted of 12 putts, in variable order, from the home position to one of the three targets. A variable order for the pretest was considered a more "real-life" test of putting proficiency. Each score was recorded and the total was calculated. On the basis of this pretest score and responses on the participant questionnaire, individuals were classified as either novice or experienced putters. Those individuals who stated that they had moderate to extended experience with putting and scored 30 points or higher on the pretest were assigned to the experienced group; 30 points was chosen because the results of a pilot study suggested this to be a natural cutoff point. Those individuals who stated that they had low or no experience with putting and scored 29 points or lower on the pretest were assigned to the novice group. Individuals not fitting the prescribed criteria were excused from further participation. For example, an individual who claimed to be an experienced putter but scored only 10 points would not fit the a priori restrictions and would therefore be excused.

After being assigned to either the novice or experienced group, participants were randomly assigned to either a constant or variable practice condition. Therefore, there were a total of four groups that were randomly assigned and equated in ability within their categories (e.g., the two experienced groups were equal). These groups included novice-constant, novice-variable, experienced-constant, and experienced-variable. Participants were screened by the method outlined earlier until each group consisted of 12 participants.

Practice (Sessions 1-4)

On each practice day, participants were required to complete 36 putts (12 to each target distance). The targets were designated by the color of the ball. For example, if the ball to be putted was white, the participant putted this ball to the near (1.8 m) target. Yellow balls were putted to the middle (3.1 m) target. Orange balls were putted to the far (4.9 m) target. The constant group putted 12 balls of the same color (e.g., white), to the same target, in a row. This was followed by putting 12 more balls of a consistent but different color (e.g., orange) to another target, then 12 more balls (e.g., yellow) to a third target. This method is consistent with traditional teaching techniques for putting mechanics. The variable practice group putted balls to each of the three targets in an experimenter-prescribed variable order, making sure that no more that two putts in a row were attempted to the same target. After each putt the ball was removed from the putting surface and the score was recorded by the experimenter.

Posttest (Session 5)

The posttest procedure was identical to the pretest in that all participants performed 12 putts, in variable order, from the home position to one of the three targets.

RESULTS

Acquisition Results

Mean score data were analyzed using a 2 [Practice Protocol (constant, variable)] × 2 [Experience (novice, experienced)] × 4 [Day (days 1-4)] analysis of variance (ANOVA) with repeated measures on the last factor. Scores were calculated by the cumulative score of the 36 practice trials completed per day.

The analysis revealed a significant main effect for practice protocol, $F(1, 44) = 33.49$, $p < 0.01$, with means being 101.3 and 91.5 for the constant and variable protocols, respectively. The analysis also revealed a significant main effect for experience, $F(1, 44) = 6.49$, $p < 0.01$, with means being 88.0 and 104.5 for the experienced and novice groups, respectively. In addition there was a significant main effect for day, $F(3, 132) = 45.38$, $p < 0.01$, with means being 91.3, 95.1, 94.4, and 104.9 for 1, 2, 3, and 4, respectively. Taken together, these findings confirm that performance increased over days of practice, experienced performers outperformed novice performers, and the constant groups outperformed their variable cohorts. All of these findings are as would be predicted.

There were no significant Practice Protocol × Experience, Experience × Day, or Practice Protocol × Experience × Day interactions. However, the analysis did reveal a significant Practice Protocol × Day, $F(3, 132) = 2.88, p < 0.05$, interaction. The means for all groups in all conditions over days of practice are plotted in figure 34.2.

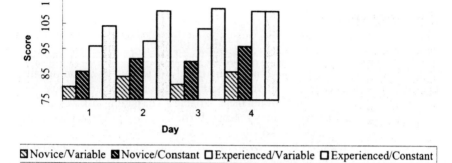

Figure 34.2   Practice protocol by experience level by day interaction.

Retention Results

Mean score data were analyzed using a 2 [Practice Protocol (constant, variable)] × 2 [Experience (novice, experienced)] × 2 [Test (pretest, posttest)] ANOVA with repeated measures on the last factor. Scores were calculated by the cumulative score of the 12 pretest putts for the pretest score and the 12 posttest putts for the posttest score.

The analysis revealed no significant main effect for practice protocol. However, the analysis did reveal a significant main effect for experience, $F(1, 44) = 95.62, p < 0.01$, with means being 24.4 and 36.6 for the experienced and novice groups, respectively. Further, there was a significant main effect for test, $F(1, 44) = 55.43$,

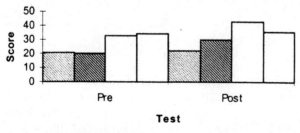

Figure 34.3   Pre- and posttest data by practice protocol, experience level.

$p < 0.01$, with means being 27.7 and 33.4 for the pre- and posttest, respectively. There were no significant Practice Protocol × Experience, Practice Protocol × Test, or Experience × Test interactions. Most importantly, the analysis revealed a significant Practice Protocol × Experience × Test interaction, $F(1, 44) = 16.07$, $p < 0.01$ (figure 34.3). Finally, a Duncan's follow-up analysis showed that novice and experienced groups differed from each other in both the pre- and posttest.

DISCUSSION

The present study investigated the extent to which differing practice techniques affect practice and retention performance in regard to a putting task. Additionally, the variable of practice technique was crossed with performer experience to assess the nature of the relationship between these variables. The putting task was utilized in the current study for two primary reasons. First, the task was chosen because it is representative of a class of skills that must be performed with a high level of movement consistency in a stable environment. Second, putting is representative of a class of skills that, in an applied setting, have traditionally been taught using a constant practice protocol, which is in contrast to theory-based teaching techniques.

Three potential hypotheses were proposed to explain the conflict between theory and application. The current data suggest that application-based putting practice techniques are more beneficial for novice participants but that theory-based practice techniques are more beneficial for experienced participants. These findings are most consistent with the third of the proposed hypotheses, which states that the factors of task difficulty, level of the performer, and practice schedule interact with efficient learning.

Guadagnoli et al. (1996) have suggested that an optimal practice schedule is based on the level of the performer and the nature of the task. They suggest that learning results from increasing the efficiency with which the system processes information. As a function of increased practice, task elements can be grouped together in memory and therefore processed in a more efficient fashion. As a result, the number of steps needed to process the same number of task elements decreases; hence learning is more efficient. When the performer is in an early stage of learning, the system is inefficient in grouping multiple task elements. In the current study these task elements include such items as putting mechanics, aiming, estimating distance, and appropriate force production. Therefore, the information needs to be presented in units small enough for efficient processing.

With a constant practice protocol, the task elements of estimating distance and the resulting appropriate force are greatly simplified, thus approximating an appropriate task element size resulting in efficient learning. However, a variable protocol includes these task elements, which may act to overload the system, making processing and learning inefficient. In viewing the acquisition data one can clearly see that the acquisition scores for those novice individuals practicing under a variable protocol are inferior to the scores of those practicing under a constant protocol. Further evidence is suggested through the acquisition/posttest data relationships. The constant group increased in performance throughout acquisition, and their performance was superior to that of the variable group on the posttest. This suggests an appropriate level of challenge. The variable group's performance was inferior to that of the consistent group in both acquisition and posttest performance. This result is consistent with the notion that the novice individuals under the variable protocol were overchallenged and thus learning was inefficient.

Experienced participants are more efficient than novice participants in grouping multiple task elements. Therefore, the information presented to experienced participants needs to be presented in units large enough to appropriately challenge the performer and thus promote efficient processing. Again, the acquisition/posttest data relationships shed light on the idea of appropriate challenge. The constant group attained performance superior to that of the variable group in acquisition but did not consistently increase in performance throughout acquisition. This would indicate that the constant group was less challenged than the variable group during acquisition. Further, the constant group attained performance inferior to that of the variable group on the posttest. This suggests that the constant group was underchallenged during acquisition. The variable group showed consistent improvement over days of acquisition, but in all cases their performance was inferior to that of the constant group. However, the variable group's performance was superior to that of the constant group on the posttest. By definition, this suggests an appropriate level of challenge and thus efficient learning (Lee 1988).

In the present study, providing variable practice for novice performers may have overwhelmed the system's ability to process information. Therefore, a constant protocol was shown to be more appropriate for novice performers. Likewise, when a performer is more experienced, the system's ability to group information improves and thus the performer can more efficiently handle a more variable practice protocol. Therefore, within a task, the overall efficiency of processing information is based on relative task difficulty, which is based on the level of the performer and the schedule of practice.

References

Adams, J.A. (1971). A closed-loop theory of motor learning. *Journal of Motor Behavior,* 3: 111-150.

Del Ray, P., Wughalter, E., & Whitehurst, M. (1982). The efforts of contextual interference on females with varied experience in open sport skills. *Research Quarterly for Exercise and Sport,* 53: 108-115.

Guadagnoli, M.A., Dornier, L.A., & Tandy, R. (1996). Optimal length for summary knowledge of results: The influence of task-related experience and complexity. *Research Quarterly for Exercise and Sport,* 67(2): 239-248.

Lee, T.D. (1988). Transfer appropriate processing: A framework for conceptualizing practice effects in motor learning. In O.G. Meijer & K. Roth (eds.), *Complex motor behavior: The motor-action controversy.* Amsterdam: Elsevier Science.

McCracken, H.D., & Stelmach, G.E. (1977). A test of the schema theory of discrete motor learning. *Journal of Motor Behavior,* 9: 193-201.

Schmidt, R.A. (1975). A schema theory of discrete motor skill learning. *Psychological Review,* 82: 225-260.

Schmidt, R.A. (1988). *Motor control and learning: A behavioral emphasis.* Champaign, IL: Human Kinetics.

Shapiro, D., & Schmidt, R.A. (1982). The schema theory: Recent evidence and developmental implications. In J.A.S. Kelso & J.E. Clark (eds.), *The development of movement control and coordination,* 113-150. New York: Wiley.

Shea, C.H., & Kohl, R.H. (1990). Specificity and variability of practice. *Research Quarterly for Exercise and Sport,* 61(2): 169-177.

Shea, C.H., & Kohl, R.H. (1991). Composition of practice: Influence on retention of motor skills. *Research Quarterly for Exercise and Sport,* 62(2): 187-195.

Shea, C.H., Kohl, R.M., & Indermill, C. (1990). Contextual interference: Contributions of practice. *Acta Psychologica,* 73: 145-157.

Stelmach, G.E. (1969). Efficiency of motor learning as a function of intertrial rest. *Research Quarterly,* 40: 198-202.

Swinnen, S.P., Schmidt, R.A., Nicholson, D.E., & Shapiro, D.C. (1990). Information feedback for skill acquisition: Instantaneous knowledge of results degrades learning. *Journal of Experimental Psychology: Learning, Memory, and Cognition,* 16: 706-716.

CHAPTER 35

The Routines and Rituals
of Expert Golf Instruction

Ken Baker, Paul G. Schempp, and Brent Hardin
University of Georgia in Athens, Georgia

Betsy Clark
Ladies Professional Golf Association in Daytona Beach, Florida

The purpose of this study was to identify the ritualized practices of expert golf instructors. Eleven expert golf instructors were selected with the assistance of the Ladies Professional Golf Association (LPGA). The experts possessed the following characteristics:

a. Ten or more years of teaching experience
b. LPGA certification
c. Formal recognition for the quality of their instruction
d. Their students' golfing success

The instructors were brought to the University of Georgia campus in Athens, Georgia, for two days. During that time, the instructors were videotaped teaching a golf lesson to a beginning golfer and also were interviewed. Selected segments of the videotape were reviewed with the instructor. During the tape review, the investigator asked the teacher to recall decisions about instructional events and teaching behavior. Data analysis revealed several consistent trends in the actions and activities of the expert golf instructors. Similarities were noted among a majority of the studied instructors in the lesson opening, verbal instruction, nonverbal instruction, positioning, pacing, and lesson closure.

Keywords: Expertise, golf instructors, antecedents, instruction routines.

INTRODUCTION

The search for the characteristics that separate the exceptional from the average is a quest that has been pursued throughout history. In the game of golf, the search for the qualities of expert instruction is a quest pursued by teacher and student alike. The research herein described represents a similar pursuit—a search to identify the ritualized practices of expert golf instructors.

Routines and rituals are characteristic and repetitive behavioral activities performed for a specific purpose. For golf instructors, routines and rituals are the tried-and-tested patterns in their instruction that offer pathways to efficient, effective, and economic student learning. The ease with which these routines are performed often masks their profound impact on student learning. To the uninitiated eye, the significance of these routines is overlooked.

The development of automatic, reflexive, and repetitive behaviors is one of the distinguishing characteristics of an expert performer (Bloom, 1986). With the attainment of a high degree of skill, both mental and physical, come both automaticity and unconscious behavior. For both simple tasks (e.g., typing) and more complex motor skills (e.g., gymnastics), experts can do things "automatically" that nonexperts can do only with much effort, or not at all. Years of experience and a familiarity with their environment have led experts to rehearse and repeat behavior patterns until they are subconscious, automatic routines. Experts appear to perform these rehearsed patterns with fluidity, elegance, and ease. It has been estimated that the development of this characteristic automaticity takes a minimum of 10 years of sustained, deliberate practice (Ericsson, Krampe, & Tesch-Romer, 1993). Extensive hours of practice are an important prerequisite for developing the automatic aspect of expert performance.

With the study of expert teaching still in its infant stages, there remain few clues as to which ritualized pedagogical routines are endemic to expert golf instructors. The research on teacher effectiveness, with its long and rich tradition in classroom study, appears to provide indicators as to which activities may account for exemplary golf instruction. In their review of teaching functions, Rosenshine and Stevens (1986) identified the following activities as having been consistently found by researchers in studies of effective classroom teachers:

- Initiating a lesson with a brief statement of goals
- Presenting information in incremental steps, with student practice following each step
- Providing clear and detailed explanations
- Offering plentiful student practice opportunities
- Asking a large number of questions to determine student comprehension of information
- Offering feedback and suggestions after student practice

Rosenshine and Stevens were quick to point out that while not all teachers used all of these routines all of the time, the more effective teachers used most of these activities most of the time. For the purposes of the current study, these characteristics offered the platform from which to investigate the routines and rituals common to expert golf instructors.

METHODS

Expert Golf Instructors

Identifying expert teachers is always a difficult task, as individuals conceptualize experts differently. Expert golf instructors were selected with the assistance of the staff of the Ladies Professional Golf Association (LPGA). The experts all possessed the following characteristics:

a. Ten or more years of teaching experience
b. LPGA certification
c. Formal recognition for the quality of their instruction (e.g., state, regional, or national teacher of the year)
d. An established record of golfing success at local, regional, or national levels on the part of their students

Procedures

The selected instructors were brought to the University of Georgia campus in Athens, Georgia, for two days. During that time, the instructors were videotaped teaching a golf lesson to a beginning golfer and were also interviewed.

Videotaped Lesson

The instructors were asked to teach a one-hour, full-swing lesson to a novice student. The students were all college-age (range in years 19-28) women volunteers with no previous golf experience. The students were recruited from University of Georgia physical education classes. The students received no compensation other than a free golf lesson.

The videotaped lesson took place at the University of Georgia driving range. Each instructor was allowed access to an unlimited number of golf balls and could choose the type and number of clubs from a selection of irons and woods. The instructors were allowed to use any training aid they chose to bring to the videotaping location.

The instructor had up to 60 minutes in which to conduct the lesson. The instructor was fitted with a cordless microphone, and the video camera was located approximately 20 yards from the point of instruction. While the cameras were mounted on tripods for improved picture stability, the instructor was free to move about the instructional site.

After the instructor was fitted with a microphone, she was brought to the instructional location, where she was familiarized with the equipment available. The assigned student was then brought to her so that the first and the last words between the student and teacher were captured on tape.

Stimulated Recall

Selected segments of the previously described videotape were reviewed with the instructor. Tape segments were selected based upon the level of pedagogical activity at various points in the lesson (i.e., introduction, information giving, student practice, feedback, activity transitions, and lesson closure). During the tape review, the investigator asked the teacher to recall decisions about instructional events and teaching behavior. This procedure has been successfully used in previous research on teaching expertise (Griffey & Housner, 1991).

Interview

A one-hour interview was conducted and structured to gain insight into the instructors' instructional practices. Questions focused on their experiences as teachers. The interviewer attempted to induce the instructors to describe, in detail, the opening and closing routines used in their classes and the instructional practices common in their lessons. Open-ended and conversational in nature, these interviews permitted the instructors to tell their stories in their own words.

Data Analysis

Analysis was completed in three steps. First, researchers observed the videotaped lessons of the 11 expert instructors. The observations were intended to identify recurring trends and patterns both within lessons and between each of the lessons. Second, examples of these trends were drawn from the data pool and examined for consistency of content, presentation style, and focus. The third and final step was a review of the audiotapes from the stimulated recall in order to identify the underlying rationale of the instructional routines and rituals.

FINDINGS

Data analysis revealed several consistent trends in the actions and activities of the expert golf instructors. The routines and rituals of these teachers may be accountable for the superior performance of these teachers and directly linked to the learning of their students. Similarities were noted between a majority of the instructors studied in the lesson opening, verbal instruction, nonverbal instruction, positioning, pacing, and lesson closure. The findings relative to each of these points are presented in the following sections.

Lesson Opening

Each of the studied lessons began with a brief conversation between the teacher and the student. The teachers had not previously met these students and were not likely to meet them again. Though the introductory remarks may have appeared casual and insignificant, the instructors revealed during stimulated recall that their questions and comments had definite purpose and would be used to shape the lesson content and teaching style.

Introductory Questions

The instructors began by asking a series of questions designed to ascertain background information about the student. In every instance, the teachers asked about

a. athletic experiences in sports other than golf,

b. previous golf exposure, and

c. injuries or physical limitations.

When one student mentioned that she had an extensive background in dance, the teacher (Wilkins) made frequent reference to this activity during her instruction.

Several of the teachers made inquiry as to whether the students had ever watched a televised golf tournament, and one teacher (Quarcelino) said later that this question was to determine whether the student had ever seen a proper swing. Another teacher (Ritson) asked her student if she considered herself to be a "detail person," explaining that this would help her determine how in-depth to be with her instruction. A third teacher began her lesson with the following sequence of questions:

> Can you tell me about other sports you have played? Can I ask you questions about your tennis experience—because it will be relevant to golf? Was your backhand or forehand better? What was your best shot in tennis? Did you take instruction in tennis? Tell me about your best instructor in tennis. Did your instructor do a lot of demonstrations for you? (Marriott)

The teacher appeared to use the student's responses to determine the content to be taught, the tenor of the lesson, and the feedback and metaphors to be used as the student practiced. The friendly, personal nature of the questions also helped establish a positive atmosphere and relaxed the apprehensive students. As was noted by this teacher's student, and others, the student felt free to ask questions and make comments throughout the lesson.

Goal Setting

After the introductory questions, each of the instructors made clear the purpose of the lesson. Teachers used the students' responses from the introductory questions to formulate goals. Some of the instructors asked the students to verbalize goals they wished to accomplish in the lesson. For example, one instructor asked, "What are your goals in golf? What would you like to accomplish in the lesson today?" (Radar). Another instructor verbally outlined the goals for her students by stating, "There are three things that you want to learn in terms of the foundation of your golf swing. These are grip, alignment, and posture" (Cole). Several of the teachers identified learning goals that would be set if they were to see the student several times, and suggested the student work toward these goals either on their own or with another instructor. It seemed that for all instructors, identifying the lesson goals was an important ritual that preceded the actual instructional portion of the lesson.

Verbal Instruction

The vast majority of the lesson was verbal instruction by the teacher. This activity dominated the lesson, and patterns of verbal interaction were consistently repeated across the lesson for all teachers. The verbal information given by the teachers appeared to appeal to the qualities and characteristics of the student that the teacher was able to discern from the introductory questions. The information was also in line with the stated goals. The instructors made several key points in the lesson and found a variety of ways to state and revisit these points throughout the lesson. While the instructors conveyed a great deal of information to the student, little of it strayed from the lesson goals. Characteristic of this information was a nontechnical language that was rich in metaphors and feedback regarding student performance and success.

Metaphors

Several of the instructors utilized metaphors and imagery to supplement their explanations of a particular teaching point. The teachers' language was rich and descriptive. Whenever possible, references were made to other sports that were specific to the background of the particular student. The teachers guided the students through the elements of the full swing with finely detailed word pictures. For example, one teacher compared the target line to a runway and the club to an airplane:

> Have you ever flown on an airplane? Here is the runway. This club face is the airplane and if it goes off the runway it will crash and burn. If I swing off the runway I burn. If I swing on the runway I am good. Keep your club face in this area. Keep your plane on the runway. (McMahon)

Later in the lesson, the same teacher used another set of word pictures to help describe the proper grip:

> Think of it this way—these fingers are the fish hooks, the club is the hot dog, your hands are the buns, and this thumb forms the cleavage. When thinking of your grip just remember hot dog—buns—fish hooks—and cleavage. (McMahon)

The effectiveness of these metaphors could be seen in the student's responses and reactions later in the lesson. The student, on several occasions, made unprompted reference to the metaphors and applied the concepts as she practiced her grip and swing.

Another teacher used the knowledge she had gathered in the originating questions about previous sport experience to create the following teaching metaphor:

> Since you are an athlete, you understand how to complete an underhand throw. Show me what it would look like if you were to throw a ball underhand to a target. In a golf swing, you want to take your right hand and throw it through to the target. (Cole)

To assist her student in handling criticism from others when playing and practicing golf, one teacher concluded her lesson with a metaphor:

I am going to give you the bubble now, and I really mean this. You have now become a golfer and since you are a young woman golfer you are now subject to advice from everyone. You have to be very very careful—so I am giving you this bubble around you. Try not to listen to this unsolicited advice. Let it hit your bubble and bounce off. (Marriott)

Feedback

The teachers consistently provided immediate and positive feedback when the students practiced and performed the skills being taught. Every single attempt by the student to perform the specified behavior elicited a response from the teacher. The feedback was overwhelmingly positive, and the teachers were often seen congratulating the students on their successful accomplishments in learning the skill components. Seldom were errors identified or corrected; rather the attention remained on what was being performed correctly.

The focus of the feedback was on the mechanical performance of the student, not necessarily the flight of the ball or the outcome of the performance. If the outcome was satisfactory, the teacher would make mention of it and congratulate the student, but the focus remained primarily on the skill components on which the student was being instructed. For example, if the student hit a poor shot that dribbled off the clubhead, yet had maintained a proper grip, the teacher would ignore the ball and comment on the placement of the hands on the club during the swing.

Whenever a correction was deemed by the instructor to be in order, it was most often initiated with a question, such as "If you needed to adjust anything, do you know what it was?" (Dengler) and "What was your assessment of that?" (Ritson). In most cases, the response from the student would reflect the points the teacher was attempting to convey to that student. In this way, it appeared that the student had learned the knowledge portion even if the performance of the skill was yet to occur.

Nonverbal Instruction

While the majority of the instruction was verbal in nature, the teachers appeared to share two common nonverbal routines in their instructional patterns. Physical manipulation of the student into proper form and demonstrations were used to supplement and emphasize the verbal instructions. In other words, the same main points made with the verbal instructions relative to the skill being learned were made with the nonverbal activities as well.

Physical Manipulation

Physical manipulation was used by the instructor to place a student into a proper position relative to the skill to be learned. Manipulation of this sort permitted the student to "feel" the proper position for activities such as the grip and posture. Every instructor touched her student while teaching the grip, though there was variance as to the sequence of verbal and manipulative instruction. For example, one teacher initially provided verbal instruction concerning the grip, allowed the student to grip the club, and then manipulated the student's hands in order to examine and provide correction (Dengler). Another, however, first manipulated her student's grip without description, then provided detailed explanation afterward (Wilkins). A third teacher began her grip instruction by grasping the hands of the student and pointing out anatomical characteristics by saying, "This is the only thing you need to know about this hand. That is called the heel pad. In this other hand . . . this area right in here, that's called the lifeline" (Ritson). She then placed the club into the student's hands while continuously giving clear explanation of how the student should hold the club.

Other facets of golf instruction that frequently elicited physical manipulation included the clarification of proper posture. For example, one teacher placed her hands on her student's lower back and said, "Bend slightly into that right hip, there" (Ritson). Another teacher pushed her student to see if balance could be maintained at the finish position (Marriott), and a third teacher shook hands with her student in order to teach the desired grip pressure (Cole).

Demonstrations

The teachers provided full-swing demonstrations sparingly and selectively. During most of the instruction, the teachers did not have a golf club in hand. However, when demonstrations were used, they were performed to supplement the verbal instruction, and students were asked to focus on one particular element of the swing. This was reflected in one episode when the instructor said:

> If you would allow me to demonstrate for a second right now just so that you can kind of see. . . . I'm going to just hit both of these golf balls, and I want you to notice that on one of them I'm going to take the grass, and on the other I won't. . . . That one I didn't take the grass, and it was like I bowled the ball. . . . This one I'm going to make sure I take some grass. . . . And that ball, you will notice really went nicely in the air. (Wilkins)

Demonstrations were also used as models of a skill. Teachers modeled posture, grip, swing, and follow-through. Teachers seldom demonstrated a full swing with ball contact. Several reasons were given regarding the selection procedures with respect to when and why to demonstrate. Because they were superior performers, several teachers stated that they did not want to intimidate the students. Most teachers stated that the focus of the lesson was the student's performance, not the teacher's. Perhaps epitomizing the student focus of demonstrations, one instructor, although naturally right-handed, skillfully modeled and demonstrated all skills left-handed for the benefit of the left-handed student (Peterson).

Positioning

During each lesson, the positioning of the student was determined by the teacher, and at no time did the student leave her position without a direct command from the teacher. The teachers stood directly in front of their students during almost all instruction. The most notable exception occurred during the instruction regarding posture. At this time, the instructors tended to stand directly beside the student, exhibiting the desired posture and encouraging the student to mimic the posture. As one teacher modeled the correct body position, she prompted her student to do likewise by saying, "Bend right here. And over. OK. Good" (Dengler). During stimulated recall, a teacher explained the importance of her position in stating, "I'm in front of her basically because she's pretty visual. Watching. Learning how to do the skill looking at me" (Quarlisimo).

Teachers appeared to position themselves relative to the student so that they could observe all critical aspects of the performance, maintain eye contact with the student, maintain proximity for physical manipulation, and ensure safety. A step or two put the teacher near the student for feedback or additional information after a student performance. The teacher's position allowed her to effectively convey information and control all aspects of the lesson.

Pacing

An important pedagogical routine for these teachers was the regulation of the lesson pace. From the start of the lesson to its close, the teachers used a variety of techniques to regulate the student performances and responses, as well as the information given, feedback provided, and time spent on each instructional activity. The teachers decided when to move from one lesson segment to another. In the beginning of the lesson, the teachers took charge by asking questions. The questions established the teacher as being in control of the lesson while also creating a positive, safe environment for the student. Closing the lesson was also a purposeful decision made by the teacher. For example, when one teacher closed a lesson by saying, "That was terrific. We are done. We're not hitting another ball," she later explained:

> We probably could have gone a few more minutes but she had just hit such a wonderful shot that I wanted her to leave with that experience. And she said, "Can I hit one more?" and I said, "We're going to hold onto that particular picture for you to take home." (Frost)

After the information was gathered for the teachers to make instructional choices and decisions, the teachers paced the lesson by prompting the student to either listen or perform. Listening prompts were given verbally, while performance prompts were given either verbally or nonverbally. For example, all the instructors teed the ball for their students and then indicated when the student should swing. The instructors would not tee a ball when they wanted the student to listen. The ball was teed only when they were ready for the student to perform. "What I'm going to ask you to do is kind of difficult. I'm going to tee the ball, but I want you to ignore the ball and hit this [pointing to the tee; instructor then tees ball]. OK, give it a whirl [instructor steps back and student swings]" (Johnson).

Lesson Closure

A ritual shared by all of these expert instructors was the closing of their lesson with a brief review during which the major points were summarized. While the style in which the reviews and summaries were given varied from teacher to teacher, the lesson goals were usually restated, the important components of the lesson reviewed, and points for future reference and practice provided. For example, one teacher prompted her student to summarize the lesson by saying, "Tell me what you got out of your lesson today" and then asked, "What will you remember that you can practice?" (Cole). Another teacher made written notes for future practice suggestions and handed them to the student at the conclusion of the lesson (Peterson). Other teachers achieved closure by reviewing the instructional objectives:

> Today, you've learned very nicely how to hold the club, and how to position your body. And you already have a basic golf swing. It looks like a golf swing. I mean it looks like mine. Maybe not so refined, but the club is going the way it should be going and your body is going the way it should be going. (Wilkins)

Finally, a common characteristic in the ritual of lesson closing was ending on a positive note. Each teacher ensured that the final performance was a successful one. The students left the lesson with the memory of their last shot being well struck.

DISCUSSION

The instructional activity of the 11 studied expert golf instructors revealed several consistencies in their behavior. These rituals and routines represented purposeful and repeated actions and events that underlined the instructional processes of expert instruction. Similarities among lesson openings, verbal instructions, nonverbal instructions, positioning, pacing, and lesson closures were noted.

Not surprisingly, several of these routines and rituals identified in the golf instructors' lessons have been consistently identified in research on other forms of teaching. In particular, initiating the lesson with a statement of goals, providing clear and detailed explanations, asking a large number of questions, offering immediate feedback following student performances, and closing the lesson with a review of the main instructional points have all been identified as activities of effective teachers (Rosenshine & Stevens, 1986). The pacing of the class also reflected instructional effectiveness of the teachers, as the teachers in this study had established routines that kept the lesson quickly paced, with brief teacher presentations interspersed with student practice opportunities (Tobin & Capie, 1982). Further, like effective coaches, these teachers made use of metaphorical language to succinctly express ideas and convey vivid images that might otherwise be inexpressible (Griffey, Housner, & Williams, 1986).

While many of the behavioral routines and rituals of these expert instructors can be identified in research on other effective teachers, the current study offers some intriguing insights that may be wholly unique to these teachers. The consistency of their instructional positioning may be unique given the performance of the golf swing. Instructors need to be conscious of the location of themselves and their students during instruction so that information can be conveyed effectively, through a variety of modalities (i.e., verbal and nonverbal instruction), and so that safety can be maintained.

Physical manipulation to convey information regarding the static positions of the golf swing (i.e., grip, posture, balanced follow-through) also represents an unprecedented finding in instructional research. While not a dominant ritual of the expert instructors, the consistency of this activity in the lessons indicates its importance in the instructional repertoire of the teachers.

Finally, the predominance of introductory questions to ascertain critical student information, followed by the use of that information throughout the lesson, is a characteristic that appears uncommon in the pedagogy of other subject areas. While this might be associated with the single-student style of teaching, the pervasiveness of this activity appears too common to indicate that it would dissipate with the addition of more students to the lesson. The teachers were skillful and consistent in the questions asked, the answers derived, and the application of the knowledge to personalize the lesson.

The study of golf instructors is only in its infancy. As more and more people aspire to teach golf, and even more demand effective instruction, it appears that interest in golf instruction will grow. To feed that interest, additional research is necessary. We hope that this study in the routines and rituals of expert golf teachers serves those who prepare and certify golf instructors, as well as those who aspire to teach well. As we discovered in the course of this investigation, there is much to learn from those who have mastered their craft.

ACKNOWLEDGMENTS

This study was supported by a grant from the Ladies Professional Golf Association.

References

Bloom, B. (1986). Automaticity. *Educational Leadership,* February, 70-77.

Ericsson, K.A., Krampe, R., & Tesch-Romer, C. (1993). The role of deliberate practice in the acquisition of expert performance. *Psychological Review,* 100(3), 363-406.

Griffey, D., & Housner, L. (1991). Differences between experienced and inexperienced teachers' planning decisions, interactions, student engagement and instructional climate. *Research Quarterly for Exercise and Sport,* 62, 196-204.

Griffey, D., Housner, L., & Williams, D. (1986). Coaches' use of nonliteral language: Metaphor as a means of effective teaching. In M. Pieron & G. Graham, eds., *Sport Pedagogy,* pp. 131-137. Champaign, IL: Human Kinetics.

Rosenshine, B., & Stevens, R. (1986). Teaching functions. In M.C. Wittrock, ed., *Handbook of Research on Teaching,* 3rd ed., pp. 376-391. New York: Macmillan.

Tobin, K., & Capie, W. (1982). Relationships between classroom process variables and middle-school science achievement. *Journal of Educational Psychology,* 74, 441-454.

CHAPTER 36

The Antecedents of Expertise in Golf Instruction

Paul G. Schempp and J.A. You
University of Georgia in Athens, Georgia

Betsy Clark
Ladies Professional Golf Association in Daytona Beach, Florida

The purpose of this study was to determine the antecedent characteristics and experiences shared by expert golf instructors. Eleven expert golf instructors were selected with the assistance of the Ladies Professional Golf Association (LPGA). The experts possessed the following characteristics:

a. Ten or more years of teaching experience

b. LPGA certification

c. Formal recognition for the quality of their instruction

d. Their students' golfing success

For collecting data, the instructors received a background questionnaire and completed two tests to assess personality traits: ego strength scales (Thomas & Zander, 1973) and philosophy of human nature scales (Wrightsman, 1964). Based on an analysis of elite LPGA instructors, several distinguishing and common background characteristics were found. These characteristics were categorized in four domains:

a. Academic antecedents

b. Pedagogical antecedents

c. Occupational antecedents

d. Psychosocial antecedents

Keywords: Expertise, golf instructors, antecedents, characteristics of expert teachers.

INTRODUCTION

The work of Sprinthall and Thies-Sprinthall (1980) suggests that psychological characteristics and development form an important foundation for teacher development. Among the qualities identified were ego development and interpersonal development. Studies from the field of cognitive psychology seem to support the notion that a stable set of characteristics underlies teacher development (Berliner, 1994). Further, it appears that skill and expertise germinate from a stable set of characteristics and grow with practice and experience (Ericsson & Charness, 1994). Unfortunately, little work has been undertaken in this area of teaching expertise (Berliner, 1994), and the psychosocial dimensions of teaching have gone largely unexplored. Specifically, whether there are common experiences and psychological characteristics shared by golf instructors, particularly expert golf instructors, has remained an unexamined concern. The purpose of this study was, therefore, to determine the antecedent characteristics and experiences shared by expert golf instructors.

METHODS

Expert Golf Instructors

Identifying expert teachers is always a difficult task, as individuals conceptualize expertise differently. Expert golf instructors were selected with the assistance of the staff of the Ladies Professional Golf Association (LPGA). The experts of this study possessed the following characteristics:

a. Ten or more years of teaching experience
b. LPGA certification
c. Formal recognition for the quality of their instruction (e.g., state, regional, or national teacher of the year)
d. An established record of golfing success at local, regional, or national levels on the part of their students

Procedures

The selected instructors were brought to the University of Georgia campus in Athens, Georgia. Data for this study were collected in the Curriculum and Instruction Research Laboratory. The instructors received a background questionnaire and completed two tests to assess personality traits: (a) ego and (b) philosophy of human nature. Prior to data collection, each instructor completed an approved Informed Consent form, as required by the Protection of Human Subjects act.

Background Questionnaire

Experience is a prerequisite to the development of expertise. The instructors, therefore, completed a personal background information questionnaire to allow cataloging of the experts' experiences. The questionnaire concerned information regarding education, teaching experience, teaching philosophy, work experience, sport involvement, and personal awards or honors. The data generated from this questionnaire were largely self-reports and qualitative in nature.

Thomas-Zander Ego Strength Scales

As suggested by Sprinthall and Thies-Sprinthall (1980), teachers' self-perceptions and ego may not only influence their teaching, but may have also influenced the selection of a teaching career. For the purpose of this study, ego strength was measured by the Thomas-Zander ego strength scales (Thomas & Zander, 1973), as the scales appear to represent qualities germane to teaching. In these scales, ego is conceptualized in two parts. An individual's ability to be self-directing and to translate intentions into behavior (i.e., executive ability) is the first part. The second part of ego, according to Thomas and Zander, is the ability to control and release tension without disturbing other psychological processes (i.e., tension control). The form used in this investigation contained 27 true/false statements. The first 20 items are intended to reflect both executive ability and tension control, as well as more general psychological functions. Seven items formed a Guttman scale thought to indicate both executive ability and tension control.

Zander and Thomas (1960) reported a test-retest reliability of 0.81 for the first 20 items and 0.72 for the 7-item Guttman scale. The reliability estimates were on data collected from 541 men who took the test twice with one week between each administration. Convergent validity was established with a manifest anxiety scale (–0. 65) and the Tennessee esteem scale (0.20).

Philosophy of Human Nature Scale

While ego was used as a measure of teachers' self-perceptions, their perceptions of others were considered equally important as a characteristic influencing why and how they taught. The Philosophy of Human Nature scale was designed to assess the expectancies that people have about the ways in which other people generally behave (Wrightsman, 1964); but in particular, this scale appeared to address issues that might influence one's pedagogical activity and orientation. Wrightsman conceptualized the perception of human nature as composed of six factors:

a. Trustworthiness
b. Altruism
c. Independence
d. Strength of will and rationality
e. Complexity of human nature
f. Variability in human nature

An overall score for favorableness toward human nature was calculated from the first four subscales. For the purpose of this study, each factor was analyzed independently.

Reliability was estimated using split-half and test-retest procedures with 530 male and female college students from six universities. Split-half reliabilities ranged from 0.58 to 0.74 for the six factors. Test-retest reliability estimates ranged from 0.52 to

0.84. Validity was determined by comparing test results with data for other similar instruments. Substantial correlations were reported with a political cynicism scale (r = –0.61), faith in people scale (r = 0.77), and the Machiavellianism scale (r = –0.68).

RESULTS

The purpose of this study was to investigate the antecedent characteristics, experiences, and traits common to expert golf instructors. Based on an analysis of elite LPGA instructors, several distinguishing and common background characteristics were found among the 11 teachers. These characteristics were categorized in four domains:

    a. Academic antecedents

    b. Pedagogical antecedents

    c. Occupational antecedents

    d. Psychosocial antecedents

Academic Antecedents

The academic antecedents reflect the degree to which the expert golf instructors were formally educated, certified, and trained. These antecedents reflect commonalities among the expert instructors in educational background, including formal education and certification programs.

Formal Education

The level of formal education of expert golf instructors is shown in figure 36.1. Eight instructors earned bachelor degrees, one instructor had a master's degree, and

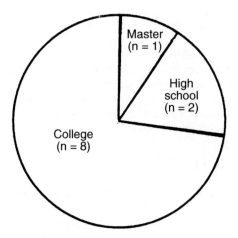

Figure 36.1   Level of formal education.

two instructors had ceased their formal education at the high school level. While a college degree does not appear to be a necessary prerequisite for golf instruction, the high number of college degrees among these instructors appears to suggest that expert golf instructors value education and are academically oriented.

As seen in figure 36.2, physical education was identified as the most common academic major of nine instructors who had a college degree. Considering that a normal course of study for a bachelor's degree in physical education includes motor learning, biomechanics, exercise physiology, pedagogical courses and experiences, and demonstrations of athletic competence, it is perhaps unsurprising that expert golf instructors chose this major and that they benefit from academic preparation in teaching golf. It appears that these golf instructors, in contrast to other sport instructors (Lawson, 1983), value an academic preparation.

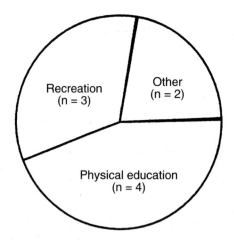

Figure 36.2   Major areas of degree (n = 9).

Certification

Of the 11 teachers, 5 instructors have PGA/LPGA certification (Class "A") and 6 instructors have LPGA certification (Class "A") as seen in figure 36.3. This means that all golf instructors are qualified and competent to teach golf. The finding that at least half of these instructors reported holding a dual certification in both the LPGA and the PGA is further evidence of the importance they place on learning and their preparation for golf instruction.

Pedagogical Antecedents

The pedagogical antecedents are those teaching characteristics and experiences common to the majority of the expert golf teachers in this study. Pedagogical antecedents included the number of years teaching golf, awards and honors won for teaching, teaching philosophy, and successful teaching experiences.

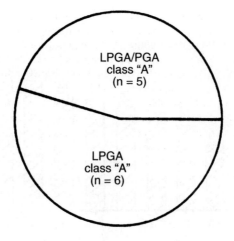

Figure 36.3   Certification.

Number of Years in Teaching

From their review of research into the acquisition of expertise, Ericsson and Charness (1994) concluded that it took at least 10 years of deliberate practice in a particular endeavor until expertise might be obtained. This finding was supported by the study by Brandt (1986), who found that experience of 10 years or longer was necessary for becoming an expert teacher. Berliner (Brandt, 1986) noted, however, that even though 10 years of experience was a requirement for becoming an expert, it was not a sufficient condition in itself to ensure pedagogical expertise.

The number of years of experience for the teachers in this study ranged from 6 to 27 years (figure 36.4). With the exception of one instructor who had but 6 years of experience, the golf instructors had over 10 years of experience. As a group, these teachers possessed extensive experience in their craft, as the mean teaching years for the total sample was 16.72 years. While the single teacher with 6 years of experience challenges previous research, the extensive experience of the other instructors seems to suggest that a minimum of 10 years' experience in the field represents a legitimate benchmark in the development of expert golf instructors.

Teaching Honors/Awards

All golf instructors in this study had received formal recognition for the quality of their instruction. The teaching honors or awards they had won included National Teacher of the Year, Section Teacher of the Year, Section Coach of the Year, and selection as one of *Golf Magazine*'s 100 Best Instructors. Because recognition by peers for superior teaching was a selection criterion for inclusion in this study, it was expected that all teachers in our sample had won one of the awards mentioned. Teaching honors and awards cannot, therefore, be objectively or logically discussed as a finding of this study.

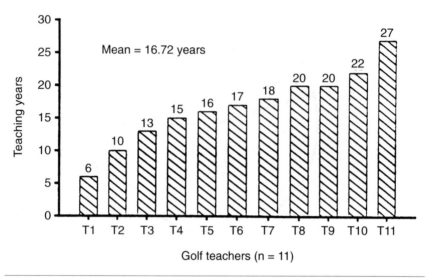

Figure 36.4   Teaching years of expert golf teachers.

Teaching Philosophy

The instructional approach of the teachers is usually guided by an instructional philosophy. Such a philosophy would include perceptions of students' needs and interests, effective teaching strategies, necessary golf knowledge, and the teachers' assessment of their own skills and abilities. Thus, one's teaching philosophy may greatly influence the instructional process and behaviors in the educational setting. Two major emerging and common themes came from the teachers' self-reports on their teaching philosophies. These data were obtained from the questionnaire. It is possible that a teacher is eclectic, subscribing to one or more philosophies or shaping a unique philosophy from several orientations. The philosophies of the expert teachers in this study are summarized next.

Student-centered approach.   This approach assumes that each student has the potential and ability to learn and play golf successfully. In addition, this approach has students actively set and achieve their goals in learning because it emphasizes that students should have motivation and fun in learning and playing golf. In a sense, teachers who emphasize the uniqueness of each student try to build upon the needs of students through smooth communication with each one. Thus, the teachers often attempt to personalize the instruction and program to fit best with each student. No two instructional programs will look alike, as no two students are exactly alike. One of the teachers described her teaching philosophy as a "students-centered model: exploring and achieving what each student wants out of the game." The other teachers described their approach as one that attempts, for example, "to honor the uniqueness of each individual and allow the humanness of teaching and learning to remain. How do they do it when they do it best?"

Fundamental approach using mechanical principles.   This approach emphasizes the basics of the golf swing in a simple way. When presenting the method of a golf swing, teachers try to deliver information regarding the most fundamental components of the swing rather than providing the student with complex and detailed information. In addition, the teachers try to explain the mechanical principles of the golf swing in a way that focuses instruction on the students' understanding of the cause and effect, as well as the sequence of physical motion in the performance of a golf swing. One golf teacher explained her philosophy in teaching as "use of a strong fundamental approach as first diagnosis and then the five ball flight laws adapted to a specific problem in swing and person's ability function." Another philosophy as stated by another teacher was "understanding of how the club works, relate it to something and then can do it!"

Successful Teaching Experiences

Previous experience has long been identified as an important antecedent in teaching (Lawson, 1983; Lortie, 1975). Teaching experience is thought to especially impact the development of teachers' skills and instructional orientations (Hammersley, 1977; Metz, 1988). It would be particularly instructive not only to understand those experiences that helped shape expert perspectives, but also to identify those experiences that the teachers deemed most successful. The majority of expert golf instructors in this study described their greatest teaching success in the form of the following points:

• Seeing students learn and enjoy the game. Teachers indicated that seeing new golfers learn and enjoy the game was the greatest success in golf instruction. For example, according to the instructors, there are some students who do not think they could play. When these students could play golf by virtue of the teaching, the teachers expressed that this experience was the greatest success in teaching. One instructor described her greatest success as happening "when the person that does not think they can do it—does it." Another teacher stated that success was "seeing people learn the game, have fun with it and share that experience with others." And a third identified teaching success by saying, "To see a new golfer enjoy the game and to see the glint of inspiration in their eye that says that they are hooked is the ultimate for me."

• The development of performance level. Teachers expressed that seeing new golfers suddenly develop a significantly higher level of performance at an early period in the instructional process is a successful experience. Further, having students establish records of golfing success at local, regional, or national levels provided the instructors with the satisfaction that they had achieved or surpassed an instructional goal. One example cited was that of "a female student in her late 30s, went from a 17 Hcp, to winning one of southern Cal's top amateur events in a 2 year period." One of the other teachers remarked, "[a] young man I have been teaching since he was 5 is joining the mini-tour this winter—Q-school [Qualifying School] next fall."

• Formal recognition as an expert teacher. Teaching success, for some, was measured in recognition from students and peers. The teachers stated that they felt success as a teacher when they received formal recognition for the quality of their instruction at state, regional, or national levels. One teacher reported that she felt "honored by my peers as their Teacher of Year in both PGA and LPGA."

Occupational Antecedents

The occupational antecedents refer to the early experiences in golf that teachers recall and carry with them today. The years spent involved in the sport of golf in various capacities and at various levels provided experiences that not only influenced the teachers' decisions to become golf instructors, but also continued to shape who these teachers are and what they do with their students. The two antecedent traits that seem to influence the majority of the expert teachers studied were their biography as a player and golf-related work experiences.

Playing Experience

When the expert golf instructors were asked to describe their playing experience, they described extensive and varied experiences that included playing as a young child, as an amateur, and for some, as a professional tour player. Most of the teachers indicated that they had started playing golf before 10 years of age. The majority of these teachers also had played in national amateur tournaments for several years and loved to compete. In addition, some actively participated in a variety of tour series including the LPGA Tour, Futures Tour, PGA section events, European Tour, and Asian Tour.

These experiences provided the expert teachers with a common quality found in other experts: early and sustained involvement in the activity in which they have become an expert. In particular, the characteristics of early playing experience, the rich experiences of national and international competitions, and longevity in the game support the research of Ericsson and Charness (1994), who found extensive experience a prerequisite for gaining expertise. It should be noted, however, that these teachers, by virtue of their involvement and achievements as players, should be identified as expert golf players. It appears, therefore, that expertise in performing the skills of golf and playing the game of golf is an important antecedent to becoming an expert teacher of golf.

Work Experience

The teachers in this study possessed a variety of golf- and teaching-related work experiences. Working as a golf instructor was obviously a common characteristic among these teachers; however, other positions they held included that of director of golf instruction for a school, head professional at a golf facility, college golf coach, assistant instructor, president of a teaching professionals' association, and assistant teaching professional. In addition, a few teachers had served as consultant, range supervisor, club manager, or owner of golf schools. These work experiences reveal a devotion to golf and its instruction by these expert teachers.

Psychosocial Antecedents

The final antecedent category investigated in this study was represented in two psychosocial characteristics: (a) ego strength and (b) philosophy of human nature. These two measures were selected as they represent important qualities in a personality. Because the research on teaching expertise has, to date, remained largely steeped in the cognitive and behavioral sciences (Berliner, 1994), little is known about the psychosocial antecedents of expert teachers. The characteristics included in this investigation consisted of ego strength and philosophy of human nature. Specifically, one represents the measure of self-perception (ego), and the other represents perceptions of others (philosophy of human nature).

Ego Strength Scales

The ego strength of the 11 expert golf instructors was assessed using the Thomas-Zander Ego Strength scales (ESS; Thomas & Zander, 1973). The scores on ESS ranged from 8 to 23 (figure 36.5). The mean scale score for the total sample was 18.45 with a maximum possible score of 26. With one teacher scoring what appears to be an uncharacteristic 8, it appears that the scores for the remaining 9 instructors reveal a relatively high level of ego strength. According to the scale authors, this would indicate that these individuals were self-directing and able to consistently translate their intentions into actions and behavior. Further, it appears these teachers were, for the most part, able to control and discharge personal psychological tension in psychologically stable and healthy ways.

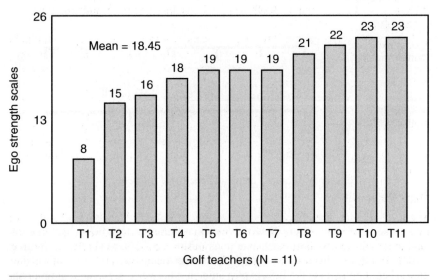

Figure 36.5   Ego strength scales of expert golf teachers.

Philosophy of Human Nature

The Philosophy of Human Nature scale (Wrightsman, 1964) was used to assess the instructors' beliefs regarding human nature. Data analysis indicates an overall favorable view toward human nature (figure 36.6). The expert teachers scored highest on variability in human nature (1.03). This indicates that the teachers held firm beliefs that there are fundamental and individual differences between people and that human nature is susceptible to change. This finding supports the previous finding of teaching philosophies that focused on the individual differences in students and the need for a student-centered approach to teaching. The high strength

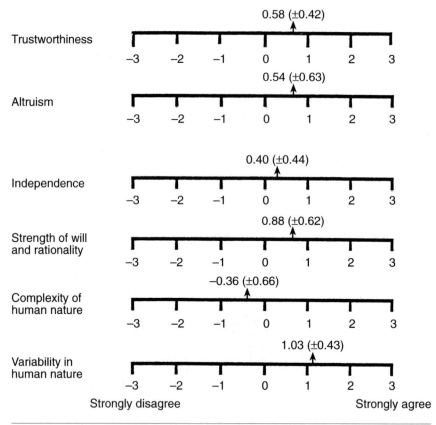

Figure 36.6   Philosophy of human nature of expert golf teachers.
Note: Mean (standard deviation).

of will and rationality score (0.88) reveals that these teachers believe that people understand the motives behind their actions and have control over both their motives and their actions. This finding would help explain the instructors' sense of satisfaction when they reverse the beliefs of a student who was convinced that he or she could not learn or play golf.

The low score on complexity of human nature (−0.36) suggests that these expert golf instructors see people as easily understood and not particularly complex. Again, this would support the view that a teacher can devise an individualized program once the teacher understands the nature of the person. Further, the importance of establishing relationships based on trust and understanding would be reflected in this finding.

On the basis of the findings, it appears that these expert golf instructors have a tendency toward a positive view of human nature. Before definitive statements regarding the personalities of expert golf teachers or antecedents of expert golf instruction can be made, more research is necessary to provide a pool of consistent and convincing evidence.

CONCLUSIONS

This study analyzed selected antecedent characteristics and experiences common to expert golf instructors. Specifically, the academic background, instructional experience, occupational history, and selected psychological characteristics (i.e., ego, philosophy of human nature) were studied. Based upon the results of this study, several conclusions were drawn.

It appears that expert golf instructors have a large variance in their educational backgrounds, with the prevailing trend toward the upper end of the educational spectrum as evidenced by the attainment of undergraduate and graduate university degrees. Variation was also noted in the instructors' teaching philosophies. It appears, therefore, that educational background and instructional philosophy are not predictors of or prerequisites for expertise in golf instruction.

The teachers in this study were quite experienced in their craft as suggested by their average of almost 17 years of instructional experience. These teachers also possessed extensive playing experience as indicated by the length of participation in the sport of golf and the success experienced in regional, national, and professional tournaments. These findings suggest that teaching and playing experience are important antecedents to becoming an expert golf instructor.

Finally, a mean score of 18.45 (score range 0-26) on the ego scale reveals that expert teachers have relatively strong egos and are thus self-directed and able to transform ideas into action. Further, with high scores on beliefs of variability in human nature (1.03) and will (0.88), and low scores on human complexity (–0.36), it appears that expert teachers believe people can change, can determine their own destiny, and can be understood. The psychological profile of an expert teacher, as revealed in the teachers in this study, is of an individual who believes in herself, as well as her students; it also suggests that the teacher and student together can accomplish the goals they set.

References

Berliner, D.C. (1994). Expertise: The wonder of exemplary performances. In J. Mangierie & Block (eds.), *Creating powerful thinking in teachers and students: Diverse perspectives,* pp. 161-186. Fort Worth, TX: Harcourt Brace.

Brandt, R.S. (1986). On the expert teacher: A conversation with David Berliner. *Educational Leadership,* 44(2), 4-9.

Ericsson, K.A., & Charness, N. (1994). Expert performance: Its structure and acquisition. *American Psychologist,* 49(3), 725-747.

Hammersley, M. (1977). *Teacher perspectives.* Milton Keynes, England: Open University Press.

Lawson, H.A. (1983). Toward a model of teacher socialization in physical education: The subjective warrant, recruitment, and teacher education (part I). *Journal of Teaching in Physical Education,* 2(3), 3-16.

Lortie, D.C. (1975). *Schoolteacher: A sociological study.* Chicago: University of Chicago Press.

Metz, M. (1988). *Teachers' ultimate dependence on their students.* Madison, WI: National Center on Effective Secondary Schools.

Pooley, J.C. (1975). The professional socialization of physical education students in the United States and England. *International Review of Sport Sociology,* 10(3-4), 97-107.

Sage, G. (1989). Becoming a high school coach: From playing sports to coaching. *Research Quarterly for Exercise and Sport,* 51, 110-121.

Templin, T., Woodford, R., & Mulling, C. (1982). On becoming a physical educator: Occupational choice and the anticipatory socialization process. *Quest,* 34(2), 119-133.

Sprinthall, N.A., & Thies-Sprinthall, L. (1980). Adult development and leadership training for mainstream education. In D.C. Corrigan & K.R. Howey (eds.), *Concepts to guide the education of experienced teachers.* Reston, VA: Council for Exceptional Children.

Thomas, E., & Zander, A. (1973). Thomas-Zander ego strength scales. In J. Robinson & P. Shaver (eds.), *Measures of social psychological attitudes.* Ann Arbor, MI: University of Michigan, Institute for Social Research.

Wrightsman, L. (1964). Measurement of philosophies of human nature. *Psychological Reports,* 14, 743-751.

Zander, A., & Thomas, E. (1960). The validity of a measure of ego strength. Manuscript. The University of Michigan, Institute for Social Research.

CHAPTER 37

The Knowledge Acquisition of Expert Golf Instructors

Paul G. Schempp and Charles L. Templeton
The University of Georgia

Betsy Clark
Ladies Professional Golf Association in Daytona Beach, Florida

The purpose of this study was to determine the sources of knowledge expert golf instructors most often used in their professional practice. Eleven expert golf instructors were identified and selected with the assistance of the Ladies Professional Golf Association (LPGA). The instructors were selected on the basis of the following criteria and characteristics:

a. Six or more years of teaching experience
b. LPGA certification
c. Formal recognition for the quality of their instruction
d. Their students' golfing success

Data were collected using the Q-Sort technique (Kerlinger, 1973), in which 11 cards, each depicting a different knowledge source, were sorted and ranked by the instructors from most important to least important. After the ranking, a semi-structured interview was used to ask the instructors to explain their ordering. The knowledge-source data from the Q-Sort were grand rank ordered and then composite ordered from most to least important. The interviews were analyzed to determine the underlying rationale for the rankings. Based on the analysis of the data, the sources of knowledge were classified into three categories: primary, secondary, and tertiary.

Keywords: Expertise, golf instructors, Q-Sort, knowledge sources.

INTRODUCTION

A distinguishing characteristic of an expert in any field is the ability to acquire, retain, recall, and recognize significantly more knowledge about their subject than virtually anyone else (Chi, Glaser, & Farr, 1988). The excellence of experts is crafted through their extensive knowledge and skills amassed over years of practice (Tan, 1997). Experts make significant investments in learning all they can about their field. One finds that experts enjoy talking almost endlessly about their subject, that they gather others' views on pertinent topics, and that they have extensive libraries devoted to their subject (Ericsson & Charness, 1994).

There is much evidence to suggest that expertise in one domain does not generalize readily to other domains (Chi, Glaser, & Farr, 1988). This is so because expert performances are dependent not only on how much experts know, but also on how they employ a strategy that is best suited to their state of knowledge. Experts are both highly knowledgeable in a particular field and eminently skilled in the application of that knowledge.

The role of knowledge in expert teaching was recently explored in a study preceding the current investigation (Schempp, Manross, Tan, & Fincher, in press). It that study, it was found that subject experts demonstrated a greater ability for planning progressive learning activities and for forming contingency plans. When teaching subjects in which they were expert, teachers were more comfortable and enthusiastic regarding their lessons and could accommodate a greater range of learner abilities. Clearly, knowledge of the subject made for better teaching.

Two particular problems are currently commanding the attention of those interested in developing better teachers: (a) what is the essential knowledge for teaching? and (b) where does this knowledge come from? (Shulman, 1987). This study was an investigation of the second of these two questions. Understanding the sources of expert golf teachers' knowledge would go a long way toward organizing and promoting programs that could directly improve golf instruction. The purpose of this study was, therefore, to identify the sources of knowledge most often used by expert golf instructors in their professional practice.

METHODS

The design of this study was both qualitative and quantitative. The quantitative portions were useful for detecting general trends across a representative sample of teachers. The qualitative portion of the study permitted the teachers' words and actions to form the essential data for analysis. Teachers' knowledge is not easily captured by traditional ways of identifying knowledge (Grossman, 1990). A mixed design study, therefore, provided in-depth and detailed information on the sources expert golf instructors looked to in gaining pedagogically pertinent knowledge.

Expert Golf Instructors

Identifying expert teachers is always a difficult task, as individuals conceptualize experts differently. Eleven expert golf instructors were selected with the assistance of the staff of the Ladies Professional Golf Association (LPGA). The experts all possessed the following characteristics:

a. Six or more years of teaching experience
b. LPGA certification
c. Formal recognition for the quality of their instruction (e.g., state, regional, or national teacher of the year)
d. A record of golfing success at local, regional, or national levels on the part of their students

Procedures

Data were collected for this study using the Q-Sort technique. Data collection took place at the University of Georgia Curriculum and Instruction Research Laboratory, Athens, Georgia. The instructors met individually and in private with one of the investigators. After the purpose of the study was explained and the teachers had read and signed an informed consent form, the data were collected as will be described. The entire process took approximately 20 minutes per instructor.

Q-Sort

The 11 expert golf teachers were asked to Q-sort (Kerlinger, 1973) a set of 11 cards, each depicting a different source of teachers' knowledge (Shulman, 1987; Fincher & Schempp, 1994). The sources of knowledge included

a. books,
b. journals and magazines,
c. films and videos,
d. playing experience,
e. teaching experience,
f. workshops,
g. students,
h. other teachers,
i. certification programs,
j. formal education, and
k. popular media.

The teachers were instructed to rank order the sources of knowledge based upon the source that had consistently proven most useful in supplying the knowledge necessary to teach golf.

The teachers first rank ordered the sources of knowledge they found most useful in their teaching. After sorting the cards, the teachers were asked to reconsider the rankings to ensure that these indeed represented a ranking from most to least important. Finally, they were asked to explain their ranking in a semi-structured interview (Goetz & LeCompte, 1984). Particular attention was directed to the teachers' use of knowledge in actual practice. The interview was audiotaped and later transcribed.

Data Analysis

Data were analyzed using a mixture of qualitative and quantitative techniques. The first level of analysis determined a grand rank ordering of knowledge sources from the Q-Sort results. The sources of knowledge were composite ranked from most to least important. The interview transcripts were analyzed in order to provide an understanding of the rationale underlying the teachers' choices of knowledge sources and their application in teaching golf.

FINDINGS

Analysis of raw score totals for the forms and sources of knowledge revealed rank orders as well as primary, secondary, and tertiary knowledge sources (table 37.1). The data indicated that the golf instructors' primary sources of knowledge were other teachers and their own teaching experiences. These instructors consistently reported gathering information regarding new and different teaching aids, drills, skill progressions, and communication techniques from informal, not formal, interactions with other golf instructors and from teachers in other disciplines. Other teachers provided models of teaching success and offered a means for discussing new information. The interactions with other teachers were informal; they usually occurred when the instructor was working with another teacher at a home course or perhaps encountered another teacher during a professional meeting. Four instructors rated other teachers as their number-one source of knowledge, and three rated this as second in importance.

Lynn Marriott, the 1992 National Teacher of the Year, cited other golf instructors as a primary knowledge source but also indicated that teachers in other disciplines

Table 37.1   Golf Instructors' Primary Sources of Knowledge

Rank	Knowledge source	Raw score	Importance
1.5	Other teachers	30	Primary
1.5	Teaching experience	30	Primary
3	Books	49	Secondary
4	Students	50	Secondary
5	Workshops	56	Secondary
6	Certification programs	67	Tertiary
7	Playing experience	71	Tertiary
8	Journals and magazines	78	Tertiary
9	Films and videos	82	Tertiary
10	Formal education	86	Tertiary
11	Popular media	95	Tertiary

provided her with a great deal of knowledge. Three instructors reported that teaching experience was their primary source of knowledge, while five ranked this second. The teachers indicated that teaching experience gave them more practice and observation time and increased their depth of knowledge and understanding of golf, thus increasing their knowledge base for teaching. They also reported that their interaction with others while teaching, particularly with students, provided them a wealth of knowledge. Interactions with students also provided feedback regarding teaching success and failure. Teaching experience also gave the teachers knowledge and experience in communicating effectively with students at all different levels. Gale Peterson, 1996 National Teacher of the Year, reported that her teaching experience gave her knowledge as well as experience in "dealing with students and learning how to be a better communicator."

Secondary sources of knowledge for the expert golf instructors were books, their students, and workshops. These sources ranked three, four, and five, respectively; but the raw scores indicated they were very close, suggesting that these sources were very similar in importance for these instructors. Books, while not a primary source of knowledge, was an important secondary knowledge source. Many of the instructors reported that reading golf books was helpful because of the availability of the information and because such reading provided an easy means of continuing education. The 1995 LPGA National Teacher of the Year, Kay McMahon, reads books as a way to continue her formal education, while Dana Rader, the 1990 LPGA National Teacher of the Year, indicated that reading books was a way of being a student of the game. Other instructors found books covering topics other than golf useful in developing the knowledge they use in their instruction. For instance, Gale Peterson indicated that she read books on motor development and physical fitness. Lynn Marriott has read books covering a variety of disciplines, and Rebecca Dengler reads books on the brain and learning. These instructors found a more holistic approach to their knowledge development important because knowledge gained from other disciplines was useful in understanding their students better and in providing more appropriate instruction.

Analysis of the data revealed that another secondary source of knowledge for these experts was the students they taught. All of the instructors were quick to acknowledge that students were very important factors to consider. Nancy Quarcelino, a Section Teacher of the Year, believed that students were the most important factor in teaching, as everything in teaching depends on the student. Other teachers found that students provided a wealth of knowledge due to the great diversity of learning styles they exhibit and the feedback they provide regarding instruction, communication, and levels of success and failure. Resoundingly, these expert instructors indicated that they valued and used the knowledge gained from their students to develop and improve their instructional skills.

Workshops were another secondary knowledge source the expert instructors found useful in their teaching. Most indicated that workshops provided a means of formal learning and sharing of information about new equipment, different instructional techniques, and more effective communication skills. They found the formal interaction with the workshop leaders, as well as with people from other professions, to be beneficial. Mardell Wilkins, Western Section Teacher of the Year for the LPGA, described a professional workshop as a "learning environment where you go and obtain different information that will be useful in teaching the game of golf."

Further analysis of the Q-Sort ranks and the interview data revealed several tertiary knowledge sources. The tertiary sources included certification programs, playing experiences, journals and magazines, films and videos, formal education, and popular media. While these sources were not highly important, the instructors did indicate they were useful. For some of the instructors, the certification programs were useful tools for developing more knowledge and extending their education. The certification programs provided opportunities for interaction with other professionals and a chance to gain, share, and explore new ideas.

The playing experiences of these instructors were also a source of knowledge. For some, playing experience was a commonality they had with their students, enabling them to better relate and express information to learners. Rina Ritson stated that her playing experience gave her knowledge about what her students were feeling, and Mardell Wilkins indicated that she used stories about her own playing experiences to better relate to her students.

As other tertiary sources of knowledge, the instructors cited journals and magazines as well as films and videos useful in their teaching practices. For some, journals and magazines provided up-to-date information, while others found reading periodicals important in order to know and understand what their students were learning through those publications. Films and videos also provided new information while offering some instructors a tool for comparing their students' skills to those of highly skilled players. Additionally, some of the instructors indicated that they used video as an instructional aid to help in the analysis of students' performance. That analysis provided the knowledge necessary to help students improve.

Finally, the sources of knowledge cited as being least important to these golf instructors were formal education and popular media. While Izzy Johnson and Kay McMahon both cited their formal education as the foundation for all of their knowledge, the majority of the instructors did not find their formal education to be of much relevance to teaching golf. Most of the teachers ranked this source very low. Popular media as a source of knowledge also ranked very low among the experts; they found the popular media to be only a way of keeping current with the golf world rather than an important source of knowledge useful in their daily instructional practices.

Overall, analysis of the data revealed a consistent finding that these expert golf instructors appeared to be very people oriented. In other words, much of the knowledge they gained was gleaned from the people with whom they worked, including students and other instructors. Their interactions with people throughout their teaching careers appeared to provide knowledge, not only about golf drills and instructional aids, but about human behavior, effective communication, and instructional strategies for students with differing personalities and learning styles. For expert golf instructors, first-hand personal interaction was critical in the development of their knowledge base for teaching.

DISCUSSION

Previous literature on the nature and characteristics of expertise indicates that experts possess extensive knowledge and skills developed over years of practice and effort (Tan, 1997). For the expert golf instructors in this study, this appears to be the case also. These instructors possessed knowledge developed and acquired over many years from a variety of primary, secondary, and tertiary sources. For these instructors, the primary sources of knowledge consisted of informal interactions with other teachers and their personal teaching experience. Secondary sources included books, work with students, and workshops. Tertiary sources of knowledge such as certification programs, playing experiences, and journals and magazines also provided knowledge and information to these golf instructors. These findings are similar to those of Fincher and Schempp (1994), who discovered that physical education teachers considered teaching experience to be a prime source of knowledge, and supplemental readings a secondary source of teaching knowledge.

A common theme linking these knowledge sources was the people factor. The expert golf instructors in this study were clearly people oriented. They learned much through a dynamic interaction process that involved many people: students, other teachers, and people from other professions. The golf instructors did not passively take in knowledge; they interacted with it and applied it.

This holds several implications for golf instructors who are striving to attain the status of expert. Instructors should look for knowledge from a variety of sources and interact with as many people as possible in their effort to develop pedagogically relevant knowledge. The high ranking of other teachers, and the continual mention of interactions with others in the teaching experience, are good indicators that new and less-experienced golf instructors should seek the counsel of more experienced and knowledgeable instructors. Those organizing certification programs and continuing education programs would do well to consider stimulating and promoting personal interaction within the context of their programs. Experts appear to draw knowledge from a variety of sources that they encounter, and they are almost always able to glean some information from such sources. With that skill, coupled with their drive to become better instructors, it is not surprising that they have assembled a vast amount of knowledge that makes them highly effective instructors and often propels them to superior performance on the lesson tee.

References

Chi, M., Glaser, R., & Farr, M. (Eds.). (1988). *The nature of expertise.* Hillsdale, NJ: Erlbaum.

Ericsson, K.A., & Charness, N. (1994). Expert performance: Its structure and acquisition. *American Psychologist, 49*(3): 725-747.

Fincher, M., & Schempp, P. (1994). Teaching physical education: What do we need to know and how do we find it? *GAHPERD Journal, 28*(3): 7-10.

Goetz, J.P., & LeCompte, M.D. (1984). *Ethnography and qualitative design in educational research.* Orlando, FL: Academic Press.

Kerlinger, F.N. (1973). *Foundations of behavioral research* (2nd ed.). New York: Holt, Rinehart & Winston.

Schempp, P., Manross, D., Tan, S., & Fincher, M. (in press). Subject expertise and teachers' knowledge. *Journal of Teaching in Physical Education.*

Shulman, L.S. (1987). Knowledge and teaching: Foundations of the new reform. *Harvard Educational Review, 57*(1): 1-22.

Tan, S. (1997). The elements of expertise. *Journal of Physical Education, Recreation and Dance, 68*(2): 30-33.

CHAPTER 38

Irish Golf Club Professionals: A Training Needs Analysis

E.P. Young, J. Granaghan, and E.S. Wallace
Department of Sport & Leisure Studies, University of Ulster, Northern Ireland

Training provides the opportunity for the individual to learn and develop new skills and competencies. The importance of staff training and development in any industry cannot be overemphasised (Torkildsen, 1992). It provides an opportunity for the individual to make a more positive contribution to the administration and operation of the organisation. The present study analysed the training needs of golf professionals in Ireland at the organisational, occupational, and individual level. Fifty-five clubs throughout the 32 counties were targeted with a postal questionnaire (60% response) that yielded both qualitative and quantitative information. The important role that the Professional Golfers Association (PGA) has in training the professional golfer is highlighted. However, the majority of the golfers had not undertaken any additional training since qualifying from the PGA course. Organisational training needs in the areas of marketing and operations management were identified. At the occupational level, budgeting, shop management, teaching methods, and golf skills are emphasised. At an individual level, the need to develop better coaching, negotiating, and communication skills is stressed. The potential barriers to training are outlined; these include aspects such as lack of refresher courses, lack of facilities, and lack of interest. The results of the research suggest that a training gap does exist for the Irish golf club professional. Continuing professional development of qualified Irish golf professionals is not a trend within the profession once they have qualified.

Keywords: Golf professional, training, training needs analysis, continuing professional development.

INTRODUCTION

In less than half a century, the game of golf has been transformed. A sport once limited to a relatively small number of participants, mostly males of high social standing, has become a game and leisure pursuit enjoyed by approximately 35 million players throughout the world (Guest, 1994). As a result of increased public interest in golf and the erosion of class barriers within the sport, the pressure on existing golf courses has become immense. Increased club membership quotas, waiting lists, queues for play, and the necessity for pre-booking have become the norm (Browning, 1990). The interest in golf as a leisure pursuit and the associated increase in the number of participants have placed demands upon golf courses and the golf professional. The training of today's golf professional has moved sharply into focus in a dynamic environment where the professional is being asked to provide a quality service and operate and perform in a dynamic business and commercial world. New technology and equipment, increased competition from other golf clubs and leisure pursuits, a focus on customer service, the emphasis on value for money, and the need to provide specialist coaching and training have translated into key objectives for the golf professional. The changing role that the golf professional undertakes has had to accommodate this commercial orientation within the golf industry. There is currently little information on the training needs of the Irish golf club professional.

The objective of this study was to identify the critical areas related to the training of the golf professional in Ireland by undertaking a training needs analysis (TNA). In an effort to establish whether training cycles have developed to cope with changes and the demands placed upon the professional by the industry, the current training regime within the profession was reviewed. Ultimately, the aim of the study was to provide a clear picture of the training areas that the Irish golf professional believes he/she requires in order to meet the demands of today's environment. Training needs can be identified in relation to three key areas:

1. Organisational
2. Occupational
3. Individual (Bee et al., 1994)

To identify the training needs at these levels, a TNA is carried out (Flemming, 1994). The Training Advisory and Consultancy Service for Industry (1994) has defined TNA as

> the systematic investigation of an organisation, its aims, objectives, procedures and the capabilities of its personnel—in order to identify specific requirements for training and recommend training strategies, plans and provision to satisfy those requirements. (p. 1)

The hypothesis is that if the training needs of the professionals are being met, then the individual should possess the necessary skills to adapt to the requirements of the rapidly changing environment. If training needs are not being met, then the golf professional is being inadequately equipped to fulfil his/her role within the club. The club is not maximising the potential of the professional and/or the professional does not have the skills or competencies to meet the demands being placed upon him/her.

EXPERIMENTAL METHODS

Postal Survey

A self-administered postal survey was used to gather primary information. This provided an economic method of targeting a variety of golf clubs throughout the 32 counties. The questionnaire was designed to establish

1. the length of time the professionals had served at their clubs,
2. their current level of professionally related training,
3. the qualifications and skills they possess,
4. the roles and activities they are involved in,
5. the organisational, occupational, and individual training needs,
6. the barriers that exist to training, and
7. the training gaps that exist.

To ensure validity and reliability, the questionnaire was piloted prior to the main survey (Cohen & Manion, 1994), and adjustments to questions were made on the basis of responses. Using the Golfing Union of Ireland's listings and the PGA yearbook, a nonprobability purposive sampling technique was used to ensure an adequate spread of club size and membership ranges from the clubs selected. To strengthen the representativeness, the sample was chosen relative to the number and size of clubs in each county. The questionnaire was posted to 16% of the golf clubs, providing a small but representative sample (Cohen & Manion, 1994). Although the administration of a postal survey often leads to a low response rate, in this case a response rate of 60% was achieved. The questionnaire generated both qualitative and quantitative data through open and closed questions.

RESULTS AND DISCUSSION

The Golf Professionals' Working Environment

Snape (1987) has noted that in the United Kingdom and Ireland the popularity of golf is "on a rising trend" (p. 32). A survey in the late 1980s indicated declining participation rates for sports such as swimming, tennis, and aerobics, while golf was still enjoying a major growth phase (Feld, 1988). In Ireland the boom of the past 20 years has increased the number of golf facilities by about 40% (Price, 1996). This is reflected in the emergence of 82 courses during the period 1990-1996. Wheat (1995) suggests that the period 1993-1994 yielded the most courses. The boom in Irish golf may be explained by the proactive approach taken by the Sports Council in promoting leisure pursuits and the increased availability of agricultural sites as declining farming incomes forced farmers to diversify (Dair & Schofield, 1994). Golf in Ireland today remains a vibrant industry, and there is even more accessibility to facilities for potential enthusiasts. Women and retired citizens have become actively involved; coverage of competitions by the media, as well as golfing exhibitions and merchandising, have prompted a rise in junior club members (PGA, 1997). Golfing academies are emerging, with specialist knowledge being applied through new technology and sport science, computer applications, simulators, and virtual reality (Ponziano, 1996). The golf professional works within a dynamic and complex environment. Eighty-five percent of the professionals surveyed worked within a club with a membership of over 600 people (figure 38.1), and 73% of these clubs have membership in excess of 800 people. Over 67% of these clubs have been opened for more than 90 years, indicating that a high proportion of the respondent professionals worked in well-established club systems. The professionals operating within the clubs were all male. Fifty-two percent had been employed by the respective clubs for over 10 years, 33% for between 5 and 10 years, and 15% for less than 5 years.

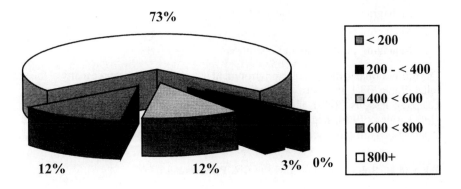

Figure 38.1   Club membership numbers.

Qualifications of Irish Golf Professionals

Seventy-five percent of the professionals had obtained the intermediate certificate or GCSE "O" levels as a minimum qualification. Forty-eight percent had completed a leaving certificate examination or GCSE "A" level. Among the respondents, 87% had served as assistant professionals, with 78% having taken recognised PGA qualifications. The PGA is a members' organisation composed of qualified professionals. For many years, membership in the association and the status of a club professional were gained simply through the ability to play to a high standard and through working as an assistant for two years without formal training. In the late 1950s formal training was discussed, and it was introduced in 1961. By 1970, the value of training was acknowledged, and compulsory training and examinations were implemented (*PGA Training Guide,* 1994). The PGA acts as the main training body, and it recognises that the professional golfer must "realise that playing is only one of the many skills and functions required" (*PGA Information Booklet,* 1996, p. 5). Trainees must serve a probation period of six months at a course or driving range prior to registering. Once committed, they undertake a three-year training programme based at the golf club under the tuition of a full-time qualified professional. The PGA syllabus contains elements such as teaching, club repair, commercial studies, and the rules of golf tournaments. Trainees must also provide evidence of their playing ability by playing to a handicap of 4 or better in no fewer than 25 PGA-approved rounds of golf.

The Golf Professionals' Role

Golf has developed in many different ways over the last century (Menton, 1991). The role of the professional has also changed considerably, from one of coach and mentor to that of business executive with a responsibility to manage and administer within the golf club environment. Economic growth has fueled the development of the services sector, and golf professionals are required to manage within this context. Donnelly et al. (1995) emphasise that managers have three broad tasks:

1. Managing work and organisations
2. Managing people
3. Managing production and operations

The professional in the golf club environment is required to undertake many of these roles. Table 38.1 indicates the variety and frequency of the roles performed. Teaching lessons (91%), shop management (97%), purchasing (88%), finance (73%), sales (79%), negotiation (70%), communication (82%), and equipment repair (82%) are activities that the professional is often or always involved in. It is

Table 38.1   Roles Undertaken by the Golf Professional

Type of activity	% of time involved			
	Always	Often	Sometimes	Never
Teaching lessons	70	21	3	0
Marketing club	6	27	52	15
Competition organisation	21	24	45	9
Shop management	88	9	0	3
Purchasing	55	33	9	3
Finance	43	30	12	15
Sales	46	33	18	3
Negotiation	18	52	24	6
Communication	36	46	12	6
Competitive participation	18	6	61	15
Golf development	24	31	39	6
Equipment repair	49	33	12	6
Monitoring of course	15	15	46	24

evident that the club professional is required to be competent in a range of areas such as business, teaching, craftsmanship, administration, and customer service.

The Professionals' Perception of Their Training for the Job

Eighty-two percent of the respondents were satisfied with the level of skill that they currently have to perform their job. Ninety-four percent indicated that they have had adequate training relevant to their job. However, Williamson (1995) and Broadwell (1993) have identified the need for training and continual professional development. Torkildsen (1992) also states that training is an input process whereby the learner is equipped with specific job-related knowledge and skills needed to carry out the job successfully. The golf professionals highlighted a number of barriers to training. The key barriers identified included a lack of training facilities, few refresher courses, and the rate of change within the golf environment. In addition, some believed that there was also a lack of interest in and finance available for training.

Training Needs Analysis

The golf professionals were given the opportunity to agree or disagree with what were perceived to be the training needs at an organisational, occupational, and individual level. At the organisational level, all of the professionals (100%) identified a need for better marketing of their organisations and 82% recognised the need for further training in operations management. Forty-eight percent recognised the need to develop training in the area of event management or the organisation of competitions. At the occupational level the professionals identified a need for training in several areas (figure 38.2).

Although 26 respondents had undertaken PGA training, 79% had not received additional training since joining their club. With 85% having been with the club for

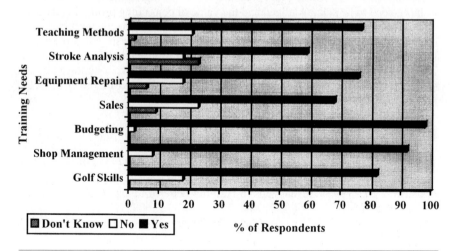

Figure 38.2 Occupational training needs.

over five years, there does not appear to be a culture of in-service training or continual professional development. It is evident from the responses in figure 38.2 that many of the golf professionals recognise the need for additional training at the occupational level in areas such as budgeting, shop management, teaching methods, and golf skills. At the individual level, three main training needs were also highlighted. Eighty-five percent identified the need to develop their communication skills, 61% highlighted the need to develop negotiation skills, and 82% identified the need to develop their coaching skills.

CONCLUSION

The purpose of this TNA was to identify key competencies, skills, and specific areas where a training gap exists for golf professionals in Ireland. As suggested, the role of the golf professional has developed over the last 20 years. Golf professionals are required to manage a business enterprise, coach, and deliver a quality service to customers who now have greater choice in how they spend their disposable income. The work of the PGA in training and development has been highlighted. However, once they have qualified, the needs of Irish golf professionals should not be set aside. Continuing professional development has become part of the training culture of many successful organisations both in business and in sport. The purpose of continuing professional development is to keep employees up to date with current technology, trends, and changes taking place within their industry. The outcome is that individuals have a better opportunity to perform their tasks efficiently and effectively, carry out their roles competently, and remain at the cutting edge of their business. The role of the golf professional has taken on a business orientation and has placed an additional burden on the professional to perform in a commercial market. A new emphasis has been placed on activities such as marketing and operations management; and the refinement of key competencies in the areas of communication, negotiating, and coaching has been highlighted. The barriers to training need to be acknowledged and the value of continuing professional development recognised as an investment in staff efficiency and effectiveness and in the organisation's overall performance. Training gaps for the Irish golf professional have been suggested, and the need for continuing professional development has been acknowledged—"the need for employees to learn new areas of knowledge and skills so that they undertake the tasks associated with their post more effectively" (Torkildsen, 1992, p. 421).

References

Bee, Roland, & Frances (1994). *Training Needs Analysis and Evaluation.* London: Institute of Personnel Management.

Broadwell, M. (1993). Seven steps to building better training. *Training Journal,* October, 75-81.

Browning, R. (1990). *A History of Golf, the Royal and Ancient Game.* London: A & C Black.

Cohen, L., & Manion, L. (1994). *Research Methods in Education.* London: Routledge.

Dair, I., & Schofield, J.M. (1994). Nature conservation and the management and design of golf courses in Great Britain. In *Science and Golf II. Proceedings from the World Scientific Congress of Golf,* ed. A.J. Cochran & M.R. Farrally. London: Chapman & Hall.

Donnelly, J.H., Gibson, J.L., & Ivancevich, J.M. (1995). *Fundamentals of Management,* 9th ed. Chicago: Irwin.

Feld, J. (1988). Sports survey. *Club Industry,* 4(12): 20–25.

Flemming, I. (1994). *Training Needs Analysis for the Leisure Industry.* London: Longman.

Guest, R.H. (1994). Golf organisation challenges of growth and change—a preliminary social science perspective. In *Science and Golf I. Proceedings of The World Scientific Congress of Golf,* ed. A.J. Cochran & M.R. Farrally. London: Chapman & Hall.

Menton, W.A. (1991). *The Golfing Union of Ireland, 1891–1991.* Dublin: Gill & Macmillan.

PGA (1997). *Show News,* January 26, 14.

PGA Information Booklet. (1996).

PGA Training Guide. (1994).

Ponziano, D. (1996). The evaluation of golf teaching. In *The 1st International Golf Theory in Practice Conference,* ed. E. Wallace, B. Deddis, & J. Hanna. Belfast: University of Ulster.

Price, R.J. (1996). The golf industry in Scotland & Ireland, retrospect & prospect. In *The 1st International Golf Theory in Practice Conference,* ed. E. Wallace, B. Deddis, & J. Hanna. Belfast: University of Ulster.

Snape, C. (1987). Golf development and directions. *Leisure Management,* October, 26–27.

Torkildsen, G. (1992). *Leisure and Recreation Management.* London: Chapman & Hall.

Training Advisory and Consultancy Service for Industry (1994). *Training Needs Analysis Manual.*

Wheat, S. (1995). Marking golf cards. *Leisure Management,* May, 26-28.

Williamson, M. (1995). *Training Needs Analysis.* London: Library Association Publication.

CHAPTER 39

Expansion of Golf Education Programs and Protection of Professional Golf Associations

D.H. Zakus
School of Marketing and Management, Griffith University—Gold Coast Campus, Queensland, 9726 Australia

A central aspect of the human basis for the sport and industry of golf is the members of the professional associations. While national golf unions also retain an important symbiotic organisation and educational role in the development and continuity of the sport, it has been the professional golfers' associations that have had the more important role in these activities. Once a professional body has been formed, this does not imply that that body will continue unchallenged. As a result, such professional bodies have taken on corporatist structures and activities. Whether this focus will help such bodies retain their power and control over the sport continues to be an issue as future challenges unfold.

Keywords: Professions, professional education, corporatism, golf academies, future challenges.

INTRODUCTION

In the beginning was the golfer. Golfers became golf specialists: people with the ability to play, to teach, to construct the game from the ground up. These specialists formed governing bodies that protected and ensured that knowledge of the game continued. They are the basis of the game, not the cadre of scientists who narrowly focus on the nature of the course, the equipment, and the swing.

In 1994, Stoddart made the case that the "scientific" study of golf must include more than the technological (e.g., biomechanical, physiological, equipment, etc.) and economic (course and real estate development, tournament, prize monies, etc.) aspects of the sport. While these topics are important, such an overly concentrated focus inverts, assumes away, or, worse yet, objectifies the human dimension of the sport. Who developed the game, its rules, and its implements? Who plays the game, and how do they come to be able to do so? Who has ensured that the game continues to develop? Who organises the sport? Simply, it is the humans involved that are central to understanding the ongoing development and continuity of golf.

While these questions point to a lengthy, voluminous study of golf, this paper focuses on the profession central to the historical development and continuity of the game, that is, the professionals who teach and direct those playing the game (as opposed to those who provide entertainment for spectators). The specific focus here is on one professional group, the Professional Golfers Association of Australia (PGA), and its education programs, which are a central focus that ensures the development of human capital for the sport and that gives the association professional status. The premise is that this PGA provides an important case study of how programs need to be extended to meet current and future challenges to the profession.

AN EXCURSUS ON PROFESSIONS

A profession is a body of individuals claiming status for, income from, and control of an area of human activity. Professionals are identified by their specialised knowledge, skills, and sensitivities, which take dedication, commitment, and years of preparation to obtain (Lawson, 1984). Cutlip, Center, and Broom (1994) identify the following as agreed upon criteria basic to all professions. Each professional

- requires specialized education to acquire a body of knowledge and skills based on theory development through scientific research. The practice is based more on unique knowledge than on performance;
- provides a unique and essential service recognized as such by the community; practitioners are identified with their profession . . . ;
- emphasizes public service and social responsibility over private interests . . . [as] private economic gain and special interests are subordinate to the public good; there is "nobility of purpose;"
- gives autonomy to and places responsibility on practitioners . . . [through the] freedom to decide and act [which] carries with it individual accountability; and
- enforces codes of ethics and standards of performance through self-governing associations of colleagues . . . [as] values are interpreted and enforced by disciplining those who deviate from accepted norms and prescribed behaviors. . . . [Thereby] professional societies provide standards for preparation, admission, and status. (p. 133)

The area of expertise of professionals is seen as a special domain that only a few can enter and that is necessary, in some form, to human existence, be it in matters of life (doctors) or leisure (golf pros).

At the heart of any human activity identifying itself as a profession is education. This pertains to both those entering the profession and those belonging to the profession. Education is an entry requirement, the central activity toward becoming a professional, and an ongoing requirement for professional credibility.

Golf has long followed the traditional mentor/apprenticeship model. PGAs of longer-established jurisdictions, however, have moved beyond this model to provide further options for those seeking full membership status. Dominant among the Australasian PGAs, the PGA of Australia has developed, expanded, and continued to enhance its education programs, providing it with a unique position in the region.

THE AUSTRALIAN CASE

The PGA of Australia coalesced in 1911. It was the second such body in the world behind that in Great Britain (1901) (de Groot and Webster, 1991, p. 39). As with many incipient professional groups of this time there was debate and conflict with the amateur body, the Australian Golf Union. Both were concerned with the development and continuity of the sport, but with different agendas. This matter is beyond the current paper and is documented well elsewhere.

While many of the PGA's concerns centered on financial issues and the incumbent ostracising of its players, there was also a central focus on ensuring the continued livelihood and income of players beyond what was attainable in competitions. De Groot and Webster (1991) noted that by the late 1920s, "the establishment of the PGA academy, lectures and the appointment of an education officer ensure[d] this continuing increase in standards required for professional golfers" (p. 42). This clearly identified and enshrined the need for golf professionals to be more than good players of the game. A body of knowledge and a set of skills beyond the actual playing of the game were required if professionals were to give themselves special status and protect that status through guidelines and continuing development of a discreet body of knowledgeable individuals.

As the body of knowledge and purview of professional expertise expanded, the requirements of golf professionals to continue their education grew. Internal struggles after the establishment of a separate headquarters in 1969, the establishment of a corporate identity (with members as shareholders), and the appointment of an executive director by the early 1980s led the PGA membership to realise the need for specialised departments for different foci in the profession.

This occurred with the formalisation of the PGA in 1984. At that time four departments were established: general administration, marketing, tournaments, and education. This formalisation led to a corporate structure and corporatist focus. The PGA was now a business that had to operate to generate revenues to ensure its future. In certain ways this has led to power struggles between the members, between the members and the staff, and between the PGA and outside or member competition. Over time the corporate image, operation, and expansion have been extended to ensure the continued viability of the organisation.

Within the education department, a key change that was demanded concerned the traditional, and increasingly outdated, traineeship program. Toward this change, a meeting with physical education specialists was held to identify and make recommendations for the types of changes necessary. Subsequently, Max Garske, himself a physical educationalist, was appointed as the next Director of Education in 1984.

First among the recommendations was one for major renovations to the traineeship program. Garske implemented a number of changes. These changes met with resistance, a situation that continues under the current Director of Education, Ian Robilliard. To ensure the continued educational development of professionals, the Professional Development Program was approved by the membership in 1997. In this program each professional is charged a fee and must show annual educational credits toward maintaining full membership status.

Under Garske and Robilliard, and in line with the changing demands of the industry and profession, alternate pathways to PGA membership were instituted. These include a "bridging year" program for tour members; university-awarded degree and certificate programs, along with a postgraduate "professional year" program; delivery of all education programs through distance modules; and ongoing academy and tertiary education program initiatives (through Griffith University). Clearly, the Australian PGA has responded to the need for the profession to continue its development, both as an organisation and as a profession. These activities are central to the fiscal, the organisational, and professional exclusivity security of the PGA.

FUTURE CHALLENGES, BY WAY OF CONCLUSION

While the PGA is incorporated, it does not have the same statutory protection that the medical or legal professions enjoy. Whereas the latter can be more self-perpetuating, insular, and secure, the PGA must face many intrinsic and extrinsic challenges to its purview. Garske (1997) and Robilliard (1997) pointed to the need to continue the expansion of varied educational programs, expansion of academy programs (varied educational programs in both the playing and business sides of the game), and enhancement of opportunities to educate and employ endorsed professionals. This being so, I have witnessed the challenges that exist among the shareholder members (PGA members), with the PGA's program initiatives (e.g., the academy, golf tourism, university degree programs, and a variety of certificate programs), and with overseas competition. Also, as programs expand in the state education system, several bureaucratic issues arise over the relationship between degree programs and industry-supported programs, as well as between degree programs in different tertiary institutions.

John Bloomfield (1997) made perhaps the most telling point, one I have confirmed by way of Asian students in Australia. In the United States there is a move afoot to establish a new professional group, the Professional Golf Teachers' Association. It is a moot point whether the market will acknowledge the difference between credentials or quality of preparation. These new "professionals" working in lucrative golf academies will provide professional golfers' associations around the world with challenges that will not be supported by the statutory protection enjoyed by many other professions. Clearly, survival for the traditional golf professionals will be based on their ability to educate and then inform clients of their status.

References

Bloomfield, J. 1997. Personal communication. 3 July. Perth, Australia.

Cutlip, S.M., A.H. Center, and G.M. Broom. 1994. *Effective public relations.* Englewood Cliffs, NJ: Prentice Hall.

de Groot, C., and J. Webster. 1991. *Pro golf: Out of the rough.* Sydney: PGA.

Garske, M. 1997. Interview. 18 August. Gold Coast, Australia.

Lawson, H.A. 1984. *Invitation to physical education.* Champaign, IL: Human Kinetics.

Robilliard, I. 1997. Interview. 20 August. Gold Coast, Australia.

Stoddart, B. 1994. Golf, development and the human sciences: The swing is not the only thing. In *Science and golf II: Proceedings of the World Scientific Congress of Golf,* ed. A J. Cochran and M.R. Farrally, 611-619. London: Spon.

CHAPTER 40

Skirting the Issue: Women, Gender, and Sexuality in the Golfing World

Marnie Haig-Muir
Deakin University, Australia

Golf as both sport and space is gendered in ways that commonly constitute it as a predominantly male environment. Value perspectives, normative language, and other, sometimes subtle, practices of exclusion and privilege grounded in social constructions of gender and gender hierarchy have constrained full and equal participation by women golfers of all levels. "Femininity" constructs associated with a limited range of body images, lifestyles, and forms of behaviour, combined with some top players' supposed lesbianism, have had particularly adverse effects on the gender division of resources, facilities, and media coverage.

Keywords: Gender, golf, sexuality, women.

INTRODUCTION

A century ago Lord Wellwood said, "If [women] choose to play . . . when the male golfers are feeding or resting, no one can object. . . . at other times . . . they are in the way" (1895: 48). Little has changed. From the days of the sand and dust of ancient Greek and Roman stadiums to the immaculate fairways and greens of Augusta today, sportswomen have remained "outsiders" because androcentric world views prevalent in sport undervalue and/or belittle their achievements. Much of the gender bias and outright sexism is invisible—often an institutionalised invisibility cloaked by specious claims of objectivity and value-neutrality driven by equally slippery (and malleable) concepts, constructs, and reifications like "the market," "viewing public," "prowess," and "femininity." Surprisingly little scholarly attention has been devoted to golf. With several notable exceptions (Cayleff 1995; Chambers 1995; Crosset 1995; Kahn 1996), women's golf has been ignored, although golf provides a special kind of cultural landscape shaped by sometimes cross-cutting currents of gender and class in which image, style, and presentation

315

all feature prominently. Like its geological counterpart, social change is rarely rapid. The first recognised female golf club in the world was formed at St. Andrews in 1867. For 30 years, activities were confined to putting on a poor piece of ground well away from male members. Even in egalitarian Australia, only the passage of the equal opportunity legislation of the 1970s and 1980s finally forced significant change on reluctant clubs and their (male) Members and (female) Associate Members, whose restricted rights were determined by men to whom they were usually related (Stoddart 1994a: 86).

Gender and sexuality become inextricably intertwined within constructions of femininity that may prove both friend and foe for female golfers. Tensions between "femininity" and the "prowess" needed for success in top-level sport create serious difficulties for sportswomen, including golfers, because sport is a key sociocultural institution in which males learn, develop, practise, and perpetuate the "manly" skills and values that conform to dominant views of masculinity (Bryson 1994). Consequently, the sporting "mainstream," perhaps more aptly, main arena, is usually depicted as male territory. Despite legislation and other initiatives, less formal gender discrimination has proved remarkably resilient. In many clubs, women players and visitors are still unwelcome on Saturdays. Deeply embedded androcentric values so prevalent in sport ensure that women's golf rates only in qualified terms. Women golfers are not golfers, but first and foremost *women* (preferably "ladies"), then golfers. Gendered ambit claims create golf and women's golf—the Australian Open and the Australian Women's Open, golf magazines and women's golf magazines, and so on. Gender and its analytical partner, value, are the principal villains here because, like beauty, they depend on the eye of the beholder. Both professional and amateur golfing spheres are shaped by constructions and reconstructions of gender created in spaces where "hegemonic masculinity" is rarely challenged by men or women (Bryson 1994; McKay 1997).

A WOMAN'S PLACE IS . . . ?

The historical context of golf's evolution to popular sport status in the late 19th century is relevant to this situation. As leisure became a reality for more privileged members of society, clubs of all kinds mushroomed. Golf clubs were seen as extensions of professional or commercial culture: places to network, or cultivate potentially advantageous business and/or social contacts. Put simply, they were a special cultivar of the crop of men's social clubs that thrived at that time. In these public, therefore "men's," spaces, women were confirmed to restricted places, roles, and times. Gender-based exclusion and control were justified by claims about, for example, their "unsettling and . . . pernicious influence" (Wellwood 1895: 48). Despite the prevalence of this kind of misogyny, women's golf was acceptable within defined limits because it "was non-threatening to male players, . . . provided the opportunity for women to mingle with males and females of the same social standing [and] was . . . a healthy form of moderate exercise . . . for ladies" (Phillips 1994: 186). Apart from exercise, golf supposedly promoted socially desirable attributes like "self-control and imperturbability of temper"—was looked on as an activity that "steadies the nerves . . . takes women out of themselves, and acts as a gentle counterpoise to tea and gossip" (Hezlet 1904: 2-3). Equal opportunity? Low markers "should be allowed to play over the men's courses at will, except on Saturdays and public holidays, it being understood that they would always be willing to allow men, coming on behind, to pass them, if the latter so desired" (Soutar 1906: 138-39). Although golf was favoured as a pastime for well-to-do females, few were considered mentally or physically capable of playing seriously.

One highly effective defence of male "superiority" has been the way value is imputed in most sports. Value-laden measures like "success" or "prowess" are generally gauged in androcentric terms. Popular standards of golfing excellence are commonly based on men's performance and/or capabilities, notably power and distance, although on average 43% of a game is putting and another 20% is short-iron shots. Since men are, *ceteris paribus*, bigger, stronger, and more powerful than women, not only are they only more likely to "succeed" in a sport, but serious participation is often declared "unfeminine," by implication, "unnatural" for women. It is a short step from there to "unnatural" women. Labels implying sexual deviance—"unfeminine," "butch," "lesbian," "second-rate men"—are used to exclude and control women's participation in sport and sporting bodies. Sports-women are in a classic double bind. If they play "like women," then their performance is, *ipso facto*, "second-rate" because it rarely stands comparison with male equivalents in terms of power, speed, distance, aggression, or similar aspects of physical prowess defined according to androcentric norms. But women who play or behave "like men"—take their sport seriously, train hard, develop muscles, display physical prowess, and so on—jeopardise their "femininity."

Sport provides critical rites of passage from boyhood to manhood but plays little part in girls' transition to womanhood. Crosset identified the territorial imperatives in this process whereby "undercutting women's athletic prowess by maligning athletes' femininity and/or sexuality allows sport to be kept a 'masculine preserve' " (1995: 94). McKay noted that trying to substitute "rambos for bimbos" is pointless. As one athlete said, it seems to be "look good or be butched" (Commonwealth of Australia 1991: 21, 21[20]) Successful women athletes may be "threatening" because they do not conform to heterosexual male images of how females *should* look and/or behave—deferential, weak, incompetent, and available. If not, accord-ing to a peculiarly warped logic, they "must" be gay! "When women are called dykes, or 'hairy legs,' or androgynous, the burden of proof falls on women themselves . . . " (Waring 1985: 89), which goes a long way toward explaining sportswomen's production of (male) partners and/or children who have little to do with the immediate moment's news except as *bona fides* of "normality."

THE "IMAGE PROBLEM"

References to the "image problem" pervade women's golf, especially professional golf. The term is a euphemism impugning players' "femininity" and refers specifi-cally to an ongoing preoccupation with lesbianism among female athletes (Nelson 1991: 132-54; Cahn 1994b; Hicks 1994). Shunned themselves, and tainting the "normal," that is, "feminine," heterosexual images of others, sportswomen whose sexuality is suspect are doubly damned because the figure of the mannish lesbian athlete has acted as a powerful but unarticulated "bogey woman" of sport, forming a silent foil for more positive, corrective images that attempt to rehabilitate the image of women athletes to resolve the cultural contradiction between athletic prowess and femininity. (Cahn 1993: 343)

Cahn's "cultural contradiction" captures the essence of the image problem. Since cultural agencies define, confirm, and consolidate power relations, so-called deviant sexuality justifies and facilitates male control of women's participation and influence in sport. Yet close friendships between women, and "mannishness," first presented serious problems for sportswomen only in the 1930s as increasingly influential sexologists, steeped in the psychology of Freud and Kraft-Ebbing, "promote[d] the ideal of companionate marriage, based on friendship and mutual sexual gratification" (Lenskyj 1986: 73-80; Cahn 1994b). Pat Griffin once referred to women's sport as something "held hostage to the 'L-word'" (Nelson 1991: 142). Sound "femininity" credentials free the hostage. The late great Mildred (Babe) Didrikson, arguably this century's greatest all-around sportswoman, was caught in the image trap. Before marrying wrestler George Zaharias in 1939, she was ostracised and ridiculed as boyish, mannish, a girl-boy child, unfeminine, unpretty, not-quite female, and a Muscle Moll who could not "compete with other girls in the very ancient and honoured sport of man-trapping" (Nelson 1996). Hounded by "reporters and members of the public as a freak" for her androgynous appearance and behaviour, Babe disowned her diverse and highly successful sporting history, claiming that her sport career began with golf. "Through golf, an unimpeachably ladylike sport, and active self-feminisation," Babe buried much of her former androgynous image. Marriage completed the "crossover" into womanhood and ended her threatening status (Cayleff 1995: 88-89, 133).

Women's sport receives slightly better coverage today, although men and horses still dominate (Stoddart 1994b). Newsworthiness and popularity are the usual reasons proffered for poor treatment of women's sport. Despite protestations to the contrary, this issue is far from value-neutral, but a clearer view of the points of departure and frames of reference means going beyond what the public wants, and like myths to challenge underlying presuppositions and values. Since masculinity is so often defined in terms of that which is not feminine, one corollary of sport's hegemonic masculinity is the relegation of women and women's sport to a separate, secondary (inferior) status (Commonwealth of Australia 1991: 157). Public perceptions of women's golf are unlikely to be lifted by Buick's hiring actor Cheryl Ladd as their first woman to work alongside well-known PGA players Crenshaw and Elkington, or U.S. equipment-maker Lynx's replacement of top tour player Michelle McGann with glamour girl Kristi Hommel (Yen 1997a,b).

The characteristics defining essential aspects of masculinity form a self-perpetuating feedback loop that excludes and/or trivialises women's sporting achievements. To date there have been two main ways out of this vicious circle. In golf, one way could be characterised as the Jan Stephenson path, the other as the Nancy Lopez route. The first flaunts and trades on physical attributes; the second establishes safely heterosexual credentials by marriage and motherhood. Of one, a journalist may write, "She is a star and the crows come to see her nipples as well as her niblick" (Kahn 1996: 287). For the other, home, hearth, husband, and a couple of well-aired kids are sufficient credentials for normality. Several other, more constructive escape routes have been opened up in recent times. In Australia, for example, Women's Golf Victoria has a highly successful program promoting golf as a fun game for both boys and girls of primary school age. Staff and volunteers also conduct clinics for teenage girls and women who want to try the game. Overseas, the USWGA is working closely with the Girl Scouts to promote golf as an active sport for girls and women, and the (British) LGU is moving to improve the image of women's golf among the broader population. Business and professional women in Australia and the United States are also making an impact on masculine monopolies of networking and doing business on golf courses.

Women's golf, especially professional golf in the United States (where women have been most successful in achieving sponsorship and public recognition), has long been dogged by sex and sexuality slurs. To optimise commercial prospects, players' images must conform to corporate executives' preconceptions, or what they think their market expects. In the mid-1980s, executive director Colin Snape urged players on the virtually bankrupt European tour "to exploit their dress sense and sex appeal" to attract sponsorship. "Pushing the pulch" was Ladies Professional Golf Association (LPGA) management's response to failing sponsorship and accusations of rampant lesbianism on the tour in the mid-1970s when "female golfers were ... too dumpy, too butch, to make Big Bucks" (Blue 1987: 109, 112). Once "jokingly referred to as the Lesbian Professional Golf Association" (Cahn 1994a: 266), the LPGA has since gone to great lengths to feminise players' images over the past 20 years. Weight, grooming, and clothes are closely monitored, and an image consultant travels with the tour. When Commissioner Volpe decided to concentrate on bustlines to revive the LPGA's flagging image in the 1970s and 1980s, Australia's golfing sex symbol Jan Stephenson was to the fore (Tresidder 1982; Taylor 1983; Lawrence 1984; Wade 1992). Never shy to exploit her physical attributes, Stephenson photographed in daring poses caused a sensation. One public relations stunt involved a scantily clad life-sized cardboard cutout. Criticism drew the retort, "I'm not ashamed of my body and if I feel like flaunting it, I'm going to" ("Dewar's 19th" 1982). Stephenson, who was and still is a talented golfer, reaped rich rewards from this approach, but merit took a back seat when mediocre but shapely Laura Baugh earned "up to half a million dollars a year off the golf course" while world record tournament winner Kathy Whitworth took 22 years and around 80 victories to make US$1 million (Kahn 1996: 185, 189).

GENDERED GOLF IN THE LAND OF OZ

Despite its undoubted effects, gender was not a burning issue in Australian golfing circles until the conservative 1950s and 1960s yielded to the more liberal 1970s. But 20 years later, women's golf still receives little public attention or credence. Television, radio, and print media all focus on men's sport (Stoddart 1994b). Womensport Australia's recent report, *Inching Forward,* shows media coverage of women's sport dropping from 10.7% in 1996 to 7.5% in 1997, reversing 16 years of steady if slow improvement (Miller 1998). Serious coverage concentrates heavily on men even where Australian sportswomen win major events. When Karen Lunn won the 1993 British (Women's) Open by eight strokes, her win rated two 6cm columns on the back page of the August 17 *Sydney Morning Herald*. Greg Norman, who lost the U.S. Open to Paul Azinger the same day, rated a large picture and two articles covering over half the page! All too commonly, frivolous, mischievous, and/ or offensive coverage of women's golf reinforces sexist prejudice. Whether Jane Crafter's boobs affected her swing preoccupied one major daily's reporter after her 1997 Women's Australian Open victory (Ramsey 1998). Reports on the 1998 Australian Ladies' Masters (ALM) included a front-page piece on Sarah O'Hare (the public figure of Wonderbra) and yet another rerun of "dykes on spikes" (Smith 1998; Pramberg 1998; Lowein 1998).

Golf is big business. Of the half-million Australian club golfers, about 25% are female. Women, especially working women, form one of golf's fastest growing market sectors. Legislation has lowered gender barriers, but worrying disparities still exist between equal opportunity principle and practice. Maisie Mooney confirms ongoing discrimination and the receipt by Women's Golf Australia and its state affiliates of more and more "requests for advice and guidance in these areas" (Mooney 1997: 46). Yet, while image and femininity reign on, sex may have taken a back seat briefly while Australian women's professional golf rides a small wave. The "worldwide" Webb's meteoric rise has booted the game, but, unlike the situation with Stephenson, her *sporting* feats dominate coverage. Ironically, her success has meant that popular press coverage treats Australian women's golf as the Karrie Webb road show, with occasional supporting acts from a few others.

Webb, winner of 1998's ALM, has lifted the game's public image hugely, but Australian Ladies' Professional Golf chief Johnston still has trouble attracting commercial interest in most of the other 90 women golfers he represents (Court 1997). With good TV coverage, attendance of nearly 40,000, and lots of favourable media attention, the 1997 and 1998 ALM tournaments should have helped. Officially cosanctioned as an LPGA tour event, the ALM's A$850,000 (US$650,000) purse makes it the world's richest event in women's golf outside the U.S. Majors. Perhaps Australian women's golf "has moved from the girdles of the last century . . . and right into the guts of mainstream sport" (Robertson 1997: 17), but hegemonic masculinity is still potent. Advertising for 1997's ALM showed a golf ball plus a provocatively sexist caption with disturbing overtones mocking domestic violence ("Have you ever been hit by a girl?"). Even more offensive cartoons advertising 1998's ALM tapped into the popular prejudice trifecta of "below the (male) belt," women as sex objects, and sportswomen as second-rate performers. The crudely sexist cartoons generated many complaints to the state and national women's golfing organisations and much disquiet among women viewers more generally. Tournament director Tuohy claimed that the response was largely positive (Happell 1998), but if the makeup of galleries actually attending the event provides any guide, the campaign made little impact on its intended target audience.

By most measures, women rank poorly in Australian golf. Compared with 13 current Australian men's tour events, there are only two on offer for women pros. The 1996 PGA tour played for around A$7.5 million while female counterparts competed for less than 10% of that sum ("Scorecard" 1996). Recent research showed that 85% of Australian teenagers could name at least one male golfer (30% could name three) but only 3% could name one female golfer (1% could name three) (Hopkins 1998). Media interest in Australian women golfers other than Webb is negligible, and the Australian Women's Open Golf championship is not on lists of so-called major events in Victorian government promotion brochures. Where to from here, *festina lente* or *carpe diem?*

References

Blue, A. 1987. *Grace under pressure.* London: Sedgewick and Jackson.

Bryson, L. 1994. Sport and the maintenance of masculine hegemony. *Women, sport and culture,* ed. S. Birrell and C.L. Cole. Champaign, IL: Human Kinetics, 47-64.

Cahn, S.K. 1993. From the "muscle-moll" to the "butch" ball-player: mannishness, lesbianism, and homophobia in US women's sport. *Feminist Studies,* 19(2): 343-68.

Cahn, S.K. 1994a. *Coming on strong.* New York: Free Press.

Cahn, S.K. 1994b. Crushes, competition, and closets: the emergence of homophobia in women's physical education. *Women, sport and culture,* ed. S. Birrell and C.L. Cole. Champaign, IL: Human Kinetics, 327-39.

Cayleff, S.E. 1995. *Babe. The life and legend of Babe Didrikson Zaharias.* Urbana, IL: University of Illinois Press.

Chambers, M. 1995. *The unplayable lie.* New York: Golf Digest/Pocketbooks.

Commonwealth of Australia. 1991. *Equity for women in sport. A joint seminar.* Canberra: House of Representatives Standing Committee on Legal and Constitutional Affairs and the Australian Sports Commission.

Court, M. 1997. It's a crying shame. *Fairway and Hazards,* 1(3): 6-7.

Crosset, T.W. 1995. *Outsiders in the clubhouse.* New York: SUNY Press.

Dewar's 19th. 1982. *Australian Golf,* March: 8.

Happell, C. 1998. Women swing into action with radical new approach. *Age,* 24 February: B11.

Hezlet, M. 1904. *Ladies' golf.* London: Hutchinson.

Hicks, B. 1994. Lesbian athletes. *Sportsdykes,* ed. S.F. Rogers. New York: St. Martin's Press, 57-74.

Hopkins, T. 1998. Golf proves to be a bogey sport for girls who just wanna have fun. *Australian Financial Review Weekend,* 2-3 March: 62.

Kahn, L. 1996. *The LPGA. The unauthorised version.* Menlo Park, CA: Group Fore Productions.

Lawrence, D. 1984. Lower those binoculars fellas! *Australian Golf,* August: 6-7.

Lenskyj, H.J. 1986. *Out of bounds. Women, sport and sexuality.* Toronto: Women's Press.

Lowein, N. 1998. The low-down. *Golf Australia,* 109: 91.

McKay, J. 1997. *Managing gender.* New York: SUNY Press.

Mair, L. 1996. The wrong message. *Women and Golf,* 5(9): 1.

Miller, C. 1998. Women still losers in sports coverage, *Age,* 7 February.

Mooney, M. 1997. Driving towards the year 2000. *Fairway and Hazards,* 1(2): 46.

Nelson, M.B. 1991. *Are we winning yet?* New York: Random House.

Nelson, M.B. 1996. Handy Olympic sexism scorecard, WISHPERD list email, 16 July.

Phillips, M.G. 1994. Golf, *The Oxford companion to Australian sport,* 2nd ed., ed. W. Vamplew et al. Melbourne: Oxford University Press, 184-86.

Pramberg, B. 1998. A gay time on tour. *Herald-Sun,* 27 February: 112.

Ramsey, T. 1998. Jane hits back in ample proportions. *Herald-Sun,* 17 November: 38.

Robertson, J. 1997. Boom: Karrie leads the new age. *Golf and Life,* 1(1): 16-19.

Scorecard, The. 1996. *Victorian Golfer,* 2(8): 1

Smith, P. 1998. When best golfers play second banana to a bra. *Age,* 25 February: 1.

Soutar, D. 1906. *Golf in Australia.* Sydney: Angus and Robertson.

Stoddart, B. 1994a. Golf. *Sport in Australia: a social history,* ed. W. Vamplew and B. Stoddart. Melbourne: Cambridge University Press, 77-92.

Stoddart, B. 1994b. *Invisible games, a report on the media coverage of women's sport, 1992.* Canberra: Sport and Recreation Ministers' Council.

Taylor, D. 1983. Vanessa who? *Australian Golf,* October: 12-14.

Tresidder, P. 1982. Turmoil and triumph for Stephenson. *Australian Golf,* August: 21-22.

Wade, D. 1992. Jan Stephenson. *Australian Golf Digest,* January: 45-59.

Waring, M. 1985. *Politics and power.* North Sydney: Unwin Paperbacks.

Wellwood, Lord. 1895. General remarks on the game. *Golf,* ed. H.G. Hutchinson, 5th (rev.) ed. London: Longmans, Green.

Yen, Y. 1997a. Marketing women's golf: dumb and dumber. GolfWeb library, 27 October.

Yen, Y. 1997b. Notes from Las Vegas: golf's latest glamour girl. GolfWeb library, 11 September.

CHAPTER 41

Behind the Image: Class and Gender in the World of Golf

Dr. June E. Senyard
History Department, University of Melbourne, Australia

Initially, golf was represented as the proper sport of the middle class. Ideally, men and women could be golfing partners, but generally women, because of their gender, were portrayed as unequal to the task. After World War II, as increasing numbers of men took up golf, the culture of the game was reconstructed. All ideas of equality were jettisoned; the golf course was repositioned as a male preserve in opposition to the suburban home. Throughout, this sporting culture, in denying women as equal participants, provided an ideological context for continued inequities of access.

Keywords: Golf, middle class, gender, race, Australia, women.

INTRODUCTION

This paper addresses the role of golf as a significant source of ideology. From the late 19th century, golf generated a wealth of published material ranging from books of rules to novels, from postcards to poetry. In Australia, although the experience of playing golf was distinctive, golfers readily accepted British and later American thinking about the game. The contradictions of a reader in Quambatook or Cottesloe sitting chuckling over golfing jokes from *Punch* or later, *The Saturday Evening Post,* were subsumed by their recognition of common ideas of class and gender expressed through them. These were not the views expressed through other sporting cultures, for golf was established and developed as a sport specifically for the middle class. The mythical golf course came to represent the world—and a round of golf, a metaphor for existence. Women, after initial acceptance to this Garden of Eden, were expelled in the post-World War II period as historical conditions changed and male authority, challenged by the demands of a consumer society, attempted to defend the world of golf as a bastion of male privilege and pleasure.

GOLF: A GAME FOR THE MIDDLE CLASS

Golf was introduced into the Australian colonies as "a fashionable game," a sport for the rich and powerful in the last decades of the 19th century. In 1893, when *The Australasian* introduced the game to its readers, the tone was benevolent and the meaning clear—the gods were at leisure: "At the close of the play the competitors in twos make for the club-house . . . the bankers, merchants, and barristers resume the habits of speed of civilised life to discuss the incidents of the day, and apply the law to doubtful cases." Only such people could pursue the game, for only they were able to comprehend and appreciate its complex rules and etiquette: "It is very difficult for the casual spectator to find out what are the fascinations of this absorbing game, for it is most absorbing." Like hunting, golf was presented as a game with fixed conventions that set the participants apart. Cartoons from *Punch,* reprinted in Australian newspapers and magazines, presented men playing golf in loud, checked outfits of baggy plus fours, kaleidoscopic fair isle jumpers, blazers, and caps and hats of all shapes. Such remarkable costumes were presented as temporary aberrations from suit and bowler hat, according to *The Australasian:* "It appears that the outer clothing is worn really as a disguise, as your bank manager who has just braved the scare, your merchant in 'the Lane,' your consul for Spain, your Crown prosecutor, etc., do not like to be recognised by strangers on the golf-ground." The voice was indulgent, with an overtone of amusement, for here were the elite, applying their substantial skills in the very different arena of sport.

The cult of athleticism and team sport has been seen as the quintessence of British bourgeois ideology in the 19th century (Hargreaves, 1986). But golf neither required strength—much of the play centred around putting on the green and a caddie carried the clubs—nor inculcated team spirit. However, golf surpassed rugby and cricket in two important respects and emerged as the preeminent sport of the middle class. Golf, it was pronounced, was a cerebral pursuit. Since the middle class possessed the intellectual capacity, they could master the skills required, regardless of their physical constitution. Self-help books became the mainstay of the publishing industry centred on golf. Soutar in *The Australian Golfer* (1906, v) announced that his "plain, direct and concise exposition of the subtleties of the game" would prove invaluable to "the vast number of men and women who have taken up the game within recent years." It was expected that readers, applying their intellect, could become proficient in the game independently.

There was much genial banter at the expense of the incompetent. Golf books were ideal Christmas or birthday presents, and P.G. Wodehouse, among other writers, enjoyed immense popularity in Australia for his golfing stories. Through Wodehouse's tales of hapless golfers, beginning with "Archibald's Benefit" ([1914] 1973), readers learned a new vocabulary of foozling, wabbling, and flopping to describe the game as played by "duffers" and "rabbits." Yet the humour was affectionate. Wodehouse invited his audience to identify with the person struggling to become proficient in the game, sustaining confidence in the idea that defects could be rationally solved. Indeed, one of the enduring jokes of golf dating from this period centres on the idea that practice will bring perfection, that golf is agreeably addictive. Delight in the golfer who would sacrifice all to the game relied on the certainty that golfers were homogeneous and that as a class, the world was theirs to be shaped as they wished—moreover, that they possessed the talent to undertake the task.

EXERCISING POWER THROUGH
THE GAME OF GOLF

More importantly, it was declared, golf was character building. Although the reporter on the *Geelong Advertiser* in 1894 acknowledged that golf did exercise the body, more significantly, golf taught "players to control themselves," for "there is no other game in which a player requires to have such complete control over his or her temper." Around this theme, countless cartoons and stories represented golf as a game that tested the player and that, above all other sports, taught self-discipline. The golf course became a metaphor for the world, the player who conquered it, the hero. In Wodehouse's "The Clicking of Cuthbert" ([1922] 1973), when a young man explodes, "What earthly good is golf? Life is stern and life is earnest. . . . All around us we see foreign competition making itself unpleasant. . . . Is golf any *use?*" The Oldest Member, also known as The Sage, responds with a story that proves the value of golf for winning in the bigger game of life. On the fairways and greens of the golf course, not to mention the rough, golfers were constantly required to exert their authority. It may have been over themselves, the course, or the opposition; different but demanding talents were required to conquer each of these. In drawing humour from those who struggled, it was assumed that golfers persevered, learning valuable moral lessons in the attempt that fitted them to exercise authority with compassion.

This idea translated easily into themes of race, and the British character was seen at its most triumphant on the golf course. Just as golf revealed the individual, so it laid bare the national type. Disregard for the rules was presented as inherent to the French or the Italians, whose flamboyance was definitely a limitation. The attitude to Americans was more ambivalent. On the golf course, the British and the American golfer shared the same preoccupations, but the American style as presented through particular examples was more aggressive and brash and a cause of tension. P.G. Wodehouse in "The Heel of Achilles" ([1922] 1973) created Vincent Jopp, the American multimillionaire, as a character who applied himself to golf with the same methodological approach as to the finance market and with the same success. In Paul Gallico's "Golf Is a Nice Friendly Game" (1936), Fowler as representative of A.R. Mallow & Co., an American sporting goods company, is witness to an excruciating ordeal, his boss playing golf in the same ruthless way he pursued business. In both stories, golf brings these men to their knees, teaching them lessons in humility and compassion. At least in the world of golf, decency could be elicited from even the most aggressive plutocrat.

THE GENDERED WORLD OF GOLF

Within this framework, the world of golf expressed middle-class aspirations that privileged leisure, the intellect, and self-control. It was an imaginative world that obtained ready assent in the Australian situation, for it affirmed the lives of those struggling on the edges of the Empire to implement the same sort of society. However, the consciousness of class defined in the culture of golf also took a gendered form. The narratives of golf expressed how the middle class conceived relationships between men and women. Ideally, women could inhabit the golf course to complement the male, to create harmonious partnerships. But this could not usually be achieved. Certain female traits precluded women from obtaining equality, confirming male authority and justifying the precedence given to the male on the course.

The culture of golf was one that elaborated on the division of the world into public and private spheres where men and women played out given roles—he, rational and confident as befitting the public stage, and she, sensitive and understanding as appropriate to the private world of home and family. Golf was offered as a site where a partnership between the sexes could be formed. As a successful golfer, a woman could support her male as both golf and life partner, truly understanding the challenges of her mate as golfer and, by analogy, as breadwinner. Through the Wodehouse stories, young women who epitomise a femininity that completes the male can be readily discerned, for they are known by their artless looks—their "beautiful eyes" the key to their romantic souls. But they were everywhere. In *Out of the Rough* (Shaw, 1934, 3) there is Jeannie, the daughter of a Scottish minister, who gradually usurps Angelica, a fashionable golfer left behind in the States, in the affections of the hero: "She is fully as tall as Angelica, but not quite so slender, and her step is more smooth and springy. Her cheek is dimpled and has rich natural colour." Because she is a child of nature, she has the rhythm to be a good golfer. When she is claimed by the hero, the two embody the ideal partnership, for their common bond of golf ensures lasting concord; they will make the perfect mixed partnership. These women were the heroines of the golf course, for through them, the proper balance of gender relationships was achieved. They were a romantic image, never the butt of the cartoonist's pen.

Approaching this heroine but with deficits to overcome were two types of women golfers who often featured as subjects for jokes: the fashionable woman and the practical woman. For the fashionable woman, golf courses were represented as part of the social whirl, and her success at golf was an extension of her grace on the dance floor. However, the fashionable girl could be shallow, equated only with glamour and glitz, earning her the cartoonists' disapproval. The practical girl, her efficiency ensuring success, could also be reproached as deviating from the feminine model. Represented as manly in her sturdy clothes and brusque approach, she was seen to imitate the male and even to challenge him on the golf course. Sometimes her common sense was amusing, but more often she was represented as a figure of fun.

THE USE OF GENDER TO DEFINE COMPETENCE

On the golf course, the acceptance of gender stereotypes was used to develop the idea that specific feminine attributes meant that women trivialised golf. Soutar (1906, 138) thought that the self-control engendered by golf was particularly useful for women, as it was a habit "which is not often consciously cultivated by women, and it steadies the nerves." Although middle-class women, like men, could learn to play, the lessons they learned from golf were less important. For men, golf was an opportunity to display their strengths in another public arena, whereas for women, golf "acts as a gentle counterpoise to tea and gossip." On the course, women's emotions might intrude. In 1893, *The Australasian* reported that "the presence of the ladies is not encouraged, except on ladies' days" because "modern golf is a serious game" and women invariably implied "flirting." Because of these traits, women disqualified themselves from equal treatment with men; as Soutar (139) wrote, "Women with a handicap of not more than five strokes should, I think, be allowed to play over the men's courses at will, except on Saturdays and public holidays, it being understood that they would always be willing to allow men, coming on behind, to pass them, if the latter so desired."

Cartoonists, in particular, relished the scope for representing stereotypical ideas about women on the golf course. In this imaginary world, women were invariably represented as frivolous, as talkative, as emotional. Consequently they were unable to master the game, to learn the requisite skills, or to understand the rules and etiquette. Usually the humour suggested that playing golf was a pretence and that women merely used the time to indulge in gossip. Another representation was that women made golf easier by not placing themselves under the mental duress of playing by the rules. But earning most ridicule was the notion that women flouted the protocol of golf. Etiquette, in both manners and language, maintained the game's traditions and separated those who understood and appreciated the game from the others. A woman who did not know a dog-ear from a dog-leg was an embarrassment, for by inference she could never understand the game. In her hands, golf would become a trivial pastime.

Most pervasive in legitimating male authority in the world of golf were the majority of jokes and cartoons that placed women solely in the private sphere as observers, playing out their gender role of domestic support. As wives and mothers, women were shown as recognising that golf was something they knew as important to their men, to be indulged, but often they did not know why. Like business, golf was a mystery to them. They were portrayed as foolish and unwilling to comprehend the complexities of the game or as innocent and oblivious of its qualities. The result was that women were represented as appendages to the male rather than equal partners in life. In its most developed form, the woman as a decorative adjunct to the enterprising male was evident in the idea of the prize, of the woman standing at the 18th green waiting to be awarded to the winner of the match. Sometimes women were presented as casualties of their husband's obsession with golf. The humour drew attention to the tensions inherent in the partnership equation, this time of the male playing out his gender role of aggressive ambition to excess.

REPOSITIONING THE GOLF COURSE

Such were the prevailing themes displayed through the pages of books and magazines published on golf in Australia up to World War II. In the postwar period, these ideas continued to have currency, but changes in Australian society also penetrated the secure world of a mythical golf course, located somewhere in the British countryside. Increased emphasis on a consumer society, and the shift whereby Australia became part of the American sphere of influence, also saw a significant change in the culture of golf. More and more, golfing material from the United States supplemented British cultural production, and the world of golf widened to include the manicured greens and golf carts found in the cartoons and stories of *The Saturday Evening Post* and *The New Yorker*.

As increasing numbers of men were enfranchised into the mass consumption of both leisure and goods in the postwar period, golf became a more popular sport and the gendered form of golf was transformed. Firstly, the golf course became identified with the male world. Golf could still be learned and it was still character building, but now golf was represented as an extension of the office and the obsession of the suburban white-collar worker. Golf became part of working life. There, on the golf course, the contest of the match became a dominant motif. Humour was derived from the stratagems devised to win and the discomfiture of the exposed. Stephen Potter in *The Complete Golf Gamesmanship* (1968) applied his theories of competition to golf and evoked the golf course as the most conspicuous site for gaining the winning edge. Women had no place in this world and were no longer shown as competitive golfers.

If the golf course became a metaphor for business life, from which women were excluded, the golf club became a refuge from the domestic demands of suburbia. Golf was no longer a site where a partnership between the sexes could be achieved. Instead, golf was set in opposition to wife, family, and home. Apart from the time devoted to the game, the "19th hole" could now be read as a poker game in the locker room or as long and loud rounds of drinking with the mates in the bar. George Houghton, who published over 20 humorous books on golf over the 1950s and 1960s, and whose books were on every public library shelf in Australia, devoted one volume to women, entitled *I Am a Golf Widow* (1965). Bob Hope, introducing Houghton's next book, *Addict in Bunkerland* (1962, 5), maintained the myth, asserting that "golf has left more women watching Westerns on television than any other sport ever conceived."

With this repositioning of the golf course, women were placed in a hostile position. There was still the wife who supported her husband without question, taking his concerns seriously and providing physical and emotional support. But mostly it was a story of conflict. Usually, the narratives of golf placed women in opposition to the sport, and instead of the older images of the wife as welcoming her husband back to the cosy haven of the fireside, new stereotypes emerged. They ranged from the wife as long-suffering martyr, to the wife as nag, to the wife as pursuing retaliation, to the most radical image—the wife as antagonist. Here, the wife was shown waging war and might be represented as sabotaging the chances of the golfer by careful strategy.

FROM A ROMANTIC PARTNERSHIP
TO SEXUAL FANTASY

To complete this reconstructed world, some women reappeared on the golf course. A whole new genre appeared, the representation of women on the golf course as sexual diversion. Cartoons of teaching curvaceous young women to play golf, of searching for balls in bushes with them, of buxom young women teeing off surrounded by a besotted gallery of men, dismissed women as there merely for men's pleasure. Sometimes, all pretence at authenticity was foregone and these young women tottered around the course in high heels and clothes stretched tightly across breast and bottom, with golf sticks as fashion accessories rather than equipment to use. In the renegotiation of gender roles in the postwar society, the world of golf was transformed into a male preserve, an oasis in a world where the privileges previously attached to their gender roles no longer exerted the authority of common sense. With the expansion of golf, based on the marketing of the game as a mass sport, women's participation was reconstructed to write them off the golf course, and golf became a site in which to resist the challenge of equity of access to the developments of a consumer culture.

CONCLUSION

For Australians, then, the culture of golf was largely constructed in Britain and the United States and has changed as historical conditions have been transformed. Yet it has always been appropriate to the Australian situation. The golf course was constructed as a metaphor for the world according to the middle class, and its readers in Malvern or Manly recognised the characters and events represented there as their own. If all readers were comfortable with the ideas of class expressed, there was a significant difference in the experience of men and women on the golf course that consigned women, in the first period, to a romantic role and, in the second, to fantasy. As women are accepted as individuals with equal rights and responsibilities, hopefully they will take their place with men across the whole spectrum of cultural images in the mythical world of the golf course.

References

Australasian, The. 24 June 1893.

Gallico, P. 1936. Golf Is a Nice Friendly Game. In *Golf Is a Friendly Game.* New York: Knopf.

Geelong Advertiser. 22 August 1894.

Hammerton, J.A., ed. 193. *Mr Punch on the Links.* London: Educational Book Co.

Hargreaves, J. 1986. *Sport, Power and Culture: A Sociological and Historical Analysis of Popular Sports in Britain.* Cambridge: Polity Press.

Houghton, G. 1962. *Addict in Bunkerland.* London: Country Life.

Illustrated Australian News. 1 September 1891.

Potter, S. 1968. *The Complete Golf Gamesmanship.* London: Heinemann.

Shaw, J.T. 1934. *Out of the Rough.* Sydney: Angus and Robertson.

Soutar, D.G. 1906. *The Australian Golfer.* Sydney: Angus and Robertson.

Stanley, D. and Ross, G.G., eds. 1956. *The Golfers Own Book.* New York: Lantern Press.

Wodehouse, P.G. 1973. *Omnibus of Golf Stories.* London: Barrie and Jenkins.

CHAPTER 42

The Americanization of Golf: 1888-1914

George B. Kirsch
Manhattan College, USA

Golf became a favorite pastime in the United States during the 1890s and early 1900s because its promoters adapted the imported Scottish game to meet native conditions. Golf's history during these years presents an example of acculturation or cultural borrowing in the world of sport. Resident Scots and Scottish immigrants introduced their favorite game in the United States. Suburbanization, topographical factors, social class structure, and entrepreneurial forces all shaped the development of the sport in the United States. Distinctive features of the game in the United States came in the development of the country clubs and clubhouses, courses, and the players' equipment (balls and clubs).

Keywords: Golf, history, United States, Americanization.

INTRODUCTION

Golf became a favorite pastime in the United States during the 1890s and the early 1900s because it was well suited to the business and social culture of middle- and upper-class American men and women. Its popularity was sustained and increased because its promoters adapted the imported Scottish game to meet native conditions. Golf's history during these years presents an example of acculturation or cultural borrowing in the world of sport. Sociologists have used the term "melting pot" to describe the process through which immigrants become assimilated into the mainstream of American society; but this metaphor has taken on many different meanings, and many scholars reject the concept completely, preferring to use such other models as Anglo-conformity or cultural pluralism (Kazal, 1995; Conzen et al., 1992; Higham, 1993; Morawska, 1994). The idea of the melting pot can still be useful as a means of describing a blending of peoples or cultural elements to create a new type with hybrid cultural characteristics. In these cases the newcomers do not melt into the dominant culture; instead they contribute to forging a new one. In sport in the United States, this leads to an examination of those athletic forms that combined elements of ethnic games and types of physical education with "Anglo" or WASP characteristics and that became widely popular throughout most levels of American society. In some cases, native-born sportsmen from the majority "Anglo" or "WASP" culture adapted immigrant pastimes to suit their own recreational needs. They selectively borrowed certain elements of the foreign sport, but rejected or transformed other aspects that did not appeal to them. The result was the evolution of new types of sports that featured elements of both the immigrant and WASP cultures. One of the most important general questions in sport history is why certain ethnic games and types of physical education (such as track and field, golf, or gymnastics) take root in American soil and evolve into mainstream sports, while others (such as cricket, curling, or Gaelic football) fail to enlist the support of the masses. It is also important to understand the process of the "Americanization" of the rules, organization, equipment, and traditions of those foreign forms of athletics that succeeded in the United States and to explain the factors that prevented the other pastimes from gaining widespread popularity.

RESIDENT SCOTS AND SCOTTISH IMMIGRANTS

To understand how native-born sportsmen adapted golf to suit American needs and conditions, one must begin with those resident Scots and Scottish immigrants who introduced their favorite pastime into the United States. John Reid (often called "the father of American golf") was a native of Dunfermline, Scotland, who earned a small fortune in the iron industry in New York. On November 14, 1888, he and a few of his friends founded the St. Andrews Golf Club of Yonkers, New York (Martin, 1936; Wind, 1956; Doyle, 1988). Another founding father of American golf was Charles B. Macdonald, a Chicagoan and second-generation Scottish-American who helped organize the Chicago Golf Club and who distinguished himself as a prominent player, golf course architect, and critic of new trends in the game.

As Reid, Macdonald, and other Scottish-Americans pioneered golf in the United States, they welcomed professional players from their homeland and England who were eager to capitalize on the sudden boom in the demand for their sporting expertise in North America. In 1891 three prosperous Long Island gentlemen (W.K. Vanderbilt, Edward S. Mead, and Duncan Cryder) invited Willie Dunn to journey to Southampton to design a 12-hole seaside links that became Shinnecock Hills. Dunn employed 150 Indians from the nearby Shinnecock reservation and incorporated their ancestral burial mounds into his layout (Wind, 1956). In 1895 an English golf magazine reported that American entrepreneurs were offering experienced club makers passage to New York and $15 per week in wages. The following year John Dunn, a Scot, recounted that during a five-month stay in the States he taught novices every day from morning until night. He especially enjoyed his three months' visit with Willie Dunn at the "Millionaires Golf Club" at Ardsley; he concluded his tour with six weeks under more spartan conditions in Buffalo, teaching even through a Scottish mist and with snow on the ground (*Spirit of the Times*, 1896). By the end of the century the trickle of British professionals became a flood as the number of new American clubs skyrocketed in the Northeast and the West. Many Scots flocked to the New World to seek their fortunes as teachers and as prize winners in open tournaments, "rashly imagining that they would pick up more gold than could be found even in the Klondike region." Although the rage for open tournaments soon faded, many newcomers did stay on as teachers, greenskeepers, and clubmakers (*New York Times,* 1898).

FACTORS AND DISTINCTIVE FEATURES

Certainly the Scottish influence had an enormous impact on the golf mania of the 1890s, which produced more than one thousand clubs and courses in the United States by the turn of the century. But at the same time the Americanization of the game proceeded relentlessly. Suburbanization, topographical factors, social class structure, and entrepreneurial forces all shaped the development of the sport on this side of the Atlantic. Even though the essence of the sport did not differ significantly in the British Isles and North America, there were some distinctive features of the game in the United States. The most important of these came in the development of the country clubs and clubhouses, courses, and the players' equipment (balls and clubs).

During the late 19th century the United States led the world in the suburbanization of its major metropolitan centers, as thousands of middle- and upper-class families purchased houses on the periphery of major cities and towns. The key to this pattern of residential suburbanization was the railroad, which made it possible for businessmen to commute to workplaces that were dozens of miles from their homes. Their desire for wholesome recreation and the availability of inexpensive land in the country made the golf mania possible (Fishman, 1987; Jackson, 1985). In 1899 the Secretary of the United States Golf Association estimated that there was $50,000,000 invested in golf in the country, with an annual expenditure of at least $10,000,000 (*Tribune,* 1899). In 1901 journalist Gustav Kobbe declared: "The Nation is beginning to find as much fascination in driving a golf-ball as in driving a bargain." He believed that the year-round, suburban golf club "exists because the American who does business in a city, or lives there, has been seized with an uncontrollable and most commendable desire to be outdoors; and it promises to be the safety-valve of an overworked Nation."

The American country club of this era was a distinctive institution that evolved according to native circumstances and social trends. In Kobbe's words, "Whoever thinks that the country club is an American imitation of something English and had its origin in Anglomania is greatly mistaken" (Kobbe, 1901). The first of these associations featured rural and field sports such as riding, hunting, and fishing, but not golf. In 1882, wealthy Bostonians founded The Country Club at Brookline, Massachusetts. Other wealthy sportsmen followed suit with similar clubs in Westchester County and Tuxedo Park, New York, and outside Boston, Philadelphia, and Washington, D.C. (Gordon, 1990). With the advent of the golf mania of the 1890s, the richest clubs spent enormous sums on their grounds and especially their clubhouses. Even a more modest club such as the one in Hackensack, New Jersey, raised $20,000 for its main building. In 1897, Theodore A. Havemeyer, president of the United States Golf Association, warned about the dangers of too many clubs and especially the lavish expenditures by some of them. He explained: "... in some cases the game has been regarded as secondary to the club itself, and this cannot help but be detrimental to the best interests of golf" (*New York Times,* 1897a,b).

Other distinctive features of American golf during these years were the location and physical characteristics of the courses. Whereas in Britain the premier grounds were seaside links, the Atlantic and Pacific coastlines were generally not suitable for golf or were inaccessible to the suburban population. The result was the creation of the inland (or "park") course, constructed out of farmland or hewed out of a primeval forest. The syndicates that built these courses around 1900 invested tens or even hundreds of thousands of dollars on land, improvements, a clubhouse, water systems, and greens and fairway maintenance. Golf course architecture progressed rapidly in the United States, as designers used natural features such as hills and dales, brooks and streams, ponds, lakes, and even rivers, along with the artificial hazards they added for extra challenges for players. H.J. Whigham, an Englishman who was United States Amateur Champion in 1896 and 1897, noted that the few seashore links in the United States were inferior to those abroad. But he added a telling point: "The desire, however, to get the best possible golf courses has manifested itself in many cases to a degree that the English golfers would call crazy. The idea of spending a hundred thousand dollars or more on the golf course, as has been done by several clubs here, would never occur to the English mind, one reason being that it would not be necessary. Inland courses, to be brought to perfection, must have water for the greens, and this is expensive, besides the cost of making the greens" (*New York Times,* 1897c). In 1903 another English visitor, J.A.T. Bramston, criticized the American courses as "distinctly easy, and rather monotonous," lacking strict requirements and characterized by mediocrity and artificiality. In his view the layouts were too similar, calling for the same shots time after time, with "nothing to make the player exert himself, to draw him out, and compel him to use his judgement." Even though many Scotsmen and Englishmen dismissed the American inland courses as "nae gowf," the game advanced significantly in the United States as a result of to these innovations in the design of golf courses (Martin, 1936).

A related phenomenon in the United States was the advent of numerous golf courses at summer colonies and vacation resorts, patronized mostly by the more affluent players. Shinnecock Hills at Southampton, Long Island, New York, was the premier example of a seasonal club founded by summer residents. The York Country Club in Maine provided a retreat for New Englanders. Hotel proprietors in the mountains and the seashore from New Hampshire to Florida were quick to see the value of constructing links at their resorts. By the late 1890s, golfers were hacking and duffing their way across the White Mountains, the Adirondacks, and the Berkshires in the North, while in the South, Hot Springs in Virginia, Pinehurst in North Carolina, and Palm Beach, Ormond, Belleair, and Tampa in Florida all attracted well-heeled players during the winter months (Wind, 1956; *New York Times,* 1897d).

American inventive genius also profoundly shaped the evolution of golf through the improvement of the game's implements—the ball and the clubs. Coburn Haskell of Cleveland and Bertram Work of the Goodrich Rubber Company together developed the rubber-wound ball in 1898, which replaced the gutta-percha ball (made of a Malay gum extracted from a percha tree). The Staughton Rubber Company then devised an improved cover made of balata, and Jack Jolly came up with the idea for a liquid center for the ball. The coming of the new liquid-centered, rubber-cored ball revolutionized the game during the early 1900s. Increasing the distance of shots put more fun into the game for all, and it also contributed to the lengthening and redesign of many courses. In Britain there was initially some stiff resistance to the introduction of the new American ball, but by the end of 1903 it was generally if grudgingly accepted. The strongest opposition came from the ranks of the professionals, who mistakenly viewed it as a threat to their status. One amateur declared that the new ball "ruins all the links in the country, destroys all science of the game, brings second-class players on a level with the first class, and encourages mediocrity at the expense of genius." British Amateur and Open Champion Harold H. Hilton thought that it "enabled the rough and tumble golfer of hard hitting propensities to range himself alongside the player who really knows the game, which he never could do with the old gutty." But in the end the English and Scottish golfers caved in. As the noted English golf writer Horace Hutchinson put it at the time: "We accept the American invention, as Britons will, of course, with grumbling, but with gratitude down in our hearts" (*Golf,* 1903, 1909; Hutchinson, 1903; McPherson, 1902).

The Scots were more resistant to innovations in club design, especially the Schenectady putter that Walter J. Travis used to win the British Amateur crown in 1904. (It had a shaft in the center of a mallet-shaped head.) In 1910 the Royal and Ancient Golf Club of St. Andrews banned the mallet putter, which set off a storm of indignation in the United States. The following January the United States Golf Association at its annual meeting refused to support the St. Andrews ruling. Its officials and leading members and supporters rejected the Scottish club's efforts to standardize the equipment of the game. The *New York Sun* proclaimed: "The time has come for the men of spirit who play golf in America to revolt against the tyranny of the Royal and Ancient Golf Club of St. Andrews if the mallet-headed putter suits them. . . . We trust the free and independent American golfers will stand for their rights and never bow the knee to St. Andrews." In *Harper's Weekly,* Leighton Calkins called on Americans to formulate their own set of golf rules, following the example of tennis, which had separate codes governing that sport on each side of the Atlantic. In later years the balanced set of clubs and steel shafts would also create much controversy *(American Golfer,* 1911; Calkins, 1911; *New York Times,* 1910, 1911; Martin, 1936; Wind, 1956; Newark *Star-Ledger,* 1980).

CONCLUSION

During the formative years of American golf, Charles Macdonald and a few other Scottish-Americans strove to retain the old Scottish style of play. Macdonald fought rule modifications that allowed the wiping of balls on muddy greens, the granting of improved lies under certain conditions, the abolition of the stymie, and even the passing of the tradition of wearing red coats during play. On the other hand, he did endorse limiting the number of clubs, the out-of-bounds rule, and the new rubber-cored ball. In the opinion of Herbert Warren Wind, who believed that moderate revision was a healthy sign for the sport in America, "Macdonald's blind allegiance to the way he had been taught the game at St. Andrews was not going to help the sport find roots in America" (Wind, 1956). But in his autobiography, written near the end of his long career in golf, Macdonald (1928) concluded that the changes wrought by Americans had not greatly violated the essence of the Scottish sport. He wrote:

> When one considers how golf has been introduced on virgin soil 3,000 miles from the fountain-head, among people who had been taught from the time of the Revolution that they were a law unto themselves and resented any enthrallment which might be dictated by the mother country, it is really extraordinary how well the game has established itself in harmony with most that was best in it in its Scotch home. Here and there there have been dissentions, but when all is said and done there are only a few unimportant diversions from the established game as fathered by the Royal and Ancient Golf Club of St. Andrews; notably, the use of the Schenectady putter and steel shafts, both of which are infinitesimally unimportant.

Perhaps it is only fitting that Macdonald should have the last word in this investigation into the Americanization of golf prior to World War I. Through the country club, the new courses, and the new balls and clubs, the sport's enthusiasts in the United States transformed the royal and ancient game of Scotland, and even Macdonald recognized the wisdom of much of this transformation.

References

American Golfer. 1911. 5: 202-208, 214, 357-361.

Bramston, J.A.T. 1903. Some reflections upon American golf-courses. *Golf* 13: 318-320. See also *Golf* 14: 16-19.

Calkins, Leighton. 1911. A crisis in golf. *Harper's Weekly* 55: 13.

Conzen, Kathleen N. et. al. 1992. The invention of ethnicity: A perspective from the U.S.A. *Journal of American Ethnic History* 12: 3-63.

Doyle, Kathleen. 1988. In John Reid's cow pasture. *American History Illustrated* 23: 34-45.

Fishman, Robert. 1987. *Bourgeois Utopias.* New York: Basic Books.

Golf. 1903, February, 12: 89; 1903, August, 13: 125; 1909, May, 24: 269.

Gordon, John S. 1990, September/October. The country club. *American Heritage,* 75-84.

Higham, John. 1993. Multiculturalism and universalism: A history and critique. *American Quarterly* 45: 195-219.

Hutchinson, Horace. 1903. American balls and British golfers. *Outing* 43: 35.

Jackson, Kenneth. 1985. *Crabgrass frontier: The suburbanization of the United States.* New York: Oxford University Press.

Kazal, Russell A. 1995. Revisiting assimilation: The rise, fall, and reappraisal of a concept in American ethnic history. *American Historical Review* 100: 437-471.

Kobbe, Gustav. 1901, June 1. The country-club and its influence upon American social life. *Outlook* 68: 253-256, 259.

Martin, H.B. 1936. *Fifty years of American golf.* New York: Dodd, Mead, 10-15, 23-24, 64-65.

Macdonald, Charles B. 1928. *Scotland's gift, golf: Reminiscences.* New York: 324-325.

McPherson, J.G. 1902. The rubber-cored ball. *Golf* 11: 312.

Morawska, Ewa. 1994. In defense of the assimilation model. *Journal of American Ethnic History* 13: 76-87.

New York Times. 1897a, January 12, 12; 1897b, April 18, 17; 1897c, December 5, 16; 1897d, June 13, 20; 1898, March 14, 4; 1910, May 9, 9; 1911, January 13, 8; 1911, January 15, 2; 1911, January 19, 13.

Spirit of the Times. 1896, December 26, 725.

Star-Ledger (Newark, NJ). 1980, June 8. Section 10, 16.

Tribune. 1899, February 18. Clipping in Washington B. Thomas scrapbook, United States Golf Association library.

Wind, Herbert W. 1956. *The story of American golf.* New York: 3-15, 29, 51, 53, 56-57, 63, 65, 70.

CHAPTER 43

Joe Kirkwood, Orientalism, and the Globalisation of Golf

B. Stoddart
R.M.I.T., Australia

Joe Kirkwood was many things to many people in many parts of the world. The point here has been to explore some possible deeper meanings and significance in his life and activities in order to show that while golf is, indeed, a global game, it is not a borderless one. Like all other aspects of globalised and globalising cultures, it can be at once invasive and protecting, developing and exploitative, recreation and business, deep and superficial. Kirkwood demonstrated all of that, and more.

Keywords: Asian golf, golf architect, golf sociology, gender, golf globalisation.

INTRODUCTION

Joe Kirkwood is remembered as golf's greatest trick-shot artist, the longtime exhibition and touring partner for Walter Hagen, a snappy dresser, and a player who never fully developed his tournament abilities (Stoddart, forthcoming). He commands little presence in golf histories, and even in his native Australia, standard references frame him as an oddity, a man associated with quirky stories (Pollard, 1990). His "autobiography" adds credence to that, being a mixture of colourful anecdote, misrepresentation of fact, and fantastic stretch of interpretation (Kirkwood, 1973).

A more "postmodernist" interpretation, however, puts Kirkwood in a different light. Specifically, the argument here is that Kirkwood played an ambivalent role in the globalisation of golf and, particularly, its spread to Asia, which has been the heartland of its modern growth. Kirkwood was a pioneer—a missionary even—in Asia, but he characterised the ambiguities and contradictions of the game's development that were present at the time and that continue today. He also typified the understanding/misunderstanding dilemma that runs through East-West golf relations as much as through economic, political, or general cultural spheres.

That prompts the reference to "Orientalism." Edward Said (1978) suggests, to oversimplify a complex case, that Western analyses of "the Orient" (which, of

337

course, itself exists only as a concept) were as much about justifying Western intervention in various Asian cultures, and Western adaptations of those cultures, as they were about trying to understand the "East." So, Northern Hemisphere views of "the Far East" and "the wily Oriental" created typologies of Asian behaviour and attitudes that in turn produced a superiority complex in the West and an inferiority one in the East. Ashis Nandy (1989, 1992) and others have elaborated this theme for specific areas of Asia to demonstrate its thoroughgoing nature and its consequences for colonial-going-into-postcolonial nations.

This is no simple academic treatise, because the Orientalism debate drives to the heart of modern East-West, North-South relations as typified in some of Said's other work, notably on Palestine (1996), in which debate he is an activist, and on the wider question of cultural imperialism (1993). His argument is that as much as having foreign values imposed upon them by intervening forces, many cultures self-imposed those values and so alienated their central sense of being and identity. Here he echoes Gramsci (1991), whose works underpin much modern cultural and postcolonial theory, and C.L.R. James (1963), whose work on Caribbean cricket has inspired some wonderfully analytical material (Beckles and Stoddart, 1995). The struggle for equal recognition and power that results from this dichotomy is seen in structures as different as the United Nations and the Olympic movement (Simson and Jennings, 1992; Stoddart, 1997). It is a struggle between metropolitan and provincial, which further reminds us of the religious themes that have endured from the Crusades through the modern Western demonising of Iran (Said, 1997) and Afghanistan.

None of which is so far away from Joe Kirkwood as might be imagined. While space precludes analysis of all the Orientalist dimensions to the Kirkwood story, one particular episode informs us about golf, life, cultural spread, and cross-cultural complexity and relates those issues to some modern trends in Asian golf and its analysis by the West. The unifying theme is that as a key cultural icon in modern life, golf and its spread both bridges and divides nations.

BALI HIGH

The most evocative Kirkwood story concerns his 1937 visit to Bali, the quintessential site for Orientalism (Geertz, 1980; Boon, 1990; Vickers, 1995). He went to the Indonesian island with the Hinduised culture (then ruled by the Dutch) to visit a man he called Le Mare, actually Adrien-Jean Le Mayeur de Merpres (1880-1958), a Belgian artist who is sometimes described as the Gauguin of Southeast Asia and who settled in Bali in 1932 to later marry Ni Polok, a local dancer who was also his main model (Sprult, 1997). His house in the now tourist area of Sanur has become a museum.[1] Presumably Kirkwood had met Le Mayeur on the continent or in Britain, because he referred to him as an old Belgian friend, once an unknown amateur painter who later exhibited "in the Orient and Paris." Whatever the reason for the visit, Kirkwood succumbed to "Bali Fever":

---

[1]For a disillusioned contemporary view of Bali, see Keith Loveard, "The Paradise Paradox," *Asiaweek*, October 3, 1997.

For it was here that I decided I had found the paradise that we all long for, but somehow find illusive [sic] in the busy commercial world. . . .

His depiction of Bali was classic Orientalism, reflecting the rich exoticism seen in his friend's paintings of people and surroundings. According to Kirkwood, Balinese people were "without problems or complexes," innocents without shame. He was instructed, according to his account, by a local chief of royal line to teach a daughter golf. The pupil turned up topless. Also, in classic style, she became a "conquest" while showing him some of the most beautiful natural surroundings in the world. It was an idyllic picture, idealised beyond recognition.

Many years later the journalist Desmond Zwar, accompanying Peter Thomson on tour, reflected Kirkwood. He claimed, for example, that golfers remembered two things about Thailand—traffic noise and the girls:

They are perhaps the gentlest, softest, most feminine females in the world. They bow their heads, hands in the self-effacing prayer position when they are told they are lovely, and they bring a lump even to the most lecherous golfer's throat. (p. 116)

For Said, this would be pure Orientalism, the ascribing of idealised characteristics to "Other" people, especially women. This attitude has continued in interesting ways. Thai women caddies, for example, were employed at a particular golf club in the Malaysian state of Kedah during the mid-1990s. Kedah is a socially conservative state (that is, more avowedly Islamic so that men golfers, for example, may not wear shorts there), and wives of golf club members had the caddies removed for fear that other services might be offered interested players.

We should add that Thomson himself was more perceptive: his comments on the evolution of Asian golf clubs and their practices reveal that (pp. 92-93, 125-126). In fact, Thomson spent considerable time in Asia during the 1950s and 1960s, doing much to popularise the game. He became a successful course designer there (some of his work was handled by his son Andrew, now Australian government Minister for Sport, who was based in Japan for many years).

Meanwhile, Kirkwood laid out a small golf course, and that attracted local attention. He was an architect forerunner, then, of Peter Thomson (Bali Handara) and Nelson-Wright-Haworth (Bali Golf and Country Club); the latter incorporates local culture into course artifacts, and the former lies in a particularly lush, "Orientalised" setting (Clarke and ffrench-Blake, 1995). Kirkwood's course ran along a beach and into an abandoned (to his eye) rice field. There was the sense of the setting's being a preserve for European pleasure, a pursuit that overrode all considerations of local practice or right. Said might have termed it "exploitation," but that would be too one-dimensional.

The nature of Kirkwood's leaving the island continued the theme. As he described it, a show was staged especially in his honour, and the temple dancers

were dressed in their traditional, fabulous costumes, made entirely of woven eighteen-carat gold studded with semi-precious stones. The girls had come from all over the island, and their dance in the firelight made a special dream of the night. The strangely beautiful fleeting music played by gongs and tiny bells still lingers in my memory and always will. That evening—in that moment of time—and the soft smile of Bali would be with me forever.

The girl, of course, was not.

POSTMODERN MODE

Amid the analytical riches here, three recurring themes present continuing symbolic importance:

1. Power
2. Gender
3. Culture

Power

The power of position in Asian sport (Stoddart, 1987) and golf, in particular, has been replaced by the power of wealth. While in former times the two were not dissociated (Thomson/Zwar, for example, noted that Tun Abdul Razak, then Deputy Prime Minister but to become Prime Minister of Malaysia, sported Kenneth Smith of Kansas City handmade clubs[2]), in the modern location the accumulation and display of wealth are a paramount feature of golf. This is best demonstrated in an advertisement for membership in a 54-hole complex in Johore, Malaysia, designed by Nicklaus, Player, and Palmer: "Don't worship the ground they walk on, buy it!" Most courses built in the region are private membership ones, with entry prices prohibitive. Those memberships are tradeable commodities in several locations, a sure sign that the game has been folded into the commercial environment. As elsewhere, business has long been done *on* the golf course, but now, too, the golf course *is* the business. For this reason, golf is much caught up in the economic turmoil that has swept Southeast Asia since mid-1997: for many developers, a golf course now is a major liability as the power to buy either property or membership has declined dramatically.

   In places like Singapore, Malaysia, and Thailand, that extraordinary growth has meant the increasing loss of valuable natural resources turned over to economic elites for use as socially restricted recreation venues (reminiscent of Kirkwood). Among other things, that has created serious environmental problems (Stoddart, 1990; TED, 1996). Membership goes along with ownership of a luxury imported car, an expensive (usually genuine Rolex) watch, brand name clothes (Zegna, Boss, and the upper-market golf brands), and the postmodern versions of Kenneth Smith-type display (Callaway is ubiquitous). In 1997, for example, a member of Royal Perak Golf Club in Malaysia was suspended after an alleged incident in the bar. He took the club to court to challenge the decision because, he claimed, he had been "shunned by various club members and friends" and evicted from his business

---

[2]My copy of Kirkwood's biography was apparently once part of a collection held by Smith, for it contains his stamp.

offices owned by a vice president of the club (*New Straits Times,* 1997). The intersection of business, position, and golf was clear.

These comments are not meant as criticism; they are simply a social reading of the uses to which golf is put in modern Asia. The state royal families (like Kirkwood's Balinese patron), for example, continue to be prominent in golf in Malaysia, and the annual rulers' conference always has a golf tournament at which the car park is full of Rolls Royces. Association with the game is still about social networking, but money rather than status is the main commodity.

In that sense, Kirkwood's idyllic view (p. 66) that golf united all community groups was not accurate then and is even less so now. Nor is it so much about fellowship as opportunity—I have spent a twelve-hour business/golf day in Malaysia, and that is a standard practice. Golf frequently serves as a location for Asian political activity: the prime photograph for a story about the 1997 succession of power in the Philippines showed President Fidel Ramos at golf with Singaporean Prime Minister Goh Chok Tong, and neither golf nor Goh appeared anywhere in the story (Tesoro and Lopez, 1997). A former Malaysian High Commissioner to Australia told me that it was mandatory for his country's foreign service officers to play golf or tennis, and that the smart ones chose golf.

Gender

Modern analysts from Kenneth Ballhatchet (1980) onward have pointed out that gender relations (for which read sexual attitudes) were a recurring theme in colonial contexts, but were overlooked (or avoided) by critics until very recently. Kirkwood exemplified many attitudes held at the time (and still held in some quarters) by males about the "Orient" as a prime place for sexual pleasure. There is evidence to support the fears held by the Kedah club wives; in Thailand there have been cases of female caddies also being involved in prostitution. Such attitudes within golf are not unique to Asia. One 1930s official of The Royal Sydney Golf Club was said to have lost his position for propositioning the wife of a member at a social function; and an Australian professional of more recent times found himself banished to Asia (an ironic fate in this context) after a more advanced operation.

Barbara Fey, compiler of the Kirkwood biography, considered her subject "a man's man," which immediately points to the construction of a male identity and the male role. What is interesting about the several photographs of Balinese women that appear in the book is not so much the fact that they invariably appear topless, but that they are all in subservient roles: housemaid, pupil, admirer, demonstration assistant. This theme is constant. Two European women appear in other photographs: one lying on her back with a tee in her mouth, Kirkwood astride her ready to hit the ball balanced thereon, and the other prostrate at his feet, one foot in the air balancing a ball about to be struck by Kirkwood. Elsewhere, both Hagen and Kirkwood appear with topless African women. And in a photograph from Japan, four women, elegant in traditional dress, wait upon Hagen and Kirkwood with umbrellas, ready to carry the bags. The prime social role in all this is male, the only possible exception being seen in a photograph in which the exiled Duke and Duchess of Windsor are seated immediately behind Kirkwood as he gives an exhibition in the Bahamas—the woman there is exalted by association with the (slightly tarnished) royal male.

Much of this remains in Asian golf, a subset of general male social dominance. At most golf sites, women appear as servants (caddies, waitresses, attendants, clerks, sales, grounds staff), and female playing membership is very low. Where such membership exists, it is almost exclusively an offshoot of an association with a man who has membership. There are very few women with independent membership. The immediate reason is obvious. Given that women have only recently begun to assert commercial and financial independence in the region, few have the financial capacity to buy a membership in the predominantly private clubs, let alone the social independence that would allow them to do so.

Culture

Le Mayeur takes us to another realm of Orientalism, that of representation, his paintings conveying a particular sense of place and in turn creating a mind-set about that place. Kirkwood's reactions to these Asian settings fall neatly within wider contemporary views of those places: of the seductive beauty of Bali, the wealth and taste of the world's titled irrespective of location. Above all, he conveys views about "civilization."[3]

There are two particular dimensions with bearing upon current practice—the depiction of Asian golf, and the creation of the golf site itself.[4]

In tourist literature, especially, Asian golf is represented as an idealised space where there are no complications. The massive Bangkok traffic problems, for example, are not mentioned in advertisements for golf courses there. The heat and humidity to be endured in many locations are similarly overlooked. Predictably, emphasis is upon beauty and mystery: one agency emphasises the "charming helpful [female] caddies" and "unique culture" to be found in Thailand (Golf Orient, 1997). Kirkwood would have appreciated that. This emphasis is most evident in modern photography because, unlike the situation in Europe or the United States, there is as yet in Asia little "artistic" representation of golf. The work of photographers like Brian Morgan (1988) reveals continuities from the Kirkwood word pictures, most spectacularly in a photograph from Kathmandu of an elephant watching as a golfer tees off. Similarly, a photograph from Calcutta displays social distance as a well-dressed golfer, supported by caddies, tees off over a stream in which more humble people wash themselves and their clothes.

This representation emanates from the courses themselves and the ways they are framed.[5] The sense and power of the golf landscape are extremely significant as in,

---

[3]While there is a very long disagreement between Kirkwood, the golfer, and Sam Huntington, the political scientist, it is interesting to note that both believe somewhat in the power and significance of transcultural elites—see Samuel Huntington, *The Clash of Civilizations and the Remaking of World Order* (New York: Simon & Schuster, 1996).

[4]This point leads on to one about resistance to globalisation, the ways in which local cultures sustain themselves in the face of intervention; but space precludes an analysis here. For an indication of some general literature, see "Cultural Resistance to Globalisation—Bibliography," **http://www.stile.lut.ac.uk/ ~ gyobs/GLOBAL/t0000064.html**

[5]While beyond the immediate bounds of this paper, there is a great deal of very interesting work to be done on the representation of golf courses around the world; Robert L.A. Adams, "Golf," in Karl B. Raitz (ed.), *The Theater of Sport* (Baltimore: Johns Hopkins, 1995) does little to move into the arena of landscape and power.

for example, the attempts to recreate specific settings in "alien" contexts—"New St. Andrews" in Japan has an "Old Course" complete with a recreation of the Swilcan bridge (Morgan, 1988). Ronald Fream, very active in the region, announced that the Silang Golf & Country Club near Manila would have a "Scottish Highlands philosophy" (*September Newsletter,* 1997), while Desmond Muirhead's Subic Bay course incorporates themes from Philippines history. While re-creation attempts are not unique to Asia, they are pronounced there and raise interesting questions about identity. Kristal Golf Resort in Penang, Malaysia, for example, is owned and operated by Japanese interests, the course itself Japanese-designed (by Hideyo Sugimoto). The water layouts and stonework remind one of Japan, as does the clubhouse with its traditional Japanese-style baths. This is a deliberate attempt to create a specific environment in an "Other" setting, because the club is a centre for expatriate Japanese social life. Asian design is much underresearched, as shown in the standard golf architecture reference (Cornish and Whitten), with Shunsuke Kato and his "distinctly American style of architecture" among the few examples mentioned.[6]

Because many Asian courses are designed by "outsiders," where they refer to local sentiment they often do so through a "foreign" prism, as did Kirkwood; the work of J. Michael Poellot is interesting here. Where there is no reference to locality, the golf course becomes a homogenised, rootless land tract. If not the "car park with flags in" decried by touring pros, it certainly has no cultural sense or symbolism. Many Asian resort courses carry this mark, such as the Penang Golf Resort in Malaysia and the more up-market Banyan Tree in Phuket, Thailand. When the cultural context is there, results can be spectacular (as in the Thomson-Wolveridge-Fream course at Malaysia's Awana resort).

Kirkwood's rudimentary layout on Bali, then, inspires much thought and analysis about the creation of the golf environment in Asia and, while he was not the first designer to work there, his reminiscences reveal the interrelationship between player, setting, and culture.

References

Ballhatchet, Kenneth. 1980. *Race, Sex and Class Under the Raj: Imperial Attitudes and Policies and Their Critics, 1793-1905.* New York: St. Martin's.

Beckles, Hilary McD., and Brian Stoddart (eds.). 1995. *Liberation Cricket: West Indies Cricket Culture.* Manchester: Manchester University Press.

Boon, James A. 1990. *Affinities and Extremes: Criss-Crossing the Bittersweet Ethnology of East Indies History, Hindu-Balinese Culture, and Indo-European Allure.* Chicago: Chicago University Press.

Comish, Geoffrey S., and Ronald E. Whitten. 1993. *The Architects of Golf.* New York: HarperCollins.

Geertz, Clifford. 1980. *Negara: The Theatre State in Nineteenth Century Bali.* Princeton, NJ: Princeton University Press.

Golf Orient. 1997. Golf In Thailand. **http://www.golforient.com**

Gramsci, Antonio. 1991. *Selections From Cultural Writings.* Cambridge: Harvard University Press.

---

[6]As a good guide, though, see the "Architects" section in *Asian Golf Review* at **http://www.asia/com.sg/ golf/designer/designt.html**

James, C.L.R. 1963. *Beyond a Boundary.* London: Hutchinson.

Kirkwood, Joe. 1973. *Links of Life.* As told to Barbara Fey. OK: R. Kirkwood).

Morgan, Brian. 1988. *A World Portrait of Golf.* New York: Gallery.

Nandy, Ashis. 1989. *The Intimate Enemy: Loss and Recovery of Self Under Colonialism.* Delhi: Oxford University Press.

Nandy, Ashis. 1992. *The Tao of Cricket: On Games of Destiny and the Destiny of Games.* Delhi: Penguin.

New Straits Times. 1997, September 20. Golfer sues club for "unlawful" suspension of his membership, p. 11.

Pollard, Jack. 1990. *Australian Golf: The Game and the Players.* Sydney: Angus and Robertson.

Said, Edward. 1978. *Orientalism.* Harmondsworth: Penguin.

Said, Edward. 1993. *Culture and Imperialism.* New York: Vintage.

Said, Edward, 1996. *Peace and Its Discontents: Essays on Palestine in the Middle East Process.* New York: Vintage.

Said, Edward. 1997. *Covering Islam: How the Media and the Experts Determine How We See the Rest of the World.* New York: Vintage.

September Newsletter. 1997. Ronald Fream Group. **http://wxvw.golfplan.com lnewslett.html**

Simson, Vyv, and Andrew Jennings. 1992. *Dishonoured Games: Corruption, Money and Greed at the Olympics.* [British edition was titled *Lords of the Rings*] New York: SPI Books.

Sprult, Ruud. 1997. *Artists on Bali: Nieuenkamp, Bonnet, Spies, Hofker, Le Mayeur, Arie Smit.* New York: Tuttle.

Stoddart, Brian. 1987. Sport, Cultural Imperialism and Colonial Response in the British Empire: A Framework for Analysis. *Comparative Studies in Society and History,* 30 (October), 4.

Stoddart, Brian. 1990. The Social Context of Golf: A Preliminary Framework. In A.J. Cochran (ed.), *Science and Golf: Proceedings of the First World Scientific Congress of Golf.* London: Spon.

Stoddart, Brian. 1997. A Transnational View. In *Report on the Sport-Culture Forum.* Lausanne: International Olympic Committee.

Stoddart, Brian. Forthcoming. Joe Kirkwood. *Australian Dictionary of Biography.* Melbourne: Melbourne University Press.

TED. 1996. (Akiko Takeda) Japan Golfcourses and Deforestation (JPGOLF Case), **http://gurukul.ucc.american.edu/TED/JPGOLF.HTM**

Tesoro, Jose Manuel, and Antonio Lopez. 1997, July. Un-Candidate. *Asiaweek.*

Thomson, Peter, and Desmond Zwar. 1969. *This Wonderful World of Golf.* London: Pelham.

Vickers, Adrian. 1995. *Travelling to Bali: Four Hundred Years of Journeys.* Oxford: Oxford University Press.

CHAPTER 44

Golf and Italian Fascism

R.J.B. Bosworth
University of Western Australia

In this paper historian Richard Bosworth investigates the nature and effect of the "failed meeting" between golf and Italian Fascism. Golf in Italy paid lip service to Fascism and its ideals—in 1939 the president of the *Federazione italiana del golf* even claimed that it was a "totalitarian" sport. However, in its appeal to a small sector of wealthy and prestigious young males (though there were some women golfers) and, simultaneously, to visiting international tourists (quite a few "milords" resided in Italy for long periods), golf was naturally distanced from Fascism's more egalitarian and xenophobic ideals.

Keywords: Golf, Fascism, Italy, class, cost, totalitarianism.

By November 1939, the times were anxious for Fascists. The Second World War had started, but Italy was still pursuing the ambiguous status of a "non-belligerent." The wording was important because, in the First World War, when, at least in Fascist eyes, the nation had been liberal, soft, corrupt and unvirile, Italy had remained neutral for nine months until May 1915. Neutrality, it was thereafter assumed, meant relegation to the second division, to use Mussolini's own metaphor. It could not be repeated.

But what did non-belligerency mean? Was Fascist Italy just steeling itself before it joined its natural ideological ally, Nazi Germany, in constructing the New Order? Or might Italy, after all, end up on the anti-German side? Fascism was proud of its inheritance from the trenches, and the last war had been fought against the *tedeschi* and alongside Britain and France. There were plenty of Italians who, however annoyed they had been about "liberal democratic" preaching, notably during the Ethiopian conflict of 1935-1936, found Nazism unattractive. Was not Hitler too fanatical, racist, naive, and German? they asked themselves.

Among those troubled by such matters were two leading figures in the regime, Galeazzo Ciano, the son-in-law of the *Duce* himself and Minister of Foreign Affairs, and Giuseppe Bottai, presently Minister of National Education. On 4 November, the 31st anniversary of Italy's "glorious" victory in the First World War, the two ministers, having first attended patriotic ceremonial, met that afternoon in the clubhouse of Rome's Acquasanta golf course (founded 1903). Ciano liked to be a dashing conversationalist, at least when away from his father-in-law. Indeed, because of Ciano's membership, Acquasanta had acquired a reputation as the best place for diplomatic leaks in Europe. Now, Ciano spoke the unspeakable: "Between domination by the Germans and domination by the English," he said, he preferred the latter. "English [sic] hegemony meant that of golf, of whisky and of comfort." As the more simple-minded Bottai would later explain in his diary with perplexity and malice, Ciano was opting for "the hegemony of the easy life."[1]

For a second vignette of golf in Fascist Italy, let us go to Venice, not so long after Mussolini had formed the first Fascist government. In 1926, one of the American tourists who came to the Lido and stayed there at the elegant Excelsior Hotel was Henry Ford. The American businessman brought his golf clubs with him, but found nowhere to play. He must have made his annoyance evident (could it have been at this particular moment that Ford muttered the unforgettable phrase "History is bunker"?), because he was taken urgently to meet Giuseppe Volpi, Count of Misurata, the president of the CIGA hotel chain to which the Excelsior belonged, then serving as Mussolini's Minister of Finance—and a man with excellent and treasured contacts with the American commercial world. Volpi was doubtless especially well disposed to rich Americans because, during the previous autumn, he had undertaken a highly successful trip to the United States, as a result of which loans from J.P. Morgan and others flowed in to replenish the Fascist treasury.

In any event, what Volpi now did was to accompany Ford on a search for an appropriate location for a Venetian golf course. They proceeded south, down the thin strip of land that composed the Lido, to Alberoni, a deserted area of dunes, marshland, and pine trees, where lay an old fort dating from the days when Austria had ruled Venice. Since 1866, this building had on occasion been utilised as a barracks and stable. Volpi and Ford decided that it would be perfect to convert into a golf clubhouse. In 1928 work began, assisted by a Glaswegian architect called Cruikshank. By September 1930, a 9-hole course, par 35, was ready, and the *Circolo Golf Venezia* was inaugurated with a membership of 25, mostly from the city's elite, indeed often from the old aristocracy of the Republic of San Marco. Among the first visitors was Queen Marie of Romania, who was entertained at the clubhouse in May 1931 by a number of local counts and countesses, a Mr. Roger Sulton, and a Major Charlton. In describing the event, the Venetian paper, *Il Gazzettino,* declared that the elegant lunch proffered to the visiting royal demonstrated that the Alberoni club was "becoming more and more Venice's ideal mondane and sporting centre for leisure activities."[2] Another visitor to the course later that summer was the English "sportsman," Kaye Don, holder of the world speedboat record. After a splendid lunch in his honour offered by the *Club Motonautico,* Don, "like all good *inglesi* a passionate lover of golf," repaired to Alberoni to play a round with a Prince Ruspoli[3] and a Major MacDonald.[4]

[1]G. Bottai, *Diario 1935-1944* (ed. G.B. Guerri), Milan, 1982, p. 167.

[2]*Il Gazzettino,* 16 May 1931.

[3]There were two golfing Prince Ruspolis, Eugenio and Edmondo. The former was the first Italian to win his nation's amateur championship (1930), beating the latter 3 and 2 at Acquasanta. In 1931, Prince Edmondo lost again, on this occasion being defeated by Count A. di Carpegna at the 37th. A. Brunialti, *Il golf. Che cosa è e come si gioca,* Milan, 1932, p. 70.

[4]*Il Gazzettino,* 26 June 1931. Don, described as bronzed and handsome and a real athlete, had, during his Italian visit, acknowledged the appeal both of Fascism and of Giuseppe Volpi (cf. also a report in *Il Gazzettino,* 8 May 1931).

Volpi himself, a great collector of offices, became the club's first president. He was succeeded by Count Giovanni Revedin (from a dogal family) 1933-1934, Count Cesare Ciccogna 1935-1936, Count Andrea Marcello (another who could claim dogal background) 1937-1940, Ing. Giovanni Ciccogna 1941-1946, and, with no hint of a break in continuity with the Fascist years, by Count Giuliano Foscari (dogal again) 1947-1950.[5] To cater for a growing postwar membership, the course was expanded to 18 holes in 1951, and eventually, Arnold Palmer, Lee Trevino, and others would compete for the "CIGA Hotels Golf Trophy," to the pleasure, no doubt, of the ghosts of Volpi and Ford.[6]

Their initiative had expressed a certain spirit of the times. In May 1927, a meeting occurred in Milan of representatives from six golf clubs (Bologna, Florence, Palermo, Stresa, Turin, and the Villa d'Este near Rome). It was agreed to establish the *Federazione Italiana Golf* under Prince Gilberto Borromeo, a scion of one of Italy's most distinguished and ancient families. In 1928 the Federation moved its offices to Rome, perhaps following the wishes of the Fascist government, which was trying to centralise Italian life as much as possible. The new president, Ardizzone Faàdi Bruno, another aristocrat who in 1908 had been a beaten finalist in the Italian amateur championship,[7] linked the federation to CONI (the Italian National Olympic Committee), the Fascist umbrella organisation for sports. Golf, it seemed, had accepted the Fascist "revolution."

But was golf in Fascist Italy different from the game played in that country before 1922? The origins of golf in Italy are shrouded in some uncertainty, but two matters are clear. The first playing was very much associated with those parts of the peninsula containing colonies of visitors from the British Isles. There were even rumours that Bonnie Prince Charlie, in exile and decay as the "Count of Albany," had hit a golf ball around the Villa Borghese in the 1700s. Certainly, in the era before 1914, the first modern clubs would betray their British connections by their names (the "Florence Golf Club," for example) or their membership lists—when the first Italian amateur title was disputed at Florence in 1905, the Hon. Denys Scott beat F.R. Lowell 4 and 3.[8] In 1915, the secretary of Acquasanta club in Rome was a "signor Young," whose remuneration was sufficient to permit him to live at the city's Grand Hotel. Also residing there was a "signor Doig," the club professional, esteemed the best teacher in Italy, and a man who could be relied on to make "unbeatable quality golf sticks."[9] In 1913, Acquasanta had been extended to 18 holes, but its English ambience was confirmed by the dispensation extended to members to bring their dogs as they strolled around the fairways.[10] Even in the early 1930s, "milords" retained a presence in Italian golf. Then Cecil Hanbury MP was the club president at Bordighera, Major H. Fife Whinney the Hon. Sec. at Lago di Garda. At Menaggio

---

[5]Circolo Golf Venezia, *Sessantacinquesimo anniversario del Circolo,* Alberoni, 1995, pp. 1-2.

[6]*Ibid.*, p. 3.

[7]A. Brunialti, *op. cit.*, p. 70.

[8]*Ibid.*, p. 70.

[9]Anon., "Vecchi campi: correva l'anno 1896 e a Varese il signor Brunelli," *Il Giornale del golf,* 1988, p. 8. The same article has, as its title implies, a charming account of the early history of the Varese course.

[10]A. Magni (ed.), "Il circolo del golf dell'Acquasanta a Roma," *Spaziosport,* XIV, September 1995, p. 42.

and Cadenabbia, Commander A.W.N. Wyatt held the presidency; his secretary was Lt. Col. P.N. Craigie.[11]

Another feature of early golfers in Italy is that where they were not foreign they were aristocratic, frequently betraying the Anglophilia of that elite, which hired British nannies (King Victor Emmanuel III himself had been instructed by one), aped British fashions, and sent its sons to English public schools. Thus Volpi's deputy at the Lido was Gr. Uff. Ing. Achille Gaggia Madonna di Campiglio. The Golf Club di Napoli boasted the Duke of Spoleto from the ruling Savoy dynasty as its president; at the Golf Club Torino, the Duke of Aosta was honorary president and Edoardo Agnelli, son of the cavalry officer who had founded Fiat, president. The ephemeral Palermo club was headed by Vannuci Girolamo, Prince of Petrulla; the more lasting Milanese one by Gr. Uff. Dr. Piero Pirelli.[12]

This mixture of aristocrats and wealthy businessmen was emblematic because golf was an expensive sport. At Acquasanta, the monthly membership charge was 50 lire (35 for the rare woman golfer),[13] a figure that amounted to more than the total monthly income for a great many Italians. Milan cost 100 lire more per year, and the top courses had formidable joining fees, 1000 lire at Milan, 1500 at Acquasanta.[14]

In this social background, golf was not unique. Indeed, virtually all modern sporting endeavours in Italy had foreign origins—the most celebrated of early football teams was that of the "Genoa Football and Cricket Club." If golf lacked native roots, so too did football, tennis, athletics, cycling, alpinism, and rowing. Socially, golf was more extreme in its appeal to the wealthiest classes, but other sports similarly found their first adherents among gilded youth and, on that account, were regularly attacked by more democratic forces. Not for nothing would socialist Elia Musatti tell his party youth group on May Day 1911: "Sporting activity is a disguised form of nationalism and irredentism. It is a war-cry, a snare and delusion for those committed to the brotherhood of the peoples. It should be opposed and rejected by workers whose labour does not match the pathetic little self-interest of the bourgeoisie, but rather defends the greater interest of the proletariat."[15]

According to its own theory, Fascism aspired to heal this class rift between Italians, forging "one Italy," which could march, resolutely, behind the *Duce* toward some imperial conquest. In this process, sport was meant to hold an important place. For Fascist historian Gioacchino Volpe, the first evidence that the new generation was coming into its own was seen with the flutterings of interest in sport before 1914.[16] Thus, when it created the "totalitarian state" in 1926-1927, the Fascist regime put major emphasis on a series of clubs, from the *dopolavoro* (or after-work) organisation to the party boy scout *Balilla* and the various girl scout associations. In turn, these bodies were emphatic in their commitment to sport, to the eugenic improvement of Italian "racial stock," and to the benefits of competition and the

---

[11]A. Brunialti, *op. cit.*, pp. 141-145.

[12]*Ibid.*, pp. 144-150.

[13]A. Magni (ed.), *op. cit.*, p. 8.

[14]A. Brunialti, *op. cit.*, pp. 147-148.

[15]*Il Gazzettino*, 1 May 1911. The futurist F.T. Marinetti noted his disdain for the "melancholy masturbation" of watching sport rather than participating in it.

[16]G. Volpe, *L'Italia in cammino: l'ultimo cinquantennio*, Milan, 1928, p. 144.

outdoors. Party propaganda, especially in the 1930s, declared, for example, that the policy of the *dopolavoro* was to engage "many participants and few spectators." As late as October 1938, Mussolini himself hailed sport in one of his speeches as necessary for the "race," denigrated only by such of its opponents as flabby members of the bourgeoisie and Jews.[17]

This apparent democratising of sport actually had many limits. It is a truism that Italy is a country of extraordinary regional diversity, and throughout the Fascist *ventennio,* many parts of the South remained as barren of sporting fields and equipment as they had always been. The national soccer title was only once won by a team from south of Bologna, and more complicated sports were impossible and even unimaginable in Sicily, Sardinia, or Calabria (and the aristocratic, "gattopardish," alleged golfers of Palermo rarely seem actually to have struck a ball on their fleeting local links).

Given the regime's fundamental sexism, there were few sportswomen in Fascist Italy. In 1934, the regime even banned female students from the *Littoriali della cultura,* an annual intellectual and sporting competition for the elite young.[18] Nonetheless, here too the regime was not altogether consistent. The Fascist fondness for parades brought girls out of doors as never before; and, with whatever second-class status, by 1940 young women, especially those from the highest social circles, were indeed engaging in a variety of sport. Mussolini's daughter (and Ciano's wife), Edda, was one; Susanna Agnelli, the granddaughter of the owner of Fiat, another. It was thus perhaps fitting that Italy's golf courses always made provision for female members, even if a residual sexism is not hard to discern. Italy's most authoritative golf writer of the 1930s plainly suspected that female golfers were oxymorons: "How often have we seen on the links during a match, women enthusing about the beauty of a sunset or a panorama and using such chatter as an excuse and justification for the poor standard of their play," he remarked reprovingly.[19]

Before Italy's somewhat inadequate performance in the Nazi-sponsored Olympics of 1936, the regime had been given to trumpeting the Fascist nation's sporting successes, claiming to have finished third in the 1928 Games and second in 1932.[20] Now politicians began to find it necessary to add a sporting dimension to their image. Even Pope Pius XI liked to be called the *"pontefice alpinista,"* and Fascist Party Secretary (1931-1939) Achille Starace is one of the few politicians in history to have deemed it advantageous to have himself photographed wearing an athletics singlet and shorts and jumping through a fiery hoop. Of course, the greatest propaganda attention was focused on Mussolini himself, who was regularly hailed as the "first sportsman of Italy."[21] Photographs proclaimed the unlimited skill of the *Duce* as a swimmer, skier, runner, equestrian, cyclist, motorcycle and racing car driver, tennis player, fencer, and rower (but he was never seen sinking, or missing, a putt).

[17]B. Mussolini, *Opera omnia* (ed. E. and D. Susmel), Florence, 1959, XXIX, pp. 185-196.

[18]V. De Grazia, *How Fascism ruled women: Italy 1922-1945,* Berkeley, 1992, pp. 162, 219-221.

[19]A. Brunialti, *op. cit.*, p. 33.

[20]See "L. Ferr"[etti], "Olimpici, Giuochi," *Enciclopedia Italiana,* XXV, p. 280. There is an entry on golf in this encyclopedia. It concentrates mainly on instruction about how to play the game. See "Il golf," *Enciclopedia Italiana,* XVII, pp. 492-493.

[21]See, for example, L. Ferretti, *Il libro dello sport,* Rome, 1928, p. 7.

Sport, Mussolini frequently remarked, allowed "the new generation of Italians to express themselves in a virile fashion" and to overcome the "lazy mentality of those who devote themselves only to brain stretching *(cerebraloidi)* and to the fatuous gossip of once upon a time [liberal] politicians."[22] Nonetheless, in this, as in other matters, an uneasy sense survived that Italy needed to catch up with the more modern powers. As Lando Ferretti, the president of CONI, pronounced, "If English schools have for centuries educated on their playing fields the cadres of British imperialism, we can use our Fascist schools for the cadres of Italian imperialism."[23] By contrast, some Anti-Fascists continued to view sport as an opiate of the masses. The great Neapolitan liberal intellectual Benedetto Croce, a *cerebraloide* indeed, bitterly condemned all sport, which, he stated, brought out man's animal instincts, damaging as a consequence both intelligence and sensibility.[24] The more civilised persons were, he averred, the more likely were they to sit in their studies and avoid the outdoor life.

Croce, then, was another never to be found at a sporting event. But how did golf fit in with the emphasis on Fascist sport, especially as, in the 1930s, the regime became more emphatically martial and xenophobic and more anxiously participatory? A proper history of Italian golf remains to be written, but we do know that the sport expanded to some degree in the interwar years. By 1934 the nation possessed 23 golf courses. Characteristically the links were confined to the North and especially were to be found in Alpine or seaside or lake resorts—Brioni (near Pola in today's Croatia), Mont Blanc, Claviere, Sestriere, Cortina, Rapallo, San Remo, Menaggio, and Varese, to name but some. Typically these courses had Scottish designers, the most active architects being the partnership of Blandford and Gannon (a later commentator would claim a certain resultant idiosyncrasy in their work that had arisen from the fact that both of these men were left-handers).[25] The clientele, too, was frequently foreign, and the game was associated with the most genteel and cosmopolitan form of tourism; by the 1930s, government propaganda regularly listed golf clubs as one of the lures for international tourists. However, there were still many tourist areas, especially south of Rome, in which playing golf was impossible. The only lasting course there was at Fiuggi, in the hills just southeast of the capital. The growing Fascist empire was also not very receptive to golfers, although a rough course existed on Rhodes in the Dodecanese islands.[26] Not all clubs survived the economic difficulties of the Depression, which struck hard, too, at the British of Italy, so dependent on their earnings from shares and property. Bologna was one city that then sold off its golfing facilities.

Given the importance of the city of Rome (and its myth) to the Fascist regime, the most prestigious course was that at Acquasanta. Positioned near the Via Appia

---

[22]L. Ferretti, *op. cit.*, p. 7.

[23]*Ibid.*, p. 110.

[24]B. Croce, *Storia d'Europa nel secolo decimono,* Bari, 1965, p. 298. Croce's list of damaging activities ran from "biciclette alle automobili, dai canotti e dai *yachts* alle aeronavi, dalla *boxe* e dal *foot ball* allo *sky* [he probably meant skiing]." The frequency of his recourse to foreign words in this passage is further proof of the point made above of the imported nature of all modern sport into Italy.

[25]V. Scionti (ed.), "Gli impianti per il golf," *Spaziosport,* XIV, September 1995, p. 45.

[26]G. Giulini, "I campi del golf in Italia," *Le Vie d'Italia,* XLII, September 1936, pp. 604-605.

Nuova, these links offered views of Emperor Claudius' aqueduct, the ruins of which ran across the flat land toward the Alban hills. The remains of some classical villas were located beside the fairways.[27] By 1927, the course had been extended to 27 holes, and club membership steadily increased, notably among the Fascist elite (Ciano and Bottai were thus typical) and international diplomats posted to Rome. In the 1930s, Acquasanta could deem itself indeed an "Italian club," no longer merely the place of pastime for wealthy or eccentric foreigners. The crises of the Second World War did, however, restrict the club's growth, and the third 9 holes were abandoned. In January 1944, the *Wehrmacht* occupied the clubhouse as Nazi German forces fought off those Allies who were landing at Anzio. When Rome was bombed, the RAF allegedly refused to make Acquasanta a target, with officers saying that they would be foolish to destroy the only golfing establishment south of Florence. In the end Acquasanta had a relatively easy Fascist war and, by 1954, was flourishing again after a major fairway reconstruction.[28] By then golf and Fascism seemed to have lost whatever connection they once may have had.

Nonetheless, during the years of the regime, there had been attempts to draw a Fascist moral from the sport: "Golf, despite its apparent simplicity, is actually a very difficult game," one commentator noted earnestly, "and long study and severe discipline are required to bring a player satisfactory results."[29] Other enthusiasts discerned that golf constituted a modern industry, which had the potential to bring prestige and remuneration to a Fascism that needed to reinforce its place in the modern commercial world (though the high cost and value of land in Italy was long a severe discouragement for a sport that occupied so much space).[30]

In 1932, *Le Vie d'Italia,* the journal of the *"Touring Club Italiano,"* Italy's senior tourist organisation, with a membership approaching one million, published an article by Paolo Stacchini on changes at the San Remo golf course. Stacchini took the chance to expatiate on the typically Fascist technological triumph involved in building a course in a steep coastal setting, and also provided a potted history of the game. It was, he said, played widely in the Anglo-Saxon world, notably in the United States and Australia (despite that country's "exiguous population"). That was appropriate because golf had been introduced to Scotland by William the Conqueror and his comrades in 1027 (sic). Tournaments were now offering considerable prize money and, generally, the "golf industry" was "giving life and business advantage to a great number of people in a way that few other [sporting] activities did." Italy, which had, for example, fewer than one-third of the golf clubs that France did, should try to catch up in this as in many other matters.[31] An even more optimistic and deferential figure, Dr. Marcello Cirillo, by 1939 president of the *Federazione Italiana del Golf,* declared that "golf is, in a certain sense, a totalitarian sport"[32] and

[27]A. Magni (ed.), *op. cit.,* pp. 40-41.

[28]*Ibid.,* p. 43.

[29]A. Brunialti, *op. cit.,* p. 31.

[30]G. Giulini, *op. cit.,* p. 602.

[31]P. Stacchini, "Sviluppi turistici: il Golf a San Remo," *Le Vie d'Italia,* XXXVIII, March 1932, pp. 197-204.

[32]M. Cirillo, "Prefazione" to A. Spalding, *Golf,* Milan, 1939, p. 115. Another Fascist authority noted that Italy was, after all, the most beautiful of all countries and, in that regard, not even St. Andrews could long compete with the potential of Italian courses. G. Giulini, *op. cit.,* pp. 602-603.

thus one doubtless fitted to that totalitarian Fascist Italy whose regime, Mussolini boasted, was in the 1930s drawing ever closer to its people.[33]

Cirillo and Stacchini exaggerated in suggesting a local readiness to convert golf into a mass and Fascist activity. In practice, the game remained a peripheral sport, too costly to be indulged in by any but the most wealthy elite, a foreign import that, still in 1945, had not been assimilated into Italian life. The two stories with which this paper began are typical. Throughout the Fascist era, golf in Italy was a game for visiting Henry Fords, for Galeazzo Cianos, for Pirellis, Agnellis, and the count of this or that, young or youngish Italians whose early education or current political or business activities had convinced them that golf was a game worth playing, either for their pleasure or to demonstrate their status and worldly wisdom.

One other matter, however, deserves comment. In the decade before his death, conservative Italian historian Renzo De Felice took to emphasising that Italy's defeat in the Second World War, and quite a few of the troubles of the Italian Republic established in 1946, flowed from the allegedly limited national sense among the highest circles. De Felice even went so far as to say that, unlike its equivalent in Nazi Germany and Imperial Japan, Italy's bourgeoisie, well embodied by Ciano and Volpi, through its lack of commitment to the Fascist war effort, had failed in its "historic task."[34] However, De Felice's conclusion can be stood on its head. In this alternative understanding, it is precisely the stubborn cosmopolitanism of Italy's rich and, indeed, if in a very different way, its poor, that has saved Italians from too direct an involvement in some of the tragedies and horrors of the 20th century's "age of violence." Perhaps Italians' tendency always to consider both the cosmopolitan and the local, and to resist the hegemony of the national, has permitted the survival in their country of what has been called the "banality of good." By this interpretation, the few Italian golfers who, between the wars and remembering sternly that their manhood required them not to enjoy the view or the weather, hacked their way from green to green, were in some small way resisting the Fascist boast of totalitarianism and, for all their frequent social class and gender insouci-ance were, while thus engaged, not damaging the rest of humankind. In this small sense, the failed meeting of golf and Italian Fascism had good aspects and helped those processes by which Italy remained Italy.

---

[33]For an introduction to the issues involved, see R.J.B. Bosworth, *The Italian dictatorship: problems and perspectives of interpretation of Mussolini and Fascism,* London, 1998.

[34]R. De Felice, *Mussolini l'alleato 1940-1945; 1. L'Italia in guerra 1940-1943,* Turin, 1990, pp. 770-771, 825-829, 959.

CHAPTER 45

Indicators of Performance Momentum
in Competitive Golf: An Exploratory Study

L.M. Landsberger and P.H. Beauchamp
Sports Performance Value Systems (SPVS), Montreal, Canada

This paper establishes quantitative indicators of performance momentum during a competitive golf round, based on the measures of Landsberger's Golf Stroke Value System. Momentum is punctuated by the results of each stroke and is based on a golfer's awareness/perception of realistic expectations for each stroke and each hole. Specific mechanisms for momentum gains and losses are established and quantified. The system is used to analyze golfers' performance in several major championships. The results support a hypothesis that a golfer's performance varies significantly with cumulative momentum.

Keywords: Performance momentum, Golf Stroke Value System, positive and negative momentum, cumulative momentum, performance analysis.

INTRODUCTION

Golfer A birdies the par 5 by sinking a 3-footer after two solid woods and a nice chip. Golfer B birdies the same par 5 by sinking a 25-footer after visiting rough and a fairway bunker. Which one is more "up" due to the results of this sequence? What will impact a golfer's state of mind more, a bad putt or a bad drive? Is there a way to quantify the effect of four missed 15-footers in a row?

These examples each point to the issue of momentum in sport performance. This research hypothesizes measures of such performance momentum in golf to address questions such as these, using the quantitative framework of the Golf Stroke Value System (GSVS) (Landsberger, 1994, 1995). The GSVS has been shown to be useful in analysis of golf performance on a stroke-by-stroke basis (Beauchamp et al., 1994, 1995; Landsberger, 1996). In the GSVS, a numerical stroke value, having two to three significant figures (e.g., 1.27), is assigned to each stroke on the basis of a scratch or personal standard (which corresponds to a value of 1.00), so that its value toward the score on the hole can be compared with the values of other strokes. Previous work with the GSVS focused on its usefulness in evaluating the performance of the various components of one's game, such as drives, short irons, and makable putts. This present study uses the GSVS in estimating the ebb and flow of factors that influence performance momentum of a golfer in competition.

BACKGROUND: MOMENTUM IN SPORT PSYCHOLOGY

Previous research in sport psychology has found psychological momentum to be an elusive concept. A growing body of research tends to support the notion that momentum exerts a powerful influence on sport performance and subsequent success (Adler, 1981). An early definition of momentum, by Iso-Ahola and Mobily (1980), suggested a unidirectional construct, according to which momentum is a gained psychological power that may change perceptions and influence physical and mental performance in a positive way. In contrast, Adler (1981) defined momentum to be bidirectional, a state of mind affecting performance in either a positive or a negative direction. Positive momentum presumes that most everything would "go right" for the athlete, while negative momentum presumes most everything would "go wrong" (Burke et al., 1997).

The model of Adler (1981) also highlights the causally cyclical nature of momentum, in which performance influences momentum, and momentum influences performance. The concept of momentum implies by its nature that early success would lead to future success (e.g., in a competitive volleyball or tennis match). Indeed this hypothesis was supported by several applied studies (Hardy & Silva, 1985; Silva, Hardy, & Crace, 1988; Weinberg & Jackson, 1989). However, other studies failed to indicate such a causal relationship (Gilovich, Valone, & Tversky, 1985; Richardson, Adler, & Hankes, 1988). This diversity of results suggests that the phenomena involved in performance momentum are subtle and complex. The point of studying momentum is to discover and characterize the psychological mechanisms by which the details of past performance and events affect future performance.

The role of perception is fundamental in this topic. It is only after the outcome of a particular event is perceived that it takes on the label of a "momentum event" (Burke et al., 1997). As Vallerand, Colacecchio, and Pelletier (1988) point out, momentum is a "perception that the actor is progressing toward his/her goal." Their early research on the antecedents and consequences of momentum defines momentum as a person (perception) and situational (event) interaction model in which subjective perceptions of the event are of critical importance in triggering cognition, affect, and behaviour that reflect this perception of momentum. "It is these perceptions which have real consequences for the person who holds them."

Vallerand et al. further explain that momentum is inherently intertwined with the perception of control by the individual, leading to feelings of competence and thus fulfilling a basic psychological need (Deci & Ryan, 1985). Positive momentum is likely to be enhanced by events that support the perception of control, while negative momentum is likely to be enhanced by events that emphasize lack of control.

MOMENTUM IN GOLF

Golf is unusual among competitive sports because the nature of the opponent is different. While there are co-competitors playing with us, their actions do not necessarily demand reactions from us on an event-by-event basis, particularly in stroke play. Rather, the most immediate and pervasive "opponents" are the golf course, "bad luck," and the golfer him/herself. The essence of the game is control over these variables in order to make the golf ball do our bidding. This involves self-control and some measure of control over the behaviour of the ball on the golf course. The precision with which we accomplish this control determines our performance (score!).

It is clear from observing golfers that their perceptions, cognitions, affect, and behaviour are affected by the results of individual strokes and that these seem to be further punctuated by the results of each hole. The results of each hole are compelling candidates as momentum-changing events, since success or failure is determined by per hole scores. Thus the golfer's anticipatory perceptions of ultimate success or failure are likely to be intensified at the end of each hole. Further, experienced golfers are keenly aware that the results of each stroke impact the likelihood of achieving a good score on a given hole. Therefore each stroke can suggest to the golfer that he/she is gaining or losing control over the situation. Moreover, these effects could be cumulative over at least several holes, resulting in "cumulative momentum" (negative or positive).

WHY PUTTS CAN AFFECT MOMENTUM SO DRAMATICALLY

Quantification by the GSVS showed that our scores are not very sensitive to fine variations in the results of most long strokes. For example, whether we make a 4 or a 5 on a given hole is not solely (or even mostly) determined by whether we get 30 yards more or less from our driver, or even whether our drive ends up in the light rough versus the center of the fairway. Similarly, it is not solely determined by whether our iron shots stop on the green or on the fringe, or even in a bunker. But whether we make a 4 or a 5 can be almost solely determined by whether our 3-footer sinks versus lips out. In other words, most of our woods and irons gain or lose small-to-medium (quantifiable) fractions of a stroke, but a putt is either in the cup or not, and the difference is a whole stroke.

Consider putts between 1.5 feet (stroke value 1.0) and 30 feet (stroke value 2.0). For example, if you make a 15-footer, your expectation was 1.75, but you took only 1 stroke, so you saved three-quarters of a stroke. On the other hand, if you missed from 5 feet, your expectation was 1.4 strokes, but you took 2 strokes, so your loss was 0.6 of a stroke. Gains and losses such as these are substantial quantities. It usually takes you at least two to three good long shots to achieve this magnitude of gain.

In the context of psychological momentum, this means that, beginning at the tee, the golfer spends several minutes and much energy to make small gains on several long strokes, but the score may be determined more in the instant when the putt either drops or stays out. If a significant putt (over 2-3 feet) drops, it can support the golfer's perception of progressing toward the goal. If a short putt stays out, it may wash out the gains achieved over several carefully executed long strokes, leading to intense feelings of lack of control and loss of momentum.

MOMENTUM INDICATORS USING THE GOLF STROKE VALUE SYSTEM

The GSVS quantifies realistic expectations for golf strokes. It is a hypothesis of this research that expert golfers are aware (at least subconsciously) of such realistic expectations for each stroke. Thus, actual outcomes can be tracked versus expectation on a stroke-by-stroke basis. Note that the average expectation for a given stroke is represented by a stroke value = 1.00.

This research hypothesizes that momentum gains are achieved by the following:

- Stroke value gains due to non-gimmie (missable: from 2 feet or longer) putts sunk. These support the golfer's perception of overall control.
- Stroke value gains due to uninterrupted sequences of high-valued strokes (having values greater than some threshold for perception, such as 1.10). These support the golfer's perception of high personal ability.
- Stroke value gains due to strokes sunk from off the green (reasoning similar to that for the other putts listed, but more intense).

Momentum losses would be incurred by the following:

- Stroke value losses due to makable (from inside about 20 feet) putts missed. These appear to "steal" from the golfer previously earned gains.
- Stroke value losses due to uninterrupted sequences of low-valued strokes (having values lower than some threshold for perception, such as 0.90). These detract from the golfer's perception of personal ability.
- Penalty strokes. These appear to "steal" previously earned gains.

(Note that lucky and unlucky breaks not captured by these categories are also likely to affect momentum, but have not been included in this analysis.)

To illustrate these measures, the examples in table 45.1 quantify the momentum issues raised by four different ways to play a par 5, two for birdie and two for par. Cases A and B correspond to the example raised at the beginning of the paper (including adjustments for rough and sand in case B).

Consider the scenario in which both players make birdie. Player A may feel the momentum of having made the three high-valued (V greater than 1.10) longer strokes, and also that of making the missable putt. For Player B, on the other hand,

Table 45.1   Examples Quantifying Stroke Values and Momentum in the Play of a Par-5

A: Bird via short putt	Distance to hole	Stroke value	Momentum
1: Teed driver	520 yds	1.14	
2: 4-Wood	260 yds	1.17	
3: Chip	18 yds	1.11	+0.42
4: Putt	3 ft	1.22	+0.22
4 Strokes		4.64	+0.64

B: Bird via mkbl putt	Distance to hole	Stroke value	Momentum
1: Teed driver	520 yds	0.96	
2: Layup iron	280 yds	0.92	
3: Short iron	80 yds	0.97	
4: Putt	16 ft	1.79	+0.79
4 Strokes		4.64	+0.79

C: Missed short putt	Distance to hole	Stroke value	Momentum
1: Teed driver	520 yds	1.14	
2: 4-Wood	260 yds	1.17	
3: Chip	18 yds	1.11	+0.42
4: Putt	3 ft	0.22	-0.78
5: Putt	1 ft	1.00	+0.00
5 Strokes		4.64	-0.78

D: Missed mkbl putt	Distance to hole	Stroke value	Momentum
1: Teed driver	520 yds	0.96	
2: Layup iron	280 yds	0.92	
3: Short iron	80 yds	0.97	
4: Putt	16 ft	0.79	-0.21
5: Putt	1 ft	1.00	+0.00
5 Strokes		4.64	-0.21

the weaker long strokes may not have been weak enough to impact his perception of his own ability, while the makable putt gains 0.79 of stroke value and thus of momentum. In this way, Player B may feel slightly more positive momentum after this sequence, although both golfers played the same hole, valued at 4.64 strokes. Note that with use of thresholds as described earlier, the momentum totals can vary differently from the total stroke values.

If Player A actually missed his 3-foot putt (case C), that would dramatically impact his momentum. Would the sequence of high-valued strokes still be felt? While this is a difficult question, we suggest that uninterrupted sequences of high-valued strokes must extend at least to the end of a hole in order for the full impact to be felt by the golfer. This is because the payoff does not occur until the end of a hole. It is only at the end of a hole that the perception of progressing toward one's goal is likely to be satisfactorily realized. The resulting contrast in momentum losses (−0.78 in case C versus −0.21 in case D) would appear to be consistent with the level of disappointment that the two players would feel if they missed their putts.

SEVERAL MAJOR CHAMPIONSHIPS ANALYZED

The momentum analysis just described was applied to televised portions of the final round of several major championships from 1995 on. The cumulative momentum data are graphically displayed in figures 45.1 through 45.8. In all cases shown, the major-championship winner had a positive and rising momentum trend on the final nine holes of the tournament. In all cases, the momentum patterns of the runner-up(s) were weaker than that of the winner. Note that momentum gains and losses are only loosely related to strokes gained and lost.

Figures 45.1 and 45.2 show Norman and Faldo in the 1996 Masters. While Norman's momentum pattern was very strong during the first three rounds, his fourth-round collapse is highly noteworthy from a momentum standpoint. He incurred substantial momentum losses on holes #9, #10, and #11. Hole #11 was particularly painful for him, since he three-putted from 12 feet. On the 12th tee he was still tied for the lead, but his momentum over the previous five holes was more than 2 strokes negative. He then made his most costly mistake, hitting into the water, incurring a double bogey. Meanwhile Faldo succeeded in maintaining positive cumulative momentum.

Figures 45.3 through 45.5 show Davis Love III, Norman, and Crenshaw in the 1995 Masters. While Crenshaw's momentum surged throughout most of the back nine, Love's and Norman's momentum patterns "couldn't get it going." The GSVS analysis showed that Norman's and Love's long woods and irons were significantly better than Crenshaw's during 9 strokes over the critical period of holes #11-15 (average stroke values: Norman, 1.295; Love, 1.312; Crenshaw, 1.05). This highlights the critical importance of putting. For example, Love and Norman left par 5 greens with birdies, but deflated after missing short eagle putts. On the other hand, Crenshaw's momentum was still high after #15, and he birdied #16 and #17 to win the tournament.

Figures 45.6 through 45.8 show the cumulative momentum in the final round for the three top finishers in the 1997 U.S. Open. On the 17th tee, Els and Montgomerie

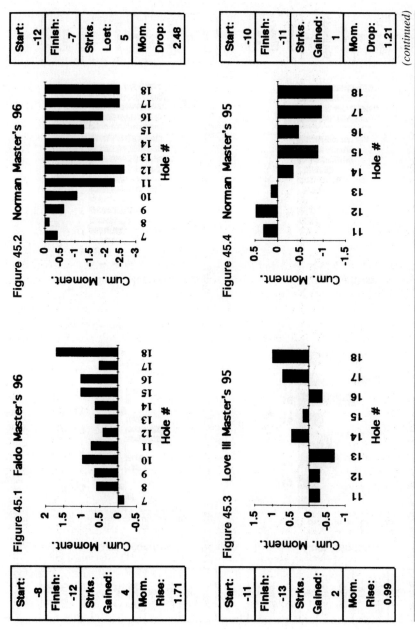

Figures 45.1–45.8   Hole-by-hole cumulative performance momentum in final rounds of selected major championships.

(continued)

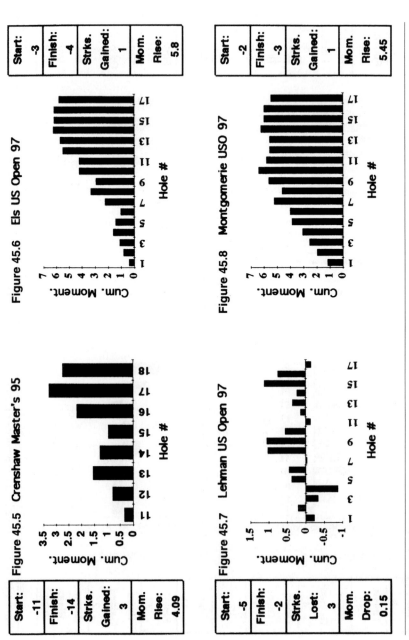

Figures 45.1-45.8   *(continued)*

led at –4, with Lehman at –3 and Maggert at –2. The results of the play of the dramatic 17th are consistent with the players' cumulative momentum at that point. Maggert's (not shown) and Lehman's cumulative momentum levels (0.27 and 0.75, respectively) were clearly much lower than Els's (6.18) and Montgomerie's (5.99). While Els's and Montgomerie's cumulative momentum levels were about equal, Els's had been surging on the back nine, while Montgomerie's had been relatively flat since hole #10. Correspondingly, Els made a two-putt par on #17, while Montgomerie bogeyed, missing a 5- to 6-footer. Lehman made a more serious mistake, hitting his ball into the water, and Maggert 3-putted for a double bogey.

CONCLUSIONS

Golf performance momentum may be quantifiable using the stroke-by-stroke measures of the GSVS, and it is likely to be cumulative from hole to hole. The catastrophic nature of putting renders it a critical factor influencing momentum in either a positive or a negative way. Momentum varies in a different way than hole-by-hole score or stroke value.

The analyses presented of major championships are consistent with a hypothesis that cumulative momentum may influence performance at critical moments in a competition. A rising positive momentum pattern late in a major championship is often characteristic of the tournament winner. Furthermore, it appears that both positive and negative momentum may be involved. Thus this study may support previous research results that characterize momentum as a bidirectional concept. Since these momentum indicators are based on the golfer's realistic expectations for each stroke and hole, the results herein would tend to support the heavy role of perception and control in influencing performance momentum.

Future research could investigate the relationship of performance momentum, as measured here, to specific accompanying behavioural, cognitive, emotional, and physiological variables (e.g., preshot routine, confidence, arousal, heart rate).

References

Adler, P. (1981). *Momentum: A theory of social action.* Beverly Hills, CA: Sage.

Beauchamp, P.H., Landsberger, L.M., Halliwell, W.R., Koestner, R., & Ford, M.E. (1994). Toward putting performance enhancement: A methodology using quantitative feedback. In A. Cochran & M.R. Farrally (Eds.), *Science and golf II* (pp. 174-179). London: Spon.

Beauchamp, P.H., Halliwell, W.R., Koestner, R., & Landsberger, L. (1995). Achievement orientation and putting improvement across varying levels of challenge in amateur golfers. *Journal Applied Sport Psychology, 1995 Conference Abstracts* (New Orleans), 7, p. 39.

Burke, K.L., Edwards, T.C., Weigand, D.A., & Weinberg, R.S. (1997). Momentum in sport: A real or illusionary phenomenon for spectators. *International Journal of Sport Psychology,* 28 (1), 79-96.

Deci, E.L., & Ryan, R.M. (1985). *Intrinsic motivation and self-determination in human behavior.* New York: Plenum Press.

Gilovich, T., Valone, R., & Tversky, A. (1985). The hot hand in basketball: On the misperception of random sequences. *Cognitive Psychology,* 17, 295-314.

Hardy, C.J., & Silva, J.M. (1985). The mediational role of psychological momentum in performance outcome. In J.R. Thomas (Ed.), *Psychology of motor behavior in sport* (p. 106). Gulf Park, MS: North American Society for the Psychology of Sport and Physical Activity.

Iso-Ahola, S.E., & Mobily, K. (1980). Psychological momentum: A phenomenon of an empirical (unobtrusive) validation of its influence in a competitive sport tournament. *Psychological Report,* 46, 391-401.

Landsberger, L.M. (1994). A unified golf stroke value scale for quantitative stroke by-stroke assessment. In A. Cochran & M.R. Farrally (Eds.), *Science and golf II* (pp. 216-221). London: Spon.

Landsberger, L.M. (1995). Evaluating your golf strokes. In A. Cochran (Ed.), *Golf the scientific way* (pp. 238-241). Herefordshire, UK: Aston.

Landsberger, L.M. (1996). Momentum indicators in a competitive golf round: An exploratory study. In *Book of abstracts of the Golf Theory in Practice Conference* (University of Ulster, Northern Ireland), pp. 33-34.

Richardson, P.A., Adler, W., & Hankes, D. (1988). Game, set, match: Psychological momentum in tennis. *The Sport Psychologist,* 2, 69-76.

Silva, J.M., Hardy, C.J., & Crace, R.K. (1988). Analysis of psychological momentum in intercollegiate tennis. *Journal of Sport and Exercise Psychology,* 10, 346-354.

Vallerand, R.J., Colacecchio, P.G., & Pelletier, L.G. (1988). Psychological momentum and performance inferences: A preliminary test of the antecedents-consequences psychological momentum model. *Journal of Sport & Exercise Psychology,* 10 (1), 92-108.

Weinberg, R., & Jackson, A. (1989). The effects of psychological momentum and performance inferences: A preliminary test of the antecedents-consequences psychological momentum model. *Journal of Sport Behavior,* 12 (3), 167-179.

CHAPTER 46

Hole Size, Luck, and the Cruelty of Putting: A Thought Experiment on the Impact of Quantization in Golf

L.M. Landsberger
Sports Performance Value Systems (SPVS), Montreal, Canada

This paper addresses the impact of quantization in golf, using the fundamentals of the Golf Stroke Value System. Subtle variations can make a whole-stroke difference in score and can wash out substantial gains or losses accrued from several previous long strokes on a given hole. This is a fundamental consequence of integer quantization of golf scores. This quantization is the main systematic avenue for the influence of luck on the game. Purposeful variation of the hole size would significantly change the proportional impact of luck, in a paradoxical way. Increasing hole size would decrease number of strokes and would lessen the role of putting, but would increase the impact of luck.

Keywords: Putting, quantization, hole size, luck, GSVS, Golf Stroke Value System.

INTRODUCTION

Drive for show, putt for dough! By using insights from the Golf Stroke Value System (GSVS) (Landsberger 1994; Beauchamp et al. 1994; Landsberger 1995), this paper traces the fundamental nature of golf scoring to the quantization of strokes in integer units.

The exploration begins with consideration of the cruelty (sensitivity) of putting in comparison to other types of long strokes. This leads to a discussion of the concept and impact of quantization. Since many golfers feel that the impact of luck is related to the importance of putting and to the diameter of the hole, this is addressed, in connection with a discussion of the effective hole area. Finally, the paper outlines the paradoxical impact of changing the hole size.

THE CRUELTY OF PUTTING

We (golfers) feel that we intuitively understand the cruelty of putting. Many times during each round that we play, we consciously confront the fact that if we miss from this humiliating distance, our score will be a whole stroke higher. But we figure that the rules of the game are the same for everyone, the hole is the same size for everyone, and that on average the greens play the same for everyone. Some putts go in, some don't.

But compare the situation of facing a short putt to the situation of facing a typical tee shot hit with a driver. If driving were like putting from about 4-6 feet (the distance at which most amateurs make half and miss half), this would be like hitting every drive over a deep sand bunker that extends out to our average carry. For example, if our average drive (average of all drives, not only those that are decent!) carried (not carried and rolled) to about 180 yards, then having a deep bunker out to 180 yards would make driving as sensitive as putting from 4-6 feet.

Similarly, to make an iron approach shot similar in nature to a 4-6-foot putt, the green would have to be completely surrounded by a deep punitive bunker, except perhaps for a narrow entry in front. If our average iron shot from 140 yards finished 35 feet from the hole, then this pseudo-island green would have to be a mere 70 feet in diameter.

These would be particularly scary situations! Any course where every shot presented such brutality with no "out" would probably be deemed too difficult. As you consider this statement, remember that the numbers given in the preceding are relative to an estimated representative performance of a certain level of amateurs. For the pros, whom we see on TV, the examples above would be transformed: (a) carry would be at least 230-250 yards on every tee shot, and (b) from 140 yards the green would be only 50 feet in diameter surrounded on all sides by deep bunkering, except for a narrow opening. Even the pros would become worn out by this level of abuse!

But we confront this type of challenge every time we address a short putt. We confront the possibility of a catastrophe—the loss of a whole stroke on the scorecard—even with a near-average (not bad) stroke. On most of our other strokes, even on "very difficult" courses, we gain or lose small-to-medium fractions of stroke value (see appendix A on the GSVS) in relation to our average performance. It usually takes us at least two to four unusually good or bad long shots to gain or lose a whole stroke. But on every green, we face the threshold: gain or lose a whole stroke on a single putt.

The sensitivity of this situation becomes most apparent on putts between about 2 feet and 10 feet. Here, there are substantial portions of the distributions of our strokes that both make and miss. Here, where sinking the putt is a realistic expectation, is where mental toughness becomes the issue. Here one needs the ability to produce a decent shot when it is really needed, in order to save a whole stroke. Note that this is not necessarily a "great" shot—all that is needed is "one of one's better shots."

THE EFFECT OF QUANTIZATION

The catastrophic sensitivity that has been described is due to quantization. Golf scores are quantized such that the player's score on each hole is necessarily an integer (e.g., 3, 4, 5, or 6). Half-strokes or 0.1 strokes do not appear on the scorecard. However, during the play of a hole, there are much more sensitive variations in the quality and value of each individual stroke. Representing these differences in value requires finer quantization. For example, to capture the difference in value between a 220-yard drive in the center of the fairway and a 200-yard drive in the rough would require quantization in units of about 0.1-0.2, depending on the severity of the rough. Such finer quantization can be examined by using the GSVS to establish either an absolute standard or a personal performance standard based on one's average stroke value (appendix A).

Quantization in integer units has a fundamental influence on the nature of golf. For example, during the play of a routine par 4, a player shapes a beautiful iron shot into the wind and stops it 6 feet from the hole. However, he makes an average putting stroke, and the ball glances off a barely visible heel mark and lips out. His competitor, on the other hand, hitting from about the same place on the fairway, pushes his iron shot to pin-high 30 feet off-line and makes an average two-putt for a tie. The first player's iron shot was much better than the second's (i.e., by about a half-stroke, according to the GSVS), they hit all other strokes in the play of this hole with equal skill, and they ended in a tie. The difference in quality of the two iron shots was not enough to overcome the integer quantization threshold, and thus the difference was washed out on the scorecard.

This washing-out effect can be called "noise." The "quantization noise" is defined as half of the quantization unit. This means that the number on the scorecard can deviate by up to a half-stroke from the stroke value that the player should have "earned." The worst-case scenario (being off by a half-stroke) occurs most often when the player has a 4-7-foot putt, depending on the skill level of the player. If, from this distance, the player makes an average stroke (i.e., one for which the probability of holing is 1/2), then if the putt lips in, its value is about 1.5, while if it lips out its value is about 0.5. Note that execution of an average stroke should earn an average personal stroke value of 1.0, while each of these results deviates from the earned 1.0 by $\pm$ 0.5.

This situation is schematically represented in figure 46.1. At left, the "earned" stroke value is assumed to be approximately normally distributed. The graph at right shows how, from this distance (i.e., that at which the probability of holing is 1/2), the "achieved" stroke value is forced either above or below the "earned" stroke value (represented by the sloped dashed line). This forced quantization would not be relevant on long-game strokes, since it would occur at a much higher "earned" stroke value (i.e., would not impact the center of the distribution).

Since this type of situation could potentially happen on all 18 holes, the maximum effect of this "quantization noise" is 9 strokes during a round of golf. The impact of this quantization noise is felt differently by players of different skill levels. For a professional, shooting in the high 60s, the impact of a half-stroke error per hole is felt significantly more than for a 100-shooter, since 9/67 = 0.134, while 9/100 = 0.09. The pro feels this effect about 50% more than the 100-shooter (since 0.134/ 0.09 = 1.5). This is a sensible insight, since a greater fraction of the 100-shooter's

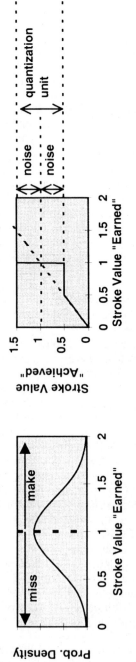

Figure 46.1 Quantization noise.

strokes do not scare the hole. In a sense, this implies that the result of a competition between two 100-shooters is determined to a greater extent by their own performance than is the result of a competition between two professionals. For the 100-shooters, the results are proportionally more determined by the vagaries of their swings than by the luck of whether or not their putts drop. In summary, the fewer the number of strokes taken, the greater the proportional impact of quantization. The greater the number of strokes taken, the less the impact of this noise.

THE EFFECTIVE HOLE AREA

A regulation golf hole is circular and has a radius of 2.125 inches (i.e., diameter = 4.25 inches). While the golf ball (eventually!) ends up confined within this hole, the effective area of the hole is actually much larger, because the hole captures many more balls than would come to rest precisely within the 2.125-inch radius if the target were merely a circular marking on the green as opposed to a hole. In fact, as Pelz (1989) and others have described, the true capture area of a golf hole is somewhat as schematically shown in figure 46.2.

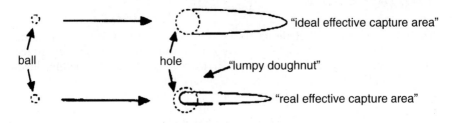

Figur 46.2 The true capture area of a golf hole.

On an ideal green (perfect putting surface with a freshly made cup that is perfectly flush with the surface of the green, with edges not raised or lowered with respect to the previous level of the ground), the capture area would look like the upper diagram in figure 46.2. The ball must reach the hole, it can fall in from the widest deviation angle at the sides of the hole, and the better your line, the harder you can stroke it. Simple mechanical calculations would show that the effective capture area would vary with green speed. It is estimated here to be at least five or more times greater than the actual hole area.

On a real green, however, there are many irregularities, leading to more random effects. Among these is the "lumpy doughnut" effect (Pelz 1989), due to golfers walking on the green near the hole, effectively raising the edges of the cup with respect to the region near the hole. Since this is a systematic effect, most putts that would just barely fall into the side of the hole on an ideal green are deflected farther away from the hole on a lumpy-doughnut green, and miss. Here, one needs to hit the ball harder just to keep it from being deflected off-line, and even so, the effective area is considerably smaller. The overall effect is that fewer putts drop.

The lumpy doughnut would be less aggravating if it were predictable and consistent. But of course it is not. It is not necessarily the same from all directions, and its exact characteristics are too difficult for the golfer to discern accurately. Thus, a real lumpy doughnut makes the effective capture area not only much smaller than it would otherwise be, but also effectively places it at an imprecise location. All the golfer is really sure of is that a "real effective capture area," smaller than the ideal effective capture area, is located roughly within the ideal effective capture area.

In golf as we know it, this is the most systematic and important influence of luck. Since we must traverse this elusive (and unfriendly!) inconsistency in green surface on every hole, it can impact scores 18 times per round. The issue is how much it can impact our scores.

For a typical range of green-surface quality, the fact that scores are quantized in integer units amplifies the impact of luck. This quantization takes a small variation in the line of a putt, caused by a green-surface irregularity, and transforms it into a whole stroke of difference on the scorecard. In this way, the impact of luck can cause differences of up to a whole stroke per hole.

THE IMPACT OF INCREASING OR DECREASING THE HOLE SIZE

The impact of doubling the hole diameter was studied quantitatively by Cochran and Stobbs (1968). They reported "(i) the near-certainty of holing from six feet, (ii) the virtual elimination of three-putting, and (iii) the very good chance of getting down in two from fifty yards. . . ." Putting from about 6 feet to a regular hole was found to be near-equivalent to putting from about 15 feet to the double-size hole. They further estimated that the scratch golfer would save a relatively small number of strokes, such as 6 strokes over the course of 18 holes.

This increase in hole size would, overall, reduce scores and reduce the number of putts taken, decreasing the relative impact of putting in golf. However, would this decrease the impact of luck on the game?

THE PARADOX OF LUCK AND PUTTING

As outlined in the preceding discussion, the element of luck appears in golf mostly in putting. Increasing the hole size would decrease the importance of putting. Clearly, any increase in the hole size would lessen the impact of any particular green irregularity such as the lumpy doughnut, thus decreasing the impact of this particular random (i.e., luck) factor.

Would this decrease the impact of luck in the game as a whole? The reasoning is not straightforward. Increasing the hole size would transfer the incidence of luck to a location farther away from the hole. Whether the player made a 3 or a 4 would be determined to a greater extent by other too-complex-to-discern, subtle factors farther from the hole, such as the texture of the green apron, the ground hardness in the landing area for a particular chip or pitch, or the integrated green irregularities over a 25-foot putt. If these irregularities were more predictable than the lumpy doughnut, would this decrease the impact of luck on the game as a whole?

It would reduce the number of strokes taken by a player of a given ability, which would increase the ratio of quantization noise to actual strokes. Since the fact of quantization amplifies the effect of luck, up to the unit of quantization, this would, in effect, increase the effect of luck. Simply decreasing the role of putting would not be sufficient to decrease the importance of luck in the game as a whole.

A way to systematically decrease the effect of luck on the overall game of golf would be to increase the number of strokes taken. This could be done either by substantially lengthening the holes or by decreasing the hole size (both likely to be unpopular suggestions!). Decreasing the hole size would increase the number of strokes taken and thus decrease the ratio of quantization unit to number of strokes.

IN A SPECULATIVE VEIN: FRACTIONAL STROKES

Since this paper is of an abstract nature, it would not be inappropriate to speculate on another way to systematically decrease the effect of luck: one could directly reduce the quantization unit. If (only if!) one were willing to change the nature of the game, one could introduce the use of half-strokes in the following manner. Draw a neatly defined circle around each hole, having a radius at or slightly greater than the "gimmie" range (e.g., a 2-foot radius). When a player's ball comes to rest inside this circle, but not in the hole, the play of the hole is deemed to be finished for that player, and a half-stroke is added to the player's score up to that point. Alternatively, the player could be required to earn the half-stroke more diligently, by sinking the remaining 1-2-footer. This type of arrangement would reduce the importance of luck by reducing the impact of a near-miss to a half-stroke instead of a whole stroke.

CONCLUSIONS

The cruelty of putting stems from its catastrophic nature. Extremely subtle variations can make a whole-stroke difference on the scorecard and can wash out substantial gains or losses accrued from several previous long strokes on a given hole. This is a fundamental consequence of the quantization of golf scores in integer units. This leads to a possible "quantization noise" of 9 strokes over the course of an 18-hole round. The lower one's aggregate score, the more significant the proportional impact of this noise.

This noise is the most significant avenue for the influence of luck on the game of golf because it amplifies the impact of green irregularities such as the lumpy doughnut effect.

Purposeful variation of the hole size would have an impact on the proportion of luck involved in the game, in a counterintuitive way. Increasing the hole size would decrease the number of strokes taken and would lessen the role of putting in golf. However, this would increase the impact of luck simply by increasing the ratio of the quantization unit to strokes taken.

References

Beauchamp, P.H., Landsberger, L.M., Halliwell, W.R., Koestner, R., & Ford, M.E. (1994). Toward putting performance enhancement: A methodology using quantitative feedback. In A. Cochran & M.R. Farrally (Eds.), *Science and Golf II* (pp. 174-179). London: Spon.

Beauchamp, P.H., Halliwell, W.R., Koestner, R., & Landsberger, L. (1995). Achievement orientation and putting improvement across varying levels of challenge in amateur golfers. *Journal Applied Sport Psychology, 1995 Conference Abstracts* (New Orleans), 7, p. 39.

Cochran, A., & Stobbs, J. (1968). *The search for the perfect golf swing.* Grass Valley, CA: Booklegger.

Landsberger, L.M. (1994). A unified golf stroke value scale for quantitative stroke-by-stroke assessment. In A. Cochran & M.R. Farrally (Eds.), *Science and golf II* (pp. 216-221). London: Spon.

Landsberger, L.M. (1995). Evaluating your golf strokes. In A. Cochran (Ed.), *Golf the scientific way* (pp. 238-241). Herefordshire, UK: Aston.

Landsberger, L.M. (1996). Momentum Indicators in a competitive golf round: An exploratory study. In *Book of abstracts of the Golf Theory in Practice Conference* (University of Ulster, Northern Ireland), pp. 33-34.

Pelz, D. (1989). *Putt like the pros.* New York: Harper & Row.

APPENDIX A: THE GOLF STROKE VALUE SYSTEM

The Golf Stroke Value System (GSVS) (Landsberger 1994; Beauchamp et al. 1994; Landsberger 1995; Beauchamp et al. 1995; Landsberger 1996) is a system for finer-quantized evaluation of golf strokes. It is a system of logic designed to objectively evaluate golf performance on a stroke-by-stroke basis. The judgments are based on the factual results of each stroke. Given where the ball started before the stroke and where it came to rest after the stroke, what was the stroke worth, compared to other strokes and compared to a defined performance standard such as the "course rating" standard? While there is often the necessity for adjustments due to wind, slope, difficulty, lie, and obstacles, this system provides an integrated framework by which the value of each stroke can be compared to the value of any other stroke.

The analysis can be done with respect to the course rating standard or another personal standard. The course rating standard is the standard of the golfer who nominally shoots the course rating. Such a golfer would have average stroke value = 1.0 versus the course rating standard. Using this standard, strokes having value near 1.0 tend to lead to pars, while strokes having value over about 1.2 are the kind needed in order to make birdies. Strokes having value less than about 0.8 tend to lead to bogeys, and so on, unless compensated for by other high-valued strokes. The total stroke value for the round is composed of the stroke values for each of the 18 holes and is based on the distance for each hole, adjusted for wind, uphill/downhill, tightness, and various other difficulty factors. On each hole, the values for all strokes taken must add up to the total stroke value for that hole.

An 18-handicap golfer would have average stroke value near 0.8 versus the course rating standard. For the 18-handicapper, a personal standard could be established, such that the average of his or her strokes on this adjusted standard was also 1.0.

CHAPTER 47

Yardage Rating by the Curve

Francis Scheid
USGA Handicap Research Team, Far Hills, NJ, USA

Golf course rating starts with the assumption that yardage is an important factor and that its influence is linear. The USGA formula for scratch men, for example, is Length/220 + 40.9. An early report (Scheid 1974) showed that the relationship between difficulty and yardage may be nonlinear. For a variety of courses and levels of playing ability hole-by-hole scoring averages did not follow a straight-line climb. Instead, over each par range they grew more slowly than the overall regression predicted. This would imply the existence of upward ramps between the par ranges, at yardages not common on ordinary courses. Recent follow-up studies (Scheid 1995, 1996) using data shot by low handicap men and women, and by women on the LPGA tour, have supported this. A study of British Open scores from 1982-1987 (Wilson 1996, 1997) and one using a small set of PGA data (Scheid 1996) also found this effect. Proceeding in a more theoretical direction, performance models have been developed by Simmons (1994) and Scheid (1995, 1997) for men and women, scratch and bogey levels, with parameters based on performance data. All these models predict the same kind of nonlinearity, a composite of modest inclines with connecting ramps. This report will describe some of the detail of these empirical and theoretical efforts and the consequences of nonlinearity for yardage rating.

Keywords: Yardage rating, nonlinearity, short courses.

THE EMPIRICAL EVIDENCE

The 1974 study used data from players of a variety of abilities, including some from the American tour. Of 33 par ranges tested, 28 showed slopes (average scores against yardage) lower than that of an overall regression. Assuming equal changes for higher and lower, such a 28 to 5 split would have extremely low probability. It was suggested by Soley at the time that course architects might be responsible, feeling obliged to be more generous with obstacles at short par 3s, 4s, and 5s, and this may be true. In fact, the argument had enough credibility to delay further study of the question for twenty years. It was Simmons' attempt at model building that brought reduced slopes and ramps back to mind. As we shall see, it explained such nonlinearity without appealing to human interference. It also triggered more data analysis. Hole-by-hole scores for twenty-three Massachusetts courses, from 352 men players with handicap 10 or less, produced these slopes for average score against yardage, all multiplied by 10,000 (Scheid 1995).

All 18 holes	Range 22 to 62	Median 54
Par 3s	Range 8 to 211	Median 47
Par 4s	Range –49 to 105	Median 42
Par 5s	Range –333 to 192	Median 70

There are some awesome figures here. Slopes for par 5s were particularly volatile. Some courses had no such holes. One course had two, lengths differing by 12 yards and a severe negative slope. Fortunately for believers in a nonlinear world, the 70 was deemed statistically insignificant by a Wilcoxon signed rank test. Unfortunately, so was the 47 for par 3s. The par 4s told a more solid story. For 16 of the 23 clubs used, par 4 slopes were less than that of the eighteen overall, with one tie. An available table for the Wilcoxen signed rank test had no suitable entry, the level of significance being too strong. For what it is worth, here are slopes obtained by pooling all 352 men (again multiplied by 10,000).

Overall 51   Par 3s 42   Par 4s 42   Par 5s 46

Using data from 21 top women's events, Amateur Championship or LPGA tour, the process was repeated with these results.

All 18 holes	Range 51 to 60	Median 55
Par 3s	Range –109 to 119	Median 40
Par 4s	Range –8 to 84	Median 33
Par 5s	Range –49 to 70	Median 36

The par 3 figure failed a signed rank test but the par 4 and par 5 results did not, scoring below 0.005. Pooling all the women's data led to these slopes.

Overall 55   Par 3s 37   Par 4s 37   Par 5s 41

MODELING

A stochastic model for scratch men has been developed for play from tee to hole (Scheid 1997). It assumes random normal errors in both length and aim. For each shot a target position is chosen. The USGA figure for average driving length by scratch men is 250 yards. If distance from tee to hole exceeds this, then 250 yards straight down the fairway is the target. Otherwise the target is the hole, the appropriate club being presumed. From the fairway the average maximal shot length is taken to be 220 yards, again the USGA figure. If distance to the hole exceeds this, then 220 yards straight out is the target position. Otherwise it is the hole. The assumption that fairways are not obstructed will be noted. A penalty for seriously off-line shots could be added but has not been included at this point. The chosen target position is central to a 2-D normal distribution pattern of stopping positions. The standard deviations for length and aim were chosen to be consistent with accepted performance data. For example, the Royal Birkdale study reported in Cochran & Stobbs (1968) found that distance remaining to the hole after an approach shot, hole within reach, was about 8% of the distance before. The figure held up well for all lengths tested. Also, the familiar straight line formula for yardage rating mentioned earlier has historical credibility and deserves refining rather than abandonment. With the Birkdale 8% and the straight-line formula as guides, numerous standard deviations were tried, eventually settling for 0.081 in length and 0.032 in aim, multiplied by target distance. It was found that using 7.5 instead of 8% brought a still better match, so this adjustment was also made. It became clear that there is not just one path to scratch play. Several parameter sets manage it, not only the (250, 220, 0.081, 0.032) chosen. Shorter but more accurate manages just as well as longer and a little wilder. And, of course, there is putting. In the 1995 models the number of putts to hole out from various distances was extracted from tables in Soley (1977). However, in Hoadley (1994) there is a stochastic model of putting which was adapted slightly and embedded in the present model. From 15 yards away this takes over to make the model fully stochastic.

With the details in place, the model made 1,000 simulations for each hole length from 20 to 650 yards. For each shot, two random standard normal numbers were generated and modified for the appropriate mean and sigma. Mean scores and standard deviations for each hole length were calculated. The deviations varied only from 0.38 for the short holes to 0.40 for the long. Means are plotted in figure 47.1,

Hole average

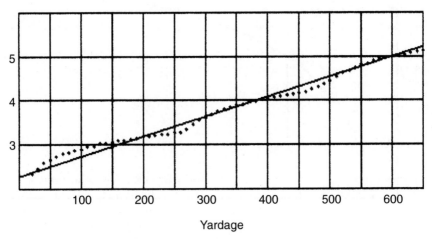

Figure 47.1 Mean scores for each hole length.

which also shows the traditional yardage rating line. Reduced slopes and ramps are evident.

SIMPLE LOGIC

One and one make true. For the first "one" take the putting curve that shows how strokes needed to hole out varies with yardage. Whatever the explanation, all data-gathering efforts have found it taking the shape, almost logarithmic in character, seen in figure 47.2. The other one will be the 7.5% rule, assumed at least roughly valid. Put them together to consider the twin problems of finishing up from, say, 20 and 40 yards away. By the 7.5% rule on average the green is reached with 1.5 or 4.5 yards of putting to do. The left of two triangles in the figure then shows a difference of about 0.8 strokes to hole out. This is where the putting curve is steep. Each of the twin problems takes one approach shot so they differ only in the putting, by about 0.8 strokes. The 0.8 measures the relative difficulty based on yardage only. Now consider a second set of twins, finishing up from 120 and 160 yards away. The rule says that average approach shots leave 9 or 12 yards of putting. The other triangle in the figure shows the difference to be only about 1/8 stroke, again a measure of relative difficulty. This is where the putting curve is nearly level. Returning to figure 47.1 we find yardage ratings rising much more between the first twins than between the second. Similar comparisons can be made elsewhere. No wonder the curve curves. The putting curve requires it.

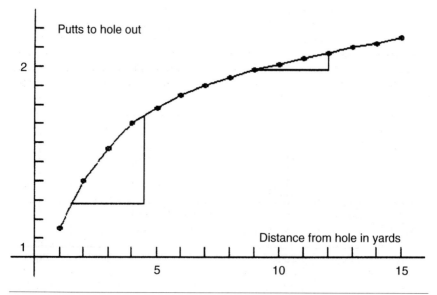

Figure 47.2   Putting curve.

Now suppose one is 370 yards away with driver in hand. An average shot (250) later the fairway has been reached and there are 120 to go, a problem just considered. Yardage ratings near 370 ought to imitate those near 120, but one stroke higher. Similarly for a 590-yard hole a drive and average long fairway shot manage 250 + 220 and there are once again 120 to finish up. The curve of figure 47.1 shows such repetitions, always one stroke higher. Presumably at 810 yards there would be another.

IMPLICATIONS

The changing slope of the curve has implications, even for courses of standard lengths. With scorecards for 23 famous ones in hand, including the U.S. Open courses, Augusta National, Pine Valley, Cypress Point, Birkdale, The Old Course, to name a few, it was possible to compare ratings from line and curve. The average difference was only 0.3 but the maximum was 1.1. It is not hard, however, to create a combination of hole lengths that adds up to something traditional but for which the discrepancy is more severe. For example, six holes of lengths 150, 350, and 550 each would total 6,300 yards but the line underestimates the curve by almost three strokes.

It is with short courses that discrepancies are abundant. A line fit to the curve over the 100- to 200-yard interval would rate holes by the formula .0028 Yardage + 2.7. The traditional line uses .0045 Yardage + 2.2 instead. In general it appears that short courses may be governed by low slopes and large constant terms. Failure to recognize this may be the principle reason for what are now suspected to be misratings of short courses.

If nonlinearity is truly present, then logic suggests using it. It is no major task to look up hole ratings in a table corresponding to the curve and add up the 18 for a given course, and this can be done for courses that are short or long, even par threes and executive courses or pitch and putt. For a fictitious Pitch & Putt CC, with two holes of lengths 30, 40, 50, . . ., 110, the rating by the curve would be 50.1. By the traditional line it would be 46.6.

SUMMARY

In hindsight there is something intuitive about the curve. Longer clubs do dispose of greater distance at the same cost (one stroke) in getting the ball to a point where the putting can dictate flattening. And getting down from 100 yards away is the same problem whether the tee is 250 or 470 yards behind, and this dictates repetition.

From a technical point of view the curve is the offspring of a simple performance model, developed from field data. It offers a theoretical explanation for observed flattening of score vs. yardage profiles over par 3, 4, 5 sectors and goes on to detail the ramps that join those flattened segments. These credentials recommend its consideration.

References

Cochran, A. & Stobbs, J. (1968) *The Search for the Perfect Swing.* J.B. Lippincott Co.

Hoadley, B. (1994) How to lower your putting score without improving, in *Proceedings of the Second Scientific Congress of Golf,* E & FN Spon, pp. 186-192.

Scheid, F. (1974) *A nonlinear feature of golf course rating and handicapping,* presented at the Kyoto meeting of TIMS-ORSA.

Scheid, F. (1995, 1996, 1997) Reports to the Handicap Research Team (HRT).

Simmons, W. (1994) Report to the HRT.

Soley, C. (1977) *How well should you putt?* Privately published.

Wilson, P. (1996, 1997) Reports to the HRT.

CHAPTER 48

All Around Improvements

Patrick D. Larkey, Anthony A. Smith, Jr.
Carnegie Mellon University, Pittsburgh, PA, USA

The U.S. PGA Tour constructs an All Around statistic from eight component measures of "skill" such as driving distance and accuracy, putting, sand saves, etc. They should reconsider the included variables and the methods for combining them.

Keywords: Golf, statistics, performance, skill, PGA Tour.

INTRODUCTION

While the PGA Tour (hereafter "Tour") reports almost forty performance statistics for each individual player and numerous player rankings (these data can be found at **www.pgatour.com**; this web site in 1997 is the source of all data used in this study), the centerpiece of their statistical system is a set of eight measures that are combined into an All Around statistic:

- Scoring Leaders (Adjusted Scoring Average = [(Σ round scores + Σ adjustments)/# of rounds played] where the adjustment for each round played = (Par – Field Stroke Average))
- Greens-in-Regulation (% of the time that players put the ball on the green of par threes in one, par fours in two or less, and par fives in three or less)
- Eagle Leaders (the "number of holes on average between eagles")
- Birdie Leaders (Birdies-per-Round [# of Birdies/# of Rounds])
- Putting Leaders (the average number of putts taken on greens-in-regulation)
- Sand Saves (% of the time that a player succeeds in getting the ball in the cup from a greenside bunker in two or less)
- Driving Leaders (yardage on the first shot as measured on two holes in each round for each player)

- Driving Accuracy (% of the time that a player's drive finishes on the fairway)
- All Around (the sum of the player ranks on the foregoing component statistics, e.g., $1^{st} + 37^{th} + 16^{th} + 101^{st} + 49^{th} + 173^{rd} + 10^{th} = 387$ which would have been good for a tie with Lee Janzen for 15th place in the All Around in 1997)

The Tour's implicit purpose for the individual skill measures is very clear. Each measure is intended to capture some important aspect of skill in golf and to enable an ordering of players on the extent to which they possess that skill in sponsored tournaments: Who is the longest driver? Most accurate driver? Best putter? Best sand player? And so on. These measures, properly done, have great potential for sparking fan interest and enabling diagnoses of player strengths and weaknesses in play.

The purpose for the All Around statistic is more difficult to discern. It is surely not intended to identify the best "all around" player when there are superior statistics based on player tournament winnings and scoring that better reflect overall player success. Bill Glasson and Tom Byrum were 1 and 2, respectively, on the All Around list in 1997; neither one was very high on any knowledgeable observer's player-of-the-year list. Without any defensible purpose, the Tour should seriously consider abandoning the All Around statistic. If they persist in providing it, the Tour should redesign it because, as it stands, it is something of a conceptual and computational embarrassment.

The two main questions in constructing any combined performance measure are:

1. What should be included?
2. How should the included elements be combined? This second question has two parts:
   a. How should the incommensurate measures problems be handled?
   b. How should the elements be weighted?

WHAT SHOULD BE INCLUDED?

The ideal set of skill measures for inclusion in the All Around statistic would be mutually exclusive (orthogonal) and exhaustive. That is, each skill measure should capture a different skill than other measures and the set of all measures should capture all of the important player skills in golf. Mutual exclusivity requires statistically insignificant correlations among the items. Exhaustiveness requires that the skill measures explain most, if not all, of the variation in outcome variables. Larkey and Smith (1997) discuss how the present skill measures might be changed to approach these goals. The discussion here centers on how the tour might improve All Around with existing measures, data that are already routinely collected.

The first significant problem with All Around is the hodgepodge of variables included; there are skills (Putting, Sand Saves, Distance, and Accuracy), a compound skill (GIR), intermediate outcomes (Eagle and Birdie), and a near-final outcome (Scoring). Player earnings are a function of scoring (and how that scoring is distributed with respect to tournaments); scoring average is a function of round scores which are a function of hole scores, i.e., eagles, birdies, pars, bogeys, and "others," which are a function of more basic skills such as how long and accurately a player hits the ball and how well he putts.

The variables in All Around seriously confound causes and effects. These relationships should be detectable. Table 48.1 shows the correlations among the final outcome variables, the intermediate outcome variables, and some other candidate variables from the large set provided by the Tour. The new variables are: Scrambling (the % of the time that a player makes par or better when missing the green in regulation.); Top 10s (the number of times in a year that a player finishes in the top ten of a tournament); Bounce (the % of the time that a player makes birdie or better following a bogey or worse); Strike (a rank sum combination of GIR and Total Driving, which is itself a rank sum combination of Distance and Accuracy). Most of the remaining variables provided by the Tour are uninteresting. There are seven additional scoring measures, five additional birdie variables, several point ranking variables, and several such as Long Drive (the longest single drive a player has hit) and Consecutive # of Cuts Made that do not sensibly capture a basic player skill and have little or no explanatory value.

Table 48.1   Correlation Matrix for Outcome and Candidate Variables (N = 195)

	Money	Scoring	Scrambling	Top 10s	Bounce	Strike	Eagle	Birdie
Money	1.000							
Scoring	−0.926	1.000						
Scrambling	0.472	−0.571	1.000					
Top 10s	0.831	−0.811	0.437	1.000				
Bounce	0.352	−0.378	0.178	0.328	1.000			
Strike	−0.617	0.645	−0.139	−0.527	−0.284	1.000		
Eagle	0.263	−0.186	−0.195	0.324	0.208	−0.297	1.000	
Birdie	0.737	−0.764	0.287	0.658	0.556	−0.532	0.280	1.000

The intermediate outcome variables, Birdie and Eagle, explain significant variation in Scoring and Money because they are part of these outcomes. If new measures on Pars, Bogeys, Double Bogeys, Triple Bogeys, and "Dreaded Others" were included, we could explain Scoring almost perfectly. So what? There are no circumstances where it is proper or interesting to mix wholes and parts in combinations. Birdie and Eagle should not be combined with more basic skills.

Top 10s is strongly related to Scoring and Money because it is a different view of final outcomes; Money is a nonlinear function of place finish and place finish is a function of relative Scoring. Top 10s is an inferior measure for explaining outcomes because it arbitrarily scores first and sole tenth as equivalent, one top ten finish, when first garners 18% of the purse and sole tenth 2.7%, and it scores sole eleventh place, worth 2.5% of the purse and only .2% behind tenth's share, as 0. The three players who tied for tenth at the Deposit Guaranty Classic in 1997 received a "1" for their effort as did Tiger Woods who won the Masters 12 shots clear of the field.

Strike also explains significant variation in Scoring and Money. As a combination of GIR and the driving variables, it confounds iron play and driving; driving actually enters twice as the effects of driving appear in both GIR and Total Driving. Strike is not a very attractive candidate variable for further combination in All Around because the variables that are its constituent parts also appear. It is also not a good replacement for the constituent parts because it conveys less information about specific skills.

From table 48.1, both Scrambling and Bounce are legitimate contenders for inclusion in All Around because they may capture "skills" and they have the proper signs and significant correlations. All that remains is to see how they perform in combination with the other skill variables. Table 48.2 gives the results of regressing Scoring on Putting, Sand Save, Distance, Accuracy, Scrambling, GIR, and Bounce.

Table 48.2   Regression of Scoring on Putting, Sand Save, Distance, Accuracy, Scrambling, GIR, and Bounce

Score	Coef.	S.E.	t	p-value	95% Confidence interval
Putting	12.298	1.299	9.467	0.000	9.735 to 14.860
Sand save	−0.012	0.005	−2.233	0.027	−0.022 to −0.001
Distance	−0.022	0.005	−4.561	0.000	−0.032 to −0.013
Accuracy	−0.023	0.008	−2.929	0.004	−0.039 to −0.008
Scrambling	−0.076	0.011	−6.859	0.000	−0.098 to −0.054
GIR	−0.130	0.012	−10.422	0.000	−0.154 to −0.105
Bounce	0.011	0.010	1.061	0.290	−0.009 to 0.030
Constant	70.120	2.807	24.981	0.000	64.583 to 75.657

N = 195; Ordinary Least Squares, $F(7, 187) = 116.19$; Prob > F-0.0000, $R^2 = 0.813$; R^2 = .806, RMSE = .363

The equation and all variables except Bounce are statistically significant. Scrambling contributes and should be included in All Around while Bounce should be excluded. (Larkey and Smith (1997) found a significant statistical relationship between driving accuracy and scrambling suggesting that players who are good at hitting the fairway are also good at getting out of trouble when they fail to hit the green in regulation. But the finding is probably an artifact of the Tour's coding rules for GIR and Putting that lead to counting successful two-putts from the fringe of greens as a successful "scramble"; the more accurate drivers have more GIRs and when they miss, they are probably closer to the green in positions like the fringe where it is much easier to get up and down.) The skill variables recommended for inclusion in a new All Around are Putting, Sand Save, Distance, Accuracy, Scrambling, and GIR. These variables are not orthogonal but substantially more so than the variables the Tour presently includes in the combination.

HOW SHOULD THE INCLUDED ELEMENTS BE COMBINED?

The two issues for constructing All Around are incommensurable measures and weighting. In illustrating a better approach, we revert to the Tour's original jumble of variables so that we can separate the impact of simply adding things up differently from possible changes in variables included.

How Should the Incommensurable Measures Problems Be Handled?

Scoring, Putting, Eagle, Birdie, Sand Saves, GIR, Distance, and Accuracy yield several different metrics. For Tiger Woods in 1997, these numbers, respectively, are 69.1 strokes, 1.776 putts per GIR (29.35 Putts-per-Round), 104.1 holes between eagles, 4.25 Birdies-per-Round, 44% Sand Saves, 70.3% GIR, 294.8 yards driving distance, and 68.6% fairways hit. Simply summing across these metrics is clearly nonsensical; that is, the answer is not 573.119 (69.1 + 1.776 + 29.35 + 104.1 + 4.25 + .44 + .703 + 294.8 + 68.6). They are in different, incommensurate units; in some cases bigger is better and other cases bigger is worse.

The Tour's solution to this problem is a rank sum computation. They rank players on each included measure. They then sum the ranks and re-rank according to the rank sum—lower is better. A player who finishes 37th, 15th, 101st, 3rd, 150th, 29th, 73rd, and 12th on the eight included measures has a rank sum of 420. 420 would have earned 18th place in 1997. Bill Glasson was "best" at 282.

The Tour's rank sum procedure surely does solve the incommensurate measures problem in the data. But it does so at a significant and unnecessary informational cost. The procedure discards the information in individual measures about the differences among players by assuming that the interval between players is a constant. In other words, the rank summing computation assumes that the measured interval between the best putter and the second best putter is equal to the interval between the second best putter and the third best putter . . . between the next to worst putter and the worst putter. Even the most cursory examination of the measures data shows that the intervals are not equal. For Driving Accuracy, for example, the distance between #1 and #2 is 1.0, between #2 and #3 is .3, between #3 and #4 is .2, between #4 and #5 is .1, between #5 and #6 is .5, and between #194 and #195 is 3.2. Every measure included in All Around has a dramatically nonuniform distribution of intervals with larger intervals among the very best and the very worst and smaller intervals in the middle of the pack. The uniformity penalizes the most skillful, rewards the least skillful, and makes too much of very small differences in the middle.

Normalization would be a better procedure for solving the incommensurable measures problem because it preserves the interval information. Each measure should be rescaled onto the 0-1 interval by assigning a "1" to the best value in the sample (195) and a "0" to the worst value. The remaining golfers' statistics are then placed on a 0-1 scale using a simple linear transformation: for example, if a golfer's statistic is 60% of the distance from the lowest statistic to the highest statistic in the sample, then this golfer's statistic is rescaled to the value 0.6.

What difference would normalization make in All Around rankings? Table 48.3 gives the results for the top 20 players ordered by the normalized measure. Column 3 is the player's ranking by the Tour's All Around statistic; column 4 is the sum of the player's eight rescaled component statistics with a theoretical maximum of 8 (if a player finishes first in all categories) and a theoretical minimum of 0 (if a player

Table 48.3   Normalized All Around versus Rank Sum All Around

Revised rank	Player	PGA Tour 1997 rank	Σ Normalized scores
1	Tiger Woods	7	6.099
2	Bill Glasson	1	5.576
3	Mark Calcavecchia	5	5.568
4	Greg Norman	3	5.439
5	Davis Love III	T11	5.438
6	Tom Lehman	4	5.365
7	Nick Price	13	5.343
8	Jim Furyk	16	5.292
9	Fred Couples	20	5.284
10	Jesper Parnevik	10	5.280
11	Steve Lowery	18	5.277
12	Scott Hoch	6	5.270
13	Lee Janzen	15	5.232
14	Phil Mickelson	14	5.194
15	Tom Byrum	2	5.179
16	David Duval	T11	5.173
17	Bob Estes	19	5.148
18	Andrew Magee	9	5.133
19	Don Pooley	31	5.069
20	Jay Haas	8	5.058

finishes last in all categories). For 1997, these sums range from 6.099 for Tiger Woods (which means that Tiger Woods' component statistic is 0.76 [6.099/8]) to .21 (1.666/8) for Chip Beck. The average value for the 195 players is .49 (3.951/8).

The new ranking produces some sensible reorderings: Tiger Woods, for example, jumps from seventh to first, while Tom Byrum drops from second to fifteenth. Moreover, preserving the quantitative information in the statistics shows that Tiger Woods finishes first by a large margin although there is not much difference between Bill Glasson and Mark Calcavecchia, who finish second and third, respectively.

In general, players at the extremes in one or more categories experience the largest changes in their rankings: for example, Don Pooley, who ranks first in Putting, jumps from 31st in the Tour's ranking to 19th in the new ranking. Similarly, John Daly, who ranks first in Distance, jumps from 80th in the Tour's ranking to 47th in the new ranking. These jumps reflect the fact that the extreme values of a given statistic tend to be more spread out than values in the middle of the range.

The New Rank and All Around are highly correlated ($r = .99$). But, as table 48.4 shows, New Rank does a much better job of explaining outcomes in terms of the logarithm of money per event. New Rank is statistically significant while the All Around rank is not.

Table 48.4   Regression of Logarithm of Money on New Rank and Tour All Around

Money	Coefficient	SE	t	p-value
New Rank	−.0187	.005	−3.645	0.000
Tour All Around	.003	.005	0.532	0.595
Constant	3.779	.082	46.195	0.000

$[R^2 = 0.7183]$

How Should the Elements Be Weighted?

The final issue in combined measures is weighting. Should component skill measures be entered as the Tour presently does with a unit weight, "1," or should some less arbitrary scheme be devised? The estimated coefficients from appropriate regressions could be used as "weights" when combining the component statistics so as to produce an overall measure of the quality of a given player's performance. That is, the coefficients in the regressions reflect the relative quantitative importance of each of the various component statistics in determining final outcomes. It is obvious in the regression results that among the current measures, Putting and GIR are the most important determinants of outcomes. Placing these two measures on a par with the other measures that are orders of magnitude less important, as the Tour currently does, doesn't make much sense. But then the skill measures as currently implemented are not very effective in capturing orthogonal player skills and the All Around statistic is such an arbitrary construct, it is hard to be enthusiastic about fine-tuning it.

CONCLUSION

The Tour is something of a model in much of what it does in running tournaments, marketing its tournaments, and developing property. The Tour deserves kudos for its attempts to measure and report on the performances of its players. The implementation of the statistical system is, however, far from satisfactory. Its statistical efforts are not comparable in quality to its other activities. It should begin repairing its statistical program immediately. This paper has provided a practical starting point.

If the Tour is determined to compute an All Around statistic, they should

1. combine only basic player skill measures;
2. include scrambling as one of those measures; and
3. use normalization in combining measures.

The recommended changes are a few hours in reprogramming. The resulting new All Around statistic will be a significant improvement.

References

Larkey, Patrick D. and Anthony A. Smith, Jr (1997). "Measuring Player Skills in Golf: Improving the PGA Tour's System," H.J. Heinz III School Working Paper, Carnegie Mellon University.
PGA Tour (**www.pgatour.com**)

CHAPTER 49

A Bivariate Probability Model
for Putting Proficiency

David E. Tierney, PhD
Richards & Tierney, Inc., Chicago, IL, USA

Richard H. Coop, EdD
School of Education, University of North Carolina, Chapel Hill, NC, USA

Traditional measures of putting skill such as "average putts per round" or "average putts per green-in-regulation" are inherently flawed because they confound ball-striking ability with putting proficiency. A more valid measure of putting skill which removes all aspects of non-putting skills is proposed. This putting proficiency index (PIX) relates actual putts taken to the expected number of putts that would be taken by a world-class putter. A simple bivariate Normal distribution is used for the positional outcome distribution of any putt. Integration over a "sink zone" region gives the probability that any putt will be made and, in sequence, the expected number of putts per hole given the initial first-putt distance. The major components of the model are directly related to a player's ability to control both the length and line of their putts. Data gathered on putts taken by PGA Tour players, under actual tournament conditions, were used to establish the model parameters and define the characteristics of a world-class putter. The model has been tested against other tour professionals, elite college team members, and amateur golfers of varying ability levels with remarkable identification and diagnostic accuracy.

Keywords: Golf, modeling, putting, probability.

INTRODUCTION

Traditional measures of putting skills such as "average putts per round" or "average putts per green-in-regulation" are flawed because they confound ball-striking ability with putting proficiency. If Player A missed every green but chipped or pitched "stone dead," taking more than 20 putts for the round would clearly involve some rather poor putting. At the other end of the spectrum, Player B hits all 18 greens in regulation but is faced with a first putt of more than 36 feet on every hole. Should Player B take 36 putts for the round we might appreciate that Player B putted very well indeed.

The PGA Tour has established, then, their own measure of putting skill. It is based on putts taken on just those holes where the green was hit in regulation or less. Interestingly, should a player hole their green-in-regulation shot (first on a Par 3, second on a Par 4, or third on a Par 5), then zero putts and a green-in-regulation (GIR) are recorded for computing this putting index even though a putt wasn't even taken on the hole. Further, on a Par 5, Player A just misses the green with his second shot, chips to a foot, and taps in for a four. Player B hits the green with his second shot, forty feet from the hole, and 2-putts, also for a four. Both players birdied the hole and created a GIR but, as far as the PGA Tour putting skill measure is concerned, Player A with a one-foot tap-in is deemed to be a better putter than Player B because Player A took only one putt from one foot whereas Player B took two putts from 40 feet. It is fair to say that a long hitter who often reaches Par 5s in two and hits a very high percentage of greens-in-regulation will have an unrealistic difficulty in having a low PGA Tour putting index, regardless of their true putting skill. Lastly, the putting measure used by the PGA Tour doesn't even consider putts taken to save par, bogey, or worse. As about a third of the holes are not hit in regulation by a tour professional, important putting information has been excluded by this measure.

As Jack Nicklaus once said when asked how to reduce the number of putts taken: "Hit the ball closer to the hole!" Except for shots holed from off the green, a holed putt ends each and every hole in a stroke play competition. Lower total scores arise out of more efficient putting regardless of where the putting process began on the green or how many strokes it took to get to the green. Therefore, the distance of the first putt is critical to the putting process and any measure of putting efficiency or skill. The closer the first-putt distance to the hole, the fewer the number of expected putts. The further the first-putt distance, the higher the number of expected putts. The proposed putting proficiency index (PIX) is:

$$PIX = 100 \times \text{Expected Putts/Actual Putts}$$

where the expected number of putts corresponds to a world-class putter. Fewer putts than expected gives a PIX value greater than 100, while more putts than expected results in a PIX value which will be less than 100. A PIX value of exactly 100 is equivalent to world-class.

If the measure of putting skill is the above, then holed shots from off the green will have no impact on such a measure. For holed shots, the actual putts taken will be zero and the expected number of putts will also be zero.

Measuring actual putts versus expected putts isolates the putting skill component of the game of golf. If all putts were tap-ins, then the expected number of putts would be just a very small fraction above 1.0 per putting opportunity. If all putts were 60-footers, then the expected number of putts must surely be above 2.0, even for a world-class putter. Given the first putt distance, the problem is then to compute the expected number of putts for a world-class putter.

MODEL

A putting green is a highly non-planar surface covered, typically, by closely mown grass. A ball rolling across the green will be deflected, diverted, slowed, and speeded by the many green imperfections, grass grain, and surface curvatures in somewhat determinable but often random ways. A skilled putter makes a mental transformation of the surface into a level plane so that the minimization of the number of putts to be taken reduces to (1) a two-dimensional problem of establishing a target line and distance (speed) down that target line and (2) an ability to physically execute the plan. Variation creeps into the putting process from any number of sources, many of which are noted above. Additional sources of variation come from the ball being imperfect and stroke mechanics: path, face angle, contact point, etc. It is fair to postulate that errors will propagate proportional to the distance of the putt and that these errors will be independent. The Central Limit Theorem of probability theory applied to the putting process, wherein the positional outcome of any putt is a result of the sum of numerous sources of variation, leads to a bivariate Normal as the approximate limiting distributional form. For the sake of simplicity, we will assume that for this bivariate Normal

1. length and line errors are uncorrelated (independent);
2. the expectation of both length and line errors relative to the player's target point are zero; and
3. the mean deviation errors in both length and line are proportional to distance of the putt to the target point.

Certainly, conditions (1) and (2) will hold for a world-class putter.

Under the above, the joint distribution of length (x) and line (y) outcomes of any putt has a reduced number of unknown parameters, just the standard deviations of s_x and s_y. Further, the joint distribution is just the product of the two marginal Normal distributions and all conditional distributions are the same as the marginal distributions. Lastly, the two standard deviations are directly proportional to an average mean absolute deviation (skill) times a putt distance.

Sink Zone Region

Figure 49.1 depicts a parametric "sink zone" for a putt. The ball travels toward the hole from the right in this level plane transformed space. The target line bisects the hole. The target length, however, is a point beyond the center of the hole, at a distance d. The target point is labeled (0,0).

The concept behind the sink zone is rather simple. If one were to put a lid on the hole, then a ball coming to rest within the sink zone is deemed to have been holed. Loewer (1992) and Diversified Technologies (1993) computed critical ball velocities which define the dividing line between putts which will go into the hole and those which will not. Critical velocities were determined for any path across the hole in "hopping out" cases and for "lipping out" cases. For center-line putts, a ball with front edge velocity of 4.3 ft/s will strike the back edge of the hole at the ball's equator and be surely holed. Should the front edge velocity increase to 5.3 ft/s, then

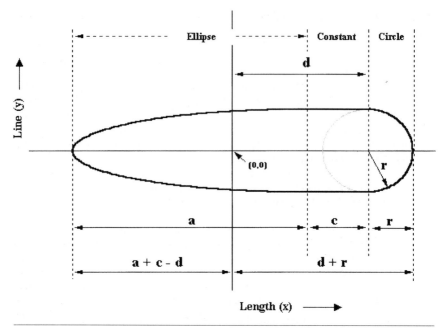

Figure 49.1　Sink zone diagram.

"hopping out" is a distinct possibility because the velocity vector at point of impact on the back edge of the hole points out of the hole.

As a ball approaches the hole parallel to the center line but closer to the side of the hole the critical velocity approaches zero because the path length from front edge to back edge decreases. The center of the ball's downward displacement also decreases.

The "surely holed" critical velocity[1] decreases quadratically as the path moves away from the center line but is only defined to within one ball radius of the side of the hole. As the path moves toward the side, conditions for lipping out increasingly occur and the complexity of a real golf hole makes an exact calculation impossible. However, we do know certain boundary conditions. At the very side edge of the hole any ball velocity will cause the putt to miss. Also, a ball that never reaches the front edge of the hole will not fall.

$$V_{critical} = (d_E - r_B)\sqrt{\frac{g}{2r_B}}$$

$$\text{but} \quad d_E = 2\sqrt{r_{H^2} - z^2} \quad o \leq z \leq r_H - r_B$$

[1]From classical mechanics, the surely holed (ball strikes the back edge at its equator) critical ball velocity is a function of the path distance (z) from the hole center line.

where r_B and r_H are the ball and hole radius and g is the acceleration due to gravity (32 ft/s^2).

As a first approximation model, the sink zone is made up of a half-circle with the hole radius attached to a constant section of length c which is then attached to a half-ellipse with major axis a and minor axis r. An ellipse was used for the back end of the sink zone because (1) a circle (front end) is an ellipse with the same major and minor axis, (2) its shape is quadratic in nature matching the surely holed critical ball velocity analysis, and (3) it has a simple mathematical form.

Together with the aim point displacement d from the hole center, the sink zone has just three unknown parameters (a, c, d). Data collected under tournament conditions were used to estimate these parameter values.

Putt Outcomes Distribution

The model used to predict putt outcomes in length and line space, should a lid have been placed over the hole, is an uncorrelated bivariate Normal distribution function with expectation (0,0) as depicted in figure 49.2.

The putt outcome distribution is centered over the sink zone surface at the aim point (0,0) so that the expectations of length and line errors are zero. If measures of putting control skill are the average absolute percentage errors (mean deviations) made in both length and line, then the standard deviation[2] parameters of the putt outcome distribution under the normality and proportionality assumptions are given by

$$\sigma_x = E_x \cdot (d + D) \sqrt{\frac{\pi}{2}}$$

and

$$\sigma_y = E_y \cdot (d + D) \sqrt{\frac{\pi}{2}}$$

where D is the distance of the putt to the hole, d is the aim point displacement beyond the hole, E_x is the length percentage error, and E_y is the line percentage error. The probability of holing a putt is then simply the probability mass of the putt outcome distribution contained within the sink zone. Under our simple model, the probability of a 1-putt, given the distance D, will be a function of five unknown parameters (a, c, d, E_x, E_y).

$$E\{|x - \mu|\} = \sigma \sqrt{\frac{2}{\pi}}$$

Learning Factor

The putting on a green does not end until the ball is holed. It is an independent, not necessarily identical, Bernoulli trial sequential process such that:

---

[2]For a Normal distribution the mean (absolute) deviation and the standard deviation are directly related.

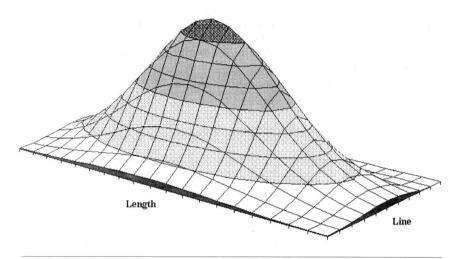

Figure 49.2   Model distribution of first-putt outcomes.

$$
\begin{aligned}
\text{Expected} \\
\text{Number of} &= \\
\text{Putts}
\end{aligned}
\quad
\begin{aligned}
& 1 \cdot \Pr\{\text{Holed}/D_1\} \\
& + 2 \cdot \Pr\{\text{Holed}/D_2\} \cdot [1 - \Pr\{\text{Holed}/D_1\}] \\
& + 3 \cdot \Pr\{\text{Holed}/D_3\} \cdot [1 - \Pr\{\text{Holed}/D_2\}] \cdot [1 - \Pr\{\text{Holed}/D_1\}] \\
& + \cdots
\end{aligned}
$$

When $D_1, D_2, D_3, \ldots$ are the distances of the first, second, third putt, etc., if required.
For our world-class putter, we truncated the process by assuming that the probability of holing any third putt was 1.0, or $\Pr\{\text{Holed}|D_3\} = 1$ for all D_3. Hence, our world-class putter never takes four or more putts on a green. In this way, our simple model needs to track just first and second putts to compute the expected number of putts. Further, we assume that our player gleaned important information on any missed first putt; information which would decrease the dispersion of second-putt outcomes by a factor k. Thus, the percentage error parameters E_x and E_y become $k \times E_x$ and $k \times E_y$ for second putts.

Probability Computations

For sink zone parameters (a, c, d, r), skill parameters (E_x, E_y, k), and a Normal frequency density function, an integration by parts routine was developed to compute the expected number of putts, 1-putt probability, and 3+ putt probability for any given first putt distance D. Problem symmetry, distributional form, and independents assumption greatly aided these calculations, though complex and tedious.

DATA AND PARAMETER ESTIMATION

First putt distances and number of putts taken were recorded for each hole played, under actual tournament conditions, by several PGA Tour players during February through June, 1996. For the purposes of this study, putts taken from the fringe were recorded as putts and the first putt distance was measured from the fringe.

Table 49.1 shows how three PGA Tour veterans putted 94 rounds (1,678 putting opportunities) of tournament golf beginning with the 1996 Buick Invitational in San Diego through the 1996 Canon Greater Hartford Open.

Table 49.1   Putting Proficiency Model Data (PGA Tour Veterans, Feb-Jun 1996)

1st Putt distance group	Number of holes	Average putts/ hole	1-Putt (%)	2-Putts (%)	3+ Putts (%)	Average distance (ft)	Expected putts/ hole	Putting proficiency index
≤ 2	70.0	1.014	98.57	1.43		1.26	1.004	98.95
2-3	42.5	1.071	92.94	7.06		2.58	1.041	97.24
3-4	60.5	1.124	87.60	12.40		3.60	1.107	98.49
4-5	61.5	1.171	82.93	17.07		4.41	1.174	100.24
5-6	55.5	1.306	69.37	30.63		5.54	1.269	97.17
6-8	127.0	1.453	55.51	43.70	0.79	7.08	1.390	95.66
8-11	191.0	1.602	40.31	59.16	0.52	9.44	1.541	96.16
11-15	217.5	1.701	30.34	69.20	0.46	13.13	1.700	99.91
15-20	250.5	1.834	18.76	79.04	2.20	17.28	1.809	98.60
20-30	283.5	1.915	10.58	87.30	2.12	24.51	1.912	99.85
30-45	223.5	2.045	7.38	80.76	11.86	35.23	1.999	97.77
45+	95.0	2.232	4.21	68.42	27.37	54.39	2.099	94.05
Total	1,678.0	1.705	33.49	62.51	3.99	18.40	1.672	98.08

Putts at distance boundaries were divided equally between adjacent groups.

The actual tournament conditions aspect of this dataset lends credibility and a rich source of research. Certainly it reflects the real world of professional golf rather than that of the laboratory.

Estimation of the unknown model parameters was done with a standard nonlinear estimation routine to fit the professional player data (see figure 49.3 for fit of 1-putt frequency). Since some parameter estimates were highly correlated (certain combinations resulted in almost identical fit statistics), practical considerations, reasonableness, and parsimony led to parameter estimates as follows:

$a = 27.6$ inches major axis of half-ellipse

$c = 0$ inches constant section

$d = 16$ inches aim point displacement behind hole

$k = 0.9$ dispersion reduction factor for second putts

The sink zone reduced to a half-circle (front) attached to a half-ellipse (back). The aim point displacement of 16 inches behind the hole is not inconsistent with the

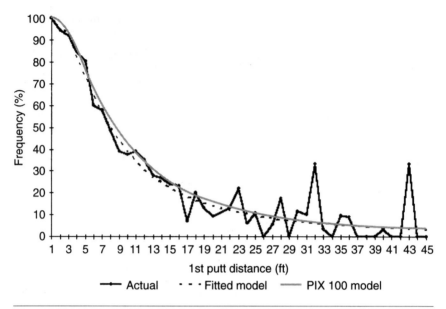

Figure 49.3   Percentage 1-putt by 1st putt distance.

findings of others[3]. The 10% increase in learning from the first putt to the second putt is also not unreasonable.

The second phase of the estimation process was to establish the percentage error attributes of a world-class putter.

Using these three PGA Tour veterans as indicative of the upper half of professional-class putters, world-class was established to be just above their skill level, especially as concerns length control. The data dictated that the world-class skill parameters be set at a 5:1 ratio:

length percentage error: 6.5%

line percentage error: 1.3%

The world-class putter expected putts per hole were computed for each first putt distance from 1 foot to 100 feet. Table 49.2 gives results for some selected distances.

Interestingly, our world-class model putter 3-putts more often than he or she 1-putts outside 36 feet, resulting in expected putts per hole over 2.0. At 15 feet, the probability of a 1-putt is only 25.2% or a 1 in 4 chance of success. As one decreases the distance inside 15 feet, the odds of a 1-putt increase markedly (see figure 49.4).

The last two columns of table 49.1 give the expected putts per hole by distance group and the putting proficiency of the three PGA Tour veterans. Within a group, the actual distances of each putt were used to arrive at expected putts.

---

[3]D. Pelz (1989) determined, through empirical studies, that the best putting speed averaged 17 inches past the hole.

Table 49.2   World-Class Model Putter (Putting Proficiency Index [PIX] = 100)

1st putt distance (ft)	Expected number of putts	Probability of 1-putt (%)	Probability of 3+ putts (%)
1	1.0003	99.97	0.00
3	1.0615	93.86	0.01
6	1.3080	69.35	0.15
9	1.5185	48.55	0.40
12	1.6627	34.46	0.73
15	1.7593	25.21	1.14
18	1.8260	19.04	1.64
21	1.8741	14.80	2.21
24	1.9108	11.80	2.88
30	1.9648	7.95	4.43
36	2.0054	5.70	6.24
48	2.0704	3.32	10.36
60	2.1261	2.17	14.78
72	2.1769	1.52	19.21
90	2.2456	0.99	25.55

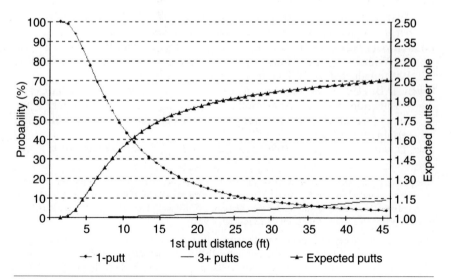

Figure 49.4   Putting proficiency model (world-class putter).

APPLICATIONS

Armed with an expected putts table calibrated to the nearest foot[4] of first putt distance, players can "score" their rounds for putting efficiency. All that is needed is for the player to record[5] the distance of the first putt and the number of putts taken on each hole played. Putting proficiency index (PIX) values can be computed for the entire round or rounds and for situations such as putting for birdie or better, putting for par, or putting for bogey or worse. One can also look at putting proficiency for short, medium, and long first putt distances. In this way, behavioral patterns of putting can be uncovered. In fact, given a nonlinear estimation routine, it is possible to fit the model to a player's putting profile data and arrive at estimates of their length control and line control skills, E_x and E_y, in addition to their overall proficiency index. Given this information, golfers can be better informed as to their specific putting strengths and weaknesses, and can adapt their practice time accordingly.

ACKNOWLEDGMENTS

The authors would like to thank the tour professionals as well as the elite college team members who faithfully recorded hole data for rounds played in actual tournaments. Their efforts have provided an extensive and fascinating research database. Also, thanks should go to John Spitzer, USGA Technical Staff, for forwarding the two papers on critical ball velocities.

References

Diversified Technologies, Inc. (1993) "The Golf Hole Target: A Theoretical Analysis to Define an Experimental Study," *Unpublished report* dated November, 1993 prepared for Mr. Dave Pelz, Independent Golf Research, Inc.

Loewer, W. (1992) "A Study of the Behavior of Golf Balls on the Putting Green With and Without the Golf Hole Target," *Unpublished working paper* dated July, 1992 conducted for U.S. Golf Hole Target, Inc.

Owen, D.B. (1957) *The Bivariate Normal Probability Integral*, Scandia Corp., Washington, DC and Ann. Math. Stat. (1956), 27, 1075 gives tables for computing the bivariate integral over regions bounded by straight lines and certain other regions.

Pelz, D. with Mastroni, N. (1989) *Putt Like the Pros,* New York: Harper & Row.

---

[4]The putting proficiency index (PIX) is very robust to distance estimation errors. An unlikely constant distance bias (under/over) of 5% would change PIX by less than 0.8%. If one used just the mid-point expected putts, rounded to two decimal places, of the twelve distance groups of table 49.1, the PGA Tour veterans' PIX value would have been 98.12 instead of 98.08.

[5]Pace of play should never be compromised by data collection activities. With a little practice, players can visually estimate the distance of their first putt with sufficient accuracy[4] to provide valid measures of putting proficiency and do so without affecting other players. Simply jot down the first putt distance in the margin of the scorecard as you walk to the next tee. The number of putts taken on a hole is easily remembered.

CHAPTER 50

Analysis of Performance
in the Open Championship 1892-1997

T. Hale and G.T. Hale
Centre for Sports Science, Chichester Institute, College Lane,
Chichester PO19 4PE, England

This paper examines whether the performance of elite golfers is improving at such a rate that the nature of the professional game is at risk. Improvement is measured by comparison of winning scores from qualifiers for all four rounds of the Open Championships since 1892. Initial analysis indicates significant lowering of raw and grouped scores over time (1-way ANOVA $p < 0.0001$). When scores are standardised against par and provisional standard scratch scores for each course, this improvement is confirmed. Regression equations derived from data arising between 1939-1993 and 1968-1993 suggest that winning scores are improving at the rate of one shot per 14 years and 10 years respectively. These rates are faster than the one shot per 21 years calculated by Thomas (1994) and suggest that improvement is continuing at an increasing rate.

Keywords: Technology, improved performance, Open Championships.

INTRODUCTION

The main issue investigated in this study arises from statements contained within two papers (Thomas 1994, Cochran 1995) which argued that performance has remained relatively stable for about the last 50 years and that the introduction of new technologies over the last 25-30 years has not resulted in improvements which give rise to concern. These statements need to be set against the changes in equipment design and manufacture, improved course preparation, increased knowledge of the mechanics of the golf swing, and enhanced education and training of professional golfers that have occurred since the inception of the Royal and Ancient Golf Club's Open Championship in 1860. Furthermore, the increased prize money available over the last 30 years has been accompanied by better conditioning of players, the use of instant feedback on swing mechanics through video recording and computerised analysis (McTeigue, Lamb, Mottram & Pirozzolo 1994), and more refined engineering processes leading to the manufacture of investment cast and perimeter weighted irons, metal-headed rather than persimmon-headed drivers and fairway clubs, and graphite as well as steel shafts.

Some golfers who have witnessed these changes have expressed concern that current courses may not present an adequate challenge to today's professionals. These concerns were implied almost forty years ago when Jones (1959) said that for the U.S. Masters Championship the holes are cut in more exacting positions and the speed of the greens is increased to counter the greater skill of the modern golfer with modern equipment.

On the other hand, Thomas (1994) argued that whilst improvements are evident they are not so great that the very nature of the game is under threat. He supported this by demonstrating the minor improvements in USPGA Tour statistics since 1968 and the relatively stable pattern of average winning scores in the USPGA tournaments since 1940. The main outcome of his analysis was that winning scores have been improving at the rate of about a shot every 21 years. This view is supported by evidence from Cochran (1995), who analysed winning scores in the R & A Medal Competitions since 1836 and argued that it is impossible to detect when major equipment changes have made the game dramatically easier. This paper addresses these conflicting views.

METHODS

With the exception of the years interrupted by the two world wars, scores of qualifiers for all four rounds (n = 5,422) of each Championship between 1892 and 1997 (n = 95) were analysed by the latest SPSS package (SPSS Inc 1996). The majority of the data (from 1892 to 1983) were taken from Ryde (1981 and 1984); the remainder came from the R & A's Official Annual Championship report. Measures of central tendency, variability, and normality of distribution were calculated for each year and for all years combined, and parametric and non-parametric (Kruskal Wallis) 1-way ANOVAs of scores over time derived. Because none of the post-hoc tests available on the SPSS package could deal with n > 50, the data were also grouped into 5-year periods (n = 19) and analysed through a parametric 1-way ANOVA and subsequent post-hoc Tukey tests. Since post-hoc tests cannot be applied to non-parametric data, serial Kruskal Wallis ANOVAs were applied to seven selected time periods to test for significant differences between the medians of winning scores for the periods 1939-1993 and 1968-1993 so that the comparisons could be made with Thomas's paper of 1994.

Information on the length and par of each course was obtained from Lewis (1995), the secretaries of the clubs hosting the Championships, and newspaper and magazine archives. Where the total length of the course was known a Provisional Standard Scratch Score (PSSS) was allocated to each in accordance with details given in Williams (1994). Comparisons over time were made between winning, median, and worst scores in absolute terms, against the stated par for the course, and against the PSSS.

RESULTS

Changes in Absolute Performance Over Time

The winning scores since 1892 are shown in figure 50.1. The performance indicators achieved during the 1997 competition, namely first, median, and worst scores, are 33, 45, and 74 strokes lower respectively than the comparable positions in the first 72-hole Championship in 1892. These differences represent absolute reductions averaging 0.35, 0.47, and 0.78 strokes respectively each year and are equivalent to an improvement rate of one stroke a round every 11.4, 8.5, and 5.1 years.

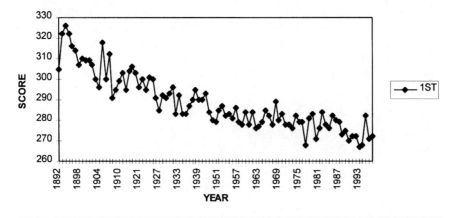

Figure 50.1   Winning scores in the Open Championships between 1892 and 1997.

The regression equations derived for 1939-1993 and 1968-1993 were

$$Y = -0.25951\ X + 790.762;\ SEE = 4.276 \qquad \text{Equation 1}$$
$$Y = -0.39829\ X + 1066.161;\ SEE = 4.410 \qquad \text{Equation 2}$$

The parametric ANOVA of all scores against time indicated a significant improvement ($F_{1,95} = 275.7$; $P < 0.0001$) in mean scores. When the grouped data were similarly analysed the improvement was still significant ($F_{1,19} = 35.265$; $P < 0.0001$). Table 50.1 shows the mean winning scores for each period and the matrix of P values derived from Tukey-test multiple comparisons.

However, further analysis of all scores revealed a strong, positively skewed (+0.973 SE ± 0.033) and leptokurtic (+0.871 SE ± 0.067) distribution. This level of a-normality could undermine the use of a parametric ANOVA. To combat this the Kruskal Wallis test for k independent samples was applied to both raw and grouped data. A significant improvement in winning scores since 1892 was confirmed ($X^2 = 4464$; 94 d.f.; $P = 0.0001$) and the average winning scores from the grouped data ($X^2 = 82.323$; 18 d.f.; $P = < 0.0001$).

Figure 50.2 shows the pattern of the median winning scores for each five-year period and this information was used to select the appropriate periods for the Kruskal Wallis serial analyses.

Table 50.1   Results of the Post-Hoc Tukey Tests on the Mean Winning Scores for Each Period Between 1892 and 1997 With the Probability (P) Values

Period	1	2	3	4	5	6	7	8	9	10	11	12	13	14	15	16	17	18	19
Dates	1892-1896	1897-1901	1902-1906	1907-1911	1912-1921	1922-1926	1927-1931	1932-1936	1937-1947	1948-1952	1953-1957	1958-1962	1963-1967	1968-1972	1973-1977	1978-1982	1983-1987	1988-1992	1993-1997
Mean	318.2	309.8	304.2	300.0	300.8	297.4	291.4	285.6	291.6	283.0	282.2	280.0	280.2	281.6	276.8	279.0	279.0	272.4	272.0
Period																			
1 (P value)		<0.001	<0.001	<0.001	<0.001	<0.001	<0.001	<0.001	<0.001	<0.001	<0.001	<0.001	<0.001	<0.001	<0.001	<0.001	<0.001	<0.001	<0.001
2			<0.001	<0.001	<0.001	<0.001	<0.001	<0.001	<0.001	<0.001	<0.001	<0.001	<0.001	<0.001	<0.001	<0.001	<0.001	<0.001	<0.001
3				<0.001	0.015	<0.001	<0.001	<0.001	<0.001	<0.001	<0.001	<0.001	<0.001	<0.001	<0.001	<0.001	<0.001	<0.001	<0.001
4					ns	0.007	<0.001	<0.001	<0.001	<0.001	<0.001	<0.001	<0.001	<0.001	<0.001	<0.001	<0.001	<0.001	<0.001
5						<0.001	<0.001	<0.001	<0.001	<0.001	<0.001	<0.001	<0.001	<0.001	<0.001	<0.001	<0.001	<0.001	<0.001
6							<0.001	<0.001	<0.001	<0.001	<0.001	<0.001	<0.001	<0.001	<0.001	<0.001	<0.001	<0.001	<0.001
7								<0.001	ns	<0.001	<0.001	<0.001	<0.001	<0.001	<0.001	<0.001	<0.001	<0.001	<0.001
8									0.006	<0.001	<0.001	<0.001	<0.001	<0.001	<0.001	<0.001	<0.001	<0.001	<0.001
9										<0.001	<0.001	<0.001	<0.001	<0.001	<0.001	<0.001	<0.001	<0.001	<0.001
10											ns	<0.001	<0.001	ns	<0.001	<0.001	<0.001	<0.001	<0.001
11												ns	ns	ns	<0.001	<0.001	<0.001	<0.001	<0.001
12													ns	ns	<0.001	ns	ns	<0.001	<0.001
13														ns	<0.001	ns	ns	<0.001	<0.001
14															<0.001	<0.001	<0.001	<0.001	<0.001
15																ns	ns	<0.001	<0.001
16																	ns	<0.001	<0.001
17																		<0.001	<0.001
18																			ns
19																			

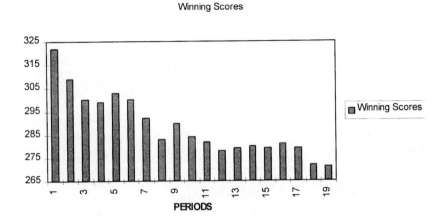

Figure 50.2   Median winning scores of each five-year period from 1892 to 1997.

The effects of the two world wars are clearly visible, with a non-significant increase in winning score between 1912 and 1921 and a significant rise between 1936 and 1946. Both immediate post-war periods were accompanied by significant improvements over 15-year time-spans. There was a plateau from 1962-1977 with median winning scores fluctuating between 279 and 281, but between 1978 and 1997 the median winning scores have fallen significantly and progressively from 281 to 271. Results of the serial Kruskal Wallis ANOVAs are shown in table 50.2.

Changes in Relative Performance Over Time

Without exception the courses which make up the current rota of Championship venues have undergone changes in the length. The changes to course lengths—and thus par figures and PSSS—make absolute comparisons over time unreliable.

Table 50.2   Changes in Median Winning Scores for Selected Groupings of Five Year Periods

Periods	Dates	Scores	P
1-4	1892-1911	322-299	0.026
4-5	1907-1921	299-303	0.599
5-8	1912-1936	303-283	0.005
8-9	1932-1947	283-290	0.042
9-12	1937-1962	290-278	0.007
13-15	1858-1977	279-279	0.792
16-19	1978-1997	281-271	0.048

Table 50.3   Recorded Changes in Course Lengths of Current Championship Courses

Course	Year	Length (yds)	Par	PSSS
St. Andrews	1900	6323	72	70
	1995	6933	72	73
Muirfield	1901	5810	71	68
	1992	6970	71	73
Royal St. George's	1904	6223	70	70
	1993	6860	70	72
Royal Troon	1923	6415	72	71
	1997	7079	71	74
Royal Lytham	1926	6456	71	71
	1996	6857	71	73
St. Anne's Carnoustie	1931	6410	72	71
	1975	7065	72	74
Royal Birkdale	1961	6844	74	73
	1991	6940	70	74
Turnberry	1977	6875	70	73
	1994	6957	70	73

Table 50.3 compares the earliest data available from courses on this rota with the latest information and gives some indication of the degree to which the courses have become more difficult over time.

Figure 50.3 shows winning scores against the 72-hole par of each course. This shows that a sub-par winning score was achieved for the first time in 1927 and that

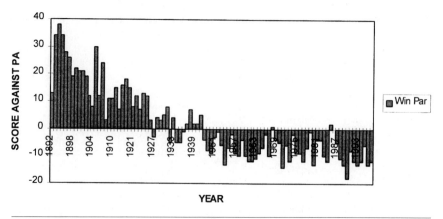

Figure 50.3   Winning scores against par between 1892 and 1997.

there have been only fourteen occasions over the subsequent 65 Championships when above-par winning scores have been posted.

Since par is set in relation to the particular conditions of each course this may not be the most useful relative measure. Provisional Standard Scratch Score (PSSS) is based entirely on the overall length of each course and provides a fixed baseline against which performances can be measured. Figure 50.4 shows the winning scores set against the 72-hole PSSS.

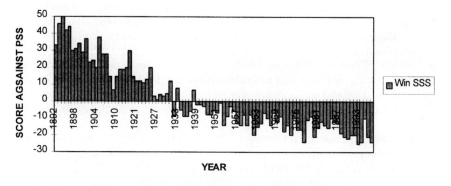

Figure 50.4   Winning scores against PSSS between 1892 and 1997.

This reveals that since 1927 only seven winning scores have exceeded PSSS and winning scores have always been sub-PSSS from 1939.

DISCUSSION

The highly significant improvement in golfing performance since 1892 is not surprising and simply mirrors the improvements seen in other sports. Figure 50.1 shows the pattern of improvement in winning scores over the last 95 Championships. However, these raw scores do not reveal the changes that have been made to all courses on the present rota. Changes have been made to the length of the courses as shown in table 50.3 and also to the designated par; some courses have increased the length and lowered the par simultaneously. Thus the improvements noted have to be set against the courses that have become progressively more difficult. Even so, winning scores against par have fallen to the point where only two winning scores (1968 and 1985) have exceeded par over the last thirty years.

However, par is not a standard measure; there are holes less than 475 yards in length which are allocated a par of 5 and those that are longer than 475 yards which are rated locally as par 4. On the other hand, Provisional Standard Scratch Score is fixed very clearly by the overall length of the course. In this sense it is the most reliable baseline measure against which to test improvements over time. Performance against PSSS (figure 50.4) reveals that winning scores have been consistently below PSSS for almost fifty years in spite of increasing overall length.

The main issue, however, is whether the improvements noted have reached a performance plateau, as Thomas and Cochran have argued, or whether winning scores are continuing to improve at a rate which may be perceived by some as a threat to the integrity of the game. Thomas's (1995) paper showed scoring averages on the USPGA Tour from 1940 to 1993 as almost flat, and regression data from 1968 and 1993 as indicating that '. . . the average winning score is improving at 1 stroke per round per 21 years . . .', and that 'A review of the data presented does not seem to indicate that there is a great need for concern.' But if the winning scores in the Open between those two sets of dates are treated in a similar way the regression equation for 1939 to 1993 represents a 1 shot improvement every 14 years—which is hardly a flat profile. For the more recent period—1968-1993—the resultant improvement is more than double the rate on the USPGA Tour at 1 shot every 10 years.

These contradictory findings may result from the questionable validity of the data presented by Cochran (1995) and Thomas (1994). The former data suffer from two problems. Firstly, analysis over ten-year periods may lead to unsustainable degradation of the data, and secondly the data are limited to the performance of amateur golfers and realistically cannot be used to monitor changes at the highest level of the game.

The statistical evidence presented by Thomas (1994) seems to be flawed on a number of counts. Firstly, the growth in the number of tournaments and prize money may result in considerable variability in the quality of the fields entering each tournament. Thus improvements made by the better golfers in the most prestigious tournaments could be counter-balanced by relatively poor performances in the weaker competitions. Under these circumstances the fairly flat average winning score shown between 1940 and 1993 is not unexpected.

Secondly, it is possible that the way courses are prepared for tournaments in the U.S. differs from that in Europe. Anecdotal evidence suggests that U.S. courses, particularly those used for the three major championships held there, are designed deliberately to make low scoring very difficult. As long ago as 1959 Jones, speaking of the U.S. Masters, indicated the need to test modern golfers 'by the introduction of subtleties around the greens;' whilst according to Feinstein (1995), '. . . [U.S.] Open courses are invariably set up to take the driver out of your hand and force you to hit irons off the tee to make sure you find the fairway . . .' and are made '. . . so unfair that it is as much luck as skill that determines the winner . . . .'

Thirdly, a *prima facie* argument can be made that until recently the restrictive practices employed by the Masters Committee and the U.S. Golf Association have led to the exclusion of accomplished golfers from other countries to the Masters and U.S. Open Championships.

Finally, the data are drawn exclusively from the United States and may be of dubious validity. It has been shown, for example (Hale & Hale 1990, Hale 1995), that the performance statistics provided by the USPGA Tour—Driving Distance, Driving Accuracy, Greens in Regulation, Sand Saves, and Putts per Round—are poor indicators of final performance and cannot be used as a measure of improvement in strokes per round analyses.

By comparison, the use of the Open Championship scores as the source of data for analysis may not be quite so easily attacked. Entry is open on a world-wide basis to anyone who can qualify; this leads to the view that over time the best golfers are likely to compete and the data on which judgements of performance can be made are likely to be more inclusive, valid, and reliable. Furthermore, the players' perception of the Open is that the R & A is not concerned how low the winning score is (Wilson 1995), implying that the courses are not made unnaturally difficult. Thus, the Open Championship is likely to reflect any changes in player performance with greater validity. This is reinforced by Watson (1995), a five-time winner of the title, who asserts that 'The winner of the Open Championship is the champion golfer of the year.'

Thus, the evidence presented here contradicts the steady-state position claimed by Thomas and Cochran and gives some weight to those who have expressed concern about the potentially damaging effect of increasing technology on the nature of the game at the highest level.

ACKNOWLEDGMENTS

The R & A for the gift of Peter Ryde's book containing the majority of the data on which this analysis was based; the Director of the British Golf Museum for information on course lengths and par figures; the Secretaries of Championship courses for their help in confirming course lengths, par, and PSSS; P. Bunyan and J. Stephens for their advice on statistical procedures.

References

Cochran, A. (1995) Statistics—impressive, surprising, ancient and sobering. (In: *Golf the Scientific Way* Ed. Cochran, A.) Hemel, Hempstead: Aston Publishing Group, pp. 248-251.

Feinstein, J. (1995) *A good walk spoiled.* London: Little Brown & Co., pp. 332-333.

Hale, T. (1995) Analysing golf performance. (In: *Golf the Scientific Way* Ed. Cochran, A.) Hemel, Hempstead: Aston Publishing Group, pp. 242-247.

Hale, T. & Hale, G.T. (1990) Lies, damned lies and statistics in golf. (In: *1st World Scientific Congress of Golf* Ed. Cochran, A.) London: E & FN Spon, pp. 151-155.

Jones, R.T. (1959) Golf is my game. (In: *1997 Masters Media Guide,* Greenspan, G.) Augusta National Inc., 1996, p. 7.

Lewis, P. (1996) Personal communication.

McTeigue, M., Lamb, S.R., Mottram, R., & Pirozzolo, F. (1994) Spine and hip motion analysis during the golf swing. (In: *Science and Golf II* Eds. Cochran, A.J. & Farrally, M.R) London: E & F N Spon, pp. 50-58.

Ryde, P. (1981) *Royal and Ancient Championship Records 1892-1980.* Royal and Ancient Golf Club of St. Andrews, pp. 22-99.

Ryde, P. (1983) *Royal and Ancient Championship Records 1981-1983 (Suppl).* Royal and Ancient Golf Club of St. Andrews, pp. 5-7.

Thomas, F.W. (1994) The state of the game, equipment and science. (In: *Science and Golf II* Eds. Cochran, A.J. & Farrally, M.R.) London: E & F N Spon, pp. 237-246.

Watson, T. (1995) (In: Feinstein, J. *A Good Walk Spoiled.*) London: Little Brown & Co., p. 373.

Williams, M. (1994) The golf course and the standard scratch score. *Golfer's Handbook 1994.* London: Macmillan, p. 748.

Wilson, G. (1995). Personal communication.

PART II

Equipment

CHAPTER 51

History and Construction
of Non-Wound Golf Balls

R.D. Nesbitt, M.J. Sullivan, and T. Melvin
Spalding Sports World Wide, Chicopee, MA, USA

Non-wound golf balls today account for about 85% of all balls sold, with wound balls clinging to the balance. While the history of golf balls can be tracked back several centuries, the timeline for the modern golf ball is only about three decades.

The "superball" patented by Wham-O Manufacturing in 1966 probably started the evolution of the non-wound golf ball. This play ball, composed of high Cis polybutadiene and sulfur cured, had extremely high drop rebound in excess of 90%, but at higher impact speeds, the Coefficient of Restitution was reduced to about .650.

This led to the one-piece Bartsch golf ball, patented in 1967. This ball, at the time, was going to revolutionize the golf ball industry—but it didn't. In 1968, Bob Molitor patented a cover blend of polyurethane/ABS that was used on a two-piece "Executive" golf ball; it proved to be short in distance but cut resistance. In 1971, Molitor replaced this cover with DuPont's Surlyn resin. This did revolutionize the golf ball industry. Today, there are now double and triple cores, multi-layer covers, soft over hard, hard over soft, oversize, low moment, high moment golf balls, and the future will bring even further combinations of new materials giving the golfer a myriad of choices.

Keywords: Non-wound golf ball, one-piece, two-piece, multilayer, coefficient of restitution.

INTRODUCTION

High Cis 1,4 polybutadiene, invented in the late 1950s by Ziegler-Natta resulted in a catalyst system that produced stereo regularity in the polymer chain. A Cis 1,4 content as high as 98% is possible using select catalysts. The higher the Cis content, the higher the resilience of the rubber. Without high Cis polybutadiene, today's non-wound top-grade golf balls would not be possible. No other polymer has the resilience of polybutadiene rubber.

"SUPERBALL" FORMULATION

In 1966, N.H. Stingley patented and assigned the Superball to Wham-O Manufacturing. This play ball, as shown in table 51.1, used polybutadiene as the base rubber.

Table 51.1 "Superball" Formulation—N.H. Stingley

	Parts by weight
Polybutadiene	100.00
Zinc oxide	4.00
Stearic acid	2.00
N-oxydiethylene benzothiazole 2 sulfenamide (Amax)	1.75
Di-ortho-tolyguanidine (DOTG)	1.00
Bismuth dimethyldithio carbonate (Bismate)	0.35
4 Methyl-6-tertiarty-butyl phenol	1.00
Hydrated silica (HiSil)	7.50
Sulfur	<u>5.25</u>
	122.85

It contained a high level of sulfur and accelerators along with a fine silica filler to increase hardness and tear resistance and minimize molding defects, such as back rinding. These balls had a drop rebound from 100 inches (254 cm) in excess of 90%, but at higher impact speeds of 125 ft. per second (38 m/s) the resilience dropped to a coefficient of restitution (COR) of about .650. If a dimpled golf ball was made from a Superball formulation, it would be at least 30 yards (27 meters) short in driver carry distance vs. a conventional modern golf ball. This is due to the fact that this ball would have 0 PGA compression and would deform too much upon impact and leave the club face too slowly.

BARTSCH ONE-PIECE GOLF BALL

In 1967, James Bartsch patented a unitary molded golf ball that had tremendous initial success and captured 10% of the U.S. market almost overnight. Table 51.2 shows one of the formulations disclosed in this patent.

Table 51.2   Unitary Molded Golf Ball—J.R. Bartsch

	Parts by weight
Cis-butadiene polymer	100.00
Butyleneglycol dimethacrylate	56.20
Fine silica filler (Hi-Sil)	37.50
60 mesh cork	6.20
Dicumyl peroxide	<u>3.13</u>
	203.03

It contains high Cis polybutadiene as the base rubber along with butyleneglycol dimethacrylate. This is a liquid unsaturated co-agent that crosslinks with the polybutadiene rubber. The fine silica filler reinforces and increases the hardness of the molded ball. The cork particles were added to increase the ball compression. Dicumyl peroxide is added to generate free radicals that initiate crosslinking and polymerization of the polymer/co-agent blend to form a highly crosslinked network, resulting in a hard, resilient golf ball. Other co-agents such as trimethylolpropane trimethacrylate (TMPTMA), a tri-functional liquid monomer; zinc diacrylate (ZDA); zinc dimethacrylate (ZDMA); and zinc monomethacrylate (ZMA) were used to improve the performance of the one-piece golf ball. ZDA gave the best COR and performance but was quite brittle and resulted in durability problems. ZDMA gives better durability but results in lower COR and performance. ZMA requires high levels of peroxide, resulting in a more stable golf ball but lacks performance and durability. One-piece golf balls are short in distance primarily due to low initial velocity off a driver. When compounded for maximum COR they lack durability. When compounded for maximum durability, they are even shorter in distance. They lose COR with time, particularly at high relative humidity. They require a white pigmented paint on the surface of the ball, as the substrate is not white enough to simply clear coat. More expensive ingredients are required for durability vs. a two-piece golf ball. One-piece golf balls today are used primarily in Japan in driving ranges where distance is not a factor.

TWO-PIECE "EXECUTIVE" GOLF BALL

In 1968 Bob Molitor patented a two-piece golf ball named "Executive." It had a urethane/ABS cover as shown in table 51.3.

The solid core contained polybutadiene, polyisoprene, and ABS and was crosslinked using ZDA and dicumyl peroxide. The ball had very good cut resistance but was short in distance, particularly off a driver at high club head speeds. To improve the COR and distance, the core was top wound with elastic thread. This improved distance but the ball lost its cut resistance. This ball was named "Executive II."

Table 51.3   Polyurethane Cover for Two-Piece "Executive Golf Ball"—R.P. Molitor

	Parts by weight
Polyester polyurethane (Texin 355D)	60.00
Polyester polyurethane (Texin 192A)	40.00
Acrylonitrile-butadiene-styrene resin (Cycolac-2502)	30.00
Titanium dioxide	8.00
Barium Stearate	1.00
	139.00

"TOP-FLITE" TWO-PIECE GOLF BALL

In 1971, Bob Molitor replaced the urethane cover with DuPont's ionomer "Surlyn" resin and this ball did revolutionize the golf ball industry. Although Stanley Harrison of Dunlop in Great Britain was the first to patent an ionomer resin for use as a golf ball cover, Bob Molitor patented an improved blend of ionomer resins. He found that blends of zinc and sodium ionomers from DuPont have synergistic properties that have superior coefficient of restitution and improved cold crack properties vs. the zinc or sodium ionomers alone.

The Top-Flite golf ball was an enormous success. It solved all the problems associated with the one-piece golf ball. The cover was tough, cut resistant, and durable. The cover protected the core from COR loss with time. It protected the core from impact failure, thus allowing the use of ZDA co-agent that has superior COR properties but is quite brittle. The hard cover also increased the COR of the core. The harder the cover, the higher the COR, the longer the distance.

MULTI-LAYER GOLF BALL

Millions of golfers used the "Top-Flite" golf ball, but better golfers and professional golfers refused to play it due to its hard cover that resulted in less backspin and poor workability. It was thought that if a soft thin cover with the Shore hardness of balata were molded around a "Top-Flite" golf ball, it would solve the spin and workability issue with the hard-covered "Top-Flite." It did and the first multi-layered golf ball was patented February 14, 1984. The soft outer cover develops maximum spin and workability of a balata-covered wound ball off irons and around the green and the hard resilient inner cover provides the increase in COR and reduced spin off the driver, resulting in maximum distance (Sullivan 1994).

DOUBLE CORES

Kasco, Sumitomo, and Bridgestone have marketed golf balls having double cores and Kasco now has a triple core named "Rockets." Double cores have certain advantages in that the weight distribution of the golf ball can be controlled. A high density inner core with a lighter outer shell results in a ball with a low moment of inertia and mimics the construction of a wound golf ball. Reversing the density gradient of a double core produces a golf ball with a higher moment of inertia, giving the ball sustained spin and roll, at least in theory.

MATERIAL SELECTION FOR NON-WOUND CORES

Table 51.4 shows a typical top-grade core formulation.

The polybutadiene rubber is usually a blend of different types from various producers. Table 51.5 shows the percent Cis content of different catalysts.

Table 51.4   Typical Top-Grade Golf Ball Core Formulation

	Parts by weight
Hi Cis polybutadiene rubber	100
Zinc oxide	3–40
ZDA (zinc diacrylate)	15–40
Zinc stearate	3–20
Ground flash (vulcanized core material)	5–30
Peroxide 40% active	0.5–5

Table 51.5   Cis Content of Various Polybutadiene Polymers

Catalyst type	% Cis content
Cobalt	96–98
Neodymium	97–98
Nickel	80–98
Titanium	92–94
Lithium	20–40

The higher the percent Cis content, the higher the COR. Lithium catalyzed polybutadiene has the lowest Cis content and is very difficult to process. Despite its low Cis content it produces a golf ball core with higher COR than natural rubber, and natural rubber has a Cis 1,4 polyisoprene structure of almost 100%. Polybutadiene types vary in (a) molecular structure (linear, branched), (b) molecular weight characteristics (number, average molecular weight Mn; weight, average molecular weight Mw; and polydispersity Mw/Mn), and (c) type of molecular weight distribution (unimodal, bimodal). All of these properties affect processing and/or final properties.

Zinc oxide is an activator and an efficient high density filler. ZDA is zinc diacrylate, a co-agent that functions as a crosslinking agent and contributes hardness and resilience. TMPTMA (trimethylolpropane trimethacrylate), a liquid trifunctional monomer, can also be added as a reactive processing aid. Zinc stearate is an activator, processing aid, and a hydrophobic diluent. Ground flash is pulverized, vulcanized core material formed as a by-product of the molding process. The ground flash increases hardness and COR and improves processing.

The peroxide crosslinks the core into a semi-rigid, resilient, thermoset polymer. There are various types of peroxides and initiators with different half-lives affecting productivity. Low levels of peroxide improve COR and durability but are more sensitive to COR loss with time. Higher levels of peroxide produce a core that is more stable but is more brittle and has lower COR vs. compression.

COVER MATERIALS

The relationship between the chemistry and physical properties of materials and their effect on golf ball performance remains an evolving science. While significant works have been presented at previous meetings and over 100 patents dealing with such topics have been issued, there remains a search for a material that better combines the properties of resilience and softness to give a golf ball maximum distance while providing high spin rates and soft feel.

Cover choices still consist of essentially three generic families of materials: ionomers, polyurethanes, and unsaturated synthetic diene rubbers such as trans-polyisoprene. While diene rubber that requires vulcanization is still in use on a few wound golf balls, its use is diminishing rapidly. This so-called synthetic "balata" suffers from poor cut resistance, relatively low resilience, and multiple-step processing that can lead to product inconsistencies. The most popular cover materials are those of the ionomer family such as those sold under the trade names Iotek (Exxon) and Surlyn (DuPont). These metal salt neutralized copolymers of ethylene and acrylic or methacrylic acid contribute outstanding resilience and durability to a wide range of golf ball types. Depending on the acid content, type and amount of cation, and molecular weight of the copolymer, golf balls with very low spin rates, good durability, and maximum allowable distance can be obtained, even at very soft PGA compressions. When the copolymer is further modified with a softening termonomer such as methyl or butyl acrylate, a wide range of moduli materials can be obtained that are useful in high-spinning golf balls, such as those described in U.S. patent 4,884,814 issued in 1988 and many others since. Ionomers are used in most golf balls because of the flexibility of design afforded the golf ball technologist as well as due to their exceptional consistency in physical properties, ease of molding, and recyclability.

Polyurethanes have been used in golf balls for decades and offer good resilience, excellent abrasion resistance, and reasonable ease of molding. They are primarily useful only in soft-covered golf balls and while they are inferior to ionomers in whiteness, resilience, and cut resistance, offer some significant performance advantages over the diene rubber covered balls.

ALTERNATE MULTI-LAYER CONSTRUCTIONS

Multi-layer golf ball covers may be soft over hard or hard over soft; both have certain advantages. A hard inner layer (or mantle) material should show increased resilience with hardness, such as ionomers or crosslinked polybutadiene. A soft mantle material should be one that shows increased resilience as the material becomes softer, such as metallocenes like "Exact" or "Engage" or polyester elastomers such as "Hytrel" or polyester amides such as "Pebax." See figures 51.1a and b.

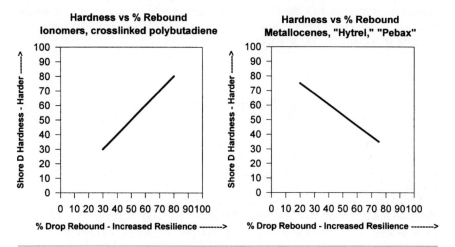

Figures 51.1a, b   Hardness vs. percent rebound.

The mantle layer can be filled with heavy materials such as powdered metals. When weight is added to the mantle layer, weight has to be removed from the core. When weight is removed from the core (zinc oxide), the COR increases and the moment of inertia of the ball increases from the weight shift.

FUTURE OUTLOOK FOR GOLF BALLS

Soft covers over hard mantles give maximum performance for low handicap golfers. We are approaching the maximum hardness using ionomers. Solid metals have higher hardness, higher flexural modulus, higher density, higher modulus of elasticity, higher resilience, and higher moisture vapor barrier properties than polymeric materials.

It is possible to form a solid metal mantle around a core via vacuum metalizing the core to produce a conductive surface, and additional thickness of the metal layer can be accomplished by electroplating, plasma deposition, sputtering, etc. As the solid metal mantle increases in thickness, a solid core will not be required and the core will become a hollow metal sphere. Hollow metal spheres may also be formed by stamping metal half shells, welding two half shells together. As the welding process anneals the metal, hardening and heat treating the metal will be necessary to prevent "oil canning" of the hollow sphere. A high temperature blowing agent may be added to the half shells that will decompose upon heat treating. This will result in a pressurized hollow metal sphere that will have increased COR and resistance to "oil canning." New shape memory metal alloys of nickel/titanium have super elastic properties and would be a good choice for the metal. This hollow metal sphere may be coated with a thin soft polymeric cover to produce the ultimate tour ball. The ultimate distance ball would not use a soft outer cover but would be a hollow metal sphere with dimples formed during the stamping of the half shells. The outer surface would be polished to a satin finish—no paint would be required. This construction is similar to metal woods and they would complement each other. Because of the complexity of these processes, future golf ball designers may need a degree in metallurgy and polymer chemistry.

References

Sullivan, M.J. (1994). The relationship between golf ball construction and performance. In *Science and Golf II* (ed. A.J. Cochran and M.R. Farrally), E&FN Spon, London, pp. 334-339.

Stingley N.H.	U.S. Patent 3,241,834	March 22, 1966
Bartsch J.R.	U.S. Patent 3,313,545	April 11, 1967
Molitor R.P.	U.S. Patent 3,395,109	July 30, 1968
Harrison S.R.	U.S. Patent 3,454,280	July 8, 1969
Molitor R.P.	U.S. Patent 3,819,76	June 25, 1974
Nesbitt R.D.	U.S. Patent 4,431,193	February 14, 1984

CHAPTER 52

The Curious Persistence of the Wound Ball

Jeffrey L. Dalton
Titleist and Foot-Joy Worldwide

Wound golf balls continue to be preferred by the game's better players because of their combination of high spin, high velocity, and low compression. These properties arise from the crystallinity of natural rubber at high strain rate and its Young's modulus. The physical properties of wound rubber thread combined with the construction variables of the center, wound layer, and the cover provide wide latitude for wound golf ball design.

Keywords: Golf ball, wound, thread, spin, velocity, compression, solid center, liquid center, ionomer, balata.

INTRODUCTION

As Mark Twain might have said, the reports of the death of the wound ball have been greatly exaggerated. An overwhelming majority of the world's best golfers play a wound ball. They play it, not merely for endorsement, or to uphold tradition, or due to an ineluctable habit, but because of its performance and because they win with it. In fact, a recent survey of tour events from around the world in mid-September 1997 showed 81% of the players on the US PGA Tour, 89% of the Nike Tour, 64% of the LPGA Tour, 67% of the Senior Tour, and 83% of the PGA European Tour played wound golf balls. In this paper I hope to show some of the technical reasons behind the continued popularity of wound golf balls.

Wound Ball History

The history of golf balls was well described by Martin in 1968. The wound golf ball was invented by Coburn Haskell in Akron, Ohio, in 1898. Haskell was a bicycle manufacturer and golf enthusiast in Cleveland, Ohio, and was a customer of the B.F. Goodrich Co., from whom he bought rubber to make bicycle tires. He was also a good friend of the plant manager, and fellow golfer, Bertram Work. While waiting in Work's office for a round of golf, and in one version, goaded by him to "do something for the game if you love it so much," Haskell spotted some rubber thread and began winding a ball. He had Work put a gutta percha cover on the wound core and the modern golf ball was born.

Another Goodrich employee designed and built the piece of equipment necessary to commercialize the new Haskell ball. John Gammeter's winding machine, which was patented in 1900, incorporated the essential features of those in use today. Gammeter's machine used spring loaded pulleys to stretch the thread to a consistent high tension. He devised a system of rollers that rotated the ball in the winding plane and in a perpendicular plane. That produces a winding pattern that he called great circle, as we do still.

The thread used in golf balls at the turn of the century was made from natural latex rubber. It was typically 0.18 cm wide and 0.06 cm thick unstretched. Those rubber threads were stretched to about 700% elongation during winding. Today, thread is thinner and wound tighter, due to improvements in rubber vulcanization chemistry, the use of synthetic rubber, and better processing. The thread used now is typically 0.16 cm wide and 0.05 cm thick, and is stretched to 1,000% elongation. Winding patterns include Gammeter's great circle and the basket weave or crisscross patterns.

Another facet of Gammeter's machine was that it required a center on which to begin winding. Solid rubber centers were an obvious choice; the early Haskell balls used a solid rubber center about 2 cm in diameter. Other materials, including celluloid, cork, and steel, were also used.

The next development in wound ball construction was made by a native of St. Andrews, Jack Jolly. In 1902 Jolly began working for Eleazer Kempshall, who had made his fortune in celluloid shirt collars. Kempshall had begun molding golf balls at his factory in Arlington, New Jersey, and was trying to improve on the Haskell design. Jolly got the idea for liquid filled centers from baby bottle nipples he saw in a pharmacy window. He filled them with water and tied off the ends, wrapped some rubber tape around them, and wound them on a Gammeter winding machine. He was awarded a U.S. patent in 1908 for his invention. Jolly made further improvements by freezing the centers with dry ice to maintain their spherical shape during winding, and experimented with various liquids, solutions, and pastes. Kempshall's company was purchased by the St. Mungo Golf Co. in Glasgow, Scotland in 1910 and they introduced the St. Mungo water core in 1911 and the Colonel, with a liquid filled center, in 1915. Finally, Frank Mingay of Berfield, Scotland received a patent in 1908 for making a liquid filled center by piercing a hollow rubber shell with a needle and injecting the liquid. That patent was licensed by Spalding and was introduced in 1919 as the Spalding Witch.

WOUND BALL TECHNOLOGY

As we have seen, the technology of wound balls is a century old. For nearly that entire period wound balls have been the preferred balls of the game's best players. The greater resilience of wound balls gave greater distance and their higher spin gave greater workability than the gutties of a century ago, and yet, in spite of the development of solid core balls, wound balls remain popular with better players to the present day.

A layer of wound thread is not just a rubber layer. Actually, a layer of solid natural rubber molded over a center would make a poor golf ball. Natural rubber is a very soft material in the unstretched state. Rubber compounds used for golf ball thread have a hardness of about 20 to 30 on the Shore A durometer scale. A ball made with a layer of natural rubber would be very low in compression and low in velocity.

Natural rubber does possess one distinctive characteristic when it is stretched. It crystallizes under tension, and that crystallization leads to high tensile strength. Natural rubber, or cis-1,4-polyisoprene has a high degree of stereoregularity. That is, as the rubber molecule is built up from its basic isoprene units the order, bonding, and orientation of each isoprene unit is the same along the chain. Rubber polymer chains are naturally coiled like springs. When rubber is stretched the springs uncoil and the molecules line up; because of its stereoregularity, polyisoprene molecules line up well enough to crystallize. Subramaniam (1995) stated the degree of crystallization could reach as high as 25-30%. The effect of crystallization is a high tensile strength that allows natural rubber thread to be stretched very tightly and wound around a golf ball core without breaking. Crystallization also leads to an increase in hardness.

The resilience of a wound ball is largely due to the high elongation of the thread. In current wound balls the thread is stretched to nearly 1,000%, or ten times its original length. At that elongation the thread is a spring stretched taut, and its ability to return the energy of an impact is high. At the same time the Young's modulus of the thread is low. Ohm (1990) gives a 300% modulus value of 14 kg/cm^2 for polyisoprene as compared with a 300% modulus value of 70 kg/cm^2 found by Kuzma (1995) for polybutadiene. The result of the high elongation and lower modulus is that a wound ball can have a higher velocity than a polybutadiene core at a lower compression.

This is illustrated in figure 52.1. A group of balls were wound at a series of thread elongations from thread 0.051 cm thick to a wound ball diameter of 3.94 cm. They were covered with a lithium/sodium ionomer blend with a cover hardness of 69 Shore D. At the same time a group of polybutadiene cores were made at a series of core compressions and molded with a core diameter of 3.94 cm. The cores were formulated to maximize the velocity at each of the compressions. They were also covered with the same lithium/sodium ionomer. The results showed that the wound balls were faster at any given compression within the range we measured.

The second element of wound ball performance is spin rate. Wound balls exhibit higher spin rates than two-piece balls at comparable compression and cover hardness. This is due to two factors. Thread is lower in density than golf ball centers or cores; this necessarily shifts weight toward the center of the ball reducing its moment of inertia. A ball with a lower moment of inertia has a higher spin rate. The effect of moment of inertia is small in this case.

A much larger factor is the torsion effect during the ball impact. Gobush (1995) describes the creation of spin during the ball impact. Spin originates in the torsional wind-up and recoil of the ball against its elastic resistance. As he states, it is "like the tightening of a coiled spring." The stiffness or modulus of that spring is a key factor in the amount of spin that is generated, a stiff spring (i.e., high modulus)

Velocity (m/sec)

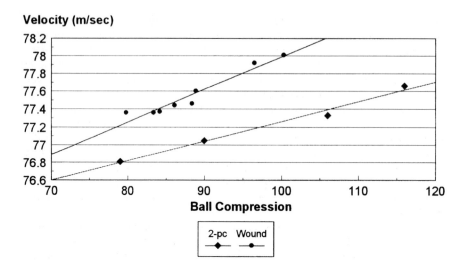

Figure 52.1   Wound versus 2-piece construction: velocity as a function of ball compression.

leading to lower spin and a soft spring generating higher spin. As we saw above, the wound layer has a lower modulus than a polybutadiene core and, therefore, will have a higher spin given the same core dimensions and cover.

Another factor identified by Gobush (1995) is the relationship of the time required for the torsional wind-up and recoil and the contact time of the ball on the club face. He states that the maximum spin is generated when the two times are the equal and that in some circumstances the contact time is shorter than the wind-up and recoil time. By inference a shorter contact time would lead to lower spin.

Ujihashi (1994) reported measurements of contact time. He found that the contact time for wound balls was 15% longer than that of two-piece balls. Scheie (1990) also measured contact time and displacement of the ball's center point. He observed that the wound ball's center point began motion later than that of the two-piece ball, implying a longer torsional wind-up time. Finally, Gobush (1990) measured normal and tangential impact forces on wound and two-piece balls. He observed that two-piece balls exhibit greater structural rigidity than do wound balls at high-speed impact conditions.

WOUND BALL DESIGN

The conclusion of these observations is that wound balls can achieve a combination of high velocity, high spin, and low compression. Of course, wound and two-piece core constructions are not the only factors used to obtain these performance characteristics. As Sullivan and Melvin (1994) point out, cover hardness, cover thickness, compression, and ball size may also be manipulated to achieve a given spin rate or velocity target. The art in golf ball design is not to maximize one performance attribute at the expense of all others, but rather to achieve a suitable balance of properties. In that regard, the balance of high velocity, high spin, and low compression provide wound constructions with a strong foundation for the design of high performance golf balls.

Among the several factors with which wound ball designers work are thread dimensions, thread elongation, the thickness of the thread layer, the composition of the rubber thread, and the winding pattern. Several variables are also related to the center: solid center, center size, solid center hardness, compression or durometer, liquid or paste center, liquid volume, liquid specific gravity, and liquid center envelope material. All these factors influence compression, velocity, and spin to some degree and may be fine-tuned to achieve the desired balance of properties. In addition to these, the same factors of cover hardness and thickness also apply to wound ball constructions, further increasing the degrees of freedom to the wound ball designer.

To illustrate the design latitude offered by wound constructions a simple matrix was constructed. Three variables were evaluated: thread thickness (0.05 cm vs. 0.06 cm), center type (liquid vs. solid), and cover hardness (69 Shore D ionomer vs. 60 Shore D ionomer). In each case the range of variables do not reflect extreme values. All other construction variables were held constant. In addition, two groups of two-piece balls of the same core size and covered with the 60 Shore D and 69 Shore D ionomers are included. The results are shown in table 52.1 and figures 52.2 and 52.3.

Table 52.1   Center Type, Thread Thickness, Cover Hardness

	Center type	Thread thickness	Cover hardness	Velocity	Driver spin	8 Iron spin
A	Liquid	0.05	69 D	77.36	57.2	136.6
B	Solid	0.05	69 D	77.61	69.9	150.5
C	Liquid	0.06	69 D	76.76	55.0	122.3
D	Solid	0.06	69 D	77.10	64.8	146.5
E	Liquid	0.05	60 D	76.89	61.7	143.0
F	Solid	0.05	60 D	77.25	71.8	156.1
G	Liquid	0.06	60 D	76.10	62.8	126.6
H	Solid	0.06	60 D	76.67	70.3	148.1
I	2-pc core	NA	69 D	77.33	51.2	126.8
J	2-pc core	NA	60 D	77.05	56.0	134.3

The golf balls produced in this experiment had spin rates ranging from that of medium hardness ionomer-covered two-piece balls to higher than balata balls. It is interesting to note that the choice of center type affects the drive spin rate by 15%, the difference in cover hardness led to a 9% difference in driver spin, and the

Driver Spin Rate (r/s)

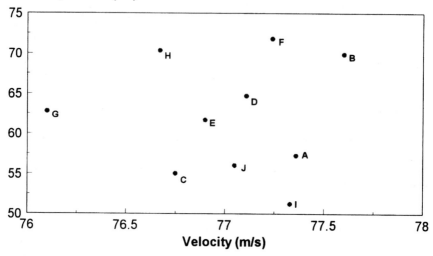

Figure 52.2   Driver spin rate versus velocity: experimental wound constructions.

8 Iron Spin Rate (r/s)

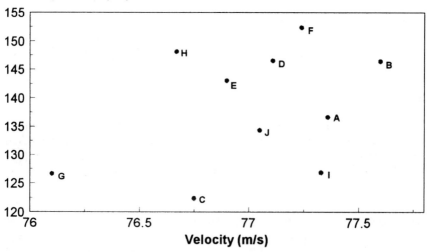

Figure 52.3   8 iron spin rate versus velocity: experimental wound constructions.

difference in thread thickness led to a 4% difference. All these differences were significant at the 95% confidence interval. The effect of center type on velocity was 0.4%, while the effects of both cover hardness and thread type on velocity was 0.6%. Again, all these effects were significant at the 95% confidence level.

The data from the 8 iron spin rate tests again show the range of spin rates attainable with wound ball constructions. As in the case of the driver data, the choice of center type affected the 8 iron spin by 15%, the cover hardness by 5.5%, and the thread thickness by 5%.

CONCLUSIONS

The enduring popularity of wound golf balls among better players is due to the balance of performance characteristics obtained from wound ball designs. The physical properties of wound rubber thread provide high velocity and spin and low compression, which translate to the golfer as workability, distance, and soft feel. Finally, the multiple construction variables associated with wound balls allow the designer wide latitude to optimize the performance for different players.

TEST CONDITIONS

Hardness

Shore hardness was measured according to ASTM Test D-2240.

Compression

Compression was measured using an ATTI compression gauge, manufactured by ATTI Engineering, Union City, New Jersey.

Velocity

Velocity was measured using a rotating pendulum device. The rotating pendulum has a length of 0.842 m and revolves at 7.56 revolutions per second. The pendulum strikes the ball and propels it through two light screens located 3.2 m apart. The time it takes the ball to pass between the screens is measured. Velocity is determined by dividing the distance between the screens by the measured time interval.

Spin Rate

Driver spin rate is measured using a True Temper hitting machine fitted with a driver and set up to achieve a ball velocity of 48.8 m/s, a launch angle of 9 degrees, and a spin rate of 50 revolutions per second using a Pinnacle Gold ball. Measurements of spin rate are made using a Titleist Launch Monitor, described in Gobush, Pelletier, and Days (1994). 8 iron spin rate is measured using a True Temper hitting machine fitted with a driver and set up to achieve a ball velocity of 35.05 m/s, a launch angle of 18 degrees, and spin rate of 150 revolutions per second using a Titleist Tour Balata ball. Measurements of spin rate are made using a Titleist Launch Monitor, described in Gobush, Pelletier, and Days (1994).

ACKNOWLEDGMENTS

A very grateful author wishes to thank the Product Development and Product Testing teams at Titleist and Foot-Joy Worldwide for their help in developing the data for this paper, and Bill Morgan and Herb Boehm for their continuing support.

References

Darrell Survey. 1997. *LPGA Tournament: Welch's Championship.* Los Angeles: Darrell Survey Company.

Darrell Survey. 1997. *Nike Tournament: Boise Open.* Los Angeles: Darrell Survey Company.

Darrell Survey. 1997. *PGA Tournament: CVS Charity Classic.* Los Angeles: Darrell Survey Company.

Darrell Survey. 1997. *Senior Tournament: Boone Valley Golf Club.* Los Angeles: Darrell Survey Company.

Gobush, W. 1990. *Impact Force Measurement on Golf Balls.* In Science and Golf: Proceedings of the World Scientific Congress of Golf, ed. A.J. Cochran and M.R. Farrally. London: E & FN Spon.

Gobush, W., Pelletier, D., and Days, C. 1994. *Video Monitoring System to Measure Initial Launch Characteristics of Golf Balls.* In Science and Golf II: Proceedings of the World Scientific Congress of Golf, ed. A.J. Cochran and M.R. Farrally. London: E & FN Spon.

Gobush, W. 1995. *Spin and the Inner Workings of the Golf Ball.* In Golf the Scientific Way, ed. A.J. Cochran, 141-145. Hertfordshire, UK: Aston Publishing Group.

Kuzma, L.J. 1995. *Polybutadiene and Polyisoprene Rubbers.* In Rubber Technology, third edition, ed. M. Morton, 235-259. London: Chapman & Hall.

Martin, J.S. 1968. *The Curious History of the Golf Ball.* New York: Horizon Press.

Scheie, C.E. 1990. *The Golf Club-Ball Collision—50,000 g's.* In Science and Golf: Proceedings of the World Scientific Congress of Golf, ed. A.J. Cochran and M.R. Farrally. London: E & FN Spon.

Sports Marketing Surveys. 1997. *1997 European PGA Tour: One2One British Masters.* London: Sports Marketing Surveys.

Subramaniam, A. 1990. *Natural Rubber.* In The Vanderbilt Rubber Handbook, ed. R.F. Ohm, 23-43. Norwalk, CT: R.T. Vanderbilt Co.

Subramaniam, A. 1995. *Natural Rubber.* In Rubber Technology, third edition, ed. M. Morton, 179-208. London: Chapman & Hall.

Sullivan, M.J., and Melvin, T. 1994. *The Relationship Between Golf Ball Construction and Performance.* In Science and Golf II: Proceedings of the World Scientific Congress of Golf, ed. A.J. Cochran and M.R. Farrally. London: E & FN Spon.

Ujihashi, S. 1994. *Measurement of Dynamic Characteristics of Golf Balls and Identification of Their Mechanical Models.* In Science and Golf II: Proceedings of the World Scientific Congress of Golf, ed. A.J. Cochran and M.R. Farrally. London: E & FN Spon.

Valin, K.A. 1990. *Synthetic Polyisoprene.* In The Vanderbilt Rubber Handbook, ed. R.F. Ohm, 44-53. Norwalk, CT: R.T. Vanderbilt Co.

CHAPTER 53

The Effects of Golf Ball Construction on Putting

L.D. Lemons and M.B. Stanczak
Dunlop Maxfli Sports Corp., Westminster, SC, USA

D. Beasley
Clemson University, Clemson, SC, USA

The effects of golf ball construction on putting, through distance, dispersion, and amount of break, are explored with the use of a putting robot. Ball construction is distinguished by cover hardness and material, core composition, and type. Three specific constructions are explored: a hard distance 2-piece golf ball, a soft high performance 2-piece golf ball, and a high performance wound 3-piece golf ball. Several distances and break amounts are tested for the construction types involved. The results show that for the same putter head velocity, 2-piece distance balls roll further by 3.2%, 5.0%, and 3.1% for 150, 450, and 900 cm putts respectively, when compared to a 3-piece wound golf ball.

Keywords: Putting, ball construction, distance, dispersion.

INTRODUCTION

Putting is one of the most important aspects of any golfer's game. Good putting can save pars or make birdies and eagles, while bad putting can cause bogies and dreaded doubles or higher. According to Pelz (1989) in a study conducted from 1975 through 1978, 43% of all golf shots played during a round of golf are putts, almost double the number in the next leading category. Also, putting is the one part of the game where all players, regardless of handicap, can greatly help their score and their overall confidence. With these issues in mind, what then is the role of golf ball construction in this important aspect of the game?

Pelz (1989) reported a study of putting distances versus ball construction which compared wound balata and ionomer covered balls, with solid ionomer covered balls. This study showed differences between all of these ball construction types to be significant. However, the face of today's ball market has changed. This study is a first step in considering some of the changes in ball construction and the effect those constructions have in putting.

The state of technology in golf ball construction today extends from a simple 2-piece distance ball, with highly resilient hard rubber core and hard thermoplastic cover, to more intricate wound products with liquid centers and soft elastomer covers. Golf ball cores can be wound, solid, or multi-piece, with covers made from synthetic rubber, thermoplastics, elastomers, or a variety of hybrid materials, and the core can be covered with more than one layer. These constructions for the most part are designed without the putter in mind. They are usually directed instead toward other shots, driver, irons, and chipping, giving the golfer the required speed, spin, or feel for the desired stance or performance, or compromise between the two.

This study intends to link putting attributes directly to today's popular golf ball constructions. Attributes such as distance, dispersion, and amount of break were examined for several golf ball construction types. A putting robot was utilized in this exercise to provide a smooth, consistent, and pendulum-like stroke. The goal was to provide some understanding of the effects of current golf ball constructions on putting.

METHODOLOGY

Putting Robot

Striking each putt consistently, with the same velocity and alignment, was essential to the study of the effects of golf ball construction on distance, dispersion, and breaking characteristics. This was accomplished through the use of a putter robot, constructed with this study in mind. This robot employed a basic pendulum type swing, relying totally on gravity for swing speed, with adjustments for lie and length. Its base is adjustable independently from the putter, to allow leveling of the apparatus with the ground surface, the horizon, or some other reference. The pendulum arm of the robot is fitted with an adjustable backswing stop, to allow repeatable swing speeds time and time again.

Test Ball Construction

This study employed golf balls of three construction types: wound 3-piece tour quality golf balls, soft 2-piece tour quality golf balls, and hard 2-piece distance golf balls. The average physical properties of each set of balls are listed in table 53.1.

These are average values for each property and ball construction type, with standard deviations for each group of balls in each property category being essentially equal. The measurements in this table are typical with industry standards, with rebound taken as percent rebound from a 250 cm drop.

Testing Methodology

The test described in this report utilized the bent grass green on the Dunlop Maxfli Sports Corporation Outdoor Research Center in Westminster, South Carolina. This

Table 53.1   Subject Golf Ball Physical Property Summary

	Ball type	Cover	Size (mm)	Wt. (gm)	Comp.	Rebound
Ball #1	2 Pc wound tour quality	55 Shore D	42.65 (pole) 42.70 (eq)	45.4	82	71%
Ball #2	2 Pc tour quality	58 Shore D	42.70 (pole) 42.65 (eq)	45.3	96	75%
Ball #3	2 Pc distance	70 Shore D	42.70 (pole) 42.72 (eq)	45.3	105	79%

green was cut to 3 mm in two directions within 3 hours of the start of each test session, equivalent to a stimpmeter reading of around 10.5. Several phases of testing were utilized in this study to gain information about distance, dispersion, and amount of break and the relationship of each to ball construction. In the initial phase of testing, two dozen balls of each construction were putted using the robot putter, for three separate distances, 150, 450, and 900 cm, and in opposite directions along the same path. The path was chosen such that these initial putts were essentially straight, and the putts were struck with constant putter head velocity. Distance and dispersion from the straight line direction of the putt were recorded. The ball types were rotated in order of testing to eliminate any effect the wear on the surface of the putting line would have on the results. Average distances and standard deviations in distances are reported. Dispersion for the different ball types were essentially the same at all distances, and thus will not be reported explicitly. In the second phase of this study, a path was chosen that produced significant break, and the break and distance of each putt was recorded for each construction type. The break amount was defined as the perpendicular distance from the line of aim and the resting point of the putt. The distance was measured as the distance traveled by the ball along the line of aim.

RESULTS

Distance and Dispersion

Distance and dispersion testing was conducted on the three balls over a two-day period. Three distances were chosen for this phase of testing, a short, medium, and long putt. For each distance, putts were struck along opposite directions of each line, to allow any uphill or downhill tendencies to be recognized. The distance averages and standard deviations for this testing are included in table 53.2.

Consideration of the data in table 53.2 leads to several apparent results. First, that the average distance for Ball #3, the hard 2-piece distance construction, was greater than the other balls in all cases, with the increased distance being statistically significant for all but the downhill 150 cm putt condition. On average, this

Table 53.2   Results From Distance Putting Test

Distance	Direction	Ball #1 distance (cm)	Std. dev. (cm)	Ball #2 distance (cm)	Std. dev. (cm)	Ball #3 distance (cm)	Std. dev. (cm)
Short	Uphill	159.5	4.3	162.8	3.9	167.1	4.3
(150 cm)	Downhill	162.6	4.4	160.5	4.8	164.8	4.1
	Average	161.1	4.4	161.7	4.4	166.0	4.2
Medium	Uphill	463.0	6.1	469.6	6.1	484.4	5.6
(450 cm)	Downhill	455.9	8.1	458.7	8.1	480.3	6.9
	Average	459.5	7.1	464.2	7.1	482.4	6.3
Long	Uphill	911.1	7.9	915.9	8.4	930.9	8.1
(900 cm)	Downhill	946.2	10.9	954.0	10.4	983.7	9.4
	Average	928.7	9.4	935.0	9.4	957.3	8.7

construction traveled about 4% farther than Ball #1, the high performance wound 3-piece construction. Since the moment of inertia of these two balls differ by less than 1%, this difference theoretically should be directly related to rebound and forces due to friction. The difference in rebound for the two balls is about 10%. Thus at first approximation, without friction, the correct order of magnitude is achieved. Secondly, the average distance for Ball #2, the high performance 2-piece construction, was greater than Ball #1 in most cases, but statistically different than Ball #1 in only one case, the uphill 450 cm case. This mathematically rigorous statement notwithstanding, it does appear that Ball #2 "tends" to travel a small amount farther than Ball #1. For all but the most consistent putters, it appears that this small amount would be lost in the inconsistency of the stroke. Lastly, the standard deviations in distance for all balls were the same within the testing parameters, and were consistent with the condition of the putt. That is, downhill putts of 450 and 900 cm had higher standard deviations than uphill putts of the same length. This would seem to be logical, since the slower moving downhill putts would be affected more by inconsistencies of each ball, putting stroke, and green than faster moving uphill putts.

Break and Distance

Break and distance testing was performed for two distances using the three golf ball constructions involved in this test. The object of this portion of testing was to determine what effect ball construction had on the amount of break a putted ball encountered. Putter speed was monitored to adjust the distance of each ball type to a common length, so that each putt traveled the same approximate line. Logically, this holds up in the realm of play, in that a player faced with a 350 cm putt tries to

Table 53.3   Results From Break and Distance Putting Test

Distance	Break	Ball #1 distance (cm)	Break (cm)	Ball #2 distance (cm)	Break (cm)	Ball #3 distance (cm)	Break (cm)
Medium (450 cm)	100 cm	449.3	108.2	450.9	113.5	447.3	106.2
Long (900 cm)	200 cm	890.5	191.8	885.7	182.9	889.8	186.2

manipulate his stroke for a specific distance, not a specified putter speed. The results of this testing are included in table 53.3.

The distance information in table 53.3 is the length measured down the line of the putt to the final resting place of the ball, while the break is the perpendicular distance from this line to the ball. The medium length putt included approximately 100 cm in break, while the long putt included a break on the order of 200 cm. The data in table 53.3 shows little differences in the relative break amount of any of the ball construction types. What differences exist follow a logical progression. For slightly longer average distances, the average breaks are slightly larger. In final analysis, this data shows that ball construction does not significantly affect break.

CONCLUSIONS

The results in distance testing showed the same trend as reported by Pelz (1989) for ionomer covered distance 2-piece balls versus high performance 3-piece wound balls, but differences were much smaller. The cover appears to play an important role in the differences between 2-piece and 3-piece wound construction. This is evidenced by the lack of meaningful distance differences between Ball #1 and Ball #2 constructions, and the significant difference between Ball #3 and Balls #1 and #2.

The results for the distance and break testing provided evidence to indicate that ball construction played no part in the break of a putt. The amount of break, as expected, depends only on ball speed and gravity.

The final analysis of this testing has to conclude that there are several important factors in putting as related to golf ball construction. Cover hardness and material probably play the most important role in the distance a ball travels, through rebound off the putter when struck. Compression seems to play a less important role as evidenced by the similar distances in Ball #2 and Ball #3 in all putts struck, despite the fact that they were 14 points apart in average compression. Rebound, typically tested from a 250 cm drop, also plays some role in putting, but is downplayed in magnitude to some extent by friction forces and the roughness of the surface of the green, as indicated by the relative distances between Ball #1 and Ball #3, and Ball

#1 and Ball #2. Clearly the inelastic response of golf balls in putting is not simply characterized by compression or rebound as measured herein.

References

Pelz, D. with Mastroni, N. (1989). *Putt Like the Pros.* pp. 3-4. New York: Harper Perennial.

CHAPTER 54

Mechanical Interaction of the Golf Ball With Putting Greens

Mont Hubbard, LeRoy W. Alaways
Sports Biomechanics Laboratory, Department of Mechanical and Aeronautical Engineering, University of California, Davis, CA, USA

A large percentage of golf shots are putts, but there has been relatively little investigation of the interaction between the ball and the green surface in putting. Previous theoretical results predict that a ball rolling on a viscoelastic surface experiences a rolling friction force which varies with velocity. To determine surface viscoelastic properties, experimental drop tests of balls and wooden blocks on a green were carried out using an accelerometer and LVDT to simultaneously measure acceleration and position. Even from small drop heights (2 cm) several bounces are observed, with contact duration increasing in successive bounces because of the increasing stiffness of the green surface with depth. Equilibrium penetration depth of 2.2 mm and peak accelerations of about 50 g's were observed. Rolling trajectories of balls were measured using 60 Hz video cameras and the coefficient of rolling friction was determined using a parameter estimation procedure. Rolling friction was found to be nearly constant, changing by only about 10% during a single roll, but in the opposite direction to that predicted by the viscoelastic theory of Flom and Beuche (1959), implying that plastic deformation of the grass blades in the soft upper surface layer or their slip on the ball is important, rather than the viscoelastic parameters of the soil subsurface.

Keywords: Rolling friction, putting, rolling resistance, green surface viscoelasticity, golf ball bounce.

INTRODUCTION

More than two-fifths of golf shots are putts and, in a typical round, three of the shots on each hole and roughly two-thirds of those in each round involve rolling of the ball on the green. In spite of this important role of putting, there has been relatively little scientific research focused on the mechanical interaction of the ball rolling on the green.

Two recent papers include models for rolling on the green which hypothesize constant rolling friction forces. Lorensen and Yamron (1992) presented a dynamic model for the ball on the green as a basis for the use of computer graphics to visualize trajectories, but with a relatively crude, piecewise-planar model for the green surface geometry. Alessandrini (1995) characterizes putting as a two-point bound-ary value problem and focuses on the choice of initial conditions which allow the trajectory to terminate at the hole with zero velocity, but also assumes constant rolling friction. Two other studies neglect rolling on the green but instead deal with the dynamics of the ball once it has reached the rim of the hole. Holmes (1991) studied the dynamics of the ball-hole interaction and how these determine capture or escape. Holmes included rolling over and along the rim, possible loss of contact and ensuing ballistic motion, and subsequent collisions with the interior surface of the hole and/or the rim again. Smith and Hubbard (1998) discuss the boundary in the velocity-impact parameter space which separates roll-in and roll-out trajectories on the rim and which corresponds to initial conditions for a set of near quasi-equilibrium roll-around trajectories.

Several references discuss putting from a mostly experimental viewpoint. The book by Soley (1977) contains a wealth of experimental data gathered over many years for both professional and amateur golfers and discusses putting from a quantitative yet practical perspective. The introduction of the Stimpmeter (Stimpson 1974) by the USGA provided a uniform method of measurement and standardiza-tion of putting surfaces. Although the device is inexpensive and relatively easy to use, it is not without its drawbacks, especially when used in research. Some of these have been noted by Holmes (1986) and by Lodge (1992). Lodge designed a ramp capable of launching a ball onto a putting surface in pure rolling at arbitrary speeds without the collisions at green contact and the slipping regions associated with the Stimpmeter. However, both these devices determine an average measure of green speed, defined as the distance rolled with a given initial velocity, implicitly assuming that the deceleration is either constant or that its variation is so small that it can be neglected. Apparently there has been no study of the ball deceleration profile in detail including the dependence, if any, of rolling friction on velocity or other variables. Such knowledge would be required as the theoretical basis of more accurate simulations of rolling (such as improvements to the models of Lorensen and Yamron [1992] and Alessandrini [1995]). Quantities of interest include instan-taneous rolling friction, surface viscoelastic properties during small velocity impacts characteristic of putting, depth of penetration into the green surface, the coefficient of sliding friction between ball and green, and rotational spin-down torque. The purpose of this paper is to present results of several experiments related to the first three of these mechanical interactions of the ball and green surface.

Although earlier measurements of rolling resistance had been done by Coulomb (1785), Reynolds (1876) apparently focused for the first time on a relatively hard object rolling on a more compliant surface and the effect of the slip and friction between the two surfaces on the rolling resistance. Much of the study of rolling friction in the last century has been motivated by losses in ball bearings and rolling of metals into sheets. Examples of this previous work are Tabor (1955), Greenwood, et al. (1961), and Merwin and Johnson (1963), all of which examined deformation losses within the surface material. A different approach of possible interest to the golf ball problem is the paper by Flom and Bueche (1959), who developed a theory of rolling friction for a sphere on a viscoelastic surface which predicted that the coefficient of rolling friction should vary with speed. Although not directly applicable to golf, a more recent series of papers (see the discussion and references in Erlich and Tuszynski, 1995) uses the drift of oscillatory nearly-circular trajectories of balls rolling on a rotating turntable as a measure of rolling friction. Because the theory of Flom and Beuche (1959) seemed most applicable, it motivated the experiments reported here. Specifically, the hypothesis was that variations of rolling friction might occur with speed and that these might be related to the viscoelastic properties (stiffness and damping) of the surface.

SURFACE VISCOELASTIC PROPERTIES

A one-piece golf ball was cut roughly in half and an accelerometer (ICSensors Model 3140-020) was rigidly mounted to its flat top surface as shown in figure 54.1. Because of the spherical ball shape, the green contact force at any instant is an

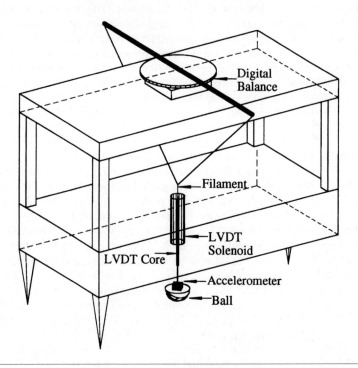

Figure 54.1   Ball bounce instrumentation and experimental setup. An LVDT and accelerometer were mounted on a ball segment (or circular block with flat bottom) to measure acceleration (dynamic green contact force) and position simultaneously. Quasi-static green contact forces were also measured using an accurate digital balance.

integral of pressures acting over a continuum of depths into the green, and is thus not indicative of the viscoelastic restoring force at a specific penetration depth. Thus, in order to obtain data which uniquely characterized viscoelastic properties of the green as a function of depth and its time rate of change, in some experiments the ball segment was replaced with a right cylindrical wooden block of equal mass and radius 4.45 cm but with a flat lower surface. The metal core of a 2.54 cm linear variable differential transformer (LVDT) (Schaevitz model DC-E 500) was rigidly mounted above the accelerometer case. The total mass of the ball (or block)-accelerometer-core combination was maintained near 45 grams so that the results would be applicable to bounces of actual golf balls. This instrumentation allowed simultaneous measurement of position and acceleration during bounce impacts with initial velocities of roughly 0.5 m/sec. Bounce characteristics during high velocity (20-30 m/sec) impacts have been described previously by Haake (1987), who used optical techniques to study the impact of approach shots with the green surface.

Figure 54.1 also shows the rest of the experimental setup for the bounce tests. A massive (10 Kg) three-legged platform constructed from a 10 cm × 10 cm× 80 cm wooden beam allowed inertial stability and precise leveling of the platform relative to the local vertical. The LVDT solenoid was press fit into a 1.9 cm vertical hole drilled in the beam. The ball (or block) was suspended and then dropped from approximately 2.5 cm above the green surface using a filament attached to the top of the core which extended upward through the center of the solenoid. Raw instrument analog outputs were sampled with a laptop computer at a frequency of 10 KHz using a LabVIEW data acquisition program. This sampling frequency allowed approximately 60 data points during the shortest bounce duration of approximately 6 msec, and hence adequate time resolution. This physical arrangement also allowed for quasi-static force-displacement measurements (see figure 54.1) by mounting an accurate (0.02 gram resolution) digital balance on top of the beam. The weight of the instrumented ball or block was transmitted to its upper surface via a stiff collar which encircled the beam and balance and partially supported the object in contact with the green surface below.

Experimental results from a typical bounce of the wooden block are shown in figure 54.2. Although the accelerometer signal is noisy, probably from rubbing of the core on the inside surface of the solenoid, the LVDT position signal is very clean. Indeed, the position resolution of the 12 bit LVDT is only 6.2 microns! Even though the final equilibrium position can be measured very accurately, the noise in the accelerometer signal prevents accurate determination of the exact time at which contact with the green begins. By relying on this accurate position measurement, however, the location of the top of the green surface was determined in the following way.

During free fall the vertical position is quadratic in time since the only substantial force acting is gravity. A segment of position-time data which includes only free fall will therefore be fit well by a quadratic in time, with the coefficient of t^2 being half the gravitational acceleration. If the segment of data includes times when green contact forces act, however, this quadratic fit will deteriorate. A segment of 300 LVDT position data points for the initial fall interval $0 < t < 0.025$ sec in figure 54.2 was extracted which clearly included both free-fall and green contact periods. Data points were then gradually removed from the contact end of the data set, computing at each stage the rms error of the fit, defined as the difference between the predicted quadratic function of time and the measured position.

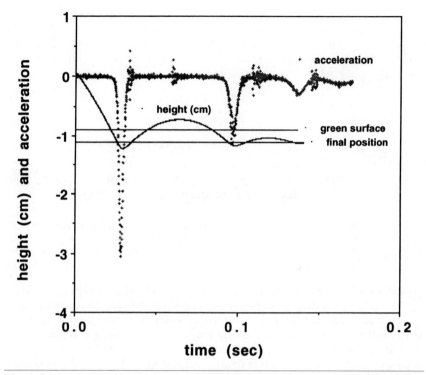

Figure 54.2   LVDT and accelerometer data for 2 cm drop of circular block with upper green surface and final resting positions shown.

Figure 54.3 shows the rms error as a function of the height h_o above which the data points were selected. This function (as well as the added rms error at each stage and the apparent value of free-fall acceleration, not shown here for brevity) changes clearly and dramatically at a value of h_o when the first significant contact forces are present. In this way it was possible to identify the height of the top of the green surface to about 0.1 mm. The final equilibrium resting position lay 2.1 mm below the top green surface, both of which are shown in figure 54.2, and the total maximum green penetration was a bit less than 3 mm. Note in figure 54.3 that the average rms position error of 4.8 microns in flight is consistent with the known LVDT position resolution of 6.2 microns. The apparent value of free-fall acceleration differed by nearly 10% from the known value of g (9.81 m/sec²), due to the electromagnetic force from the LVDT solenoid of roughly 0.04 N on the core.

In figure 54.2 further note that while the first bounce results in loss of contact with the surface, the second and third are merely damped oscillations about the eventual equilibrium position without loss of contact. If we define the duration of each of the bounces as the time spent below the final equilibrium position in an oscillation, successive bounce durations increase (8.77, 10.9, 11.3 msec) as the amplitude decreases. This same trend is apparent in the acceleration signal and results from the hardening spring nature of the nonlinear surface stiffness. Note also that the maximum depth of penetration below the eventual equilibrium position decreases

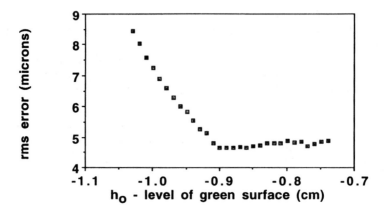

Figure 54.3   Rms position error in quadratic fit of position data in flight versus vertical position below which data is excluded. The top of the green surface lies at the sharp break in the curve $h_o = -0.9$ cm where the rms reaches its steady value of 4.8 microns.

in successive bounces as the energy of the block is lost from the dissipation provided by the surface. The bounce duration and decay can be used to calculate rough approximations for the linearized stiffness and damping (not shown here due to space limitations) of the surface about the final equilibrium position. Bounce results for balls (also not shown here) are very qualitatively similar to, but clearly distinguishable from, the results in figures 54.2 and 54.3. The major differences for balls are slightly larger penetration depths, narrower acceleration pulses during green contact, and less quickly decaying bounce depth, due probably to the decreased importance of the damping provided by the no-longer uniformly thick air layer between the green and ball.

Quasi-static measurements of the force-deflection characteristics of a ball into the green surface in the 2.1 mm deep surface region above equilibrium are shown in figure 54.4a. The ball was placed at several positions partially supported by both the green contact force and force balance. Force measurements were read from the digital balance and subtracted from the weight to obtain the surface contact force. Rather than a constant force as had been expected, force relaxation in time was observed (see figure 54.4b) with a time constant of from 30 to 50 sec. The direction of the relaxation depended on whether the previous position was below or above the set position. Shown in figure 54.4b are four traces corresponding to successively raising the set position, and one in which the position was lowered. Although the force relaxation is too slow to be relevant to rolling, it is interesting and apparently has not been observed previously. Its cause is not known. Apparent in figure 54.4a is the strong nonlinearity of the force-deflection profile.

ROLLING FRICTION MEASUREMENT

Figure 54.5 shows the experimental setup for the rolling friction measurements. Motion of rolling balls was measured using digitized 60 Hz video images (with resolution of 240×256 pixels). A straight rolling line 7.32 m long was laid out on a nearly flat section of green surface on the local El Macero Country Club private course with bent grass greens mowed daily to a height of 3.6 mm (0.140 in). The elevation z(x) as a function of distance x along the rolling line was measured to an accuracy of 1 mm every 0.305 m (1.0 ft) using a surveyor's theodolite. Although visually the green appeared flat, a monotonic change of elevation of 0.089 m was

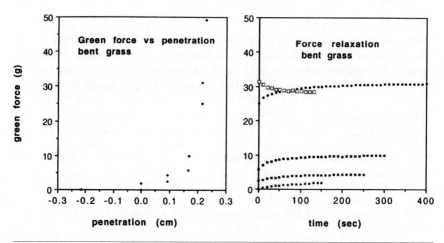

Figure 54.4   (a) Quasi-static green-ball contact force vs. penetration depth in the upper 2.1 mm region, and (b) force relaxation vs. time at given positions. In figure 54.4a two values of force, the initial value and the relaxed value, are shown at each position.

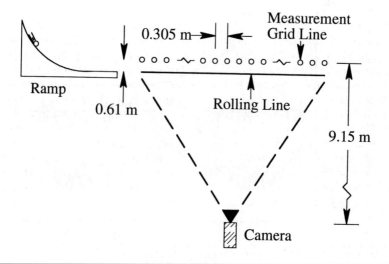

Figure 54.5   Top view of rolling measurements setup. Balls were launched perpendicular to camera axis using a ramp (shown in frontal view) and viewed simultaneously with a grid of balls in background.

observed over the 7.32 m, resulting in a green slope which varied from 0.0110 to 0.0162 about its average of 0.0122. A measurement grid line was constructed parallel to and 0.61 m from the rolling line by placing 25 balls on tees on this line at intervals of 0.305 m. The camera was placed 9.15 m away from the rolling line with its horizontal optical axis in the perpendicular bisector plane of the rolling and grid lines but high enough so that both the rolling ball and the grid balls were visible simultaneously, ensuring that the distance scale grid always lay within the field of view.

Balls were launched repeatedly in pure rolling using a specially constructed ramp similar to the one described by Lodge (1992) (i.e., with a circular region of transition from the constant slope section to the horizontal section), but made from a clear acrylic thermoplastic tube. The 60 Hz images of the fixed balls and rolling ball were updated at each frame and scaled using a scale factor determined from the grid. By zooming the camera it was possible to increase the position resolution for shorter rolls. A typical position vs. time plot for a 4.3 m roll is shown in figure 54.6. Although very little noise is apparent in the position data versus time, successively differentiating this data twice to obtain estimates for the rolling friction force was not feasible because the amplification of the noise swamped the force estimates. Rather, estimates for the rolling friction were obtained in the following way. The two first order differential equations describing position x and velocity v of the ball

$$\dot{v} = -\mu g + g \sin(s(x)) \quad \text{and} \quad \dot{x} = v$$

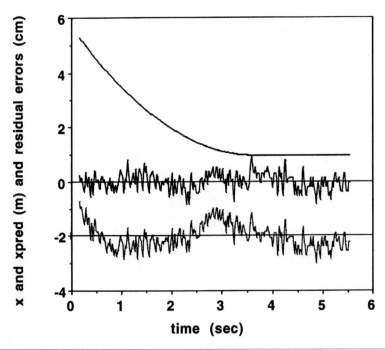

Figure 54.6 Measured and predicted rolling displacement and residuals (magnified 100×) vs. time for two models of rolling friction, constant and linearly varying in time.

were numerically integrated until $v = 0$ as a function of presumed unknown parameters X_o, V_o, and m describing the position and velocity initial conditions and the rolling friction model. The position X_o was assumed to be unknown since the video position data did not include all frames from first ball-green contact. The rolling line slope $s(x)$ was determined from the surveyed elevations according to $s(x) = a \tan (dz/dx)$. Using a nonlinear Newton's-method parameter estimation scheme similar to that described by Hubbard and Alaways (1989), initial guesses for these parameters were iteratively varied and the equations integrated again until a converged best fit of the experimental data was achieved. In this way the substantial and changing effect of gravity (which, even though the green was visibly flat, is here of the order of 20% of the rolling friction coefficient) is able to be removed from the data at every instant rather than in an average sense as proposed by Brede (1991).

The parameters for two different rolling friction models estimated using the rolling data in figure 54.6 are shown in table 54.1. The first model assumes that the rolling friction coefficient μ is constant. The difference between the predicted and measured positions is not able to be detected with the resolution of figure 54.6, although both are plotted in the upper trace. The zero mean error for this model magnified by a factor of 100 is shown in the lowest trace (centered about –2 for distinguishability). Although one is tempted to be satisfied that its rms value of only 4.5 mm is small enough to conclude that rolling friction is indeed constant, the error has clear correlation in time.

Table 54.1   Nonlinear Least Squares Parameters Determined From Data in Figure 54.6

Model	x_o (m)	v_o (m/sec)	μ_o	β (sec-1)
Constant rolling friction	5.286	–2.474	0.0842	0
Linearly varying rolling friction	5.276	–2.440	0.0793	0.00237

The second model allowed the rolling friction coefficient μ to vary linearly with time according to $\mu = \mu_o + \beta t$ (and also approximately linearly with velocity since velocity is nearly linear in time). The two best fit coefficients μ_o and β were identified in the same manner and are also shown in table 54.1. The residual error for this model, plotted as the middle trace in figure 54.6 centered about 0, is clearly less correlated (although still not perfectly white noise) and its rms value decreases significantly to 3.1 mm. The positive value of the coefficient $\beta = 0.00237$ however, which over the motion interval $0 < t < 3.654$ sec leads to variations in friction force of the order of the gravity effects, indicates that the rolling friction actually increases as time increases and the velocity decreases. This variation is opposite to what is predicted from the theory of Flom and Beuche (1959). This analysis suggests that it may be plastic deformation of the grass blades or their slip on the ball rather than viscoelastic surface effects which account for the substantially constant rolling friction force. The source of the smaller variation of rolling friction with time and velocity is not known.

It is of interest to correlate the rolling friction coefficient μ, used in this paper and defined as the weight-specific friction force, with the other commonly used determinant of green rolling friction, Stimpmeter distance x_s or "green speed." It is relatively easy to show that the assumption of constant friction force leads to the relation that $\mu = V_o^2/2gx_s$ so that green speed and friction coefficient are inversely related. If V_o is chosen to be 1.83 m/sec (Holmes 1986), which is very roughly the initial velocity of the ball launched by the Stimpmeter, then rolling friction μ and green speed x_s satisfy $\mu = 0.171/x_s$. Some typical values of x_s and μ are shown in table 54.2.

Table 54.2   Rolling Friction μ as a Function of Stimpmeter Rolling Distance x_s

Stimpmeter distance x_s (ft)	4.5	5.5	6.5	7.5	8.5	9.5	10.5
Stimpmeter distance x_s (m)	1.37	1.68	1.98	2.29	2.59	2.90	3.20
Rolling friction μ	0.125	0.102	0.0862	0.0745	0.0659	0.0589	0.0533

CONCLUSIONS

Although rolling friction of golf balls on green is roughly constant, it does vary by about 10% over the course of a 4.3 m putt. Thus the assumption that rolling friction is constant appears to be a reasonable approximation for average measurements but perhaps not adequate for dynamic simulation of rolling trajectories. It is probably plastic deformation of the grass blades or their slip on the ball rather than viscoelastic surface effects which account for the substantially constant rolling friction force. The small variation of rolling friction (which increases as the velocity decreases) is opposite to that expected from the theory of rolling on viscoelastic surfaces of Flom and Beuche (1959), which predicts that rolling friction should decrease with decreasing velocity.

References

Alessandrini, S.M. 1995. A motivational example for the numerical solution of two-point boundary-value problems. *SIAM Review* 37: 423-427.

Brede, A.D. 1991. Correction for slope in green speed measurements of golf course putting greens. *Agronomy Journal* 83: 425-426.

Coulomb, C.A. 1785. Theory of simple machines. *Memoire de Mathematique et Physique de l'Academie Royale*.

Erlick, R. and J. Tuszynski. 1995. Ball on a rotating turntable: comparison of theory and experiment. *American Journal of Physics* 63: 351-359.

Flom, D.G. and A.M. Beuche. 1959. Theory of rolling friction for spheres. *Journal of Applied Physics* 10: 1725-1730.

Greenwood, J.A., H. Minshall, and D. Tabor. 1961. Hysteresis losses in rolling and sliding friction. *Proceedings of the Royal Society, London* 259A: 480-507.

Haake, S.J. 1987. An apparatus for measuring the physical properties of golf turf. *Journal of the Sports Turf Institute* 63: 149-152.

Holmes, B.W. 1986. Dialogue concerning the Stimpmeter. *The Physics Teacher* 24:401-404.

Holmes, B.W. 1991. Putting: how a golf ball and hole interact. *American Journal of Physics* 59:129-136.

Hubbard, M. and L.W. Alaways. 1989. Rapid and accurate estimation of release conditions in the javelin throw. *Journal of Biomechanics* 22:583-595.

Lodge, T.A. 1992. An apparatus for measuring green "speed." *Journal of the Sports Turf Institute* 68:128-130.

Lorensen, W.E. and B. Yamron. 1992. Golf green visualization. *IEEE Computer Graphics and Applications* 12(4):35-44.

Merwin, J.E and K.L. Johnson. 1963. An analysis of plastic deformation in rolling contact. *Proceedings of the Institution of Mechanical Engineers* 177: 676-688.

Reynolds, O. 1876. On rolling friction. *Philosophical Transactions of the Royal Society, London* 166:155-174.

Soley, C. 1977. *How well should you putt?* San Jose, California: Soley Golf Bureau.

Smith, T. and M. Hubbard. 1998. Dynamics of golf ball-hole interactions: rolling around the rim. *ASME Journal of Dynamic Systems, Measurement and Control.*

Stimpson, E.S. 1974. Putting greens – How fast? *USGA Golf Journal* 27:28-29.

Tabor, D. 1955. The mechanism of rolling friction; II the elastic range. *Proceedings of the Royal Society, London* 229A: 198-220.

CHAPTER 55

Observations on the Wake Characteristics of Spinning Golf Balls

Matthew B. Stanczak and Lane D. Lemons
Dunlop Maxfli Sports Corporation, Westminster, SC, USA

Donald E. Beasley and James A. Liburdy
Clemson University, Clemson, SC, USA

The lift and drag characteristics of spinning golf balls are the primary determining factor in aerodynamic performance. In the present study, extensive hot wire velocity measurements were made in the turbulent wake of the golf ball to characterize differences in wakes resulting from changes in dimple pattern or design. The measurements were made in a low-turbulence wind tunnel having a 0.7 m square cross-sectional area. The golf ball was held on an aerodynamic sting and spun at 3000 RPM. Time-resolved velocity measurements allowed examination of the fundamental statistics of the velocity as a function of spatial location in the wake.

Wake characteristics are presented for three dimple patterns. Aerodynamic performance of the three golf balls was significantly different, as determined from machine testing using a driver. The wake characteristics are presented in terms of the size of the wake, streamwise mean velocity distribution, and RMS values of the fluctuating velocity component. The three dimple patterns exhibit markedly different wake characteristics. Observations are made concerning the correlation between the measured wake characteristics and the aerodynamic performance.

Keywords: Golf ball, aerodynamics, dimple pattern, wake characteristics.

INTRODUCTION

Aerodynamic force on a golf ball in flight is a result of both frictional and pressure forces acting over the surface of the spinning ball. For convenience, the single resultant aerodynamic force is resolved into components along the flight path and normal to it; these components are termed drag and lift, respectively. Because

440

essentially all high-performance golf balls are near the maximum allowable launch speed, aerodynamics is the primary determining factor in carry distance on driver shots. The dimples uniquely determine the aerodynamic performance of a golf ball under specific launch conditions.

Wakes are formed behind objects that have a shape or orientation that causes the flow to separate. As the air flows around the surface of the ball, it does not have enough momentum to overcome the adverse pressure forces created by the curvature of the surface, and the flow will separate from the surface and rejoin the free stream. The point at which this occurs is called the separation point. The region behind the sphere, between the two separation points, is an area of low pressure. In other words, the average pressure on the golf ball on the downstream half of the ball is considerably less than on the side facing the airflow, or the upstream side. The net result of the force created by this pressure difference is called form drag, and is essentially a resistance to the movement of the ball through the air. The form drag is directly related to the location of the points of separation on the ball and the formation of the wake. Wakes are characterized by velocities less than the velocity in the undisturbed, or freestream, flow and grow laterally in the downstream flow direction. The edges of the wake are regions of high shear due to large changes in velocity over small distances.

In the present study, extensive hot-wire velocity measurements were made in the wake of a spinning golf ball to examine differences in the wake characteristics of balls having significantly different lift and drag characteristics. These differences in lift and drag are characterized by ball performance on driver shots measured on the test range at the Dunlop Maxfli Sports Corporation Outdoor Research Center in Westminster, SC, USA.

EXPERIMENTAL FACILITY AND MEASUREMENTS

The subsonic flow examined here was generated in a variable-speed, suction type, open-circuit wind tunnel located in the Department of Mechanical Engineering, Clemson University. The wind tunnel has a contraction ratio of 9:1. The range of velocity used during testing was 62.98 to 65.43 m/s, corresponding to Reynolds numbers based on ball diameter from 174,329 to 181,103. The wind tunnel test section dimensions are 57 cm (22.4 inches) square by 240 cm (94.5 in) long. Honeycomb and screens, followed by a settling section, are used to reduce turbulence levels in the test section and promote a uniform velocity distribution in the wind tunnel. The tunnel is driven by a Buffalo Forge centrifugal blower having a 1.13 m wheel diameter (size 890) with a rated capacity of 1130 (40,000 cfm) at 14 cm (5 + in) of water. The wind tunnel exhibited a minimum working turbulence intensity of 0.44% at 20 m/s. A sting was employed to hold the ball in the air stream and to spin it at a known rate. The spinning sting provided a drive rod encased in a streamlined housing. Balls were mounted on the drive rod by drilling a stepped hole through the center of the ball. A DC variable-speed motor and a variable, regulated DC power supply controlled the spin rate. Using a stroboscope to measure the peripheral velocity, the ball was set to 3000 rpm ± 25 rpm.

Hot-wire anemometry was used to measure the component of the velocity in the downstream direction, or the streamwise velocity component. Hot-wire anemometry employs an electronic circuit to maintain a noble metal wire at an elevated, constant temperature. The power required is a direct indication of the air speed. A single TSI tungsten 1260-TI.5 constant-temperature hot wire was used to measure velocity. A traversing mechanism was employed to accurately locate the hot wire in the wake of the spinning golf ball. The ball was spun around its vertical axis. Velocity measurements were made in a horizontal plane located at the center of the ball, and perpendicular to the vertical spin axis. Streamwise velocity data was obtained in the horizontal plane at the vertical center of each ball. Velocity measurements were made at x/D of 0.2, 0.5, 0.75, 1, 1.25, 1.5, 1.75, and 2, where D is the ball diameter, and x is the distance measured in the streamwise direction, with $x = 0$ at the rear (downstream) surface of the ball. At each x/D location, twenty-four velocity measurements were made on a base grid having 5 mm intervals. During these measurements the probe was moved in a direction perpendicular to the flow and in a horizontal plane; this direction is termed the spanwise direction. Relative to the center of the ball, this grid was displaced 1.5 cm toward the side of the ball spinning against the wind to account for the wake deflection in that direction. In addition, more detailed measurements were made in the wake based on information gained from the initial measurements made on the base grid described above. A refined wake region was identified based on an increase in the RMS value of the velocity, and a corresponding decrease in the mean velocity from the freestream data. The number of spanwise measurements ranged from a minimum of 48 to a maximum of 64 measurements over the 11.5 cm traversing span.

RESULTS

As summarized in table 55.1, flight testing of Balls 1, 2, and 3 indicated significant differences in the aerodynamic performance, with a resulting range of variation in carry distance for driver shots from 7 to 8%. As such, these balls should provide an opportunity to examine whether significant differences in lift and drag correlate with measurably different wake characteristics.

As previously discussed, flow separates from the surface of the ball creating a low-pressure region at the rear of the ball. Separation points located further toward the rear of the ball yield smaller drag forces due to pressure, and smaller wakes. An important fundamental characteristic of flow around a golf ball is related to the spin,

Table 55.1   Aerodynamic Performance From Flight Testing

| Ball identification | Normalized Distances and Trajectory Height | | |
	Carry distance	Total distance	Trajectory height
Ball 1	0.919	0.884	1.000
Ball 2	1.000	1.000	0.74
Ball 3	0.934	0.969	0.60

and the way the spin changes the relative velocity between the surface of the ball and the air. Assuming the ball has been struck with sufficient skill to impart backspin, the relative velocity between the top of the ball and the air is lower than the relative velocity at the bottom of the ball. Pressure forces resulting from these differences in relative velocity result in a force normal to the direction the ball is traveling, typically termed lift. The same effects that cause lift cause the wake of the golf ball to be deflected downward. This in fact is required to satisfy Newton's second law! It should be noted that lift and drag are defined in flight path coordinates, and are not, in general, horizontal and vertical forces.

Figure 55.1 shows wakes for the three golf balls listed in table 55.1. The edges of the wake are defined as the point in the flow where the decrease in velocity is 50% of the maximum decrease relative to the speed in the undisturbed flow. There are dramatic differences in the size of these wakes in the lateral, or spanwise, direction with the widest wake corresponding to the ball with the shortest carry distance. In fact, the wake of Ball 1 grows so rapidly that it is outside the range of the measurements at 1.5 ball diameters downstream. It is reasonable to assume that Ball 1 has relatively higher lift and drag than Balls 2 and 3, based on the trajectory height data in table 55.1. Ball 2 has a highly optimized dimple pattern; the resulting wake is clearly the smallest in lateral extent.

Figure 55.2 shows a contour plot of Root-Mean-Square (RMS) values of the streamwise velocity in the wake. These RMS values measure the degree of velocity fluctuations in the wake in a form appropriate to the description of turbulent kinetic energy. The plot shows significantly higher turbulence near the ball on the side

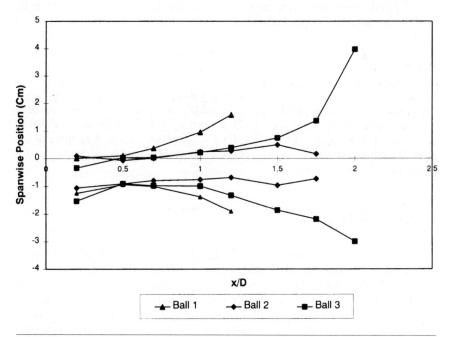

Figure 55.1   Wake size as a function of streamwise distance for Balls 1, 2, and 3. Spanwise origin is located at the center of the ball.

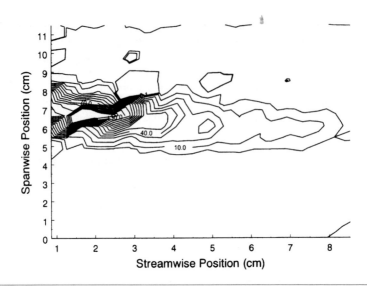

Figure 55.2   Contour plot of RMS values of streamwise velocity in the wake of Ball 2; the center of the ball is at a spanwise position of 6.5 cm.

spinning against the wind direction. Such characteristics may be useful in understanding the role of dimples in controlling lift and drag. Clearly, the pressure and velocity in the wake determine the resulting aerodynamic forces on the golf ball.

If the momentum changes in the flow are appropriately quantified, the forces on the ball may be determined from Newton's second law. Diaz et al. (1983 and 1985) suggested a means of determining a relative measure of drag from velocity measurements in the wake of a spinning cylinder. The drag force is proportional to the product of the wake width, w, and the maximum velocity deficit, ΔU_m, in the self-similar region of the wake. Employing this method of characterizing drag, figure 55.3 may be constructed; the figure plots $w \times \Delta U_m$. This relative estimate of the drag is most valid at the highest value of x/D in figure 55.3, because the proportionality assumes the wake is self-similar. The relative magnitude of the drag force determined by this method is clearly in agreement with the observed flight characteristics of the three balls.

CONCLUSIONS

Three methods of characterizing the wake of a spinning golf ball have been employed to examine the relationship between measurable characteristics of the wake and the aerodynamic performance of dimple patterns. The results suggest that the lateral extent of the wake varies dramatically among dimple patterns having significant differences in aerodynamic performance. Turbulence levels in the wake, as measured by RMS values of the streamwise velocity, clearly show that regions of high shear and turbulence occur near the ball on the side spinning against the free stream. Estimates of the drag based on measured characteristics of the velocities in the wake correlate well with observed flight characteristics.

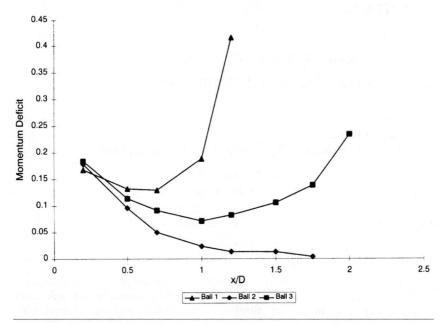

Figure 55.3   Momentum deficit ($w \times \Delta U_m$); this value represents relative values of drag as determined from momentum considerations.

References

Diaz, F., J. Gavalda, J. G. Kawall, and F. Giralt, 1983, "Interpretation of the Complex Turbulent Flow Generated by a Rotating Cylinder," in *Structure of Complex Turbulent Shear Flow*, edited by R. Dumas and L. Fulachier, Springer Verlag, New York, 175-184.

Diaz, F., J. Gavalda, J. G. Kawall, J. F. Keffer, and F. Giralt, 1985, "Asymmetrical Wake Generated by a Spinning Cylinder," *AIAA Journal*, 23: 49-54.

CHAPTER 56

Flow Characteristics of a Golf Ball Using Visualization Techniques

K. Aoki and Y. Nakayama
Department of Mechanical Engineering, Tokai University, Japan

T. Hayasida, N. Yamaguti, and M. Sugiura
Yokohama Rubber Co. Ltd., Kanagawa, Japan

This paper describes flow characteristics of a golf ball using visualization techniques. This experiment shows the flow visualization around a rotating ball using the spark tracing method and the pressure distribution brought about when the ball is rotated at the rate of 0 to 5000 rpm in a case where Re Numbers are $2 \times 10^4 \sim 1.2 \times 10^5$ (flying speed: $6 \sim 42$ m/s). From these results, it is found that in the range of flying speed 6 ~ 42 m/s, the flow around a spherical body is laminar, whereas a golf ball shifts to be turbulent at 21 m/s ($Re = 6 \times 10^4$). With respect to a golf ball in rotation, as the Re numbers became greater, the amount of the transfer of the removal point was made smaller as the rotational frequency became greater. Furthermore, lift coefficient (C_L) is found to increase spin, and drag coefficient (C_D) also increased as a result of induced drag effects associated with C_D.

Keywords: Flow characteristic, flow visualization, pressure distribution, golf ball.

INTRODUCTION

The discovery of Magnus force on ball lift (Magnus force) is familiar to us as the curve of a baseball and the slice and hook of golf balls. It goes back to the age of Newton and, it is said, two centuries before the discovery by Magnus of the lift on a spinning column.[1] As to a smooth ball, there is a very interesting report that in Macoll's experimental result[2] negative lift occurred when the spin rate was small; Taneda[3] also related this phenomenon to a problem of transition of turbulent flow in the boundary layer on the surface of a smooth ball. In the case of balls having seams and dimples, there are the experimental results of Tani about a baseball[4] and of P.W.

446

Bearman about a golf ball,[5] in which the drag and lift were measured. But a golf ball flying at high speed or a spinning golf ball is complicated and its flow mechanism is not clear at the practical flow velocity. In this report the lift and drag were measured by changing the ratio of flow velocity and rotational speed using a golf ball, which gave a uniform turbulent boundary layer in any rotating direction, and a smooth ball of the same diameter. The pressure distribution of the rotating golf ball was measured at rotating speed from 0 to 5000 rpm. The phenomena of separation in laminar boundary layer and turbulent boundary layer were visualized using the oil film method and spark tracing method and the mutual relationship was investigated.

EXPERIMENTAL APPARATUS AND METHOD[6, 7]

Drag and Lift

The measurement of the drag and lift developing on a golf ball and a smooth ball was performed using the device shown in figure 56.1. A golf ball on the market (made by Yokohama Rubber Co., Ltd., PRGR M-43) was used for the experiment; its diameter was 42.7 mm. Putting putty into the dimples of a golf ball and polishing it makes a smooth ball. This ball was set up in a uniform flow of the wind tunnel. As the measuring section of the wind tunnel is 300 mm × 300 mm, the blockage ratio is 0.016, so the wall effect is almost negligible. The golf ball was supported by

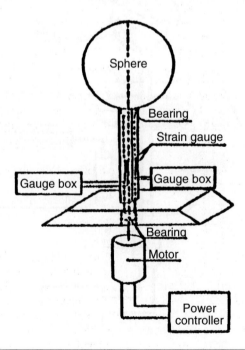

Figure 56.1   Experimental apparatus for drag and lift measurement.

a square pillar of side length 5 mm, which gave some effect to the measuring results of lift and drag. But it is difficult to estimate the value. Two strain gauges were stuck on two faces intersecting at the right angle of this pillar. These output voltages were amplified by a strain gauge amplifier, and the measured values were obtained by a F.F.T. The rotation was given by a motor set up underneath, and was controlled by a power controller, and the spin rate was regulated by using a stroboscope. The drag and lift were calibrated by giving a standard force at the end of the pillar.

Visualization of Separation Point

Figure 56.2 shows an experimental apparatus for flow visualization. Two sets of electrodes, one a needle electrode on a sphere face and the other a line electrode, were set up (see figure 56.3). Spark trains were made on a sphere surface at the same time, supplying as high as 125 kV with a high voltage, high frequency, pulse generator, and the separation points were visualized clearly. A photopickup was set on a disk so as to generate spark lines at a fixed position of the electrodes when a ball rotates. The maximum output voltage is 250 kV. The pulse width is $0.5 \sim 1 \mu$ s, the repetition frequency is 100 kHz. The number of pulses, the pulse intervals, the time of generating pulses, etc. can be set freely. The circuit diagram of the pulse generator is shown in figure 56.4.

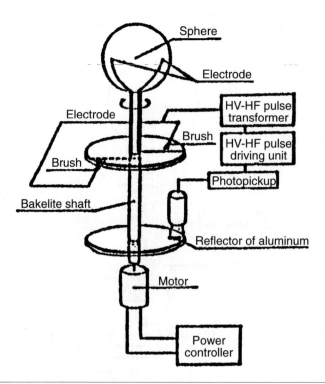

Figure 56.2   Experimental apparatus for flow visualization.

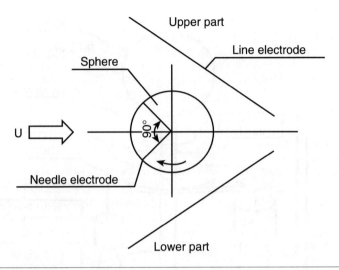

Figure 56.3   Layout of electrodes.

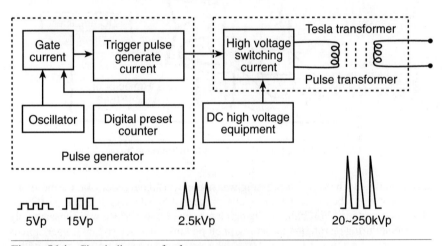

Figure 56.4   Circuit diagram of pulse generator.

Pressure Measurement and Method

In measuring the pressure distribution on the surface of a spherical body (its typical example is a golf ball), the device as shown in figure 56.5 was used. For the pressure on the surface of the spherical body, a semiconductor pressure detector with compensation circuits for sensitivity and temperature (made by Toyota-Koki Inc., rating pressure—0.1 ~ 0.1 kgf/cm^2) was used. The detector was buried inside the spherical body, and the pressure from the pressure-measuring hole on the spherical surface was transmitted to the detector through an injection needle. The transmission of the electric pulse from the rotary system to the static system was made through a slip ring using

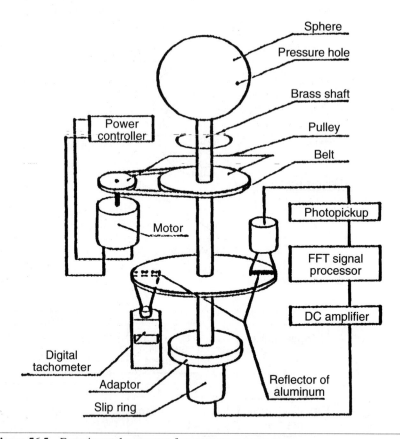

Figure 56.5   Experimental apparatus for pressure measurement.

a DC amplifier. The signal processing was made by a signal processor. Furthermore, the output from the meter was computer-processed to calculate pressure coefficient (Cp). For a rotating golf ball, the changing pressure on its surface was consecutively measured during its rotation by setting photopickups on a disc so that trigger signals are generated when o is 0° and 360°. The averaging computation was made with a signal processor to eliminate disturbing elements. The revolution was given to a pulley set on the shaft from a monitor through a belt. The revolving cycle was read on a digital revolution counter and was controlled by a power controller. Figure 56.6 shows the rotating direction and the nomenclature as seen from above the rotating shaft.

EXPERIMENTAL RESULTS AND CONSIDERATIONS

Drag Coefficient and Lift Coefficient[6, 7]

Drag coefficient (C_D)and lift coefficient (C_L) were obtained by determining a drag and a lift

$$C_D = \frac{D}{1/2 A p U^2} \qquad C_L = \frac{L}{1/2 A p U^2}$$

where A: projected area of sphere (π $d^2/4$), p: density, U: flow velocity. As seen in figure 56.7, the C_D value complies with the Reynolds numbers of the sphere body and golf ball in a static state. The solid line, dotted line, and single-point dotted line are measured with a strain gauge. The C_D value in figure 56.7 indicates an almost

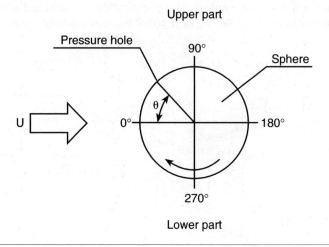

Figure 56.6   Rotating and flow direction.

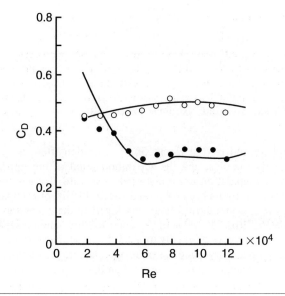

Figure 56.7   Drag coefficient C_D for Re.

settled amount. No value reaches the critical Re with respect to the Re in this range, from which it is believed that the inside of the boundary layer maintains the state of laminar flow. However, the C_D value of the golf ball gives the minimum value with the Re in a vicinity of 6×10^4, and the value maintains a settled amount at almost $C_D = 0.3$ even if the Re is increased. This might be caused by the fact that turbulent flow was induced inside the boundary layer by the dimple on the surface, and the critical Re is lowered. Figure 56.8 shows the relation of C_D and C_L to the ratio of rotation speed $\alpha = V/U$ ($V = \pi \, dn/60$: peripheral speed) about a sphere ball. The values of C_D exist in the range from 0.4 to 0.5, and the value of C_L becomes negative with decreasing Reynolds numbers. This phenomenon is considered as following: the peripheral velocity of the C_L of a golf ball becomes large with increasing

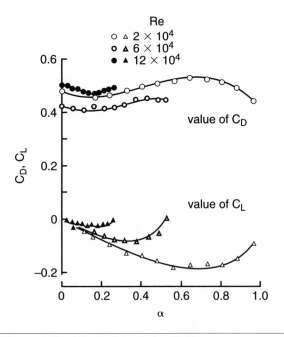

Figure 56.8   Characteristic of C_D, C_L for α (sphere ball).

Reynolds numbers and α (see figure 56.9). Turbulent flow is induced in the boundary layer by dimples, and the separation point of the upper part moves downstream, so the separation area is distorted downward. Besides, the flow around a golf ball is affected by its high rotational speed; the lift of comparatively large value develops with asymmetrical boundary layers in the upper and lower layers, shown in figure 56.12(b). The value of C_D seems to show laminar separation still in Re $= 2 \times 10^4$, and increases gradually to $\alpha = 0.5$. This is because the influences of dimples and rotation are large, and the value of C_D becomes small by the shifting of a separation point, when α becomes larger than 0.5.

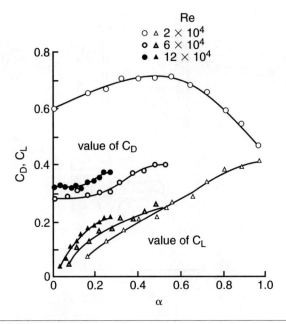

Figure 56.9   Characteristic of C_D, C_L for α (golf ball).

Pressure Distribution

Where the pressure at point θ is p_θ and the static pressure of uniform flow is p_∞, coefficient Cp is given by the following formula:

$$C_p = \frac{2(p_\theta - p_\infty)}{\rho u^2}$$

Figures 56.10a, b, and c show the pressure distribution brought about when the ball is rotated at the rate of $0 \sim 5000$ rpm in a case where the Reynolds number is $2 \sim 12 \times 10^4$. In cases where the Reynolds number is 2×10^4, the boundary layer around the golf ball is a laminar flow when the ball is in a static state. However, when rotating the removal point is shifted to 130° at the top (i.e., in a side where the rotational direction and the direction of the homogeneous flow rate conform to each other). Furthermore, as the rotational frequency is increased, it is conceived that the said point shifted downstream to the vicinity of 150°. In cases where the Reynolds number is 6×10^4, the inside of the boundary layer is shifted to turbulence owing to the dimples, even in a static state different from the case where Re is 2×10^4. This compels the removal point to shift to the vicinity of 110°. When rotation is given in such a state, the shift of the removal point on the top is not so large in comparison with the case where Re is 2×10^4. Despite the above, the shift in the downstream direction is seen in the vicinity of 130° to 150°. However, the lower separation point

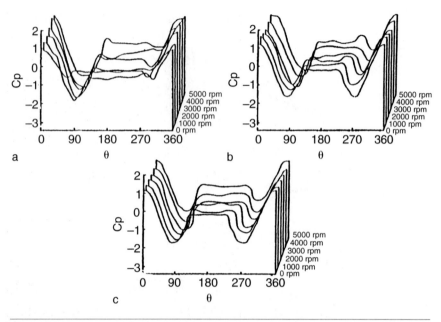

Figure 56.10   Pressure distribution Cp for rotational frequency: (a) Re = 2 × 10⁴; (b) Re = 7 × 10⁴; and (c) Re = 12 × 10⁴.

locates at the 100° point (counterclockwise) for a nonrotating ball, but at the 90° point (counterclockwise) for a ball rotating at 5000 rpm (moving upstream by 10°). This tendency is seen too when Re = 6 × 10⁴, but the distance of shift is smaller. This is due to the fact that the effect of rotation is small as the rotation speed ratio α is small.

Visualization of Separation Points by Spark Tracing Method

The result for a sphere ball is shown in figures 56.11a and b, and the positions of separation points are approximately 80°. The result for a golf ball is shown in figures 56.11c and d, and the separation points are approximately 110°. By these experiments, it was made clear that the separation point can be obtained by the spark tracing method in the case of a rotating ball. Figures 56.12a and b show the flow visualization photographs of a ball rotating at Re = 7 × 10⁴, (a) showing the movement to a downstream separation point of the lower part, and (b) showing the movement to the upstream side of a separation point of the lower part.

CONCLUSION

In this experiment, the behavior of flow around the golf ball was made clear, especially for the shift of separation point.

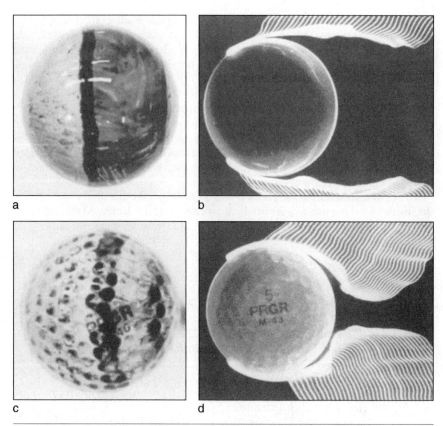

Figure 56.11   Comparison of separation points by oil film method [(a) Sphere ball and (c) Golf ball] and the spark tracing method [(b) Sphere ball and (d) Golf ball]. (Re = 7 × 10⁴).[6, 7]

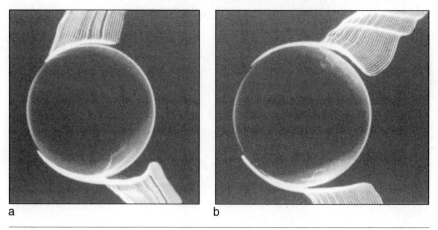

Figure 56.12   Visualization of separation points in spinning ball by spark tracing method: (a) Sphere ball and (b) Golf ball (Re = 7 × 10⁴, N = 4000 rpm).[6, 7]

It became clear that a turbulent boundary layer was made compulsory by the function of dimples; the separation point moved toward downstream and the separation area became small. According to these effects, it became clear that the value of C_D became small and the value of C_L became large with increasing value of α.

In a range of the flying speed 6-42 m/s, the flow around a spherical body is laminar, where a golf ball shifts to be turbulent at 21 m/s (Re $6 = 10^4$).

With respect to a golf ball in rotation, the removal point on the top was transferred downstream and the one on the bottom was transferred upstream. As the Reynolds numbers became greater, the shift amount of the separation point was made smaller. Meanwhile as the rotational frequency became greater, the amount of the transfer was made greater.

The C_D obtained during the rotation was increased to the extent of $\alpha = 0.6$ when the inside of the boundary layer is a laminar flow and was decreased thereafter. At the turbulent state, a tendency was for the said value to increase. Furthermore, as α increased, C_L increased.

References

[1]Tsuji, S. et al. (1986), *Trans. Japan Soc. Mech. Eng.* (in Japanese), vol. 52, No. 474, B557.

[2]Macoll, J.H. (1982), *J.R. Aeronant Soc.,* 32, 777.

[3]Taneda, S. (1957), *Rep. Res. Lnst. Mech.* (Kyushu Univ.), 5-20, 123.

[4]Tani, I. (1950), *Science* (in Japanese), vol. 20, No. 9, 405.

[5]Bearman, P.W. and J.K. Harvey. (1976-5), 112.

[6]Nakayama, Y., K. Aoki, M. Kato, K. Ohmura, and T. Okumoto., *Flow Visualization Around Golf Ball,* 2nd International Symposium on Fluid-Control, Measurement, Mechanics, and Flow Visualisation, Sept. 1988, Sheffield, England, 10-13.

[7]Aoki, K. and T. Kobayasi, *Flow Visualization of a Golf Ball,* Symposium on Sports Engineering '93. No. 930-69, Nov. 1993, 99-102.

CHAPTER 57

The "Row Effect" Anomaly in the 336 Octahedron Dimple Pattern

S. Aoyama
Titleist and Foot-Joy Worldwide, Fairhaven, MA, USA

An orientation specific anomaly in the aerodynamic characteristics of the classic 336 octahedron dimple pattern is identified and quantified through wind tunnel testing. Its effects on lift and drag coefficients are measured throughout the ranges of spin rates and Reynolds numbers encountered by a golf ball during a typical driver trajectory. An evaluation is made of the possible flight performance effects of the anomaly, and the possible effect on a player's game.

Keywords: Aerodynamics, lift, drag, wind tunnel, dimple pattern, 336 octahedron, symmetry, trajectory, orientation.

INTRODUCTION

During the 1970s, the dimple patterns typically used on golf balls began to change quite rapidly. The previous several decades had been dominated almost exclusively by the 336 octahedron dimple layout, sometimes referred to as the "Atti" pattern (see figure 57.1). This layout was based on a division of the ball's surface into eight identical spherical triangles, which were filled with dimples in concentric triangular rings. Assembly of these eight triangles into a complete sphere resulted in a pattern dominated by nearly straight, spaced latitudinal rows and columns of dimples. One of the reasons this layout began to fall out of favor was the presumption of a "row effect": that these latitudinal rows would generate anomalous aerodynamic behavior at certain specific spin axis orientations. Specifically, if the spin axis should happen to fall precisely along the polar axis of these latitudinal rows, then the dimples would simply follow one behind the other as the ball rotated, leaving narrow bands of ball surface (the spaces between the rows) undisturbed by the passage of dimples.

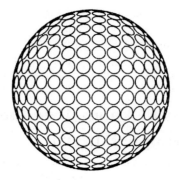

Figure 57.1   336 octahedron dimple pattern.

The patterns which replaced the 336 octahedron were predominantly icosahe-dron based (see figure 57.2). In their purest forms, such layouts are completely devoid of continuous straight rows of dimples. In practice, however, the intrusion of a mold parting line usually creates at least one pair of nearly straight rows.

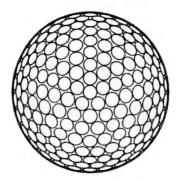

Figure 57.2   392 icosahedron dimple pattern.

However intuitive the notion of a row effect in the 336 octahedron dimple pattern may be, there has been little if any direct evidence presented to support it. This research is intended to determine whether or not such an effect actually exists, and if so, to quantify it and assess its potential impact on a player's game.

EXPERIMENTAL METHODS

Wind Tunnel Test Method

The wind tunnel testing of golf balls presents some unusual challenges. Primary among these is the need to spin the ball while measurements are made, and to do so without using any physical attachments to the ball that might alter the flow field. Davies (1949) presented a clever solution to this problem, sometimes called the "ball-drop" method. Using a specially constructed mechanism, he suspended and spun the ball above the wind tunnel test section, then dropped it through the airstream and recorded its impact point on the tunnel floor. By successively spinning the ball in opposite directions, and making some simplifying assumptions, he was able to estimate the lift and drag forces.

A substantially updated version of Davies' method was reported by Aoyama (1990). The entire drop trajectory, rather than just the endpoint, was recorded with a video camera, while a digital computer provided a means of solving the equations of motion, thus determining the lift and drag forces without the need for any compromising simplifications. This was the method employed in this study.

Wind Tunnel Facility

The updated ball-drop method requires a specialized low turbulence wind tunnel equipped with a ball spin mechanism and a vertically elongated test section to provide adequate drop distance. Appropriate video equipment, computer, and software are also needed for data capture and reduction. The Titleist wind tunnel facility includes all of these features, and was used for all lift and drag measurements in this study.

Test Specimens

Since golf balls having the 336 octahedron dimple pattern are not easily found today, reproductions were made of the Titleist "K2" model of the early 1970s. The dimples were formed in original production molds, guaranteeing an accurate representation of a pattern that was at one time in popular use. Each dimple was nominally spherical in shape with a diameter of 3.52 mm and a depth of 0.33 mm.

To facilitate accurate spin axis orientation, each ball was marked with a great circle stripe approximately 0.3 mm wide, accurately centered between two latitudinal rows of dimples. With this dimple pattern, there are three possible locations for such a great circle, all substantially identical with regard to dimple layout geometry. However, one of the locations corresponds to the mold parting line, which has been buffed as part of the manufacturing process to remove mold flash. Since this buffing can have a small effect on the dimensions of adjacent dimples, the parting line location was not used for striping.

Test Procedure

Using the methods described by Aoyama (1990), lift and drag coefficients were measured over a spin rate range of 1500 to 4500 rpm and a Reynolds number (Rn) range of about 60,000 to 200,000. This covers the envelope of conditions encountered by golf balls during the typical drive trajectories of a large majority of golfers.

A complete set of test data was recorded for each of two spin axis orientation conditions: (1) random, and (2) aligned perpendicular to the great circle stripe (and thus perpendicular to latitudinal dimple rows). For this row-aligned condition, the ball's spin axis was carefully oriented so that the runout of the great circle stripe was less than 0.3 mm. This resulted in a spin axis orientation within 0.4 degrees of perpendicular to the latitudinal dimple rows.

RESULTS AND DISCUSSION

Lift and Drag Coefficients

The measured differences in drag coefficient (C_D) between the random and row-oriented conditions are presented in the contour plot of figure 57.3. Positive numbers indicate that the row-aligned orientation is greater, a convention which will be followed throughout this study. It can be seen that the differences are rather small over much of the ranges, especially at the important higher Rn region. However, the row-aligned condition creates substantially more drag at some low spin/low Rn conditions and substantially less drag at high spin/high Rn conditions. This mimics an effect observed in some less aggressive types of dimple geometry, which are less effective at tripping the boundary layer into a turbulent state. At lower speeds and spin rates, the boundary layer is not effectively transitioned to turbulent form, and thus the drag is greater. On the other hand, such dimpling is well suited to higher speeds and spin rates, where it is sufficient to cause turbulent transition without excessively disturbing the flow. This results in very low drag.

Figure 57.4 shows similar data for lift coefficient (C_L). Again, the differences are rather small over a substantial portion of the spin and Rn ranges, but there are localized areas of greater effect. Specifically, the row-aligned orientation generates

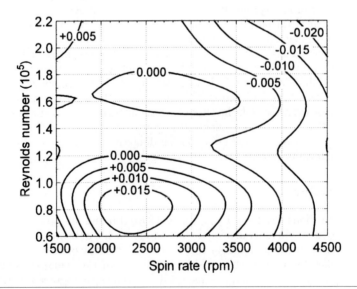

Figure 57.3   Difference in drag coefficient between row-aligned and random orientations.

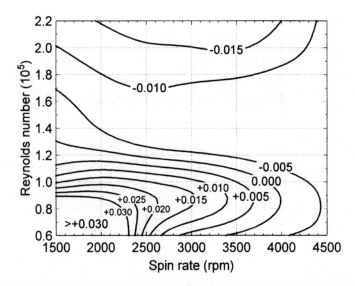

Figure 57.4   Difference in lift coefficient between row-aligned and random orientations.

somewhat less lift across most spin rates at high Rn, and much greater lift at low spin/low Rn. This is a further similarity between the row-aligned orientation and less aggressive dimpling. Under low spin/low Rn conditions, aggressive dimpling can encourage the "negative Magnus effect," in which a negative lift force is created by boundary layer transition which is asymmetrical between the upper and lower surfaces of the ball. Under the same conditions, less aggressive dimpling may not create this effect, resulting in lift which is comparatively much greater.

For both C_L and C_D, perhaps the most interesting finding is the relative sameness of the two orientations over a majority of the tested conditions. Although this may tend to contradict the long held assumption of a significant row effect in the 336 octahedron dimple pattern, it is not entirely unexpected. In order to maximally manifest such an effect, the flow must be substantially two-dimensional in nature. In other words, the air must flow in substantially parallel planes perpendicular to the spin axis. In reality, however, the flow around a spinning sphere satisfies this condition only at or near the equatorial plane. Thus, only the dimple rows adjacent to the equator are likely to contribute to a row effect, and these constitute less than 20% of the dimples on the ball.

Driver Trajectories

From a practical standpoint, the golfer is only interested in what, if any, impact this may have on his or her game. To this end, it is a rather cumbersome but relatively straightforward problem to calculate the flight path of a golf ball (Aoyama 1994). There are only two forces acting on a ball in flight: the aerodynamic force (resolved into lift and drag components), and the ball's weight. By knowing these, and specifying initial conditions (initial velocity and spin vectors), a ball's flight path can be incrementally built up over small time intervals until the elevation reaches

0, indicating ground impact. This procedure was automated using a personal computer and specially written software, which were used for all of the performance calculations in this study.

It is well known that the effect of most any aspect of a golf ball's performance can vary substantially depending upon the particular launch condition characteristics of the golfer. See, for example, Aoyama (1994). Thus, to fairly assess the orientation effect it is necessary to perform trajectory calculations over a wide range of launch conditions. To keep the scope manageable, the initial ball speed was limited to a relatively high single value of 70 m/sec (assuming that the greatest effect would be seen at higher ball speeds), while the initial spin rate and launch angle ranges were quite broad. Figures 57.5 and 57.6 present the findings in the form of contour plots of maximum trajectory height and carry distance, respectively.

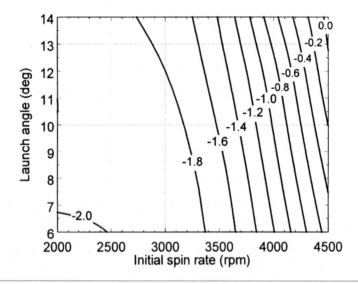

Figure 57.5   Difference in maximum trajectory height (in yards) between row-aligned and random orientations.

In figure 57.5, it can be seen that the trajectory height differences between the row-aligned and random orientations are 2 yd or less over the entire range of launch conditions. While more perceptive golfers might be able to detect a 2 yd height difference, it would not be expected to significantly alter the ball's playing characteristics.

Carry distance differences, as shown in figure 57.6, are somewhat greater with a maximum absolute value of 6 yd. A large majority of golfers would see less than a 4 yd difference either way. Some might consider this to be a significant difference, but in a practical sense it is less than 2% and would be substantially masked by the swing-to-swing variations of even an accomplished player.

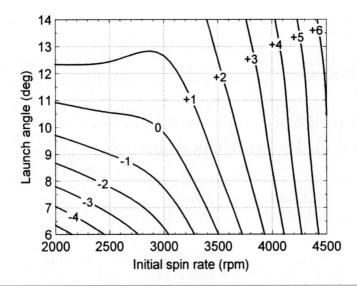

Figure 57.6   Difference in carry distance (in yards) between row-aligned and random orientations.

CONCLUSIONS

The long held assumption of a dimple row effect in the 336 octahedron dimple pattern has been placed in question. While the effect on C_L and C_D does exist and can be measured, its magnitude is, in general, surprisingly small. More importantly, its consequences for the golfer are not very significant in a practical sense. Even on the rare occasions when the spin axis happens to assume one of the row effect orientations, it is not likely to substantially alter the outcome of a golfer's shot, nor to affect his or her score for the round.

References

Aoyama, S. 1990. A modern method for the measurement of aerodynamic lift and drag on golf balls. In *Science and Golf: Proceedings of the First World Scientific Congress of Golf*, ed. A.J. Cochran, 199-204. London: E. & F.N. Spon.

Aoyama, S. 1994. Changes in golf ball performance over the last 25 years. In *Science and Golf II: Proceedings of the World Scientific Congress of Golf*, eds. A.J. Cochran and M.R. Farrally, 355-361. London: E. & F.N. Spon.

Davies, J.M. 1949. The aerodynamics of golf balls. *Journal of Applied Physics* 20: 821-828.

CHAPTER 58

Golf Ball Spin Decay Model
Based on Radar Measurements

G. Tavares, K. Shannon, and T. Melvin
Spalding Sports World Wide, Chicopee, MA, USA

Measurements have been made of golf ball spin rates using a radar based device. Through Fourier analysis of the radar signal, spin decay rate has been extracted. Measurements have been acquired for golf balls having significantly different dimple patterns, but of the same overall construction. Measurements have also been acquired for golf balls of different constructions, but with identical dimple patterns. The dependence of spin decay on dimple pattern and moment of inertia is presented as is a spin decay model which includes the effects of both moment of inertia and dimple pattern.

Keywords: Spin, radar, aerodynamics, moment of inertia.

INTRODUCTION

In order to understand the trajectory of a spinning golf ball it is necessary to consider all the aerodynamic forces involved. These include lift, drag, and torque. Davies along with Bearman and Harvey (1976) considered only lift and drag. Lieberman (1990) suggested an exponential decay model. Smits and Smith (1994) applied an empirical model based on spin decay measurements of a spinning ball mounted in a wind tunnel. This model assumes spin decay to be a function of the ratio of spin velocity to ball velocity. The data used for the model covered spin ratios up to 0.3, typical of a driver simulation. In general, aerodynamic torque has been either ignored, or has been addressed through spin decay models that assume spin decay to be a function of spin ratio alone.

Although shown to be adequate in the case of low spin ratio, a model that assumes spin decay is independent of dimple pattern and ball construction may become inaccurate under higher spin conditions. A spin decay model that includes the coefficients of moment and mass moment of inertia is presented.

THEORETICAL BACKGROUND

In order to solve for the full trajectory of the golf ball we must consider all the aerodynamic forces involved. A solution to the general equations on motion is sought.

$$\Sigma F = ma \qquad (1)$$

$$\Sigma T = I\alpha \qquad (2)$$

Where:

F = translational forces

$$F_{drag} = C_d \frac{1}{2}\rho V^2 A$$

$$F_{lift} = C_l \frac{1}{2}\rho V^2 A$$

T = rotational forces

$$T = C_m \frac{1}{2}\rho V^2 A d$$

m = mass

a = linear acceleration

I = mass moment of inertia

α = angular acceleration

ρ = density

V = velocity

A = ball projected area

d = ball diameter

C_d, C_p, C_m = coefficients of drag, lift, and moment

In order to simplify the computations it is convenient to assume the rotational forces are small and ignore equation 2. Changes in lift and drag forces due to spin decay can be expressed by semiempirical models. Both the Lieberman study and Smits and Smith suggest an exponential spin decay model based on experimental data. Smits and Smith show spin decay measurements that take the following form.

$$\alpha \frac{R^2}{V^2} = \frac{cR}{V}\omega \qquad (3)$$

Where:

V = velocity (m/sec)

R = ball radius (m)

ω = spin rate (rad/sec)

c = experimental constant

That is, the spin decay is a function of the spin ratio only. Effects of dimple pattern and moment of inertia are lumped into the experimental constant. Equation 3 should look more familiar as a linear 1st order differential equation with constant coefficients.

$$\frac{d\omega}{dt} + \frac{cV}{R}\omega = 0 \tag{4}$$

Which has a solution of the form

$$\omega(t) = \omega_0 e^{-\frac{cV}{R}t} \tag{5}$$

Where:

t = time

ω_0 = initial spin rate

If applied over a small range of spin ratios, equation 5 is a good approximation for golf balls having similar constructions and dimple patterns. Smits and Smith data cover a range of spin ratios from .025 to 0.275. This represents low spin, high velocity conditions typical of a driver.

However, at higher spin rates rotational forces increase and the effects of aerodynamic torque and moment of inertia become increasingly important. In this case equation 2 must be considered in more detail. The following approach is used to consider the individual effects of both aerodynamic torque and mass moment of inertia.

1. Measure the mass moment of inertia of the ball.
2. Measure the spin decay rate over a large range of spin ratios (up to 0.7).
3. Solve for the aerodynamic torque, and thus the coefficient of moment (C_m).
4. Define C_m as a function of spin ratio.
5. Solve equations 1 and 2.

EXPERIMENTAL PROCEDURE

Moment of Inertia

The mass moment of inertia of the ball is measured using instrument model 5050 made by Inertia Dynamics of Wallingford, Connecticut. The instrument consists of a horizontal pendulum with a top-mounted cage to hold the ball. The moment of inertia is calculated using the measured period of oscillation. The moment of inertia can also be calculated with reasonable accuracy if the material densities are known.

Spin Decay

Spin decay is measured during the initial part of flight using an outdoor test range. In order to control the initial spin and velocity of the golf ball, the USGA type ball launcher (UBL) was used. The UBL was designed and developed by Wilson Sporting Goods and Automated Design Company of Chicago, Illinois. The UBL allows spin to be applied to the ball without impact, or externally mounted devices.

The device used to measure the spin decay rate is a radar based instrument developed by ENCORE of Jacksonville, Florida. A one-inch diameter circle of thin metallic based material is adhered to the golf ball. The UBL is aimed downrange with the radar instrument positioned at the UBL ball exit, also aimed downrange. Figure 58.1 shows a schematic of the experimental setup.

The radar instrument tracks the rotation of the metallic spot as it travels downrange. An example of a typical signal is shown in figure 58.2.

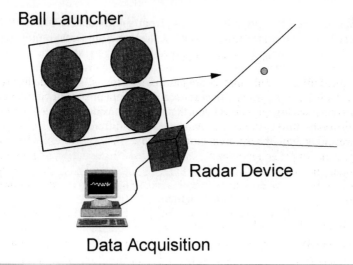

Figure 58.1   Experimental setup.

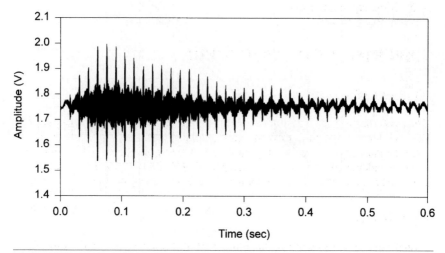

Figure 58.2   Typical signal of a spinning golf ball acquired from radar device.

Each "spike" in the signal represents a revolution of the ball. From the amplitude vs. time signal the mean spin rate along with spin decay can be extracted using Fourier methods. Velocity can also be extracted by applying a Doppler frequency shift to the signal. Spin measurements of the radar device were compared to those made using conventional high-speed video. The radar measurements were within 2%-4% of the video measurements. The higher spin rates (9000 rpm) having better agreement.

RESULTS

Data was acquired for spin ratios ranging from approximately 0.05 to 0.70. The lower end represents driver conditions while the higher spin ratio is more representative of short iron shots. Figure 58.3 shows spin decay vs. spin ratio for three golf balls having the same dimple pattern, but different constructions. (The dimple pattern chosen has 422 dimples arranged in a hexagonal group having five fold symmetry.) A linear regression fit was used on all data presented here. There does appear to be some higher order effects that are not considered here. Note each ball has a distinctly different curve. This is due to the different values of moment of inertia resulting from the different constructions.

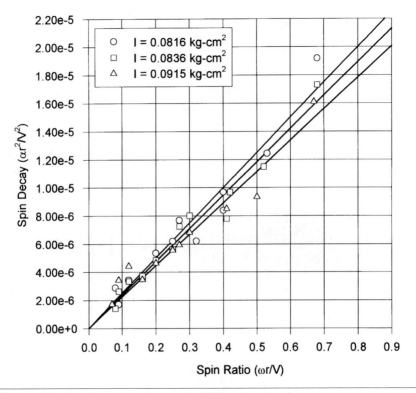

Figure 58.3   Spin decay vs. spin ratio for different inertia values.

If the aerodynamic performance of the dimple pattern is truly the same for all three balls, the coefficient of moment will collapse to a single curve for all three constructions. Figure 58.4 shows C_m vs. spin ratio for the three different golf ball constructions. As expected the slope of each curve is nearly the same and C_m is dependent only on dimple pattern.

Dimple pattern also affects the spin decay. Figure 58.5a shows the coefficient of moment vs. spin ratio for two golf balls of the same construction, but different dimple patterns. Both dimple patterns have 422 dimples arranged in a hexagonal grouping. The only difference is the depth of the dimples (0.2565 mm and 0.2972 mm). The figure shows the deeper dimple pattern has a higher C_m, and therefore higher spin decay. Figure 58.5b shows C_m vs. spin ratio for several different dimple patterns. For high spin ratios a 30% difference between the high and low C_m can be seen.

A relation between the coefficient of moment and spin ratio can be formed for any particular dimple pattern. Once this is done, solving the angular equation of motion becomes straightforward. Effect of moment of inertia and dimple pattern on flight can now be addressed. Figure 58.6a shows spin vs. time for three different values of inertia. As expected, balls having higher moments of inertia retain more spin over time. Figure 58.6b shows spin vs. time for two golf balls having the same construction, but different dimple patterns. The combined effects of both dimple pattern and construction can have a significant effect on spin decay rate.

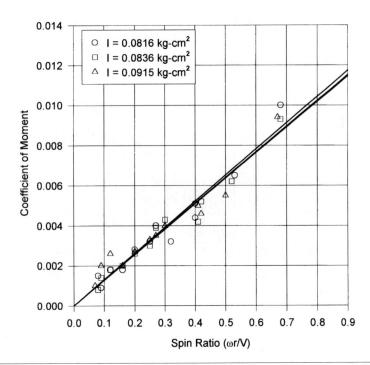

Figure 58.4   Effect of construction on aerodynamic coefficient of moment. (C_m vs. spin ratio for different inertia values.)

470   Tavares, Shannon, and Melvin

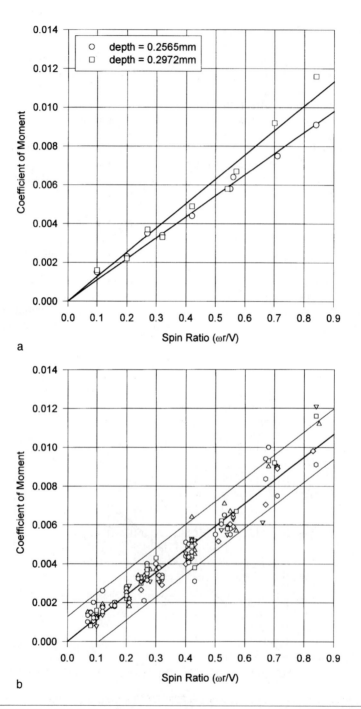

Figure 58.5 Combined effect of dimple and construction on aerodynamic coefficient of moment. (C_m vs. spin ratio for dimple patterns.)

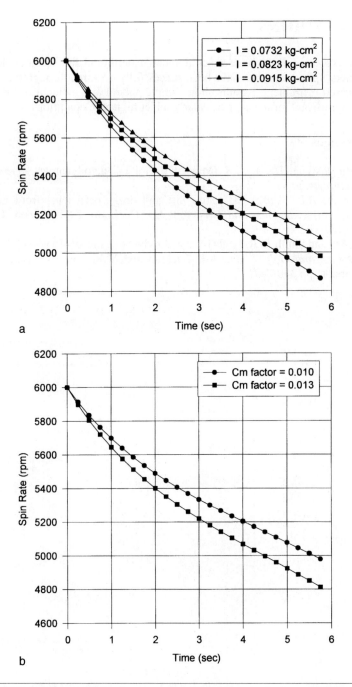

Figure 58.6   Predicted effects of construction and dimple on spin decay (a) Effect of construction on spin rate during flight (5 iron simulation). (b) Effect of dimple pattern on spin rate during flight (5 iron simulation).

CONCLUSIONS

A spin decay model which addresses moment of inertia and dimple pattern has been presented. Spin decay data have been successfully acquired through the use of a radar-based instrument. Results show dimple pattern and moment of inertia can have a significant influence, particularly under high spin conditions.

References

Bearman, P.W. and Harvey, J.K. (May 1976) Golf ball aerodynamics. *Aeronautical Quarterly*, pp. 112-122.
Lieberman, B.B. (1990) Estimating lift and drag coefficients from golf ball trajectories. *Science and Golf*, (ed. A.J. Cochran), E&FN Spon, London, pp.187-192.
Smits, A.J. and Smith, D.R. (1994) A new aerodynamic model of a golf ball in flight. *Science and Golf II*, (ed. A.J. Cochran and M.R. Farrally), E&FN Spon, London, pp.340-347.

CHAPTER 59

Use of Finite Element Analysis in Design of Multilayer Golf Balls

G. Tavares, M. Sullivan, and D. Nesbitt
Spalding Sports World Wide, Chicopee, MA, USA

The advantages of solid multilayer vs. conventional two-piece performance construction golf balls are investigated. Results of a Finite Element Analysis are compared to force plate impact measurements to verify the model. Analytical studies are presented showing some of the benefits of multilayer constructions. A soft outer cover over a hard inner layer is shown to be a preferred choice of construction to produce optimum spin characteristics.

Keywords: Finite elements, multilayer, impact.

INTRODUCTION

In recent years significant advances have been made in golf ball materials and manufacturing processes. These advances have led to a relatively new category of golf ball construction, the non-wound multilayer golf ball.

Historically golf balls have been classified as either solid two-piece or three-piece thread wound constructions. Two-piece golf balls consist of a solid rubber core with an ionomer or ionomer blend cover. Two-piece balls were initially well known for their performance in distance and durability. The modern two-piece ball of the mid 1980s and 1990s added feel and spin through advances in materials.

The three-piece, or thread wound, golf ball has a solid rubber or liquid filled core wrapped in a layer of rubber windings and covered with synthetic balata, ionomer, or other polymeric material. From the early 1900s thread wound balls were the players' ball of choice for two reasons.

1. The balata covered ball had excellent spin and feel around the green, a preferred feature by touring professionals.

2. Two-piece balls developed in the late 1960s, although having outstanding driver distance and durability, were deficient in feel and spin, particularly around the green.

Recently a new category of multilayer non-wound construction has been introduced. Such multilayer constructions consist of three or more solid layers of different materials, including the core. This is not a new concept (1984 Nesbitt patent), but only through advances in materials has it recently become a practical construction for achieving excellent feel and spin without sacrificing distance and durability.

The Finite Element Method (FEM) is used here to demonstrate the added benefits of the three-piece multilayer construction. In particular, the super soft cover over hard mantle layer is investigated.

EXPERIMENTAL PROCEDURE

In order to gain confidence in any numerical or analytical model a calibration to experimental data is required. Similar to Gobush (1990) and Ujihashi (1994), impact reaction forces and contact times have been measured. The device used is a force plate

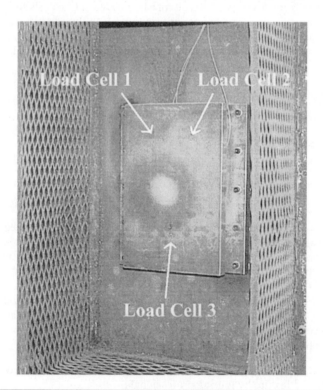

Figure 59.1   Experimental force plate apparatus.

consisting of three Kistler load washers positioned in a triangular pattern, sandwiched between two rigid plates. The force plate is 24.5 cm × 16.5 cm and is mounted to a 61 cm × 61 cm× 6.4 cm plate located 1.83 m in front of an air cannon from which the golf balls are fired. Figure 59.1 shows the experimental impact plate. The experiment only measures the normal component of impact. This method was selected for its simplicity. The force plate has been calibrated using a 7.94 kg mass concentrated on each of the three load washers. Balls are fired at the plate. Response of all three load cells is measured simultaneously. The total force is the summation of the response of all three load cells during the impact. As noted by Gobush, velocity and displacement can be calculated by integration of the load-time curves (not shown here). Although adequate for normal impact measurements, an angled impact experiment such as described by Gobush (1990) is more desirable. Calibration to normal impact data does not necessitate a calibrated model under oblique impacts. It should also be noted here that the data acquisition rate is 33 kh per load cell. This is adequate for low to moderate impacts, but gives poor results at higher impact velocities (>35 m/s).

FINITE ELEMENT MODEL

The Finite Element Analysis (FEA) was done using the commercially available code, LSDYNA. This code was also used by Iwata et al. (1990). LSDYNA was chosen primarily for its explicit numerical method, most suitable for short duration contact problems. Other codes with the same capabilities include ABAQUS, DYTRAN, and nonlinear ANSYS. Chou et al. (1994) used a circular cylinder approximation for an FEA model of a golf ball, considering only two-dimensional effects. The two-dimensional model, although giving good results, does not consider the out of plane hoop stresses. The model considered here is three-dimensional. A half sphere model is used in order to take advantage of symmetry since side impacts are not considered here. Figure 59.2 shows the FEA mesh of a two-piece ball.

Measured stress-strain properties are included in the material constitutive model, along with viscous shear and damping through LSDYNA's shear relaxation method.

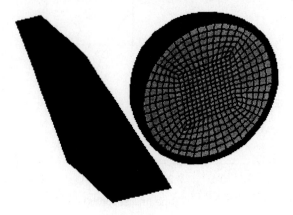

Figure 59.2   FEA mesh of a two-piece golf ball.

Stress-strain properties are measured using simple tensile and compressive testing performed on an MTS servo-electric tensile machine. Shear modulus is taken from the measured stress-strain data. Damping is empirically derived from the normal impact test. Static and kinetic coefficients of friction are measured using a friction plate fixture designed to work with the MTS tensile tester. Friction coefficients range from 0.30-0.60. Rate and load dependence were not considered in the friction measurements.

Model Calibration

Normal impacts were simulated for two different forward velocities (18.3, 27.4 m/s). Figure 59.3 shows predicted reaction forces vs. time for a two-piece golf ball. The calibration golf ball is identified as type 1. Cover hardness and core compression are given in table 59.1. Results are in reasonable agreement with those published by Chou (1994), Gobush (1990), and Ujihashi (1994). It should be noted that the FEA model stress-strain and shear modulus are the same for each case. The viscous damping value is the only variable that changes since it is dependent on the impact velocity. Chou et al. (1994) also treated viscous damping in a similar manner.

RESULTS

An FEA study has been performed on five golf ball constructions under four types of impact conditions. Table 59.1 shows the construction types.

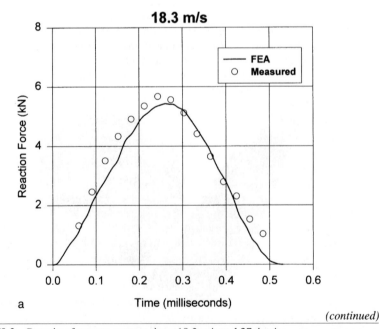

a

(continued)

Figure 59.3   Reaction force vs. contact time, 18.3 m/s and 27.4 m/s.

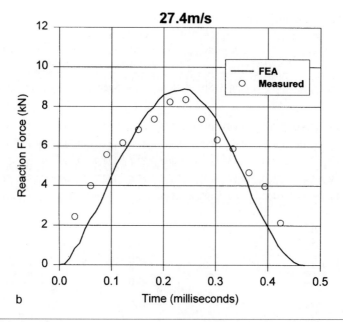

Figure 59.3   (*continued*)

Table 59.1   Construction Types

Case type	Cover Shore D	Mantle Shore D	Core Compression (PGA)
Type 1—two piece	56	None	63
Type 2—two piece	47	None	63
Type 3—two piece	70	None	63
Type 4—multilayer	47	70	63
Type 5—multilayer	70	56	63

The impact simulations are for a driver, 5-iron, 9-iron, and pitch shot. Club head velocity is typical of professional golfers. Table 59.2 compares FEA predicted launch conditions for the different constructions. Type 1 is a commercially available high performance two-piece ball. To give the FEA model more credibility, comparisons of predicted and measured launch conditions were made. Figure 59.4 compares measured launch conditions of professional golfers with FEA predicted results for type 1 construction. Player measurements were made using two-dimensional high-speed photography (only 2-D component is of interest here). Player measurements are shown with error bars. FEA predicted ball speed and spin rates are in good

Table 59.2   Summary of FEA Results

Type	Driver			5 Iron			9 Iron			Pitch shot		
	Angle	Speed	Spin	Angle	Speed	Spin	Angle	Speed	Spin	Angle	Speed	Spin
1	8.7	240	2,700	13.8	192.1	6,775	26.4	142.3	10,000	33.7	55.1	5,100
2	8.5	235	3,400	13.4	192.2	7,600	26.5	142.2	10,500	29.5	55.5	6,500
3	9.1	243	2,200	14.5	192.6	5,800	27.1	141.9	9,200	36.2	53.8	3,750
4	8.9	240	2,500	13.4	193.6	6,800	26.4	142.7	10,500	28.3	56.7	6,500
5	9.1	243	2,400	14.7	192.9	4,175	27.3	141.6	9,300	36.2	52.9	3,750

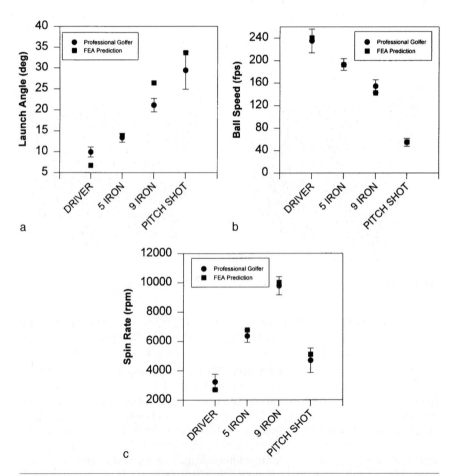

Figure 59.4   FEA results vs. live player measurements.

agreement with measurements launch. Launch angle does not agree as well, but is not considered to be unreasonable. The error is attributed to the FEA simulated club motion and dynamic angle at impact.

Type 2 is the two-piece ball with the softest cover and has excellent spin on the short pitch shot. Unfortunately the full shot spin rate of Type 2 is extremely high, making it difficult to control. This is where multilayer construction becomes advantageous.

The soft cover is necessary to achieve spin and feel on short shots. A problem occurs in the two-piece golf ball on full shots. The extremely soft cover on a two-piece ball transfers more energy into core "wind-up" since there is less sliding taking place from friction during impact. The result is excessive spin. By adding a rigid shell (mantle layer) between the cover and core, "wind-up" is reduced (Type 4), producing low spin off the driver as a result of the firm mantle layer, and high spin on the pitch shot from the soft cover. Figure 59.5 shows the effect of a multilayer vs. two-piece construction. Stress contours are shown at maximum deformation during a 5-iron impact simulation. The mantle layer of the multilayer construction is shown to absorb some of the impact forces that can generate excessive spin due to shear "wind-up" in a two-piece golf ball's core.

Figure 59.5   Stress distribution in two-piece and multilayer golf balls.

In the case of a hard cover over a soft mantle (Type 5), multilayer is not as beneficial. Type 5 shows low spin for all shots. This is due to the low friction and rigid cover material. The result is more slipping at impact, and therefore less spin. This may be achieved as well by using a hard covered two-piece construction like Type 3.

CONCLUSIONS

An experimental and Finite Element Analysis of two-piece and multilayer construction golf balls has been presented. The FEA model has been shown to agree well with experimental results. FEA studies have shown that the soft cover over hard mantle is the best construction for a high performance multilayer golf ball. That is to say, low spin off the tee for distance, with high spin and feel around the green. At this point hard covered multilayer balls don't appear to have significant benefits beyond those achieved in a conventional two-piece construction. As golf ball constructions and materials become more advanced, the use of Finite Element Analysis as a design tool will become useful in identifying potential new benefits.

References

Chou, P.C., Gobush, W., Liang, D., and Yang, J. (1994) Contact forces, coefficient of restitution, and spin rate of golf ball impact. *Science and Golf II,* (ed. A.J. Cochran and M.R. Farrally), London: E&FN Spon, pp. 296-301.

Gobush, W. (1990) Impact force measurements of golf balls. *Science and Golf* (ed. A.J. Cochran), London: E&FN Spon, pp. 219-224.

Iwata, M., Okuto, N., Satoh, F. (1990) Designing of golf club heads by Finite Element Method (FEM). *Science and Golf* (ed. A.J. Cochran), London: E&FN Spon, pp. 274-279.

Ujihashi, S. (1994) Measurement of dynamic characteristics of golf balls and identification of their mechanical models. *Science and Golf II,* (ed. A.J. Cochran and M.R. Farrally), London: E&FN Spon, pp. 302-308.

CHAPTER 60

Methods for Developing New Polymers for Golf Ball Covers

R. J. Statz
DuPont Packaging and Industrial Polymers, Wilmington, DE, USA

J. F. Hagman
Retired

Methods used for designing the cover materials for golf balls are described and some of the materials recently introduced to the golf ball industry are disclosed. These new materials have allowed manufacturers to develop golf balls which spin more or less, go further, and feel softer.

Keywords: Golf ball covers, ionomers.

INTRODUCTION

Ethylene copolymer ionomers were invented at DuPont in 1965 and introduced in the late 1960s as a thermoplastic material for packaging applications. Ionomers were first put on golf balls in the 1970s and made the game of golf more friendly to the average golfer. Ionomer-covered golf balls were relatively indestructible; however, these ionomer-covered indestructible golf balls were not used by professionals and better players because they were relatively hard, did not take the proper spin, and had a somewhat harsher, sharper sound when hit.

In the 1980s DuPont introduced a number of ionomer materials which produced golf balls which would mimic the spin of a balata covered ball and still be relatively resistant to cutting and lumping. It was also possible to produce high-spin two-piece golf balls with this material. Later DuPont introduced a number of ionomer resins which made it possible to make golf balls which would go further and spin less.

The same methods used to develop new ionomer materials were found to be useful in evaluating all thermoplastic resins, and this resulted in the introduction of several polyester ether based materials useful in golf ball construction.

METHODS DEVELOPED TO DESIGN NEW MATERIALS

In 1990 researchers developed a method that would enable them, without producing a golf ball, to determine if polymeric materials were more or less resilient. This method involved the injection molding of spheres out of neat resins or resin blends and the measuring of the coefficient of restitution (C.O.R.) and ATTI compression of the sphere. In addition, the hardness and the flexural modulus of the materials could be determined. This method can be applied to a limitless number of materials that might be useful for golf balls.

CORRELATION OF NEAT RESIN RESILIENCE AND GOLF BALL RESILIENCE

Generally, neat sphere resilience and the resilience of the material on a golf ball are directly correlatable. A material which gives a higher C.O.R. value in a sphere will generally give one-half to one-third of this improvement in the cover of a two-piece ball. Figure 60.1 plots the relationship of the neat sphere C.O.R. versus the C.O.R. of a standard two-piece golf ball.

RELATIONSHIP OF SPIN TO ATTI COMPRESSION OF THE COVER MATERIAL

There is some correlation of cover hardness and spin of a nine iron or a pitching wedge. Generally, softer lower modulus materials will give higher spins; but this relationship is clouded by the hardness and the size of a core in a two- or three-piece ball. Figure 60.2 shows the relationship of the ATTI compression on a neat sphere versus the spin off a nine iron.

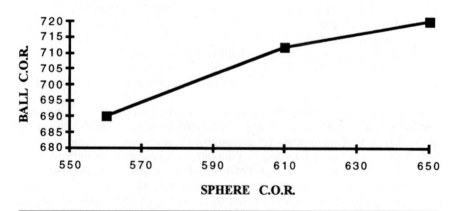

Figure 60.1   Ball C.O.R. versus sphere C.O.R.

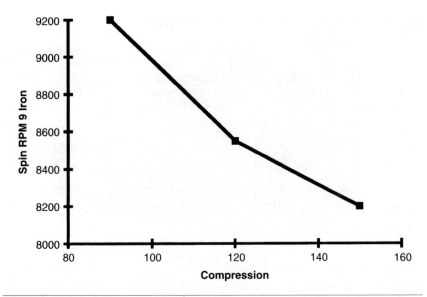

Figure 60.2   Spin versus ATTI compression.

In addition, more recent work has indicated that harder, stiffer materials might give better spin responses if they do not come off the club face as fast. Evaluating coefficient of restitution at low speeds or possibly drop rebounds might lead to better correlations.

GENERALIZATIONS ABOUT IONOMER STRUCTURE AND GOLF BALL PROPERTIES

The structure of ionomers can be varied by changing the chemistry used to produce them. The resulting changes give differences in physical properties; hence, materials that are very hard and stiff are possible. Materials which are soft and flexible are also available. The data generated in the studies of spheres indicate that polymers containing high levels of acid and lithium ions are the most resilient (see figure 60.3), and that soft ionomers are the least resilient. The data also indicates that there is synergy in mixed ionomer systems (see figure 60.4).

RELATIONSHIP OF HARDNESS, STIFFNESS, COMPRESSION, AND RESILIENCE

These properties are not independent but appear to be dependent upon the polymeric type. Generally, ionomers get harder and stiffer as they get more resilient. Other thermoplastic materials such as polyester ethers and polyamide ethers get softer and more flexible as they get more resilient. Polyolefinic materials such as the metallocene

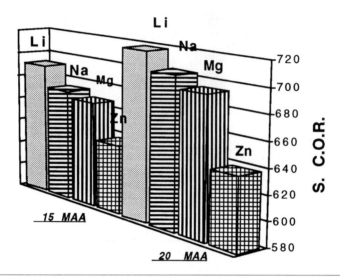

Figure 60.3   Sphere C.O.R. versus acid level and ion type.

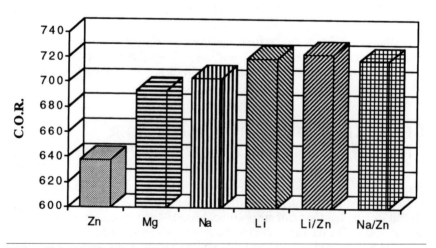

Figure 60.4   C.O.R. for mixed ion covers.

and EPDM materials are similar to polyether based TPEs. Figure 60.5 shows the relationship between the ATTI compression and the C.O.R. for a number of ionomers. Non-ionomeric materials will display a relationship defined by a line with the opposite slope.

MATERIALS FOR MULTILAYERED GOLF BALLS

The latest trend in the golf ball industry seems to be the desire to produce solid golf balls with more than two layers. The intermediate layers can be both hard and

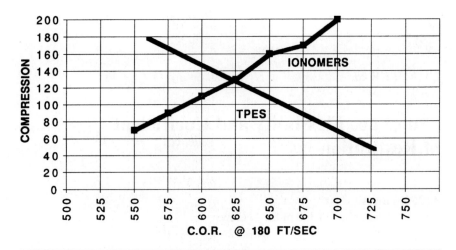

Figure 60.5   Compression versus C.O.R.

resilient and soft and resilient. The cover materials in such a case are usually complementary, soft ionomer covers on stiff mantles and stiff covers on soft mantles. These types of constructions appear in some cases to give golf balls which are more resilient but feel softer and have a lower ATTI compression.

References

E. I. du Pont de Nemours & Co (Inc) *Golf Balls Based on Lithium Ionomers or Blends with Lithium Ionomers, Research Disclosure*, Dec 1986.

E. I. du Pont de Nemours & Co (Inc) *Ionomer Blends for Golf Ball Covers, Research Disclosure,* Nov 1986.

Molitor, R. P., U.S. Patent 3,819,768 *Golf Ball Cover Compositions Comprising a Mixture of Ionomer Resins.*

Shinichi Nakade, U.S. Patent 4,526,375 *Golf Ball.*

Statz, Robert J., U.S. Patent 4,690,981 *Ionomers Having Improved Low Temperature Properties.*

CHAPTER 61

Club Face Flexibility and Coefficient of Restitution

A. J. Cochran
Royal & Ancient Golf Club of St. Andrews

The possibility that flexible club faces, particularly in oversize drivers, might impart more speed to the ball than clubs with rigid faces has been the subject of conjecture in recent years. This theoretical study models the club face as a thin plate which behaves as a linear spring, and models the ball as a non-linear spring in parallel with a non-linear viscous resistance. It is shown that, under certain conditions, coefficient of restitution may increase by 6% to 12% by virtue of the plate flexibility. Experiments would be needed to show whether the effect can happen with actual golf clubs.

Keywords: Golf club face, spring effect, coefficient of restitution, mathematical model.

INTRODUCTION

The collision between a golf ball and a golf clubhead is not perfectly elastic because of energy losses in deformation and recovery. Even the hardest club face materials are not completely rigid, and the club face must deform slightly, but in most analysis of impact it has been (correctly) assumed that for practical purposes all the deformation, and therefore all the energy loss, takes place in the ball. When we talk about the "coefficient of restitution" it is commonly treated as being a property of the ball alone.

The popularity of metal woods, which are effectively thin shells of steel or titanium, has raised the conjecture again that deformation in the clubhead could perhaps replace some of that in the ball. This could reduce the total energy loss, and so increase the speed imparted to the ball, if the material and construction of the clubhead is such that less energy is lost in *its* deformation than in that part of the ball's deformation which it replaces, and if no other energy-losing mechanism is created (such as significant residual vibrations in the clubhead).

Any thorough study of this needs proper experimental investigation, but simple theoretical models may be able to indicate qualitatively the circumstances, if any, in which enhancing ball speed in this way might occur, and perhaps put some limits on its extent.

REBOUND FROM A FIXED PLATE–PLATE MODEL

The physical reality modelled here is of a ball impacting normally on the centre of a thin plate mounted rigidly at its edges, but free to deform and to recover. A one-dimensional model of the deflection under load of such a plate regards it as a linear spring, in parallel, if we wish to consider its dynamic behaviour, with a dashpot damping resistance (figure 61.1a), whose equation of motion is:

$$m\ddot{x} = -kx - c\dot{x}$$

where 'dots' as usual indicate differentiation one or two times with respect to time. The mass m represents the effective mass of the plate. The spring constant's value will depend on several parameters, such as plate thickness, area, shape, mass, and material properties, but we need not be concerned with these at this stage.

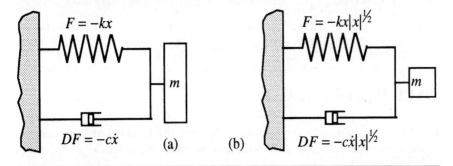

Figure 61.1   Model adopted for flexible plate (a); and for ball (b).

BALL MODEL

To simulate how a golf ball rebounds from this idealised plate we need a ball model which reproduces the observed behaviour of a real golf ball at impact. It should give approximately correct values of such things as coefficient of restitution and duration of contact, and the variation of these with impact speed. (Both of them increase slowly as speed decreases.)

The very simplest two-element visco-elastic models do not meet all these criteria (see, for example, Simon 1967, Cochran 1974, Lieberman and Johnson 1994); more complicated combinations of three or more linear elements (springs and dashpots) in series and parallel give better agreement (Ujihashi 1994, Johnson and Lieberman 1996). The more parameters there are to be fitted to observations the better the correlation will be, but, it may be argued, the more difficult will it be to understand the underlying processes.

For the purposes of this study a two-parameter model of the golf ball is used—similar to that for the plate, but with a non-linear spring and dashpot. Figure 61.1b shows this model as it depicts rebound from a massive rigid plane. The "Hertzian" spring—with restoring force proportional to (displacement)$^{3/2}$—is known to reproduce the purely elastic properties of the ball quite well, and indeed is theoretically correct for small deformations of a uniform sphere (Goldsmith 1960). The non-linear viscous element is postulated on the same qualitative grounds as the Hertzian spring. The spring becomes stiffer as the deformation (x) increases because the volume of material involved increases, so in the Hertzian spring we introduce a further factor $x^{1/2}$, to the $F = -kx$ of the linear spring. By analogy we multiply the linear dashpot resistance, $F = -cv$, by the same factor $x^{1/2}$.

$$m\ddot{x} = -kx\,|\,x\,|^{1/2} -c\dot{x}\,|\,x\,|^{1/2}$$

The mass m in this case is the mass of the ball (46 gm); because of the extra factor $x^{1/2}$ the constants k and c have different dimensions from the corresponding constants in Equation 1. Systematic fitting of this to observations has not been carried out, but, as will be seen in later results, values of k and c can be found that predict coefficient of restitution, duration of contact, deformation, and their variation with impact speed which are realistic enough for the purpose of this study. The values used are:

$$k = 2.5 \times 10^{7}\,\text{N/m}^{3/2} \quad \text{and} \quad c = 850\,\text{N} - \text{s/m}^{3/2}$$

BALL PLATE IMPACT

Combining the plate and ball models given in figures 61.1a and 61.1b and equations 1 and 2, we can model impact of the ball on the plate (figure 61.2).

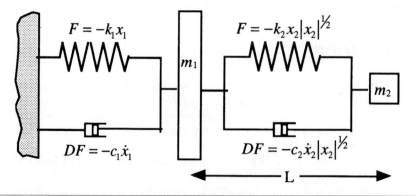

Figure 61.2   Model of combined ball and plate during impact. The "ball" comes in from the right and rebounds to the right.

The equations of motion governing this collision are:

$$m_1\ddot{x}_1 = -k_1 x_1 - c_1 \dot{x}_1 + k_2 (x_2 - x_1 - L) |x_2 - x_1 - L|^{1/2} + c_2 (\dot{x}_2 - \dot{x}_1) |x_2 - x_1 - L|^{1/2}$$

$$m_2\ddot{x}_2 = -k_2 (x_2 - x_1 - L) |x_2 - x_1 - L|^{1/2} - c_2 (\dot{x}_2 - \dot{x}_1) |(x_2 - x_1 - L|^{1/2}$$

In these (see figure 61.2) the variables and constants with suffix 1 apply to the plate, those with suffix 2 to the ball. The origin for x_1 and x_2 is taken to be the point of contact on the plate, and the centre of the ball, where its mass is located, is at a distance L from there (= 0.023 metres).

These equations have been solved numerically for values of k_1 ranging from extreme flexibility of the plate to virtually complete rigidity; and for three values of c_1 which represent no damping in the plate, small (realistic?) damping, and heavy damping. The effective mass of the plate, m_1, has been fixed at 25 gm.

RESULTS

The results are shown in figures 61.3 and 61.4 for an impact velocity of 30 m/s. It can be seen (figure 61.3) that, in a particular range of plate stiffness, flexing of the plate can indeed add to the ball rebound velocity obtained from the usually assumed

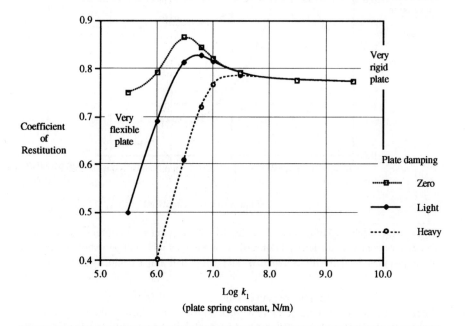

Figure 61.3   Calculated coefficient of restitution on rebound of a golf ball from plates with different stiffnesses and three amounts of damping (c_1 = 0, 40 and 400 N per m/s). Impact velocity is 30 m/s.

rigid body provided damping is not too large. If the low damping case (middle curve in figure 61.3) is a reasonable estimate of reality then the coefficient of restitution could be raised from 0.774 to 0.827. In a real golf drive a C of R increase like this would increase ball speed by about 3%. The maximum possible gain (zero damping—top curve in figure 61.3) would raise the C of R by about 12% to 0.865—converted to a golf drive, a gain of 5% in ball speed.

Intuition suggests that the conditions most likely to enhance rebound speed arise where some kind of matching occurs between the flexing and recovery of the plate, and ball compression and recovery. Figure 61.4 confirms this. The duration of contact of the ball impacting a rigid surface—far right in figure 61.5—is 0.5 msec (at the velocity in question). The plate stiffness which has 0.5 msec as its half period of vibration (when loaded with its own mass plus that of the ball) gives near optimum C of R in the lightly damped case, and almost exact optimum in the zero damping case.

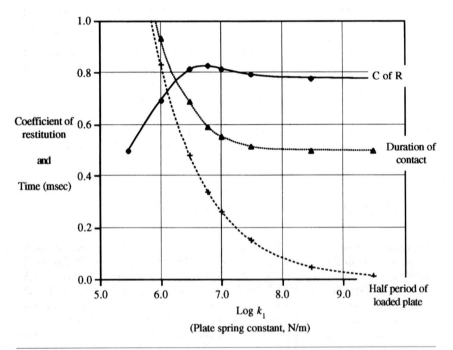

Figure 61.4   Rebound of golf ball from lightly damped plates with different stiffnesses. Duration of contact and coefficient of restitution, together with half period of vibration of undamped plate loaded with its own mass and that of ball. Impact velocity is 30 m/s.

Figure 61.5 shows that the region of enhanced C of R is not greatly dependent on the impact velocity. The peak moves a little to the right—stiffer plate—as velocity increases, (as expected since the time of contact decreases), but in general it would be easy to find a stiffness that gives near maximum enhancement over the range of velocities achieved in a golf drive. The effect of changing the effective mass, m_1, of the plate has not been systematically investigated.

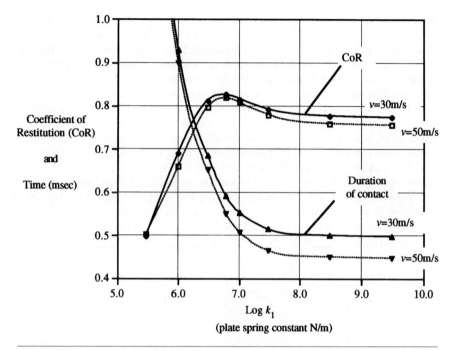

Figure 61.5   Rebound of ball from lightly damped plates of different stiffnesses, showing effect of two different impact velocities, 30 m/s and 50 m/s, on coefficient of restitution and duration of contact.

CONCLUSIONS AND LIMITATIONS

We cannot yet deduce from the above analysis that a 3% to 5% increase in ball velocity is obtainable in practice by virtue of a "trampoline" effect in drivers. The analysis uses a simplified model of the impact of a ball on a flexible plate, which is itself a simplification of the club/ball impact. The deformation in the real club is almost certainly more than just flexing of the face, and even in the face there will be more than one mode of vibration, particularly if impact is off-centre.

Nevertheless, whatever the deformation of the club, if it is reasonably well represented by a linear spring, then for some values of the material properties and the physical dimensions the phenomenon shown in the graphs of figures 61.3, 61.4, and 61.5 will occur. The present analysis does not say whether these values are obtainable in practice in a swingable club that does not collapse at impact. However, calculations on idealised circular plates of roughly "jumbo" driver face area suggest that thicknesses of a few millimetres would give spring constants of the right magnitude.

More sophisticated theoretical models might throw more light on this, but it is likely that experimenting both with plates and ultimately with actual clubs will be the best way to determine whether the effect predicted in theory can happen in practice.

References

Cochran, A.J. (1974). The impact of an imperfectly elastic ball on a hard plane surface. Part I: Normal impact. Acushnet Company report.

Goldsmith, W. (1960). Impact. London, Edward Arnold.

Johnson, S.H. and Lieberman, B.B. (1996). Normal impact models for golf balls. In *The Engineering of Sport*, ed. S.J. Haake, 250-256. Rotterdam, A.A. Balkema.

Lieberman, B.B., and Johnson, S.H. (1994). An analytical model for ball-barrier impact. Part I: Models for normal impact. In *Science and Golf II*, ed. A.J.Cochran and M.R. Farrally, 309-314. London, E.& F.N.Spon.

Simon, R. (1967). The development of a mathematical tool for evaluating golf club performance. ASME Design Engineering Conference, New York, May 1967.

Ujihashi, S. (1994). Measurement of dynamic characteristics of golf balls and identification of their mechanical models. In *Science and Golf II*, ed. A.J.Cochran and M.R. Farrally, 302-308. London, E.& F.N.Spon.

CHAPTER 62

Golf Ball Rebound Enhancement

S.H. Johnson
Mechanical Engineering and Mechanics Department, Lehigh University, Bethlehem, PA, USA

J.E. Hubbell
Research and Test Center, United States Golf Association, Far Hills, NJ, USA

New materials and manufacturing processes applied to golf equipment produce endless variations that may or may not affect the performance of professional or amateur golfers. To assess the present and future impact of titanium-alloy club heads, a series of impact experiments with golf balls of two common constructions was conducted at the USGA Research and Test Center in Far Hills, New Jersey, USA. Balls were fired at free-standing target plates using an air cannon until fifty central impacts were obtained. The targets were planar, cavity-back disks with various membrane thicknesses. Thicknesses were selected arbitrarily with no attempt to optimize the ball construction/target design combination. Results show velocity ratio improvements for cavity-back plates in comparison to the flat-plate base case of 13% for the two-piece balls used in the test and comparable increases for the wound balls used. The results of the five experiments reported here can be simulated reasonably well by combining Lieberman and Johnson's five-parameter model of normal impact with a linear two-mass/one-spring representation of the elastically deforming target.

Keywords: Spring-like effect, trampoline effect, golf ball launch conditions, ball-club matching.

INTRODUCTION

The possibility of building a golf club head with elastic characteristics that interact with the viscoelastic behavior of golf balls to produce greater launch velocities than would a rigid head has been judged unlikely. New materials, manufacturing methods, and optimizing design techniques dictate that the possibility of spring-like behavior be revisited. Simulated normal impacts by Cochran (1997) showed enhanced launch velocities to be possible.

The rules of golf specify that the club head shall not have a spring-like effect on the ball, nor shall the club head have moving parts. Recent numerical simulations of normal impact between two-piece balls and an elastically deforming cavity-back flat plate indicate that the ball and a titanium target can be matched in such a way as to reduce the ball deformation rate, increase the contact time, and launch the ball off a face that is moving forward relative to the movement of the center of mass of the simulated driver. Similar results are obtained using the ball models of Ujihashi (1994), Lieberman and Johnson (1994), Johnson (1996), and Cochran (1997).

The air cannon at the USGA Research and Test Center in Far Hills, New Jersey, USA, was used to fire balls at a free-standing, unrestrained disk 101.6 mm in diameter with a mass of 0.23 kg. An α-β alloy of titanium has been used for all target disks thus far. A 76.2 mm diameter cavity was machined into the back of two flat-plate targets and the rim thicknesses were adjusted to keep the masses of the targets the same. Two target suspension methods have been tried, two membrane thicknesses used, and two ball constructions tested. A third target with simulated bulge and roll was tested. Comparisons are made on the basis of the ratio of the outgoing or rebound velocity of the ball to the incoming ball velocity with no adjustments for drag or gravity.

SIMULATIONS

A simple two-mass, one-linear spring model of a club head is coupled to the lumped-mass, viscoelastic models of ball normal impact by Lieberman and Johnson (1994) using parameters reported by Johnson (1996). The left sketch in figure 62.1 is the cross-sectional view of a cavity-back target. The right sketch is the lumped-parameter representation of the target for the simulation of normal impact. Imagine the target moving from left to right. The leading mass of the model is some fraction of the mass of the membrane portion of the target. One of the uncertainties with such a simple model is how much of the membrane mass to assign to the sprung mass,

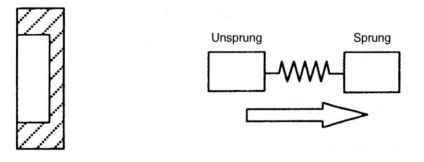

Figure 62.1   (a) Cross-sectional view of a cavity-back target. (b) Simulation of normal impact.

leaving the remainder of the mass of the simulated club head to be assigned to the unsprung mass of the model. The spring is assigned the elasticity of a centrally loaded, uniform circular plate with a continuous, clamped boundary (see Timoshenko [1959]). The schematic of the complete simulation is shown in figure 62.2.
    The equations to be integrated numerically are

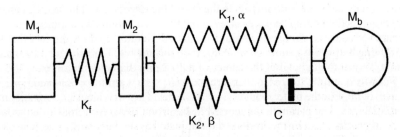

Figure 62.2   Model schematic. The three elements labeled M_1, M_2, and K_f form the model of the target, and the remaining elements constitute the nonlinear ball model for normal impact of Lieberman and Johnson (1994). The spring forces are proportional to the deformations raised to the power α or β as indicated. The damping force is proportional to the rate of deformation. The simulations yield the target plate and ball deformations and the post-impact velocities of the mass and the target masses.

Motion of mass M_1: $\qquad\qquad\qquad \dot{x}_1 = x_2 \qquad \dot{x}_2 = K_f(x_3 - x_1)/M_1$

Motion of mass M_2: $\qquad\qquad\qquad \dot{x}_3 = x_4$ $\qquad\qquad\qquad\qquad\qquad$ *and*

$$\dot{x}_4 = K_f(x_1 - x_3)/M_2 + K_1 \mid x_6 - x_3 \mid^\alpha sgn(x_6 - x_3)/$$
$$M_2 + K_2 \mid x_5 - x_3 \mid^\beta sgn(x_5 - x_3)/M_2$$

Motion of ball mass M_b: $\qquad\qquad\qquad \dot{x}_6 = x_7$

$$\dot{x}_7 = -K_1(x_6 - x_3) \mid^\alpha sgn\,(x_6 - x_3)/M_b - C(x_7 - \dot{x}_5)/M_b \ .$$

The representation of energy dissipation introduces one additional equation

$$\dot{x}_5 = -K_2 \mid x_5 - x_3 \mid^\beta sgn\,(x_5 - x_3)/C + x_7 \ .$$

The variables x_1, x_3 and x_6 are the displacements of the three masses M_1, M_2 and M_b. The variables x_2, x_4, and x_7 are the corresponding velocities.
    The target plate equivalent spring constants calculated from

$$K_f = \frac{16\pi\,(1+v)\,D}{(3+v)\,a^2} \qquad D = \frac{E\,h^3}{12\,(1-v)^2} \qquad M_2 = \frac{\pi a^2 h\rho}{g}\,f$$

for a simply supported circular plate and for a clamped edge

$$K_f = \frac{16\pi D}{a^2}.$$

The apparent moving mass M_2, is that part of the membrane mass that is assumed to be moving as a unit with respect to the rest of the target plate. The factor f is some fraction less than one. The uncertainty about the actual boundary condition and the arbitrariness of the choice of f reduce the model fidelity, as does the fact that the impacting ball is not a static point load. At 49 m/s the ball footprint on the target is about 25 mm in diameter at the center of a 76.2 mm diameter membrane.

For α-β titanium, the parameters are $\rho = 4.67 \times 10^6$ kg/m^3, $v = 0.34$ and $E = 1.03 \times 10^{11}$ N/m^2. For the plate geometry, a = 38.1 mm. The two values of h are 2.54 mm and 3.18 mm. The parameters reported in Johnson (1996) for liquid-filled wound balls allow the model to reproduce the flat plate results very well. The two-piece parameters as reported do not do as well. The linear constitutive relationship for damping probably is inadequate. If the damping coefficient is reduced somewhat (about 35%) the five-parameter model fits the plate data well for the two-piece ball also. Then the factor f is adjusted to fit the cavity-back data. A value of 0.4 works well for both ball constructions and both membrane thicknesses.

Experimental determinations of the membrane stiffnesses using a compression test machine and a 7.62 mm diameter plunger yielded 4,407,000 N/m for the 2.54 mm thick membrane as compared to theoretical values of 5,529,000 N/m for ideal clamped boundary conditions and 2,218,000 N/m for a simply supported boundary. For the 3.18 mm thick membrane, the experimental value was 7,763,000 N/m as compared to 10,800,000 N/m (clamped) and 4,333,000 N/m (simply supported). The simulated stiffness is the average of the calculated simply-supported and clamped-edge stiffnesses. The fundamental natural frequencies of the two plates are 3880 Hz and 4530 Hz respectively. The natural frequencies are obtained by performing an FFT analysis on accelerometer output after the plate is struck sharply in the center. The simulations show that there is very little launch velocity enhancement until the membrane thickness is reduced to about 4 mm. The beneficial effect increases rapidly and is limited only by the onset of plastic deformation as the thickness is reduced to 2.5 mm. The model predicts a similar pattern for 302 stainless steel, except the membrane thickness must be reduced to 1.8 mm for significant benefit.

EXPERIMENTS

In all experiments, the USGA R&T Center airgun was used to fire golf balls horizontally at selected targets. The base case target is a 76.2 mm diameter disk of α-β titanium 11.0 mm thick. The mass is 0.23 kg. The airgun is set to fire golf balls at a nominal velocity of 48.8 m/s and without significant spin. Ballistic light screens measure the ball approach velocity and rebound velocity. Carbon paper taped to the face of the target records the impact location. If the impact is in the center of the plate, the ratio of the rebound velocity over approach velocity is recorded. The largest credible recorded ratio out of fifty central impacts is taken to be representative of that ball and target combination (see figure 62.3). The conclusions would be the same if averages of the fifty were used.

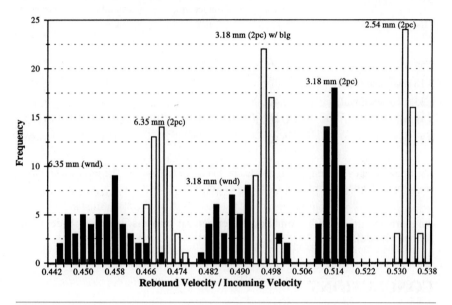

Figure 62.3   Experimental velocity ratios. Only data from central impacts were recorded to accumulate fifty ratios plotted for each experiment. The experiments match the rows of Table 62.1 with the addition of fifty shots at a titanium plate with a membrane thickness of 3.18 mm and a convex shape with a radius of curvature of 254 mm labelled *w/blg*.

Two methods of positioning the target in front of the airgun were tried. In the first configuration the plate was suspended from two light metal chains and fifty central impacts recorded. In the second configuration the target was supported by two horizontal pins with freedom for the target to slide in the direction of ball travel. The pins were 6.4 mm in diameter, 6.4 mm long and parallel with 19.1 mm between centers. Fifty central impacts recorded for the second configuration produced the same average velocity ratio as the first configuration (0.4693 ± 0.0064 versus 0.4676 ± 0.0052). The second, free-standing configuration was used for all subsequent testing of circular targets.

Four additional α-β titanium targets 101.6 mm in diameter were constructed. Cavities of 76.2 mm inside diameters were machined into the backs of two of the disks, leaving membrane thicknesses of 3.18 mm and 2.54 mm. The peripheral rings were adjusted in thickness to maintain the masses at 0.23 kg. Fifty central impacts were recorded for each target using matched two-piece Surlyn-covered balls. About 200 shots were required to get fifty central impacts. At the completion of these tests, the 2.54 mm thick flat membrane was found to have a permanent deformation of approximately 0.15 mm. These results are summarized in Table 62.1 and

Table 62.1   Simulated Results Using the Lieberman-Johnson Lumped-Parameter Model With Comparisons to Experiments

Thickness h in mm	Factor f	Contact time μsec	Velocity ratio	Measured ratio
2.54 (two-piece ball)	0.40	526	0.554	0.538
3.18 (two-piece ball)	0.40	468	0.526	0.518
6.35 (two-piece ball)	0.40	402	0.475	0.474
3.18 (wound ball)	0.40	500	0.505	0.502
6.35 (wound ball)	0.40	427	0.474	0.466

The ratios are the rebound speeds divided by the approach speeds. The measured ratios are computed without corrections for drag or gravity.

comparisons made with simulated direct central impacts using the Lieberman-Johnson model.

CONCLUSIONS

As analytical and experimental evidence of possible launch velocity enhancements accumulated, it became essential that the basic properties of ball-target interactions be investigated and suitable test procedures and baseline comparisons be established.

Direct central impact tests on planar membranes with supporting peripheral rings show that velocity ratios increase as thicknesses decrease for two ball constructions. Relatively simple lumped-parameter models successfully simulate the observed behavior and, in turn, can be used to estimate the effects of changed thickness or material. Bulge and roll are seen to alter the stiffness versus mass distribution of the flat membrane and the amount of velocity enhancement. An actual golf club head, with its nonuniform face thickness, unequal bulge and roll, and smaller, noncircular membrane performs still less like a circular, cavity-back flat plate. Nevertheless, it is easy to imagine durable club head designs, optimized for a launch-velocity enhancement, with the performance of the 2.54 mm thick, 76.2 mm diameter flat membrane.

ACKNOWLEDGMENTS

The authors wish to express their sincere gratitude to Mr. Frank Thomas, technical director of the United States Golf Association, for his generous support of this work and to thank Pete Ball, Stan Chaprapowicki, Bob Tygar, Len Anfinsen, and Henry

Thumm-Borst from the staff of the USGA Research and Test Center for their invaluable contributions.

References

Cochran, A.J. 1997. Discussions held at the USGA Research and Test Center, Far Hills, New Jersey, USA, in April, 1997.

Johnson, S.H. 1996. Normal impact models for golf balls. In *The Engineering of Sport: Proceedings of the 1st International Conference on the Engineering of Sport, Sheffield, UK, 2-4 July 1996,* ed. S. Haake, 251-256. Rotterdam: A.A. Balkema.

Lieberman, B.B., and S.H. Johnson. 1994. An analytical model for ball-barrier impact, Parts I and II. In *Science and Golf II,* ed. A.J. Cochran and M.R. Farrally, 309-320. London: E. & F.N. Spon.

Timoshenko, S. and S. Woinowsky-Krieger. 1958. *Theory of Plates and Shells, 2nd edition.* New York: McGraw-Hill, Inc.

Ujihashi, S. 1994. Measurement of dynamic characteristics of golf balls and identification of their mechanical models. In *Science and Golf II,* ed. A.J. Cochran and M.R. Farrally, 303-308. London: E. & F.N. Spon.

CHAPTER 63

Optimum Design of Golf Club Considering the Mechanical Impedance Matching

Tetsuo Yamaguchi
Sports Goods Research Dept., Sumitomo Rubber Industries Ltd., Kobe, Japan

Takuzo Iwatsubo
Faculty of Engineering, Kobe University, Japan

This paper proposes the method to design a golf club which gives the maximum restitution coefficient based on the concept of the mechanical impedance matching between golf club and golf ball. First of all, the mechanism of the impact phenomena between golf club and golf ball is clarified by time series analysis and the concept of mechanical impedance in the frequency domain. Consequently the optimum combination of golf club and golf ball which gives the maximum restitution coefficient and the maximum energy transfer efficiency is investigated. Second, the optimum combination for the maximum restitution coefficient between golf club and golf ball is related to the mechanical impedance.

Furthermore, a few experiments on hitting golf balls are performed, and the results of the experiments are compared with those of the numerical analysis. Finally, the material properties for club heads which are suitable to design a high-restitution golf club are discussed from the viewpoint of the mechanical impedance matching.

Keywords: Mechanical impedance, restitution coefficient, energy transfer, impact mechanism, golf club, golf ball, golf club head material.

INTRODUCTION

Since the impact between two bodies is an instantaneous phenomenon, its analysis is very difficult. So in the usual analysis of impact, the impact mechanism is regarded as a black box and a restitution coefficient is used as a variable. There are many investigations about the wave propagation problem, but the theory of impact mechanism is little studied. Doi and Asano (1976) treated the impact problem of a uniform bar by using the finite element method. Yagawa et al. (1983) analyzed the dynamic contact problem by the penalty function. Nakagawa et al. (1977) investigated the propagation of waves which are partly reflected at the interface of semi-infinite elastic and viscoelastic bars, and obtained an exact solution by means of the Laplace transform. There is, however, little study (Yamaguchi, 1986, Iwatsubo, 1990) of both the mechanism of impact and the combination of a golf club and a golf ball which gives the maximum restitution velocity from the standpoint of mechanical impedance in the frequency domain.

In this paper the impact phenomena are analyzed by time series analysis and frequency domain analysis by replacing golf ball and golf club with a lumped mass system. The optimum condition which gives the maximum restitution coefficient and the maximum impact transfer efficiency is investigated. Then a few hitting tests are performed, and the results of the above numerical analysis are proved.

Next, the material properties for club heads which are suitable to design a high-restitution golf club are discussed from the viewpoint of the mechanical impedance matching.

NUMERICAL ANALYSIS OF IMPACT PHENOMENA

The Definition of Problem and Modeling

It is possible to analyze impact phenomena by the wave propagation theory. In this paper, however, a finite-degrees-of-freedom model, as shown in figure 63.1, is adopted in order to analyze the impact problem from the viewpoint of the mechanical impedance of golf balls and clubs. Golf balls and clubs are assumed to be uniform in axial direction for the sake of fundamental research of impact phenomena.

In Figure 63.1, golf ball and golf club are divided into equal m and n elements respectively, and masses of golf ball and club are denoted by M_{b1}, M_{b2}, ... M_{bm}, and M_{c1}, M_{c2}, ... M_{cn}, respectively.

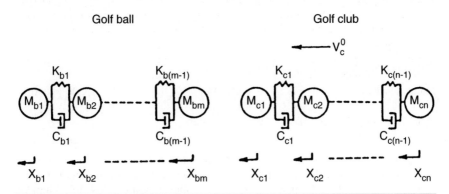

Figure 63.1   Model of lumped mass system.

As written in the reference (Yamaguchi et al. 1986), the equations of finite-degrees-of-freedom system for the golf ball and golf club are given as follows, respectively.

$$[M_b]|\ddot{X}_b| = -[K_b]|X_b| - [C_b]|\dot{X}_b| + f_b(t)|$$

$$[M_c]|\ddot{X}_c| = -[K_c]|X_c| - [C_c]|\dot{X}_c| + f_c(t)|$$

Then it is assumed that M_{c1} collides with M_{bm} in the axial direction.

Time Domain Analysis of Impact Phenomena

The boundary conditions and calculating conditions were investigated in Yamaguchi, et al. before. Impacting end masses of two bodies maintain contact during impact. The standard calculating condition of masses, material constants, initial velocities, and numbers of partition of golf club and ball are shown in table 63.1. The restitution coefficient RE is defined by the following equation:

$$RE = (V'_b - V'_c)/V_c^0$$

where V^0 denotes the velocity before impact, and V' denotes the velocity after impact.

Table 63.1   Values of Standard Calculating Conditions

	Impacting body	Impacted body
Number of partition N	11	10
Lumped mass M (kg)	$M_{c1} = M_{c11} = 0.01$ $M_{c2}, \ldots, M_{c10} = 0.02$	$M_{b2} = M_{b10} = 0.0025$ $M_{b2}, \ldots, M_{b9} = 0.005$
Spring constant K(N/m)	6.6×10^7	1.35×10^7
Damping ratio(ζ)	0.1	0.01
Initial velocity (m/s)	$V_{c1}(-0) = 40$ $V_{c1}(+0) = 32$ $V_{c2}, \ldots, V_{cn} = 40$	$V_{b1}, \ldots, V_{b(m-1)} = 0$ $V_{bm}(-0) = 0$ $V_{bm}(+0) = 32$

Figure 63.2 shows the influence of the spring constant of golf club K_c on the restitution coefficient RE for some parameters of the damping ratio ζ. It is found for each case that an optimum combination of golf club and golf ball which gives the maximum restitution coefficient exists. It is also found that the smaller the damping ratio is, the larger the restitution coefficient becomes.

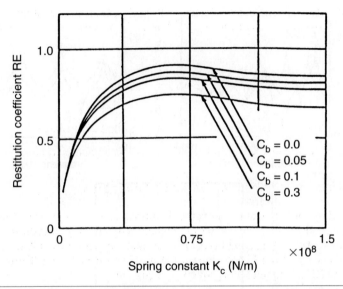

Figure 63.2   Influence of spring constant of golf club on the restitution coefficient.

Frequency Domain Analysis of Transfer Characteristics

The mechanical impedance is considered with regard to golf club and golf ball separately. The mechanical impedance of golf ball and golf club, Z_b, and Z_c are defined as follows, as shown in Yamaguchi et al. 1986 before.

$$Z_{bi} = f_{bm}(t) / \dot{X}_{bm} = f_{bm}(t)/j\omega \dot{X}_{bm}$$

$$Z_{cl} = f_{cl}(t) / \dot{X}_{cl} = f_{cl}(t)/j\omega \dot{X}_{cl}$$

Figure 63.3 shows the mechanical impedances of golf club and golf ball for the model used in figure 63.2, where damping ratio is set to $\zeta = 0.05$.

Figure 63.3(b) shows the case that the value of K_c is set to 6.6×10^7(N/m), which shows the maximum restitution coefficient in figure 63.2. Figure 63.3(a) shows the case that the spring constant of golf club K_c is set to 3.0×10^7(N/m), which is smaller than the optimum value. And Figure 63.3(c) is the case that K_c is set to 9.0×10^7(N/m), which is larger than the optimum value. It is seen from figure 63.3(b) that the restitution coefficient becomes maximum in the case that the frequencies at the minimal value of the mechanical impedances of golf club and golf ball coincide with each other.

EXPERIMENTS OF SIMULATED GOLF CLUB HEAD

In the actual collision between golf club and golf ball, the impact face of the golf club is not perpendicular to the collision direction and collides with the golf ball

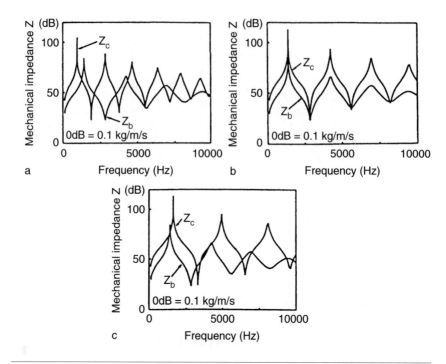

Figure 63.3   Mechanical impedances of golf club and golf ball (a) K_c=3.0 × 10^7 (N/m). (b) K_c=6.6 × 10^7 (N/m). (c) K_c=9.0 × 10^7 (N/m).

with a certain angle, which is called loft angle. This causes a spin motion of the golf ball, and then it becomes difficult to evaluate true restitution. Therefore a simulated club head composed of an aluminum cylinder and a spacer fixed at the impact face, as shown in figure 63.4, was used. In the test apparatus shown in figure 63.4, the simulated golf club is projected by an air gun and collides with the

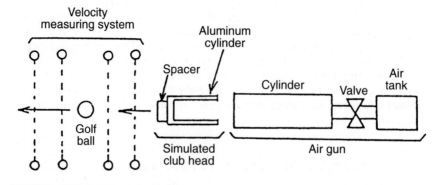

Figure 63.4   Schematic test apparatus for measuring restitution coefficient.

golf ball. The velocities of the simulated golf club and the golf ball before and after impact are measured by using optical sensors. The weight of the simulated golf club is adjusted to 200 grams so as to be nearly equal to the weight of the actual golf club head.

The mechanical impedances of golf ball and simulated club head are measured, respectively, by the method as shown in figure 63.5; that is, sinusoidal vibration is given to the specimen, and the accelerations of the vibrator and the specimen are measured by acceleration pickup A_1 and A_2, and then the transfer function and the mechanical impedance are calculated by the F.F.T. analyzer.

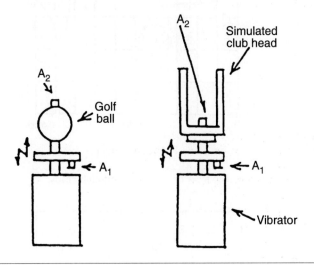

Figure 63.5   Schematic figure for method of measuring mechanical impedance.

Figure 63.6 shows the mechanical impedances of the golf ball and the simulated club heads which are used in the measurements of the restitution coefficient. The spring constant of each spacer of the simulated club heads (A, B, . . . F) is different from each other, so the simulated club heads (A, B, . . . F) show various values of the natural frequencies as in figure 63.6. It is found from figure 63.6 that the mechanical impedance of the simulated club head (B) becomes minimal near the region in which the mechanical impedance of the golf ball has the minimal value.

Figure 63.7 shows the results of the restitution coefficient between the simulated golf club and the golf ball whose mechanical impedances are shown in figure 63.6, and also shows the mechanical impedance of the golf ball, where the accuracy of the restitution coefficient is ±0.1%. It is found from figure 63.7 that the optimum stiffness of the golf club exists, and the simulated club head (B) whose mechanical impedance coincides with that of the golf ball shows the largest value of the restitution coefficient. Thus, these results agree with those obtained by the numerical analysis.

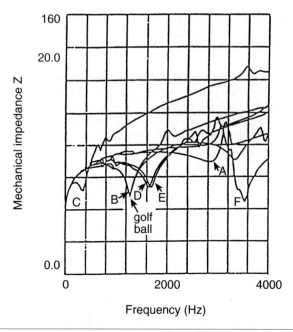

Figure 63.6   Mechanical impedances of simulated golf club heads.

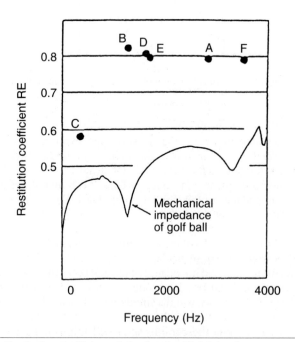

Figure 63.7   Restitution coefficient of simulated golf club heads.

MATERIAL PROPERTIES OF CLUB HEAD
FOR IMPEDANCE MATCHING

In this section, the materials of the club heads for high restitution efficiency are discussed from a viewpoint of natural frequencies of mechanical impedance. As mentioned in figure 63.2, there is an optimum spring constant of the club head (i.e. natural frequency of mechanical impedance) for the restitution efficiency.

Figure 63.8 is the schematic figure that shows the relation between the club head volume and the natural frequency of each club head for various materials. In these twenty years, the materials of club heads have mainly changed from persimmon via stainless steel to titanium alloy. With the changes in materials, club head volume has become larger and the frequency of the mechanical impedance has become smaller. On the other hand, the values of the natural frequencies of golf balls also have a tendency to decrease today. The natural frequencies of first-generation two-piece golf balls are from 1100 Hz to 1300 Hz, but those of so-called soft two- piece balls at the present time are from 800 Hz to 1000 Hz. Generally speaking, hard golf balls show higher restitution coefficients than soft golf balls. However, soft feeling at impact is also a very important characteristic of golf balls, and the harder golf balls are generally disadvantageous in this respect. It has been a target for us to achieve both performances of high restitution and soft feeling.

Figure 63.9 shows the relation between the tensile strength and the Young's modulus for various materials used for club heads. It is found from this figure that

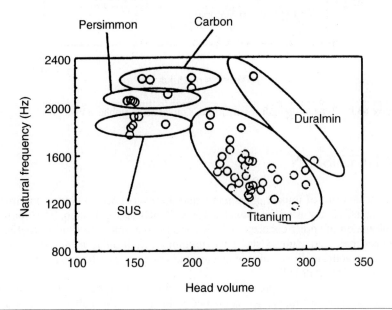

Figure 63.8 Schematic figure of relation between clubhead volume and natural frequency.

the titanium alloy has higher strength for its Young's modulus than stainless steel or dulalmin. This is the reason why the titanium club head can be designed to have a large head volume, large face area, and small thickness of club face, and consequently shows lower natural frequency and higher restitution coefficient than the stainless steel or dulalmin head. Furthermore, figure 63.9 also shows a superior characteristic of the amorphous metal as club head material in respect to high restitution coefficient. Although the amorphous metal was only available for fiber or thin film till recently, there is much current research to develop the bulk amorphous metal. In this sense, the amorphous metal is expected to be a more superior material for club heads to the titanium alloy in the near future, considering the tendency of golf balls being softer and softer.

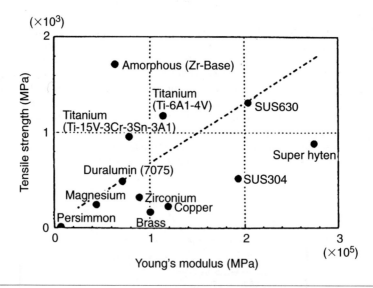

Figure 63.9   Tensile strength versus Young's modulus of clubhead materials.

CONCLUSION

The mechanism of impact phenomena and the factors which control the impact transfer efficiency were investigated for golf ball and golf club. The optimum combination of spring constants which gives the maximum restitution coefficient between ball and club exists. This optimum condition is achieved when the frequency at the minimal value of mechanical impedance of the golf club coincides with that of the golf ball.

The above result was proved by the experiments that the simulated golf club whose mechanical impedance coincided with that of the golf ball showed the maximum value of restitution coefficient.

As for the materials of the club head, the properties of low modulus and high strength are important in the viewpoint of the impedance matching theory. In this sense the titanium alloy is most popular for designing the club head in the above concept. The amorphous metal is expected to be more suitable for designing the high restitution club head.

References

Iwatsubo, T., Nakagawa, N., and Yamaguchi, T. (1990) *Optimum design of golf club* (in Japanese). Trans. Jpn. Soc. Mech. Eng. Vol. 56, No. 524, pp. 1053.

Doi, O. and Asano, N. (1976) *Study on dynamic contact of tooth of gear* (in Japanese). Prepr, Jpn. Soc. Mech. Eng., Vol. 17, No. 760, pp. 144.

Nakagawa, N., Kawai, R., and Akao, M. (1977) *Behavior of impact waves at the interface of a viscoelastic bar.* Bull. Jpn. Soc. Mech. Eng., Vol. 20, No. 149, pp. 1402.

Yagawa, G., Kanto, Y., and Ando, Y. (1983) *Analysis of dynamic contact problem by penalty function method.* Trans. Jpn. Soc. Mech. Eng., Vol. 49, No. 488, pp. 1581.

Yamaguchi, T., Tominaga, I., and Iwatsubo, T. (1986) *Transfer characteristics in collision of two visco-elastomers under mechanical impedance.* Theoretical and Appl. Mech., Vol.34, pp. 153.

CHAPTER 64

Experimental Determination of Golf Ball Coefficients of Sliding Friction

Erik A. Ekstrom
Mechanical Engineering and Mechanics Department, Lehigh University, Bethlehem, PA, USA

A coefficient of sliding friction test apparatus was designed, calibrated, and used to determine the coefficient of sliding friction between golf balls and club head materials. The device was used in conjunction with a compression/tension machine and a computer program to generate the coefficient of sliding friction online. The fixture can test any golf ball/club head material combination. Twenty different golf balls were tested. The golf balls varied in compression rating, ball construction, and cover material. Three club head inserts were used during testing. All were stainless steel: smooth (25-30 μ in. RMS), medium (100 μ in. RMS), or rough (150 μ in. RMS). Results indicated that the higher the club face roughness, the higher the coefficient of sliding friction. However, the coefficient of sliding friction was about the same for the medium and rough plates. The compression rating had little or no correlation with the coefficient of sliding friction. Neither the Rockwell R nor the Shore D hardness had any apparent correlation to the coefficient of sliding friction. The coefficient of sliding friction was determined to be lower for Balata balls than for Surlyn-covered balls.

Keywords: Coefficient of sliding friction, coefficient of rolling friction, coefficient of static friction, friction tester, compression rating, ball construction, cover material, Rockwell R hardness, Shore-D hardness.

INTRODUCTION

The coefficient of friction between a club face and a golf ball is needed to compute the spin rate and velocity of the ball after impact (see Johnson and Ekstrom [1998] for application). Cochran and Stobbs (1968) reported that "the ball reaches its maximum speed of spinning at the split second at which it completely stops sliding and begins to do nothing but roll." Gobush (1994) modeled the golf ball with many concentric layers, as if it were an onion. When this model is used, the outer covering moves as if it were attached to the club head while the inner core winds up. Backspin is affected by how easily the ball can unwind and release from the club head. In both cases the coefficient of friction is a key characteristic that needs to be determined. The coefficient of friction is the tangential force over the normal force.

$$\mu = \frac{F_T}{F_N}$$

There are three types of coefficient of friction: the coefficient of rolling friction, the coefficient of static friction (Coulomb static friction), and the coefficient of sliding friction (Coulomb kinetic friction). Rolling friction occurs when the ball rolls across the club head. The difference between static friction and sliding friction is due to the fact that the tangential force needed to start the ball sliding is greater than the tangential force needed to keep the ball sliding, given the same normal force. Gobush (1996) uses Maw's equation (1981) and the Titleist Flight Analysis system to determine the coefficient of friction. Maw's equation is:

$$\mu = \frac{V_X^A - V_X^B}{(V_Z^A - V_Z^B)(1 + 1/K^2)}$$

where μ = coefficient of friction, $K^2 = I/MR^2$, I = moment of inertia of the golf ball, M = mass of the golf ball, R = radius of the golf ball, V_x^B = tangential speed of ball before impact, V_x^A = tangential speed of ball after impact, V_z^B = normal speed before impact, V_z^A = normal speed after impact.

In order to use Maw's equation, several assumptions need to be made:

1. The contact area is regarded as small compared with the general sizes of the impacting bodies.

2. The coefficient of static friction is equal to the coefficient of dynamic friction and remains constant.

3. The material of the impacting bodies behaves in a linearly elastic manner.

4. The theory follows Hertz in being quasi-static.

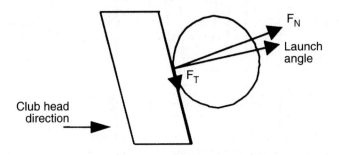

Figure 64.1   Ball and club head impact diagram (from Gobush [1994]).
Reprinted, by permission, from B. Gobush, 1994, "Spin and the Inner Workings of a Golf Ball." In *Golf the Scientific Way*, edited by A. Cochran (Hertfordshire, UK: Aston Publishing Group), 141-145.

5. The distribution of tangential traction (surface shear stress) is axisymmetric.

Gobush also compares his results to force transducer data. The values that are determined from this technique are more of an average of the entire event, which may include sliding, rolling, unsticking, and sliding again. This problem exists when using the transducer method as well. The Friction Tester used in this study is able to calculate the coefficient of sliding friction directly.

DESIGN

The Friction Tester has five parts: a frame (1), two identical insert seats (2), two identical inserts (3), two clamps (4), and a ball holder (5) (see figure 64.2). The frame was made out of a 10.5" × 7"× 1.5" piece of cold-rolled stainless steel. The insert seats were made out of 7" × 3" × 1" pieces of cold-rolled stainless steel. The tester can accommodate any insert less than 6" × 5" × 0.5". The inserts that were designed for testing were made out of 5.5" × 3" × 0.5" pieces of cold-rolled stainless steel. The clamps were made out of 2" × 2" × 1.5" pieces of aluminum. The ball holder has two sections. One section was made out of a 3" × 3.625" × 1" piece of cold-rolled stainless steel. This section was drilled out so a ball could rest within it. The

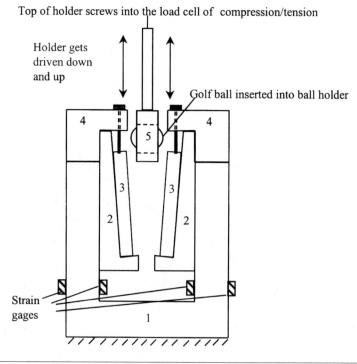

Figure 64.2   Coefficient of friction tester: frame (1), insert seats (2), inserts (3), clamps (4), ball holder (5)

other section was made from a 7" solid aluminum cylinder with a 1" diameter, which allowed the first section to be driven further down between the inserts. The ball holder is attached to a compression/tension load cell, which measures the forces in the vertical direction. There are two pairs of strain gages located on each arm of the frame. The strain gages are of type CEA-06-125UW-120. They have a 120.0±0.3% resistance in Ohms at 34 °C (75 °F) and a gage factor of 2.090±0.5% at 34 °C (75 °F). The gage factor was not used in our experiment because a conversion was determined that correlated volts to pounds. The strain gages have a K_1 value of (+1.1 ± 0.2%).

CALIBRATION

The first step was to calibrate the strain gages. The Friction Tester was placed on its side, and loads were applied using the compression/tension machine. The load and strain voltages were recorded. Using Hooke's Law, the relationship between strain and load can be determined:

$$F = \frac{\varepsilon EI}{yd}$$

where ε = strain, E = Young's modulus, y = half the width of the cross-sectional area of an arm of tester frame, I = area moment of inertia, F = force applied to tester frame, d = distance from force location to strain gage.

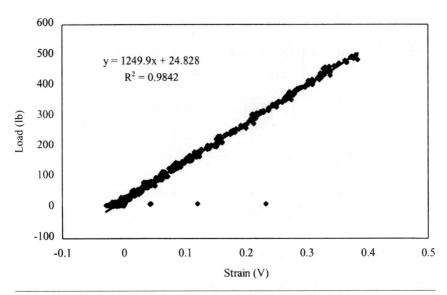

Figure 64.3   Plot of load versus strain from a calibration data set

A typical data set for load versus strain in voltage can be seen in figure 64.3. The data is linear and makes calibration easy. The full bridge constant EI/y was determined to be 1914.56-lb. in./V.

There is a difference in the equations, depending on whether the ball is being driven down or up. This is due to the fact that the x-directional force is always spreading the frame, whereas the y-directional force spreads or closes the frame depending on the direction in which the ball is traveling (see figure 64.4).

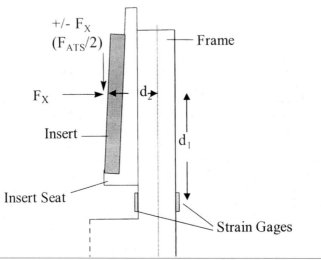

Figure 64.4   Diagram of forces on the friction tester.

Note in Figure 64.4 that d_1 is a function of the ball location and d_2 is a function of the insert thickness. These factors are accounted for in the program used during testing.

The change in the y-directional force can be accounted for by changing the F_x equations to:

Down
$$F_x = (\varepsilon * \frac{EI}{y} + \frac{F_{ATS}}{2} * d_2)/d_1$$

Up
$$F_x = (\varepsilon * \frac{EI}{y} - \frac{F_{ATS}}{2} * d_2)/d_1$$

where: F_x is the force applied on the fixture in the x direction and F_{ATS} is the force applied on the fixture in the y direction.

TESTING

A test requires the fixture to be upright, the strain gages to be attached in a full bridge, and the ball holder to be attached to the load cell. A ball is placed in the ball holder and the ball and ball holder are driven down between the insert plates, compressing the ball. When the ball holder reaches the bottom of the fixture, the compression/ tension machine changes direction and pulls the ball holder up until it reaches its starting point. A test cycle takes about 35 seconds to run. The strain gage, load cell, and displacement readings are recorded and used to calculate the coefficient of sliding friction based on the equation:

$$\mu = \frac{(F_{ATS} \cos\theta - 2F_x \sin\theta)}{(2F_x \cos\theta + F_{ATS} \sin\theta)}$$

where: F_{ATS} = force read from the load cell, F_x = forces determined above, q = angle of taper on the insert seats.

Typically during testing the normal forces varied from 0 to 2000 lbs., while the tangential forces varied from 0 to 300 lbs.

Twenty different golf balls of various compression ratings, ball constructions, and cover materials were tested. The three compression ratings used were 100, 90, and 80. The three classifications of ball construction were wound, two-piece, and other. The three classifications of cover materials were Surlyn, Balata, and other (as defined by the Conforming Golf Ball List 1997). Note that only two 80-compression balls were used; therefore, only 20 balls were tested as opposed to 27 balls. Six balls from each of the 20 lots were tested. Six balls were determined to give a tolerance of 0.05 based on the approximation:

$$\left(\frac{S_x}{tolerance}\right)^2 = \# \, of \, samples$$

where: S_x is the standard deviation of a trial set.

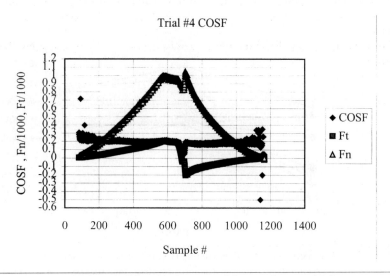

Trial #4 COSF

Figure 64.5   Coefficient of sliding friction, normal force and tangential force versus sample number (can be converted to seconds by multiplying by .0303)

With these 20 balls, three different inserts were used. Each of the inserts was made out of sandblasted stainless steel, but the surface roughnesses varied. The three surface finishes were smooth (25 μ in. RMS), medium (100 μ in. RMS), and rough 150 μ in. RMS). A typical data set is shown in figure 64.5.

The data match theory because theory states that the coefficient of sliding friction is a constant regardless of the magnitude of the normal forces applied. It also can be seen that the coefficient of sliding friction is not a function of area of contact between the golf ball and the insert plates. There was more contact area when there were higher loads, but the coefficient of sliding friction remained constant. Trial tests were performed driving the compression/tension machine at different speeds. No effect was observed. The compression/tension machine was driven at its maximum speed, however, in order to reduce the possibility of viscoelastic effects, like creep. The dip in the data is where the ball and ball holder reach the bottom of the fixture and change direction. There is no y-component load during this period of time. A computer program was written to filter the data such that these points were not averaged with the rest, thus eliminating the need to view each set of data.

Hardness of the golf balls was tested using the Rockwell R scale and a Shore D durometer to see if a correlation between hardness and coefficient of sliding friction could be determined. These scales were used because they are the tests recommended for testing elastomers (ASTM D 785-93, ASTM D 2240-91). For both the Rockwell R and the Shore D tests, the hardness was determined at the seam of the balls.

RESULTS

Several relationships are illustrated in figure 64.6. As roughness increases, so does the coefficient of sliding friction. There is a roughness at which the coefficient of

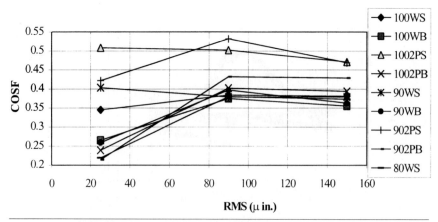

Figure 64.6   The coefficient of sliding friction (COSF) versus roughness. The legend shows the compression rating, ball construction, and cover material. Ex: 100WS stands for a 100 compression, wound, Surlyn ball.

sliding friction levels out. This supports the findings by Cochran and Stobbs (1968), in which grooves had no effect on the golf ball's performance. The compression rating appears to have little or no effect on the coefficient of sliding friction. Also, the coefficient of sliding friction is higher for Surlyn-covered balls than for balata-covered balls. This is an interesting result because balata balls usually have a greater backspin than Surlyn balls. This may be due to the release of the golf ball from the club head. The higher coefficient of friction may slow down the release of the ball, thus causing lower backspin.

Figure 64.7 shows that there is little or no relationship between Rockwell R hardness and the coefficient of sliding friction. This is also apparent by looking at the R^2 values for the regression lines.

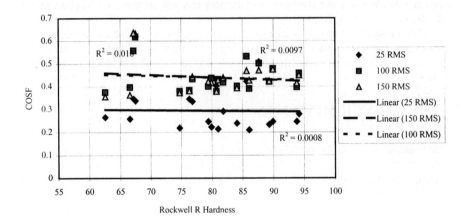

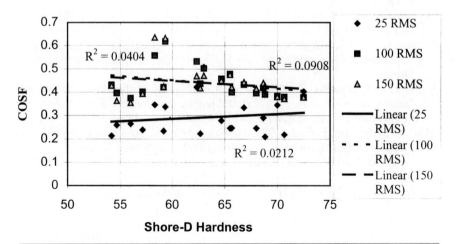

Figure 64.8   The coefficient of sliding friction versus Shore D hardness.

Figure 64.8 shows that there is little or no relationship between Shore D hardness and the coefficient of sliding friction. This is apparent by looking at the R^2 values of the regression lines.

CONCLUSION

We reach several key conclusions from this research. As the roughness of the insert material increases, the coefficient of sliding friction increases and then levels off. The compression rating has little or no effect on the coefficient of sliding friction, and the coefficient of sliding friction is higher for Surlyn balls than for balata balls. Neither Rockwell R nor the Shore D hardness has any apparent correlation to the coefficient of sliding friction.

This paper also establishes a quick and easy way to determine the coefficient of sliding friction. The device used in this paper can determine the coefficient of sliding friction between any golf ball and the club head face material in less than a minute.

ACKNOWLEDGMENTS

The author of this paper would like to thank Frank Thomas and all of the technical staff at the United States Golf Association for funding and supporting this research. Also, special thanks to Stan H. Johnson, PhD for all of his advice and contributions to this paper.

References

Cochran, A. & Stobbs, J. 1968. *The search for the perfect swing.* The Golf Society of Great Britain.

Conforming of golf balls 1997. The United States Golf Association and The Royal and Ancient Golf Club of St. Andrews, Scotland.

Gobush, B. 1994. Spin and the Inner Workings of a Golf Ball. In *Golf the Scientific Way.* Edited by A. Cochran, pp. 141-145. Hertfordshire, U.K.: Aston Publishing Group.

Johnson, S.H. Ekstrom, G. 1998. Experimental Study of the Golf Ball Oblique Impact. In *Science and Golf II.* Edited by A. Cochran and M. Farrally. Hertfordshire, U.K.: Aston Publishing Group.

Maw, N. Barber, JR., Fawcett. 1981. The Role of Elastic Tangential Compliance in Oblique Impact. *Journal of Lubrication Technology.* 103: 74-80.

Rockwell Hardness of Plastic and Elastomeric Materials. ASTM Standard D 785-93.

Rubber Property-Durometer Hardness. ASTM Standard D 2240-91.

CHAPTER 65

Experimental Study of Golf Ball Oblique Impact

S.H. Johnson
Mechanical Engineering and Mechanics Department, Lehigh University, Bethlehem, PA, USA

E.A. Ekstrom
Packaging Division, Harris Corporation, Mountaintop, PA, USA

After a review of models of normal impact and their estimated parameters, the same models are shown to produce almost identical parameters using data from oblique impacts. The analogous models of transverse and rotational motion of Johnson and Lieberman do not well reproduce the transverse impact data, but coefficients of rolling friction determined directly from the data are shown to be consistent with ball construction, independent of approach conditions, and capable of representing the rebound spin rates up to values of about 100 revolutions per second. Such calculations depend on accurate coefficients of sliding friction as well, and a separate, parallel experimental study was carried out to design an appropriate technique and apparatus for measuring the static and sliding characteristics of golf balls in contact with sandblasted stainless steel plates.

Keywords: Impact model, oblique impact, coefficients of sliding and rolling friction, spin rates.

INTRODUCTION

Lieberman (1990) and Lieberman and Johnson (1994) have proposed ordinary differential equation models of normal and oblique golf ball impact, and Johnson and Lieberman (1996) presented numerical values for the parameters of normal impact models obtained from tests performed on representative two-piece and wound balls. The entire ball mass was assumed to be concentrated at the center of the ball and the deformation arising from impact on a massive rigid barrier was represented by a parallel combination of lumped-parameter elastic and dissipative constitutive elements. The two elastic parameters were determined from compression tests and the remaining three parameters of the generalized Maxwell model of viscoelasticity were obtained by gradient-based searching until the predicted force on the barrier is an optimal match to measured normal force-time histories. The normal impact data were obtained from experiments conducted at the United States Golf Association Research and Test Center in Far Hills, New Jersey, USA, using an air-driven ball cannon and a Kistler model 9067 three-axis force transducer mounted on a massive barrier.

The same equipment was used for oblique tests with the barrier rotated 15°, 25°, 35°, 45°, or 55° from the normal impact orientation, and the balls were fired at nominal approach velocities of 30.5 m/s, 36.6 m/s, and 42.7 m/s, with two ball constructions: wound, liquid-filled with balata covers, and two-piece with Surlyn covers.

A separate series of tests were performed to determine the coefficients of static and sliding friction and to determine the influences of loading and contact area on these coefficients. Twenty combinations of compression, construction, and cover material were tested for friction and stiction at three roughnesses of sandblasted stainless steel foundation.

SUMMARY OF NORMAL-IMPACT MODELING

Comparison With Data From Normal-Impact Experiments

Johnson and Lieberman (1996) compared their generalized Maxwell normal-impact model with five parameters to three- and two-parameter Maxwell models and the two-parameter model of normal impact by Simon (1967). A model has been proposed by Cochran (1997) with nonlinear Kelvin viscoelasticity (x is the radial ball deformation, m is the ball mass, and c, β, and k_2 are parameters to be estimated from impact data).

$$m(dx^2 / dt^2) + c(dx / dt) \mid x \mid^{\beta} + k_2 x \mid x \mid^{1/2} = 0$$

See Findley, et al. (1976) for classical models of viscoelasticity. Numerical values for the three parameter Cochran model have been determined from the same data as were used for the Johnson and Lieberman model-parameter determinations. The fitting algorithm has been simplified and improved and a reporting mistake corrected; hence, there are some differences between Johnson and Lieberman (1996) and table 65.1.

Application to Normal Components of Oblique Impact Experimental Data

The same parameter-estimation algorithm and the Johnson and Lieberman model when applied to the normal component of the oblique-impact force-time histories for two-piece balls and approach velocity normal components ranging from 21.4 m/s to 42.5 m/s yielded values for k_2 of 50,271,000 ± 59,500 N/m$^{\beta}$, values for c of 364.10 ±

Table 65.1   Experimentally Determined Parameters for Mathematical Models of Normal Impact

	Ball model with Maxwell viscoelasticity		Ball model with Kelvin viscoelasticity	
	5 parameter 2-piece	5 parameter wound	3 parameter 2-piece	3 parameter wound
k_1 N/m$^\alpha$	15.92×10^6	4.701×10^9	For the Kelvin model the units of	
α	1.5034	2.6804	k_2 are N/m$^{3/2}$ and N-s/m$^{1+\beta}$ for c	
k_2 N/m$^\beta$	$47.71/85.69 \times 10^6$	$5.708/9.047 \times 10^6$	$33.59/33.17 \times 10^6$	$25.08/26.37 \times 10^6$
β	1.6436/1.7613	1.3390/1.4043	0.8232/0.9346	0.1459/0.1816
c N-s/m	635.96/581.79	219.57/205.83	5,949.8/11,941.5	84.35/111.72

Where pairs of parameters are listed, the left values are based on data obtained at a nominal approach velocity of 36.6 m/s and right-hand values are obtained from 42.7 m/s data. The Kelvin model permits use of a simpler parameter-estimation algorithm.

48.16 N-s/m, and β values of 1.6882 ± 0.0225. The narrow ranges for k_2 and β, when used with the k_1 and α from static tests, support the use of the Maxwell model and the assumed nonlinear form for the elasticity. But the range of resulting values for c as the normal component of the approach velocity changes indicates that dissipation is not adequately represented by the linear viscous damping term presently in use.

The results for the wound balls are qualitatively the same. Over a similar range of normal components of approach velocity—16.8 to 42.6 m/s for the wound balls—the parameter values are $5,359,600 \pm 218,250$ N/m$^\beta$ for k_2, 1.3117 ± 0.0583 for β, and 135.01 ± 59.88 N-s/m for the damping parameter c. Again the narrow ranges for k_2 and β validate the form of elastic terms in the model, and the spread of the damping values indicates that linear damping is inadequate for wound balls also. There are no apparent differences in agreement between the models and experimental data for normal impact and the normal components of oblique impact.

STATIC TESTING

A test apparatus, calibration procedure, and data reduction program were created and are in the process of being patented for the measurement of golf ball coefficients of static and sliding friction. A conventional compression/tension test machine is used to drive the golf ball down between convergent, roughened test plates and then reversed to extract the ball. The normal and transverse force time histories are used to compute the coefficient of sliding friction and to verify that stiction is not significant (see Ekstrom, 1997). Figure 65.1 shows a typical data set. Thus far, twenty balls of three compression ratings (80, 90, and 100), three constructions

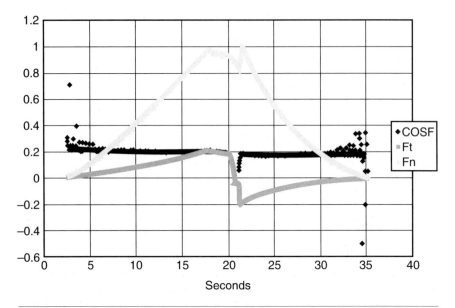

Figure 65.1   Example of sliding-friction results. The measured normal and transverse forces, F_n and F_t respectively, have been divided by 4448 N for plotting on the same vertical scale as the COSF or coefficient of sliding friction. For the first 17 seconds the ball is being compressed and it is expanding after the reversal of direction between 17 and 22 seconds. Note the typical lack of static friction or stiction after the pause during the reversal process.

(wound, two-piece, and other as established by the USGA Conforming Golf Ball List), and three cover materials (Surlyn, balata, and other) have been tested. Three roughnesses of sandblasted stainless steel plates were used (25, 100, and 150 μ in rms surface roughness—given in U.S. Customary units as measured according to ASTM procedures and for comparison to USGA Standards). No correlation has been observed between compression rating, cover material hardness—as measured by Rockwell R and Shore D test equipment—and coefficients of sliding friction. There has been no evidence of significant stiction even at reversal of motion under load. No coefficient of static friction is warranted.

DYNAMIC IMPACT TESTING

An oblique model was constructed in Johnson and Lieberman (1994) by appending a torsional linear Maxwell model to the normal model above. The ball was separated into a rigid core and a concentric shell with the relative angular movement governed by the viscoelastic constitutive relations. The difficulty of obtaining transverse force-time data from oblique ball-barrier impact tests make differentiating between viscoelastic models inconclusive (see figure 65.2). However, the data is sufficient to identify coefficients of rolling friction during oblique impact.

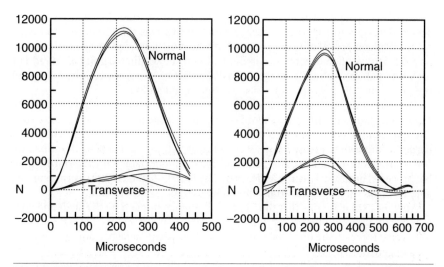

Figure 65.2   Typical sets of force-transducer data. The left plots are for three shots of two-piece Surlyn-covered balls fired at 42.7 m/s and at an angle of 45° from normal to the barrier. The right plots are for three liquid-center, wound, balata-covered balls fired at the same velocity and approach angle.

If the coefficients of sliding friction obtained by Ekstrom (1997) are used to estimate when sliding stops and rolling begins, then by dividing the subsequent instantaneous measured transverse force by the corresponding instantaneous measured normal force, one calculates the coefficient of rolling friction. The values obtained are consistent, mildly velocity dependent, and less than the coefficient of sliding friction for the appropriate ball construction (see table 65.2).

The coefficients of rolling friction in table 65.2 are averages computed over periods of 180μs for the two-piece balls and 189μs for the wound balls. The

Table 65.2   Experimentally Determined Coefficients of Rolling Friction

Approach angle	55°	45°	35°	25°	15°
2-pc time to roll	Approximately 2% of contact time				
wnd time to roll	Approximately 10% of contact time				
2-pc CORF (early)	$0.097 \pm .032$ averaged over 180μs following predicted onset of rolling				
2-pc CORF (later)	$0.146 \pm .076$ averaged over 180μs from late in the contact time				
wnd CORF (early)	$0.213 \pm .018$	$0.219 \pm .042$	$0.216 \pm .032$	$0.197 \pm .066$	$0.092 \pm .018$
wnd CORF (later)	$0.268 \pm .028$	$0.238 \pm .012$	$0.088 \pm .115$	$0.068 \pm .051$	$-.017 \pm .158$

Time to roll is computed using a rigid-body model and coefficients of sliding friction for a smooth plate of 0.484 for the two-piece balls with Surlyn covers and 0.262 for the wound balls with balata covers.

insensitivity to approach angle and approach velocity and the relatively small standard deviations support the scenario that sliding was short lived and followed by an extended period of rolling contact of a heavily deformed viscoelastic sphere on a rigid foundation. Energy dissipation takes place within the golf ball at radii of high internal shear strains. Images of ball contact on the faces of lofted clubs by pressure-sensitive polymers fail to show significant sliding.

The later-time coefficients of rolling friction exhibit less consistency, including negative values, and greater standard deviations, exceeding 100% on some cases. One explanation is that the extraction of data from the noisy Kistler signals becomes harder as more time elapses. This was the case with normal data as described by Johnson (1996). The suppression of noise in the oblique data is much more difficult but proceeds backward in time as described by Huerta-Ochoa (1997). As a result the data from late in the contact time should be as valid as earlier data.

Another explanation is that the internal dynamics implied by the shell and core models of various authors or Gobush's (1996) onion model are altering the transverse force on the transducer from that of classical inelastic rolling contact of a homogeneous sphere.

RESULTS

Coefficients of sliding and rolling friction can be used to compute post-impact spin rates. As Cochran and Stobbs (1968) noted, the spin rate is a maximum at the instant

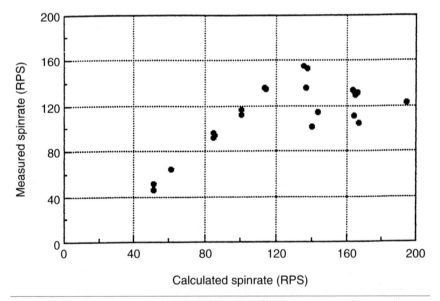

Figure 65.3 Comparison of calculated and measured launch spin rates for two-piece balls with Surlyn covers. Similar results were obtained from liquid-center, wound balls with balata covers. The calculated values depend on the coefficients of rolling and sliding friction and contact time. A rigid-body model is used to compute the time of sliding cessation and rolling onset.

that sliding stops and rolling ensues. Subsequent energy loss during viscoelastic rolling continuously reduces that spin rate until loss of contact. As an overall verification of the normal and transverse and torsional model with sliding and rolling friction, figure 65.3 shows good agreement between simulated and measured post-impact spin rates resulting from the firing of golf balls against a rigid, oblique barrier at various approach velocities and angles of approach. For moderate spin rates the coefficients of sliding and rolling friction produce good agreement. Above about 100 rps, the sliding and rolling coefficients are insufficient to represent the observed behavior and one suspects that internal dynamic behavior of greater complexity than can be described by coefficients of friction is taking place.

ACKNOWLEDGMENTS

The author wishes to express his gratitude to Mr. Frank Thomas, technical director of the United States Golf Association, for his generous support, cooperation, and encouragement. Thanks also to the outstanding technical staff of the USGA Research and Test Center for their assistance.

References

Cochran, A.J. 1997. Private conversations at the USGA Research and Test Center, Far Hills, New Jersey, USA in April 1997.

Ekstrom, E.A. 1997. *Experimental Determination of Golf Ball Coefficients of Sliding Friction.* M.S. thesis, Lehigh University.

Findley, W.N., J.S. Lai, and K. Onaran. 1976. *Creep and Relaxation of Nonlinear and Viscoelastic Materials.* Amsterdam: North-Holland Publishing Co.

Gobush, W. 1996. Spin and the Inner Workings of a Golf Ball. In *Golf the Scientific Way,* ed. A. Cochran, 141-145. Hemel Hempstead: Aston Publishing Group.

Huerta-Ochoa, R. 1997. Identification of a piezoelectric transducer under an impact load. In *Control '97 Proceedings of the IASTED International Conference at Cancun, Mexico,* 211-214. Anaheim: IASTED-ACTA Press.

Johnson, K.L. 1985. *Contact Mechanics.* Cambridge: Cambridge University Press.

Johnson, S.H. and B.B. Lieberman. 1996. Normal impact models for golf balls. In *The Engineering of a Sport,* ed. S. Haake, 251-256. Rotterdam: A.A. Balkema.

Johnson, S.H. and B.B. Lieberman. 1994. An analytical model for ball-barrier impact, Part 2: a model for oblique impact. In *Science and Golf II,* ed. A.J. Cochran and M.R. Farrally, 315-320. London: E. & F.N. Spon.

Lieberman, B.B. 1990. The effect of impact conditions on golf ball spin-rate. In *Science and Golf,* ed. A.J. Cochran, 225-230. London: E. & F.N. Spon.

Lieberman, B.B. and S.H. Johnson. 1994. An analytical model for ball-barrier impact, Part I: models for normal impact. In *Science and Golf II,* ed. A.J. Cochran and M.R. Farrally, 309-314. London: E. & F.N. Spon.

CHAPTER 66

Computational and Experimental Analysis of the Golf Impact

A. Hocknell, R. Jones and S.J. Rothberg
Loughborough University, Leicestershire, UK

An approach to modelling and experimental validation is presented which produces accurate finite element models, validated by experimental measurements during impact. The experimental data represents a greater level of detail than achieved previously and strong agreement with the impact behaviour of the finite element model provides validating evidence for the approach taken to club head and ball modelling. The detailed analysis capability afforded by a validated, accurate finite element impact model is then discussed by presenting behaviour of the club face and ball in the contact region during and immediately after impact.

Keywords: Finite element, impact, validation, experimentation.

INTRODUCTION

A validated, detailed finite element golf impact model is a powerful design analysis tool for both club heads and balls. However, several previous studies have been limited by inaccuracies in modelling the sculptured shape or by difficulties in obtaining detailed experimental data to validate the model behaviour during impact. In this paper, sculptured surface geometry modelling and finite element mesh generation techniques are used to generate an accurate representation of a hollow metal club head. The impact model is then validated using experimental data obtained from a measurement system based on non-contacting transducers. The lateral deformation of the ball and the generation of rotational velocity components from rest are presented as examples of the detailed experimental information which can be obtained during impact and which provide validating evidence for the finite element model impact behaviour. The usefulness of a validated finite element model is then discussed and deformation of the club face and ball in the contact region are presented as examples of parameters which are difficult to obtain experimentally but which can be extracted

526

readily from a validated model. The club-ball combination under investigation is a hollow metal driver with 10.5° loft and a 2-piece ball; however, the techniques discussed in this paper are equally applicable to other club-ball combinations.

FINITE ELEMENT MODEL

Geometrical accuracy is essential if the model is to be used in a predictive capacity, but accurate models of sculptured surface structures are generally more difficult to produce than prismatic structures. In this study, an established feature-based approach (Mitchell, 1996) is applied to the accurate representation of hollow golf club head surface geometry in a CAD model. The discretisation of the geometry model into a mesh of finite elements well suited to the physical situation under investigation is crucial to the quality of the analysis solution. The sculptured nature of the golf club head makes mesh generation difficult if the entire club head is considered as a single surface because elements are produced with excessive warp and taper or with aspect ratios unsuitable for finite element analysis. A feature-based approach to quadrilateral mesh generation on sculptured surface bodies has been reported previously (Hocknell et al. 1997a) and the finite element mesh created using this procedure is shown in figure 66.1. The mesh was constructed within the MSC/PATRAN pre/post processing environment and contains 701 2-dimensional quadrilateral shell elements with thicknesses determined from pointed anvil micrometer measurements on the real club head. The Young's Modulus of the material was determined by static tensile tests on a specimen cut from a stainless steel investment cast club head and was found to be 207 GN/m². The density of the material is 7850 kg/m³, which when applied to the finite element model, gives a club head model a mass of 190 grams.

The finite element ball model shown in figure 66.1 is based on an icosahedron shape which is subdivided into 320 facets and projected onto the surface of a sphere.

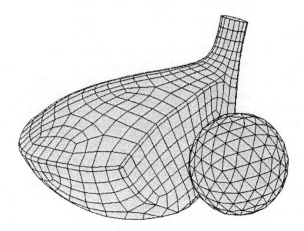

Figure 66.1   Hollow club head and ball finite element representation. 701 elements in the club head. 2880 elements in the ball.

The outer sphere is composed of 320 wedge elements of thickness equal to that of the cover material in a 2-piece ball, and the core of the ball is filled by several concentric hollow spheres of decreasing radius, each containing 320 wedge elements. This arrangement is necessary to prevent the finite element mesh from introducing asymmetry into the behaviour of the ball model. The core and cover material properties were determined from compression tests of material samples at a strain rate of 10 ms^{-1} and the resulting stress-strain curves were supplied to a Mooney-Rivlin hyperelastic material model. The Abaqus Explicit finite element code was used to analyse the impact.

EXPERIMENTAL IMPACT ANALYSIS FOR MODEL VALIDATION

The golf impact is characterised by large elastic deformation of the ball and significantly smaller elastic deformation of the club head. In addition to attaining a forward velocity of up to 60 ms^{-1} during the impact, the ball is observed to undergo significant deformation in the contact region. Other, smaller extremes of deformation are recorded diametrically opposite the contact site and also perpendicular to the direction of the intended line of flight. Additionally, the golf club–ball collision is an example of an eccentric impact. Backspin is generated on the ball due to the 10.5° loft of the golf club face and misalignment of the impact can produce sidespin. High speed video images taken as part of this study show little appreciable spin of the ball whilst in contact with the club; however, the generation of backspin and sidespin velocity components during the impact is of importance.

The laser Doppler vibrometer is a non-contacting velocity transducer which is generally employed in vibration measurement systems where the target object is hot, light, or rotating. Its non-contact operation makes the instrument well suited to measurements of motions on impact and a measurement system has been reported previously in which a vibrometer is used to analyse both the whole body velocities and localised deformations of elastic bodies during impact (Hocknell et al. 1996a). Application of this measurement technique to the golf impact is shown in figure 66.2 and is used in this study to provide experimental validating evidence for the detailed behaviour of the golf impact finite element model.

The vibrometer is sensitive only to the component of the target velocity which lies along the axis of the incident laser beam. Relevant components of target velocity can therefore be selected and the vibrometer aligned to measure only these. In figure 66.2, two vibrometers are shown aligned to make measurements initially at point D on the ball. A vibrometer positioned at an angle $\alpha = 75°$ from the x-axis makes a measurement, $V_{D,\alpha}(t)$, which contains components of velocity due to whole body forward motion, forward deformation and lateral deformation of the ball. The component of velocity due to lateral deformation in this measurement is determined by making a simultaneous measurement at the same point on the ball, $V_D(t)$, using the vibrometer aligned perpendicular to the x-axis. The two measurements can then be used to extract components of both the whole body forward velocity of the ball and the deformation of the ball in the forward and lateral directions.

The ball moves forward a distance of approximately 11.5 mm during the impact, causing the illuminated point on the surface of the ball to move toward the contact site during the period of measurement. A method which compensates for relative whole body displacement between the target and a remote transducer fixed in space has been reported previously (Hocknell et al. 1997b). In this study, the displacement compensation technique is applied to remote measurements made during impact using laser vibrometers at five points of interest, A-E, across the equator of the golf ball, as shown in figure 66.2. In this case the five data sets are not simultaneous and their use in displacement compensation relies on the good repeatability of the impact conditions created using a golf robot. Several measurements were taken in order to demonstrate that the results presented here are representative. This data, when combined with a measurement of the whole body ball displacement, produces a close estimate in time of the measurement which would have been made by a transducer fixed to a point on the ball. Direct comparison can be made between the behaviour of nodes in a finite element model and close estimates of the behaviour of equivalent fixed points on the real ball. This permits a significantly more detailed comparison of computational and experimental data than is possible using either high speed video techniques or transducers actually fixed to the ball.

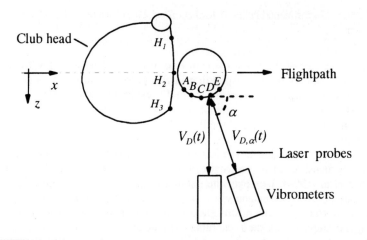

Figure 66.2   Alignment of two laser vibrometers to determine whole body ball forward velocity and deformation of the ball in the x and z directions.

An example of a displacement compensated lateral deformation velocity measurement, $V_c(t)$, taken by the vibrometer during an impact in which the club struck a ball at 35.5 ms[-1] is shown in figure 66.3. It can be seen that in the first half of the impact the lateral deformation velocity of point C on the ball is toward the vibrometer. In the second half of the impact, the ball attempts to recover its original shape and the measured velocity is negative. The equivalent finite element result for point C is shown dotted in figure 66.3. Close agreement between these results and those from points A, B, D and E provides strong evidence for the validity of the

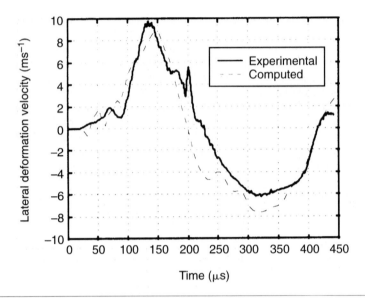

Figure 66.3   Experimental lateral deformation velocity measurement and finite element equivalent.

impact behaviour of the finite element ball model. Integration of $V_c(t)$ over the contact time allows the corresponding lateral deformation to be calculated and reveals how at the end of the impact the ball 'over recovers' to a lateral dimension less than that of the un-deformed ball. This is the start of a heavily damped oscillation which is a feature of the initial ball motion.

The golf club–ball collision is an example of an eccentric impact, with backspin generated on the ball due to the loft of the club head. The rotational velocity is commonly measured in the first metre of flight using stroboscopic video techniques (Gobush et al. 1994). However the detailed mechanics occurring during impact which cause the rotation can only be inferred from these post-impact measurements. High speed video systems afford the capability to observe the motion of the ball during the impact, but their usefulness in detailed analysis is limited by the resolution of the captured images and no appreciable rotation of the ball is observed whilst the ball is in contact with a club face of 10.5° loft angle.

The rotational velocity of the golf ball during impact can be determined if the measurement arrangement in figure 66.2 is applied to points on the ball which lie above and below the equator. The result is shown as a solid line in figure 66.4, where the low rotational velocity in the early stages of the impact increases rapidly after approximately 100 μs and a slight oscillation is observed about a slowly increasing rotational velocity over the remainder of the impact. The mean value of the final rotational velocity, 2750 rev/min, agrees closely with the value measured by a stroboscopic video system in the first metre of flight and the experimental observations of the rotational velocity increasing from rest during the impact represent a level of measurement detail not previously achieved.

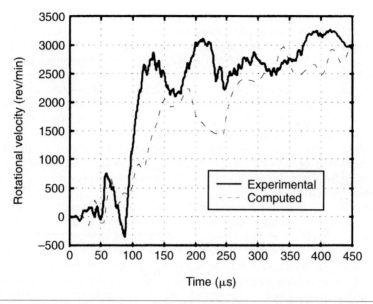

Figure 66.4   Experimental rotational velocity measurement and finite element equivalent.

The rotational velocity of the ball calculated using the finite element model is shown dotted in figure 66.4. The model slightly underestimates the rate of increase in rotational velocity in the interval $100 \leq t \leq 150$ μs. However, the rotational velocity in the second half of the impact is in close agreement with the experimental result. These measurements and others pertaining to the velocity and deformation of the ball in the forward direction, the contact approach and contact duration, captured using this measurement system but not presented here, provide a wealth of detailed model validating evidence from a relatively small number of measurements.

USEFULNESS OF A VALIDATED FINITE ELEMENT GOLF IMPACT MODEL

A validated, detailed finite element golf impact model is a powerful design analysis tool. By providing the capability to change parameters quickly and analyse their effects, the validated finite element model can assist in reducing design iterations and hence the cost of introducing a new product. Design analysis examples include the study of off-centre impacts, the use of alternative material properties and re-distribution of the wall thickness in the club head. This impact analysis capability, allied to the steady state vibrational analysis, identified previously as being important in the understanding of 'feel' (Hocknell et al. 1996a & 1997c), gives the

validated finite element model considerable functionality in new product development. Additionally, having proven the modelling procedure, models of different
club heads and ball constructions can be created, following the same rules, with
considerable confidence in the ability to predict closely the dynamic behaviour of
the real product.

In the pursuit of improved knowledge of the detailed mechanics occurring during
impact, a validated finite element model is particularly useful to interrogate
parameters which would be extremely difficult to measure experimentally. In the
golf impact, it is particularly difficult to capture experimental data from points on
the club head or ball near to the contact site. However, the range of measurements
made elsewhere on the club head and ball suggest strongly that the behaviour of
those areas for which there is no experimental data is also represented accurately in
the finite element model.

The relative displacement across the face of the golf club head during impact is
an example of an important parameter which is extremely difficult to measure
experimentally. This can be determined from the finite element model by considering the displacement in the x-direction of three nodes which all lie on the face of
the club head. In figure 66.2, node H_2 lies in the centre of the face, equidistant from
nodes H_1 and H_3, which are chosen to lie at the edges of the face. In this arrangement
the forward displacements of nodes H_1 and H_3 are assumed not to include any
component of deformation, such that the average of these two displacements
represents the displacement of the un-deformed face centre, in the x-direction, in the
presence of whole body rotation of the club head about the normal to the xz-plane.
The deformation of the centre of the club face is therefore given by displacement of
node H_2 relative to the average of nodes H_1 and H_3. The result is shown in figure 66.5,

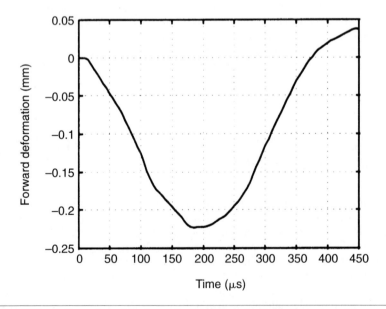

Figure 66.5   Deformation of the face calculated from the finite element model.

where a peak deformation of 0.22 mm is predicted at a time 200 μs into the impact. The timing of the peak deformation is consistent with that of the maximum forward deformation of the ball and the face deflection and recovery data is of value in further studies which may seek to analyse the effect of face thickness on the transfer of energy to the golf ball.

The localised deformation of the golf ball in the contact region can be investigated using the finite element model by analysing the forward velocities of the finite element node pair on the club head and ball which are first to make contact and last to break contact, as shown in figure 66.6. The finite element model suggests strongly that the ball contact surface, shown in a solid line, accelerates rapidly at the start of the impact then actually slows down during contact with the club face. This localised region of the ball must again accelerate rapidly at the end of the impact in order to attain the whole body velocity of the ball, shown dotted in figure 66.6. In fact, a deformation and recovery oscillation is established in this localised region of the ball in the forward direction and the associated velocity component can be observed on top of the 52 ms^{-1} final velocity of the whole ball in the period $t > 450$ μs, after the end of the impact. This is an example of the insight which a validated model can provide into parameters which are difficult to measure experimentally. Additionally, the intersection of the two lines at a time 200μs into the impact is evidence for all points on the equator of the ball having the same instantaneous forward velocity at the time of maximum forward deformation of the ball. This is confirmed in further experiments performed using the measuring system described in the section above on experimental impact analysis for model validation.

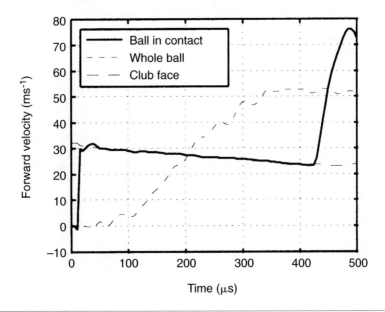

Figure 66.6   Forward velocity of the club head and ball calculated from the finite element model.

CONCLUSIONS

The modelling and experimental analysis approach presented in this paper provides accurate golf impact finite element models which are validated to a greater level of detail than has been possible previously. Accurate club head representation is achieved through application of sculptured surface geometry modelling and finite element mesh generation techniques and the golf ball model is based on an icosahedral node pattern. The validity of the model during impact is tested using experimental data obtained by remote measurement techniques. The experimental data represents a superior level of measurement detail in the golf impact, and close agreement with the finite element model impact behaviour provides strong evidence for the validity of the modelling approach taken. A validated finite element golf impact model is a valuable design analysis tool and this paper has demonstrated a capability to investigate parameters using the model which are difficult to measure experimentally. This provides the basis for greater understanding of the detailed mechanics occurring during impact leading to improved equipment design.

ACKNOWLEDGMENTS

This study was carried out as part of an Engineering and Physical Sciences Research Council grant investigating the design analysis of sculptured surface products. The authors would like to acknowledge the assistance of Dunlop Slazenger International Limited and Dr. Séan Mitchell of Loughborough University.

References

Gobush,W; Pelletier,D; Days,C (1994): Video monitoring system to measure initial launch characteristics of a golf ball. *Proceedings of the Second World Scientific Congress of Golf*, St Andrews, UK, 327-333.

Hocknell,A; Jones,R; Rothberg,SJ (1996a): Experimental analysis of impacts with large elastic deformation. Part 1: Linear motion. *Measurement Science and Technology* 7(9), 1247-1254.

Hocknell,A; Jones,R; Rothberg,SJ (1996b): Engineering 'feel' in the design of golf clubs. *Proceedings of the First International Conference on the Engineering of Sport*, Sheffield, UK, 333-337.

Hocknell,A; Mitchell,SR; Underwood,DJ; Jones,R (1997a): Feature based quadrilateral mesh generation for sculptured surface products. Submitted to the *Transactions of the IIE*.

Hocknell,A; Jones,R; Rothberg,SJ (1997b): Remote vibration measurements: Compensation of waveform distortion due to whole body translations. Accepted for publication in the *Journal of Sound and Vibration*.

Hocknell,A; Mitchell,SR; Jones,R; Rothberg,SJ (1997c): Hollow golf club head modal characteristics. Determination and impact applications. *Experimental Mechanics*, June 1998.

Mitchell,SR (1996): *A feature based approach to the computer aided design of sculptured products*. Ph.D. Thesis, Loughborough University.

CHAPTER 67

The Initial Trajectory Plane After Ball Impact

K. Miura
Institute of Space and Astronautical Science, Sagamihara, Kanagawa, Japan

F. Sato
Mizuno Corporations, Osaka, Japan

This paper presents a study on the initial trajectory plane immediately after ball impact and its relation to the direction of the swing and the direction of the club face. The explicit formulae describing the above relations are presented. These formulae provide a tool for understanding the effects on the resulting trajectory of the swing direction, the club face direction, and the loft of the club.

Keywords: Trajectory, impact, swing, club face, diagnosis.

INTRODUCTION

The slicing and hooking trajectories are essentially the direct result of the impact condition that consists of the normal vector of the club face and the swing vector. The practical explanation of the problem was given by Cochran and Stobbs (1968), for example, although their discussion was limited to the pure sidespin around a vertical axis. In reality, a ball spins around a single tilted axis which is in effect equivalent to a combination of pure backspin and pure sidespin. It is, therefore, very difficult to find the direct relation between the cause (the normal vector of the club face and the swing vector) and the effect (trajectory).

In 1994, Jorgensen proposed the idea of the initial trajectory plane called "the D plane" for this problem. (In this paper we use the Greek letter Δ for D.) The Δ plane for a golf swing is defined by a plane that contains the path along which the club head is moving at impact (the Δ swing vector) and the normal vector to the club face. The Δ plane includes the initial trajectory of the ball after impact. The Δ plane also contains a lift force since the lift force is perpendicular to the axis of spin, which is perpendicular to the Δ plane. The Δ plane is extremely useful for us to understand the pattern of resulting trajectory based on the impact condition, or vice versa.

535

To use Jorgensen's Δ plane for a quantitative study, however, the Δ plane must be expressed in terms of the swing vector and the normal vector of the club face. The purpose of this paper is to present exact and explicit formulae describing the Δ plane in terms of the swing vector and the normal vector of the club face. These formulae provide an indispensable tool for understanding the effects on the resulting trajectory of the swing direction, the club face direction, and the loft of the club. To demonstrate the validity of the tool for practical applications, a limited number of examples are shown in this paper.

COLLISION OF A BALL ON A RIGID PLANE

A Case Where a Ball Collides With a Rigid Plane

Let us consider the case where a ball having the velocity vector V_i collides with an oblique rigid and massive plane. Throughout this study, we treat the impact phenomenon from a macroscopic viewpoint. The rebound ball velocity vector V_o should lie on the plane that is common to V_i and the normal vector N on the impact point on the plane. This is because there is no force to break the symmetry condition. Let us call the plane the "initial trajectory plane," or the "Δ plane."

A Case Where a Rigid Plane Hits a Ball

Though the physical phenomenon is identical between the case where a flying ball collides with a rigid plane and the case where a traveling rigid plane collides with a ball, the treatments of the motions of these cases are different. Let us consider the case where a club face having a swing velocity vector V_{si} collides with a ball at the point 0 (figure 67.1). If we view the motions of the ball and the club face based on

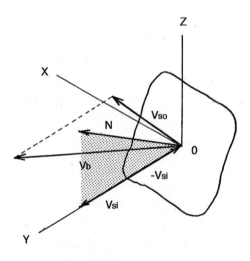

Figure 67.1   Impact of a club and a ball.

the coordinate system fixed in the 3-space, we are faced with a considerable difficulty. This is because both the club and the ball are moving.

To simplify the problem, let us treat it with the coordinate system fixed on the club face. For this purpose, we add the vector $-V_{si}$ to the whole system. In this way the problem is transferred to that of the ball traveling with velocity vector $-V_{si}$ colliding with the stationary club surface. Here, the normal to the club face is called the "face vector." The restitution velocity vector V_{so} is given as shown in figure 67.1. To view V_{so} based on the coordinate system fixed in space, we simply add the vector V_{si} to V_{so} and finally the ball velocity vector V_b is obtained. This treatment does not include the influence of finite mass of the rigid plane; however, the following discussion of angular properties is not substantially affected.

Conclusively, the following information about the ball velocity vector V_b is obtained.

1. The ball velocity vector V_b lies on the Δ plane (shown by shaded area).

2. The ball velocity vector V_b lies slightly under the normal vector of the club face.

3. The axis of the spin is normal to the Δ plane.

INCLINATION OF THE Δ PLANE

A Case Where the Swing Vector Points to the Target

In this section, we treat the case where the swing vector points precisely to the target. Throughout this study, it is assumed that the swing vector at impact is on a horizontal plane, and that the leading edge of the club face is on a horizontal plane. In figure 67.2, the Cartesian coordinates X, Y, Z are set so that the impact point is on the origin $(0, 0, 0)$, and the target is located on the Y axis. In this figure, the face vector points toward the right of the target, and the swing vector V_s is on the Y axis. The angle between the face vector N and its projection on the X-Y plane is the loft angle λ, and the angle between the projections of the face vector and the swing vector V_s is α. The Δ plane is defined by an inclined plane formed by the face vector N and the swing vector V_s. On careful inspection of figure 67.2 with the aid of the principle of triple normals (Hokari et al. 1959), the angle of inclination δ of the Δ plane is obtained as follows.

$$\delta = \arctan[\sin\alpha / \tan\lambda] \qquad (1)$$

The ball vector V_b is located on the slightly lower position on the Δ plane as shown in figure 67.2. To understand the practical meaning of this equation, we shall apply it to a few examples for different values of α with the identical loft $\lambda = 11$ degrees.

1. $\alpha = 0$, thus $\delta = 0$

The Δ plane is vertical and the spin axis is horizontal. The flight trajectory is straight to the target.

2. $\alpha = +3°$

This is the example where the club face is open to the right as much as 3 degrees.

$$\delta = \arctan[\sin(3)/\tan(11)] = +15.06°$$

The Δ plane is inclined approximately 15 degrees to the right. This is the situation which appears in the model in figure 67.2, and the position of the ball vector is similar to it. Therefore, at least during the initial stage of free flight of the ball, the trajectory will be within the extension of this inclined plane.

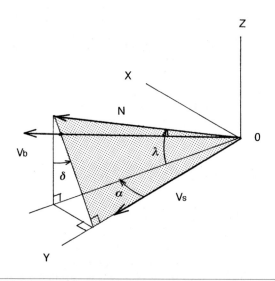

Figure 67.2 Δ plane: a swing vector points to the target.

Let us consider the trajectory of the ball after the initial stage. The external forces applied to the ball during free flight are the aerodynamic drag and lift forces and the gravity force. We neglect the wind effects in the present problem. Since the spin axis of the ball is perpendicular to the Δ plane, aerodynamic forces act within the Δ plane. As a result, these forces do not affect the ball deviation from the Δ plane. On the other hand, the gravity force has a component normal to the Δ plane. Because the Δ plane is inclined as much as 15 degrees in the right side, the gravity component acts also in the right direction. This makes the ball fly rightward. This is exactly what happens in a slice.

3. $\alpha = -3°$

This is the mirror condition to the previous example. The result is a hook.

A Case Where the Face Vector Points to the Target

Let us consider the case where the projection of the face vector points exactly to the target. Naturally, the angle α equals zero. Contrary to the previous case, the direction of swing vector is as much as β deviated from the target line (figure 67.3). A similar approach to the previous section allows us the following result.

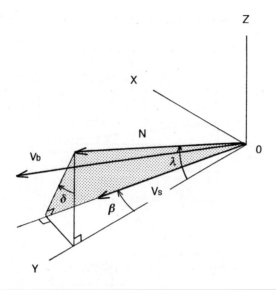

Figure 67.3   Δ plane: a face vector points to the target.

$$\delta = -\arctan[\sin \beta / \tan \lambda] \qquad (2)$$

We assume the sign convention about δ such that the clockwise screw rotation along the face vector N is positive. If we compare Equations (1) and (2), we can find that the effect of α and β, at least on the inclination of the Δ plane, are identical in magnitude but with opposite signs. An example is as follows.

1. β = +3°, α = 0, λ = 11°

$$\Delta = -\arctan[\sin(3) / \tan(11)] = -15.06°$$

Due to the sign convention, the negative angle means counterclockwise rotation along the normal vector N. Therefore, the Δ plane is inclined leftward as much as 15 degrees. The direction of the ball vector V_b is close to the normal vector N. However, it is slightly deviated to the right. The following flight is influenced by the leftward inclination of the Δ plane, and the ball curves to the left. This is a draw. Equations (1) and (2) indicate the similar effects of α and β on δ; however, the effects on the resulting flight are different. The initial flight direction is predominantly governed by the direction of the face vector N and not by the direction of the swing vector V_s.

General Cases, α and β Are Non-Zero Values

When the angles α and β are not zero, the inclination δ of the Δ plane is given by the following formula (figure 67.4).

$$\delta = \arctan[\sin(\alpha - \beta) / \tan \lambda] \qquad (3)$$

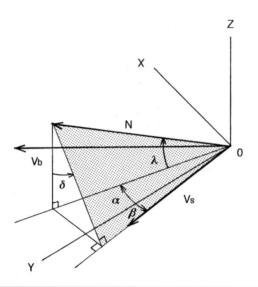

Figure 67.4   Δ plane: general case.

The model in figure 67.4 represents α > 0 (face open) and β < 0 (outside in). The resultant of the swing is a typical slice. The direction of the ball vector is right to the target, and the inclination of the Δ plane produces the rightward curve of the trajectory.

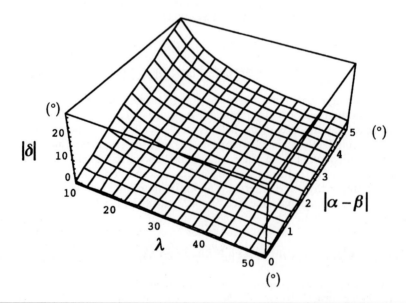

Figure 67.5   Inclination δ of the Δ plane vs. |α − β| and loft λ.

EFFECT OF α, β, AND λ ON δ

Equation 3 gives the explicit relation of the inclination δ to the parameters (α – β) and λ. Let us examine the effects of these parameters quantitatively. Figure 67.5 is a 3-D representation of Equation 3 for |α – β| = 0 ~ 5 degrees, and λ = 9 ~ 52 degrees. We can observe from this figure that δ is large for a low loft angle and that it increases linearly as the deviation of the swing vector β increases.

The effects of β = 1 degree error in the direction of the swing vector on δ for different lofted clubs is shown by the curve in figure 67.6. The value of δ significantly increases as the loft λ decreases. For example, if you use a driver with 11 degree loft, a one degree error in the swing direction will result in the inclination of the trajectory plane by as much as 5 degrees. Because it increases linearly, it reaches 25 degrees for 5 degrees error in your swing. The value of δ reduces as the loft increases. This is one reason why the more lofted clubs are less sensitive to an error in the swing direction.

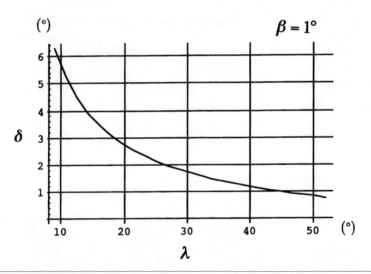

Figure 67.6   Inclination δ (β = 1°) vs. loft λ.

CLASSIFICATION OF TRAJECTORY

It is shown in this study that we can use a priori knowledge on angular properties of a swing to predict the trajectory of a ball. In a similar way, we can diagnose our own swing based on the information of the trajectory of a ball. As a simple application of this study, the classification of the ball trajectory by means of the angular properties, α and β, is shown in the following.

(1) The curve of a trajectory is determined by the quantity (α – β): (α – β) > 0, slice; (α – β) = 0, straight; (α – β) < 0, hook. In other words, the type of curve is

determined by the relative magnitude of α and β. For example, if you hit a ball with your club face open ($\alpha > 0$) and inside out swing ($\alpha < \beta$), you hit a push hook.

(2) The ball vector immediately after impact is on the Δ plane and slightly below the face vector N. The projected angle α of the face vector determines the initial path as follows: $\alpha > 0$, right direction; $\alpha = 0$, center direction; $\alpha < 0$, left direction.

In more detail, a curved ball leaves a club face slightly deviated to the direction of the swing vector and then gradually curves to the other side.

With a combination of the two parameters ($\alpha - \beta$) and α, the $3 \times 3 = 9$ types of trajectory of the ball are determined as shown in figure 67.7.

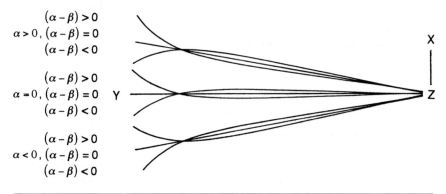

Figure 67.7   Nine types of trajectories projected on the horizontal plane.

CONCLUDING REMARKS

The explicit formulae describing the relations between the initial trajectory plane and the angular properties of the clubs and the swing are presented. Since angular properties of the swing and the club face are more perceivable than the scalar properties, this information is useful for the diagnosis of the swing.

References

Cochran A. and J. Stobbs. 1968, *Search for the Perfect Swing*, The Golf Society of Great Britain.
Hokari, Y. et al. 1959, *Handbook of Mathematics*, Tokyo: Kyoritsu Publishing.
Jorgensen, T. P. 1994, *The Physics of Golf*, New York: American Institute of Physics.

CHAPTER 68

Clubhead Speed and Driving Distance: 1938 vs. 1998

R. Stewart
Trends and Traditions, New York, USA

Given the many discussions of the increase in driving distance and whether or not the ball is livelier, an anomaly appears. In the year 1938 Gene Sarazen and Sam Snead were apparently more successful at "getting more for less" than many golfers today. Their drives went 25% further per unit of clubhead speed than occurs today. An examination of the literature provides pieces of the puzzle, but not a solution.

Keywords: Clubhead speed, driving distance, Sam Snead, Gene Sarazen.

INTRODUCTION

How did golfers such as Gene Sarazen, Sam Snead, and Harry "Lighthorse" Cooper drive the ball so far with a relatively slow clubhead speed velocity? Conversely, if the amount of energy available in the clubhead speed has doubled or tripled why doesn't the ball go even further than today's statistics record? Data and discussion from Smits and Smith (1994), Sullivan (1994), Jorgensen (1994), Lieberman (1994), Robinson (1994), McKirdy (1990), Aoyama (1990), and others provide pieces of the puzzle, but not the solution.

THE BACKGROUND

Engineers from the General Electric Company in Schenectady, New York, developed an instrument to measure clubhead speed (figure 68.1). They chose the Glens Falls Country Club (in Queensbury, New York) to demonstrate the instrument during the 1938 Glens Falls Open. Sarazen, Snead, Ben Hogan, Cooper, and other touring professionals were in town. Unfortunately, most of the patent (research) books have been lost or destroyed. Fortunately, the *Glens Falls Times* reported that Gene Sarazen had a clubhead speed of 69 mph (31 m/s) and Sam Snead 81 mph (36 m/s). Another newspaper reported that the fastest speed by a woman was 57 mph (26 m/s). Gene Sarazen stated that the better golfers of his time averaged between 225 and 240 yds (206-220 m) (personal communication). Harry "Lighthorse" Cooper, the leading money winner in 1937, confirmed Sarazen's estimates when he reported the average was between 225 and 240 yds. Both agreed that Jimmy Thomson could outdrive them both by ten to twenty yards. Thomson was in the top ten in scoring and earnings and averaged 250 m (275 yds). A simple calculation shows that Sam Snead achieved up to 6.1 m/m/s (3 yds/mph) of club speed, and Gene Sarazen 7.1 m/m/s (3.5 yds/mph). Thomson also participated in an interesting demonstration. He drove a gutty 182 m (200 yds), an early 1.62 oz-1.62 in. ball 226 m (248 yds), a 1930s 1.55 oz-1.68 in. ball 182 m (255 yds), and a 1937 1.62 oz-1.68 in. ball, 280 m (308 yds). This progression convinced Robert Trent Jones (1937) that golf course architects needed to adapt to the new, livelier, ball. (Aging of each ball was not considered.)

Figure 68.1   General Electric Company engineers H.D. Philips and Elmer Finger (with club) test their first instrument to measure clubhead speed. The device uses two electric eyes and will measure to a fraction of one mph.

THE LITERATURE

A review of the literature provides a series of measurements and estimations of clubhead speed/initial velocity and/or driving distances. Horwood (1994) provides a starting point: "Assuming that good contact is made with the ball, simple physics shows that for a given head weight, clubhead speed will govern distance." McKirdy's (1990) review of Professor Tait's research provides the early data that a well-hit gutty could travel 140-160 m at a clubhead speed of 45-50 m/s. Lieberman, using 235 fps (71 m/s) for initial velocity, reported the ball would carry about 252 yds (231 m), based upon two-piece construction and 324 dimple calibration balls. Note that some distances include carry and roll, others just carry. This is true for the data on Sarazen and Snead. Robinson (1994) separated the amateurs from the professionals while reporting clubhead mean speeds of 41.8 m/s (93 mph) for the amateurs and 48.3 m/s (108 mph) for the professionals. This is somewhat faster than Barrentine's (1994) measurements, which were divided into three parts: Professionals 39.27 m/s (88 mph), low handicaps (0-15) 37.62 m/s (84 mph), and high handicaps (16+), 33.52 m/s (75 mph).

The average distance (carry and roll) for the top ten professionals on the US PGA Tour in 1997 was 263 m (287 yds). The difficulty is to obtain coincident clubhead speeds, which are just not available. Additionally the distance measurements are averages for a year while the clubhead speeds may be a one-off, or from a small sample. To work within a reasonable range we do know that the USGA uses 109 mph (48.9 m/s) when testing with Iron Byron, that Karsten considers speeds at 115-120 mph (53 m/s) in some driving tests, and a golfer such as Davis Love III has a clubhead speed between 125 and 130 mph (57 m/s). Therefore an estimate of clubhead speed and distance will give about 4.8 m/m/s (2.3 yds/mph). Allowing for the estimations and limitations the basic premise does not change—Snead and Sarazen achieved a fine distance to clubhead speed ratio. Another factor to be considered is the lift/drag ratio. Recognizing that the number of dimples on a 1930s golf ball is less than at present, the conclusion by Aoyama (1990) comparing the flight of the 336 Atti vs. the 384 icohedron is valid: "Lower drag dissipates less energy, while lower lift keeps the trajectory at optimum height." Then apply Sullivan's comment, "While studies have been limited in this area, wider dimples generally contribute reduced drag for greater carry distance." Were the dimples on the 1930s balls wider than those of the 1990s? Yes. Jorgensen provides a more generic statement: "A larger spin produces a larger drag which makes the ball slow down more rapidly and thus keeps the ball from going so far, but a larger spin produces a larger lift which keeps the ball in the air for a longer time, and thus allows the ball to travel further. Experience tells us that the latter effect is predominant." This experience is probably modified slightly for the 1938 data as both the lift coefficient and the drag coefficient reach maximums in the 100 f/s (30.5 m/s) range, especially at the mid-range of spin (Aoyama 1990), which is closer to the conditions at the time. Unfortunately, none of these factors are large enough individually or in concert to explain the anomaly. Objectively we must omit the analysis of clubhead rotation, as it was not considered in 1938. We do know that we are comparing professionals from both eras, but that the early golfers who learned on hickories had a flatter swing to sweep the ball, and thus probably had less clubhead rotation. The analysis by Mather and Cooper (1994) provides some insight into the difficulties and limitations of such shaft/swing analysis.

Thus the Sarazen/Snead era golfers used golf balls with less dimples, swung the club more slowly, used steel shafts and persimmon heads, slept in the car (apparently Ben Hogan did so at the aforementioned Glens Falls Open), and yet drove the ball 25% further per unit of clubhead speed.

DISCUSSION

It seems that there must be a series of factors which have conspired to produce the Snead/Sarazen result. A few points will add a bit more fuel. Golf courses in 1938 did not have sprinkler systems unless they dragged them around by hand, but neither did the greenkeeper cut the fairways as often or as short. Today's golfer shapes shots more than in 1938, thus using some of the increased energy available with the increase in clubhead speed. However, on the par fives used for driving distance statistics, little is held back. John Daly averaged 277 m (302 yds) in 1997. Additionally, there were more fairway bunkers in 1938 thanks to Donald Ross (who designed the Glens Falls Country Club) and his colleagues, who installed many fairway bunkers. Although there were complaints about the distance a golf ball would travel since the introduction of the "bounding billie," little was done until 1931. At that time the USGA standardized the size and weight of the golf ball to be used at official tournaments in the United States. The intent was to decrease the length of a 228 m (250 yds) drive by 5.5 m (6 yds). Thus in 1938 Sarazen and Snead played under those rules, but the manufacturers were free to continue fine-tuning the golf ball to increase initial velocity.

In 1932 the North British ball was advertised as averaging fifteen yards longer than other brands. Based upon tests by American professionals the North British ball traveled an average of 243 m (267 yds). Three other brands averaged approximately 228 m (250 yds). These are very respectable numbers given the technology of the day. The USGA did not apply initial velocity requirements for golf balls until 1942. Could the General Electric engineers be mistaken? Yes, but their measurements are reasonable for that era, and they had tested the technology for several years. This same technology which was used by the General Electric engineers was used three years later by the United States Golf Association to begin testing the initial velocity of golf balls.

CONCLUSIONS

We are left with the anomaly, but we should heed the words of Julian Curtiss of Spalding, who in 1935 said, "Golf balls have reached their limit, so far as distance is concerned . . ." Effectively that became true when the USGA began controlling initial velocity, but that was after Gene Sarazen and Sam Snead teed up the golf ball of their choice in the Glens Falls Open.

ACKNOWLEDGMENTS

The author gratefully acknowledges the efforts of the reviewers. A thank-you is extended also to Michael Daniels of Albany, NY, USA, for his discovery of the General Electric photograph and related magazine articles.

References

Aoyama, S. 1990. A modern method for the measurements of aerodynamic lift and draft on golf balls. In: *Science and Golf,* A.J. Cochran (ed.) July 1990. E. & F.N. Spon, London. pp. 199-204.

Barrentine, S.W., Fleisig, G.W., Johnson, H., and Woolley, T.W. 1994. Ground reaction forces and torques of professional and amateur golfers. In: *Science and Golf II,* A.J. Cochran & M.R. Farrally (eds.) E. & F.N. Spon, London. pp. 33-39.

Horwood, G.P. 1994. Golf shafts—a technical perspective. In: *Science and Golf II,* A.J. Cochran & M.R. Farrally (eds.) July 1994. E. & F.N. Spon, London. pp. 247-258.

Jones, R.T. 1937. Start pushing your traps around. *The National Golf Review,* December 1937. p. 47.

Jorgensen, T.P. 1994. *The Physics of Golf.* American Institute of Physics, New York.

Lieberman, B.B. 1990. Estimating lift and drag coefficients from golf ball trajectories. In: *Science and Golf,* A.J. Cochran (ed.) July 1990. E. & F.N. Spon, London. pp. 187-192.

Mather, J.S.B. and Cooper, M.A.J. 1994. The attitude of the shaft during the swing of golfers of different ability. In: *Science and Golf II,* A.J. Cochran & M.R. Farrally (eds.) July 1994. E. & F.N. Spon, London. pp. 271-277.

McKirdy, A.S. 1990. Professor Tait and the physics of golf. In: *Science and Golf,* A.J. Cochran (ed.) July 1990. E. & F.N. Spon, London. pp. 213-218.

Robinson, R.L. 1994. A study of the correlation between swing characteristics and club head velocity. In: *Science and Golf II,* A.J. Cochran & M.R. Farrally (eds.) E. & F.N. Spon, London. pp. 84-90.

Smits, A.J. and Smith, D.R. 1994. A new aerodynamic model of a golf ball in flight. In: *Science and Golf II,* A.J. Cochran & M.R. Farrally (eds.) July 1994. E. & F.N. Spon, London. pp. 340-347.

Sullivan, M.J. and Melvin, T. 1994. The relationship between golf ball construction and performance. In: *Science and Golf II,* A.J. Cochran & M.R. Farrally (eds.) E. & F.N. Spon, London. pp. 334-339.

CHAPTER 69

Golf Club and Ball Fitting
Using Launch Condition Measurements

Douglas Clay Winfield
Titleist and Foot-Joy WorldWide, Fairhaven, MA, USA

An important aspect of today's golf equipment market is to provide the golfer with a way to get the best possible club and ball combination. Measuring golf ball velocities and spins in three dimensions after impact with a club can give information such as the launch velocity, launch angle, push/pull angle, backspin, and sidespin. Different golf balls exhibit different launch conditions when hit by "Iron Byron," which is a golf swing simulator, or by an actual golfer. The launch conditions and predictions of total distance give actual objective data that can be used to fit the golfers for club and ball combinations that suit their game and desires.

Keywords: Golf ball, launch conditions, launch angle, backspin, equipment fitting.

INTRODUCTION

Golf consumers are interested in getting the best possible equipment to match their game. The golf ball is an important part of the golfer's equipment and should properly fit his or her game. There are currently in the marketplace wide ranges of ball types and performance options in terms of feel, spin, and distance. Also, there is a wide range of golfers in terms of swing speeds, swing patterns, and approaches to the game. For instance, one player may desire a soft feeling ball, another player wants distance off the tee, and other players want more spin for their short games. Also, fitting the proper ball to the player depends on their clubs and swing characteristics. Measuring and calculating the launch conditions of the ball with the players swinging their own clubs can provide useful insights into choosing equipment. Therefore, the aim is to provide the golfer with a way to get the best possible club and ball combination for use in playing golf.

MEASURING AND CALCULATING THE LAUNCH CONDITIONS OF A BALL

There are several devices commercially available to measure the velocity of the ball coming off the clubhead, but there are few devices that are capable of measuring ball velocity and spin in three dimensions. Gobush, Pelletier, and Days (1994) described a launch monitor that uses two cameras that each take two pictures of the ball just after it is struck by a club. The ball has a pattern of retroreflective markers which are automatically digitized into a computer after being lit by two strobe flashes separated by a short interval in time. Photogrammetric techniques are used to calculate the coordinates of the retroreflective markers from each of the two images. The three-dimensional launch velocities and launch spins of the ball can then be calculated from the two images.

Once the velocities and spins of the ball have been calculated from the launch monitor, other useful information can be obtained. Consider a right-hand Newtonian reference frame XYZ where the X axis is down the middle of the fairway, the Y axis is in the vertical direction, and the Z axis is normal to the XY plane. The magnitude of ball velocity V is

$$V = \sqrt{V_X^2 + V_Y^2 + V_Z^2} \; .$$

The launch angle θ of the ball is calculated as

$$\theta = \tan^{-1}\left(\frac{V_Y}{\sqrt{V_X^2 + V_Z^2}}\right)$$

where V_X, V_Y, and V_Z are the components of the ball velocity in the X, Y, and Z directions, respectively. The launch angle relates the amount of vertical ball velocity with respect to the amount of horizontal ball velocity in both the X and Z directions. The push/pull angle f of the ball can be defined as

$$\phi = \tan^{-1}\left(\frac{V_Z}{V_X}\right)$$

and relates the angle in the horizontal plane away from the X axis that the ball is launched. The spin components in the X, Y, and Z directions represented by ω_X, ω_Y, and ω_Z, respectively, can be used to calculate backspin and sidespin of the ball. Backspin is defined as the component of spin that is normal to the vertical plane that contains the velocity vector of the ball. Backspin or ω_{BS} is calculated as

$$\omega_{BS} = -\omega_X \sin(\phi) + \omega_Z \cos(\phi)$$

Sidespin or ω_{SS} is defined as the spin component normal to the velocity vector and the backspin direction, which is

$$\omega_{SS} = -\omega_X \cos(\phi)\sin(\theta) + \omega_Y \cos(\theta) - \omega_Z \sin(\phi)\sin(\theta)$$

There are no significant impact forces to create rifle spin or a spin component in the direction of the velocity vector of the ball. It is important to note the three-dimensional nature of the definitions of launch angle, sidespin, and backspin. A two-dimensional measurement, meaning only the X and Y components of velocity and the Y and Z components of spin, would require that the golfer hit the ball precisely in the XY plane to get true measurements of launch angle, sidespin, and backspin. In reality, this condition rarely exists in player testing due to misalignment.

Trajectory simulations can be used to predict the landing position of the ball, which can be useful information in helping fit the player with a ball and club. Aerodynamic information such as the drag, lift, and spin decay properties of the ball have to be known in order to simulate its trajectory. Various techniques for measuring aerodynamic information of the ball such as that by Aoyama (1990), Smits and Smith (1994), and Zagarola, Lieberman, and Smits (1994) have been used. The differential equations of motion necessary to perform a three-dimensional trajectory simulation have been outlined by many authors including Winfield and Tan (1996). Once the ball lands, a roll model can be used to predict where the ball comes to rest after it has stopped rolling. Aoyama (1994) has presented results of trajectory simulations including a roll model to calculate the total distance the ball travels; this model will be used to perform calculations in this work.

TESTING RESULTS WITH DIFFERENT GOLF BALL TYPES

The launch conditions of various balls were measured after being hit with the robot "Iron Byron" using a driver, 5 iron, 8 iron, and a half wedge, meaning a wedge swung at half speed. The backspin verses launch angle was plotted for four balls as shown in figure 69.1. In each case Ball 1 had a lower backspin rate than that of Ball 2, Ball 2 had a lower backspin rate than that of Ball 3, and Ball 3 had a lower backspin rate than that of Ball 4. Also, for the driver and 5-iron shots, the balls that had a higher backspin also had a lower launch angle; the 8-iron and half wedge shots did not show that trend. The balls hit with the half wedge did not have as much range of launch angles or backspin as that of the other clubs. For slower swing speeds and higher lofted clubs, the ball does not deform as much on the club face. Therefore, the material properties of the cover of the ball have a greater impact on the launch conditions of higher lofted clubs and slower clubhead speeds. For the lower lofted clubs and faster clubhead speeds, the material properties of the entire ball, the cover and core for 2-piece balls, and the cover, windings, and core for 3-piece balls, can affect the launch conditions.

When testing a golfer, one must consider the ball velocity leaving the clubhead. The United States Golf Association sets an initial velocity limit on balls based on a measurement made by a rotating striker. Because of this limit, golf balls do not generally exhibit a large range of ball velocities when struck on "Iron Byron." However, launch velocity is a factor with player testing since the location of impact on the club face and the presentation of the clubhead to the ball can affect the launch

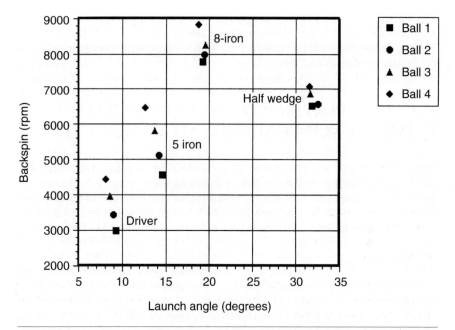

Figure 69.1   Launch conditions of four balls hit on "Iron Byron" with a driver, 5 iron, 8 iron, and a half wedge.

velocity of the ball. The presentation of the clubhead to the ball is dependent on several factors such as the length of the club, the flexing characteristics of the shaft, and the ability of the player to swing the club. Therefore, it is important to test different club and ball combinations when trying to find an optimal arrangement of a club and ball. Table 69.1 shows the average ball velocity, average launch angle, average backspin, and average total distance in the X direction with a club professional golfer using combinations of two drivers and two balls where each club combination was hit five times. It should be noted that Ball 1 and Ball 3 in table 69.1

Table 69.1   Average Launch Conditions of a Golfer Hitting Combinations of 2 Drivers and 2 Balls

	Average V (m/s)	Average θ (deg)	Average ω_{BS} (rpm)	Average total distance (m)
Ball 1 / Driver 1	69.8	10.7	3413	245
Ball 3 / Driver 1	70.1	9.5	3913	241
Ball 1 / Driver 2	71.9	12.0	3578	253
Ball 3 / Driver 2	71.7	11.6	4107	248

correspond to Ball 1 and Ball 3 in figure 69.1. Driver 2 gave the golfer more ball velocity than Driver 1, which resulted in greater total distance for Driver 2. Also, Ball 1 gave the golfer a higher launch angle with lower backspin and gave the golfer more distance than that of Ball 3.

FITTING A PLAYER WITH A CLUB AND BALL USING LAUNCH CONDITION MEASUREMENTS

When fitting a ball to a player, one must consider the swing characteristics and desires of the player as well as the launch condition testing results. For instance, if a player wants more spin in the short game, a higher spin ball such as Ball 3 or Ball 4 in figure 69.1 might be appropriate. Having launch condition test results from "Iron Byron" is useful in distinguishing ball spin characteristics. One can also compare the spin results from various clubs to determine which club tends to allow the golfer to obtain greater spin.

If the player wants longer drives for a particular driver, one must consider the combination of launch angle and launch spin to achieve maximum distance. It has been shown by Winfield and Tan (1994) and others that relatively high launch angles and low spin rates will produce longer drives. In table 69.1, Ball 1 was better suited for both drivers since it resulted in a higher launch angle and lower spin than that of Ball 3. Another player with less spin off the tee might be better suited to Ball 3 than Ball 1. It is important to perform launch condition tests since different ball types can produce a wide range of launch conditions.

When testing different club and ball combinations, ball velocity can also be an important factor. Based on the results in table 69.1, Ball 1/Driver 2 clearly gave the golfer the most ball velocity and total distance and could be considered the best fit out of the four combinations. The increase in ball velocity from Driver 1 to Driver 2 could be the result of several factors such as club length, shaft flex, or the overall comfort level the golfer feels with that particular club. Sometimes values of sidespin along with ball velocity can be important determining factors in deciding why a club does not perform as well as another club. If a player does not consistently hit the "sweet spot" of the club, the ball velocity will be lower and the amount of sidespin will be higher. Increased sidespin due to missing the "sweet spot" of the clubhead could be the result of several factors such as improper lie angle or length of the club. With player testing, it is difficult to make statistically valid judgments because of the human factor in the test as well as the large number of club and ball variables. However, the use of launch conditions and predictions of total distance gives objective data and can help the decision making in equipment fitting.

CONCLUSIONS

The ball velocities and spins in three dimensions after impact with a club can give interesting information such as the launch velocity, launch angle, backspin, and total distance as well as other useful quantities. One must consider the desires of the player when attempting to fit a club and a ball. The launch conditions and predictions of total distance give objective data that can be used to fit golfers for club and ball combinations that suit their game.

ACKNOWLEDGMENTS

I would like to acknowledge the efforts of the Product Research team at Titleist including Bill Gobush, Diane Pelletier, Charlie Days, Ed Hebert, Jim Silvera, Kieran Andre, Larry Bissonette, and Steve Aoyama for their work and effort in this study.

References

Aoyama, S., 1990, A modern method for the measurement of aerodynamic lift and drag on golf balls. In *Science and Golf*, ed. A. J. Cochran, 199-204, London: E & FN Spon

Aoyama, S., 1994, Changes in golf ball performance over the last 25 years. In *Science and Golf II*, ed. A. J. Cochran and M. R. Farrally, 348-354, London: E & FN Spon

Gobush, W., Pelletier, D., and Days C., 1994, Video monitoring system to measure initial launch characteristics of golf ball. In *Science and Golf II*, ed. A. J. Cochran and M. R. Farrally, 327-333, London: E & FN Spon

Smits, A. J. and Smith, D. R., 1994, A new aerodynamic model of a golf ball in flight. In *Science and Golf II*, ed. A. J. Cochran and M. R. Farrally, 340-347, London: E & FN Spon

Winfield, D. C. and Tan, T. E., 1994, Optimization of clubhead loft and swing elevation angles for maximum distance of a golf drive. *Computers and Structures*, 53: 19-25

Winfield, D. C. and Tan, T. E., 1996, Optimization of clubface shape of a golf driver to minimize dispersion of off-center shots. *Computers and Structures*, 53: 1217-1224

Zagarola, M. V., Lieberman, B., and Smits, A. J., 1994, An indoor testing range to measure the aerodynamic performance of golf balls. In *Science and Golf II*, ed. A. J. Cochran and M. R. Farrally, 348-354, London: E & FN Spon

CHAPTER 70

A Study of Clubhead Speed as a Function of Grip Speed for a Variety of Shaft Flexibility

Tiejun Miao, Makato Watari, Masatake Kawaguchi, and Masakazu Ikeda
Nippon Shaft Co., Ltd., Kanagawa 236-0003, Japan

This paper shows how the grip speed applied to the club shaft affects the clubhead speed at impact. Data are recorded for clubhead speed in experiments where grip speed is increased gradually in both machine tests and live golfer tests. Our investigation reveals that there are highly systematic variations of clubhead speed in relation to grip speed for a variety of stiffnesses of club shaft. In order to reach a better understanding of the correlation between the grip speed and the clubhead speed, a model of deflection of the clubhead during downswing is developed. By the use of an oscillating curve obtained according to the model, a consistent description is found for the data in machine tests. The model has also been proved useful in discussion of the live golfer test, where a peak of clubhead speed appears in the range of a player's grip speed in which he hits the ball. The oscillating curves are employed to interpret the players as having the ability to adjust their phase shift in making good use of the merits of clubhead deflection.

Keywords: Grip speed, clubhead speed, flexibility, oscillation frequency.

INTRODUCTION

Interactions between golf swing and golf club have been investigated extensively with regard to the parameters relating to physical exertion by the golfer (Kaneko 1992, Iwatsubo et al. 1990, Budney and Bellow 1979). The force and torque applied to the club shaft over the period of the downswing were emphasized in order to gain insight into the dynamics of the swing of the club and to help the golfer to increase the distance in his shot. However, even though high-speed video is available to give kinematics data of the golf swing, information that can be extracted on the golfer's torque is limited (Ronald and Davis 1992). In addition, there is no way of independently determining the various golfers' variables and complicated wrist actions. It then remains an unclear and open question concerning how the swing and golfer's hand influences the performance of the clubhead at impact.

In view of these difficulties, we propose a method to investigate kinematics dependence of clubhead performance on a golfer's wrist movement during gripping the club shaft (Miao et al. 1997). The wrist movement is estimated according to grip speed observed from a reflecting marker attached to a position on the shaft near the grip. Also, from the fact that the grip speed is proportional to the momentum applied by the player to the club shaft during the swing, studies on interactions of the grip speed with the clubhead speed will shed some light on actions of the golfer's hand on the resulting clubhead speed achieved under variations in flexibility of a club shaft in impacting a golf ball.

METHOD

Both the experimental method and the model chosen for this study should now be discussed.

Experimental Method

The tested clubs were drivers in lengths of 44", 44", 44", and 48", with shaft reflexes of X, R, LL, and Super L. The oscillation frequency f_0 of clubs for these shafts was 4.74 Hz (X-shaft), 4.13 Hz (R-shaft), 3.79 Hz (LL-shaft), and 2.97 Hz (Super L), which was the frequency of oscillations of the club when it was clamped in a vice and was pulled to one side and released. Each club was subjected to both machine tests using a swing machine (ShotRobo-III, Miyamae Co., Ltd.) and live golfer tests. A reflecting marker was placed on the club shaft at a point 279 mm from the grip end. The marker speed was recorded just before the impact of clubhead on golf ball. In the machine test, a speedometer (Miyamae Co., Ltd.) with a laser switch was placed on the path of the swing of the machine arm and club grip. The reflective light from the marker triggers the laser switch at impact and gives a record of speed. Simultaneously, the clubhead speed was measured in the same way according to another speedometer placed on the path of the clubhead. Experimental data of the clubhead speed was plotted against the grip speed in figures 70.2 and 70.3, using solid dots.

In live golfer tests, in order to reduce uncertainty and give a more accurate measurement for the grip speed, a set of two laser sensors 2 cm apart was placed on a support. Signal from the reflecting marker was sensed and directed onto a processing system in a computer via an A/D converter, enabling traveling speed of the marker to be read with high accuracy. The players were tested with handicaps ranging from 1-5. Players were asked to hit clubs in succession with one shot recorded for each player with each club. The sequence of the four clubs was randomized to help reduce experimental error from player performance variations. These recordings were collected, but the mis-hit that is clearly understandable is excluded and plotted in figure 70.4.

Model

The model chosen for study is shown in figure 70.1, a view of the assumed plane of the motion of the golf club. Hinge A moves about fixed center of rotation O, and the arm $\overline{AB}$, which connects to the club at B, rotates about the hinge A. The angle ϕ measured counterclockwise relating to rod $\overline{OA}$ that has the angle θ counterclockwise from horizontal. C' corresponds to clubhead C, and especially when a perfectly stiff shaft of $f_0 = \infty$ is used, the club becomes a rod in the place of $\overline{BC'}$. Differentiating the vector d two times with respect to time derives the acceleration component $\ddot{d}_2$ of C', as shown in equation (1), along the direction e_2 perpendicular to $\overline{AC'}$.

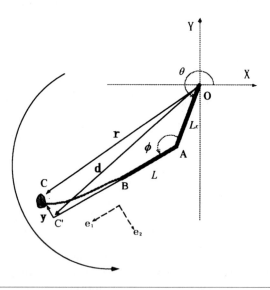

Figure 70.1   Model of swing machine.

$$\ddot{d}_2 = L(\ddot{\phi} + \ddot{\theta}) - L_K(\dot{\theta}^2 \sin\phi + \ddot{\theta}\cos\phi) \tag{1}$$

where L_K represents the length of rod $\overline{OA}$, and L is the length of $\overline{AC'}$.

As shown in figure 70.1, vector y is deflection of the clubhead, and is approximately vertical to the $\overline{AC'}$. The major source causing club shaft lateral bending comes from $\ddot{d}_2$, the inertial acceleration shown in equation (1). Contrarily, the shaft flexibility tends to recover the clubhead deflection produced by $\ddot{d}_2$. If damping of the club is assumed to be negligible, then a linear oscillator without damping term, i.e., $\ddot{y} = -\omega_0^2 y$, can be taken into account to represent the recovering process for the clubhead deflection. The angular frequency ω_0 relates to the oscillation frequency f_0 of the club with a relation: $\omega_0 = 2\pi f_0$. Combining this recovering term and the term expressed by equation (1), the final equation governing the deflection of y of the clubhead is given by

$$\ddot{y} + \omega_0^2 y + L(\ddot{\phi} + \ddot{\theta}) - L_K(\dot{\theta}^2 \sin\phi + \ddot{\theta}\cos\phi) = 0 \tag{2}$$

In the swing machine, it is noted that $L = \overline{AC} \gg L_K$ and that the swing machine swings the club in an approximately constant angular acceleration. These allow reducing the angle-dependent term in equation (2) to $L(\ddot{\phi} + \ddot{\theta}) = Const.$ Such treatment produces a great simplification in calculations without introducing significant error. Finally, by the use of initial conditions at the swing top, the deflection of the clubhead as a function of t, $y(t)$, is yielded from solving equation (2):

$$y(t) = \frac{L(\ddot{\phi} + \ddot{\theta})}{\omega_0^2}(\cos(\omega_0 t) - 1) \tag{3}$$

The deflection velocity $\dot{y}(t)$ of the clubhead is easily derived from a differentiation of $y(t)$.

On the other hand, suppose the tested club shaft is replaced by a perfectly stiff shaft; because this rigid club $\overline{AC}$ follows a rotational motion of rigid body, the speed of point C', denoted as V_{h0}, has a simple relation with speed V_{g0} of point B at impact. Concretely there is the relation as $V_{h0} = \alpha + (l_h/l_g)V_{g0}$, where α is a constant, distance l_h is measured from C' to hinge A, and distance l_g is from B to A. Such linear dependence obtained for a perfectly stiff shaft is plotted in figures 70.2, 70.3, and 70.6 using a straight dashed line. It is due to the clubhead speed V_{himp}, at impact which is given by a superimposition of the speed V_{h0} and the deflection velocity $\dot{y}(t)$ of clubhead. Using downswing time t_d, V_{himp} becomes

$$V_{himp} = V_{h0} - \frac{L(\ddot{\phi} + \ddot{\theta})}{\omega_0}\sin(\omega_0 t_d) \tag{4}$$

It is noted that $\overline{OA}, \overline{AB}$ and B in figure 70.1 will correspond to the shoulder, elbow, and wrist of a real golfer. Because this paper is primarily interested in what happened

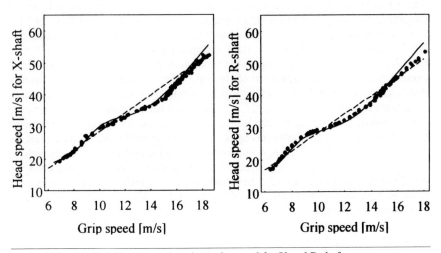

Figure 70.2   Plot clubhead speed against grip speed for X and R shaft.

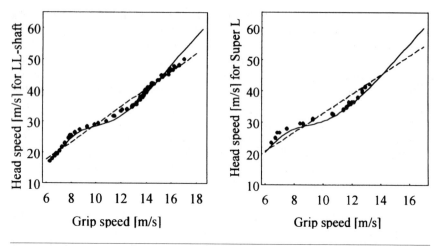

Figure 70.3   Plot clubhead speed against grip speed for LL and super L shaft.

just before impact, the wrist B that cannot "break" is a reasonable assumption for the results of the investigation.

RESULT

Both machine and live tests yielded results which will be discussed.

Results of Machine Test and Comparison With Simulations

Data of experiments on the correlation between clubhead speed and grip speed under different shaft flexibility are plotted, as indicated by dots, in figure 70.2 for X shaft club with $f_0 = 4.74$ Hz and R shaft club with $f_0 = 4.13$ Hz, and in figure 70.3 for LL shaft club with $f_0 = 3.97$ Hz and Super L shaft club with $f_0 = 2.97$ Hz. Furthermore, parameters in equation (4) are evaluated to create simulations of these experimental tests. That a motion of the rod $\overline{OA}$ up to impact travels an angular displacement of Ω_0 with a constant angular acceleration ($\ddot{\phi} + \ddot{\theta}$) gives estimated equations: $(\ddot{\phi} + \ddot{\theta}) = V_{g0}/(d_g t_d)$ and $t_d = 2\Omega_0 d_g/V_{g0}$, with a distance d_g from center O to the reflecting marker. However, it should be noted that the presumed constant of Ω_0 will undergo a slight variation due to the flexibility of the shaft. To account for this difference in Ω_0, the term $\omega_0 t_d$ in equation (4) is changed to $\omega_0 t_d + \Delta\mu$ by a phase shift $\Delta\mu$ that is assumed as dependent on the oscillation frequency of the club. We comment that the physics cause of the phase shift can be understood by full analysis of the inertial delay of the massive clubhead at golf top. All of these parameters have been combined with measurements of the swing machine and tested clubs for doing numerical computations. The simulations are plotted in figures 70.2 and 70.3 using solid curves, along with experimental data. $\Delta\mu$ used in the simulations are: -0.05π, $0, 0.11\pi$, and 0.45π for X, R, LL, and Super L shaft. The theoretically obtained curve is defined, in this paper, as the oscillating curve in order to emphasize the oscillations along the dashed line obtained for a perfectly stiff shaft in speed space spanned by clubhead speed and grip speed.

Results of Live Test

Plots of clubhead speed in relation to grip speed are shown in figure 70.4 in the live golfer test. As the player's grip speed is increased up to 15 [m\s], there appears a peak located in the range of 13-14 [m/s] for LL shaft and 11-12 [m/s] for Super L shaft. In comparison with machine tests displayed in figure 70.3, such peak is in the range corresponding to a negative region of oscillating curves relating to the straight dashed line, for either LL shaft or Super L shaft.

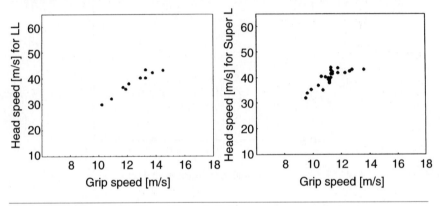

Figure 70.4   Live test for LL and Super L shaft

DISCUSSION AND CONCLUSION

It can be seen clearly from equation (4) that the oscillating curve is largely dependent on oscillation frequency f_0 of the club. Accordingly, shaft flexibility may play an important role in interactions of deflection velocity of the club with clubhead performance. Miao et al. (1997) has evidenced that the oscillating curve, owing to its relation to f_0, predicts a possible optimum choice of stiffness or shaft for a certain value of grip speed of the swing machine, by which the shaft deflection can contribute to an additional increment of clubhead speed.

In spite of the difference of a machine swing from a golfer's swing, their similarities suggest an applicability of the oscillating curve to understand the effect of a golfer's grip speed on his clubhead speed. It should firstly note that the phase shift $\Delta\mu$ in oscillating curves used in simulations of the machine test correlates closely with the oscillation frequency of the club. As depicted in figure 70.5, $\Delta\mu$ decreases with an increase of f_0. In other words, a larger phase shift arises in a flexible shaft. This tendency provides a useful clue to formulate data obtained from live tests by making use of a proper phase shift. It is found that an additional phase shift of π is needed to describe data of live tests. The difference in angular acceleration between machine and real swing may give a cause for the additional phase shift of π. Figure 70.6 shows a comparison of the formulated curve with experiments on an LL and Super L shaft. The good agreement suggests that the relationship between the golfer's grip speed and his clubhead speed is determined partly by shaft flexibility and partly by the player's ability to adjust during the swing such that he tunes the phase shift so as to move his oscillating curve in a peak when hitting a ball with a certain grip speed.

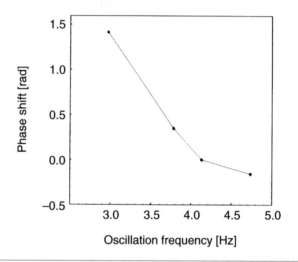

Figure 70.5   Phase shift vs. frequency f_0.

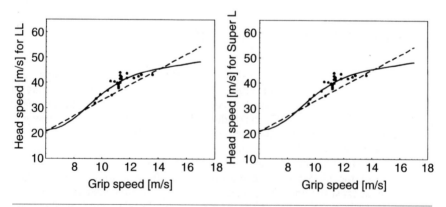

Figure 70.6   Compare results of live test with oscillating curve with an extra phase shift.

In conclusion, as demonstrated in machine and live tests, there is the correlation between grip speed and clubhead speed at impact under a variety of shaft flexibility. The oscillating curve obtained from a model is proved generally applicable to describe and simulate the experiments, and therefore to guide systematically and optimally designing of the club. The oscillating curve is also helpful in gaining an understanding of the relationship between a golfer's grip speed and clubhead speed. Particularly, the appearance of a peak of clubhead speed, which is evidenced experimentally in a range of a player's grip speeds at which he or she hits the ball, can have a reasonable explanation in terms of the oscillating curve.

REFERENCES

Budney, D.R., and D.G. Bellow. 1979. Kinetic analysis of a golf swing. *Res Quart Exercise Sports* 50:171-179.

Iwatsubo, T., N. Konishi, and T. Yamaguchi. 1990. Research on optimum design of a golf club. *J Japan Society of Mechanical Engineers* C56:2386-2391.

Kaneko, Y. 1992. The application of biomechanics to the optimum golf club design. *Proc 11th Meet Japan Soc Biomech.* 4451-4455.

Miao, T., M. Kawaguchi, M. Watari, Y. Ebina, and K. Shimohera. 1997. The relationship between grip speed and clubhead speed at impact. *JSME Dynamics and Design Conference '97.* No.97-10-2: 104-108.

Ronald, D.M., and J.P. Davis. 1992. The role of the shaft in the golf swing, *J Biomechanics* 25:975-983.

CHAPTER 71

Does It Matter What Driver You Use?

T. Hale, P. Bunyan, and S. Squires
Chichester Institute, United Kingdom.

This study compared driver performance, measured by distance and accuracy, between a wooden-headed and three popular metal-headed drivers. Six low handicap golfers (mean $2.67 \pm$ SD 1.97) volunteered. Six trials with each club were performed in a randomised order, with their own drivers acting as a baseline measure. A 1-way ANOVA of the means of all subjects combined showed a significant difference between clubs (P = 0.048). The greatest distance, 195.1 ± 11.73m, was achieved with the subjects' own drivers (OD), followed by the wooden-headed driver (WD) at 190.4 $\pm$ 12.6m; the three metal-headed drivers (M1, M2, M3) averaged 190.4 ± 12.2m, 189.5 ± 14.3m, and 186.1 ± 11.6m respectively. Group mean for accuracy data showed WD producing the lowest dispersion (13.2 ± 8.3m), followed by M2 (13.6 ± 10.5m), OD (14.3 ± 10.4m), M3 (14.6 ± 10.8m), and M1 (14.9 ± 8.2m). There was no significant difference in dispersion measures (P>0.05). However, a 2-way ANOVA with 1 repeated measure, the club, with the subject as the independent variable, showed significant differences in distance within (P<0.011) and between subjects (P<0.001) and an interaction between club and subject (P<0.021). There was no significant difference in dispersion errors within (P = 0.936) or between (P = 0.079) subjects and no significant interaction between clubs and subjects (P = 0.183).

Keywords: Drivers, wooden-headed, metal-headed, distance, accuracy.

INTRODUCTION

Jepson (1995) argues that a fundamental purpose of equipment manufacturers is to provide better equipment so that the golfer's desire to drive the ball ever increasing distances can be met, scores can be improved, and enjoyment enhanced. The introduction of metal-headed drivers around 1980, according to Mahaffey & Melvin (1995), has resulted in considerable benefits—the ball becomes airborne more easily and consistently and greater distance is achieved on miss-hits, for

562

example, when compared with the performance produced by traditional wooden-headed drivers. These benefits are explicable in theoretical terms and are also supported by the buying habits of golfers generally. Proctor (1995) describes the growth in metal-headed drivers from 1984 and reveals that 30% of European Tour professionals were using oversized metal drivers, and 75% of the drivers used have a graphite shaft. At the same time—1993—about 70% of amateurs were playing with graphite-shafted metal drivers. However, Jepson (1995) also warns about exaggerated claims and asserts that it is common practice for marketing personnel to introduce products that are accompanied by evidence that is claimed to be scientific but that may be of dubious validity.

This study aimed to compare the performance of a graphite-shafted wooden driver (WD) with three popular graphite-shafted, oversized, perimeter-weighted metal drivers (MD) and hypothesised that there will be no significant differences in distance or accuracy between the wooden and metal clubs.

METHODS

Six golfers with a handicap of 5 or below volunteered to take part in the study and were allocated one of six time slots on a single day. Attendance time was dependent on availability and therefore random. The subjects were kept ignorant of the true purpose of the study. They were given a 10 min free warm-up period and allowed time to familiarise themselves with a wooden-headed driver (WD) fitted with a graphite shaft and three popular metal drivers (MD)—Callaway Big Bertha, Ping Zing 2, and Taylor Made Bubble. Static and dynamic characteristics of all clubs were recorded using a Flex board (Diamond Golf, Littlehampton UK) and a Brunswick FM Frequency Analyser (Brunswick Golf, Torrington CT, USA).

A target was set at 200m and surrounded by marker cones 20m from the center target. The ball-target line ran from a 2m marked teeing area through the flag and was marked with further cones at 50m intervals. Several dozen balata golf balls of a single type were heated to approximately 23°C and stored in insulated tubing during the test procedure.

Subjects were then asked to hit six shots with each driver at the target in a random order determined by a random number table (Altman, 1991). The position of the ball on the club-face at impact was recorded by SureSpot (Staple Leisure Products, Chichester UK) indicators. A recorder stood behind the target area and recorded the error distance and direction at right angles to the ball-target line. The actual distance driven was derived by triangulation. All distances were recorded in metres.

RESULTS

The mean (± SD) age and handicap of the group was 23 ± 8 years and 2.7 ± 1.97 respectively. The weather on the day of the test was cool—between 7 and 10°C with a left to right wind of about force 3-4; ground conditions were soft with little roll after pitching. The grouped data, shown in table 71.1, revealed that the greatest

564 Hale, Bunyan, and Squires

mean distance was achieved by the subjects' own drivers (OD) followed by the wooden driver (WD), and the three metal drivers MD1, MD2, and MD3; the difference between the highest and lowest mean values was 9.8m. The lowest dispersion was achieved with the WD, followed by MD2, OD, MD3, and MD1; the difference between highest and lowest was 3.1m. A 1-way ANOVA showed no significant difference in distance or dispersion between the clubs.

Table 71.1   Group Means (±SD) for Distance and Dispersion for Each Club

	OD	WD	MD1	MD2	MD3
Distance (m)	195.1 ± 11.7	190.4 ± 12.6	190.4 ± 12.2	189.5 ± 14.3	186.0 ± 11.6
Dispersion (m)	14.3 ± 10.4	13.2 ± 8.3	14.9 ± 8.2	13.6 ± 10.5	14.6 ± 10.8

Individual performances for mean distances of each individual with each club are shown in table 71.2. Ranking each club by subject the most effective with a mean rank of 1.8 was the OD; this was followed by WD (2.7), M1 (2.8), M2 (3.5), and M3 (4.2). Four of the six subjects performed best with their own driver, but in one case this club was the least effective for distance.

Table 71.2   Individual Means (±SD) for Distance (m) Achieved With Each Club

Subject (Handicap)	OD	WD	MD1	MD2	MD3
1 (4)	185 ± 17.5	199 ± 5.6	190 ± 19.0	207 ± 22.8	199 ± 9.1
2 (4)	194 ± 5.1	184 ± 15.2	191 ± 5.6	181 ± 10.4	180 ± 15.7
3 (1)	193 ± 6.5	185 ± 8.3	188 ± 5.7	189 ± 5.4	182 ± 9.4
4 (0)	194 ± 4.0	179 ± 1.9	185 ± 8.1	177 ± 3.3	178 ± 7.9
5 (2)	211 ± 8.9	200 ± 11.1	200 ± 16.1	196 ± 5.0	189 ± 7.2
6 (5)	195 ± 8.7	196 ± 8.7	189 ± 11.9	187 ± 9.6	191 ± 9.4

Table 71.3 shows the mean dispersion distances for each individual with each club. The most effective was M2 with a mean rank of 2.75 followed by the subjects' OD (2.8), M3 (2.9), M1 (3.2), and WD (3.3).

The data were then analysed to take account of the differing abilities of the subjects as well as their interaction with the clubs. A 2-way ANOVA with one repeated measure (clubs) and the subjects as the independent variable was applied firstly to distance and then to dispersion data. There was a significant difference ($F_{1,4}$ = 3.407; P = 0.011) between clubs and a significant interaction ($F_{1,20}$ = 1.869; P =

Table 71.3   Individual Means (±SD) for Dispersion for Each Club

Subject (Handicap)	OD	WD	MD1	MD2	MD3
1 (4)	16.1 ± 11.2	21.7 ± 11.5	14.8 ± 10.5	20.6 ± 14.8	21.6 ± 8.6
2 (4)	8.6 ± 6.2	10.9 ± 5.6	15.0 ± 10.7	15.1 ± 8.3	19.4 ± 18.2
3 (1)	9.2 ± 4.4	10.0 ± 7.3	13.3 ± 9.9	16.5 ± 12.6	10.4 ± 6.1
4 (0)	23.8 ± 12.9	8.1 ± 4.2	18.7 ± 4.5	7.3 ± 7.5	15.9 ± 9.3
5 (2)	11.2 ± 9.6	15.3 ± 7.8	14.7 ± 9.1	11.0 ± 8.0	9.0 ± 6.4
6 (5)	16.7 ± 10.8	13.2 ± 6.7	13.1 ± 4.4	11.3 ± 8.0	11.3 ± 9.4

0.021) for distance. The observed power, based on alpha = 0.05, was 0.840 and 0.965 respectively. A post-hoc Scheffe test located significant differences between subjects 1 and 5 using their ODs (P = 0.003), and between subjects 1 and 2, and 1 and 4 when using M2 (P = 0.030 and 0.008 respectively). There was also a significant between subjects effect ($F_{1, 4}$ = 10.747; P<0.001); observed power in this case was 1.0. There were no significant differences in dispersion between clubs (P = 0.936) or subjects (P = 0.079), and there was no significant interaction effect (P = 0.183).

The static and dynamic characteristics of each club are outlined in table 71.4. There is considerable variability between clubs in length, flexion, and frequency in spite of the fact that seven of the clubs had stiff shafts; the remaining three had

Table 71.4   Static and Dynamic Characteristics of the Clubs

Club	Flex	Length (m)	Deflection (cm)	Frequency (min)
OD1 (4)	Stiff	1.105	14.5	230
OD2 (4)	Stiff	1.067	11.7	257
OD3 (1)	Stiff	1.072	10.4	251
OD4 (0)	Stiff	1.082	13.5	235
OD5 (2)	Stiff	1.120	10.9	252
OD6 (5)	Stiff	1.105	11.4	248
WD	Stiff	1.108	10.7	256
M1	Regular	1.082	15.5	230
M2	Regular	1.086	16.3	219
M3	Regular	1.086	14.0	243

regular flexes. There were low correlations between length and degree of flexion, and length and frequency; but a high negative relationship (-0.9 $P<0.05$) existed between flexion and frequency.

An attempt was made to monitor the position of the ball on the club-face at impact. There were five delineated areas on the SureSpot indicator; top, bottom, left, right, and an overlapping area in the centre. The greatest number of centre strikes were achieved with M2 ($n = 17$); this was followed by M3 ($n = 10$). The remaining three clubs had 7 centre strikes each.

DISCUSSION AND CONCLUSION

The finding that four out of the six subjects produced a slightly greater mean distance with their own clubs is unsurprising, but two of the subjects stand out as anomalies. S 1 not only drove 22m farther with the M2 club than his own driver but also farther with every other club. The longest drive for S 6 was the wooden club, but there was only a small difference of 1m between the WD and OD. If performances for both distance and dispersion are ranked—1 for first down to 5 for fifth— and the ranks combined, the subjects' own clubs are clearly ahead with 28 points; but the WD, M1, and M2 clubs scored 36, 36, and 37.5 points respectively. M3's score of 42.5 points is largely the result of poor distance performance. A recent advertising campaign has extolled the virtues of this club in terms of added distance.

The more important result is the lack of significant difference in either distance or dispersion between the wooden-headed and metal-headed drivers. Wood & Wood (1995) described tests conducted by Yamaha in the late 1980s that concluded 'that all drivers performed similarly in regards to distance and accuracy.' It may be argued that insufficient time was allowed for the subjects to become accustomed to the new clubs. This may be so and is probably reflected in the differences between their own and the trial clubs; but if the claims that the metal drivers are intrinsically superior to wooden clubs are to be sustained these results might have been expected to show some evidence of this. However, there is no significant difference; indeed, the evidence tends to favour the wooden club.

Another argument may be based on the different characteristics of the various clubs. Clearly the trial clubs, bought at random from local outlets, are not matched to the subjects' needs, whereas their own drivers are likely to be. It is important to note here that the subjects' own drivers, as befits low handicap golfers, are fitted with stiff shafts and that the wooden club was also fitted with a stiff shaft with the second-highest frequency. This might suggest that the shaft, rather than the shape or material of the head, is the more important feature. However, the strength of this argument is difficult to test rigorously because of the variability in the overall characteristics of the clubs. Frequency will be affected not only by the stiffness but also by the length of the shaft, but there is no relationship between length and frequency in the clubs used here.

This study supports the notion that although these metal drivers are designed on a sound technical basis that theoretically may give golfers potential benefits, even these low handicap golfers seem unable to take immediate advantage in terms of distance or accuracy. It is still possible that tour professionals have the necessary techniques to maximise the benefits arising from design and manufacturing developments, but the likelihood that the average 18 handicapper—the great majority of the golfing community—can also benefit seems remote. In this sense the manufacturers may be fulfilling their objective, set out at the beginning of this paper, but only to the most privileged sector of the golfing community—the tournament professional. The choice of driver for the great majority of golfers is likely to be determined by fashion and marketing skills rather than valid scientific evidence. It is quite likely that there will be a driver that suits an individual's technique better than most other drivers, but it may not be the latest metal-headed, perimeter-weighted model, no matter how attractively packaged.

References

Altman, D G (1991) *Practical statistics for medical research*. Chapman Hall London

Jepson, J (1995) Golf equipment development—science v marketing. (In: *Golf the Scientific Way*. Ed. Cochran A) Aston Publishing Hemel Hempstead pp. 191–194

Proctor, S (1995) The golf equipment market 1984–1994 (In: *Golf the Scientific Way*. Ed. Cochran A) Aston Publishing Hemel Hempstead pp. 188–190

Mahaffey, S & Melvin, T (1995) Metal woods or wooden woods? (In: *Golf the Scientific Way*. Ed. Cochran A) Aston Publishing Hemel Hempstead pp. 27–30

Wood, D & Wood, C (1995) Modern persimmon clubheads. (In: *Golf the Scientific Way*. Ed. Cochran A) Aston Publishing Hemel Hempstead pp. 33–36

CHAPTER 72

Ground Reaction Forces in Regular-Spike and Alternative-Spike Golf Shoes

K.R. Williams and B.L. Sih
Department of Exercise Science, University of California, Davis, USA

Ground reaction forces were measured as golfers hit shots on an artificial surface in a laboratory hitting station. Shots were made in two shoe conditions, one with regular-spike shoes, and the other with alternative-spike shoes, where metal spikes are replaced by what are generically called "softspikes." The ratio of shear to vertical force, an important factor in determining whether slip will occur, was calculated from the force-time curves and compared to a traction coefficient measured for each shoe type using a traction test. No significant differences were found for maximum and minimum ground reaction force component measures between the regular-spike and alternative-spike shoes. Force patterns were very consistent within subjects but varied considerably between subjects. No significant differences were found for the ratio of shear to vertical force between shoe conditions. The shear to vertical force ratio averaged across shoe conditions was 0.77 for the left foot, peaking 0.31 s before ball impact, and 1.47 for the right foot, peaking 0.1 s after ball impact. The left foot ratio was smaller than the left foot traction coefficients of 1.38 for the regular-spike shoe and 0.96 for the alternative-spike shoe, and the right foot ratio was lower than the traction coefficients during the downswing but exceeded it after ball impact. Subjects showed no indications of slip except in the right foot after impact.

Keywords: Golf, ground reaction forces, traction, shoes.

INTRODUCTION

A successful golf swing is dependent on appropriate transmission of forces between the feet and the ground. Forces exerted at the feet provide the foundation for movements of the legs, trunk, and arms that occur during the swing. Anything that interrupts the transmission of forces to the ground will have an effect on movements in other regions of the body. Traditionally, golfers have used spiked shoes to provide sufficient traction between the shoes and the ground to prevent the feet from slipping during the swing. The penetration of the spikes into the ground provides resistance to movement between the shoe and surface that normal frictional forces might not provide.

In recent years there has been a trend toward the use of alternative-spike systems in response to concern by greenskeepers that a major contributor to turf problems on greens was wear resulting from spiked shoes. In alternative-spike systems traction is usually provided by surface protrusions that penetrate only several millimeters into the turf rather than the 6 or 8 mm spikes used in most traditional golf shoes. The alternative outsole designs are generically referred to as "softspikes." A question of interest to golfers is whether or not the changes in spike design will alter the forces acting at the feet, which could then influence the swing. It is likely that an outsole design with features that protrude less into the ground would be more susceptible to slip, which could have adverse effects on the swing. This study examined ground reaction forces for golfers hitting golf balls in regular-spike shoes and in alternative-spike shoes to examine whether there were any changes in the patterns of forces exerted by the feet on the ground and whether slip was more likely to occur in alternative-spike shoes. A simple traction test was used to identify differences in a static frictional coefficient between the shoes.

There have been very few scientific studies of forces acting at the feet during the golf swing. Ground reaction forces during the golf swing were measured by Williams and Cavanagh (1983) for 10 golfers hitting in an indoor hitting station on artificial turf. The pattern of change in the three components of force were measured while hitting with different clubs, and a number of design features for the outsole to enhance traction were identified. The patterns of change in forces in the anteroposterior direction at the start of the downswing were found to be important forces providing the kinetic base for rotations occurring at the trunk during the downswing. Center of pressure patterns identified the locations on the outsole where forces were most important, allowing design features on the outsole to be localized and devised in relation to the applied forces. Frictional characteristics between sport shoes and surfaces have been measured for a variety of shoe and surface conditions, but golf has not been studied extensively (Stucke, Baudzus, & Baumann 1984; Valiant 1993). Recently Slavin and Williams (1995) measured traction of golf shoes and showed that considerably less traction is provided by outsoles with alternative-spike designs compared to traditional spiked outsoles. Traction coefficients (the ratio of shear force to vertical force when slip occurs) ranged from 1.53 for 8 mm spiked shoes to 1.05-1.15 for alternative-spike shoes. A flat golf shoe with spikes removed gave a traction score of 0.73. The effect of using alternative-spiked outsole designs on ground reaction forces has not been identified. If the outsole design causes alterations to the pattern of forces exerted at the feet, or if a greater probability of slip occurs, the alternative-spike designs might be a disadvantage to golfers.

EXPERIMENTAL METHODS

Ground Reaction Force Measurements

Five subjects with handicaps ranging from 8 to 35 hit golf shots in a laboratory hitting station standing on an artificial "Astroturf" surface. Five shots were hit in each footwear condition. A rectangle of artificial turf was fixed to each of two Kistler force platforms (Type 9281), and ground reaction forces from each plate were collected at 1000 Hz into a Macintosh computer using National Instruments hardware and LabView software. An analog signal from a photocell was measured simultaneously so that the time of impact with the ball could be determined. Subjects hit golf balls wearing both Etonic Stabilizer shoes with 8 mm spikes (regular-spike) and Etonic Difference (alternative-spike) golf shoes. In addition, one subject hit shots with a shoe having a smooth leather outsole so that a shoe with minimal traction could be compared to golf shoes.

Reflective markers on the clubhead and on both shoes were filmed at 200 Hz using four Motion Analysis cameras. 3D coordinates for the markers were obtained using the DLT algorithm (Abdel-Aziz and Karara, 1971) by use of Motion Analysis ExpertVision software. The marker on the clubhead was used to calculate the speed of the clubhead at ball impact, and markers on the shoes were used to locate the position of the shoes relative to the force platform coordinate system so that center of pressure patterns could be put in reference to shoe position. Video and force platform systems were triggered simultaneously so that the two sets of data could be temporally synchronized.

Each component of the force-time curves was analyzed for maximum and minimum values during the time period before and after impact to identify any significant differences in force magnitudes. The ratio of shear to vertical force was also calculated. Data for each trial were obtained and then averaged across the five trials for each shoe condition for each subject. Data were analyzed using a one-tailed t-test between shoe conditions to identify any significant differences between shoes.

Traction Measurements

A static coefficient of friction, termed here the traction coefficient, was determined for each type of golf shoe using a Kistler force platform and a wheeled cart system through which a vertical load could be applied to the shoe with minimal rolling resistance (figure 72.1). The shoe was placed on an artificial surface that was attached to the force platform, and a shear load was applied using a high torque, fixed-gear motor that applied a relatively slow but fixed velocity pull through a

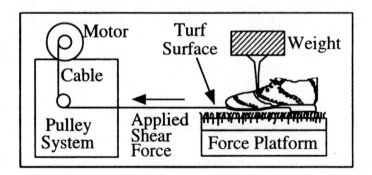

Figure 72.1   Traction test experimental setup.

cable to a bolt mounted in a shoe last placed in and projecting out from the shoe. The pull was applied to the left shoe in a forward direction in the horizontal plane along the long axis of the shoe to mimic the orientation of the force vector seen during the downswing. The data acquisition system described previously was used to acquire vertical and shear forces at 200 Hz while the shear load was applied. The traction coefficient of friction for each trial was the ratio of horizontal to vertical force at the instant the shoe began to slip (at either peak shear F_s or an inflection point on the F_s-time curve). Tests were done with vertical loads of 143, 254, and 366 N and averaged across loads.

RESULTS AND DISCUSSION

Subjects had average clubhead speed at ball impact ranging from 26.4 to 36.9 m·s^{-1} across individuals. Figure 72.2 shows the anteroposterior, side-to-side, and vertical forces during the golf swing for a representative subject hitting in each type of shoe. The averages of curves from five shots for each shoe condition are shown. The center of pressure patterns for each shoe conditions is also shown. Within a subject the ground reaction force patterns were very repeatable across the five shots in each condition, as illustrated in figure 72.3 by the vertical force curves for five trials from one subject in alternative-spike shoes.

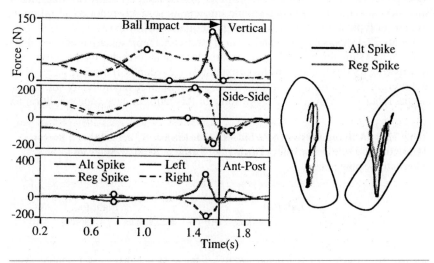

Figure 72.2   Anteroposterior, side-to-side, and vertical ground reaction forces and center of pressure patterns during the golf swing for subject 1 for regular-spike and alternative-spike shoe conditions.

Table 72.1 shows the mean and SD for maximum and minimum values from the anteroposterior, side-to-side, and vertical forces during the swing. There was considerable variability between subjects in these maximum and minimum values,

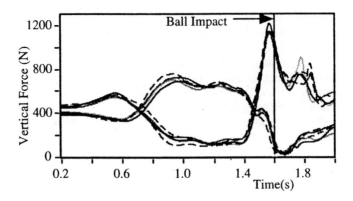

Figure 72.3   Vertical force curves for subject 2 in alternative-spike shoes.

as indicated by standard deviations. The dots on figure 72.2 show the approximate location of these maximum and minimum values during the swing. No significant differences were found between the alternative-spike and regular-spike conditions for any of the maximum or minimum measures. Because shots were hit on a flat, dry surface in an indoor laboratory facility, the conditions under which these tests were conducted are ones for which the likelihood for slip would be considered minimal. The flat artificial Astroturf surface, similar to that used on many driving ranges, provides good traction, and none of the subjects subjectively reported any slipping except for typical movements of the right foot after ball impact.

Figure 72.4 shows the shear and vertical forces for a representative subject, along with a curve showing the ratio of shear force to vertical force during the swing. The downswing for this trial began at approximately 1.2 seconds. If the ratio exceeds the traction coefficient for a given shoe/surface combination, theoretically slip should occur. Table 72.2 shows the average value of this ratio for each shoe condition for

Table 72.1   Anteroposterior (AP), Side-To-Side (SS), and Vertical (Vert) Forces Maximum and Minimum Values During the Swing in Regular-Spike and Alternative-Spike Shoes

	Left foot			Right foot		
	Reg spikes	Alt spikes	Diff (%)	Reg spikes	Alt spikes	Diff (%)
AP max (N)	166.3 (61.2)	168.8 (62.5)	−1.5%	58.1 (30.3)	58.7 (29.1)	−0.9%
AP min (N)	−39.6 (17.5)	−34.1 (12.9)	15.1%	−142.6 (46.4)	−142.6 (45.0)	0.0%
SS max (N)	37.8 (26.4)	36.8 (22.9)	2.6%	160.9 (27.9)	159.0 (28.5)	1.2%
SS min (N)	−142.3 (25.2)	−143.1 (22.8)	−0.6%	−103.4 (48.0)	−95.4 (46.6)	8.1%
Vert max (N)	1095.9 (188.2)	1099.7 (177.2)	−0.4%	728.8 (76.9)	724.8 (67.0)	0.5%
Vert min (N)	56.5 (48.5)	49.6 (45.2)	13.0%	31.9 (5.6)	24.8 (16.5)	24.8%

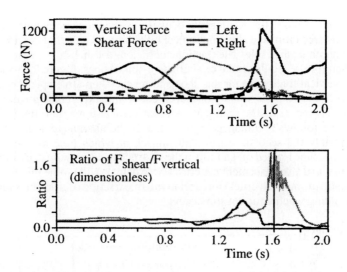

Figure 72.4   Shear and vertical forces, and the ratio of shear/vertical force, for subject 1 in regular-spike and alternative-spike shoes.

left and right feet, along with the times of the maximum ratio. The shear to vertical force ratio was highest for the left foot shortly after the downswing begins, 0.31 seconds before ball impact, with no significant differences between shoe conditions. Both the shear and vertical forces were relatively low at this time. For the right foot, the ratio was typically lower than the ratio for the left foot until near the time of impact, when it increased quickly.

The traction coefficients measured for the shoes used in this study were 1.38 for the regular-spike shoes and 0.96 for the alternative-spike shoes. In previous traction tests for these shoes using a bluegrass-rye real grass surface coefficients were slightly higher, 1.50 and 1.13 respectively (unpublished data). The lower traction coefficients indicate a slightly greater chance of slip on the artificial surface than on real turf. The average shear to vertical force ratio for the left foot in both shoe conditions was less than the corresponding measured traction coefficient. The ratio for the right foot became higher than the traction coefficient at or just following ball impact, and in many trials the right foot moved slightly following impact.

Table 72.2   Maximal Values the Ratio of Shear to Vertical Force and the Time of Maximum Averaged Across Subjects

	Left foot		Right foot	
	Alt spike	Reg spike	Alt spike	Reg spike
$F_{shear}/F_{vertical}$ ratio	0.80 (0.34)	0.73 (0.22)	1.53 (0.58)	1.42 (0.46)
Time of ratio max (s)*	−0.31 (0.13)	−0.31 (0.10)	0.07 (0.05)	0.13 (0.13)

* Times are relative to the time of ball impact.

To further examine the relationship between the traction coefficients, the shear to vertical force ratio, and slip, one subject hit additional golf shots wearing shoes with a smooth leather sole. The traction coefficient for this shoe was 0.39, much lower than for the regular-spike or alternative-spike shoes. Figure 72.5 shows the shear to vertical force ratio for this shoe and for the alternative-spike shoe, along with curves showing the x and y displacement of a marker on the toe of the shoe during the swing. It can be seen that the shear/vertical force ratio for the smooth leather sole follows a similar pattern to that of the alternative-spike shoe until approximately 0.2 seconds before ball impact, at which time the ratio for the smooth-sole shoe leveled off and slip of the shoe occurred, as indicated by the sharp change in x and y displacement patterns. These data provide some initial evidence that the ratio of shear to vertical force relative to the traction coefficient is important to determining whether or not slip occurs.

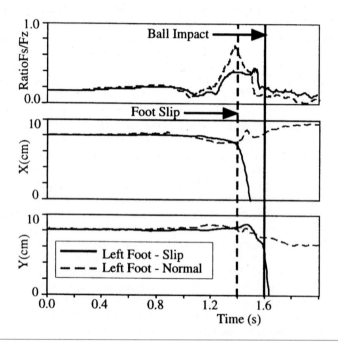

Figure 72.5   The ratio of shear/vertical force for the shoe and the alternative-spike shoe and a shoe with a smooth leather surface, along with curves showing the x and y displacement of a marker on the toe of the shoe showing slip during the swing.

CONCLUSIONS

No significant differences were found in the three components of ground reaction forces between regular-spike and alternative-spike golf shoes when hitting on an artificial surface in an indoor hitting facility. Within subject force patterns were very consistent, with marked variability between subjects in the pattern and magnitudes of forces. The ratio of shear to vertical force during the downswing was less than the traction coefficient for both spike conditions, and as would be expected, slip did not occur in the left or right feet prior to ball impact. The shear to vertical force ratio for the left foot, which peaked shortly after the downswing began, was lower than the ratio for the right foot, which peaked shortly after ball impact. Further tests are needed using a natural grass surface and conditions where slip is more likely to occur to further define any effect alternative-spike outsole designs may have on golf swing dynamics.

References

Abdel-Aziz, Y.I., & Karara, H. M. (1971). Direct linear transformation from computer coordinates into object space coordinates in close-range photogram-metry. *Proceedings Symposium on Close-Range Photogrammetry*, Urbana, 1971. A.S.P. Falls Church Va, pp. 1–18.

Slavin, M.M., & Williams, K.R. (1995). Golf shoe traction: The effect of different outsole surface designs on the static coefficient of friction. In K.R. Williams (ed.) *Proceedings of the American Society of Biomechanics Annual Meeting,* Stanford University, Palo Alto, CA, October 1995. Stanford University & American Society of Biomechanics, Palo Alto.

Stucke, H, Baudzus, W., & Baumann, W. (1984). On friction characteristics of playing surfaces. *Sport shoes and playing surfaces*, ed. E.C. Frederick, pp. 87–97. Human Kinetics Publishers, Champaign, IL.

Valiant, G.A. (1993). Friction—slipping—traction. *Sportverletzung Sportschaden* 7(4):171–178.

Williams, K. R., & Cavanagh, P.R. 1983. The mechanics of foot action during the golf swing and implications for shoe design. *Medicine and Science in Sports and Exercise* 15(3):247–255.

CHAPTER 73

The Effects of Golf Shoe Tread Types on Putting Green Quality

G.W. Hamilton, J.S. Gregos, D.S. Sinkus, L.P. Tredway, and A.E. Gover
Penn State University, Pennsylvania, USA

New golf shoe tread types are being developed to minimize the damage to putting green surfaces. Golf shoe spikes are being developed in new designs and materials and are being widely accepted. This study evaluated a conventional 8 mm metal spike, new soft plastic spike, and a spikeless tread for their effects on ball roll distance and turfgrass wear. Traffic was applied at 20 and 40 traverses per day and the study was conducted on an all sand rootzone and a modified rootzone. The spikeless tread reduced ball roll distance more often than the other two tread types. All of the tread types caused unacceptable wear at the high traffic intensity on both rootzones, and there was more wear on the all sand rootzone. The metal spikes usually caused more wear than the other two tread types. The effects that tread types have on ball roll distance and wear appear to be directly related to the amount of sand in the rootzone and traffic intensity.

Keywords: Putting green, golf green, golf shoe spike, SoftSpikes, green speed.

INTRODUCTION

Many types of golf shoe treads have been developed to help alleviate the damage caused by conventional metal spikes. Changes in spike design and materials have significantly increased the number of tread types that are commercially available.

Only a few studies have been conducted to evaluate the effects of shoe types on turf quality and ball roll. In 1958, Ferguson reported on a study conducted by Gipson and Potts at Texas A&M College. He reported that ripple sole and rubber cleated shoes caused significantly less damage to a Seaside bentgrass turf when compared to a shoe with conventional metal spikes. Gibeault et al. (1983) evaluated four different types of shoes including metal spikes, two different types of multi-stud soles, and suction-type cleats. This study showed that the authors conclude that the metal spikes caused the most damage when compared to the other styles of shoes, and the suction-type cleats caused the least amount of damage. Morrow and Danneberger (1995) evaluated the effects of metal spikes and soft plastic spikes (SoftSpikes) on ball roll. They concluded that both soft plastic spikes and metal spikes caused ball roll distance to increase when compared to an untreated control. They also stated that the metal spikes appeared to cause more turf damage than the soft plastic spikes, although this was not quantified.

OBJECTIVE

This study was conducted to evaluate the effects of three tread types on putting green turf wear and ball roll distance (BRD).

MATERIALS AND METHODS

The first study was conducted at the Valentine Memorial Turfgrass Research Center at Penn State University, University Park, PA. Two Penncross creeping bentgrass (*Agrostis palustris* Huds.) greens maintained at a cutting height of 3.8 mm, one having an all sand (99% sand) rootzone and the other a slightly modified (74% sand) rootzone, were used for the study.

The turf on the all sand rootzone was 6 yrs old with 17 mm of thatch, and the turf on modified rootzone mix was 18 yrs old with 17 mm of thatch. The thatch on the all sand root zone had a significant amount of sand incorporated throughout. The areas were mowed five to seven times per week and irrigated as needed to encourage good turfgrass growth. The areas received a seasonal total of 195 Kg of N/ha, and fungicides were applied as needed to control diseases.

Individual plots (0.8 × 3 m) were arranged in a randomized complete block design with three replications. Treatments consisted of three tread types: conventional 8 mm metal spikes; soft plastic spikes (SoftSpikesLTK); and spikeless (Footjoy 98593FU). Traffic was applied at two intensities (100 and 200 traverses per week) by people wearing the various shoes and walking directly back and forth across the plot, without turning on the experimental areas. The three people providing the traffic were of similar shoe size (women's size 8) and body weight (55 to 60 Kg) and applied approximately equal amounts of traffic throughout the duration of the experiment. Traffic was applied Monday through Friday at 20 and 40 traverses per day.

Traffic was started on June 12 and June 17 and finished on September 5 and September 9 (12 weeks), in 1995 and 1996, respectively. BRD for all plots was measured with a Stimpmeter (USGA, 1979) on Fridays following traffic applications. Three balls were rolled in one direction with the Stimpmeter and an average distance was determined. Three balls were then rolled (from the average distance point) of the first three balls in the opposite direction of the first rolls. The BRD for the plot was calculated by averaging the distances of the six ball rolls. The 12 weekly BRD measurements of each year were averaged together for statistical analysis.

Wear was rated on a scale of 0 to 5 with 5 being full cover and 0 being bare. A cover rating of 3 or above was considered to be acceptable as a putting surface. Wear was rated 12 weeks after the initiation of traffic treatments in both years.

All data were subjected to Analysis of Variance (ANOVA) statistical procedures, and means were compared using Duncan's New Multiple Range Test with p = 0.05. Since the control plots were not subjected to traffic, the control data was not included in the ANOVA of the wear data.

RESULTS AND DISCUSSION

In 1995, on the modified soil plot the spikeless tread at the high traffic intensity was the only treatment to cause BRD to be significantly less than the control (table 73.1). On the all sand plot, the spikeless tread at both traffic intensities and metal spikes at the high traffic intensity caused BRD to be significantly less than the control.

Results were slightly different in 1996 (table 73.1). On the modified soil, the soft plastic spikes significantly reduced BRD at the low traffic intensity and the spikeless tread significantly reduced BRD at the high traffic intensity. The metal spikes significantly reduced BRD at both traffic intensities. All treads significantly reduced BRD at both traffic intensities on the all sand plot.

These data suggest that BRD can be affected by tread type. The spikeless tread reduced BRD more often than the other two tread types and the metal spikes reduced

Table 73.1   Average Ball Roll Distances for All Treatments, Traffic Intensities, and Soil Types

Tread type	Traffic intensity (traverses per week)	Ball roll distance			
		1995		1996	
		Modified soil	All soil	Modified soil	All soil
		cm			
Metal	100	225 ab	235 bcd	216 c	215 d
Soft plastic	100	226 ab	239 abc	221 bc	213 d
Spikeless	100	227 ab	232 cd	228 ab	233 b
Metal	200	232 a	230 d	215 c	224 c
Soft plastic	200	230 a	244 a	228 ab	230 b
Spikeless	200	220 b	232 cd	218 c	228 bc
Control	0	233 a	241 ab	232 a	242 a

*Means within the same column followed by the same letter are not statistically different according to Duncan's New Multiple Range test with p = 0.05.

BRD more often than the soft plastic spikes. It also appears that the composition of the rootzone and thatch and traffic intensity influence the effect that tread types have on BRD.

In 1995, the wear from all treads was acceptable on the modified soil at the low traffic intensity. (Table 73.2); and only the metal spikes caused unacceptable wear on the all sand rootzone at the low traffic intensity (1,200 traverses). All tread types caused unacceptable wear on both soil types at the high traffic intensity (2,400 traverses). The spikeless tread usually caused significantly less wear than the metal and soft plastic spikes on both soil types.

In 1996, the wear from the spikeless tread and the soft plastic spikes was acceptable on both soil types at the low traffic intensity (Table 73.2). All tread types caused unacceptable wear on both soil types at the high traffic intensity, and the spikeless tread caused significantly less wear than the metal spikes and soft plastic spikes on both soil types and the low traffic intensity. The spikeless tread also caused significantly less wear than the metal spikes on both soil types at the high traffic intensity.

Table 73.2   Wear Ratings for Both Soil Textures After 1,200 and 2,400 Traverses

| Tread type | Traverses | Wear* | | | |
| | | 1995 | | 1996 | |
		Modified soil	All sand	Modified soil	All sand
Metal	1,200	3.3 b**	2.5 bc	2.3 c	2.8 b
Soft plastic	1,200	4.1 a	3.1 ab	3.0 b	3.0 b
Spikeless	1,200	3.9 a	3.5 a	4.0 a	3.8 a
Metal	2,400	1.3 c	1.3 d	1.3 d	1.3 d
Soft plastic	2,400	1.8 c	1.1 d	1.7 d	1.5 cd
Spikeless	2,400	2.8 b	2.3 c	2.7 c	2.1 c

*0 = bare, 5 = full cover, ≥ 3 = acceptable.
**Means within the same column followed by the same letter are not statistically different according to Duncan's New Multiple Range test with p = 0.05.

CONCLUSIONS

The golf shoe tread types used in this study did affect putting green quality. The tread types significantly decreased ball roll distance and caused some level of wear on both rootzones.

The turf wear appears to be very dependent on the type of rootzone mix that the putting surface is constructed from. On the modified soil the spikeless shoe caused significantly less wear than the metal or soft plastic spikes, which performed very similarly. On the all sand rootzone, the metal spikes usually caused significantly more wear than the soft plastic spikes and spikeless treads.

A general observation was that the metal spikes, because of the creation of the hole in the turf, made the traffic much more noticeable. Although the holes make the traffic more apparent, the effect on putting green quality may not be significantly different from that of tread types that do not create holes.

References

Ferguson, M. (1958). Effects of Golf-Shoe Soles on Putting Green Turf. *USGA Journal and Turf Management* (November), pp. 25–28.

Gibeault, V., V.B. Youngner, and W.H. Bengeyfield. (1983). Golf Shoe Study II. *USGA Green Section Record*, 21(5):1–7.

Morrow, J. and K. Danneberger. (1995). A Look at Ball Roll. *Golf Course Management*, 63(5):54–55.

United States Golf Association. (1979). *Stimpmeter instruction booklet*. Golf House, Far Hills, NJ.

PART III

The Golf Course

CHAPTER 74

Scientific Approach to Golf Course Design

M. Hurdzan
Hurdzan/Fry Golf Course Design, Columbus, Ohio, USA

Scientific information, technologically improved materials, and environmental management concepts are being combined to change modern American golf course design. This new direction was promulgated by increases in environmental regulations, public concern about the environment, and the golf industry's commitment to lead rather than be led. Therefore, research and development are finding practical application on the golf course through a scientific planning method.

Keywords: Golf course design, environment, planning, design.

INTRODUCTION

Golf course design principles had their genesis in Great Britain during the late 1800s, were nurtured and refined on links and lands in harmony with natural physical and biological forces, and were exported to North America. In America, for various reasons those principles of "natural" golf course planning, construction, and maintenance evolved into more "artificial" methodologies that lately have been suspected of having negative environmental impacts. Specifically, North American golfers came to expect and demand lush, green playing surfaces, and turfgrass scientists were happy to give them the tools and skills necessary to achieve that. Recently, however, environmentalists saw the penchant for perfect turf as excessive and wasteful, epitomized by the golf course conditioning efforts at Augusta National, and subsequently coined the term "Augusta Syndrome" to represent excessive use of water, fertilizer, pesticides, and fossil fuels (Whitten, 1994). Turfgrass scientists, golf course architects, and superintendents began cooperative efforts to examine those concerns.

In 1995, a select group of international leaders from golf and environmental organizations were invited to a conference at Pebble Beach. After three days of meetings to discuss points of agreement and disagreement about the environmental impact of golf, three initiatives for future cooperation were identified:

1. a set of environmental principles for golf courses in the United States
2. better education of golfers to environmental concerns
3. demonstration project golf course(s)

After more than a year, and many meetings, a set of "Environmental Principles for Golf Courses in the United States" was agreed upon and published (Center for Resource Management, 1996). Two demonstration projects were selected: Widow's Walk, a new course built south of Boston, Massachusetts, and the Presideo, a remodeled course near the Golden Gate Bridge in San Francisco, California. It is too early to draw conclusions about how successful in terms of management practices the application of these environmental principles to these demonstration courses has been. It is, however, possible to show how scientific advances are allowing American golf courses to return to the "natural" principles of planning, construction, and operation. That methodology can be broken down into sequential and distinct phases and labeled as follows:

Research → Schematic → Design Development → Permit and Review →

Construction Documents → Bidding → Construction → Grow-In → Operations

Figure 74.1   Methodology broken into sequential phases.

DISCUSSION

The research phase begins by scientists evaluating a potential golf course site for its resource areas and possible impacts. Along with a golf course architect, the owner should include in his project team a soil scientist and civil engineer, plant and animal specialist familiar with endangered species, water testing specialist, representative from a local environmental organization, experienced greenkeeper or superintendent, lawyers, accountants, and other specialists as needed (Hurdzan, 1994).

Site surveys for natural resource areas, or areas of special environmental value, conducted by scientists are tailored to fit that site. They are often aided by satellite pictures that can show seasonal or longer term variations in vegetation patterns, water bodies, or surrounding influences. Using increasingly sophisticated methods of testing and monitoring, scientists prepare baseline readings on plant and animal communities, soils and groundwater, possible irrigation water quality and quantity, and the health, age, distribution and diversity of biological systems. Site surveys also may include very sophisticated means of archeological investigations with ground wave technology and infrared photography (Maier, 1995).

Such accurate assessment of high value resource areas allows the designer to first avoid those areas, or where impacts are unavoidable to accurately quantify them. As the accuracy of satellite imagery improves, it can be used to monitor migration patterns of animals through or to the golf course site, assess the health of the turf, and evaluate the efficiency of irrigation systems, after completion of the golf course (Corbley, 1996).

During the next phase of the golf course design process, schematic design, computer science is called upon to generate maps of various combinations of information generated during the research phase. With this computer information, the golf course designer can try different routings of holes and evaluate them quickly for their environmental impacts, and then if necessary make modifications to those routings.

The product of the design development phase is a master plan, which is then ready for the approval and review process, where scientists can further validate the impact of the plan through the environmental impact study (E.I.S.). The team should establish maintenance input goals for that particular golf course in terms of expected usage of water, fertilizers, and pesticides. These goals should be referred to often for they will influence many choices and decisions throughout the following phase of design and preparation of construction documents (Hurdzan, 1996).

Perhaps nowhere is this more dramatic than in the field of plant breeding and genetic engineering. Scientists are developing turfgrass cultivators that have been selected or genetically designed to provide better adaptability to heat, shade, drought, compaction; better resistance to weeds, disease, insect and mechanical injury; and require less water, fertilizer, and cultural manipulation. Planting better adapted and genetically superior plants means less maintenance inputs and hence less environmental impact, while producing outstanding playing conditions. It is truly "doing more with less."

Through genetic engineering and using a gene gun, selective properties of one type of plant can sometimes be passed to a different genus and species of plant, such as transferring the gene for drought tolerance in corn to a variety of turfgrass (Schumann, 1995). Developing symbiotic relationships to improve turfgrasses is already common using the endophyte fungus to increase insect and disease resistance (Sun, 1996). Planting varieties of turfgrass that are better suited to each site-specific combination of microclimate, soil, and water quality can save enormous amounts of water, pesticides, fertilizers, and fossil fuels in long-term maintenance.

In the future, in some areas, irrigation water will be in short supply and of poorer quality, and will require specialists to tackle the problem in several ways. One solution is to produce turfgrass varieties that can cope with the limitations of lower quality irrigation water—such as increased tolerance to salt and/or heavy metals. Another solution is to improve the quality of irrigation water through bio-remediation or passing it through a series of ponds planted with selected vegetation capable of cleansing the water (Cooke, 1995). Perhaps irrigation water will be improved by passing it through inexpensive osmotic filters or an electromagnetic field that changes the polarity and hence the properties of the water. Such techniques are in their infancy, but show promise.

Water conservation through using new plant varieties is fast becoming a standard technique, but determining how much water to apply is not precise and hence subject to overapplication errors. The use of weather stations to determine each day's water loss through evapotranspiration does not allow for different soil or micro-climates on the golf course. Scientific and engineering research have recently produced the first economically priced and easily calibrated soil moisture sensors for golf course use (Leslie, 1997). Installed at various depths in the rootzone, these sensors and associated computer software programmes allow irrigation applications to be matched to soil moisture reserves in small areas around the golf course, resulting in enormous water savings by tailoring water application to each small area.

Irrigation head design and control systems continue to advance, so water can be placed exactly where it is needed, in the proper amount, and at a rate that the soil and plants can absorb it. Variable frequency pumping equipment saves energy, as well as wear and tear on the hardware and controls. All of these environmental measures are possible through advances in science and engineering.

Alterations to improve the chemical and physical characteristics of rootzones use a great variety of materials ranging from clacine clay to diatomaceous earth to various minerals like zeolites (Allen and Andrews, 1997). Polyacrylamide gels to retain water and nutrients are finding application in turfgrass culture as they did in agriculture in arid areas. Systems for pumping air under rootzones of greens or applying a vacuum to drain greens down have made troublesome micro-climatic sites more predictable, healthier for the plants, and hence reduced the need for artificial cures like preventative pesticide treatments (Sub Air). The "seeding" of soil organisms that increase the health of turfgrasses and act as an antagonist to pests may soon be standard practice in golf course construction.

Golf course construction itself has evolved as scientists showed contractors how to better control silt, manage topsoil, re-vegetate and stabilize slopes, and reduce dust, noise and air pollution. Planting nurse crops of companion and noncompetitive species such as fine fescues has reduced grow-in requirements for water. Improved methods of growing sod, often soil-less on plastic, or on a thin layer of compost, have made it more cost effective to specify larger acres of sod (turf), thus far shortening the maturation time from bare soil to established sod. Root washing of sod is popular in the United States and allows sodding of greens without soil layering.

Research on transplanting native vegetation, endangered plants, or ancient trees has allowed contractors to save important plants and plant associations. Further, once they have been transplanted the golf course superintendent or greenkeeper will assume responsibility for nursing these plants along with his other responsibilities during the final phase of the scientific approach called operations.

Inexpensive fertilizers used by agriculture are often quick release, large particle, and subject to leaching. However, through research the most widely used fertilizers on golf courses are small particle, slow release or encapsulated in a sulfur on plastic coating, designed to release nutrients at the same rate as plants can use it. Turf grade fertilizers have nearly eliminated any possibility of nutrient leaching. Fertigation, or the application of minute amounts of soluble fertilizer through the irrigation system, is another method for eliminating nutrient loading of soil. Similarly, acid or gypsum injection at the pump house can neutralize water or soil limitations, and hence improve turf quality without fertilizers. In the United States, it is becoming more common to use a system of injecting selected bacterial populations into the irrigation water to fight diseases, fix atmospheric nitrogen, reduce thatch, and control nematodes. Biological turf pesticides and growth stimulants are being developed and refined rapidly, so it is possible that sometime in the future no chemical pesticides may be required.

Through science we know not only much more about biological interactions and complexes, but we also know much more about the fate of pesticides and fertilizers applied to golf courses. Scientists can now measure or assay down to the "ppt" (parts per trillion), so tracking chemicals is much easier. Today's pesticides are found to be rapidly absorbed by the target species and residuals, will quickly photodegrade, will be broken down by beneficial organisms, or will be held by the turfgrass profile until weathered or rendered harmless (Kenna, 1995). Properly applied, modern pesticides and fertilizers used on golf courses pose no significant health threat to golfers, greenkeepers, neighbors or the environment. I welcome any peer reviewed research to the contrary, and in fact, I have challenged the U.S. Environmental Protection Agency at the highest levels to do that, and none has come forth.

CONCLUSION

So what kind of golf course will our scientific effort to save water, fertilizers, pesticides, and fossil fuels produce? It will permit golf courses of the year 2020 to have the same magical charm and character of golf courses created in the nineteenth century, a "natural" look and feel. The magic of golf lies not in the greenness of the turf. It is the connection of the human spirit in a physical and tangible way to the earth and wind. It is the full range of human emotions played out with a small ball in a pure, wholesome landscape. Golf represents one of the few opportunities for modern man to find solitude and himself.

It is our charge as responsible scientists to continue to improve and protect that mystical experience in golf by finding even better ways for a golf course to continue as a healthy environment produce.

References

Allen, E. and Andrews, R. (1997). Space age soil mix uses centuries old zeolites. *Golf Course Management,* 65(5): 61–66.

Center for Resource Management. (1996). Environmental Principles for Golf Courses in the United States.

Cooke, R. (1995). Using plants to clean up contamination. *Newsday.*

Corbley, K. (1996). One meter satellites: Practical applications by spatial data users. *Geo Info Systems,* July 1.

Hurdzan, M. (1996). *Golf course architecture: Design, construction and restoration.* Sleeping Bear Press, Chelsea, Michigan, USA.

Hurdzan, M. (1994). Team approach to golf course development. Hurdzan/Fry Golf Course Design, Columbus, Ohio, USA.

Kenna, M. (1995). What happens to pesticides applied to golf course. *USGA Green Section Record,* 33(1):1–9.

Leslie, M. (1997). Taking irrigation into the future. *Golf Course News,* 9(2).

Maier, T. (1995). Radar of the lost ark: High-tech digs. *Newsday,* February, 28.

Schumann, G. (1995). New possibilities for disease resistant turfgrasses. *Golf Course Management,* 63(10):56–59.

Sun, S. (1996). Endophites for creeping bentgrass and Kentucky bluegrass. *Golf Course Management,* 64(9):49–52.

Whitten, R. (1994). Perfection versus reality. *Golf Digest.*

CHAPTER 75

An Architect's Name—What's It Worth?

M.R. Judge
Golf Research Group, London, England

Using past and present data on the income streams of a golf course—green fee revenues, membership sales and real estate sales—it is possible to evaluate its probable future income using specially adapted present value formulae. By collating and analysing these values for the projects of an architect, it is possible to make valid and important comparisons between two or more architects.

Keywords: Architect, present value, income streams.

INTRODUCTION

While green fees, joining fees, annual subscriptions and real estate prices alone can be good indicators of the standard of course and standard of architect, they cannot convey how successful that course is financially. Other factors have to be looked at. Are golfers willing to pay the green fee? Do golfers feel the member privileges are worth the asking price? Is the real estate of sufficient quality to attract home buyers? If the answer is 'No' to any of these questions, the course could be losing money. If the course was designed by an architect with a large fee (effectively a promotional cost), requiring a large construction budget and needing expensive maintenance and if the answers are still 'No,' it could be haemorrhaging money. Along with other factors, such as good location and sound management, choosing the right golf course architect greatly influences the financial success of the project. Could the decision be made easier if we knew that architect B will, on the whole, design you a course that will give greater returns on your investment than architect A?

The need for research into valuing the uplift generated by using a certain architect was highlighted in Siegal (1995), which looked at the varying performances of the three real estate developments at PGA West in La Quinta, California.

The ideal way to quantify what an architect's name is worth would be to analyse the financial accounts of every course and collate the income and cost items for each architect. This method, unfortunately, is unworkable, as courses are, on the whole, reluctant to part with their accounts. Assuming a significantly large number of accounts could be collected further, problems arise. For instance, it is very unlikely they will contain the same line items as one another, hence making direct comparisons very difficult.

It is, however, possible to estimate the past income streams of each golf course—how many rounds, how many memberships and how much real estate has been sold and at what price, estimate its future income streams based on membership and real estate levels, rates of sale and growth of prices, then value everything back to the year of opening of the facility. By identifying the designer of each course, it is possible to create an average income value for each architect.

The main objective was to derive a formula or formulae that would calculate such a figure using the data collected—green fee prices, membership prices and numbers, and real estate sales and inventories.

The primary concept was one of present value—how much an item will be worth sold at some point in the future in today's money. It is well known that £1 next year is worth less than £1 this year; inflation devalues it. The same is true for subscriptions—a subscription worth £500 in 10 years time is worth £307 (£500/1.0510) now, if inflation is level at 5%. That is, 'the present value of a £500 subscription paid in ten years time is £307, assuming an inflation rate of 5% pa.' As the time span increases to infinity, the present value of each payment decreases to zero.

Figure 75.1 represents the present value of the cumulative income to the course

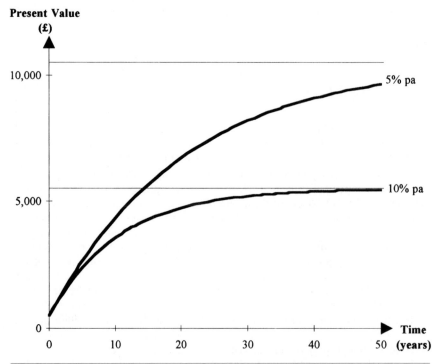

Figure 75.1   Present values of one annual subscription, priced at a fixed £500, at discount rates of 5% pa and 10% pa.

of a single member paying annual subscriptions of £500. If the time axis was extended to infinity, the two curves would become horizontal, leveling out at £10,500 for the 5% discount rate and £5,500 for the 10% discount rate. The discount rate is not the same as inflation but is the interest rate at which developers may lend or borrow their money and does not include the growth rate of prices.

Thus we can say that, if we assumed a discount rate of 5% pa and subscription growth rate of 0%, each member paying £500 pa subscriptions is 'worth' £10,500 to the course owner.

Applying this concept to the other key income items, it can be seen that the most financially successful courses will be those who can sell their memberships and real estate quickly and at a reasonable price as the present value of those sales falls rapidly with time.

DATA COLLECTION

The data applied to the present value formulae was collected during the spring months of 1997 by means of a telephone survey of the 2,163 new developments built in the United States since 1988. Follow-up calls were made to the real estate offices of the 43% of courses claiming to have such schemes. Well over 3,000 separate interviews were conducted to complete the survey. The data were collected originally for a report into the development of golf courses in the United States by Judge and Hegarty (1997), a follow-up to Hegarty (1994).

The following data items were collected from each course and used in this study: the golf course architect; year of opening; midweek and weekend green fees; joining fee; annual subscription; number of members; type of course—private, semi-private or public; average house price; houses sold to date; size of real estate master plan. From these, using the assumptions given in chapter 3, rates of sale of memberships and real estate were calculated. Analysis of the data also provided the concept of different 'full' membership levels at private and semi-private clubs. By analysing the data from courses appearing in both the 1997 and 1994 surveys, growth rates of green fees, joining fees, subscriptions and real estate can be established.

DERIVATION OF FORMULAE

Writing down the Present Value equations, one makes the following assumptions:

1. Linear sales of memberships and real estate.
2. Green fees, joining fees, subscriptions and house prices will continue to grow at surveyed rate in perpetuity.
3. Memberships become 'full' at 400 members for private clubs and 150 members for semi-private clubs, after which no more will be sold.
4. Those clubs already with more than 'full' memberships sell no more.
5. Memberships do not lapse—they are simply passed on to a new member, i.e., no resales.

6. Real estate master plan sizes do not change over time.
7. The course is not involved in the resale of real estate.

The fundamental element of each formula is a geometric progression *(x + ax + a2x + a3x + ..)* with *x* representing the yearly income streams associated with each course (green fees, subscriptions, etc.) and *a* representing the ratio between the income growth rates *ix* and discount rates *dx*. Other formula elements deal with the rates of sale of memberships and real estate. It is vital to ascertain how long a course will take to fill its memberships or sell out its master plans, as this can significantly alter its present value. For example, Southern Woods CC, Florida, and Renaissance Vinoy GC, Florida, are both private clubs, were both opened in 1992 and both have joining fees of $3,500. However, Southern Woods has 142 members compared with Renaissance Vinoy's 350. With the assumptions made above, Southern Woods would sell its last (400th) membership in early 2006 whereas Renaissance Vinoy would be full by the end of 1997. After inputting the above data and the discount and growth rates into Eq. (2) it can be seen that the Present Value of Joining Fees for Southern Woods ($808,000) is less than three-quarters that of Renaissance Vinoy ($1.132 m). The Tx's in Eqs. (2), (3) and (4) represent the period after which new membership and real estate sales will cease.

In the main the formulae were derived from first principles, using standard calculus processes. No approximations were used and the assumptions made are listed above. The formulae have been simplified greatly and are applicable to any course where the income stream discount rate *dx* is greater than the income stream growth rate *ix*—otherwise the income streams rise to infinity. The calculations incorporate an infinite time period.

Present Value of Green Fees (PVGF)

$$PV_{GF} = \frac{(1+d_{GF})RG_{97}}{(d_{GF}-i_{GF})(1+i_{GF})^{97-Y}} \tag{1}$$

Present Value of Joining Fees (PVI)

$$PV_I = \frac{[(1+d_I)^{T_I} - (1+i_I)^{T_I}]I_{97}m_{97}}{(97-Y)(d_I - i_I)(1+i_I)^{97-Y}(1+d_I)^{T_I-1}} \tag{2}$$

Present Value of Annual Subscriptions (PVD)

$$PV_D = \frac{D_{97}}{(1+i_D)^{97-Y}} \left[\frac{m_{97}}{97-Y} \left(\frac{r_D - T_D r_D^{T_D} + (T_D-1)r_D^{T_D+1}}{(1-r_D)^2} \right) + \frac{m_{max}r_D^{T_D}}{1-r_D} \right] \tag{3}$$

Present Value of Real Estate Sales (PVRE)

$$PV_{RE} = \frac{H_{97}S_{97}\left[(1+d_{RE})^{T_{RE}} - (1+i_{RE})^{T_{RE}}\right]}{(97-Y)(d_{RE}-i_{RE})(1+d_{RE})^{T_{RE}-1}(1+i_{RE})^{97-Y}} \tag{4}$$

where

$$T_I = T_D = \begin{cases} \dfrac{m_{max}(97-Y)}{m_{97}} & \text{if } m_{97} < m_{max}, \\ 97-Y & \text{if } m_{97} \geq m_{max}. \end{cases}$$

$$T_{RE} = \frac{F(97-Y)}{S_{97}},$$

$$m_{max} = \begin{cases} 400 & \text{for private courses,} \\ 150 & \text{for semi - private courses.} \end{cases}$$

$$r_D = (1+i_D)/(1+d_D),$$

and

Y = year opened

G_{97} = 1997 green fee

D_{97} = 1997 annual subs

F = master plan size

m_{97} = no. of members in 1997

d_{GF} = green fee discount rate pa

d_I = joining fee discount rate pa

d_D = annual subs discount rate pa

d_{RE} = real estate discount rate pa

R = annual green fee roundage

I_{97} = 1997 joining fee

H_{97} = average 1997 house price

S_{97} = houses sold by 1997

m_{max} = full membership

i_{GF} = green fee growth rate pa

i_I = joining fee growth rate pa

i_D = annual subs growth rate pa

i_{RE} = real estate growth rate pa

RESULTS

The Golf Value in table 75.1 is the sum of the Green Fee, Joining Fee and Subscriptions Values. The Adjusted Real Estate Value is the estimated value of the incomes from a 300 lot development. This adjustment was made to reduce the dependency on the master plan size. If an architect designed ten or more courses in the eight-year study period he or she was classed as a 'Top 33 Architect.' 'Other Architects' designed between two and nine, and 'Not Recognised Architects' were involved in just the one development—the majority being the local pro or land-owner.

Table 75.1 shows that, on the whole, it is the repeat sales items (green fees and subscriptions) that provide the greatest revenue. The 'Famous Five' selected appear able to sell joining fees quickly and at a high price, as are most of the Top 33. Using lesser known architects, or indeed designing it yourself, has a tendency to decimate the income from the membership sector. Real Estate is the big money spinner, worth more than the course itself.

Table 75.1   Average Present Value of All Past and Future Income Streams Over an Infinite Time Period at a Single Course ($ millions)

Architect	No. of projects	Green fee value $ m	Joining fee value $ m	Subscriptions value $ m	Golf value $ m	Adj. real estate value $ m
Nicklaus	31	13.0	13.2	18.5	44.7	116.0
Tom Fazio	42	11.0	8.2	12.5	31.8	57.5
Weiskopf & Morrish	13	10.0	8.2	13.3	31.5	56.0
RTJ Junior	28	9.0	8.1	11.6	28.7	59.5
Palmer	37	11.0	6.5	11.0	28.4	78.5
Top 33 architect	606	8.0	4.5	4.0	16.5	53.0
Other architects	522	5.0	0.7	1.8	7.5	35.0
Not recognised architect	1,064	3.0	0.1	0.8	3.9	27.0

On average, a course designed by a leading architect will achieve golf-related income premiums of 120% over one designed by a lesser known architect and 323% over one designed without a qualified architect. Real estate income premiums are 51% and 96% respectively.

CONCLUSIONS AND REFINEMENTS

The analysis highlights the stark contrast between courses designed by the top professional architects and those of lesser notoriety. This difference is an important one and should be considered by those included in the decision processes involved in developing a new course. The results point strongly in the direction of building a 'Big Name' course, although it should be noted that this paper has touched only upon the income side of the coin and does not include any costing analysis. While a 'Nicklaus' or 'Jones' course will bring in the money, how much will it take out? How much will it cost to build and maintain? (Design 'signatures' inevitably lead to high-budget projects.) Also, if real estate is a consideration, are the income premiums sufficiently large to warrant using a 'Name'?

Before using this analysis, a developer must first decide into which niche of the market to put the new course. Not every market can absorb a 7,000-yard, signature-designed, championship golf course. A 5,500-yard, Par 67 course could easily bring in a greater return on investment if built in the right location.

Some element of costing analysis needs to be introduced to the equation to get a true perspective on the relative merits of each architect. A tighter figure on the number of green fee rounds played at each course needs to be found, although past experience indicates this will be extremely difficult. Continuing the surveys on a yearly basis will provide more accurate pricing growth rates. Frequent surveys may be able to identify an accurate membership and real estate sales curve, thereby eliminating the assumption that all sales are linear over time.

References

Hegarty, C J (1994). *Financial Performance of US Golf Developments*. Golf Research Group, London, England and Orinda, California, USA.

Judge, M R & Hegarty, C J (1997). *The US Golf Development Report*. Golf Research Group, London, England, and Martinez, California, USA.

Siegal, Robert L (1995). *The Jack Nicklaus Private Course PGA West*. Robert L. Siegal & Associates, Kenner, Louisiana, USA.

CHAPTER 76

Golf Course Provision, Usage, and Revenues in Scotland

R.J. Price
Kirkintilloch, Glasgow, UK

The provision, usage, and revenues generated by the three sectors (members clubs, municipal, and commercial facilities) of the Scottish golf industry are described and analysed. Changes taking place in the relative importance of each sector are assessed and possible implications for the future suggested.

Keywords: Golf course, provision, usage, revenues, Scotland.

Between 1880 and 1990, 152 new golf courses were opened for play in Scotland, bringing the total number of courses in 1990 to 195 (Price, 1989). Eighty percent of these courses were operated by members clubs, and 20% were provided by municipal authorities. This pattern of golf facility provision continued to characterise Scottish golf for the next 60 years, except that a few golf courses were constructed by commercial companies usually in association with hotels (e.g., Turnberry, 1903; Gleneagles, 1924).

Golf in Scotland was generally an egalitarian game despite the existence of about a dozen all-male exclusive members clubs. The average golfer played at a members club that welcomed males, females, and juniors and also extended a warm welcome to non-members to play on payment of a visitors green fee. Many of the courses were laid out rather than constructed, and clubhouses often provided only very basic facilities. Golf was cheap with annual membership fees in 1960 often being less than £5 and visitors green fees 10p to 20p per round.

By 1960 there were 69 municipal golf courses (including courses operated by Links Management Committees in Scotland [19%]). They ranged from the championship courses in St. Andrews and Carnoustie to very basic, heavily-used and cheap nine-hole courses in Glasgow and Edinburgh.

Commercial golf, i.e., the construction of golf facilities by profit-oriented companies or individuals, was very limited in Scotland until after 1990 (Price 1993, 1997; Scottish Sports Council 1991). In that year 16 commercial courses existed, representing only 5% of all golf courses in the country, and 12 of them were associated with hotels. The commercial golf boom, which in 1990 was well underway in England, Wales, and Ireland, was late arriving in Scotland. The main reason for this was that golf in Scotland was still relatively cheap and apart from certain areas in Edinburgh, Glasgow, and Aberdeen, access to golf either via membership of a club or as a visitor to a members club or to a municipal golf course was relatively easy. However, since 1980 visitor green fees and, to a lesser extent, annual membership fees at members clubs have increased significantly (table 76.1).

Table 76.1   Average Mid-Week Visitors Green Fees

	1980	1985	1990	1995	1997
All courses	£3	4	8	14	16
Members clubs	£3.5	4.5	8	16	19
Municipal courses	£2	2.6	5.7	10.2	14
Commercial courses	£3.6	5.2	10	20	25
Old Course, St. Andrews	£5	15	23	55	70

While visitors green fees have been increasing rapidly over the past 17 years, annual membership fees at members clubs have risen much less dramatically. Green fees have increased fivefold, while membership fees have increased threefold. Over the same period the retail price index has increased by 130%.

Before proceeding to an analysis of the course providers, users, and revenues in 1997 it is necessary to clarify some complicated changes that have taken place over the last decade. Many members clubs have become much more commercialised in that it is estimated that some 60% of members clubs receive at least 25% of their total annual income from visitor fees, 50% obtain over 33% from that source, and there are probably some 40 members clubs (11%) that obtain over half of their total revenue from non-members. No longer can all the members clubs be regarded as consisting of purely nonprofit making, mutual trading organisations. Many members clubs use visitor fee income to subsidise members' annual fees.

The public sector providers have also changed radically over the past decade. While relatively high green fees are charged by the Links Management Committees at St. Andrews and Carnoustie because of the huge demand to play their famous golf courses, many local authorities have also increased their green fees as they now regard the golf courses they operate as commercial assets rather than public liabilities (table 76.1). Some authorities have launched official membership clubs attached to their courses (e.g., the City of Glasgow Golf Club created by the Dept of Parks & Recreation) and actively promote the courses to tourists.

Commercial golf facilities range from very basic 9-hole facilities through 18-hole good quality pay-and-play facilities to major golf resorts such as Dalmahoy or Gleneagles. While green fee income from visitors is often the prime source of revenue, many such commercial facilities have membership clubs attached to them (members clubs attached to municipal facilities). Such members clubs organise competitions and establish players' handicaps. However, the members of these clubs have no control over the operation of the courses, allocation of tee times, or the green fees charged. The fee such members pay to the course operator for the use of the course is not a membership subscription but is a season ticket for access to the course (season ticket sold to regular players on municipal courses).

From the above comments it can be seen that any attempt to categorise golf facilities is difficult, as the aims and objectives of the various types of providers overlap. Nevertheless, the core types of members club, commercial, and municipal facilities still exist.

Table 76.2 is an attempt to identify the relative importance of each sector in terms of provision, usage, and revenue. The data on usage and revenues must be regarded as tentative as accurate statistics on these items do not exist. The writer has used various surrogate measures and sample statistics derived from a variety of sources. Nevertheless, the relative (%) values are useful indicators. A golf facility is defined as one or more golf courses at one location operated by one management. Visitor rounds at a course are defined as rounds of golf played by persons who are not members of a club attached to that course.

Table 76.2   Relative Importance of Each Sector in Terms of Provision, Usage, and Revenue (Scotland 1996-97)

	No. of facilities	%	No. of courses	%	Total holes	%	No. of members	%
Municipal	65	14	82	16	1249	16	27,000	11
Commercial	60	13	67	13	937	12	13,000	5
Members club	340	73	365	71	5619	72	208,000	84
Total	465		514		7805		248,000	

	Total rds	%	Visitor rds	%	Total revenue (£m)	%
Municipal	2,400,000	21	1,600,000	50	22	20
Commercial	1,200,000	10	600,000	19	18	16
Members club	8,000,000	69	1,000,000	31	73	64
	11,600,000		3,200,000		£113	

In 1997 there were 514 golf courses (31% of nine holes) in Scotland—16% were municipal, 13% commercial, and 71% members club courses (table 76.2). Of the 248,000 registered golfers (i.e., members of golf clubs registered with the Golf

Unions) 11% played their golf on municipal courses, 5% on commercial courses, and 84% at members clubs.

Detailed data on the usage of Scotland's golf courses do not exist. It is estimated that 11,600,000 rounds of golf are played each year—21% on municipal courses, 10% on commercial courses, and 69% on members club courses. In contrast, of the estimated 3,200,000 rounds played by visitors, 50% are played on municipal courses, 19% on commercial courses, and 31% on club courses.

Based on a sample survey of members clubs' annual financial statements and average membership fees and green fees charged by commercial facilities and local authorities, an attempt has been made to estimate the total revenue—£113 million—received from membership and green fees by all the golf courses in Scotland in 1997. Twenty percent was generated by municipal courses, 16% by commercial courses, and 64% by members clubs.

It is concluded that while members clubs provide 71% of Scotland's golf courses, they only generate 64% of the total revenue. Together, the municipal and commercial sectors generate 36% of the revenue, and accommodate 31% of the total rounds played and 69% of the visitor rounds. It is estimated that approximately 34% of the total fee revenue received by members clubs is not in the form of annual membership fees. While the members clubs served the Scottish people well during the first 80 years of this century, they are now no longer such a dominant force. It could be argued that the members clubs are not assisting the continued development of golf in Scotland. In generating an estimated £20 million per year from visitors fees (34% of their fee income) they are subsidising their members' annual fees while at the same time restricting membership (many clubs with high income from visitors have long waiting lists) and offer only restricted use of their facilities to women and juniors (albeit for reduced fees). These same clubs have in recent years received £20 million in VAT refunds and some £5 million from the Scottish Sports Council Lottery Fund to improve their facilities.

It is estimated that it costs approximately £250,000 per year to operate an average 18-hole members club. If that club has 600 members then the annual membership fee should be £417 (i.e, each member pays £10.42 per round for 40 rounds per year). In reality such clubs subsidise their members fees with income from visitors fees and other sources so that the annual membership fee is £316 (i.e., £7.90 per round for 40 rounds) while at the same time charging 3,000 visitors a green fee of £20 (£60,000). Ironically, it has been the increase in the price of visitors green fees charged by members clubs that has allowed commercial golf facilities to be developed in Scotland over the past decade.

Scotland is the oldest and most mature of golf markets. Following the introduction of the gutty ball in 1876 cheap golf became widely available and the first golf boom occurred. Partly as a result of two world wars and a period of economic stagnation, there was no significant expansion either in the number of golfers or the number of golf facilities until the late 1980s. The advent of the worldwide television coverage of golf championships at St. Andrews, Turnberry, Muirfield, Carnoustie, Troon, and Gleneagles created a new demand from golf tourists. Similarly, the golf boom in England and Wales, France, Sweden, and Germany had an impact on demand in Scotland. Initially, this increased demand was absorbed by the members club courses and the municipal courses, but since 1990, 28 new commercial golf facilities have been opened so that by 1997 commercial facilities represented 13% of the total (table 76.3).

Table 76.3   Golf Courses

	1930			1960			1990			1997		
	MC	MU	CO	MC	MU	CO	MC	MU	CO	MC	MU	CO
Scotland	81	17	2	79	19	2	78	17	5	71	16	13
England & Wales							75	12	13	52	8	40
Ireland				88	8	4				68	2	30
USA	78	10	12	50	12	38	33	19	48	31	17	52

% Members (MC); Municipal (MU); Commercial (CO).

It is interesting to speculate what future developments will take place in Scotland. If similar trends to those that have occurred in England and the USA (table 76.3) occur in Scotland then a considerable expansion in commercial golf facilities will take place. Between 1990 and 1997 the percentage of commercial courses in England and Wales (table 76.3) increased from 13% to 40%. Currently in the USA, 67% of all golf facilities are classed as public access (daily fee commercial plus public/municipal courses).

The trends identified in this paper in the provision, use, and fee revenues of Scotland's golf courses raise many issues that need to be addressed by those who administer and market golf in Scotland. At present, the game and its administration is controlled by members clubs and the National Unions, and remains male dominated—84% of registered golfers and only 12% of members are juniors (1% female). Twenty-eight percent of all rounds of golf are played by visitors. Unless members clubs are willing to open up the use of their facilities, i.e., end sex and age discrimination, and improve and expand their facilities out of green fee income rather than subsidise their members fees, they will tend to discourage the further growth of the game. The facts that 36% of golf revenue, 31% of total rounds, and 69% of visitors rounds in Scotland are already concentrated in the municipal and commercial sectors indicate that the dominant status of the club sector is in decline.

The increased commercialisation of golf in Scotland by all three types of providers is likely to cause tensions within the current administrative structure of the game that is dominated by the members clubs and the national Golf Unions. VAT is not charged on membership fees levied by private clubs but is charged on annual fees (season tickets) charged by commercial facilities. Those members clubs generating large incomes from visitors fees are possibly putting their mutual trading status at risk. The members clubs will continue to dominate the provision and management of golf facilities in Scotland for the next decade. Whether this dominance is good for the continued growth and prosperity of the game is questionable.

The EMAP Golf Futures report produced by the Henley Centre in 1997 concludes that the UK golf industry must turn potential growth into real growth by promoting golf tuition and junior and female participation. This can only be achieved by increasing access to existing golf facilities and creating new and appropriate golf facilities. There are some 15 new golf courses under construction in Scotland, 14 of which are in the commercial sector. Within five years, Perth and Kinross region will have over half of its golf facilities provided by the commercial sector. Over the same period South Ayrshire, East Ayrshire, Angus, and Fife regions will have over half of their courses in the commercial and municipal sectors. If these trends are maintained, within ten years it is probable that half of the fee income generated by Scottish golf facilities will be from the municipal and commercial sectors. A change in the Scottish golf culture is in progress that will require administrators to adapt to the increased commercialisation of both the provision and use of golf facilities. On a national scale, initiatives such as the World Golf Foundation's First Tee programme (Callander, 1998), which will create 100 golf learning facilities in the USA during the next three years, should be replicated in Scotland, if the future development of the game is to be ensured.

References

Callander, C. 1998. Excellent New Initiative. *Golf Monthly,* February, p. 7.
Price, R.J. 1992. *Scotland's Golf Courses.* Mercat Press, Edinburgh, p. 235.
Price, R.J. 1993. Is the Golf Boom Bunkered? *The Scottish Banker,* May, pp. 2–4.
Price, R.J. 1997. Performing Below Par. *The Scottish Banker,* February, pp. 33–36.
Scottish Sports Council. 1991. *Study of Golf in Scotland.* Research Report 19, p. 78.
The Henley Centre. 1997. *EMAP Golf Futures.* EMAP Pursuit Publishing, p. 122

CHAPTER 77

Golf Tourism: Measurement and Marketing

M.G. Williamson
M.W. Associates, P.O. Box 6677, Edinburgh, EH14 3YB, Scotland

The paper describes two studies carried out for Scottish Enterprise and Fife Enterprises. The Golf Tourism Monitoring System tested various survey methodologies and developed a better database and understanding of golf tourism in Scotland, while the Fife Golf Study applied this new information, together with supply/demand and SWOT analyses, to the development of a golf tourism strategy for the region.

Keywords: Golf tourism, survey methodologies, new information, marketing, development strategy, Scotland.

INTRODUCTION

Tourism is one of Scotland's biggest industries (Scottish Tourist Board, 1997), and is one of Scottish Enterprise's target industries in terms of its growth potential. The national tourism strategy identifies activity holidays as a growth market (Scottish Tourism Coordinating Group, 1994, and Scottish Enterprise, 1996), and Scotland is universally recognised as "The Home of Golf."

Scotland has more golf holes per head of population than almost anywhere in the world, has been a destination for golfing holidaymakers for a century or more, and gets huge publicity whenever it hosts The Open Champions. So far, so good.

But supply has been growing faster than demand. Fifty-six new courses have been added to Scotland's already large stock since 1990 and a further 15 are under construction (Price, 1997), the Scottish Sports Council's figures show local participation in golf to be broadly static (Scottish Sports Council, ongoing), and the best available data on golf tourism (though limited) suggests that the number of visitors who play golf while on holiday in Scotland has remained at around 3–4% of total visitors for some years (NOP, 1997, and Office of National Statistics, 1995). In golf tourism, international competition is also intense—in Scotland's case, most particularly from Ireland.

Scottish Enterprise (SE) and Highlands and Islands Enterprise, and their networks of local enterprise companies (LECs), of which Fife Enterprise is one, are the government's lead agencies for economic development in Scotland. This paper describes two studies carried out for Scottish Enterprise and Fife Enterprise, with the aims of:

- establishing for the first time a robust database on levels and trends in golf tourism in Scotland, and a better understanding of the profile, behaviour, and attitudes of Scotland's golfing visitors;
- developing a golf tourism strategy for one part of Scotland (Fife) where golfing visitors are particularly significant to the regional economy.

GOLF TOURISM MEASUREMENT

SE and its LEC partners identified a need for better baseline information for golf tourism planning and decision-making in Scotland, and commissioned the author to set up a Golf Tourism Monitoring System as an important new tool for the work of the SE/LEC network in developing this sector of the Scottish tourist industry.

Following a 1996 pilot, the 1997 Golf Tourism Monitoring System collected information on visitors to 31 golf courses in Dumfries and Galloway, Scottish Borders, Lothian, Fife, Tayside, and Grampian. Funding and supervision were provided by SE and the LECs in the six areas involved, and the participating golf courses provided assistance in kind by supplying data on visitor rounds in a standard format and by helping with visitor questionnaires.

The courses selected (25 members' club courses and 6 commercially run courses) covered a reasonable cross-section of those involved in golf tourism. Municipal courses were not included at this stage in the development of the monitoring system; nor were major urban members' clubs with few visitors other than members' guests, or small 9-hole courses without the staffing resources to participate.

Methodology

The different elements of the system, and their effectiveness, were as follows.

- Visitor Rounds Figures: Collected for each month of the survey period (May to September 1997 inclusive) from all 31 courses—86% of the 36 courses that had originally agreed to participate—using standard forms that divided visitors into three types: visiting parties, individual visitors, and members' guests.
- Visiting Party Questionnaires: Short questionnaires to be completed by course operators, based largely on information provided by visiting parties at the time of booking, with supplementary information to be provided where possible by the party organiser on arrival at the course. Information collected on 628 visiting parties, but pattern of response skewed, with almost half the participating courses providing no questionnaires.
- Self-Completion Questionnaires: Questionnaire cards, to be distributed by course operators to individual visitors on arrival, and designed either to be left at

courses on completion or returned reply-paid to the researcher. Although 487 questionnaires were returned, most courses reported that this method was inefficient in terms of both the practicalities of persuading golf course staff to distribute the cards and the reaction of visitors to receiving such questionnaires just before commencing their rounds. (Contact with visitors *after* their rounds is too sporadic for this to be an acceptable alternative method of distribution.) This element of the survey was therefore discontinued in August.

• Postal Survey: To replace the questionnaire cards. Participating courses were asked instead to collect the names and addresses of visiting golfers during August and September 1997, and the author sent these golfers a postal questionnaire in October. This method proved much more effective, with a response rate of 70% being achieved—305 completed questionnaires from the 434 sent out. This very high response rate is attributed to the fact that recipients were volunteers rather than a random sample and the questionnaire was user-friendly, sent when the visit was still fresh in recipients' minds, and was accompanied by a promotional pack of golf tees as an incentive. Additional benefits compared to the questionnaire cards were that the postal questionnaire could obtain factual information about the whole trip (since it was completed after the visit rather than partway through it), and could include many more questions than could be incorporated on the questionnaire card.

In summary, the collection of standard-format data on visitor rounds and the postal survey worked well, and the visiting party questionnaires and self-completion questionnaire cards less well. The visitor rounds data collection could now form the basis of ongoing data gathering, to provide a robust database on golf tourism in Scotland plus reliable annual trend data and a basis for aggregate volume and value estimates, analogous to the hotel occupancy surveys that have been running for many years. The postal survey, piloted in 1997, could be extended to cover visitors to more courses and over a longer season, and the questionnaire itself extended to include more behavioural/attitudinal questions of direct relevance to those involved in golf tourism development and marketing policies.

The relative lack of success of the visiting party questionnaires and the self-completion questionnaire cards is not serious. The general profile of visiting parties is now well-established (the results of the 1996 pilot and the 1997 survey being consistent in this regard), and at least some data can be retrieved from individual courses' bookings records where particular course operators wish to use such data. The questionnaire cards have been superseded by the postal survey, which is more effective in several respects as noted above.

RESULTS

Table 77.1 is a summary of the most significant results from the 1997 monitoring system.

As the table shows, there was little monthly variation in total visitor rounds per course, but there were significant monthly variations in visitor types—with visiting parties prevalent in May, June, and September, and the balance shifting towards individual visitors and members' guests in July and August.

Table 77.1   Average Levels and Distribution of Visitor Rounds per Course

	May %	June %	July %	Aug. %	Sept. %	Average %
Visiting parties	52	48	33	34	47	43
Individual visitors	32	34	42	43	36	37
Members' guests	16	17	25	23	17	20
Total	100	99	100	100	100	100
Average total rounds	1,334	1,195	1,237	1,340	1,257	1,273

About half of the courses provided figures on a weekly rather than monthly basis; July was a five-week month, which means its monthly total will be slightly overstated relative to June and August.

There were no discernible regional variations in the figures as such, as distinct from the variations between individual courses, which ranged widely from a low of about 200 visitor rounds a month to a monthly high of about 3,000. On average, commercially run courses attracted 15–20% more visitor rounds than members' club courses. Overall, the relatively high numbers of visitor rounds reflect the composition of the sample of participating courses, as noted earlier.

From the courses' point of view, there is a good mix in the visiting golfer market between first time and repeat visitors, between day trip and holiday visitors, and between parties, individual visitors, and members' guests. Larger parties tend to be on day trips, which makes this accessible market an attractive one for courses because of the substantial revenue generated by attracting one party; individual holiday visitors, however, are also an attractive market—though requiring more marketing and organisational effort—because holiday visitors each play about four different courses on average during their visit.

On average, visiting golfers on holiday in Scotland spent about £275 per head in total (i.e., covering accommodation etc. as well as golf) during their visit. Those on a holiday where the main purpose was playing golf played more courses, were more likely to stay in hotels, but had shorter holidays than those playing some golf as part of a general holiday. Visitors generally were middle-aged males, and experienced golfers who had been playing golf for 19 years on average. Eighty-four percent of them were club members. Their average handicap was 16, which suggests that visitors are at least as proficient players as the average member at the courses they visit.

Seventy-two percent of respondents to the postal survey took at least one golf holiday a year, and the following tables highlight their golf holiday destinations and their rating of features of Scotland in this regard—the kinds of information from the golf monitoring system that relate directly to Scottish golf tourism development and marketing policies.

The figures in table 77.2 are percentages of respondents, not responses; the fact that the figures add to almost 200% in each case indicates that respondents had

Table 77.2   Countries Visited, or Likely to Be Visited, on Golf Holidays

	Visited in last 3 years %	Likely to visit in next 3 years %
England	45	34
Scotland	72	59
Ireland	15	26
France	8	12
Mediterranean	27	30
USA	15	18
Far East	—	—
Other	7	6
None	8	13
Total	**197**	**198**

visited, or planned to visit, two different countries each on average over each three-year period. Measuring competition for Scotland by comparing future intentions with past practice shows Ireland as the destination with the fastest growth rate, followed by France and the USA respectively. (The apparent drop in the popularity of Scotland itself may at least partly reflect the fact that visitors were in Scotland during 1997—the one year not asked about in this question.)

Respondents were asked to rate each feature as very poor (−2), poor (−1), average (0), good (+1), or very good (+2). As shown in table 77.3, all features were rated somewhere between good and very good, but with a clear ranking order.

- The number and quality of golf courses are Scotland's strongest features as a golf holiday destination, ranking significantly higher than anything else.
- Access to golf courses for visitors and the value for money of the golf itself are the next best features—ranking about equally, well behind the number and quality of courses but well ahead of the other features.
- The final group of features decreases steadily in visitors' ratings from making bookings for golf to the value for money of accommodation and getting information about golf holidays.

These results are from a relatively small-scale postal survey, and the questions should be repeated—and extended to cover perceived strengths and weaknesses of competing golf holiday destinations, responsiveness to different types of marketing, etc.—in future larger-scale surveys. Nonetheless, even the pilot results suggest some important pointers for golf tourism marketing in Scotland, as well as adding to the golf tourism database generally.

Table 77.3   Rating of Features of Scotland as a Place to Visit on a Golfing Holiday

	Rating	Rank
Number of courses to choose from	+ 1.84	1
Quality of golf courses	+ 1.75	2
Access to courses for visitors	+ 1.33	3 =
Value for money—golf	+ 1.30	3 =
Making bookings for golf	+ 1.19	5
Making bookings for accommodation	+ 1.15	6
Standards of accommodation	+ 1.10	7
Value for money—accommodation	+ 1.05	8 =
Getting information about golf holidays	+ 1.04	8 =

GOLF TOURISM MARKETING

Scotland has a regional structure of local enterprise companies and area tourist boards, and work is continuing to link national golf research and other initiatives to regional golf tourism development and marketing strategies. Fife is at the heart of Scottish golf, and, on the basis of a detailed assessment of supply and demand, the 1996/97 Fife Golf Study identified the need for a marketing-led golf tourism strategy in the region. This was because the best available figures suggested broad stability in local and visitor demand at a time when new courses, i.e., those opened in the previous five years and under construction, had added 20% to the number of golf holes in Fife—but had added an estimated 40% to the capacity available to visitors, since all the new courses are more visitor-oriented than most of the members' club courses that make up the bulk of existing provision.

"Ground-up" analysis of visitor use of each course in Fife, cross-checked against "top-down" estimates of numbers of golfing visitors to Fife from the national surveys referred to earlier, confirmed that golf is disproportionately important to the region's tourism economy, with direct golfing visitor spending of around £18 million a year.

The study therefore devised a strategy for golf tourism in Fife based on a detailed analysis of the region's strengths, weaknesses, opportunities, and threats (SWOT analysis), and including suggested roles in implementing the strategy for the many agencies involved in golf in Fife.

In particular, given the need to segment both the Fife golf tourism produce and its markets as a basis for effective implementation of a marketing-led strategy, the author devised a framework for matching supply and demand, and identifying possible groupings of courses and target markets for marketing purposes. (The accommodation sector of the product could be similarly segmented, to identify groupings of courses and accommodation establishments that would effectively work together in targeting golf tourism markets.)

Given the uniqueness of every golf course, the fluctuating policies of course operators, and the overlap between market segments, none of the assessments in the framework is quantitative or even objective, i.e., ticks represent subjective rankings rather than empirical measures. Nonetheless, the framework does provide a starting point for more detailed assessments, and a structure for decisions on partnerships and the allocation of marketing resources—as well as identifying the well-known Catch-22 that the courses most in demand (and least able to be replicated) are the traditional links courses with least capacity to take more visitors. (A hypothesis of the study is that, at least to some extent and over the longer-term, the clubs that control such courses may need to try a bit harder than they currently do to attract visitors—given the overall trends in supply and demand highlighted earlier.)

The full framework covered all 40 courses in Fife, including the six courses managed by the St. Andrews Links Trust. For reasons of space, only a section is shown in table 77.4. The framework shows:

- the type of course, i.e., MC (members' club), LA (local authority/municipal), or CO (commercial), since the nature of the body controlling each course has a strong bearing on the policy towards visitors;

Table 77.4   Fife Golf Courses—Matching Supply and Demand?

Name of course	Type of course	Spare capacity for visitors (Physical or policy)	Attractiveness to visitors (Course & location)	Target market segments
Aberdour	MC	√√	√√	2,3,4
Anstruther	MC	√√	√√	2,4
Auchterderran	LA	√√	√	4
Balbirnie Park	MC	√√	√√	(1),2,3,4
Balcomie (Crail)	MC	√√(√)	√√√	1,2,3,(4)
Burntisland	MC	√	√√	2,3
Canmore	MC	√√	√	(2),4
Charleton	CO	√√√	√√	2,3,4
Cupar	MC	√√	√	4
Dora	LA	√√	√	4
Drumoig	CO	√√√	√√(√)	(1),2,3
Dunfermline	MC	√√	√√	2,3,4
Dunnikier Park	LA	√	√√	(3),4
Elie	MC	√	√√√	1,2,3
Elie Sports	MC	√√	√√	4

- the author's assessment of each course's spare capacity, whether defined by available physical capacity or by the policy of the body controlling the course towards additional visitors; the additional (√) against Balcomie reflects the additional capacity that will be available when the new course there is completed;

- a similar—and subjective—assessment by the author of each course's general attractiveness to visitors based on the nature of the course and its location; the addition (√) against Drumoig in this instance reflects its additional appeal once the new course is fully established;

- finally, the author's view of the appeal of each course to various golf tourism market segments, identified as North America (1), Europe (2), UK golfing holidaymakers (3), and UK holiday golfers (4); where a segment is shown as ( ) in the framework, this indicates only moderate appeal to that segment.

The study then went on to suggest specific marketing initiatives appropriate to each of the product groupings and market segments identified in the framework. The implementation of such initiatives can also draw on the results emerging from the Golf Tourism Monitoring System, in which Fife participated.

SUMMARY

Taken together, and related to other work (including a 1997 Survey of Visiting Golfers at St. Andrews, and the preparation of a Highland Golf Strategy), the golf tourism monitoring system and the methodology used in the Fife Golf Study are steadily improving both the quality of information on Scotland's golf tourism and the effectiveness of its golf tourism planning and management—at a time when such initiatives are necessary if Scotland is to hold its own in a very competitive international market.

ACKNOWLEDGMENTS

Funding and supervision for the Golf Tourism Monitoring System was provided by Scottish Enterprise and a group of six local enterprise companies, while the Fife Golf Study was sponsored by Fife Enterprise. The resulting reports are the property of these bodies. The author is particularly grateful to Nicky Yule of Scottish Enterprise and Sandra Macrae of Fife Enterprise for their assistance during the carrying out of the studies and with the preparation of this paper.

References

NOP (1997) *The United Kingdom Tourist—Statistics 1996* Report prepared for the English Tourist Board, Northern Ireland Tourist Board, Scottish Tourist Board, and Wales Tourist Board.

Office for National Statistics (1995) *International Passenger Survey.*

Price, R.J. (1997) The Scottish Golf Industry. *The Scottish Banker*, February, and personal communication with the author.

Scottish Enterprise (1996) *Network Tourism Action Plan.*

Scottish Sports Council (Ongoing) *Sports Participation in Scotland.*

Scottish Tourism Co-ordinating Group (1994, 1996, 1997) *Scottish Tourism Strategic Plan* and subsequent *Progress Reports.*

Scottish Tourist Board (1997) *Annual Report.*

CHAPTER 78

Golf Course Development in Japan II: Business in the Period of Depression

S. Takeshita
National Institute of Fitness & Sports, Kagoshima, Japan

T. Meshizuka
Japan Society of Golf Sciences, Tokyo, Japan

K. Kawashima
Nihon University, Tokyo, Japan

H. Zaitsu
Prague Golf Course Construction Project, Prague, Czech Republic

We introduced the history of golf course development in Japan at the 1994 World Scientific Congress of Golf. In this paper, we intend to present the unique circumstances surrounding Japanese golf courses and membership in comparison with the USA and the UK. The Japanese golf business has suffered from the country's economic depression since 1990. Data is presented in this paper that indicates how income and expenditure in the golf business has changed as a result of changes in the economy. It is suggested that golf businesses can only be successful by reducing operating costs and expanding the local markets. Developing golf course businesses in other countries should be able to learn in the future from these suggestions.

INTRODUCTION

At the 1994 World Scientific Congress of Golf, we presented a paper entitled "Golf Course Development in Japan: Its Abnormal Supply and Demand" (Zaitsu et al., 1994). The main points of the discussion in the paper were to explain the so-called yotaku membership and the reason why the membership became popular, along with an analysis of the history of Japanese golf courses. The yotaku membership system was being conducted like a stock market. This led to golf not being regarded as "a sport for all people" in Japan: golf is seen not only as a sport but in a commercial context.

The period of economic prosperity in Japan, "the bubble economy," came to an end in 1989 because of the cutting of the official interest rate. Along with business in general, the golf business went into decline. In particular the number of players who played golf in courses declined. Business receptions held at golf courses were popular during the bubble economy. After the bubble burst, the number of such business receptions declined so that the total number of visitors to golf courses dropped during the economic stagnation that followed the bursting of the bubble economy. Recently, the total number of visitors has decreased.

The purpose of this paper is to analyze the changes in the number of golf courses and visitors, and also to look at management systems, operating systems and the business expenses of golf courses based on statistical data so as to clarify the problems and find a way of tiding over periods of economic depression. Therefore, the conclusion of this paper should give useful information to countries that are developing golf businesses.

THE NUMBER OF GOLF COURSES AND VISITORS IN THE PERIOD OF ECONOMIC DECLINE

According to the census conducted by the Japan Golf Course Association (1994), the number of golf courses in Japan grew from 1,818 courses in 1991 to 2,200 in 1994 (figure 78.1). That means that 382 new courses were constructed during these three years although the economic situation was bad. Many of these courses had received planning approval during the bubble economy but were constructed after the bubble burst in 1990. The annual total of players including both members and visitors in courses remained the same between 1991 and 1994.

On the other hand, the line in figure 78.1 shows that the income of courses fell after the peak of 1990. It can be supposed that the increase in the numbers of golf courses will not be so rapid from now on. Also the green fees fell after the peak of

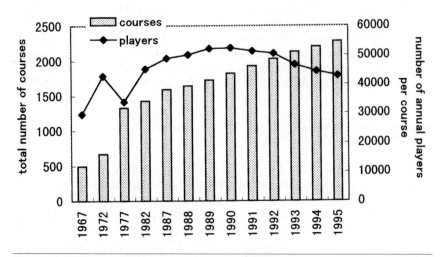

Figure 78.1   The number of golf courses and annual players.

1993 (Japan Golf Course Association, 1995) so that reduction in the income of a golf course will result in serious financial difficulties. Managers engaged in the golf course business need to understand the chronological change in supply and demand.

BALANCE, OUTFLOW AND INFLOW AREAS

In Japan, every visitor has to pay a playing-tax when she or he plays on a course. The Japan Golf Course Association collects data by calculating the playing-tax in cooperation with the Ministry of Home Affairs. So we can see the actual number of visitors and courses. Based on this data, the relation between the number of visitors and the population of those over 15 years old in all of Japan's 47 prefectures is shown in figure 78.2.

In figure 78.2, the prefectures around Line 1 are in an area that maintains a good balance between population and visitors. On the other hand, prefectures around Line 2 are in an area in which the ratio between the two is unbalanced. Prefectures near the right side of Line 2, such as Tokyo and Osaka, are in an outflow area in which the population is in excess in relation to the number of visitors. On the other hand, prefectures near the left side of Line 2 are in an inflow area in which visitors are in excess in relation to population. Managers need to understand the location of their golf courses.

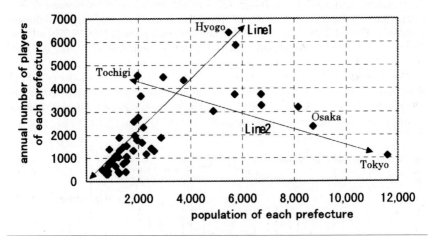

Figure 78.2   Relation between 47 prefectural populations and golf players (1 unit = 1,000 persons).

CHANGES IN THE MANAGEMENT OF COURSES DURING THE PERIOD OF ECONOMIC DECLINE

The Ministry of International Trade and Industry published in 1991 and 1994 "Specific Service Industry Inquiry Report: Golf Courses." The reports are based on questionnaires sent to every golf course that has more than 9 holes and with each hole over 100 m. The 1991 report was based on 1,670 responses (86.7%) and the 1994 report on 1,954 responses (88.9%) and the data are therefore regarded as reliable. Moreover, the Journal of "Golf Courses Seminar," published monthly by Japan Golf Digest, Inc., is circulated to most courses as a journal of management study. These reports indicated that during the economic depression many courses that previously did not accept visitors decided to accept visitors in order to increase income. Similarly, many courses which previously insisted on visitors hiring a caddy allowed golfers to carry their own bags (Kato, 1996).

INCOME AND EXPENDITURE OF COURSES DURING ECONOMIC DECLINE

According to the Ministry of International Trade and Industry (1991), business data came from the 1,670 responses out of the total of 1,954 courses. The data indicated income of US$12,821 million in 1991. The expenditure was US$10,798 million. Therefore, the rate of expenditure was 84.2% of the income. The number of annual players including members and visitors was almost 91 million. The total number of holes was 33,885. The number of members holding individual memberships was 1,830,731. The number of memberships owned by companies (the so-called "corporation membership") was 465,422. The number of employees was 183,731.

The data of the Ministry of International Trade and Industry (1994) indicated income of US$14,230 million in 1994. The expenditure was US$12,778 million. Therefore, the rate of expenditure was 89.8% of the annual income. This is a 5.6% rise in comparison with 1991. The number of annual players was a little over 90 million. The total number of holes was 39,676. The number of members holding individual memberships was 1,990,659. The number of memberships owned by companies was 523,771. The number of employees was 206,388. The data per golf course in terms of the above is illustrated in table 78.1 and figure 78.3.

Table 78.1   Income and Expenditure per Course

	Income	Expenditure
1991	7,676	6,485
1994	7,283	6,539

(1 unit = $1000/$1 = ¥120)

The items of expenditure at 1991 and 1994, which include labor costs, course maintenance costs, land rents, restaurant and pro-shop purchases (material costs) and others, are shown in table 78.2 and figure 78.4. The labor costs were US$42,867 million in 1991, representing 39.7% of the entire business expenses. The course

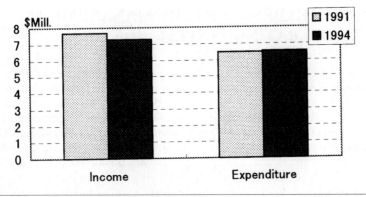

Figure 78.3   Income/expenditure per course.

maintenance costs were US$12,450 million which was just over 10% of the expenses. Both percentages were basically the same for the both years. Labor costs in 1994 were about 40% of the entire expenditure, much the same as in 1991. The course maintenance costs for 1994 were also the same rate as in 1991. The 1991 and 1994 annual income and expenditure per course indicate that although annual income declined, expenditure on course maintenance and labor was reduced.

Table 78.2   Division of Expenditure of a Golf Course

	Labor costs	Maintenance costs	Land rent	Material costs	Others
1994	2,789	726	256	468	2256
1991	2,567	746	242	544	2304

(1 unit = $1000/$1 = ¥120)

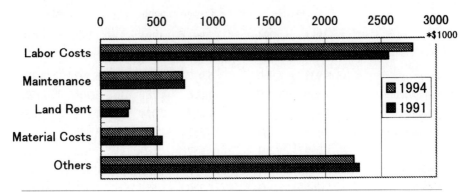

Figure 78.4   Division of annual business expenses per course.

BUSINESS EXPENSES IN THE MANAGEMENT STYLE/OPERATING SYSTEM

Tables 78.3 and 78.4 provide data on the income and expenditure of golf facilities with various types of management styles and operating systems. According to the Ministry of International Trade and Industry (1991, 1994), the management style of golf facilities is divided into three types; company (a joint-stock corporation), corporate body (a nonprofit making foundation) and individual ownership. On the other hand, the ministry also divides the three operating types according to whether or not a membership system is in operation (private, private and public, or public).

Table 78.3   Business Expenses of a Course on Management Style

	Company		Corporate body		Individual owner	
	1991	1994	1991	1994	1991	1994
Income	7,817	7,383	5,517	5,575	908	1,108
Expenditure	6,565	6,630	4,948	5,024	652	1,208
Labor costs	2,593	2,817	2,203	2,350	186	328
Maintenance costs	751	731	662	646	258	247
Land rent	303	296	349	379	33	33
Material costs	563	483	232	210	100	122
Others	2,355	2,303	1,502	1,439	75	478

(1 unit = $1000/$1 = ¥120)

Table 78.4   Income and Expenditure of a Course on Operation System

	Private		Private & public		Public	
	1991	1994	1991	1994	1991	1994
Income	8,932	7,900	5,917	5,475	5,592	5,767
Expenditure	4,850	7,210	4,626	4,781	5,708	4,591
Labor costs	2,882	3,112	1,887	2,074	1,452	1,665
Maintenance costs	815	783	537	502	585	658
Land rent	299	294	187	182	522	503
Material costs	594	514	445	372	352	304
Others	260	2,505	1,570	1,651	1,345	1,461

(1 unit = $1000/$1 = ¥120)

The division of expenditure of table 78.3 is divided based on management style. Comparing the company and the corporate body, the former was much worse than the latter. The business profits of the company were reduced by about 40% from 1991 to 1994. In addition, labor costs of the company increased nearly 10%. According to the Ministry of International Trade and Industry (1994), 75% of all golf courses out of a sample of 1,818 apply this company management style. Therefore, companies have the doubled pressure of declining profits and increasing labor costs.

Looking at the operating system of private, private and public, and public golf courses, it appears that total income of both private and public courses are declining (table 78.4). The number of private golf courses is 73.3% out of the total sample of 1,818 (Ministry of International Trade and Industry, 1994). So, the labor costs of all systems have increased. Thus, reducing or holding down the labor costs should be the most important factor when considering golf course management.

SUMMARY ABOUT GOLF BUSINESS DURING ECONOMIC STAGNATION

An analysis of the statistical data about golf course management in this study provides some implications. The relationship between players to courses (demand) and the courses themselves (supply) has been changing as is clearly shown in figure 78.1. People who engage in the management of golf courses must pay attention to the chronological change in supply and demand. In terms of regional supply and demand that is illustrated in figure 78.2, there are three types of areas: balance, outflow and inflow.

Depending on the types of areas, we need to collect information and we should learn from this information concerning chronological changes and regional differences that affect supply and demand, especially in times of economic decline. On the other hand, there was information about changes for the better management of golf courses; for example, many courses which previously did not accept visitors decided to accept visitors in order to increase income. Similarly, many courses which previously insisted on visitors hiring a caddy allowed golfers to carry their own bags.

Eventually, reducing labor costs in business is the main factor for all golf courses whether they have a company or a corporate management style, or are private or public in their system of operation. In addition to the main factor, it is important for golf business to create service and marketing based on statistical data concerning chronological changes and regional differences.

References

Japan Golf Course Association. (1995). *The Number of Visitors to Golf Courses and Tax.*

Kato, Y. (1996). "Arithmetic for Golf Courses: Survival Strategy." *Journal of Golf Course Seminar* 29(29): 90–93.

Ministry of International Trade and Industry. (1991). *Specific Service Industry Inquiry Report: Golf Courses.*

Ministry of International Trade and Industry. (1994). *Specific Service Industry Inquiry Report: Golf Courses.*

Takeshita, S. (1997). "Regional Characteristics of Golf Courses in Kyushu Based on 1994 Statistical Data." *Annals of Fitness and Sports Science*, 18:1–7.

Zaitsu, F., Takeshita, S., Meshizuka, T., & Kawashima, K. (1994). "Golf Course Development in Japan: Its Abnormal Supply and Demand." *Science and Golf II* (A. Cochran & M. Farrally, eds.), pp. 562–568.

CHAPTER 79

Closing the U.S. Golf Facility Supply Gap: A Geographic Analysis of Metropolitan Change, 1988–1997

J.F. Rooney, Jr., and G.A. Finchum
Oklahoma State University, USA

H.J. White
Golf Digest, New York, USA

The recent surge in golf course construction in the United States has been enhanced by the recent interest of large portions of the mass population to engage in golf as a participation sport. With this growth in interest by large numbers of urban and young population, the golfing community must investigate the current supply situation of golf in metropolitan areas, and determine which areas need additional supply to meet both the current and expected demand for golf as the twenty-first century approaches. This paper provides an analysis of recent changes in golf course supply in metropolitan areas of the United States, with an eye on which areas are in the greatest need for new course development in the immediate future.

Keywords: Golf course, construction, development, supply and demand.

INTRODUCTION

The recent cyclical surge in golf course construction, in association with the immense presence of Tiger Woods, has positioned golf to become a mass participation sport. Though U.S. developers have built nearly one new course a day since 1992, and there are over 1,400 courses under construction throughout the United States, access to golf facilities lags far behind other American sports. Most U.S. cities have plenty of playing fields, basketball and tennis courts, swimming pools, and gymnasiums. As a result cities produce far more basketball, football, baseball, softball and track athletes than golfers. This is particularly true for the minorities who are clustered in the inner cities where playgrounds abound and golf facilities are scarce.

If golf is to reach its potential as a sport, many more courses and practice facilities must be constructed. The recently announced World Golf Foundation First Tee Program has the lofty goal of constructing 100 golf courses and learning facilities within the next three years. Their long-term goals are building 1,000 centers nationwide, and bringing golf to large numbers of children who have hitherto been totally unfamiliar with the game.

Everyone familiar with the geographic distribution of U.S. golf courses is aware of the long-term and acute shortages that characterize markets like New York City, Washington D.C., Los Angeles, and San Francisco. Since high land costs and extreme population pressures will persist in these and other markets, it is vital to add First Tee facilities and programs to increase urban access to the game.

The purpose of our paper is to analyze the geographic patterns associated with the growth of U.S. golf facilities during the period 1988–1997. Our primary focus is on growth within large urban markets where shortages have been most persistent. We will compare relative access to golf in 1988 and 1997. We will also factor in the results of the courses under construction, most of which will open within the next two years.

Our analysis establishes a facilities per population base for each of the three time periods. We compare urban areas of similar sized population against the U.S. base and the metropolitan urban base.

Access in 1988 was far from equal across the United States (Adams & Rooney, 1989). Golf has historically been a northern game, an important part of the sports participatory culture in states within the Midwest and Northeastern regions. Access has always been much lower in the Southeast and South central regions. Thus there was a concentration of high golf facilities to population base in the North and many low base cities in the South. Much of the West Coast was low base, with the Southwest and Mountain West around the national average.

Using this base analysis methodology allows us to evaluate the development of courses in a new light. It allows us to evaluate the locational decisions relative to need, and to compare urban accessibility and change in accessibility much more objectively. Were the new courses built in the right places? Where is relative accessibility increasing? Where is the situation getting worse? Where should First Tee and other developers concentrate their efforts?

Our earlier research confirmed the strong relationship between participation and public access to golf. It is really very simple! States and cities with the highest per capita supply of public courses have the greatest rates of participation across the demographic spectrum. And so the World Golf Foundation is correct: if golf is to truly become a mass participation sport, access must be dramatically improved.

A secondary purpose of our research is to pinpoint the cities with the greatest access problems and the greatest potential for new facility impact. The following analysis will detail the metropolitan access bases and changes in those bases.

ANALYSIS OF GOLF SUPPLY: 1988-1997

Golf course supply in the urban United States has grown substantially in the past ten years. Many of the country's largest urban areas were the major beneficiaries of this growth. We have focused our analysis of golf facility expansion on the metropolitan areas of the United States, as defined by the U.S. Census Bureau. These 31 metropolitan areas contain 79.5% of the population. This constitutes over 211 million inhabitants, many of whom would appreciate greater access to golf and golfing facilities.

Metropolitan Statistical Areas (MSA) consist of counties containing a city or agglomeration of cities with a population over 50,000, as well as surrounding counties from which a notable proportion of the population works or conducts regular business in the central county. For this study, we examine the entire population of MSAs, as well as a subset of the largest 30 MSAs. By dividing the metropolitan areas in this manner, it is possible to deal with the unique land cost and congestion problems associated with the largest MSAs, problems that do not impact the smaller MSAs to the same degree.

For this study, we have calculated new and sophisticated measurements of the supply of golf, the growth of golf supply, and the rate of growth in metropolitan areas. These include the 18-hole equivalents per 100,000 population for the years 1988 and 1997. We have also calculated the change in the base during the study period and the growth rate of courses during the period. These measures were then normalized around the average for the various groups outlined in this study (all MSAs and the largest 30).

For this study, a "low base" is one with a low proportion of courses per person or a poor supply, while a "high base" region is one with a strong course supply. For the various groups of metropolitan areas the exact ranges for low and high base sub-groups vary in relation to the average base for that grouping. The ranges were consistently calculated using a three group quantile method. The ranges calculated for 1988 base groupings were 0–77.1 percent of the average for the Low Base group, 77.2–113.8 percent for the average base group, and greater than 113.8 percent of the national average for the high base group. While these percentage breaks vary slightly for each sub-group, the representation of the various population groups into three equal size sub-groups remain constant throughout the study.

1988 AND 1997 COURSE SUPPLY DATA

The 1988 and 1997 course supply base and growth rates for the various groupings outline above are depicted in table 79.1. The MSA base for all metropolitan areas was the strongest for the metropolitan areas, while the 30 largest MSAs showed the worst course supply ratio. Though the largest MSAs had the weakest supply, as a group they experienced the fastest growth rate. Non-MSAs had the strongest overall supply ratio, while the ratio for all MSAs was far stronger than for the large MSA subset. This can be primarily explained through population density and land values. The per capita supply of golf in the non-MSA counties and the smaller cities is much higher due in large part to the lower population densities and lower land values. Many small towns support nine-hole courses with less than 200 local golfers providing superb access to virtually all residents. The availability of cheap land makes course construction much less expensive than in larger cities where suitable parcels of land are both scarce and expensive.

Table 79.1   Golf Supply Base* and Growth Rates

AREA	1988 Avg. base	1997 Avg. base	Base change	Pop change
All MSA	27,214.25	23,998.94	+11.16%	+6.8%
Big 30	35,946.11	31,503.77	+12.35%	+5.7%
Entire US	23,322.38	20,719.51	+11.16%	+6.4%
Non-MSA	14,929.85	13,423.49	+10.10%	+5.6%

*Base calculated at persons per 18-hole equivalent course.

In 1988, course supply analyses verified the existence of broader course supply regions as outlined by Adams and Rooney (1984, 1989), and Rooney and White (1990, 1994).

They also identified considerable variance between the largest and smallest groups of metropolitan areas. As can be interpreted in figure 79.1, two high base areas stand out. The high base MSAs in the Northern Heartland include those from Upstate New York, through western Pennsylvania, to Michigan. A second high base area is the peninsula of Florida. This golfing region differs from the Northern Heartland region in that most of the MSAs are geared to winter tourists and second-home owners.

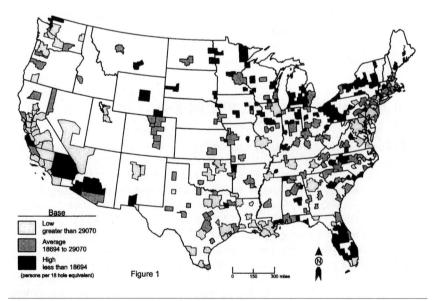

Figure 1

Figure 79.1   1988 golf supply base (all MSAs).

In contrast, the Mid-Atlantic and western Golf coasts and the majority of California contain a strong concentration of low base MSAs. There are also a large number of other major cities across the United States with low golf supply bases. Atlanta, Dallas, St. Louis, Dallas and Seattle are exemplary.

BASE CHANGES

In comparison to 1988, the calculations for course supply in 1997 changed significantly. While the strength of the eastern and central Great Lakes region persisted (the proportion of high base metropolitan areas in the region remains high), the strength of western Pennsylvania seems to have weakened. The MSAs in the western Lakes states of Wisconsin and Minnesota have improved their relative standing. Florida metropolitan areas have maintained their relative strength.

The most notable improvement in base ranking occurred in the regions that Adams and Rooney (1992) classified as "The Southern Void" and the "South Atlantic." Numerous MSAs in these areas had a jump in the course supply base, while most others at least maintained their position in relation to the national average. This indicates that course supply for these areas is keeping up with the overall growth rate (table 79.1). Most of North and South Carolina, particularly the piedmont urban crescent and Myrtle Beach, SC, recorded a marked rise in relative supply. The majority of MSAs in Kentucky, Virginia, West Virginia, Tennessee, Georgia, and Alabama also fall into the same category. While few of these areas (the tourist cities of the coastal region are the exception), had a high base, several MSAs

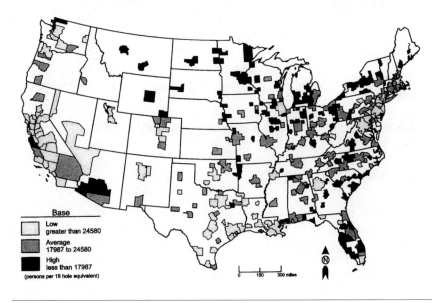

Figure 79.2   1997 golf supply base (all MSAs).

moved from low to average supply base (figure 79.2). The eastern Megalopolis region, the western Gulf Coast, and California continue to lag behind the national average in course supply. The majority of MSAs in these regions have a very low base ranking and experienced little growth off their low bases. Bad golfer access has actually worsened in these metropolitan areas.

Figures 79.3 and 79.4 pinpoint the changes in 18-hole equivalents per 100,000 between 1988 and 1997, as well as new course construction in 1977. In relation to the 1997 national average for course supply, the eastern and central Great Lakes had a number of MSAs with a relative base decline (figure 79.3). Most notable among those metropolitan areas are those in upstate New York and western Michigan. As noted earlier, these regions showed a slight decline in the proportion of MSAs with a high base. This can be attributed to a low to moderate number of new courses being built in this region since 1988 (figure 79.4).

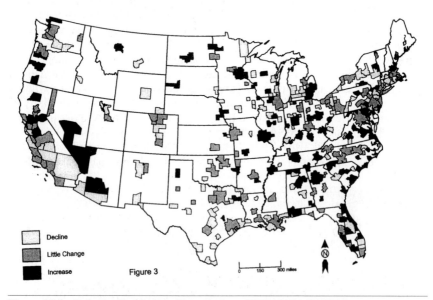

Figure 79.3   Relative change in golf supply base 1988-1997 (all MSAs).

NEW CONSTRUCTION

During 1996–1997 all MSAs had at least 0.5 18-hole equivalent courses under construction (figure 79.4). New construction projects in MSAs underway during 1996–1997, totaled approximately 730 18-hole equivalents. These construction projects ranged from 0.5 to 20.5 new 18-hole courses, and included at least one new development in every U.S. metropolitan area. Several very large metropolitan areas are experiencing the greatest surge in new development (Atlanta, St. Louis, Chicago, Kansas City, Cincinnati, Minneapolis, and Washington). This rapid

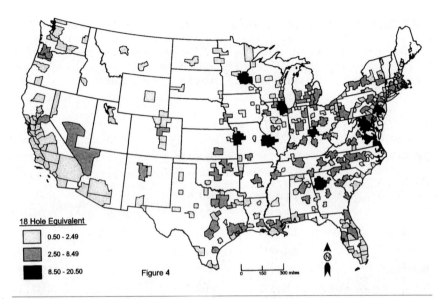

Figure 79.4   Courses under construction 1996-1997 (all MSAs).

growth in the large metropolitan areas was desperately needed to service poorly supplied golfing populations (by 1988 base standards).

The supply problem has been exacerbated with low base MSAs in California being pushed even lower in the relative rankings. High land and building costs and pressures from environmentalists continue to inhibit golf development in this area. Metropolitan areas in Florida, a previously noted high supply region, is an area of limited new course development, along with several MSAs in the Great Lakes regions. The southern regions are generally characterized by moderate growth.

AMERICA'S 30 LARGEST MSAS

After analyzing all of the MSAs as a single group, we then isolated the largest 30 metropolitan areas to determine what changes occurred in this unique group (table 79.2). The "Big 30" MSAs contain over 98 million inhabitants; 37 percent of the U.S. population. These MSAs had by far the worst overall supply base in 1988 in comparison to the entire group. The average base calculation for all MSAs was one 18-hole equivalent per 23,322 persons in 1988, versus one equivalent per 35,946 persons for the largest 30 MSAs. Golfers in the "Big 30" had 50% less access to facilities than those living in other MSAs.

In 1988, the "Big 30" MSAs with the best supply base were either in the Heartland region (Pittsburgh, Cincinnati, Minneapolis, Kansas City), or the resort areas of the far west (San Bernadino-Palm Springs, Phoenix, Denver) (figure 79.5). In contrast, they display only average base calculations when compared to the total universe of

Table 79.2   "Big 30" MSAs: Population Change per 18-Hole Equivalent

Name	Pop 1996	Base 88	Base 97	Base change
New York	8598042	113957.94	99977.23	13980.71
Los Angeles	9323890	89077.03	90523.20	−1446.18
San Jose	1593746	59903.08	59027.63	875.45
San Francisco	1674940	61679.92	56777.63	4902.30
Orange County, CA	2615046	61026.73	50289.35	10737.39
Miami	2060795	57823.70	50263.29	7560.41
Oakland	2234452	52732.00	49108.84	3623.16
Seattle	2163731	44840.02	37960.19	6879.83
Baltimore	2483818	50150.99	34983.35	15167.64
San Diego	2701572	38728.93	34197.11	4531.82
Houston	3779977	41786.48	33901.14	7885.34
Dallas	2632462	39544.46	31908.63	7635.83
Washington, DC	4519415	43394.39	31494.18	11900.21
Philadelphia	4956508	35539.17	30690.45	4848.72
Boston	3795774	32902.75	29086.39	3816.37
Newark	1939890	29475.81	27322.39	2153.42
Chicago	7768495	31943.35	26741.81	5201.55
Denver	1867195	28225.73	26485.04	1740.70
Atlanta	3482438	38440.90	24963.71	13477.20
Long Island, NY	2669473	25209.78	23314.17	1895.60
St. Louis	2550372	35607.50	21164.91	14442.59
Kansas City	1672863	27290.95	20525.93	6765.02
Detroit	4313114	26016.18	20489.85	5526.33
Riverside, CA	3024128	19686.64	19961.24	−274.60
Cleveland	2123896	19926.52	17773.19	2153.33
Cincinnati	1600967	22442.53	17690.24	4752.29
Pittsburgh	2401614	19629.60	17154.39	2475.21
Phoenix	2570938	19809.56	16220.43	3589.13
Minneapolis	2747878	21245.47	16163.99	5081.48
Tampa	2188062	18972.10	16088.69	2883.41

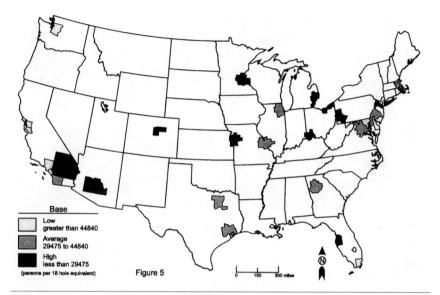

Figure 5

Figure 79.5   1998 golf supply base (30 largest MSAs).

MSAs, with the exception of the travel destinations of San Bernadino-Palm Springs and Phoenix. The highly overcrowded cities of Megalopolis and their West Coast counterparts (New York, Baltimore, Los Angeles, San Francisco, Seattle), along with a surprising entry, Miami, have the lowest bases.

SHIFTS IN BASE LEVELS FOR THE LARGEST MSAS

Atlanta and St. Louis moved up to the high golf base group of the "Big 30," while Denver and Newark fell from the high to average base group (figure 79.6). These four cities moved relative to their peer group because of either very rapid or very slow growth in new golf facilities, or because of exceptionally rapid population growth. Atlanta and St. Louis were among the national leaders in new facility construction in 1996–1997 (figure 79.7). These growth-led base changes are countered by Denver, which experienced moderate golf facility growth, combined with rapid population growth (over 15 percent between 1990 and 1996). One issue providing both good news and bad news for Denver is that there is great potential for new facility growth outside the central Denver MSA, but as in many of the largest MSAs, that is where most of the rapid population growth is occurring, thus increasing demand for recreational facilities.

Overall growth in new facilities for the group of largest MSAs was highest in the Northern Heartland region, a small number of Megalopolis cities, and in Atlanta. The Heartland cities, with the exception of Chicago and St. Louis, were among the best supplied of the "Big 30," so that while the improvement in golf supply there was undoubtedly welcomed by golfers, new opportunities for the least served inner-city

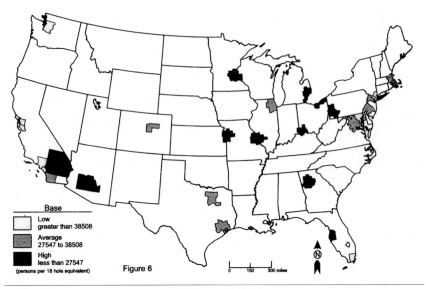

Figure 79.6   1997 golf supply base (30 largest MSAs).

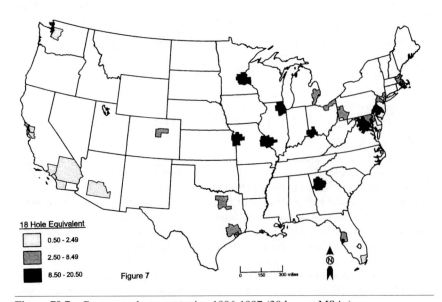

Figure 79.7   Courses under construction 1996-1997 (30 largest MSAs).

golfers were not adequately provided. Atlanta and Washington D.C., are two cities with a recent history of rapid supply growth much needed to serve the new golfers generated by their exploding metropolitan populations. Lastly, the golfers of urban Southern California continue to languish. They are blessed by great golf weather, but burdened by worsening golfer access. Few new courses have been built or are under construction in Southern California, providing little relief. The only saving grace to this dilemma is that existence of yearlong golfable weather. While the Heartland cities have an eight- to nine-month season (even shorter in parts of the upper Midwest), golfers in California can play year-round, thereby slightly offsetting the facility shortage.

CONCLUSIONS AND RECOMMENDATIONS

In summary, aside from the Southern Void region, those who reside in non-metropolitan/small town America have much greater access to golf. Their fellow urban citizens, generally, have decreased access as the size of their MSA increases.

Golf supply is now growing faster than the U.S. population. Supply ratios have improved for almost all markets. But most importantly the greatest improvement has been in the largest 30 MSAs, where the golf supply base has expanded at a rate of 2.2 times the population base. Our largest MSAs now have one 18-hole equivalent per 31,500 people. Just nine years ago that number was one per 35,900. But though the golfer pressure on facilities has eased a bit, it is still nearly three times greater than that in nonmetropolitan America.

The real crisis, however, remains in and around our largest cities: New York, Washington D.C., Philadelphia and Miami in the East, and Los Angeles and San Francisco on the West Coast. Golf there, and in most of the larger MSAs, has been forced to the periphery, at least a half hour's drive from the inner cities. Thus in order to grow, the game will have to find cheap parcels of land in close proximity to the young people who want to follow in Tiger Woods' footsteps. First Tee is a long overdue program. But as the name suggests, it is just the first move toward golf reaching its potential as a mass participation sport.

References

Adams, R.L., and J.F. Rooney, Jr. (1985). Evolution of American Golf Facilities. *Geographical Review*, 75(4):419–438.

Adams, R.L., and J.F. Rooney, Jr. (1989). American Golf Courses: A Regional Analysis of Supply. *Sport Place International*, 3(1):2–17.

Rooney, J.F., Jr., and H.J. White. (1990). The Utilization of the U.S. Golf Data Base for the Optimal Location of New Golf Facilities; in Cochran, A.J., and M.R. Farrally, eds. *Science and Golf: Proceedings of the World Scientific Congress of Golf*. London: E & FN Spon.

Rooney, J.F., Jr., and H.J. White. (1994). The Database of Golf in America: A Guide to Understanding U.S. Golf Markets; in Cochran, A.J., and M.R. Farrally, eds. *Science and Golf II: Proceedings of the World Scientific Congress of Golf*. London: E & FN Spon.

CHAPTER 80

The Home of Golf: The Role of St. Andrews in Scottish Golf Tourism

Steven Lawther
Scottish Tourist Board, Edinburgh, Scotland

Mike Williamson
MW Associates, Edinburgh, Scotland

The paper describes a study of visiting golfers at St. Andrews carried out for the Scottish Tourist Board. The study profiled the visitors to St. Andrews during the summer of 1997 and obtained information on their spending and travel patterns while in Scotland. The paper explores the nature of golf tourism to St. Andrews and examines the willingness of visiting golfers to play golf at other locations throughout Scotland.

Keywords: Golf, tourism, St. Andrews, market research, Scotland.

INTRODUCTION

Scotland is widely accepted as the country where golf took root and developed. The town of St. Andrews in Fife is at the heart of Scottish and international golf, being home to the Old Course and the Royal and Ancient Golf Club. St. Andrews therefore presents Scottish tourism with a strong image worldwide and a unique selling point to promote golf tourism to the world (Arthur Young Management Consultants, 1987).

Tourism is important to the Scottish economy, currently employing approximately 177,000 people, equivalent to 8% of the Scottish workforce, contributing £2.4 billion to the Scottish economy (Scottish Tourist Board, 1997). Golf tourism can be classified into two categories: visiting on a holiday where golf is the main purpose of the holiday trip, and visitors who play golf while on a more general holiday. An examination of the market for golf tourism in the United Kingdom (NOP, 1997) shows that during the period 1993 to 1995 some 100,000 holiday trips were taken in Scotland by U.K. visitors each year specifically for the purpose of golfing (this equates to around 2% of total holidays).

Expenditure on these golfing trips to Scotland amounted to £29 million (3% of total holiday expenditure in Scotland). When U.K. holidaymakers who included golfing as part of their holiday are included a further 300,000 trips and £69 million of expenditure annually can be attributed to golf tourism. In the U.K. context, golf is therefore a significant niche market for Scottish tourism.

Although no precise figures on trips and expenditures are available for Scotland's overseas markets, approximately 3% of all overseas visitors played golf on their holiday in Scotland in 1996, while in a previous survey some 5% of North American visitors stated they played golf on their holiday in Scotland (Office for National Statistics, 1995). Overseas visitors spend approximately three times as much as U.K. visitors (in 1995 overseas visitors spent, on average, £445 per trip, compared to £142 per trip for domestic visitors) (Office for National Statistics, 1995). Golf tourism is therefore a significant market for Scotland, both from within the United Kingdom and from overseas.

A previous study into visiting golfers at St. Andrews, undertaken for the Scottish Tourist Board by the University of St. Andrews in 1989 (Jackson, 1989), provided a profile of visiting golfers to the town at that time. This showed that golfing visitors at St. Andrews were not typical of the average visitor to Scotland. They tended to be older, higher spenders, and included a higher proportion of overseas (particularly North American) travelers. Furthermore, most were visiting St. Andrews for the first time, having been attracted purely on the strength of its reputation.

In order to update aspects of the 1989 survey and, in particular, to examine the role of St. Andrews in the development of golf tourism throughout Scotland, the Scottish Tourist Board commissioned TMS to carry out a survey of visiting golfers at St. Andrews in 1997. This survey is part of STB's ongoing programme of research into Scottish golf tourism.

The new St. Andrews survey also related to a general study of golf in Fife carried out by TMS for Fife Enterprise (TMS, 1997). The joint author of this paper, Mike Williamson, was consulting director with TMS when the survey was undertaken.

RESEARCH OBJECTIVES

The 1997 survey of visiting golfers to St. Andrews sought to provide practical information on the current state of the market for those involved in golf tourism and had the following specific objectives:

- to profile visitors and obtain information on the spending patterns of visiting golfers to St. Andrews,
- to obtain information on travel patterns of visiting golfers to determine the current role of St. Andrews in encouraging visitors to play golf in other parts of Scotland, and
- to determine the willingness of visiting golfers at St. Andrews to play golf at other secondary courses in Fife and throughout Scotland.

METHODOLOGY

The research adopted a quantitative, face-to-face interviewing approach, a methodology frequently used in other golf studies and widely recognised to be suitable for exploring a range of issues among a sample population (Aaker and Day, 1986; Witt and Moutinho, 1989). The sample focused on:

- Tourist and day trip golfers visiting St. Andrews. (As a main focus of the study was dispersal issues, local players from Fife and Dundee were excluded.)
- A cross-section of the courses in St. Andrews was covered, with relatively higher coverage of golfers on the Old Course. This ensured that issues surrounding the role of St. Andrews and the Old Course could be explored in-depth.
- Interviewing took place during the main golf tourism season, from mid-June to early August.

Based on experience of previous golfer surveys, the methodology was based on 10–15 minute interviews with randomly selected visiting golfers as they completed their rounds. Interview dates were selected in collaboration with the course operators, with the aim of achieving a good spread of days of the week over each course and over the period of the survey. Specific dates were avoided when it was known that local players would predominate because of established booking arrangements or specific tournaments. In total, 504 interviews were conducted—132 in June, 196 in July, and 176 in August (see table 80.1).

Table 80.1   Interviews Undertaken per Course

Course	No. of interviews
Old Course	169
New Course	121
Jubilee Course	85
Strathtyrum Course	38
Dukes Course	91

The sample approach attempted to take account, where possible, of potential sources of bias. Conducting interviews across a selection of locations, dates, and times of day, and randomly selecting individual respondents ensured that the sample was as representative as possible. The resultant profile of the sample was similar to the profile obtained in the 1989 St. Andrews survey, suggesting that the sample chosen was reflective of the actual population.

Golfers interviewed were typically middle-aged males, with the majority (88%)

Table 80.2   Profile of Respondents

	%
Age of visitor	
Under 25	6
25-34	14
35-44	21
45-54	31
55+	27
Gender of visitor	
Male	87
Female	13
Type of visitor	
Day trip visitor	12
Tourist visitor	88

Base: All respondents (504)

staying at least one night away from home rather than being on a day trip from home. Table 80.2 below shows the exact breakdown.

The remainder of this paper focuses on the tourist golfers in the sample of holidaymakers, i.e., those staying away from home for at least one night. The vast majority of these (92%) were on a holiday trip—the others being on a business trip or visiting friends and relatives. Staying visitors are obviously of most interest to Tourist Boards and the tourist industry as their use of accommodations and overall spending generates much greater economic impact than do day visitors. The next section summarises the main survey findings relating to the tourist golfers interviewed.

RESEARCH FINDINGS

The Visitors

Tourist golfers were predominantly from the United States of America, accounting for almost half of respondents (49%). This may be a reflection of St. Andrews' reputation as the 'home of golf' and the fact that more interviews were conducted on the Old Course. Of the remaining respondents, 26% were from the United Kingdom (predominantly England), and 25% came from other overseas countries.

These included Canada, Australia, Germany, Sweden, and Japan but with no single country accounting for more than 3% of respondents. Respondents tended to be experienced golfers, with most being club members (84%) for 21 years on average.

The average handicap among visiting golfers was around 15, relatively high in relation to the degree of difficulty of some of the course played, but significantly lower than the average (17) of all golfers who have handicaps.

Again, reflecting the experience of the market, the majority of the overall sample (82%) had been on a previous golfing holiday in the last three years. The high number of golf visitors to Scotland was also evident, with a fifth of visitors loyal, Scottish golf converts, having taken more than five previous golf holidays in Scotland.

The Trip

The average party size was around six people, with overseas visitors tending to travel in rather larger groups than U.K. visitors. The average length of stay in Scotland for overseas visitors was nine nights, while the average length of stay for U.K. visitors was six nights.

During the interview, respondents were asked to indicate their spending levels during the previous 24 hours. On average respondents spent around £220 per person, highlighting the high spending nature of the market. The difference between overseas and U.K. visitor spending was marked, with the average figure being £170 for U.K. visitors, £240 for U.S.A. visitors, and £220 for other overseas visitors.

Comparing these figures to average expenditure for general tourism spending (Office for National Statistics, 1995) and examining previous research into European golf spending (Hegarty, 1993), the golf tourism market to St. Andrews is a significantly higher spending market. This difference can be attributed in part to the high levels of golf-specific spending (green fees, equipment, and golf souvenirs), accounting for 40% of spending and the high use of serviced accommodations.

Daily itineraries were completed for respondents' visits to Scotland. This included collecting detailed information on accommodations, cities, towns, or locations visited and whether they had played (or planned to play) golf the following day. Not surprisingly, 53% of all nights were spent in St. Andrews, however, the fact that almost half of visitor nights were spent elsewhere in Scotland is encouraging in terms of the dispersal of the benefits of golf tourism around the country. The following patterns emerged from an analysis of the individual itineraries.

Visitors from the U.S.A. and the other overseas countries tended to be on tours, staying an average of two to three different locations during their nine-day stay in Scotland. More than half of U.S.A. visitors interviewed were on a tour of famous courses and expensive hotels, staying several nights in each of a selection of locations including Turnberry, Troon, Gleneagles, Edinburgh, and Dornoch. This confirms the high spending and 'famous courses' focus of the U.S.A. market, which is clearly a very valuable one for Scottish tourism. Visitors from other overseas countries had more dispersed itineraries, with less focus on famous courses.

U.K. visitors were more likely to be on a centered holiday often either on a short break of two to four nights or on a longer stay, typically of seven to fourteen nights. They were generally based in St. Andrews itself or within easy traveling distance, for example elsewhere in Fife, Dundee, or in Edinburgh. Visitors tended, on average, to play golf on two days out of three during their trip, again re-emphasising the importance of golf to visitors during their trip.

The Role of the Old Course and St. Andrews

The Old Course is the most famous golf course in the world, and it is central to Scotland's acknowledged status as the home of golf. A number of questions were asked of those interviewed at the Old Course itself, and related questions were asked of those playing at the other courses.

From table 80.3 it can be seen that for two-thirds of those interviewed at the Old Course, the chance of playing the course was a very important factor in their decision to visit Scotland.

Table 80.3   Importance of Playing Old Course in Decision to Take Holiday

	%
Very important	67
Fairly important	15
Not very important	4
Not at all important	4
Don't know/not stated	11

Base: All respondents interviewed at Old Course (169)

While this does highlight the strategic importance of the Old Course, the result is not surprising. The Old Course is an unconventional course, and the green fee is very high by general Scottish standards, so it can be assumed that visitors who do play the course have a very definite wish to do so. The result may also reflect the dominance of U.S.A. visitors who are on a first trip to Scotland. Visitors interviewed at courses other than the Old Course were asked the importance of playing golf in St. Andrews and the chance to play the Old Course. The results can be seen from table 80.4.

The possibility of playing in St. Andrews was important to 89% of respondents, while the possibility of playing the Old Course was important to 56% of respondents. Therefore, even for those not actually playing on the Old Course, the attraction is still relatively significant. These results highlight the importance of both St. Andrews and the Old Course in bringing visitors, particularly overseas golfers, to Scotland. This reinforces the view that many are visiting St. Andrews having been attracted purely on the strength of its reputation.

Table 80.4   Importance of St. Andrews/Old Course in Decision to Take Holiday

	Possibility of playing in St. Andrews %	Possibility of playing Old Course %
Very important	65	41
Fairly important	24	15
Not very important	7	14
Not at all important	4	26
Don't know/not stated	1	4

Base: All respondents interviewed at courses other than the Old Course (257)

Future Intentions

Encouragingly, 87% of U.S.A. visitors said they were very or fairly likely to take a future golf holiday in Scotland, with the figure rising to 89% for both U.K. and other overseas visitors. Although repeat visits from U.S.A. visitors are likely to be infrequent, the figures are still encouraging and suggest that the majority of visitors have a positive golfing experience in St. Andrews and Scotland. These respondents were then asked which parts of Scotland they were likely to visit on their next golf holiday and which courses they would like to play.

From table 80.5, it can be seen that the results are generally encouraging in terms of the geographical spread of golf holidays, with two-thirds indicating that they would combine St. Andrews with other areas on their visit. U.S.A. and other overseas visitors were more likely to revisit St. Andrews on their next visit. Therefore, while St. Andrews is still an important attraction for repeat visits, there appears to be potential to 'disperse' the benefits of golf tourism more widely throughout Scotland.

Table 80.5   Parts of Scotland Likely to Visit on Next Golf Holiday

	%
Just St. Andrews	19
St. Andrews and other areas	67
Other areas but not St. Andrews	12
Don't know/not stated	3

Base: All respondents intending to holiday in Scotland in the future (436)

The golf courses visitors wish to play on their next visit reflect the predominance of Open Championship and other 'famous' courses. Troon was mentioned by 26% of respondents and Gleneagles by 20% of respondents. Other frequently mentioned courses included Muirfield (15%), Turnberry (15%), Carnoustie (12%), and Royal Dornoch (11%). The international profile these courses already have highlights the difficulty of creating a similar profile for Scotland's many other fine courses, which are often more accessible and less expensive for visitors to play.

DISCUSSION

This survey has again demonstrated that visitors to St. Andrews tend to be male, middle-aged, travel in relatively large groups, and are likely to be on a specific golfing holiday. The golf product in St. Andrews attracts a significant proportion of visitors from the U.S.A. and other overseas countries, reflecting the strength of the St. Andrews brand throughout the world. The St. Andrews visitor spends significantly more than the general Scottish tourist and stays in Scotland for a longer period of time. Although 40% of spending is golf-related, visitors also spend significant amounts on accommodations, food and drink, travel, and other shopping, thus benefiting the wider economy. The detailed consideration of itineraries highlights the importance of St. Andrews and other famous golf locations in Scotland for the U.S.A. market, but also provides evidence that visitors do travel widely throughout Scotland. There is still considerable potential for encouraging golfing visitors to visit Scotland's lesser known golfing areas to generate a wider spread of economic benefits beyond the St. Andrews area.

The research reinforces the view that many are visiting St. Andrews purely on the strength of its reputation and on the reputation of the Old Course. The possibility of playing golf in St. Andrews and/or of playing on the Old Course act as a significant trigger to encourage people to visit Scotland in the first instance, while their experience here further creates a willingness to return, maintaining Scotland as a 'front of mind' destination for future golf holidays.

Both this survey and the 1989 survey demonstrate the relative strength of the current Scottish golf tourism market to St. Andrews. At the same time there are obvious challenges for the future to consider in golf tourism. It is important for Scottish golf to take account of the international competition in the world marketplace. A number of competing countries, such as Ireland and Portugal, have recently been very active in developing their golf product to encourage tourism, and Scotland must continue to develop golf facilities to stay ahead of its competitors.

The interrelationship between golf and tourism is important. For those in tourism, golf is an important element of the Scottish product. It is a niche market that has developed a strong, worldwide reputation, particularly in one of Scotland's main markets, the United States of America. Partnership efforts involving STB and other tourism and golf organisations will be required if Scotland is to build on its clear golf tourism strengths and thus maximise the benefits golfing visitors can bring. This survey of visiting golfers at St. Andrews has contributed to a greater strategic understanding of the golf market, allowing those involved in tourism to ensure that resources are used to best effect in further developing Scotland's golf tourism market.

In conclusion, golf has a lot to offer tourism, both in terms of promoting Scotland on a macro level and encouraging golf tourism to Scotland. Scotland as a tourist destination also has a lot to offer golfers, encouraging high spending visits from overseas markets. Golf and tourist organisations must work together in the future to encourage tourism for the benefit of the Scottish economy and for the game of golf in Scotland.

References

Aaker, D.A. and Day, G.S. (1986). *Marketing Research,* John Wiley.
Arthur Young Management Consultants (1987). *Study of Golf Facilities in Scotland,* Report prepared for the Scottish Tourist Board.
Hegarty, C. (1993). *European Golfer Spending,* Golf Research Group Report.
Jackson, A.A. (1989). *Visiting Golfers to St. Andrews, Research Report No. 1, September,* Report prepared for the Scottish Tourist Board.
NOP (1997). *The United Kingdom Tourist Statistics 1996,* Report prepared for the English Tourist Board. Northern Irish Tourist Board, Scottish Tourist Board and Wales Tourist Board.
Office for National Statistics (1995). International Passenger Survey.
Scottish Tourist Board (1997). *1997 Annual Report.*
TMS (1997). *Fife Golf Study,* Report prepared for Fife Enterprise.
Witt, S.F. and Moutinho, L. (1989). *Tourism Marketing and Management Handbook,* Prentice-Hall.

CHAPTER 81

Organic Amendments for Sand-Dominated Golf Green Rootzones

A. Cook and S.W. Baker
The Sports Turf Research Institute, Bingley, West Yorkshire, BD16 1AU, UK

In light of the increasing environmental concerns about peat extraction, a laboratory study was conducted to examine the properties of non-peat organic amendments for sand-dominated golf greens with regard to the United States Golf Association (USGA) recommendations for rootzone mixes. Ten organic amendments were mixed at different ratios with two different sands. Most of the rootzones were successful in meeting at least one of the USGA recommendations for physical properties; however, the number of mixes that complied simultaneously with all recommendations was considerably less.

INTRODUCTION

Environmental concerns have been expressed about the future sustainability of peat extraction and thus the utilisation of mined peat may ultimately be more restricted. However, the use of peat in golf green construction and maintenance is still popular. Peat is used in rootzones because it improves the water and nutrient retention of the freely draining sands (Kussow 1987) and its low pH may reduce risks of disease and weeds on the green. However, if the average green size is taken as 540 m^2 (Anonymous 1977) then a USGA green construction with a 300 mm rootzone of a 70:30 sand:peat mix would use almost 50 m^3 of peat. This would mean using 900 m^3 of peat for an eighteen-hole golf course and this does not include any peat used for tees, topdressing and landscaping.

The properties of various non-peat organic and non-organic materials have been studied as amendments to sand for turfgrass rootzones including slag, composted soil (Waddington et al. 1974), clinoptilolite zeolite (Ferguson et al. 1986), bark (Baker 1984) and perlite (Baker 1984; Crawley and Zabcik 1985), lignified sawdust, ground rice hulls, calcinced clay and vermiculite (Paul et al. 1970) and sandy loam topsoil (Baker and Richards 1993). However, many of these studies are removed from the current need to satisfy the recommendations of the USGA Green Section Staff (1993) that are widely regarded in the United Kingdom as the definitive specification that indicates the impending success or failure of a rootzone mix once on a green. In this study, the aim was to test different non-peat organic amendments in the laboratory and compare the physical properties of the mixes to the USGA recommendations for rootzones.

MATERIALS AND METHODS

Rootzone Mixes, Cylinder Preparation and Measurements

The rootzone mixes comprised ten organic amendments mixed with two sands at four different mixing ratios. The two sands used were a medium-coarse sand (particle size distribution: 27% 1.0–0.5 mm and 73% 0.50–0.25 mm) and a medium sand (particle size distribution: 6% 1.0–0.5 mm, 70% 0.50–0.25 mm, 23% 0.25–0.15 mm and 1% 0.15–0.05 mm) and were selected to represent the finer end and the centre of the recommended USGA particle size range. In practice, the medium sand had fractionally more fine sand than is recommended by the USGA for rootzone mixes. Each sand was mixed with each organic amendment at the following ratios; 90:10, 80:20, 70:30 and 60:40 (sand:amendment by volume). Table 81.1 shows the amendments used in the rootzone mixes. Numbers 1 to 7 are non-peat organic products and were chosen to contain a range principal ingredients. Numbers 8 to 10 are more conventional organic amendments used in golf green construction.

Each mix was placed into a metal cylinder of dimensions 72 mm diameter and 100 mm height, under which a layer of permeable voile fabric had been secured. The cylinders were prepared in accordance with the USGA method (Hummel 1993) for determining saturated hydraulic conductivity (K_{sat}), after rootzone compaction at –3 kPa matric potential. The bulk density (D_b) of each rootzone mix was calculated by dividing oven dry weight by volume after compaction. Loss on ignition was calculated by dividing the loss in weight of a dried sample after ignition in a furnace at 360°C for 2 hours by its oven dry weight. Loss on ignition was then used to calculate particle density (D_p) as described by Baker and Isaac (1987). Total porosity was calculated thus: Total porosity = $(1- D_b / D_p) \times 100$. Capillary porosity was measured at a matric potential of –3 kPa to the USGA method (Hummel 1993). Total porosity minus capillary porosity gave air-filled porosity. Particle size analysis was performed in accordance with the USGA method (Hummel 1993) on the 70:30 mixes only.

Experimental Design and Statistical Analyses

The experiment comprised a randomised block design with five replicate blocks. There were 80 cylinders within each replicate block; however, each block was split into eight separate runs due to space limitations on the tension tables. Each of the eight runs per block was accompanied by a control rootzone mix (70:30 medium

Table 81.1 Organic Amendments Included in the Rootzone Mixes

	Principal ingredient	Product name	Manufacturers
1	Greenwaste	Fendress Greentop	Banks Horticultural Products
2	Bark, timber & paper pulp	Ecocompost	Woodgrow Horticulture Ltd.
3	Coir	Cocopeat	Wessex Horticultural Products
4	Sewage and straw	Terra Compost	Terra Eco Systems
5	Rape residue	Fi Pro	Fi Pro
6	Pine wood fibre	Silvafibre	Melcourt Industries Ltd.
7	Woodchip	Screened woodchip	Boughton Loam Ltd.
8	Peat	Sphagnum peat	Shamrock Peat Ltd.
9	Fensoil	Fensoil	Banks Horticultural Products
10	Sandy loam soil	Topsoil	STRI Trial Ground

sand:peat) that underwent the same analyses as the experimental treatments. The values obtained from the controls were used as a covariate in an analysis of covariance so that block splitting effects would be accounted for.

RESULTS

The rootzone mixes comprising medium-coarse sand had significantly ($P<0.001$) higher K_{sat} rates than those made with medium sand, with values, averaged over all amendments and rates, of 676 mm h^{-1} and 283 mm h^{-1}, respectively. The rate at which the amendment was added had an overall significant ($P<0.001$) effect of reducing K_{sat} by approximately 30% with each increasing addition of organic amendment.

Almost half of the rootzones failed to comply with the USGA recommendations for K_{sat} by falling outside both the normal and accelerated ranges (figure 81.1). The majority of the failures were mixes made with medium-coarse sand where all 90:10 mixes exceeded the upper limit for the accelerated range and 60% of the 80:20 mixes were also above this threshold. All treatments made with medium-coarse sand and coir, rape residue and pine wood fibre exceeded the accelerated range at all mixing ratios. More than half the treatments containing medium sand fell within the ranges recommended for K_{sat} (figure 81.1). Only the 90:10 mixes of coir and rape residue exceeded the accelerated range. Most of the failures with medium sand were with amendments mixed to 70:30 and 60:40 ratios. Only bark/timber/paper and pine wood fibre mixes were within the USGA guidelines at all mixing ratios with medium sand.

All rootzone treatments apart from three had total porosities that came within the USGA recommended range of between 35% and 50% (data not shown). The 90:10 coir mixes with both sand types marginally exceeded the upper recommended limit

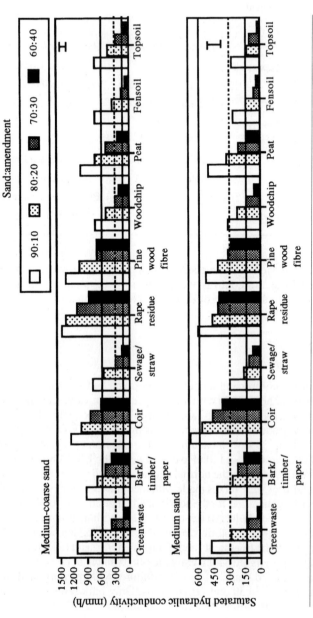

Figure 81.1 K_{sat} of the rootzone mixes. The bold horizontal lines represent the limit recommended by the USGA. The broken horizontal line delimits the top of the 'normal' USGA range and the bottom of the 'accelerated' range. The vertical bars represent the LSD (P=0.05). n=5.

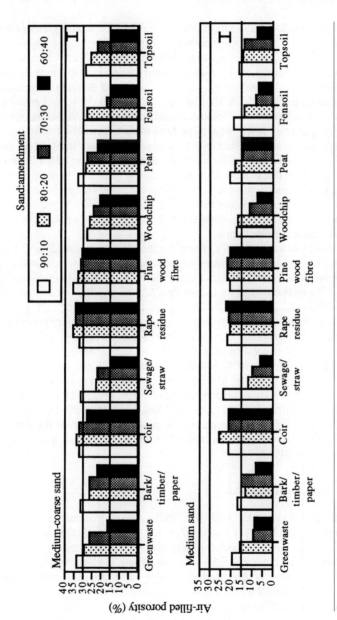

Figure 81.2   Air-filled porosity of the rootzone mixes. The horizontal lines represent the limits recommended by the USGA. The vertical bars represent the LSD (P=0.05). n=5.

for total porosity, and the 90:10 mix of medium sand with topsoil had slightly less total pore space than the lower limit of 35%. In most cases an increase in the amount of organic amendment added resulted in an increase in the total porosity of the rootzones.

The rootzones made with medium-coarse sand had in general greater air-filled porosities than those made with medium sand (figure 81.2). Averaged over all amendments and rates, the medium sand rootzones had 16% air-filled pore space compared with 27% for the medium-coarse sand rootzones. Moreover, in general, as the rate of organic amendment increased, the air-filled porosity decreased. The USGA recommended range for air-filled porosity is 15–30%, and many of the rootzones containing medium-coarse sand especially at the 90:10 incorporation exceeded the upper limit, whereas many of those made with medium sand especially at the lowest rates of sand inclusion did not reach the lower limit. More failures against the USGA requirements for air-filled pore space occurred for the medium sand rootzones than those made with medium-coarse sand. However, amendments such as coir, rape residue and pine wood fibre were more successful at all rates in meeting the USGA recommendations for air-filled porosity when mixed with medium sand than with medium- coarse sand, but the opposite was true for the more conventional organic amendments.

Capillary porosity was generally greater for those rootzones made with medium sand than for those made with medium-coarse sand. Averaged over all amendments and rates the medium-coarse sand rootzones had 19% capillary porosity compared with 29% for the medium sand rootzones. In addition, capillary pore space tended to increase with the amount of organic amendment added (figure 81.3). With either sand the mixing ratio of 60:40 resulted in rootzones with capillary porosities that exceeded the USGA recommended range of 15–25% with only two exceptions (rape residue and pine wood fibre with medium-coarse sand). For the medium-coarse sand, the mixing ratio of 90:10 with all amendments failed to reach the lower limit of 15% capillary porosity; however, for the medium sand, all of the amendments at this rate were within the recommended range. Moreover, rootzones mixed to a ratio of 70:30 with medium-coarse sand had nine out of the ten amendments comply with the USGA recommendation. In contrast, nine out of the ten amendments mixed with medium sand at a ratio of 70:30 exceeded the upper threshold of 25% capillary porosity.

USGA Recommendations

Many of the mixes complied with the USGA recommendations for one or a combination of factors but very few rootzone mixes fell within the recommended ranges for K_{sat}, total, air-filled and capillary porosity simultaneously (table 81.2). Most of the mixes that complied fully were made with medium sand at the rates of 90:10 or 80:20. Fewer of the medium-coarse sand mixes complied fully in comparison, and were of the 80:20 and 70:30 mixing ratios.

The particle size distributions of the 70:30 mixes were compared with the USGA recommendations for rootzone mixes. Seven out of the twenty rootzones failed to comply with the recommendations and all of the failures were mixes made with medium sand. In each of the seven cases, the fine sand fraction exceeded the

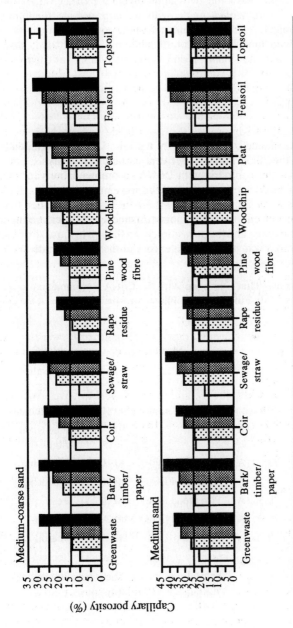

Figure 81.3 Capillary porosity of the rootzone mixes. The horizontal lines represent the limits recommended by the USGA. The vertical bars represent the LSD (P=0.05). n=5.

recommended limit of 20% by 1–3%, but the other fractions of these mixes met the USGA recommendations (data not shown). By averaging the measured parameters of the rootzone mixes over the two sands types, the mean values indicate the potential values for rootzones made with an intermediate medium-coarse to medium sand. Table 81.2 shows that only ten of the potential forty rootzones would have complied with the USGA recommendations for K_{sat}, total, air-filled, and capillary porosity simultaneously, if an intermediate sand was used.

DISCUSSION

Most of the mixes failed to fully comply with the USGA recommendations for rootzones. Only the 70:30 mixes underwent particle size analysis, but out of the thirteen rootzones that complied with USGA recommendations for particle size distribution, only three complied to all recommendations for K_{sat} and the various porosity parameters. In contrast, none of the 70:30 mixes that failed to comply to the particle size distribution recommendations succeeded in performing within the USGA guidelines for K_{sat} and the porosities, even though in the case of each failure, the fine sand fraction was just 1–3% in excess of the recommended limit.

Table 81.2   Rootzones That Complied With the USGA Recommendations on all Counts of K_{sat}, Total, Air-Filled and Capillary Porosity. n = 5 (n = 10 for intermediate sand)

Medium-coarse sand		Medium sand		Intermediate sand[+]	
Amendment	Mix ratio	Amendment	Mix ratio	Amendment	Mix ratio
Bark/timber/paper	70:30 (A)*	Bark/timber/paper	90:10 (A)	Greenwaste	80:20 (A)
Sewage/straw	80:20 (A)	Coir	80:20 (A)	Pine wood fibre	70:30 (A)
Sewage/straw	70:30 (A)	Sewage/straw	90:10 (N)	Woodchip	90:10 (A)
Woodchip	80:20 (A)	Rape residue	80:20 (A)	Woodchip	80:20 (A)
Woodchip	70:30 (A)	Pine wood fibre	90:10 (A)	Peat	80:20 (A)
Peat	70:30 (A)	Pine wood fibre	80:20 (A)	Fensoil	90:10 (A)
Fensoil	80:20 (A)	Woodchip	90:10 (A)	Fensoil	80:20 (N)
		Peat	90:10 (A)	Topsoil	90:10 (A)
		Fensoil	90:10 (N)	Topsoil	80:20 (N)
		Topsoil	90:10 (N)	Topsoil	70:30 (N)

[+]Results averaged between the medium-coarse and medium sands. *(A) and (N) = satisfying the accelerated (300-600 mm h[-1]) and normal (150-300 mm h[-1]) range for K_{sat} respectively.

This study has shown that in terms of soil physical properties there is potential for the use of non-peat organic amendments in sand-dominated rootzones. For the two sands used, the majority of amendments that complied with USGA recommendations, including peat, were mixed at a ratio of 90:10 for the medium sand and 70:30 or 80:20 for the medium-coarse sand. A 90:10 rootzone mix may have performed well in the laboratory, but under field conditions such a sandy rootzone may not be able to support healthy growth without very careful management due to a low cation exchange capacity and therefore low amounts of available nutrients. Chemical properties of some of the rootzones are reported elsewhere (Cook and Baker, in preparation).

A valid assessment of the success of non-peat organic materials as sand amendments can only be made after a long-term, replicated field trial using a suspended water table golf green construction. The performance of various organic amendments in mixes with appropriate sands could be monitored, and assessments of soil physical properties, grass cover and playing quality characteristics under conditions of wear could be made.

ACKNOWLEDGEMENTS

Thanks to the Royal and Ancient Golf Club of St. Andrews for funding this research and the companies that supplied the organic amendments and to R.S. Taylor , M.A. Baines, M.J. Sugden and P.S. Lowe for their assistance.

References

Anonymous (1977). *Amenity grasslands—the needs for research*, Natural Environment Research Council. Publications series C, No. 19, NERC, London, p. 64.

Baker, S.W. (1984). Long-term effects of three amendment materials on moisture retention characteristics of a sand-soil mix. *J. Sports Turf Res. Inst.*, 60:61–65.

Baker, S.W. and Isaac, B.J. (1987). The assessment of soil porosity in sports turf rootzones using measured and calculated values of particle density. *J. Sports Turf Res. Inst.*, 63:141–144.

Baker, S.W. and Richards, C.W. (1993). Rootzone composition and the performance of golf greens. III. Soil physical properties. *J. Sports Turf Res. Inst.*, 69:38–48 .

Crawley, W. and Zabcik, D. (1985). Golf green construction using perlite as an amendment. *Golf Course Management,* July, 44–52.

Ferguson, G.A., Pepper, I.L., and Kneebone, W.R. (1986). Growth of creeping bentgrass on a new medium for turfgrass growth: Clinoptilolite Zeolite-amended sand. *Agron., J.* 78:1095–1098.

Hummel, N.W. (1993).Rationale for the revisions of the USGA green construction specifications. *USGA Green Section Record*, March/April, 7–21.

Kussow. W.R. (1987). Peat in greens: knowns, unknowns and speculations. *USGA Green Section Record*, September/October, 5–7.

Paul, J.L., Madison, J.H. and Waldron, L. (1970). Effects of organic and inorganic amendments on the hydraulic conductivity of three sands used for turfgrass soils. *J. Sports Turf Res. Inst.*, 46:22–32.

USGA Green Section Staff (1993). *USGA Green Section Record*, March/April.

Waddington, D.V., Zimmerman, T.L, Shoop, G.J., Kardos, L.T. and Duich, J.M. (1974). Soil modification for turfgrass areas. I. Physical properties of physically amended soils. *Pennsylvania Agri. Exp. Stn. Prog. Rep.* 337.

CHAPTER 82

Effect of Plant Growth Regulators on Suppression of Poa Annua Ssp. Reptans in a Creeping Bentgrass Putting Green

A.H. Bruneau, F.H. Yelverton, J. Isgrigg, and T.W. Rufty
North Carolina State University, Raleigh, NC, USA

Two experiments were conducted on two unamended creeping bentgrass (*Agrostis palustris* Huds.) putting greens to compare the effectiveness of flurprimidol, paclobutrazol, and trinexapac-ethyl applied at various rates and application frequencies in suppressing annual bluegrass (*Poa annua* ssp. *Reptans* [Hausskn.] Timm.) plant populations and seedheads. One of the putting greens was overseeded with bentgrass and the other was non-overseeded. Paclobutrazol applied twice in the fall and once in the spring at 0.42 kg ai/ha/application provided the greatest suppression of annual bluegrass populations and seedheads on both overseeded and non-overseeded putting greens. Flurprimidol applied once in the fall and spring at 0.28 kg ai/ application as well as trinexapac-ethyl applied twice in the fall (0.19 and 0.06 kg ai/ ha respectively) and again in the spring (0.19 kg ai/ha) provided some seedhead suppression but did not reduce annual bluegrass populations. Trinexapac-ethyl applied at a low rate twice in the fall (0.11 and 0.06 kg ai/ha respectively) and once in the spring (0.11 kg ai/ha) did not provide any seedhead suppression of annual bluegrass in the non-overseeded bentgrass putting green.

Keywords: Plant growth regulators, creeping bentgrass golf green, annual bluegrass.

INTRODUCTION

The perennial biotype of annual bluegrass (*P. annua* ssp₁ *Reptans* [Hausskn.] Timm.), hereafter referred to as PAR, is a major problem in creeping bentgrass (*Agrostis palustris* Huds.) putting greens (Breuninger, 1993). Preemergence herbicides are ineffective in controlling PAR since this biotype has a perennial growth habit, a strong fibrous root system, more prostrate growth, and produces seedheads throughout the season compared to the annual (*Poa annua* ssp. *Annua* [L.]) biotype (Williams and Neal, 1993). The plant growth regulators paclobutrazol and flurprimidol have been used by golf superintendents to suppress PAR and increase the lateral growth of creeping bentgrass (Breuninger, 1993). Population shifts from PAR to bentgrass depend on rate and timing of the two plant growth regulators (Johnson and Murphy, 1995a). The application of flurprimidol at 0.14 active ingredient (ai) and 0.28 kg ai/ha in early spring and again in the fall at three- to six-week intervals resulted in a 20 percent conversion from PAR to bentgrass (Breuninger, 1993). Johnson and Murphy (1995a) did not see a shift from PAR to bentgrass two months after the end of a flurprimidol application program, which involved two spring and two fall applications for two years at a total of 1.8 kg/ha annually. In another study, where higher rates (2.6 kg ai/ha annually) of flurprimidol were applied more frequently (four vs. six weeks), they did observe suppression of PAR three weeks (approximately 47 percent) and 3.5 months (approximately 20 percent) after the final application (Johnson and Murphy, 1995b).

Wu et al. (1992) showed that paclobutrazol applied in two applications six weeks apart reduced total dry weight of PAR in the greenhouse 12 weeks following the initial application. Johnson and Murphy (1995a) showed a transitory suppression of PAR when paclobutrazol was applied twice in the fall and again in the spring at a total annual rate of 1.8 kg ai/ha for two consecutive years. Suppression was 52 percent and 28 percent one and four months after the final treatment, respectively. In a later study, they observed increased suppression of PAR using paclobutrazol three weeks (approximately 72 percent) and 3.5 months (approximately 57 percent) after the final application when the plant growth regulator was applied more frequently (thrice in spring and in the fall) using either of two (1.8 vs 2.6 kg ai/ha) total annual rates (Johnson and Murphy, 1995b). Flurprimidol was not as effective as paclobutrazol in suppressing PAR.

A relatively new plant growth regulator, trinexapac-ethyl, suppresses growth of cool- and warm-season grasses and may be useful in the suppression of PAR. The objective of this study was to compare the effectiveness of flurprimidol, paclobutrazol and trinexapac-ethyl applied at various rates and application frequencies in suppressing PAR plant populations and seedheads.

EXPERIMENTAL METHODS

Experiments were conducted on two unamended creeping bentgrass putting greens located at the Wake Forest Country Club near Raleigh, North Carolina, USA. One of the putting greens was overseeded with bentgrass and the other was not overseeded. Two application programs for trinexapac-ethyl and a single program for both paclobutrazol and flurprimidol were initiated in the fall of 1995 on both putting greens (table 82.1). Each plot was 1.5 by 1.5 m replicated four times using a randomized complete block design. Trinexapac-ethyl was applied at 309 L/ha and paclobutrazol and flurprimidol were applied at 608 L/ha, using XR8002 flat fan nozzles (TeeJet Spraying Systems Company, Wheaton, Illinois, USA). The PAR rating were estimated visually at experiment initiation (5 September 1995) and four weeks after (16 April 1996) the last application. The PAR ratings were converted to percent change in PAR populations to quantify the degree of PAR suppression. Seedhead suppression ratings were visually estimated at four weeks after the last application (16 April 1996). Both PAR and seedhead suppression ratings were analyzed via analysis of variance using the Statistical Analysis System (General Linear Model Procedure). Treatment means were compared with the LSD at the 0.05 level of significance.

Table 82.1   The Rates and Timings for Three Plant Growth Regulators Applied to an Overseeded (Bentgrass) and Non-Overseeded Bentgrass Putting Green

Treatment	Total Applied	Rates	Timing*
	---------------kg ai/ha---------------		
Nontreated	–	–	–
flurprimidol (Cutless 50 WP)	0.560	0.28	Fall + Spring
paclobutrazol** (TGR 2 SC)	1.263	0.421	2 Fall + Spring
Trinexapac-ethyl			2 Fall + Spring
(Primo 1EC)	0.280	0.112 + .056 + 0.112	
(Primo 1EC)	0.438	0.191 + .056 + 0.191	

*Fall applications made 4 weeks apart.
**Paclobutrazol was applied with 12.23 kg N/ha.

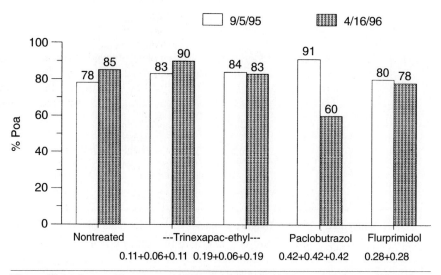

Figure 82.1   Percent *Poa annua* ssp. *Reptans* (Hausskn.) Timm. visually present before and after the application of plant growth regulators (kg ai/ha) to a bentgrass putting green overseeded with bentgrass.

RESULTS AND DISCUSSION

Putting Green Overseeded With Bentgrass

Figure 82.1 shows PAR present before and after treatments on the overseeded bentgrass putting green. In the absence of a plant growth regulator in nontreated plots, the PAR populations increased from 78 to 85 percent (figures 82.1 and 82.2) from early September to mid-April. This eight-month period is when PAR competes most effectively with creeping bentgrass on putting greens in North Carolina. At four weeks following the last treatment applications, paclobutrazol was the only plant growth regulator that exhibited the ability to reduce the presence of PAR (figure 82.2). The suppression observed using paclobutrazol was approximately 30 percent compared to the population observed the previous fall. Neither trinexapac-ethyl or flurprimidol treatments suppressed PAR in this experiment.

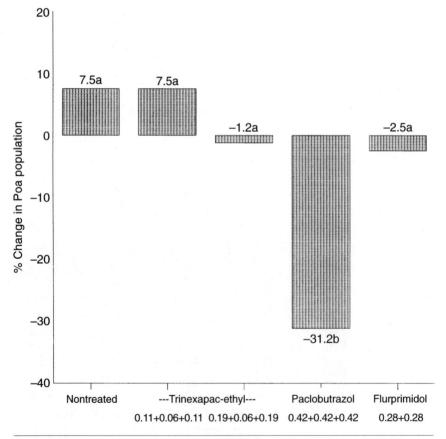

Figure 82.2   Percent change in *Poa annua* ssp. *Reptans* (Hausskn.) Timm. from 5 September 1995 to 16 April 1996 following application of plant growth regulators (kg ai/ha) to a bentgrass green overseeded with bentgrass.

All plant growth regulators reduced the presence of PAR seedheads compared to the nontreated plots (figure 82.3). The best suppression occurred with paclobutrazol and the high rate of trinexapac-ethyl (0.44 kg ai/ha) applied twice in the fall and once in the spring, which suppressed seedheads by 98 and 71 percent, respectively. Trinexapac-ethyl applied at the low total rate (0.28 kg ai/ha) gave the least control with 38% suppression. Flurprimidol applied once in the fall and spring at the total rate of 0.56 kg/ha decreased seedheads by 55%, intermediate between the two trinexapac-ethyl treatments.

Putting Green Not Overseeded With Bentgrass

Figure 82.4 shows the PAR ratings before and after treatment applications in the study on the non-overseeded bentgrass putting green. At treatment initiations, PAR present in the non-overseeded green was lower than in the overseeded green. The

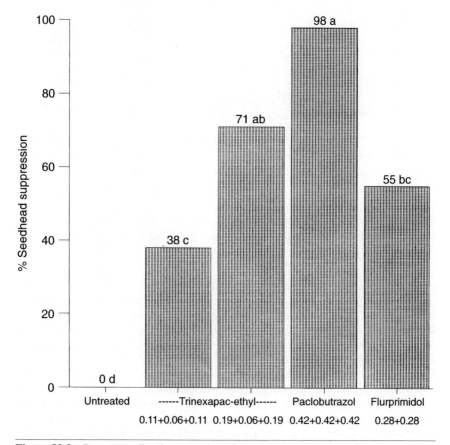

Figure 82.3   Percent seedhead suppression of *Poa annua* ssp. *Reptans* (Hausskn.) Timm. On 16 April 1996 following the application of plant growth regulators (kg ai/ha) to a bentgrass green overseeded with bentgrass.

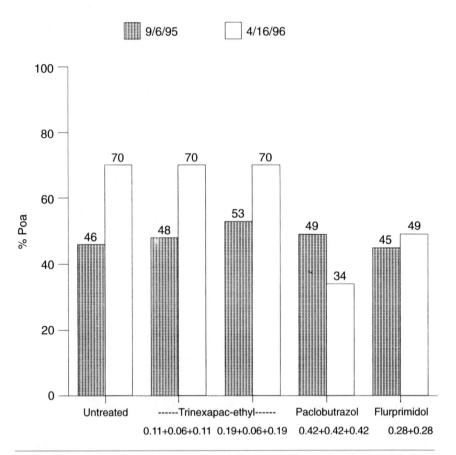

Figure 82.4   Percent *Poa annua* ssp. *Reptans* (Hausskn.) Timm. visually present before and after the application of plant growth regulators (kg ai/ha) to a bentgrass putting green not overseeded with bentgrass.

PAR in nontreated plots increased from 46 to 70 percent during the eight-month period of study (figure 82.4). These data indicate the relative competitive advantage PAR can have on creeping bentgrass putting greens in this geographical area. Paclobutrazol was the most effective plant growth regulator in reducing the presence of PAR four weeks after the last application (figure 82.5). The suppression observed using paclobutrazol was approximately 15 percent compared to the PAR population present the previous fall. Flurprimidol also suppressed PAR compared to the nontreated bentgrass but still had more PAR present compared to the previous fall. Trinexapac-ethyl did not exhibit the ability to suppress PAR populations.

Paclobutrazol, flurprimidol and the high rate (0.44 kg ai/ha) of trinexapac-ethyl were able to reduce the presence of seedheads compared to the nontreated plots (figure 82.6). Paclobutrazol provided the best control, showing an 80 percent reduction in seedheads, followed by flurprimidol and the high rate of trinexapac-

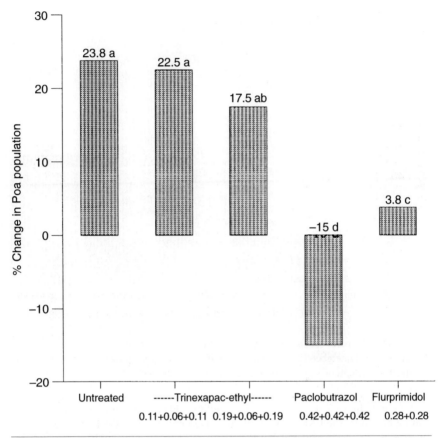

Figure 82.5   Percent *Poa annua* ssp. *Reptans* (Hausskn.) Timm. populations following the application of plant growth regulators (kg ai/ha) to a bentgrass green not overseeded with bentgrass.

ethyl that were comparable. Trinexapac-ethyl at the low (0.28 kg ai/ha) total rate did not suppress seedheads.

CONCLUSION

The main finding of this study is that paclobutrazol is the most effective growth regulator for the control of PAR in bentgrass greens. This was true for reductions in PAR populations and seedhead suppression on both overseeded and non-overseeded greens. With the paclobutrazol treatment regime used in this study, a significant conversion from PAR to bentgrass occurred. Flurprimidol and a high rate of trinexapac-ethyl also were effective in seedhead suppression, indicating that they also might have a role in PAR control programs.

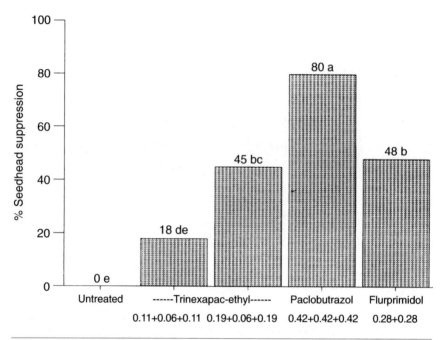

Figure 82.6   Percent seedhead suppression of *Poa annua* ssp. *Reptans* (Hausskn.) Timm. from 5 September 1995 to 16 April 1996 following the application of plant growth regulators to a bentgrass green not overseeded with bentgrass.

Although direct comparisons of overseeding and not overseeding with bentgrass cannot be made, the PAR population increased more (24 percent vs. 7 percent for overseeded vs. non-overseeded respectively) in non-overseeded bentgrass putting greens. This may indicate overseeding with bentgrass in combination with a paclobutrazol program may be advantageous.

References

Breuninger, J.B. (1993). *Poa annua* control in bentgrass greens. *Golf Course Management* 61(8):68–73.

Johnson, B.J. and Murphy, T.R. (1995a). Effect of paclobutrazol and flurprimidol on suppression of *Poa annua* spp. *reptans* in creeping bentgrass (*Agrostis stolonifera*) greens. *Weed Technology* 9:182–186.

Johnson, B.J. and Murphy, T.R. (1995b). Suppression of a perennial subspecies of annual bluegrass (*Poa annua* spp. *reptans*) in a creeping bentgrass (*Agrostis stolonifera*) green with plant growth regulators. *Weed Technology* 10:705–709.

Williams, N.D. and Neal, J.C. (1993). Annual bluegrass biology and control. *Weed Facts: Weed Management Series No. 7.* Cornell Coop. Ext, Cornell University.

Wu, L., Harding, J.A., Borgonovo, M., and Harivandi, M.A. 1992. The versatile *Poa annua* L.; wanton weed and/or golf turf. *California Agriculture* 46(3):24–26.

CHAPTER 83

Comparative Assessments of Turf Characteristics and Stress Resistance for Three Cynodon Hybrids Used on Putting Greens

J.B Beard and S.I. Sifers
International Sports Turf Institute, Texas, USA

Three dwarf *Cynodon dactylon* × *Cynodon transvaalensis* hybrids were assessed in terms of six turf morphological-growth characteristics, plus for wear stress tolerance and direct low temperature hardiness. Compared to Tifgreen and Tifdwarf, the recently released Champion cultivar represents a new generation of what can be described as a vertical dwarf genotype, in that it has a much slower vertical leaf extension rate than the other two cultivars but with the capability of much more intense lateral stem development with an associated higher shoot density even under extraordinarily close mowing heights. A 3.2 mm mowing height results in significant thinning of Tifdwarf and a major reduction in shoot density of Tifgreen. In addition, the vertical dwarf cultivar Champion had a more narrow leaf width than the other two cultivars. The higher shoot density and finer leaf width contribute to excellence in surface quality in terms of ball roll on putting greens. Champion also exhibited better wear stress tolerance, which is most probably associated with the much higher shoot density. In addition, Champion exhibited significantly better direct low temperature stress hardiness than either Tifdwarf or Tifgreen.

Keywords: Lateral stem number, internode length, shoot density, leaf width, vertical leaf extension rate, turf recovery rate, wear stress tolerance, direct low temperature kill hardiness, Champion, Tifdwarf, and Tifgreen.

INTRODUCTION

The *Cynodon* species (L.C. Rich) encompass one of the most important and widely used warm-season turfgrasses (Beard, 1973). It is adapted to the warm- and subtropic-climatic regions of the world. The turf-type *Cynodon* species are C$_4$, perennials that originated in southeastern Africa, and include: *Cynodon dactylon* (L. Pers.) or dactylon bermudagrass which is a tetraploid, and *Cynodon transvaalensis* (Burtt-Davy) or African bermudagrass which is a diploid. The *C. dactylon* as a group are characterized by a more coarse leaf width and lower shoot density, while the *C. dactylon* × *C. transvaalensis* hybrids tend to have a narrower leaf width and higher shoot density. Both are relatively low-growing via vigorous lateral stems, both rhizomes and stolons. The dominant turfgrass used on putting greens in the warm-humid climatic regions is the *Cynodon* hybrid (Beard, 1982). With only a few exceptions, the *Cynodon* hybrid cultivars used on putting greens since the mid-1960s have been either Tifgreen or Tifdwarf. However, there have been major problems for these hybrid cultivars, especially at the mowing heights now being used. Tifgreen and Tifdwarf do not have the ability to maintain adequate shoot density at sustained mowing heights of 4 mm and lower. Champion is a new vertical dwarf hybrid *Cynodon* released in 1995.

The objectives of this study were to conduct comparative turfgrass morphological-growth and stress resistance assessments of three dwarf hybrid *Cynodon dactylon* × *C. transvaalensis* cultivars: Champion, Tifdwarf, and Tifgreen.

EXPERIMENTAL METHODS

Morphological-Growth Assessments

In June 1995, quantitative assessments of stolon number, stolon internode length, shoot density, leaf blade width, vertical leaf extension rate, and turf damage recovery rate of three low-growing hybrid *Cynodon dactylon* × *C. transvaalensis* cultivars, Champion, Tifdwarf, and Tifgreen, were conducted in College Station, Texas. Assessments were conducted on turfs grown in four replicate 150 mm diameter, 3.8 liter volume, black plastic pots filled with sand within the USGA Method specifications. All turf treatments were established by transplanting mature, washed sod into each of the four replicate sets of containers, which were then placed in a glasshouse and maintained for three months before the assessments were initiated. The turfs were mowed at a cutting height of 6.4 mm at two-day intervals using electric shears. The turfs were watered as necessary to prevent visual wilt and fertilized weekly with liquid fertilizer to provide 0.5 kg each of N/P/K 100 m^{-2} per growing month.

Stolon number measurements were made by counting the number of lateral stems extending outward laterally from the edge of the 638 mm perimeter of each replicate container after 16 days of growth. The internode length was measured between the second and third youngest nodes of six stolons extending outward from the perimeter of each container.

Shoot density counts were conducted on a 64.5 mm^2 area of turf for each replicate treatment. Leaf blade width assessments were made at the linear midpoint of the youngest, fully expanded leaf blade on a shoot, with six blade measurements made per replicate treatment. Assessments of the vertical leaf extension rate were made by measuring the leaf growth that occurred over a 24-hour period on 10 leaves per replicate treatment for an 18-day growth period.

Assessments of the turf recovery rate from mechanical injury were conducted on an opening of 2500 mm^2 in each of the replicate turf treatments made by removing a portion of mature turf using a soil sampling tool. Turf recovery was visually estimated weekly as percent turf recovery in the opening over a four-week period.

These six turf morphological-growth assessments were repeated in a second study conducted in July of 1995. Both assessment periods produced comparable results. Thus, only the June data are presented herein.

Wear Stress Resistance Assessments

Replicated quantitative assessments of shoot density and of wear stress tolerance were made on a putting green turf in Bay City, Texas, that had been planted with the same three low-growing hybrid *Cynodon* cultivars. The putting green zone was a 400 mm deep, 90/10 sand/peat mix that was within the specifications of the USGA Method. The green was sectioned into 6 × 3 m plots for each cultivar, and established in April of 1995 by sprigging. The cultivars were separated by wood dividers placed vertically into the rootzone until mowing was initiated, which was four weeks after sprigging.

The experimental green was initially mowed daily at a 6.4 mm cutting height using a Jacobsen 55.9 cm walking greensmower with clippings removed. Six weeks after sprigging, the height of cut was lowered to 3.2 mm, with the mowing performed daily. At nine weeks after sprigging, a Turfgroomer attachment was used daily with the groomer blades set to 1.5 mm below the bedknife. A water-soluble fertilizer was applied during the grow-in period at 1.0 kg each of N/P/K 100 m^{-2} wk^{-1}. An organic fertilizer containing 6% N was applied monthly at 14 kg 100 m^{-2}.

Replicated quantitative assessments of shoot density were made in early November of 1995 on cores removed from the putting green. Shoot counts were made on four 865 mm^2 replicate samples of turf for each treatment. The procedure involved separating the turf into individual shoots, with one shoot being a stem that had both a root and a leaf attached.

Quantitative assessments of the wear stress tolerance of Champion and Tifdwarf were conducted on the putting green in early November of 1995. Wear was imposed by placing a wear simulator between each replicate of two 6 × 3 m plots of Champion and Tifdwarf (Shearman et. al., 1974). The wear stress simulation was terminated after 1,900 revolutions, as the Tifdwarf leaf blades had been worn away.

Low Temperature Stress Hardiness Assessment

Assessments of the low temperature stress hardiness of the Champion and Tifdwarf hybrids grown on the previously described experimental putting green were conducted in February of 1996. After dormancy had occurred, five replicate sets of 100 mm diameter by 200 mm deep turfed plugs per cultivar were taken from the green, placed into plastic cups, and transferred to the cold stress simulator in the Turfgrass Field Research Laboratory at Texas A&M University in College Station, Texas. The cold stress simulation chamber was maintained at a temperature of −1.1C for 48 hours, after which one replicate set of each cultivar was removed (Beard, 1966). Then the simulator was programmed to lower the temperature to −3.8C and held at this temperature for 24 hours, when another set was removed. This procedure was continued in 2.7C increments through the last temperature treatment at −12C. By this procedure the monitored temperatures of the turfed plugs were uniform throughout the entire soil column and were the same as the air temperature in the cold stress simulation chamber. The turfed plugs were thawed slowly in the shade and placed in a glasshouse at a 35/25C day-night temperature regime. Green shoot recovery was monitored weekly for four weeks to assess the shoot injury sustained from low temperature stress. The turfs were rated visually as a percentage of their potential, which was the nonstressed treatment.

All data were evaluated by Analysis of Variance Procedure T Test (LSD) with alpha + 0.05.

RESULTS AND DISCUSSION

Morphological-Growth Assessments

Lateral Stem Development

The rates of stolon formation and development were quantitatively assessed based on the number of lateral stems extending outward from the perimeters of replicate containers. Direct comparisons revealed that Champion exhibited significantly greater lateral stem development in the order of 2.6 times that of Tifdwarf and 2.8 times that of Tifgreen (table 83.1). This intense lateral stem development is the morphological mechanism that contributes substantially to more rapid rates of turf establishment and turf recovery from damage in comparison to the other two cultivars.

The internode length did not vary significantly among the three cultivars. This indicates that the higher shoot density of Champion is attributed primarily to a greater number of lateral stems and their vigorous lateral growth.

Shoot Density

Champion exhibited a significantly higher shoot density than the two other hybrid *Cynodon* cultivars at the 6.4 mm, with shoot numbers being in the order of 27.4% greater than Tifdwarf and 118.7% greater than Tifgreen (table 83.1). Under field plot conditions in the autumn of 1996 with a 3.2 mm cutting height, Champion had a significantly higher shoot density at 2,842 shoots dm^{-2} in comparison to Tifdwarf at 1,472 shoots dm^{-2}. The Tifgreen cultivar was not evaluated for shoot density as this cultivar was severely thinned under frequent mowing at 3.2 mm. This higher shoot density contributed to a superior, more consistent turf surface for closely mowed putting greens.

Leaf Blade Width

Quantitative assessments of the leaf blade width revealed Champion to have a comparatively narrow leaf blade width. The leaf blade width of Champion was found to be significantly finer than the other two dwarf hybrid cultivars, being 13.8% less than Tifdwarf and 36.3% less than Tifgreen (table 83.1).

Table 83.1   Comparisons of Six Turf Morphological-Growth Characteristics Among Three Dwarf Hybrid *Cynodon* Cultivars Maintained at a 6.4 mm Mowing Height

Morphological-growth characteristics	Cultivar		
	Champion	Tifdwarf	Tifgreen
Stolon development (no. 100 mm^{-1})	12.2a*	5.4b	4.4b
Internode length (mm)	12.8a	17.0a	12.8a
Shoot density (no. dm^{-2})	2,093a	1,643b	915c
Leaf blade width (mm)	1.00a	1.16b	1.57c
Vertical leaf extension rate (mm d^{-1})	0.7a	1.6b	4.0c
Turf recovery rate:			
%3 WAT	68.3a	20.0c	38.3b
%4 WAT	95.0a	76.7ab	65.0bc

*Numbers followed by the same letter in the same row are not significantly different based on the Duncan Test (p = 0.05).

Vertical Leaf Extension Rate

A detailed quantitative assessment of the vertical leaf extension rate revealed that Champion had a significantly slower rate, being in the order of 56% slower than Tifdwarf and 82.5% slower than Tifgreen (table 83.1). This characteristic contributes to less ball roll resistance that allows a more rapid speed of ball roll on closely mowed turf surfaces. The net result has been measurements of ball roll distance in the range of 3.0 to 3.3 m when mowed at 3.2 mm or lower.

Turf Recuperative Rate

In comparison to the two other hybrid *Cynodon* cultivars, Champion was found to be significantly superior in turf recuperative rate (table 83.1). It exhibited in the order of 1.8 times more rapid turf recovery rate than Tifgreen and 3.4 times more than Tifdwarf. This rapid rate of turf recovery should provide a better quality turf surface under intense use, including less persistent ball marks and less proneness to weed invasion.

Wear Stress Resistance Assessment

After 1,900 revolutions with a wear stress simulator, Champion and Tifdwarf were visually and quantitatively assessed for damage from wear. Visually, Champion had sustained less damage, having a substantial quantity of green shoots evident after 10 days, whereas Tifdwarf had practically none. Quantitatively, Champion was found to have retained 32% more green shoot biomass than Tifdwarf after imposition of wear stress simulation (table 83.2). Tifgreen was excluded from this study

Table 83.2   Comparative Assessments of Wear Stress Resistance, Expressed as Shoot Dry Weight Per Square Decimeter after 1,900 Revolutions of a Wheel Wear Simulator, of Champion and Tifdwarf Maintained at a 3.2 mm Mowing Height

Cultivar	Pre-wear stress	Post-wear stress
Champion	5.2a*	1.9a
Tifdwarf	2.2b	1.3b

*Means followed by the same letter in the same column are not significantly different at the 5% LSD t Test.

because of the severe thinning under the very low mowing height. The weight of the shoot biomass of Champion was 58% greater than the weight of the Tifdwarf shoot biomass before imposition of wear stress. This was a factor contributing to the differential in wear stress tolerance.

Low Temperature Stress Assessment

Evaluations of low temperature stress hardiness were made at one, three, four, and five weeks after treatment. Champion showed significantly better survival from cold stress than Tifdwarf at the –1.1C, –3.8 C, and –6.5C treatments at five weeks after treatment (WAT), with canopies fully recovered from the stress treatments, whereas Tifdwarf had survived to only 83, 74, and 77 percent, respectively (table 83.3). Tifgreen was excluded from this study because of the thinning it had exhibited under the very low mowing height. In previous studies conducted at Texas A&M

Table 83.3   Comparative Low Temperature Stress Hardiness Assessments, Expressed as Percent Green Shoots, of Champion and Tifdwarf Maintained at a Mowing Height of 3.2 mm

Recovery Assessment (WAT)	Cultivar	Stress temperature (°C)				
		–1.1	–3.8	–6.5	–9.2	–12.0
4	Champion	100 a	98 a	100 a	3 c	0 c
	Tifdwarf	80 b	68 b	65 b	0 c	0 c
5	Champion	100 a	100 a	100 a	3 c	0 c
	Tifdwarf	83 b	74 b	77 b	0 c	0 c

*Means followed by the same letter in the same row and column are not significantly different at the 5% level LSD t-Test.

University using the same methods, the low temperature hardiness of Tifgreen was found to be less than that of Tifdwarf (Beard et. al., 1992). These results and those reported early would indicate that Champion possesses greater hardiness to low temperature stress than either Tifgreen or Tifdwarf.

References

Beard, J.B. (1966). Direct low temperature injury of nineteen turfgrasses. *Quarterly Bulletin of the Michigan Agricultural Experiment Station.* 48:377–383.

Beard, J.B. (1973). *Turfgrass: Science and Culture.* Prentice-Hall, Inc., Englewood Cliffs, New Jersey, USA, p. 658.

Beard, J.B. (1982). *Turf Management for Golf Courses.* Burgess Publishing Company, Minneapolis, Minnesota, USA, p. 642.

Beard, J.B, Sifers, S.I., and Griggs, S.D. (1992). *Genetic diversity in low temperature hardiness among 35 major warm-season turfgrass genotypes.* Texas Turfgrass Research—1991.

Consolidated Research Report PR-4878, 56–58.

Shearman, R.C., Beard, J.B, Hansen, C.M, and Apaella, R. (1974). Turfgrass wear simulator for small plot investigations. *Agronomy Journal.* 66:332–334.

CHAPTER 84

Water Release Curve Evaluation
of Golf Green Construction Materials
and Field-Collected Samples

D.K. Otto, C.R. Dixon, and S.B. McWilliams
Turf Diagnostics & Design, Inc., Olathe, Kansas, USA

The current protocol (Hummel, 1993) for evaluating the performance of rootzone materials provides the minimal amount of technical data needed to properly assess the suitability of materials. Water release curves allow for a more complete evaluation of a rootzone's performance by determining the water release characteristics over a predetermined range of tension points. The generated data can be used as a diagnostic tool of existing rootzones and for the assessment of greens construction materials under various conditions and climates. Water release curves not only allow for laboratory simulation of naturally occurring conditions but can also determine the actual impact of applied turf management programs. By expanding the soil physical assessment of the growing medium, potential environmental and economic patterns may be identified and optimized.

Keywords: Water release, tempe, greens construction, USGA rootzone evaluation.

INTRODUCTION

Greens are physically, as well as chemically and biologically, dynamic. The current United States Golf Association (USGA) method (Hummel, 1993) of rootzone evaluation does not assess the dynamics of water retention in rootzone materials. The USGA method determines water- and air-filled porosities at only one energy level. The USGA porosity values are determined at the moment of field capacity at the surface. The aim of this research was to develop a more thorough method of evaluation using water release curves. Water release curves allow the analysis of air-

and water-filled pore space through a range of energy levels that occur in the putting green.

Evaluation of the dynamic physical properties provides a better risk assessment process for material selection and diagnostic assessment of putting green rootzones. The curve also helps to assess the suitability of materials in various climatic regions.

MATERIALS AND METHODS

The water release curve represents how the soil releases water over a range of tensions. Pressure cells were used to determine water content at each tension. This method was first described by Reginato and van Bavel (1962).

The brass cores used in the pressure cells also fit equipment for taking field samples as well as the compactor in the lab for repacking cores with disturbed soil samples. Field cores are collected from representative areas of the green. The collection equipment allows the removal of the thatch layer without the disruption of the soil core. Field cores can be taken from additional depths if desired. Field cores were first shaved to provide good contact with the porous plate that will allow the water to pass through. Various types of porous plates were used depending on the tension range and the flow rate of the sample. The porous plates each have an air entry value dependent on the material of the plate. Typical plates include ceramic, stainless steel, wettable porous plastics and nylon. Tensions were not applied greater than the air entry value for each plate. Although the flow rate of the plates do not affect the results of the test, they can affect the timing of the test. By matching the flow rate of the plate and sample, the length of the test can be optimized.

After the cells were put together, the soil was saturated. A 0.005 M CaSO$_4$ solution was used as a buffer for the saturation of the soil cores (Klute, 1986). The cores were saturated from the bottom by backflooding the cells. The cores were weighed at saturation and then connected to the manifold. The pressure cells were weighed after each equilibration point.

Rootzone organic matter content was analyzed using a wet oxidation method (American Society of Testing and Materials [ASTM] Method F 1647-95, Method B) and is expressed on a dry weight basis. The particle size analysis was analyzed following the USGA method (ASTM Method F 1632). See table 84.1 for results.

RESULTS AND DISCUSSION

The water release characterization test provides paired values of water content and tension that are used to generate a water release curve. The water release curve is the relationship between the soil water content and the soil water tension. The data are graphed with tension versus degree of saturation (DS). The DS represents the percentage of pore spaces filled with water. The pore spaces not filled with water are filled with soil gases. Figure 84.1 illustrates the water-air relationship of a field collected core.

Table 84.1   Rootzone Organic Matter Content and Particle Size

Sample name	% Sand >0.05 mm	% Clay <0.002 mm	>1.0 mm	Coarse 0.5 (35)	Medium 0.25 (60)	<0.25 mm	Uniformity coefficient
Fig 84.1	99.4	<1.0	9.1	15.1	50.2	24.7	2.3
Fig 84.2 Surface	100.0	<1.0	3.9	18.1	60.4	17.8	2.1
Fig 84.2 Original	97.9	1.4	5.0	18.4	54.6	19.8	2.2
Fig 84.3 Sample #1	97.4	1.0	9.3	13.7	38.7	35.7	2.7
Fig 84.3 Sample #2	95.1	2.0	41.2	21.6	21.6	10.8	6.2
Fig 84.3 Sample #3	95.6	1.9	8.4	29.1	35.4	22.8	3.8

There are three types of soil water—gravitational, capillary, and adhesion. The gravitational water is the free flowing water from a saturated soil. Capillary water is the water held by the capillary forces within the soil. These forces are influenced by soil structure and pore-size distribution. Adhesion water is the water held by the adsorptive forces that are influenced by the particle size and specific surface of the

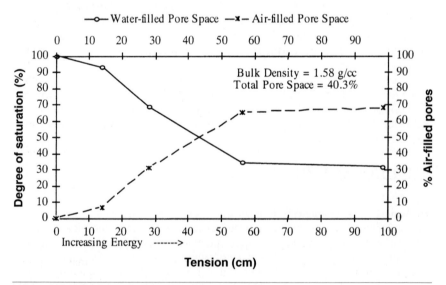

Figure 84.1   Water release curve showing the relationship of air- and water-filled pore spaces in a field collected core.

soil. Water release in the 0–1000 cm range is strongly influenced by the capillary forces. At higher tensions, the absorptive forces are more dominant (Young, 1994).

Typically, a low tension range (0 to 100 cm) is used for the test as this is the common working tension range for golf greens, especially with daily irrigations. Two major driving forces of the working tension range are evapotranspiration (ET) and precipitation events (including irrigation). This lower range also allows the risk assessment of casual water (standing water after a precipitation event). The risk of casual water would be indicated by the rate of change in the degree of saturation. The presence of casual water will typically reduce the playability of the course. Higher tension ranges are used when the working tension range is known, or suspected, to be greater than 100 cm.

Water release curves are useful as a diagnostic tool. Water release curves indicate the effect of organic matter accumulation in the surface of a green. Figure 84.2 illustrates one example of field cores collected from the same green showing the difference in water retention due to the organic matter accumulation at the surface. The accumulation of organic matter in the surface layer impacts the water retention and the air-filled pore spaces. More water is retained throughout the entire tension range in the sample with the higher organic matter content. The higher water content implies lower air-filled porosities at each tension. An adjustment in management practices (i.e., fertility or core aerification programs) may be needed to control the rate of organic matter increase at the surface.

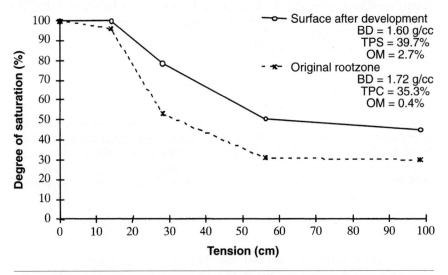

Figure 84.2   Effect of organic matter development on water release characteristics.

Water release curves are also useful as an assessment tool for greens construction materials and topdress selection. Soils may exhibit similar performances at one tension point, but may exhibit marked differences at other tensions. Figure 84.3 illustrates three different soils that have acceptable DS values at 30 cm tension for a USGA system, but have different retention characteristics under the 30 cm tension.

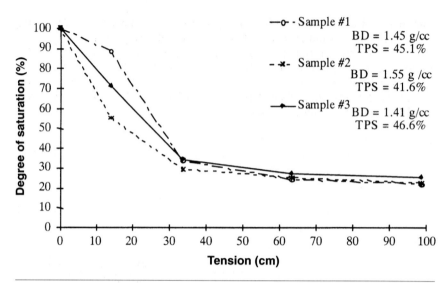

Figure 84.3   Water release curves for material assessment of three different sands.

This is important to know for assessing the climatic suitability of the soils. These samples will have different risks of casual water. The decision on which sand to use would depend primarily on the level of traffic after precipitation events and climatic conditions of the location.

CONCLUSION

Water release data expands the knowledge of the physical properties of the rootzone. This data can be useful in material selection for varying climatic regions. Water release is also useful in assessing and diagnosing needs for putting green management. Due to the effect of excessive water retention on the traffic potential, disease, and chemical management, we believe the method to be a valid and important risk assessment tool.

References

American Society of Testing and Materials. 1995. *Standard test method for organic matter content of putting green and sports turf root zone mixes*. F1647-95. ASTM. Philadelphia, PA.

American Society of Testing and Materials. 1995. *Standard test method for particle size analysis and sand shape grading of golf course putting green and sports field root zone mixes*. F1632-95. ASTM. Philadelphia, PA.

Klute, A. 1986. Water Retention: Laboratory Methods. In *Methods of Soil Analysis. Part 1*. ed. A. Klute, pp. 687–734. 2nd ed. American Society of Agronomy, Madison, WI.

Hummel, N.W., compiler. 1993. Standard Test Methods for Saturated Hydraulic Conductivity, Water Retention, Porosity, and Bulk Density on Putting Green Root Zone Mixes. *USGA Green Section Record.* March/April pp. 23–27.

Reginato, R.J., C.H.M. van Bavel. 1962. Pressure cell for soil cores. *Soil Science of America* 26:1–3.

Young, M.H. 1994. *Soil Water Release Curve in the Wet Range (0–0.3 bar).* University of Arizona.

CHAPTER 85

Agrostis Cultivar Characterizations for Closely Mowed Putting Greens in a Mediterranean Climate

P. Croce and M. Mocioni
Federazione Italiana Golf, Green Section, Sutri, Italy

J.B. Beard
International Sports Turf Institute, College Station, Texas, USA

Seventeen *Agrostis* cultivars were assessed in terms of turfgrass quality, shoot density, leaf width, *Poa annua* invasion, and moss invasion when maintained under extraordinarily close mowing on a putting green in a Mediterranean climate. Four recently released *Agrostis stolonifera* cultivars, Penn G-1, A-1, G-6, and G-2 had a higher turfgrass quality and shoot density and a lower leaf width and degree of *Poa annua* and moss invasion after 5+ years of assessments. Four *Agrostis* cultivars, National, Emerald, Seaside, and Astoria provided unacceptable turfgrass quality and shoot density for golf putting greens. After the cutting height was lowered from 4.8 to 4.0 mm and the nitrogen nutritional level raised at the end of the 1994 season, there was a general increase in shoot density and a decrease in leaf width of most *Agrostis* cultivars. Generally, those cultivars with higher shoot densities exhibited the least proneness to *Poa annua* and moss invasion. In the case of *Poa annua* invasion there tended to be a general increase over the years 1995 through 1997, particularly in the case of the lower shoot density cultivars. In contrast, the moss invasion did not exhibit an increasing trend over time, but rather varied from year to year and from cultivar to cultivar, which suggests that the variations were more a response to climatic conditions. There also was a intra-seasonal variation in extent of moss coverage, with the peak occurring in June.

Keywords: *Agrostis stolonifera*, turfgrass quality, shoot density, leaf blade width, moss invasion, *Poa annua* invasion, bentgrass.

INTRODUCTION

Agrostis stolonifera L. (creeping bentgrass) is widely used as the preferred turfgrass species on putting greens in Italy. It is uniquely adapted morphologically for use on putting greens (Beard, 1982). Extensive, prostrate lateral stem development and a high shoot-leaf density can be sustained under frequent, close mowing of 4 to 6 mm. Lateral stem growth speeds turf recovery from ball marks and other damages to the turf surface. *Agrostis stolonifera* is a cool-season, C_3, perennial turfgrass that has an optimum growing temperature of 16 to 24°C. It responds to nitrogen fertilization and irrigation, especially under intense traffic stress. Penncross has been the cultivar most widely accepted and used throughout the world for the past 35 years.

In the past five years, a number of new *Agrostis stolonifera* cultivars have been released. Thus, there is a need to assess their potential for use under golf course putting green conditions in Italy. Accordingly, the Federazione Italiana Golf (F.I.G.) initiated an *Agrostis* cultivar characterization study on a closely mowed putting green in cooperation with the Torino Golf Club located northeast of Torino, Italy (Croce et al., 1994) in a Mediterranean climate.

This paper represents the final conclusions concerning the adaptation and performance of these *Agrostis stolonifera* cultivars under the conditions of the study in Italy after six years of evaluation. This duration is required for the turf-soil ecosystem to stabilize in terms of the soil physical characteristics, rooting, thatch, microorganism population, disease causing fungi, insect pests, and nematode populations.

EXPERIMENTAL METHODS

Establishment

Eleven commercially available cultivars of *Agrostis stolonifera* and one cultivar of *Agrostis capillaris* L. (Astoria colonial bentgrass) were planted onto a 600 m² specially constructed experimental putting green located at the Torino Golf Club. The plot size was 2.0 × 3.5 m, arranged in a randomized block design with four replications. In addition, five genotypes that at the time were advanced experimental selections of *Agrostis stolonifera* from Pennsylvania State University were planted in an adjacent area. These plots were 2.0 × 1.75 m in size, with two replications in a randomized block design. The root zone profile construction was a high-sand composition meeting Texas-USGA specifications, including a subsurface drainage system.

The experimental area was planted on May 4, 1992. Preplant fertilization consisted of 1.0 kg 100 m⁻² each of N, P, and K incorporated into the upper 100 mm of the root zone. All cultivars were planted at a seeding rate of 0.5 kg 100 m⁻², with the seed lightly raked into the surface. Vertical barrier boards were used to avoid contamination of seed between plots. No lateral seed movement occurred and successful turfgrass establishment was achieved with distinct perimeters between individual cultivar plots.

Cultural Practices

Cultural practices on the experimental putting green involved mowing five times per week in multiple directions at a 5 mm cutting height during 1992 through 1994 and subsequently from 1995 through 1997 at a cutting height of 4 mm by means of a triplex greensmower with a groomer attachment, with clippings removed. The nitrogen fertilization program consisted of 0.35 kg 100 m^{-2} per growing month from May through September, totaling 1.75 kg 100 m^{-2} annually in 1993 and 1994. The nitrogen fertility program was increased in 1995 through 1997 to 3 kg 100 m^{-2} annually divided into 8 applications from March through October. The base phosphorus (P) and potassium (K) levels were applied as needed to maintain these nutrient levels in the high range based on an annual chemical soil test. The pH of the root zone was 6.8. Supplemental water was applied as needed to prevent visual wilt of the turf via gear-driven, pop-up heads arranged in a tight spacing that sustained uniform moisture conditions across the experimental area. Topdressing was prac-ticed at two-month intervals during the growing season at a rate of 0.16 m^3 100 m^{-2}, using the same mix composition as the underlying root zone. No turf cultivation or vertical cutting was practiced on the turfed plots, to avoid interplot genotype contamination.

Disease and insect problems were minimal, except for dollar spot (*Sclerotinia homoeocarpa* F.T. Bennett) which was allowed to develop, with no fungicide applications made during the 1993 growing season. A modest preventive fungicide program has been followed since 1995. No insecticides or herbicides have been applied. All emerging weeds were manually removed during the 1992 growing season. Subsequently after the turfs had fully stabilized, weeds were allowed to develop across the experimental area.

Assessment

Both turfgrass quality and morphological assessments were made. The turfgrass quality assessments involved visual estimates made by two F.I.G. Green Section Agronomists at intervals throughout the growing season. The visual estimates were based on a composite of two primary components: (a) uniformity of appearance and (b) shoot density. The rating scale used was 9 = best and 1 = poorest. A rating of 5.5 or higher represented an acceptable quality putting surface.

Morphological assessments were made in September of each growing season. They consisted of actual shoot density counts conducted on a 1,600 mm^2 area of turf. Measurements of lead width were based on a midpoint measurement of the second youngest leaf, with 10 leaves measured per replication. In addition, visual assess-ments were made of the comparative extent of moss and *Poa annua* invasion. All data were summarized at the end of each growing season and processed for statistical assessment involving the analyses of variance for the 12 older cultivars being separate from that for the five new cultivars.

Any occurrences of disease or insect damage were noted, including identification of the causal organism. If the turf damage was sufficiently uniform across the plot area, assessments were made as to the percent of turf area damaged. This occurred only in 1993 and involved dollar spot disease (*Sclerotinia homoeocarpa*). These data were of a unique quality, such that they are presented in a separate F.I.G., Green Section Final Research Report No. 201 (Croce et al., 1994).

RESULTS AND DISCUSSION

Turfgrass Quality

Visual estimates of turfgrass quality, although subjective, remain the best effective means of assessing the composite turfgrass quality at frequent intervals over a growing season. The primary components assessed are the shoot-leaf density, and the uniformity of leaf width, growth habit, and color. The specific color should be described and not judged as part of turfgrass quality in terms of a color preference. Turfgrass quality estimates above 5.5 indicate an acceptable quality putting green. The comparative seasonal means of visual turfgrass quality of 17 *Agrostis* cultivars maintained under closely mowed putting green conditions in a Mediterranean climate are shown in table 85.1 for 1992 through 1997.

After five full years of being maintained under closely maintained putting green conditions the turfgrass quality ranged from 7.95 down to 2.80. Ranking highest of the older cultivars in visual turfgrass quality after 5+ years were Providence, Penneagle, Southshore, PennLinks, and Penncross, with SR 1020, Cobra, and Putter not being significantly different. Ranking inferior and unacceptable as a putting green surface after 5+ years were Emerald, Seaside, and Astoria. Among the newer Penn series, the G-1, A-1, G-6, and G-2 all had turfgrass quality values ranking higher than Providence at the end of 5+ growing seasons.

The individual seasonal means varied from year-to-year, due to the influence of seasonal variations in climate. It should be noted that no control of dollar spot was practiced during the 1993 season and the height of cut was lowered from 4.8 to 4.0 mm at the start of 1995.

Shoot Density

A high shoot density usually is preferred for putting greens as it results in a more narrow leaf width and more vertical leaf orientation that contribute to a more uniform surface for ball roll. A high shoot density also results in the turf being more competitive against weed, moss, and algae invasion. In contrast, certain cultivars with a very high shoot density may tend to form a puffy surface over time, especially if not mowed daily at a very close mowing height of less than 4 mm. The comparative shoot densities of 17 *Agrostis* cultivars maintained under closely mowed putting green conditions in a Mediterranean climate are shown in table 85.2 for 1993 through 1997.

The comparative shoot densities of the 13 most dense cultivars ranged from 1,522 to 3,003 shoots per square decimeter in 1997, a 1.97-fold differential. There was a decrease in shoot density from 1993 to 1994, except for Astoria and Seaside. This was most probably the result of a very modest fertilization program. The fertilization rate was adjusted upward in 1995, along with a lowering of the cutting height

Table 85.1   Comparative Seasonal Means of Visual Turfgrass Quality of Seventeen *Agrostis* Cultivars Maintained Under Closely Mowed Putting Green Conditions in a Mediterranean Climate

Genotype	Turfgrass quality annual season means (9-best; 1-poorest)					
	1992	1993	1994	1995	1996	1997
Providence	7.25	6.13	6.25	6.69	7.22	7.10 a
Penneagle	6.87	6.42	6.38	6.54	7.18	6.91 a
Southshore	—	6.38	6.49	6.81	7.18	6.86 a
PennLinks	7.01	6.15	5.88	6.45	6.99	6.57 a
Penncross	7.11	5.76	5.78	6.29	6.99	6.48 a
SR 1020	6.70	5.03	5.19	6.57	6.57	6.37 ab
Cobra	6.81	5.60	5.73	6.22	6.56	6.31 ab
Putter	7.15	6.15	5.89	6.40	6.69	6.29 ab
National	6.31	4.85	4.91	5.61	6.16	5.36 bc
Emerald	6.39	4.20	4.53	5.43	5.72	4.75 c
Seaside	5.18	3.41	3.87	4.58	4.38	3.61 d
Astoria	4.35	3.50	3.48	3.80	2.79	2.80 d
LSD value*	0.61	0.47	0.78	0.53	0.39	1.05
mean	6.46	5.30	5.37	5.95	6.20	5.78
Penn G-1	7.48	7.22	6.89	7.13	8.10	7.95 a
Penn A-1	7.46	7.37	6.65	6.73	8.06	7.87 a
Penn G-6	7.34	6.72	6.80	6.94	7.38	7.54 ab
Penn G-2	6.80	6.54	6.54	7.33	7.86	7.40 ab
Seaside II	6.39	5.75	5.46	6.23	6.90	7.04 b
LSD value**	0.75	0.48	0.88	0.52	0.42	0.68
mean	7.10	6.72	6.47	6.87	7.66	7.56

*To determine the statistical differences among the above 12 cultivars, subtract one cultivar's mean from another cultivar's mean; a statistically significant difference occurs when this value is larger than the corresponding LSD value (LSD 0.05).

**To determine the statistical differences among the above five cultivars, follow the procedure described in (*).

Table 85.2   Comparative Annual Shoot Density Counts of Seventeen *Agrostis* Cultivars Maintained Under Closely Mowed Putting Green Conditions in a Mediterranean Climate

Cultivar	Shoot density count (shoots dm⁻²)				
	1993	1994	1995	1996	1997
PennLinks	1,504	1,301	1,553	1,793	2,186 a
Providence	1,425	1,093	1,395	1,799	2,080 a
Southshore	1,509	1,126	1,692	2,040	2,037 a
SR 1020	1,419	1,204	1,523	1,799	1,876 ab
Cobra	1,195	1,007	1,363	1,521	1,873 ab
Putter	1,272	1,093	1,356	1,681	1,814 ab
Penncross	1,022	987	1,358	1,642	1,631 b
Penneagle	1,240	1,088	1,383	1,651	1,522 b
National	1,013	759	1,156	1,320	—
Astoria	835	943	1,048	1,307	—
Seaside	755	765	1,020	1,268	—
Emerald	1,010	796	1,172	1,212	—
LSD value*	224	174	214	354	376
mean	1,183	1,014	1,335	1,587	1,877
Penn G-6	2,378	1,306	2,700	2,662	3,003 a
Penn A-1	2,240	1,540	2,325	2,656	2,868 a
Penn G-2	2,546	1,793	2,366	2,225	2,725 a
Penn G-1	2,612	1,902	2,228	2,912	2,675 a
Seaside II	2,053	1,309	1,475	2,762	2,550 a
LSD value**	650	259	538	534	1,333
mean	2,366	1,570	2,219	2,643	2,764

*To determine the statistical differences among the above 12 cultivars, subtract one cultivar's mean from another cultivar's mean; a statistically significant difference occurs when this value is larger than the corresponding LSD value (LSD 0.05).

**To determine the statistical differences among the above five cultivars, follow the procedure described in (*).

from 4.8 to 4.0 mm. Subsequently from 1995 through 1997 the shoot density for most cultivars increased, with a few exceptions over the 3 years. Ranking highest in shoot density among the older turfgrass cultivars after 5+ years were PennLinks, Providence, and Southshore, with SR 1020, Cobra, and Putter not being significantly different. All the newer Penn series cultivars were higher in shoot density after 5+ years.

The newer *Agrostis* cultivars sustained very high shoot densities under a close mowing height, which can be a positive from a quality playing surface standpoint. However, they may require new approaches in terms of cultural practices such as weekly turf cultivation by means of closely spaced, 6.4 mm, solid tines, plus periodic vertical cutting to properly manage the canopy biomass.

Leaf Blade Width

A narrow leaf blade width usually is associated with a uniform, fast surface for ball roll due to less leaf resistance. This assumes that the leaf blades among cultivars do not vary in stiffness, which is another component of resistance to ball roll. The comparative leaf width measurements of 17 *Agrostis* cultivars maintained under closely mowed putting green conditions in a Mediterranean climate are shown in table 85.3 for 1993 through 1996.

In 1996 the leaf blade widths among the 17 cultivars ranged from 0.62 to 0.92 mm. The most narrow leaf blade widths were found among the Penn series cultivars, ranging from 0.62 to 0.69 mm. These five cultivars also possessed the highest shoot densities. This contrasts with the older *Agrostis* cultivars where only SR 1020 and Southshore were under 0.75 mm, with the remainder being wider than 0.81 mm.

Poa Annua Invasion

Poa annua seed requires sunlight for germination. Thus, the higher the canopy density and biomass the less light will penetrate to the soil surface where the *Poa annua* seeds are located. In addition, a high shoot density provides greater competition to the emerging *Poa annua* seedlings. *Agrostis* cultivars vary in their ability to impair *Poa annua* invasion, which in turn affects the extent of herbicide use required for control. The comparative *Poa annua* invasions among 17 *Agrostis* cultivars maintained under closely mowed putting green conditions in a Mediterranean climate are shown in table 85.4 for the third through fifth years of the study.

The older *Agrostis* cultivars can be aligned in three groups in terms of the extent of *Poa annua* invasion, with Southshore, PennLinks, Providence, SR 1020, and Penneagle exhibiting the least *Poa annua* invasion, with Penncross, Putter, and Cobra being intermediate after 5+ years. National, Emerald, Seaside, and Astoria exhibited the greatest *Poa annua* invasion, being 12.5, 17.5, 35, and 50%, respectively, after 5+ growing seasons. Ranking lowest in *Poa annua* invasion as a group were the Penn series, which also possessed the highest shoot densities.

Generally, those cultivars with higher shoot densities exhibited the least proneness to *Poa annua* invasion. Over the third through fifth years the amount of *Poa annua* tended to increase for most of the *Agrostis* cultivars.

Table 85.3   Comparative Annual Leaf Width Measurements of Seventeen *Agrostis* Cultivars Maintained Under Closely Mowed Putting Green Conditions in a Mediterranean Climate

Cultivar	Turfgrass leaf width (mm)			
	1993	1994	1995	1996
SR 1020	0.84	0.80	0.77	0.73 a
Southshore	0.84	0.84	0.77	0.74 a
Providence	0.96	0.85	0.87	0.81 ab
Putter	0.94	0.86	0.78	0.82 abc
Penncross	0.89	0.85	0.83	0.85 bc
PennLinks	0.93	0.80	0.81	0.85 bc
Penneagle	0.95	0.96	0.86	0.87 bc
Seaside	0.96	0.90	0.97	0.87 bc
Cobra	0.93	0.88	0.88	0.89 bc
Astoria	0.96	0.85	0.86	0.90 bc
National	0.94	0.90	0.85	0.91 c
Emerald	0.95	0.96	0.88	0.92 c
LSD value*	0.10	0.05	0.09	0.09
mean	0.92	0.87	0.84	0.85
Seaside II	0.76	0.79	0.79	0.62 a
Penn G-6	0.73	0.70	0.62	0.63 a
Penn G-2	0.73	0.63	0.70	0.66 a
Penn A-1	0.75	0.70	0.68	0.67 a
Penn G-1	0.69	0.72	0.69	0.69 a
LSD value**	0.18	0.16	0.13	0.08
mean	0.73	0.71	0.70	0.65

*To determine the statistical differences among the above 12 cultivars, subtract one cultivar's mean from another cultivar's mean; a statistically significant difference occurs when this value is larger than the corresponding LSD value (LSD 0.05).

**To determine the statistical differences among the above five cultivars, follow the procedure described in (*).

Table 85.4   Comparative *Poa annua* Invasion Estimates of Seventeen *Agrostis* Cultivars Maintained Under Closely Mowed Putting Green Conditions in a Mediterranean Climate

Cultivar	Percent of turf cover as *Poa annua*		
	1995	1996	1997
Southshore	0.8	2.5	2.0 a
PennLinks	2.0	4.3	2.8 a
Providence	1.5	2.8	3.0 a
SR 1020	1.0	2.0	3.5 a
Penneagle	0.5	2.0	3.5 a
Penncross	2.3	5.3	7.0 ab
Putter	3.0	3.8	7.7 ab
Cobra	4.8	5.3	8.0 ab
National	3.3	6.8	12.5 bc
Emerald	4.0	10.0	17.5 c
Seaside	9.3	20.0	35.0 d
Astoria	15.0	41.3	50.0 e
LSD value*	3.76	5.89	8.47
mean	4.00	8.80	12.70
Penn G-1	0.5	1.0	1.2 a
Penn A-1	1.0	1.0	1.3 a
Penn G-6	0.0	1.0	1.3 a
Penn G-2	0.5	1.0	1.8 ab
Seaside II	3.0	3.0	2.1 b
LSD value**	0.70	0.66	0.70
mean	1.00	1.40	1.50

*To determine the statistical differences among the above 12 cultivars, subtract one cultivar's mean from another cultivar's mean; a statistically significant difference occurs when this value is larger than the corresponding LSD value (LSD 0.05).

**To determine the statistical differences among the above five cultivars, follow the procedure described in (*).

Table 85.5   Comparative Moss Invasion Estimates of Seventeen *Agrostis* Cultivars Maintained Under Closely Mowed Putting Green Conditions in a Mediterranean Climate

| Cultivar | Percent of turf cover as moss | | | |
	1994	1995	1996	mean
Providence	3.3	8.8	10.0	7.4
SR 1020	6.0	10.0	9.3	8.4
Penneagle	7.0	13.0	7.5	9.2
Putter	7.3	10.5	10.0	9.3
Southshore	5.3	9.8	15.5	10.2
PennLinks	10.0	9.3	16.8	12.0
Cobra	11.7	11.8	17.5	13.7
National	16.7	18.8	12.5	16.0
Penncross	13.3	20.0	15.0	16.1
Emerald	26.7	21.3	16.3	21.4
Seaside	30.0	26.3	18.9	25.1
Astoria	54.0	27.5	35.0	38.8
LSD value*	13.06	8.77	8.54	
mean	15.90	15.60	15.40	
Penn G-6	2.5	5.0	4.0	3.8
Penn G-1	1.0	9.0	4.0	4.7
Penn G-2	2.5	7.5	7.5	5.8
Penn A-1	2.5	16.5	2.5	6.2
Seaside II	6.5	15.0	9.0	10.2
LSD value**	3.35	5.54	3.60	
mean	3.00	10.00	5.40	

*To determine the statistical differences among the above 12 cultivars, subtract one cultivar's mean from another cultivar's mean; a statistically significant difference occurs when this value is larger than the corresponding LSD value (LSD 0.05).

**To determine the statistical differences among the above five cultivars, follow the procedure described in (*).

Moss Invasion

A moss invasion is most severe generally in those turfs with a thinned turf canopy that allows radiant light penetration to the soil surface. The comparative moss invasion among 17 *Agrostis* cultivars maintained under closely mowed putting green conditions in a Mediterranean climate are shown in table 85.5 for the third through fifth years of the study.

Generally, *Agrostis* cultivars with a high shoot density had the lowest moss invasion, while those with the lowest shoot densities had the highest moss invasion. It can also be noted that the extent of moss invasion varied from year to year within individual cultivars. There were no distinct trends across the cultivars as a whole. The greatest moss invasion generally occurred in June in most years. The cultivars that were particularly prone to moss invasion included National, Pennross, Emerald, Seaside, and Astoria. In contrast, the new cultivars Penn G-6, Penn G-1, and Penn G-2 were characterized by a moss invasion of less than ten percent in all three years.

ACKNOWLEDGMENTS

This turfgrass research initiative was developed and sponsored by the Federazione Italiana Golf under the leadership of President Giuseppe Silva and Roberto Livraghi. Special appreciation is given to the Torino Golf Club under the leadership of Presidents Alberto Brignone and Sergio Pininfarina and its Club Secretary Renato Bianco and Golf Course Superintendent V. Merlo Pich for providing the host experimental site and day-to-day turf maintenance of the research putting green.

References

Beard, J.B. (1982). *Turf Management for Golf Courses*. Macmillan Company, New York, NY, USA. p. 642.
Croce, P., Mocioni, M., Pich, V.M., and Beard, J.B. (1993). *Comparative dollar spot susceptibility of seventeen bentgrass (Agrostis spp.) cultivars under putting green conditions*. Federazione Italiana Golf, Green Section—Final Research Report No. 201. p. 4.
Croce, P., Mocioni, M., Pich, V.M., and Beard, J.B. (1994). *Bentgrass (Agrostis spp.) cultivar characteristics for 1993 under closely mowed putting green conditions near Torino, Italy.* Federazione Italiana Golf, Green Section—Research Progress Report No. 301. p. 9.

CHAPTER 86

Long-Term Differences in Thatch Development, Soil Bulk Density, and Water Infiltration in Bentgrass Fairway Turf Related to Core Aerification Method and Intensity

S.E. Brauen, W.J. Johnston, and R.L. Goss
Department of Crop and Soil Sciences, Washington State University, Puyallup, WA, USA

Shallow core aerification is an effective method of relieving surface compaction in turf and enhancing thatch decomposition, rooting depth, stress tolerance, turf uniformity, and water infiltration. A negative effect may be the development of a compaction zone below the depth of tine penetration. Hollow-tined coring (HTC), solid-tined coring (STC), and alternate hollow/solid-tined coring (H/STC) were conducted for five years at zero, two, four, or six times annually from March to October on an established bentgrass [mixed stand of colonial bentgrass (*Agrostis tenuis* Sibth.) and creeping bentgrass (*Agrostis palustris* Huds.)] fairway turf at Puyallup, Washington. The objectives of the study were to identify the effects of coring methods on thatch development, soil bulk density below the level of tine penetration, and water infiltration. Thatch levels as measured by depth, ashed dry weight, and density after five years were not different between aerification methods. Aerification intensity (number of times core aerification was carried out annually) was effective in reducing the rate of increase of thatch depth and ashed dry weight. Six aerifications annually were insufficient to keep thatch depth in check relative to pre-study levels. HTC was more effective than STC or H/STC systems in controlling net change of thatch ashed dry weight. Thatch density increased with aerification intensity. Soil bulk density at 10 to 13 cm below the compressed turf surface was not changed by method of aerification, but increased as aerification intensity increased. Field-saturated hydraulic conductivity decreased as aerification intensity increased. STC was more favorable than HTC in retaining the ability of the soil to conduct water in the potential compaction zone below aerification depth under a hydraulic potential gradient.

Keywords: Coring, field-saturated hydraulic conductivity, hollow tine, solid tine.

INTRODUCTION

Turf cultivation by core aerification has many beneficial and few negative effects on turf. Assisting in thatch control, relieving soil surface compaction, improving uniform water infiltration, and improving surface aeration and rooting are often observed (Carrow et al., 1987; Erusha et al., 1989; Dunn et al., 1995; Lederboer and Skogley, 1967; Shildrick, 1985; White and Dickens, 1984). Since thatch substantially increases pesticide sorption, reduction in thatch by coring may increase the potential for pesticides to move off site (Dell et al., 1994). Soil compaction in heavily trafficked areas of golf fairways is often a problem, especially on heavy, wet soils, as often occur in the Pacific Northwest, USA. Aerification with hollow tines sometimes followed by sand topdressing is commonly used to relieve this stress, but the aerification frequency needed, the turf disturbance caused, and the time and labor required are not always appreciated. Use of solid tines rather than hollow tines has been used to some degree to overcome some of the labor requirements and reduce surface disturbance. However, core aerification may enhance turfgrass injury due to stress, increase weed establishment, decrease turf quality through disruption of the turf surface, and possibly slow water percolation through creation of a compacted zone of soil below the depth of coring tines (Erusha et al., 1989; Murphy et al., 1993; Shildrick, 1985). A compaction zone, if present, may be dissimilar between hollow-tine coring (HTC) and solid-tine coring (STC) due to the differences in downward forces imposed by tine structure on soils. This study was designed to measure the effects of HTC and STC over several years on thatch development, soil bulk density, and hydraulic conductivity in fairway-type bentgrass turf.

EXPERIMENTAL METHODS

The study was conducted on a Puyallup fine sandy loam soil (coarse-loamy, mixed mesic, Fluventic Haploxerolls) (Cogger and Kennedy, 1992) with a composition of clay, 7.3%; silt, 24.7%; and sand, 68%, at the Turfgrass Field Research Laboratory at the Washington State University-Puyallup Research and Extension Center. Core aerification was performed by HTC or STC on a well-established, mixed colonial bentgrass (*Agrostis tenuis* Sibth.) and creeping bentgrass (*Agrostis palustris* Huds.) fairway turf. The turf consisted of 5% to 10% annual bluegrass (*Poa annua* L.). At the beginning of aerification treatments in 1983, there was 4.1 to 4.8 cm of thatch (SD 0.3 cm). The turf was routinely clipped at 1.9 cm, fertilized at 147 kg ha[-1] annually with 21-7-14, and irrigated to prevent stress. A factorial array of aerification treatments was applied in a completely randomized design in four replications for five years. A Greensaire II vertical action aerifier (Ryan/Ransomes America Corp., Lincoln, NB) was used in aerification and was equipped with 12.7-mm diameter hollow or solid tines and operated so tine aerification holes were spaced 5.1×7.6 cm apart. Intensity of aerification treatments consisted of zero, two, four, or six aerifications annually between March and October via HTC, STC, or alternate H/STC. Plot aerifications were applied at the following times: two times annually during March and October; four times annually during March, May, August, and

October; and six times annually during March, May, June, August, September, and October. Aerification treatments were applied when soil moisture was below field capacity and never when the soil was considered to be wet. Soil cores following HTC were removed and turfs, including non-aerified treatments, were topdressed with 823 hl ha^{-1} of sand (1 to 2 mm, 3.6%; 0.5 to 1.0 mm, 32.2%; 0.25 to 0.5 mm, 52.9%; 0.1 to 0.25 mm, 8.4%; and <0.1 mm, 1.3%) following each core aerification treatment.

Thatch depth and ashed dry weight estimates were made from two 10-cm diameter cores from each experimental unit (plot) on July 12, 1983, and from four cores per plot on November 11, 1988. Thatch depth was estimated from six random measures from each compressed core (1.7 kPa) and thatch density calculated as (ashed dry weight)/(volume of compressed thatch). Thatch cores were oven dried at 38 C for 96 h, weighed, ashed at 538 C for 12 h, and reweighed to determine ashed dry weight. Field-saturated hydraulic conductivity estimates were made during July and August 1989 from three 6.35-cm-deep wells per plot using a Guelph permeameter (Soil Moisture Equipment Corp., Santa Barbara, CA) modified to maintain well head heights in surface thatch (Reynolds and Elrick, 1985a and 1985b).

RESULTS AND DISCUSSION

After five years of core aerification treatments, there were no differences associated with method of aerification on thatch depth, ashed dry weight, or thatch density compared to initial measurements. Yet, the net increase in ashed dry weight of thatch between initial and final levels was different between coring methods. HTC was more effective than STC in mitigating net thatch buildup (figure 86.1). The number

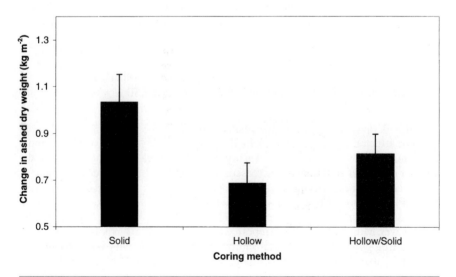

Figure 86.1   Net change during 5 years in ashed dry weight of thatch as affected by coring method. Bar = 1 SD.

of aerifications annually was highly effective in controlling net change in thatch depth and ashed dry weight (table 86.1). However, six corings annually did not completely maintain thatch depth or ashed dry weight at pre-study levels. Thatch density increased markedly with increasing intensity of aerification over the five-year period. High density thatch provides a more tortuous path for water, which increases resistance and allows for greater infiltration and reduced surface runoff from golf course bentgrass fairways (Linde et al., 1995). No significant interaction in thatch measurements occurred between aerification intensity and aerification method. Cores from HTC were removed from the plots after aerification and before sand topdressing. Since HTC, to some extent H/STC, and increasing the number of annual core aerifications were effective in reducing net thatch development, it seemed that physical removal of cores was an important factor controlling thatch development in bentgrass fairway turf. Improved soil biological activity due to frequent aerification plus sand topdressing following each aerification may have been important in reducing thatch in these treatments.

Table 86.1   Net Change in Bentgrass Thatch Depth, Thatch Ashed Dry Weight, and Thatch Density After Five Years Due to 0 to 6 Core Aerifications Per Year

Number of annual core aerifications	Net change in thatch		
	Depth	Ashed dry weight	Density
	cm	kg m^{-2}	kg m^{-3}
0	3.0 a	1.6 a	−2.7 d
2	2.7 ab	1.0 b	2.5 c
4	2.2 bc	0.6 c	6.4 b
6	2.0 c	0.2 d	11.0 a

Mean of 36, 10-cm cores averaged over coring methods. Means within columns not followed by the same letter are different by Fisher's protected LSD ($P = 0.05$).

Soil bulk density, following five years of coring, at the 10- to 13-cm soil depth was not affected by aerification method or by increasing the intensity of annual aerification. However, soil bulk density steadily increased numerically as the number of annual aerifications increased, which may indicate the development of a compaction zone below the depth of tine penetration over a period of time (figure 86.2). Field-saturated hydraulic conductivity below the aerification zone (10 cm below the turf surface) was higher with STC than HTC or H/STC (figure 86.3).

However, Murphy et al. (1993) reported that when aerifying a moist or wet loamy sand putting green soil profile that saturated water conductivity was 49% greater with HTC than STC. They also report that STC provided short-term benefits, required repeated applications, and exhibited the potential for development of a cultivation pan. Field-saturated hydraulic conductivity was, in general, inversely related to the intensity of aerification annually (figure 86.4). Two corings annually had a marked reduction in hydraulic conductivity compared to the control with little additional decrease caused by additional coring annually. White and Dickens (1984) have also reported that four to six core aerifications annually are required to have a major effect on thatch or related soil properties.

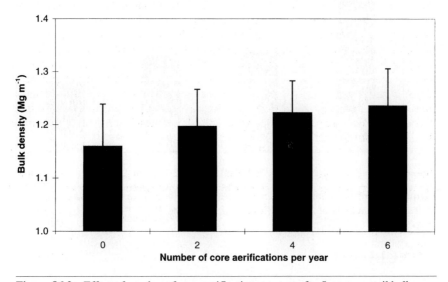

Figure 86.2   Effect of number of core aerifications per year for 5 years on soil bulk density 10 to 13 cm below the surface of compressed bentgrass turf. Bar = 1 SD.

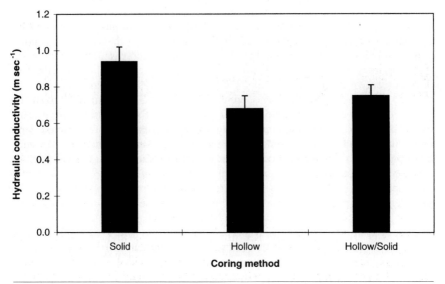

Figure 86.3   Effect of core aerification method for 5 years on field-saturated hydraulic conductivity of soil below the aerification zone. Bar = 1 SD.

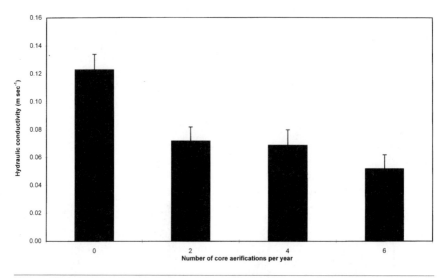

Figure 86.4   Effect of number of annual aerifications for 5 years on field-saturated hydraulic conductivity of soil below the aerification zone. Bar = 1 SD.

CONCLUSIONS

HTC was more effective than STC in controlling net change of thatch ashed dry weight over a five-year period. H/STC tended to be intermediate in performance. Two aerifications annually had a positive impact on net change in thatch; however, six aerifications annually were required to have a major effect on thatch or soil properties. Soil bulk density below the depth of tine penetration was not changed by method of coring. However, soil bulk density below the aerification zone consistently increased as the number of annual corings increased, which suggests that long-term use of core aerification, especially in heavy soils, may result in development of a compacted zone. Field-saturated hydraulic conductivity was reduced by increasing the number of annual corings, but STC retained the ability of soil to conduct water through the soil area 10 cm below the turf surface to a greater extent than HTC. Hydraulic conductivity values suggest that a compacted zone below the depth of tine penetration may be an earlier factor with HTC than with STC, particularly when STC is conducted on soils that are dry and easily fracture in the compaction zone.

References

Carrow, R.N., B.J. Johnson, and R.E. Burns. 1987. Thatch and quality of Tifway bermudagrass turf in relation to fertility and cultivation. *Agronomy Journal* 79:524–530.

Cogger, C.G., and P.E. Kennedy. 1992. Seasonally saturated soils in the Puget lowland. I. Saturation, reduction, and color patterns. *Soil Science* 153:421–433.

Dell, C.J., C.S. Throssell, M. Bischoff, and R.F. Turco. 1994. Estimation of sorption coefficients for fungicides in soil and turfgrass thatch. *Journal of Environmental Quality* 23:92–96.

Dunn, J.H., D.D. Minner, B.F. Fresenburh, S.S. Bughrara, and C.H. Hohnstater. 1995. Influence of core aerification, topdressing, and nitrogen on mat, roots, and quality of 'Meyer' zoysiagrass. *Agronomy Journal* 87:891–894.

Erusha, K.S., R.C. Shearman, and D.M. Bishop. 1989. Thatch prevention and control. *Turfgrass Bulletin* 10(2):10–11.

Lederboer, F.B., and C.R. Skogley. 1967. Investigations into the nature of thatch and methods for its decomposition. *Agronomy Journal* 59:320–323.

Linde, D.T., T.L. Watschke, A.R. Jarrett, and J.A. Borger. 1995. Surface runoff assessment from creeping bentgrass and perennial ryegrass turf. *Agronomy Journal* 87:176–182.

Murphy, J.A., P.E. Rieke, and A.E. Erickson. 1993. Core cultivation of a putting green with hollow and solid tines. *Agronomy Journal* 85:1-9.

Reynolds, W.D., and D.E. Elrick. 1985a. In situ measurement of field-saturated hyraulic conductivity, sorptivity, and the alpha-parameter using the Guelph permeameter. *Soil Science* 140:292–302.

Reynolds, W.D., and D.E. Elrick. 1985b. A method for simultaneous in situ measurements in the vadose zone of field-saturated hydraulic conductivity, sorptivity and the conductivity-pressure head relationship. *Groundwater Monitoring Review* 6(1):84–95.

Shildrick, J.P. 1985. Thatch: A review with special reference to UK golf courses. *Journal Sports Turf Research Institute* 61:8–25.

White, R.H., and R. Dickens. 1984. Thatch accumulation in bermudagrass as influenced by cultural practices. *Agronomy Journal* 76:19–22.

CHAPTER 87

Relative Effectiveness of Soil Acidification and Pesticide Application as Methods to Control Earthworm Casting on Golf Courses

S.W. Baker, D.J. Binns, and A. Cook
Sports Turf Research Institute, Bingley, UK

Heavy rates of casting by earthworms can cause muddy, moisture retentive, uneven and weed-infested playing surfaces on golf courses. Two methods of control of casting were examined: first, modification of soil pH using sulphur and, second, chemical control using either carbendazim or gamma-HCH + thiophanate-methyl (γHCH+TM). On a sandy loam soil with a pH of 5.5, casting was effectively eliminated for five months using carbendazim and γHCH+TM. At this site the effect of sulphur, applied in a powdered form, was not significant at $P = 0.05$, although at the highest application rate (20 g m^{-2} sulphur) casting rates were reduced to 70% of those on untreated turf. On a clay loam soil, 40 g m^{-2} of sulphur, applied as an aqueous suspension, reduced the pH of the surface 25 mm from 5.8 to 5.2, and the pH of the 25–75 mm depth fell from 6.7 to 6.4. Casting was considerably reduced by sulphur and pesticide applications and one year after the initial applications, rates of casting relative to the untreated turf were 21% for carbendazim, 25% for γHCH+TM, and 48% and 36% respectively for sulphur applied at 20 and 40 g m^{-2}. There were problems of scorch when sulphur was applied as two dressings of 20 g m^{-2}. It is suggested that on suitable sites, careful use of sulphur could reduce the need for, or frequency of, pesticide applications.

Keywords: Earthworms, casting, sulphur, carbendazim, gamma-HCH + thiophanate-methyl.

INTRODUCTION

Until the 1960s casting by earthworms was a significant problem affecting the quality of turf on golf courses (Escritt and Arthur 1948, Jefferson 1958). However, the subsequent widespread use of chlordane gave relatively long-term control of casting (Lidgate 1966) and thus for two or three decades the problem of smeared casts producing uneven, water retentive, and sometimes weed-affected surfaces was not a major issue facing greenkeeping staff. In the United Kingdom, the approvals for use of chlordane, a persistent, organochlorine material, were revoked in 1992, and alternative methods of earthworm control on golf courses have to be considered.

There are two main strategies for earthworm control on areas of sports turf, one being based on pesticide application, the other based on cultural practices, most notably the manipulation of food supply and soil pH (Kirby and Baker 1995). Under current United Kingdom legislation (Anonymous 1997) three pesticides are still permitted for use on turf/amenity grass, these being carbendazim, gamma-HCH + thiophanate-methyl (γHCH+TM) and carbaryl, and of these the first two materials appear to have greater persistency of control (Baker et al. in preparation).

Earthworms are highly sensitive to the pH of the soil (Lee 1985) and on turf Jefferson (1956) has shown that earthworms are scarce on acid soils (pH<5.0) but populations rise with increasing pH, reaching maximum numbers at pH values between 6.5 and 7.0 before decreasing again on more alkaline soils. In particular, two of the main casting species of earthworm, *Apporectodea longa* and *A. caliginosa*, are intolerant of acid conditions (Satchell 1955). Acidifying fertilisers such as ammonium sulphate or ammonium nitrate are known to reduce earthworm activity (Escritt and Lidgate 1964, Potter et al. 1985) and reductions in casting have also been associated with the use of iron sulphate (Jefferson 1961, Escritt and Legg 1969). Sulphur has also been used to acidify soil and, for example, Goss et al. (1977) found no earthworm activity on their sulphur-treated plots. More recently, Baker et al. (1996) examined the effects of soil acidification on earthworm activity using sulphur and aluminium sulphate. Total applications of approximately 65 g m^{-2} of aluminium sulphate were required to reduce casting by approximately 50% on a sandy clay loam soil with an initial pH of 5.7.

The objective of the current study was to assess the relative effectiveness of two pesticides (carbendazim and γHCH+TM) and soil acidification using sulphur on earthworm casting and to assess any effects on turf quality.

MATERIALS AND METHODS

Research Sites

The study was carried out at two sites: firstly on the practice ground at Silkstone Golf Club, Silkstone, South Yorkshire (NGR SE304060) and, secondly, in an area adjacent to a green at Bracken Ghyll Golf Club, Addingham, West Yorkshire (NGR SE068504). The soil at Silkstone was a clay loam with a pH of 6.7 in the upper 150 mm of soil. The site at Addingham was a sandy loam with a pH in the top 150 mm of 5.5. At both sites, preliminary assessments were made to identify areas with relatively heavy and uniform rates of casting activity.

Experimental Design

At both sites, the trial was a factorial design incorporating pesticide and sulphur treatments in four randomised blocks. The pesticide treatments consisted of an untreated control and single applications of carbendazim at 8 litre ha^{-1} and γHCH+TM (41.7% w/w thiophanate-methyl, 5.0% w/w gamma-HCH) at 10 litre ha^{-1}. The material was applied by watering can using 5.0 liter and 8.1 liter of water for each 9 m^2 plot for carbendazim and γHCH+TM respectively. The sulphur treatments at Addingham were based on material in a powdered form. At Silkstone, the material (Headland Sulphur) was applied as an aqueous suspension containing 800 g litre^{-1} of elemental sulphur (58.8% w/w). This is based on finely milled particles and contains surfactants to aid efficient application. At both sites, the elemental sulphur was applied at rate of 0, 5, 10, and 20 g m^{-2} and plot size was 3 m×3 m. At Silkstone, the sulphur was applied on 20 November 1995 and washed in using approximately 4 litre m^{-2} of water applied by watering can. This was helped by light rain the following night. A second application of sulphur applied at the same rates was made on 27/28 March 1996. The applications of carbendazim and γHCH+TM were made on 22 November 1995. At Addingham, the sulphur was applied on 1 November 1995 and washed in using approximately 4 litre m^{-2} of water applied by watering can. The carbendazim and γHCH+TM was applied on the same date.

Data Collection and Analysis

Rates of casting were assessed by counting the number of casts within a 1.5 m × 1.5 m frame quadrant placed centrally within each plot. Monthly assessments were carried out throughout the autumn, winter, and early spring. No attempt was made to record casting during the summer when casting activity is generally very low.

Soil pH was measured at Silkstone using cores taken on 19 March 1997. The cores were divided into depths of 0–25 mm, 25–75 mm, and 75–150 mm. The soil material was screened through a 2 mm sieve and pH was measured using a glass reference electrode after equilibration of 20 ml of soil with 50 ml of distilled water.

Visual appraisal of turfgrass quality was made on a number of dates by two observers acting independently using a 1–10 scale, 10 = best. Values below 5 are considered unacceptable. On some dates, visual assessments were supported by measurements of reflectance ratio using the principle described by Haggar et al. (1983). Four measurements were made in each plot.

Data collection at Silkstone was carried out for two years, but the trial at Addingham had to be abandoned in October 1996 because of changes in the position of the semi-rough during the summer months.

The data were examined using analysis of variance and differences in treatment means were identified using the least significant difference (LSD) at P = 0.05.

RESULTS

Rates of Casting

On the sandy loam soil at Addingham the main effect on casting rates was brought about by the application of carbendazim and γHCH+TM (table 87.1). Twenty-three days after the initial application, casting rates on plots treated with both pesticides had fallen to less than 8% of rates on the control plots. For all subsequent measurements up to March 1996 the treated plots were effectively free from casting

Table 87.1   Effect on Applications of Carbendazim and γHCH + TM on Casting Rates at Addingham

Date	Casts m^{-2}		
	Control	Carbendazim	γHCH + TM
23 November 95	41	3	3
18 December 95	35	Tr	Tr
18 January 96	39	0	Tr
29 February 96	44	Tr	Tr
22 March 96	27	Tr	Tr

Tr = trace (<0.5 casts m^{-2})

Note: LSD values are not presented because of the highly skewed nature of some of the data sets.

activity with no more than 0.5 casts m^{-2} being recorded. No significant effects of sulphur application were recorded, although at the highest rate (20 g m^{-2} of sulphur) there was some evidence of a reduction in casting. For those plots where no pesticides were applied, casting rates on the 5, 10, and 20 g m^{-2} sulphur treatments were respectively 89%, 98%, and 70% of values recorded for the zero sulphur treatment, when averaged over all five sampling dates.

On the clay loam soil at Silkstone both pesticide and sulphur treatments brought about major reductions in casting (figure 87.1). In December 1995 rates of casting were particularly high, with the untreated plots having 76 casts m^{-2}. On the same date, casting rates for carbendazim and γHCH+TM averaged 21 and 19 casts m^{-2}, while casting rates on the sulphur-treated plots ranged from 14–28 casts m^{-2}. Results averaged for the assessments of January–March 1996 showed a good level of control on the plots treated with carbendazim and γHCH+TM, with values averaging 5% and 6% respectively of the untreated control. For those plots where no pesticides were applied there was a progressive decrease in casting activity as the rate of sulphur application increased. For plots receiving 10 and 20 g m^{-2} of sulphur, casting rates were 20% and 15% respectively of the untreated control.

For both the pesticide and sulphur applications there was a progressive increase in casting activity over time. For results averaged over the period October–December 1996 (i.e., approximately one year after application), casting rates for the carbendazim and γHCH+TM treatment were 21% and 25% of the untreated control and corresponding figures for 20 g m^{-2} and 40 g m^{-2} of sulphur were 48% and 36% respectively. By the autumn of 1997 there was still a significant, although much reduced, effect of the carbendazim and γHCH+TM treatments but no significant effect of the sulphur applications was observed.

Soil pH

Soil pH data for the Silkstone site from March 1997 show a reduction in pH with increasing additions of sulphur for the upper layers, although not at the 75–150 mm

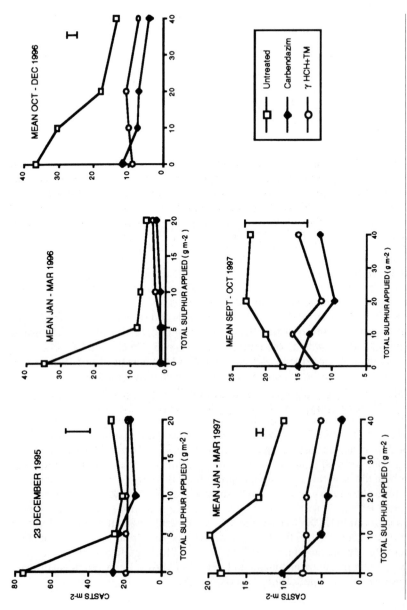

Figure 87.1   Changes in casting rates at Silkstone in relation to pesticide and sulphur applications. (Note: an LSD value for January to March 1996 is not shown as the data were highly skewed.)

Table 87.2   Soil pH at Silkstone in Relation to Total Sulphur Applied (March 1997)

Depth (mm)	Total sulphur applied (g m^{-2})				
	0	10	20	40	LSD (5%)
0–25	5.8	5.7	5.3	5.2	0.23
25–75	6.7	6.6	6.6	6.4	0.14
75–150	7.0	6.9	6.9	6.9	NS

NS = Not significant.

depth (table 87.2). For the 0–25 mm depth, pH fell to 5.2 with 40 g m^{-2} of sulphur compared to 5.8 where no sulphur was applied. The corresponding figures for the 25–75 mm depth were a reduction from 6.7 to 6.4. A significant reduction of pH was also recorded for the γHCH+TM treatment at the 0–25 mm depth, i.e., a value of 5.3 compared to 5.7 for the untreated control (data not shown). No significant differences were recorded lower in the profile or with carbendazim.

Turf Quality

There were no apparent effects of either the sulphur or pesticide treatments on turf quality at Addingham, however there was a significant decrease in visual scores of turf quality at Silkstone, especially at the highest sulphur rate (table 87.3). Reflectance ratio measurements at Silkstone in February 1996 and January 1997 suggested a significant decrease in the amount of green leaf tissue with increasing applications

Table 87.3   Visual Assessment of Turfgrass Quality in Relation to Application of Sulphur at Different Rates (Visual Score 1–10 scale, 10 = best)

Site and date	No. of applications of sulphur	Rate of sulphur (g m^{-2})				
		0	5	10	20	LSD (5%)
Silkstone						
28 February 96	1	7.3	7.3	6.3	6.1	0.35
20 December 96	2	6.2	6.1	5.9	4.2	0.47
23 January 27	2	6.0	5.9	5.8	4.6	0.41
15 September 97	2	5.6	5.5	5.0	4.6	0.49
Addingham						
29 February 96	1	8.3	8.1	8.0	8.1	NS

NS = not significant.

of sulphur (data not shown). A visual assessment of live grass cover at Silkstone in July 1996 suggested a small decrease in live grass cover when the total amount of sulphur applied increased from zero to 20 g m^{-2} (ground cover figures 85% and 80% respectively). However, for plots where a total of 40 g m^{-2} of sulphur had been applied in two applications, there was a highly significant reduction in grass cover to 66%, with a notable invasion of broad-leaved weeds, especially clover, into areas that had been weakened by scorch.

In general, there was no significant effect of the pesticide treatments on scores of turf quality. However, in February 1996 significant effects were recorded with average scores of 6.3 for the control plots, 6.9 for carbendazim, and 7.2 for γHCH+TM. On the same date, reflectance ratio values were significantly higher on the pesticide-treated areas than on the control plots. It is not possible to be certain that these higher visual scores and reflectance ratio values associated with the pesticide applications represented a significant improvement in grass quality or were an artifact of the reduction in casting.

DISCUSSION

There appeared to be differences in response to the pesticide and sulphur applications at the two sites. With both carbendazim and γHCH+TM virtually no casting was recorded in the five months of monitoring at Addingham. At Silkstone, control over a similar time period was good, with casting rates after five months being 4% and 6% of the untreated plots for carbendazim and γHCH+TM respectively. In general, there was no significant difference in the level of control by carbendazim and γHCH+TM. It should be noted, however, that carbendazim was applied at the relatively high rate of 8 litre ha^{-1} which is normally used for disease control rather than specifically for worm cast control, for which a rate of 4 litre ha^{-1} is recommended.

The response to sulphur varied between the two sites and may have been a result of both site conditions, particularly existing pH, and the form of sulphur used. At Silkstone, the initial pH was 5.8 for the 0–25 mm depth and over 6.5 for the underlying layers. In contrast, the initial pH at Addingham was lower, i.e., 5.5 averaged through the top 150 mm. The effect of a given quantity of sulphur on earthworm casting may be greater on more alkaline soils because of a proportionately greater reduction in pH or because populations of casting earthworm species respond more to reductions in pH when pH is around 6.5 (Jefferson 1961).

At Silkstone there was a gradual increase in casting activity over time after both the pesticide and sulphur treatments. The gradual loss of the effect of pesticide applications on casting activity is well documented (see Kirby and Baker 1995), but the increase in earthworm activity on the sulphur-treated plots is perhaps more surprising. In the earlier study by Baker et al. (1996) there was little evidence of loss of effectiveness of sulphur applications over time. As neither alkaline irrigation water or alkaline fertiliser were used on the practice area at Silkstone, the main possibilities are either conversion of the sulphur to sulphuric acid and subsequent leaching from the surface or a reduction in surface pH because of casting by earthworms gradually bringing more alkaline material (e.g., pH 6.9 for the 75–150 mm depth) to the surface. This would suggest that on some sites further applications of sulphur may ultimately be needed. However, on most sites soil acidification should have a relatively permanent effect on earthworm populations rather than the more transient effect of carbendazim or γHCH+TM. As such, the use of soil acidification on suitable soils may reduce the need for, or the frequency of, pesticide applications. There are, however, possible problems associated with sulphur application, such as scorch or long-term effects on sward quality. In the light of differences in response to sulphur application recorded in this study and previous work (Baker et al. 1996), information is needed from a greater range of soils on the effects of acidification on earthworm activity and sward quality.

ACKNOWLEDGMENTS

The authors wish to thank the Royal and Ancient Golf Club of St. Andrews for financial support for this work.

References

Anonymous. (1997). *The UK Pesticide Guide*. CAB International/British Corp Protection Council, p. 645.

Baker, S.W., Hunt, J.A., and Kirby, E.C. (1996). The effect of soil acidification on casting by earthworms. I. Preliminary trials using sulphur and aluminium sulphate. *J. Sports Turf Res. Inst.* 72:25–35.

Escritt, J.R. and Arthur, J.H. (1948). Earthworm control. *J. Board Greenkeeping Res.* 7(24):162–172.

Escritt, J.R. and Lidgate, H.J. (1964). Report on fertiliser trials. *J. Sports Turf Res. Inst.* 40:7–42.

Goss, R.L., Brauen, S.E., Gould, C.J., and Orton, S.P. (1977). Effects of sulphur on bentgrass turf. *Sulphur in Agriculture* 1:7–11.

Haggar, R.J., Stent, C.J., and Isaac, S. (1983). A prototype hand-held sprayer for killing weeds, activated by spectral differences in crop/weed canopies. *J. Agric. Engng. Res.* 28:349–358.

Jefferson, P. (1956). Studies on the earthworms of turf. B. Earthworms and soil. *J. Sports Turf Res. Inst.* 9(32):166–179.

Jefferson, P. (1958). Studies on the earthworms of turf. C. Earthworms and casting. *J. Sports Turf Res. Inst.* 9(34):437–452.

Jefferson, P. (1961). Earthworms and turf culture. *J. Sports Turf Res. Inst.* 10(37): 276–289.

Kirby, E.C. and Baker, S.W. (1995). Earthworm populations, casting and control in sports turf areas: a review. *J. Sports Turf Res. Inst.* 71:84–98.

Lee, K.E. (1985). *Earthworms: Their Ecology and Relationships with Soils and Land Use*. Academic Press, New South Wales, Australia, p. 411.

Lidgate, H.J. (1966). Earthworm control with chlordane. *J. Sports Turf Res. Inst.* 42:5–8.

Potter, D.A., Bridges, B.L., and Gordon, F.C. (1985). Effect of N fertilisation on earthworm and microarthropod populations in Kentucky bluegrass turf. *Agron. J.* 77(3):367–372.

Satchell, J.E. (1955). Some aspects of earthworm ecology. In *Soil Zoology* (Ed. D.K. McEkevan), Butterworth, London, pp. 180–202.

CHAPTER 88

Preliminary Assessment of the Effects of Golf Course Pesticides on Golfers

M. P. Kenna

United States Golf Association, Green Section Research, Stillwater, Oklahoma, USA

The testing protocols used to develop the reported findings simulated golfing environments and provided greater exposure than is ever likely for any one golfer, and far in excess of the exposure expected by almost all golfers. Under this scenario, the research summarized indicates certain pesticides, when applied to golf course turf, result in inhalation, dermal or oral exposures that cannot be considered completely safe as judged by the United States Environmental Protection Agency (US EPA) hazard quotient (HQ) determination. Clark (1996) estimates the critical vapor pressure, below which no turfgrass pesticide will volatilize to produce an HQ greater than one, to be between 3.3×10^{-6} and 5.6×10^{-5} mm Hg. Clark (1996) determined the chronic reference dose (RfD) above which no turfgrass pesticide will result in a dermal HQ greater than one to be between 0.0005 and 0.0009. Borgert (1994) reported that a golfer playing every day would have received about one-third of the lifetime reference dose considered safe by the US EPA while playing on a golf course treated with three insecticides. Star et al. (1997) found that a golfer placing a golf ball or tee in their mouth could result in a HQ greater than 1.0 for certain herbicides. Because the HQ is a conservative estimate of hazard, and because golfer exposure was based on worse-case scenarios, more realistic exposure estimates are necessary to predict the health implications, if any, of pesticide exposures to golfers. The evidence provided suggests the need for biological monitoring to determine actual dermal and inhalation exposures of golfers following the application of selected turfgrass pesticides to a golf course. The results would provide a realistic risk assessment, since the behavior of golfers while playing golf is unique compared to pesticide applicators or agricultural workers.

Keywords: Volatile residues, dislodgeable residues, pesticide exposure, chronic reference dose (RfD), hazard quotient (HQ), biological monitoring, turfgrass.

Abbreviations: HQ, hazard quotient; RfD, chronic reference dose; US EPA, United States Environmental Protection Agency; USGA, United States Golf Association.

INTRODUCTION

The use of pesticides for the control of turfgrass pests, in conjunction with other cultural practices, has had a tremendous positive effect on the function and quality of turfgrass grown for golf courses. Despite the obvious cultural and economic benefits, conflicts have developed over pesticide use in relation to environmental quality issues. Pesticide residues found in golf course environments have been implicated as the cause of ill-health effects. However, until recently, the effects of golf courses on humans had not been addressed scientifically.

In 1990, the United States Golf Association (USGA) initiated the Environmental Research Program to quantify and document the impact of turfgrass management on the environment. There were three research goals in the environmental research program. First, use the scientific method to understand the effect of turfgrass pest management and fertilization on water quality and the environment. Second, begin to evaluate valid alternative methods of pest control to be used in integrated turf management systems. Last, estimate the human, biological, and environmental factors that golf courses influence. The purpose of this paper is to summarize available research results from the third objective dealing with human exposure to pesticides used on golf courses.

RISK ASSESSMENT

This is a preliminary risk assessment. It should not be considered as a thorough and complete examination of the health risks related to pesticide exposure in golf course situations. It is intended to present some of the USGA-sponsored research results in terms of health risk, as applied to golf course situations, and help to ascertain the need and future direction of research dealing with pesticide risk assessment.

The studies summarized determined pesticide residues that may or may not lead to exposure through inhalation, contact with the skin (dermal), or ingestion (orally by licking the golf ball or putting a tee in the mouth). The amount of pesticide inhaled would depend on how much of the product in question volatilized. The amount of pesticide present for dermal exposure or ingestion would arise from residues in the turfgrass or soil that easily dislodge onto the skin or other objects (i.e., clothing, shoes, grips, ball, tee, etc.). For the purposes of this article, volatilization and dislodgeable foliar residues are discussed in separate sections.

The hypothetical golfer's expected inhaled, dermal, or oral doses were estimated and compared with the United States Environmental Protection Agency (US EPA) Office of Pesticide Programs (OPP) chronic reference dose (RfD) to produce a hazard quotient (HQ). The chronic RfD takes into account that toxicity can accumulate in some human organ systems when the chemical is received as frequently as every day. The acceptable dose is determined from daily doses that cause no observable effects on laboratory animals over their lifetime multiplied by a safety factor of 10 to 10,000 (US EPA, 1993). The hazard quotient for the exposed golfer is the expected dose divided by the chronic RfD.

Hazard quotients less than one indicate that the residues present are at concentrations below those that would cause effects in humans. A HQ greater than one does not necessarily infer that the residue levels will cause adverse effects, but rather that the absence of adverse effects is less certain. The situations posed in the research reviewed for this article constitute worse-case scenarios and likely overestimate the potential dose a golfer would receive. The references cited should be thoroughly studied before broad generalizations about risks are communicated to the public. The reported HQ values greater than one should be interpreted with this overestimation of dosage in mind.

VOLATILE RESIDUES

Volatilization is the process where chemicals transform from a solid or liquid into a gas and is dependent on the vapor pressure of the compound. Pesticide volatilization is more likely as the vapor pressure of the chemical increases. As surface wind turbulence and ambient temperature increase during the day, so does the chance for volatilization losses.

Volatile residues of pesticides were measured in several USGA-sponsored studies (Murphy et al. 1996a, Murphy et al. 1996b, Yates 1995, Yates et al. 1996, Snyder et al. 1996). The total measured losses of volatile residues, expressed as a percent of the total pesticide applied, are summarized in tables 88.1 and 88.2. The large majority of detectable volatile residues were lost within the first two days after the pesticide was applied. Diurnal patterns of volatility were observed, and when surface temperature and solar radiation were greatest, volatile loss reached a maximum. Generally, the insecticides were more prone to volatilization than fungicide or herbicide products tested.

Inhalation exposures were estimated using measured air concentrations of volatile residues (Clark 1996, Murphy et al. 1996a, Murphy et al. 1996b). Inhalation exposure (i.e., dose) divided by the chronic reference dose (RfD) estimates the inhalation hazard quotient (HQ). A HQ less than one indicates that the residue level is below a concentration that might reasonably be expected to cause adverse effects in humans. Among the twelve pesticides (and their important metabolites) evaluated ethoprop, diazinon, and isazofos were the only three products with calculated HQs greater than one. The combination of high vapor pressure and low chronic RfD values increases the health risks associated with these products. Murphy et al. (1996a) reported that isazofos volatile residues resulted in a calculated HQ greater than one for three days after the product was applied. Trichlorfon, its metabolite DDVP, mecoprop, and triadimefon all had calculated HQs less than one three hours after the products were applied. Clark (1996) estimates the critical vapor pressure, below which no turfgrass pesticide will volatilize to produce an HQ greater than one, to be between 3.3×10^{-6} and 5.6×10^{-5} mm Hg (table 88.3).

Table 88.1   Summary of Volatile Insecticide Residues Recovered From Putting Green and Fairway Plots

Pesticide	Volatile residues (% of applied)	Comments	Reference
Trichlorfon	11.6	Applied 9/28/91 on bentgrass fairway, no irrigation following application. Sampled for 15 days.	Murphy et al. 1996a
	9.4	Applied 7/7/93 on bentgrass fairway, 1.3 cm of irrigation after application. Sampled for 15 days.	Murphy et al. 1996a
	0.09	Applied 6/4/96 on bentgrass green. Sampled for 29 days.	Yates et al. 1996
Isazofos	11.4	Applied 8/22/93 on bentgrass fairway, 1.3 cm of irrigation after application. Sampled for 15 days.	Murphy 1996a
	1.04	Applied 10/4/96 on bermudagrass green, 0.6 cm of irrigation followed by 3.94 cm of rainfall over 24 hrs. Sampled 48 hours during cloudy, rainy conditions.	Snyder et al. 1997
	9.14	Applied 10/10/96 on bermudagrass green, 0.6 cm of irrigation after application. Sampled 22 hrs, no rainfall.	Snyder et al. 1997
Chlorpyrifos	2.7	Applied 10/4/96 on bermudagrass green, 0.6 cm of irrigation followed by 3.94 cm of rainfall over 24 hrs. Sampled 48 hours during cloudy, rainy conditions.	Snyder et al. 1997
	11.6	Applied 10/10/96 on bermudagrass green, 0.6 cm of irrigation after application. Sampled 22 hrs, no rainfall.	Snyder et al. 1997
	15.7	Applied 6/4/96 on bentgrass green. Sampled 29 days.	Yates et al. 1996.
Fenamiphos	0.04	Applied 10/10/96 on bermudagrass green, 0.6 cm of irrigation after application. Sampled 22 hrs, no rainfall.	Snyder et al. 1997
	0.25	Applied 10/4/96 on bermudagrass green, 0.6 cm of irrigation followed by 3.94 cm of rainfall over 24 hrs. Sampled 48 hours during cloudy, rainy conditions.	Snyder et al. 1997
Carbaryl	0.03	Applied 8/93 to bentgrass green and bermudagrass fairway plots. Value is average over turfgrass and soil types.	Yates et al. 1995

Values expressed as the percent of total insecticide applied.

Table 88.2   Summary of Volatile Fungicide and Herbicide Residues Recovered From Putting Green and Fairway Plots

Pesticide	Volatile residues (% of applied)	Comments	Reference
Triadimefon	7.3	Applied 8/23/91 on bentgrass fairway, 1.3 cm of irrigation after application. Sampled 15 days.	Murphy et al. 1996b
Metalaxyl	0.08	Applied 9/27/96 on bentgrass green. Sampled 8 days.	Yates et al. 1996
Chlorothalonil	0.02	Applied 9/27/96 on bentgrass green. Sampled 8 days.	Yates et al. 1996
Mecoprop	0.08	Applied 9/24/92 on bentgrass fairway, no irrigation following application. Sampled 15 days.	Murphy et al. 1996b
2, 4-D	0.67	Applied 8/93 to bentgrass green and bermudagrass fairway plots. Value is average over turfgrass and soil types.	Yates et al. 1995

Values expressed as the percent of total pesticide applied.

DISLODGEABLE FOLIAR RESIDUES

Following the application of a pesticide, especially liquid materials, there remains a residue of the pesticide on the turfgrass foliage. The quantity and duration of dislodgeable foliar residues for pesticides were evaluated in USGA-sponsored investigations (Clark 1996, Murphy et al. 1996a, Murphy et al. 1996b, Borgert et al. 1994, Star and Smith 1997). Generally, these studies indicate less than one percent of the pesticides could be rubbed off immediately after application. After the pesticides dried on the turf, only minimal amounts could be rubbed off. Borgert et al. (1994) conducted a preliminary risk assessment on putting greens treated with insecticides. The study included several dermal and oral pathways (table 88.4). They assumed that the golfer knelt on every green to align putts, handled golf grips laid on the green, touched the soles of leather shoes when cleaning them, and cleaned the ball after every hole by licking it. In addition, the greens were sprayed every day with three insecticides and the golfer played golf 365 days a year for 70 years. Under these assumptions, the golfer would have received about one-third of the lifetime reference dose considered safe by the US EPA.

Murphy et al. (1996a) reported that trichlorfon/DDVP and isazofos dislodgeable residues resulted in a HQ greater than one for three days after the pesticides were applied. In a second study, Murphy et al. (1996b) reported dermal HQs for triadimefon and MCPP calculated from dislodgeable residues remained below one

Table 88.3   Inhalation Hazard Quotient (HQ) for Turfgrass Pesticides in the High, Intermediate and Low Vapor Pressure Group Over a Three-Day Post-Application Period[a]

Pesticide	Vapor pressure	RfD[b]	Day 1	Day 2	Day 3
	mmHg	mg kg^{-1}d^{-1}	----------Hazard quotient[c]----------		
High vapor pressure					
DDVP	1.6×10^{-2}	0.0005	0.06	0.04	0.02
ethoprop	3.5×10^{-4}	0.000015	50.0	26	1.2
diazinon	9.0×10^{-5}	0.00009	3.3	2.4	1.2
isazofos	5.6×10^{-5}	0.00002	8.6	6.7	3.4
chlorpyrifos	2.0×10^{-5}	0.0003	0.09	0.1	0.04
Intermediate vapor pressure					
trichlorfon	3.8×10^{-6}	0.002	0.02	0.004	0.004
bendiocarb	3.4×10^{-6}	0.005	0.02	0.002	0.002
isofenphos	3.3×10^{-6}	0.0005	nd[d]	0.02	nd
chlorothalonil	5.7×10^{-7}	0.015	0.001	0.001	0.0003
propiconazole	4.2×10^{-7}	0.0125	nd	nd	nd
carbaryl	3.1×10^{-7}	0.014	0.0005	0.0001	0.00004
Low vapor pressure					
thiophanate-methyl	7.1×10^{-8}	0.08	nd	nd	nd
iprodione	3.8×10^{-9}	0.061	nd	nd	nd
cyfluthrin	2.0×10^{-9}	0.025	nd	nd	nd

[a]An average daily dose of pesticide for a 70 kg adult playing a 4-h round of golf.

[b]US EPA Office of Pesticide Programs Reference Dose Tracking Report, January, 1993.

[c]The HQs reported are the maximum daily HQs measured during the sampling period.

[d]nd = non-detect

Reprinted, by permission, from John M. Clark, 1998, "Evaluation of Management Factors Affecting Volatile and Dislodgeable Foliar Residues." In *1997 Turfgrass and Environmental Research Summary*, edited by Michael P. Kenna (USGA).

for the entire 15-day experiment. Clark (1996) determined the chronic RfD above which no turfgrass pesticide will result in a dermal HQ greater than one to be between 0.0005 to 0.0009 (table 88.5).

Star et al. (1997) estimated the toxic dose of three herbicides on a golfer that habitually licks the golf ball or chews on a wooden tee. Putting green plots were treated with herbicides 2,4-D, mecoprop, and dicamba at treatment rates of 0.56, 1.40, and 0.28 kg ha^{-1}, respectively. Simulated putts were performed at 0, 6, 30, 54, 78, and 102 hours after treatment. To represent the human tongue and lips, small pieces of chamois leather (2.5×2.5 cm) were treated with artificial saliva for 12 hours. These pieces of leather were used to wipe the golf ball or tee and the amount

Table 88.4   Hazard Quotient (HQ) for Total Dose (Dermal and Oral) of Three Insecticides Expected From Exposure to Putting Greens During a Round of Golf

Pesticide	RfD[b]	Dose[a]			Hazard quotient
		Dermal	Oral	Total	
	mg kg^{-1} d^{-1}	mg kg^{-1}			
Diazinon	0.0009	1.73×10^{-5}	1.25×10^{-5}	2.98×10^{-5}	0.0331
Isazofos	0.00002	1.0×10^{-6}	3.9×10^{-6}	4.9×10^{-6}	0.2450
Chlorpyrifos	0.003	2.0×10^{-7}	3.9×10^{-6}	4.1×10^{-6}	0.0014

[a]Dose based on adjusted life-time male body weight of 62 kg.

[b]US EPA Office of Pesticide Programs Reference Dose Tracking Report, January, 1993.

Reprinted, by permission, from C.J. Borgert, S.M. Roberts, R.D. Harbison, J.L. Cisar, and G.H. Snyder, 1994, "Assessing Chemical Hazards on Golf Courses." *USGA Green Section Record* 33 (2): 11-14.

of pesticide on the leather was determined. It was assumed that the entire amount recovered from the leather was absorbed through the lip or mouth tissues.

The herbicide residue recovered from the leather used to simulate licking the golf ball decreased for the three products during the 102 hours after treatment (table 88.6). The maximum amounts collected from the leather were 0.2, 0.6, and 0.9 mg of dicamba, mecoprop, and 2,4-D, respectively, and occurred immediately after treatment. The HQ for dicamba was never greater than one. Mecoprop and 2,4-D had HQ values greater than or near one at zero hours after treatment application. The HQs for exposure to the three herbicide residues resulted in values less than one 30 hours after treatment application.

CONCLUSIONS

This article is a very preliminary risk assessment of the effects of golf course pesticides on golfers. The testing protocols used to develop the reported findings simulated golfing environments and provided greater exposure than is ever likely for any one golfer, and far in excess of the exposure expected by almost all golfers. The research summarized indicates certain pesticides, when applied to golf course turf, result in inhalation, dermal, or oral exposures that cannot be considered completely safe as judged by the US EPA hazard quotient determination. However, because the HQ is a conservative estimate of hazard, and because golfer exposure was based on worse-case scenarios, more realistic exposure estimates are necessary to predict the health implications, if any, of pesticide exposures to golfers.

The evidence provided suggests the need for biological monitoring to determine actual dermal and inhalation exposures of golfers following the application of selected turfgrass pesticides to a golf course. The results would provide a realistic risk assessment. The behavior of golfers while playing golf is unique compared to

Table 88.5   Dermal Hazard Quotients (HQs) Over a Three-Day Post-Application Period for Turfgrass Pesticides Listed by Increasing RfD[a]

Pesticide	RfD[b]	Day 1 15 min	Day 1 5 hours	Day 1 8 hours	Day 2 12:00 p.m.	Day 3 12:00 p.m.
	mg kg^{-1} d^{-1}					
Ethoprop	0.000015	16.0	1.64	1.35	0.23	0.34
Isazofos	0.00002	10.5	1.17	0.97	0.16	0.21
Diazinon	0.00009	3.0	0.28	0.22	0.04	0.05
Isofenphos	0.0005	0.32	0.05	0.05	0.01	0.01
DDVP	0.0005	0.06	0.003	0.003	nd[d]	nd
Trichlorfon	0.002	0.64	0.007	0.009	0.008	0.005
Chlorpyrifos	0.003	0.17	0.02	0.016	0.003	0.004
Bendiocarb	0.005	0.31	0.006	0.01	0.006	0.0008
Propiconazole	0.0125	0.0002	0.003	0.0002	0.0005	0.0002
Carbaryl	0.14	0.03	0.0008	0.001	0.0006	0.00002
Cyfluthrin	0.25	—[c]	—	—	—	—
Iprodione	0.61	0.0004	0.0003	0.0003	0.0004	0.0003
Thiophanate-Methyl	0.08	—	—	—	—	—

[a]An average daily dose of pesticide for a 70 kg adult playing a 4-h round of golf.
[b]US EPA Office of Pesticide Programs Reference Dose Tracking Report, January, 1993.
[c]— = no data available at the time of this report.
[d]nd = not detected.

Reprinted, by permission, from John M. Clark, 1998, "Evaluation of Management Factors Affecting Volatile and Dislodgeable Foliar Residues." *In 1997 Turfgrass and Environmental Research Summary*, edited by Michael P. Kenna (USGA).

pesticide applicators or agricultural workers. A comprehensive evaluation of the exact exposure that a golfer receives is a necessary step in determining the environmental impact of golf courses on humans. At this time, there is no data available on exactly what proportion of dislodgeable and volatile residues are actually transferred to golfers resulting in dermal and inhalation exposures. It also is unknown what proportion of these residues actually penetrates into the individual resulting in the real absorbed body dose.

The procedures used for the research projects reviewed in this article inflate and exaggerate risk. Other industry and agricultural groups who use pesticides have already adopted the use of biological monitoring to estimate actual exposure. For example, the State of California estimated indoor insecticide exposure ranged up to 2.2 mg kg^{-1} but the actual measured levels using biological monitoring were between 0.1 and 30 µg kg^{-1} or less (Krieger, personal communication). The more

Table 88.6   Oral Hazard Quotient (HQ) for a Golfer Who Places a Golf Ball or Tee in Their Mouth During a 102-Hour Post Application Period of Three Herbicides[a]

Pesticide	RfD[b]	0 h	6 h	30 h	54 h	78 h	102h
	mg kg^{-1} d^{-1}						
Golf ball							
Mecoprop	0.001	9.013	0.271	0.486	0.500	0.029	0.443
2,4-D	0.03	4.254	0.119	0.152	0.343	0.024	0.395
Dicamba	0.003	0.094	nd	0.002	0.008	nd	0.004
Golf tee							
Mecoprop	0.001	1.586	1.743	0.386	0.857	0.143	0.043
2,4-D	0.03	0.867	0.714	0.224	0.481	0.090	0.076
Dicamba	0.003	0.021	0.030	0.001	0.023	<0.001	nd

[a]The dose of pesticide was calculated for a 70 kg adult.
[b]US EPA Office of Pesticide Programs Reference Dose Tracking Report, January, 1993.

than 100-fold difference between actual measurements and worse-case scenarios is the consequence of reliance on unvalidated procedures and assumptions. Validated biological monitoring can avoid such errors that periodically alarm the public and regulatory community.

As the risk assessment process is applied to more and more activities in modern life, it is important to stress the need for accuracy and defensibility. Overstated risk, which may be the case of results reported in this article, erodes confidence. On the other hand, understated risk could represent a threat to the health of golfers. The accurate exposure assessments produced from biological monitoring will demonstrate that today's safe pesticide use practices minimize golfer exposure.

References

Borgert, C.J., S.M. Roberts, R.D. Harbison, J.L. Cisar, and G.H. Snyder. 1994. Assessing Chemical Hazards on Golf Courses. *USGA Green Section Record* 33(2):11–14.

Clark, John M. 1996. Evaluation of Management Factors Affecting Volatile Loss and Dislodgeable Foliar Residues, In *USGA 1996 Annual Turfgrass and Environmental Research Summary*, pp. 60–63. USGA Green Section Research, Stillwater, Oklahoma, U.S.A.

Murphy, K.C., R.J. Cooper, and J.M. Clark. 1996a. Volatile and Dislodgeable Residues Following Trichlorfon and Isazofos Application to Turfgrass and Implications of Human Exposure. *Crop Science* 36(6):1446–1454.

Murphy, K.C., R.J. Cooper, and J.M. Clark. 1996b. Volatile and Dislodgeable Residues Following Triadimefon and MCPP Application to Turfgrass and Implications of Human Exposure. *Crop Science* 36(6):1446–1454.

Snyder, George H., and John L. Cisar. 1996. Measurement and Model Prediction of Pesticide Partitioning in Field-Scale Turfgrass Plots, In *USGA Environmental Research Program: Pesticide and Nutrient Fate Annual Project Reports*, pp. 109–140. USGA Green Section Research, Stillwater, Oklahoma, U.S.A.

Star, Jennifer, and Al Smith. 1997. Potential Pesticide Dose from Licking a Golf Ball and Placing a Tee in the Mouth. USGA Green Section Research, Stillwater, Oklahoma, U.S.A.

U.S. Environmental Protection Agency. 1993. Office of Pesticide Programs Reference Dose Tracking Report. Washington, D.C.

Yates, Marylynn V. 1995. The Fate of Pesticides and Fertilizers in a Turfgrass Environment, *USGA Green Section Record*, 33(1):10–12.

Yates, Marylynn V., Robert L. Green, and Jianying Gan. 1996. Measurement and Model Prediction of Pesticide Partitioning in Field-Scale Turfgrass Plots, In *USGA Environmental Research Program: Pesticide and Nutrient Fate Annual Project Reports*, pp. 80–94. USGA Green Section Research Office, Stillwater, Oklahoma, U.S.A.

CHAPTER 89

Dynamics of Heathland Conservation on a Golf Course

A.C. Gange
School of Biological Sciences, Royal Holloway, University of London

Many golf courses in the United Kingdom possess areas of heathland. This type of habitat is now internationally endangered, as a great deal of it has been lost to farmland or urbanization in the last 150 years. Golf courses have the potential to act as reservoirs of this important habitat. This paper suggests that the ecological theory of metapopulation dynamics needs to be applied to courses in order to understand their conservation value and to enhance it. The theory states that an overall population of a species will persist if there is movement of individuals between fragmented pieces of habitat or patches. With golf courses, there are two aspects of scale to consider, namely the movement of individuals between patches within a course, and the movement between courses. An experimental study is presented that examined invertebrates on patches on one course. It was found that the degree of isolation of patches was much more important in affecting invertebrate diversity than was patch size.

Keywords: Heathland, conservation, population dynamics, insects.

INTRODUCTION

The term 'heathland' is used to describe an open landscape, generally on nutrient-poor, acid soils with a vegetation dominated by low, woody shrubs of the heather family. The commonest of these are usually ling heather (*Calluna vulgaris*), cross-leaved heath (*Erica tetralix*) and bell heather (*Erica cinerea*). Tall shrubs and trees are usually absent, but other species such as bracken, gorse and broom are often present. In Britain, lowland heath has declined greatly in its extent over the past 150 years. For example, in southern England, 72% of the area has been lost to farming or urbanization, while the figure for the county of Surrey is even more alarming at 85% (Gimingham, 1992). Britain has over 20% of the total area of heathland in

Europe, but the recent declines have meant that this habitat type has now been designated as internationally rare and endangered. There is therefore an urgent need to review our conservation strategies, as many species of animals and plants depend on heathland for their survival. In addition to becoming smaller in total area, heathland has become broken up into fragments, as urbanization and farming have increased in area. For example, in the county of Dorset, the once large areas of heath have now become fragmented into about 800 patches, set in a matrix of farmland, forest and urban areas (Webb and Hopkins, 1984).

Ecologists are now aware of the urgent need to conserve our heathland remnants, and guidelines for their protection have been produced (e.g., Gimingham, 1992). There is a growing recognition that golf courses can play a vital role in the conservation of many natural habitats, and some practical reviews have been published (Taylor, 1995). It has been recognised that golf courses can secure areas of heathland, and that when properly managed these can be an important resource. Indeed, effort has been directed at finding ways of restoring areas of heathland on courses (Taylor, Stefanyszyn and Canaway, 1994).

Recently, theoretical ecologists have worked with conservationists to identify strategies by which habitats fragmented into patches may be conserved. A number of features of patches have been studied, including size, distance between them (which influences the degree of movement of species between patches), botanical diversity and habitat structure. The critical point appears to be whether there are interactions between populations of one species on different patches. This concept has been termed 'metapopulation dynamics' (Hanski and Gilpin, 1991). A metapopulation can be described as a population of populations, in which local populations are connected by dispersing individuals (Gotelli, 1995). The important feature of a metapopulation is that if a population on a patch becomes extinct, then

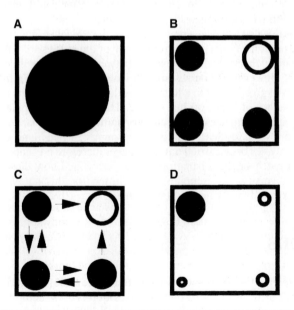

Figure 89.1   The concept of metapopulation dynamics applied to golf courses.

the patch can become populated again by migrants from another patch. In this way, the overall population of the species is maintained, with a much lower probability of extinction than if all the patch populations were completely isolated or 'closed' (Gotelli, 1995).

I suggest that it is now time to apply this conceptual framework to the conservation of heathland on golf courses. There are two aspects of scale to this problem, namely whether individual courses support interacting patches (i.e., the course acts as the metapopulation), and whether there are interactions between courses (i.e., the local area acts as the metapopulation). If both of these criteria are fulfilled, then golf courses will be shown to be vitally important in the maintenance of this habitat. The theoretical concept is displayed graphically in figure 89.1.

The square represents a large area of land; circles represent patches of habitat that may be occupied by a species (filled circles) or unoccupied (open circles) at any given time. Arrows represent movement of individuals between patches. Diagram A represents the situation in southern England 150 years ago when there were large tracts of heathland. Diagram B represents the fragmented situation that we have today. However, the overall population is in danger of extinction, because if an environmental disaster (e.g., fire) defaunates a patch, then recolonization of that patch will not occur (there might be an urban barrier between patches, for example). In C, the overall population of a species will persist if there is movement between the patches; the set of interacting population islands is called a metapopulation. Note that not all of the patches may be occupied at any one time, but the unoccupied ones ('sinks') can be recolonized at any time from other nearby patches ('sources'). Diagram D (which can easily lead on from B) represents a recipe for rapid extinction: there is only one occupied patch and no movement between any of them, because they have become too isolated. In addition, some patches are too small to support viable populations. Any environmental disaster could wipe out the only extant population and the species becomes extinct.

My proposal is that today at a regional scale, the square in diagram C represents a large area, (e.g., the county of Surrey), some of the circles are golf courses, and some are natural heathland. Movement between courses will ensure species conservation. However, if courses are too isolated (diagram B), then eventually populations will go extinct. On a local scale, the square represents one course and the circles patches of heath on that course. The same metapopulation argument applies for the maintenance of a species population on that course.

In order to test these ideas, a preliminary survey of heathland patches on one course in Surrey has been carried out. This paper therefore presents the first results of a study of patch size and isolation on one course and how these factors affect invertebrate diversity. Invertebrates were chosen for this study, because their diversity is extraordinarily high on heathland (Usher, 1992).

METHODS

The course selected for this study was the Berkshire Club, Ascot, Berkshire. The club is typical of well-managed older courses in this area, being built on acidic, sandy soil overlying the Bagshot Sands. Natural habitat areas between the fairways are composed of Scots pine or birch woodland, rough grassland or heathland. Twenty heather patches were selected at random in an area adjoining a number of fairways. The heather on this course is managed by periodic cutting, and all patches selected were uniform in appearance and age. The area of each patch was measured, to the nearest square metre, and the distance between each patch and its nearest neighbour was also recorded. Invertebrates (mainly insects and arachnids) were sampled with a Vortis insect suction sampler (Arnold, 1994). This machine removes arthropods from the vegetation, but leaves the vegetation intact. It is a very efficient means of sampling foliar-dwelling invertebrates. Five suction samples were taken in each patch and each sample was sorted under a binocular microscope to record the number of individuals in each arthropod group. The numbers of invertebrates in each sample were converted to numbers per m² in each patch, and the mean for each patch calculated from the five replicate samples. The data set is extensive, and for simplicity, the relations between patch size and patch isolation and the total invertebrate density per m² are presented here. Linear regression analysis was used to examine these relations.

RESULTS

The smallest patch size studied was 5m² and the largest was 1162m². There was no relation between the abundance of invertebrates per unit area and the size of the heather patch ($F_{1,18} = 0.38$; $P>0.05$, $r^2 = 0.021$). Indeed, one of the smallest patches had the highest density of arthropods.

In contrast, there was a highly significant negative relation between the degree of patch isolation (nearest neighbour distance) and the invertebrate density ($F_{1,18} = 21.16$; $P<0.001$; $r^2 = 0.528$) (figure 89.2). Therefore, patches that were some distance from others supported much lower invertebrate populations than those which were close to other patches. In this study, it appeared that the critical inter-

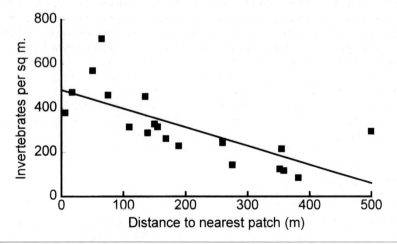

Figure 89.2   Isolated patches have fewer invertebrates than those near to others.

patch distance may be about 100m, as above this figure, invertebrate density began to decline rapidly.

DISCUSSION

It is clear from this preliminary study on one golf course that for heathland management to be effective, course managers will need to take into account how the patches of heather are arranged on the course. Excellent guidelines have been produced for the way in which heather should be managed (Taylor, 1995), but, up to now, the physical sizes and spatial orientation of heather patches have never been considered. This study shows that such considerations are crucial; there is little point in following accepted practice for heather management if the patches are so isolated that they do not support viable populations of any animals.

Similar studies on the role of isolation in fragmented heathland have been carried out on naturally occurring areas of habitat. It is interesting that den Boer (1981) came to a similar conclusion to that reported here, when studying ground-dwelling beetles on heather patches in the Netherlands. The beetles moved only short distances per day, often less than 100 m, meaning that many patches were effectively isolated, because dispersal of the beetles was not sufficient for inter-patch movement to occur. Thomas and Harrison (1992) found that the silver-studded blue butterfly was able to colonize patches of heath if these were less than 1 km apart. While the dispersal abilities of invertebrates in the current work have not been considered, the fact that the negative relation was found between total invertebrate density and patch isolation strongly suggests that large inter-patch distances may prevent dispersal of less mobile species. This would then lead, over a period of time, to reduced overall populations of these species, because they would be absent on the most isolated patches.

The single course study reported here must now be scaled up, to investigate whether whole courses can act as islands in a metapopulation 'sea.' Given that mobile species can migrate over distances of at least 1 km and often much more, the density of golf courses in areas such as the Surrey Heath in southern England may mean that much dispersal is taking place between courses. This is the subject of our current research on this system.

ACKNOWLEDGEMENT

I am grateful to the Berkshire Golf Club, and in particular to Mr. Robert Moreton for permission to undertake this study.

References

Arnold, A.J. 1994. Insect suction sampling without nets, bags or filters. *Crop Protection* 13:73–76.

den Boer, P.J. 1981. On the survival of populations in a heterogeneous and variable environment. *Oecologia* 50:39–53.

Gimingham, C.H. 1992. *The lowland heathland management handbook.* Peterborough: English Nature.

Gotelli, N.J. 1995. *A Primer of Ecology.* Sunderland, Massachusetts: Sinauer Associates.

Hanski, I., and M. Gilpin. 1991. Metapopulation dynamics: brief history and conceptual domain. *Biological Journal of the Linnean Society* 42:3–6.

Taylor, R.S. 1995. *A Practical Guide to Ecological Management of the Golf Course.* British and International Golf Greenkeepers Association and the Sports Turf Research Institute.

Taylor, R.S., O. Stefanyszyn, and P.M. Canaway. 1994. Reinstatement of heather on the golf course using physical and mechanical methods. *Journal of the Sports Turf Research Institute* 70:7–12.

Thomas, C.D., and S. Harrison. 1992. Spatial dynamics of a patchily distributed butterfly species. *Journal of animal Ecology* 61:437–446.

Usher, M.B. 1992. Management and diversity of arthropods in *Calluna* heathland. *Biodiversity and Conservation* 1:63–79.

Webb, N.R., and P.J. Hopkins. 1984. Invertebrate diversity on fragmented *Calluna* heathland. *Journal of applied Ecology* 21: 921-933.

CHAPTER 90

The Importance of Environmental Management for Golf

David Stubbs (MIEEM)
Executive Director, European Golf Association Ecology Unit

Golf is a major outdoor recreational activity that has experienced substantial growth in popularity in the last decade. Through the professional game at major tournaments, golf has attracted a huge global audience. Such a massive activity inevitably has important interactions with the environment. Questions have been raised from many sources—environmental groups, public authorities, academics, the media—concerning land use issues, water consumption and the possible adverse effects from overuse of fertilisers and pesticides.

There is, however, another side to golf. It owes its origins to nature. Contact with the natural environment is an essential part of really appreciating the game. This is reflected in both the construction and management of golf courses, where the intensively managed playing surfaces have to be integrated within the natural landscape. The environmental debate is of crucial importance to golf, both internally and in its relations with the wider community.

If golf is to continue to develop over the coming years, expanding to new areas and attracting more players, especially juniors, the game's authorities will have to be seen to be addressing environmental issues in a thorough and professional manner. That is the basis behind "Committed to Green." This initiative introduces the concept of Environmental Management Systems to golf. Its purpose is to encourage people to take a more active and constructive role in improving the environmental quality of golf courses.

The incentive for individual golf clubs will be official recognition for implementing a comprehensive Environmental Management Programme, which has been subject to independent verification. This is designed to raise the environmental performance of the golf industry and, as a result, its wider acceptance.

Keywords: Environmental management programme, awareness, environmental performance, recognition, independent verification.

INTRODUCTION

Among all the major land-based sports, golf has probably the strongest interaction with the environment. Certainly no other sport exclusively occupies and manages such large areas of greenspace. In Europe alone, there are 5,200 golf courses covering 250,000 hectares and serving a golfing population of nearly 5,000,000 people. Golf is a sizable industry in its own right and continues to grow. Any activity on this scale cannot function in isolation and it is important to understand the game's responsibilities towards the wider community.

In common with many other major sports, golf owes its origins to nature. The first golf courses were formed entirely by natural elements: earth, wind and water, and grazing animals, each of which contributed to creating the tight, short grass sward of the original golf links. The game evolved to fit what nature provided.

The elemental contact and association with the natural environment is also one of the fundamental pleasures of golf, whether consciously or not. Take away the varied landforms, remove the rough, tame the weather, iron out the imperfections and what is left—a flat, indoor playing field? It would certainly not be a golf course (Royal & Ancient Golf Club of St. Andrews and European Golf Association 1997).

However, as with many other sports, golf has gradually moved away from its natural origins. In many respects this has been an inevitable consequence of the game's popularity. Golf courses have had to be built more closely associated with where people live, rather than necessarily on the best golfing terrain.

The demand for golf has also spread the game far beyond its natural climatic region. It is no coincidence that the maintenance of fine turfgrass dominated by bents and fescues is most successful in the cool temperate climate of northwestern Europe, where the game evolved. The expansion of golf into warmer, even arid, climatic regions has had a fundamental effect on golf course management and how the game is played and perceived.

All this means a certain amount of compromise from the original ideal of natural golf. New courses are designed and constructed. No matter how carefully this is done, there must inevitably be a tendency to make the site fit the game. Challenges are increasingly in the form of designed impediments whose creation requires some modification of the site.

While there is nothing inherently wrong in a more artificial sporting environment, this creates greater uniformity that is at odds with the diversity so central to the appeal of golf. This tendency towards the artificial disconnects golf from its natural environment. Chernushenko (1994) states:

> . . . the move away from nature as a sporting environment has been a principal contributor to the sports community's diminishing understanding of and concern for the environmental health upon which it is in fact highly dependent.

This is most vividly seen in the professional game, where the competitive pressures for high prizes and greater performances overrule the charm of unpredictability inherent in a natural setting. Instead, the needs and expectations of competitors, sponsors, media and eventually spectators govern the "quality" of tournament venues. In turn these influences have a strong effect on management, often leading to greater reliance on extra water resources, chemicals and intensive use of machinery.

However, we must acknowledge that golf would not be the popular sport it is today without the massive interest spawned by major events, star players and the associated media coverage. Modern golf has to be managed in a present-day and forward-looking context. But we should always remember the natural origins of the game and consider just how important environmental quality is to the golfing experience.

CHALLENGES AND OPPORTUNITIES

Environmental factors are certainly among the most significant external influences affecting the future development and operation of golf facilities. (European Golf Association Ecology Unit 1995a). It is wrong to think of golf-environment issues being related solely to land use and natural heritage. Golf course turfgrass management is fundamentally linked to environmental factors: climate, soils, availability of natural resources. Consideration must therefore extend to subjects like water resource management, use of chemicals, energy efficiency and waste management.

The key environment-related limiting factors affecting the golf industry are:

- Water
- European Union Directives and Regulations
- Cost of compliance
- Environmental pressure groups
- Public perception of golf
- Environmental attitudes of the young

Water

The quality and supply of water available for golf course irrigation will be the primary technical challenge facing the game across most of Europe. Present attitudes and methods will not be sustainable in the face of anticipated social, political and economic pressures.

There are four main consequences facing golf:

- Cost—the price of water supply will continue to rise substantially.
- Availability—supply restrictions will become more frequent. In times of shortage, this may mean temporary cutoffs.
- Quality—golf courses will be expected to look to alternative sources of nonpotable water supply, such as treated wastewater. This is now widespread in the western United States of America and is likely to develop in Europe in the coming years.
- Public opinion—golf courses that continue to irrigate when local residents

suffer hose pipe bans inevitably attract much public hostility. This does not help the image of the game.

Each of these will have either direct or indirect economic implications for golf. It is generally accepted by industry experts that golf courses continue to be overwatered. There is considerable scope for reducing the quantity of water used for irrigation but this may well involve clubs in initial investment costs to upgrade irrigation systems and equipment, consultant fees and staff training. In the long run these would be wise investments.

Alternative sources of supply, such as treated wastewater, as well as extra storage provision and rainwater farming, also impose considerable initial cost burdens. Further down the line, there is the European Water Framework Directive. At the core of this is the notion that all water should be charged at its full economic cost. This could have fundamental consequences for water pricing and drastically alter our perceptions of this vital natural resource. The days of cheap water are numbered and golf clubs must plan accordingly.

On a related matter is the issue of water quality. There is a common perception that golf courses use considerable amounts of chemicals, and that some of these must leach into the groundwater, or run off into surface waters. Research evidence shows that golf courses are generally small users of pesticides and fertilisers, and turfgrass is such a good biological filter that the risk of leaching is minimal (United States Golf Association 1995). Runoff is a greater potential risk but can be minimised through basic good practice of defining buffer zones and appropriate application methods. However, there is one significant loophole: the standard of maintenance facilities. Many golf clubs have inadequate containment provision for spills and leaks of turf chemicals and fuels. In some cases wash pads, mixing and loading areas drain directly into water courses. If a pollution incident is traced back to a golf course, there is a likelihood of punitive fines and enforcement of remedial measures.

European Union Directives and Regulations

The increasing influence of European Union institutions in environmental, social and economic fields has important implications. These arise through Directives and Regulations on water resource management, pollution control, health and safety, nature conservation, energy efficiency, Environmental Assessment and standards (through the European Committee of Normalisation—CEN), as well as policies and instruments relating to tourism, regional development, agriculture and social affairs. The European Commission has been a driving force for much of the environmental legislation to have arisen in recent years. While none of this has been targeted specifically at golf courses, the effects have been more far-reaching.

Cost of Compliance

Health and safety regulations and the potential risk of pollution infringements have already had an impact on golf course management. Clubs are having to pay more attention to workplace facilities and employment conditions. Greenkeeper qualifications and opportunities for continuing professional development are also rising up the agenda. These all have cost implications to be factored into management budgets, which in turn will become more significant as a proportion of a club's overall budget.

Golf clubs will need to think in terms of upgrading fuel and chemical storage and containment, building oil separators and other waste management facilities, such as settlement ponds. Investment in these environmentally driven measures will be a vital consideration for many clubs in the next few years. On the benefit side, clubs that adopt effective risk management strategies are likely to gain more favourable insurance terms.

Environmental Pressure Groups

Much of the tangible opposition to golf—and this applies essentially to new golf course developments—has been led by environmental pressure groups, supported by local community interests. Right or wrong, the majority sentiment among environmentalists, especially in continental Europe, is that golf courses are generally bad for the environment.

This is an image problem for the game. Although opposition may be directed towards new developments on the basis of their potential impact on existing environmental conditions, much of this stems from perceptions of what golf courses constitute. Accusations have covered the destruction of natural habitats, suburbanisation of the countryside, depletion of water resources, overuse of chemicals and restrictions on public access. Although not universal realities, examples can be found to support all of these criticisms.

In the U.K., golf is much longer established, and because of the heritage conservation function of many of the older courses, the game has a better relationship with the professional environmental community. Even so, there are many who hold strong reservations.

Further afield, but by no means irrelevant, there is the Global Anti-Golf Movement (GAGM). Operating out of Japan and Malaysia, its focus is primarily against major resort developments in the Pacific Rim. However, it claims to monitor golf development worldwide, and in 1993 it instituted "World No Golf Day." It would be wrong to give the group too much credence but equally it would be a mistake to ignore such activities. Yesterday's fringe groups are today's mainstream. The lesson for golf is to stay one step ahead.

Public Perceptions

The problem for golf has been that just through having these arguments, a large chunk of public opinion can be turned against the game. This feeds through to the political level and eventually regulatory restrictions. That has been very much the case in Germany, Switzerland and Belgium—in Flanders there is currently no possibility for golf development, although a current regional review of the structure plan may allow some limited provision.

Some say that the real antipathy to golf is based on social and political reasons and is not strictly environmental. The fact is that environmental arguments have been consistently used against the game and there are sufficient cases of insensitive projects to give this credence in the public eye.

Environmental Attitudes of the Young

Today's young are tomorrow's generation of golfers. Whenever they come into the game, future golfers are going to be more informed and opinionated about green issues. It is very easy for environmental opponents to paint the game in a poor light: it is said to be ecologically destructive, elitist and a selfish use of land. These are powerful sentiments, likely to influence the young. If they perceive golf as an environmentally unfriendly activity, that has potentially long-term consequence for the game.

The environmental image of the game will be a strong determining factor on future growth patterns, not simply through legal and planning constraints, but also through consumer choice.

RESPONSE OF THE GOLF AUTHORITIES

The rise of environmental issues has certainly been recognised by the main golfing bodies. In 1994 the R&A, PGA European Tour and European Golf Association joined together to establish a specialist Ecology Unit. This provides a clearing house for environmental information relevant to golf. It was set up to address the subject on a technical level, to develop guidelines on Best Management Practice and the development of new golf courses (European Golf Association Ecology Unit 1995a and 1995b). The remit covers the whole of Europe. In this way it was intended to avoid duplication of effort and to provide a coordinated approach to environmental issues.

A number of countries have engaged their own environmental specialists to provide a more direct, hands-on service for their member clubs. In the U.K., the lead has been taken by the Scottish Golf Union, in the appointment of a Golf Course Wildlife Advisor in May 1996. This is a joint project with Scottish Natural Heritage and a number of voluntary environmental groups (Scottish Golf Course Wildlife Group 1997).

In addition to the necessary continued leadership role to be shown by the golf authorities in this matter, there is a responsibility of all clubs and golf facility operators to take a more active environmental stance. The credibility of golf's environmental case will depend on its ability to demonstrate a collective commitment, backed up by tangible results on the ground: i.e., on golf courses.

BENEFITS OF AN ENVIRONMENTAL APPROACH

Potential benefits can be grouped into two categories, 'hard' benefits that have a clear and direct link to cost, and 'soft' benefits that have some indirect effect on overall performance.

Hard Benefits

1. Cost savings through improved efficiency:
   - reduced water, chemical and fuel consumption due to revised irrigation, fertiliser applications and mowing regimes;
   - introduction of Integrated Pest Management strategies to cut down on pesticide use and other controls;
   - introduction of energy saving policies;
   - waste reduction, reusing and recycling;
   - maintenance of equipment and machinery.
2. Cost avoidance through compliance:
   - environmental regulations (e.g., protected species, pollution controls);
   - health and safety regulations.
3. Protection of property asset value:
   - appropriate silvicultural management of trees and woodland blocks;
   - maintenance of ponds, lakes, streams, ditches and other wetlands;
   - general landscape management.
4. Reduced premiums for environmental liability insurance.
5. Cost and time savings through accelerated approval process for extensions or new facilities.
6. Environmental improvement grants:
   - grants for tree planting, hedgerow restoration, habitat management;
   - environmental awards;
   - local authority environmental improvement schemes.

Soft Benefits

1. Employee motivation
2. Membership/visitor satisfaction
3. Improved aesthetic quality
4. Improved local community relations
5. Enhanced public image

While this is an impressive list of potential benefits, there might still be reticence from clubs not wishing to embark on significant changes. There may be worries that anticipated savings could lead to greater costs in other areas; e.g., less chemicals but more labour, or more expensive equipment. Management savings might be offset by revenue loss. High capital start-up cost is another frequently cited disincentive to adopting environmental measures, even though long-term operational benefits would accrue (Chernushenko 1994).

There is at present insufficient hard evidence to quantify the cost-effectiveness of environmental management in a golf course context. However, experience from other industries, and indeed from some other sports (Roskam 1995), does point to there being a positive relationship between environmental management and cost-efficiency.

COMMITTED TO GREEN

To be "Committed to Green" is to demonstrate environmental awareness and responsibility. This is a new campaign by the EGA Ecology Unit launched during the 1997 Ryder Cup Matches at Valderrama, southern Spain. The campaign encourages everyone involved in golf to participate in improving the environmental quality of golf courses (European Golf Association Ecology Unit 1997).

The rationale behind "Committed to Green" is to introduce the concept of Environmental Management Systems to the golfing world (European Golf Association Ecology Unit 1996). In this respect the structure of the programme very closely matches the Eco-Management and Audit Scheme (EMAS), but packaged specifically for golf clubs. Inspiration has been drawn from the Audubon Cooperative Sanctuary Program for Golf Courses, a programme of Audubon International in the United States of America (Audubon International 1996). In this way "Committed to Green" is based on recognised international systems and proven initiatives aimed at golf clubs.

"Committed to Green" aims to show how well-managed golf courses can be of benefit to the environment and the community. This will help golf clubs by offering cost-effective means of enhancing environmental quality, without compromising turfgrass quality and playing conditions.

A key premise of "Committed to Green" is that all golf courses, whatever their situation, have the potential for improving their environmental performance. This can span a wide range of management activities and policies. Environmental benefits will embrace:

- Conservation of biodiversity—through improving the value of golf courses for wildlife
- Conservation of landscape quality and cultural heritage features associated with golf courses
- Application of sustainable development principles in the location, design and construction of new golf courses
- Conservation of water resources and maintenance of high quality standards in surface and ground waters
- Safe and appropriate usage, storage and disposal of fertilisers and pesticides
- Energy conservation and minimising waste
- Awareness and knowledge of environmental management principles and techniques among golf course managers
- Public awareness of golf's role in the wider environment

Although each golf course is a relatively small, independent entity, the cumulative effect of many clubs undertaking environmental improvements will be significant. This multiplier effect, along with the awareness raising potential of "Committed to Green," is a primary motivation for the programme over the long-term.

There are initially three targets for "Committed to Green":

- Existing golf clubs: to encourage the improvement of environmental performance
- New golf course projects: to ensure they are developed in accordance with appropriate environmental guidelines
- Major golf events: to use the media to promote environmental awareness

Real improvements in environmental performance will only be achieved through the active involvement of golf clubs. The first priorities, therefore, are to build awareness and to encourage golf clubs to participate. "Committed to Green" is open to all types of golf facility on a voluntary basis.

Emphasis is on continual improvement. Clubs that implement a full Environmental Management Programme can qualify for "Committed to Green" recognition. To guarantee objectivity and credibility, the setting of environmental criteria and awarding of recognition will be subject to independent verification.

There is a series of basic steps to "Committed to Green."

1. Policy: To participate in the programme, a golf club will first need to make a policy commitment endorsed by its membership. It should include the following points:
   - Statement of intent to improve environmental performance
   - Establishment of a "Committed to Green" team to manage the project
   - Commitment to carry out an environmental review of the site and current management, and to implement appropriate conservation measures.
2. Environmental review: This provides a baseline picture of the current environmental performance of a golf facility and forms the basis for developing the environmental management programme.
3. Environmental Management Programme: This should build up to be a comprehensive and integrated plan, combining environmental and golf management objectives appropriate to the site.
4. Audit: After a maximum of three years, progress will be evaluated to assess whether a club has achieved its initial environmental management targets.
5. Recognition: A "Committed to Green Award for Environmental Excellence" will recognise and support golf clubs that have made significant achievements across eight specific environmental categories. These should cover the entire property under the golf club management, including the golf course, club house, ancillary buildings and related facilities. They are:
   - Nature conservation
   - Landscape and cultural heritage
   - Water resource management
   - Turfgrass management
   - Waste management

- Energy efficiency and purchasing policies
- Education and the working environment
- Communications and public awareness

Recognition is a reward for effort and commitment, not a direct comparison of widely different golf course situations. This is a continuous programme aimed at sustaining environmental commitment. Clubs that achieve "Committed to Green" recognition will be expected to continue to follow the programme in order to maintain their status.

New golf courses may join "Committed to Green." To be eligible, projects will have had to follow the *Environmental Guidelines for Golf Course Development in Europe* (European Golf Association Ecology Unit 1995b). A key requirement will be an Environmental Assessment, specifying any necessary site safeguards for the design and construction. It will also set out policy and management commitments, so the new course can link into the "Committed to Green" programme for existing golf clubs.

CONCLUSIONS

To quote European Commission President Jacques Santer at the official launch of "Committed to Green" on 28 September 1997 at Valderrama Golf Club:

> Sport and recreation which occupy so much of our leisure are increasingly important in environmental terms, and it is vital to ensure that pressures involved in terms of land use, resource consumption and, sometimes, pollution, be continuously minimised. Respect for the environment goes hand in hand with human well-being and, indeed, sporting excellence. This is certainly true for golf, in which harmony with nature is part of the game's heritage and its enjoyment. The wise use of natural resources is the proper goal of all responsible managers. Golf has a great opportunity to serve as a role model for good environmental practice.

The "Committed to Green" campaign will foster a closer dialogue between everyone connected with golf: players, course managers, officials, NGOs, environmental specialists and local interest groups. Eventually, one may hope that the themes developed here will come to apply in other spheres of human activity. One thing is clear: it will be through the effective implementation of environmental programmes that golf will be best placed to gain greater recognition and acceptance among the European public.

References

Audubon International (1996). *A Guide to Environmental Stewardship on the Golf Course—Audubon Cooperative Sanctuary System.* Audubon International, Selkirk NY.

Chernushenko D. (1994). *Greening our Games—Running Sports Events and Facilities That Won't Cost the Earth.* Delphi Group, Ottawa.

European Golf Association Ecology Unit (1995a). *An Environmental Strategy for Golf in Europe.* Pisces Publications, Newbury.

European Golf Association Ecology Unit (1995b). *Environmental Guidelines for Golf Course Development in Europe* (revised edition). EGA Ecology Unit, Brussels.

European Golf Association Ecology Unit (1996). *An Environmental Management Programme for Golf Courses.* Pisces Publications, Newbury.

European Golf Association Ecology Unit (1997). *The "Committed to Green" Handbook for Golf Courses.* Pisces Publications, Newbury.

Roskam F. (1995). *Sports Infrastructure.* Paper presented to the World Conference on Sport and the Environment, Lausanne, 15 July 1995. International Olympic Committee and United Nations Environment Programme.

Royal & Ancient Golf Club of St. Andrews and European Golf Association (1997). *A Course for All Seasons.* R&A St. Andrews.

Scottish Golf Course Wildlife Group (1997). *Golf's Natural Heritage: An Introduction to Environmental Stewardship on the Golf Course* (revised edition). Scottish Golf Course Wildlife Group.

CHAPTER 91

The Passion for Green: Experimental Insights Into the Power of Golf's Primary Color Over the Mind of the American Golfer

J.R. Hansen
Auburn University, Alabama, USA

A number of opinion polls and surveys have elicited golfer attitudes about golf course playing conditions, but no instrument has specifically tested the role of golf course *color* in shaping attitudes about the overall excellence of a golf course. This paper reports the unpublished results of an experiment into this aspect of golfer psychology. The results confirm what environmentalists and other critics of the modern, high-maintenance American-style golf course have been observing in recent years—that is, that golfers in the United States have come to identify excellent golf with one color, dark green. Environmental ramifications of this influence of color are discussed.

Keywords: Environment, golfer psychology, aesthetics.

INTRODUCTION: GOLF AND THE ENVIRONMENT

The United States Golf Association, eight other major American golf organizations, and a dozen environmental groups have recently endorsed a document entitled *Environmental Principles for Golf Courses in the United States*. The product of two unprecedented national meetings on the environmental impact of golf (held at Pebble Beach, California, in January 1995, and Pinehurst, North Carolina, in March 1996), this historic document provides a framework under which environmental excellence may be stressed in all aspects of golf course planning and siting, design, construction, maintenance, and facility operations (*Environmental Principles*, 1996). Hardly revolutionary and essentially an expression of environmental common sense, the principles offer a road map from which to chart a more sustainable course for American golf.

One principle in the document is, in fact, revolutionary, and underscores the need to go far beyond mere compliance with environmental regulations: it calls for golfers to "Accept the natural limitations and variations of turfgrass plants growing under conditions that protect environmental resources." In other words, golfers are going to have to accept more brown turf, thinning of grass, and loss of color (Japenga, 1997). As simple as it may sound, this is going to be a very difficult environmental principle for American golfers to accept.

DATA FROM RECENT POLLS AND ATTITUDE SURVEYS

Results from four recent opinion polls and attitude surveys clearly demonstrate how passionate the American golfing public has become about ultra-green, carpet-like playing conditions.

1. In 1990 and 1991, the National Golf Foundation conducted two surveys that included questions aimed at measuring the attitudes of golfers towards golf and environment issues. Significantly, when asked whether "to reduce water and chemical usage, I would accept somewhat poorer golf course playing conditions," nearly half of the 1,389 golfers answered no. In fact, in two sections of the country where golf has grown the most in the past half century, the South and the West, 53% and 54%, respectively, answered no, preferring better playing conditions to a more environmental approach. Similarly, 57% of the respondents nationwide answered no when asked whether "Golf courses use too much water for conditioning" (NGF, 1991). Perhaps attitudes on these issues have changed since 1990-91, due to increasing environmental awareness. But the golf industry has not reported new data indicating any dramatic change.

2. In 1992, the National Golf Foundation engaged Vinson & Elkins L.L.P., a Houston law firm with a substantial environmental law practice, to undertake a comprehensive examination of the impact of environmental regulation on golf. The firm interviewed turf chemical manufacturers, course owners, superintendents, architects, builders, major golf association officials, golf product manufacturers, and golf industry publishers. Many of those interviewed admitted that golfers needed to lower their expectations about turfgrass and pointed to the distorting influence of television. "Amateur golfers who see tournaments played at lush golf courses under these artificial conditions develop unrealistic expectations about the conditions of their golf courses," the report argued. Golfers "need to be educated that reduced chemical use may result in different turf appearance, but fine playing conditions" (NGF, 1992). The *Environmental Principles* document of 1996 repeated this call for golfer education, and some of the organizations endorsing the principles document (including the USGA and the Golf Course Superintendents Association of America) have looked for ways (i.e., advertising campaigns, environmental awards programs) to effect adjustments in golfer thinking about playing conditions. To date, however, there is no evidence that these efforts have provoked any major change in attitudes or expectations.

3. In December 1994, *Golf Digest* magazine published a report, *Golf & The Environment: An Attitudinal Survey*, done in cooperation with the National Wildlife Federation as background information for the first Golf & Environment Conference held at Pebble Beach. Several results reflected the American golfer's passion for green. Twenty-one percent of the 332 *Golf Digest* respondents disagreed that "Golfers should be willing to play on brown grass (even) during periods of low rainfall" (*Golf Digest*, 1994). Another 10% were not sure. The response from another group filling out the questionnaire, 358 subscribers to *E Magazine*, an environmental publication, was significantly different; only 11% disagreed with this statement.

Only 46% of *Golf Digest* respondents agreed with the following statement, "The amount of water used on a golf course should only be enough to keep the grass alive, not make it green and lush." On the other hand, 67% of the *E Magazine* respondents agreed with it.

Only 34% of *Golf Digest* respondents disagreed with the statement, "Golf courses should be uniformly maintained (the green grass consistently kept) throughout the year for the enjoyment of golfers and enhancement of scenery in the community." Another 13% were not sure. On the other hand, 52% of *E Magazine* subscribers disagreed.

In response to a question asking whether they were willing to "play golf under less manicured conditions" if it helped the environment, nearly a third of *Golf Digest* respondents (30%) failed to answer yes.

4. A fourth opinion poll demonstrated the American golfer's aesthetic ideal. In April 1996, in its pre-Masters issue, *Golf Digest* reported that 36% of golfers surveyed picked Augusta National—the best groomed, most immaculate and verdant course in the world—as the one course to play for the rest of their lives (*Golf Digest*, Apr. 1996).

CRITICAL VOICES

It has not just been environmentalists condemning American golf's "green syndrome." In the 1990s, a growing number of people inside the golf industry have also criticized the American golfer's obsession with immaculate, emerald-green playing conditions. So bothered was PGA professional Lee Rinker by the lush conditions and meticulous handmowing of stripes on the fairways at the 1997 U.S. Open played at Congressional that he wrote a fiery letter published by *Golf Digest*. "I could not believe they were mowing the fairways by hand," Rinker stated in disgust. "What they should be doing is turning off the sprinklers, letting some of the grass turn a little brown so we can get some more bounce and roll back into the game" (Rinker, 1997).

Perhaps the most devastating published indictment of the passion for green came in *Golf Digest*'s April 1994 Master's issue. In a stinging indictment of Augusta National, entitled, "Perfection vs. Reality: Why Augusta National Sets a Bad Example for American Golf," architecture editor Ron Whitten declared that Augusta today is "more of a TV studio than a golf course." Its grass seems so perfect we envision a legion of workers on hands and knees, clipping away with tiny scissors.... Given the chance to wander around the place, you'd be amazed at [its] utter perfection.... There's not a blade of grass out of place." In person or on television, Augusta National is "as good as it gets." But, as Whitten argued, "that's precisely what's wrong with the golf course." It sets a standard impossible to emulate, and promotes a landscape aesthetic of "fastidious spotlessness, scrupulous conditioning," and manufactured green-ness that is resource-intensive, tremendously expensive, and ultimately one of the reasons why American-style golf has become unnecessarily unfriendly to the environment.

Michigan-based golf course architect Tom Doak has also expressed biting criticisms of the recent trends. In his 1992 book, *The Anatomy of a Golf Course*, Doak suggested that the chemically maintained area of golf courses in many regions of the United States could be decreased by as much as 90% if golfers only accepted somewhat lower standards for fairway turf. However, "it is hard to imagine the pampered American golfer ever relaxing his expectations." "The average golfer has little understanding of the science of golf course maintenance" (Doak, 1992); moreover, there are powerful economic forces—and class values—deeply embedded within American society actively promoting the vanity of emerald-green turf, not just for golf courses but for home lawns, gardens, and parks.

THE PSYCHOLOGY OF COLOR

Scientists have explored the affective values and psychophysiological effects of color (e.g., Goldstein, 1942; Sharpe, 1974; Kaiser, 1984; Reeves, 1985; Mahnke & Mahnke, 1987; Walker, 1989). It is clear from their research that color influences decision-making, affects mental outlooks, impels emotions, persuades purchasing, predisposes people to perform in all manner of behavior, and perhaps even offers healing power.

In these studies, special attention is given to the color green. Findings suggest that green "represents a withdrawal from stimulus." Because the lens of the eye focuses green light exactly on the retina, it is also "the most restful color to the eye" (Mahnke & Mahnke, 1987). Green is "soothing, healing, peaceful, and cool" and has "great healing power." On its negative side, green represents "selfishness, jealousy, and laziness" (Walker, 1989). Green stabilizes the emotions and stimulates the pituitary. Known disorders treatable with the color green include: asthma, back problems, heart problems, insomnia, irritability, nervous disorders, and ulcers (Walker, 1989). Forest green, hunter green, and similar shades "cause an anti-allergic or desensitizing reaction" in certain groups of people, such as hay-fever sufferers (Walker, 1989). Green is the most popular color in hospitals, clinics, and operating rooms because people feel secure around green (Walker, 1989). It is also the color favored by NASA in its interior designs for space stations (Kaiser, 1984).

Research into the sociological effects of color suggests that emerald green is "the symbol of hope and growth" (Walker, 1989). One who adopts green as a personal color is "a good citizen and a pillar of the community" and "sensitive to social customs and etiquette" (Walker, 1989). Green is the second most popular color with American consumers, only behind red (Walker, 1989). Green "provides a good environment for meditation and tasks involving high concentration" (Mahnke & Mahnke, 1987). In a green environment, time seems to pass more slowly (Goldstein, 1942).

Whether this research provides insights into the power of green over the golfer is questionable. Beyond stating the obvious—that "green is nature's color" and that "nature has probably conditioned most people to feel safe around green" (Walker, 1989)—science does not tell us much about the historical forces at work driving the passion for green in a particular cultural context, i.e., American golf. It does provide a context from which to devise an experiment into the role of *color* in shaping golfer attitudes.

BACKGROUND TO THE AUBURN EXPERIMENT

During spring 1997 the author of this report was one of three instructors at Auburn University responsible for teaching a brand new course entitled "Swinging into the Evolving Golf Course in America: A Golfer's Delight." The course, organized by Auburn's Outreach Division, was offered as part of the international Elderhostel program, an independent, non-profit organization that offers short-term, on-campus academic experiences to individuals 55 years of age and older. The curriculum of the course consisted of three parts: eight hours of classroom presentation on the history of the golf course taught by the author of this report; another eight hours of classroom presentation and field trips on turf science taught by an assistant professor in the department of agronomy and soils; and a third involving eight hours of golf instruction, taught by the PGA professional and director of golf at Grand National on the Robert Trent Jones Golf Trail in nearby Opelika, Alabama. Designed to attract golfers from throughout the U.S. to an Elderhostel whose curriculum included opportunities for inexpensive daily play and practice at the highly rated championship courses at Grand National, the Elderhostel easily filled all 35 spots allotted for students during the two weekly sessions (May 11–16 and May 18–23) offered in spring term 1997.

DEMOGRAPHICS

The 70 Elderhostel "students" (57% male, 43% female) represented an avid group of American golfers (63% play golf at least three days a week). As a control group, they served well because, as senior citizens (average age 67.5) they had lived through significant changes in golf course playing conditions over the past half century. They had also been exposed to television and other media influences relative to golf virtually their entire adult lives (60% watch golf on TV every weekend; 55% subscribe to golf magazines; 64% belong to the USGA). Of all golf groups in America one might have tested to evaluate the power of green over golf course perceptions, however, one might have thought that the Elderhostelers (64% college educated; 56% have lived abroad) were less likely to demonstrate an obsession with dark-green playing conditions than other, especially younger, control groups.

CONDUCT OF THE EXPERIMENT

The experiment involved showing the students a series of 36 35mm color slides. Each slide showed a picture of a golf course, almost always a view of a particular hole. Students were asked, after seeing each slide for 30 seconds, to rate what they had seen. Students were not advised on criteria by which to base a rating. They were told only to rate the course on a scale of 0-10, with 10 representing "Great Golf— Or Golf at Its Very Best" and 0 representing "Terrible Golf—Or Golf at Its Worst." Students were told not to talk to one another or to let their neighbor see their ratings sheet. The slides were numbered 1 through 36, the equivalent of two 18-hole rounds.

Crucial to the concept of the experiment was the sequence of course material leading up to the experiment. The experiment took place on Day 3 of the curriculum (Wednesday). It was critically important to the experiment not to bias or predispose the students in any way that would make them conscious of environmental issues or help them rationalize attitudes about color. Day 1 was spent in the historical presentations on "The Origins of Golf and the Early History of the Golf Course," and Day 2 on "The Evolution of Golf Course Architecture and the Modern Schools of Golf Course Design." During Day 2, students saw slides in which they were asked to identify "Penal," "Strategic," or "Heroic" designs. The experiment took place at the beginning of the historical presentation for Day 3, which dealt with "The History and Evolution of Augusta National." Given that the previous day had just been devoted entirely to matters of course architecture, it was suspected that the students, in rating the slides, would be thinking in terms of the landscape features inherent to design, and not about color. In such a context, the nonverbal psychological influence of color might become apparent.

The selection of the 36 slides and the order in which they were to be shown was also crucial to the experiment's success. There was one criteria for selection: color. Eighteen of the slides depicted courses of lush green color; the other 18 depicted courses of various colors, including all shades of green but also tawny tints, buff-browns, yellows, golds, and reds. Some slides showed courses where turf, due to drought, was turning a little brown. Others showed golf courses featuring native grasses and plants of various colors, including browns. Special effort was made to assure that the courses depicting "not-so-green" golf represented courses that were rated just as highly as a group as those chosen for their "ultra greenness." To assure a general equivalency, different "Top 100" listings and other published ratings of golf courses done by acknowledged experts in the field were consulted. Also, every effort was made to ensure that the two groups of slides were equivalent in their overall aesthetic (i.e., sunny vs. cloudy days, blue vs. gray skies) and production values (i.e., quality of the photographic print). Also, it was important to pick views of courses not instantly recognizable to the average golfer from television. The order of slides was also arranged so that there was an irregular mix of "ultra-green" and "not-so-green" pictures, with 9 holes of each color genre per 18.

EXPERIMENTAL FINDINGS

The data clearly support the hypothesis that golfers exhibit a significant preference for ultra-green conditions. For the 18 slides showing ultra green, the average rating per slide was 8.1, compared to 5.9 for the slides depicting not-so-green golf. Women were somewhat less influenced by ultra green than men: 7.9 average compared to 8.3. Individuals playing the most years, playing the most frequently, (curiously) who did not belong to the USGA, and rarely watched televised golf or read golf publications rated ultra-green conditions lower than did their opposites: averages of 7.8, 7.6, 7.9, 7.7, and 7.7, respectively, compared to 8.4, 8.3, 8.3, 8.1, and 8.3. Still, even these groups rated ultra green appreciably higher than not-so-green, which rated 6.2, 6.4, 6.0, 6.1, and 5.9 in these groups, respectively. People living in the South and West rated ultra-green conditions higher than those in the Northeast and Midwest: 8.3 and 8.2, respectively, compared to 7.9 and 7.8. Those who had lived abroad rated ultra green slightly lower than those who had not: 8.0 average compared to 8.2. The demographic groups that rated not-so-green golf the lowest were the beginning golfer (5.6), those from the South (5.6) and West (5.5), and those playing golf only occasionally (5.0).

CONCLUSIONS

The sample size was only 70 people, so one must be circumspect in drawing conclusions. Moreover, the experiment involved a control group made up entirely of American golfers between 59 and 84 years of age. No data exist to compare with golfers of different ages or elsewhere in the world, so generalizations are difficult. One might speculate that the control group was typical of the general American response, but that if the experiment were conducted with golfers in Britain, where courses are not as artificial, the data would not show such a strong preference for ultra-green conditions. The results clearly demonstrate the power of golf's primary color over the mind of the Elderhostelers and they seem to confirm that TV and other media images of golf are a powerful influence. The results reinforce the concern of environmentalists and other critics of recent trends in American golf, and they demonstrate that it will be very difficult for American golfers to accept more brown turf.

AESTHETICS AND ENVIRONMENT

As difficult as it will be for golfers to accept, a turning away from the demand for lush green playing conditions is essential to the future health of golf. As architect Tom Doak has argued, reduced water and chemical use would curtail public apprehension about the environmental impact of golf and lower the cost of playing the game. It might even encourage a higher percentage of the population to become devotees of the game, who would be more sympathetic to the needs of the sport. Golf will not suffer if course maintenance standards are scaled back; it will survive more flexible standards and perhaps even grow stronger. "The vanity of eye-appealing green turf is all that has to be sacrificed" (Doak, 1992).

As the results of the Auburn experiment suggest, however, it will take a revolutionary change in landscape aesthetics and the psychology of color for golfers to make the sacrifice. How such a rupture might take place in American golf—short of Augusta National going back to 1950s-style agronomic practices, a public rejection of the White House lawn, a return to black and white TV, a government takeover of the chemical and lawn-care industries, a crisis of conscience within the PGA, or a monumental environmental disaster—is almost impossible to imagine. Definitely, it will take more than organizational endorsements of an environmental principles document for American golfers to back off their demands for lush green playing conditions. Without a fundamental change in golfer attitudes about what makes good playing conditions, it is likely that golf will continue to threaten the environment in ways that will be increasingly unacceptable to the public, no matter what the golf industry does to mitigate environmental concerns.

References

Doak, Tom (1992). *The Anatomy of a Golf Course*. New York: Lyons & Burford.

Environmental Principles for Golf Courses in the United States; Golf & The Environment: Charting a Sustainable Future (1996). Salt Lake City: Center for Resource Management.

Goldstein, K. (1942). "Some Experimental Observations Concerning the Influence of Colors on the Function of an Organism." *Occupational Therapy and Rehabilitation* 21:147—51.

Golf Digest (1994). *Golf & The Environment: An Attitudinal Survey*. New York: New York Times Sports/Leisure Magazines Research Resource Center.

Japenga, Ann (1997). "Can you golf—and care about the environment?" *USA Weekend,* July 27.

Mahnke, Frank H. and Mahnke, Rudolf H. (1987). *Color and Light in Man-Made Environments.* New York: Van Nostrand Reinhold Co.

National Golf Foundation (1992). *Golf and the Environment: A Status Report and Action Plan.* Jupiter, FL: National Golf Foundation.

Reeves, I.S.K (1985). *Color and Its Effect on Behavior Modification*. Winter Park, FL: Green Apple Publishing.

Rinker, Lee, letter to editor (1997). "Brown Can Be Beautiful," *Golf Digest* 48:12.

Sharpe, Deborah T. (1974). *The Psychology of Color and Design*. Chicago, IL: Nelson-Hall Co.

Walker, Morton (1989). *The Power of Color*. Garden City Park, NY: Avery Publishing Group.

Whitten, Ron (1994). "Commentary: Perfection vs. Reality—Why Augusta National Sets a Bad Example for American Golf," *Golf Digest* 45:123–135.

CHAPTER 92

The Role of Golf Clubs in the Conservation of Scotland's Natural and Cultural Heritage

J.A. Smith
Scottish Golf Course Wildlife Adviser, Glasgow, UK

This paper provides an overview of the relationship between golf and the environment in Scotland and specifically seeks to demonstrate why golf clubs should consider environmental issues, how they can effectively undertake stewardship of their environment, and the benefits to be gained.

Much of the discussion focuses on the golf club and the opportunities for integrating environmental issues into the management of existing golf courses. The following aspects are addressed—summary of the golf/environment debate, structure for Integrated Management, the benefits of such an approach, and the role of the Scottish Golf Course Wildlife Initiative.

The paper is prepared from the research and experience of the Scottish Golf Course Wildlife Group, a partnership of golfing and environmental organisations established in 1993.

Keywords: Golf clubs, environmental stewardship, Scotland.

THE GOLF/ENVIRONMENT DEBATE

Historically, golf courses have utilised natural features and landscapes, taking advantage of existing topography and vegetation. Due to the close compatibility of early courses with the environment, golf and nature coexisted in relative harmony. Over the past 20 to 30 years technological improvements have allowed greater manipulation and intensity of management of the natural and cultural environment to meet the changing demands of the golfer.

However, the interdependent relationship between golf and the environment is still widely recognised. As areas of permanent, managed green space, all golf courses constantly interact with the environment, and the management practices of clubs have a direct bearing on environmental quality. With over 450 golf courses in Scotland, and in the light of increasing pressure on our natural and cultural heritage, the importance of understanding and evaluating this relationship has become an issue of greater urgency.

To some, the design, construction and management of golf courses symbolise negative environmental impact. Opinion of this sort is often based on misunderstanding, drawn from publicised examples of bad practice. The positive contribution golf courses are providing, in terms of conservation, is often overlooked.

Significantly, golf clubs have the opportunity to take a proactive role in ensuring that environmental considerations are built into the design and management of golf courses. Efforts by clubs to demonstrate such stewardship of their environment will benefit not only the club itself but also the standing of the golfing industry as a whole.

It is important to consider that golf courses are not perceived to be inherently at odds with the principles of sustainability and stewardship, and that through environmentally sensitive management they have the potential to conserve wildlife and habitats (biodiversity), water resources, historical features, cultural heritage and much more. Indeed golf courses have demonstrated the capacity to exist in harmony with the environment. Testimony to this are the 33 courses in Scotland that contain Sites of Special Scientific Interest (SSSI). Countless others contain Wildlife Sites, and many contribute to the conservation of Historic Designed Landscapes and National Scenic Areas. Such examples indicate that in principle, golfing and environmental quality are not mutually exclusive. In practice, golf clubs can demonstrate this fact by integrating environmental issues into their existing management policies and objectives.

INTEGRATED MANAGEMENT PLANNING

Integrated Management Planning is about balance. It is a process that enables golf clubs to give consideration to a wide range of issues, and integrate them into a single, long-term plan for the course. It provides a framework through which golfing and environmental issues can be reconciled within a forward looking plan of management. Integrated Management Planning is relevant to all golf clubs, regardless of size or location. As golf course management becomes increasingly complex and the range of issues requiring consideration broadens, all clubs will need to develop management systems that are able to reconcile golfing, environmental, health and safety, education, and training issues. As businesses, golf clubs will plan ahead, budget, and allocate resources. An Integrated Management Plan can contribute greatly to achieving all of these requirements of the modern golf club.

The production of an Integrated Management Plan is initiated and carried out by a small working group within the club, which has the support of the full committee. Representation from the head greenkeeper and greens convenor is essential, along with other past committee members and interested individuals from the club's membership. Within most clubs there are members who have an environmental background, and their experience and advice are an extremely productive addition to the working group. The structure for producing such a plan can be summarised as follows:

1. Club prepares policy statement: setting out its vision for the course, its aims and goals. It expresses commitment to the integration of environmental issues into the management of the course.

2. Introduction:

General Factors	Location map, size of area, ownership, brief history of course, legal designations, current access
Physical Factors	Geology, soils, rainfall, drainage, topography, aspect, etc.

3. Environmental review:

Golf Course Management	Detail current practices, Irrigation programme, Turfgrass management, Chemical applications, Cultural techniques
Nature Conservation	Survey of habitats, Survey of wildlife, Evaluation of findings, Conservation management already undertaken, Identifies scope for further study
Landscape and Cultural Heritage	Assess landscape character, Survey archaeological features, Gather historical information, Evaluate findings
Waste Management, Energy Efficiency, and Purchasing Policies	Recycling policies, Fuel and energy saving measures, Management of waste products, Use of environmentally friendly products, etc.
Education and Awareness	Promote environmental policies within and without the club, Consult with external advisors, Assess environmental management and training needs for greenstaff, Raise awareness among members

4. Evaluation of information

5. Production of future management objectives and policies

Having undertaken such a comprehensive review of the club's management policies and golfing and environmental qualities, it is possible to evaluate the interaction between current practices and the environmental attributes of the course and its surrounds. This may result in the identification of both positive and negative impacts on the environment.

The review provides not only the reasoning behind future policies and objectives for course management but it also creates a valuable baseline of information to which future enhancements and efficiency can be measured. Gathering and evaluating information as a basis for structuring the future management of the course enables the club to gain an understanding of the golfing, ecological, landscape and historical needs of the course.

Discussion and evaluation of the information should then lead to the creation of future management objectives. In many respects this is the Action Plan, which can be worked through over a period of three to five years. Many clubs are already implementing management objectives that will integrate golfing, nature conservation, landscape and historical issues. The most obvious example is probably tree planting, where golfing and environmental quality can be enhanced through the selection of appropriate species, mixes, densities, and design. However, a club's Integrated Management Plan may demonstrate that tree planting may only be suitable in certain locations. It may be that planting is to be avoided in certain areas due to the value of existing habitat, e.g., wetlands or heather. It could also be the case that tree planting may detract from the atmosphere and character of designed parkland. Only through fully understanding its environment can a golf club be sure that its future management will retain or enhance golfing and environmental quality.

Following implementation of these environmental objectives, a full internal review of the Action Plan is undertaken to assess progress, successes and further opportunities. This is a vital aspect of the planning process, and should be the point at which the club prepares a further set of objectives for the next three or five years. Through the implementation of those objectives, the club can continue its demonstration of environmental stewardship—in a way that also enhances the golfing quality of the course, increases efficiency, improves members' appreciation, and generates respect for the club from environmental organisations and the public.

The success of any management plan depends upon communication and discussion. This could be internally between committees and individuals, from committees to the membership, and from the club as a whole to outside organisations. Technical advice should be sought when required. Indeed many aspects of the plan may relate to technical issues such as turf management, pest control, ecology, water resource management, forestry, landscape character assessment, etc. By seeking advice the club can ensure that the policies and objectives they finalise are the most appropriate for the course. Communicating policies will help ensure that committees and members understand the projects the club is implementing and how they contribute to the environmental and golfing quality of the course.

THE BENEFITS OF INTEGRATED MANAGEMENT PLANNING

By producing a long-term plan for the golf course, which pulls together a range of different issues, the golf club will potentially experience a number of benefits. Those clubs that have already set out on this process have found that;

- The club has been able to give balanced consideration to a wide range of diverse, but related and relevant issues;

- Forward planning assists in the creation of a strategy for the management of the course. This can help avoid fragmented and inconsistent management;
- Management costs can be reduced through evaluating and prioritising current management;
- Management can become more efficient with potential for reductions in grass cutting regimes, chemical and water applications, energy costs, etc.;
- Clubs can generate local recognition and respect by creating quality golfing conditions in a way that also enhances environmental quality;
- At a National and European level, the efforts of golf clubs will combine to highlight the environmental sensitivity of the industry as a whole;
- The playing experience can be tangibly enhanced by the quality of the surrounding environment. Conservation of the natural and cultural heritage can therefore play an important role in the development of exciting and challenging golf courses.

CONCLUSIONS

This paper has not attempted to provide a fully comprehensive account of the golf/ environment debate in Scotland. However, it is important to consider the contribution to the conservation of Scotland's natural and cultural heritage that golf clubs can make. In practical terms this can be achieved through a number of actions, ranging from nature conservation, adoption of environmentally sound policies and practices for water and chemical use, raising awareness of environmental issues within the club, and so on. Any objectives must be specific to each course. The key to environmental stewardship lies in understanding and appreciating the golf course environment, and based on that awareness, making informed judgments on the best management practices. The process of Integrated Management Planning enables golf clubs to achieve this. Such stewardship will go far to ensure a sustainable relationship between golf and the environment. It will also contribute towards maintaining the inherent natural qualities on which the challenge and enjoyment of golf so greatly depends.

ACKNOWLEDGMENTS

This research was funded by the Scottish Golf Union, the Royal and Ancient Golf Club of St. Andrews, Scottish Natural Heritage, and the Scottish Greenbelt Foundation.

References

Mackay, J. (1996). *A Guide to Environmental Stewardship on the Golf Course.* Audubon International.

Royal and Ancient Golf Club of St. Andrews, European Golf Association (1997). *A Course for all Seasons.* R&A St. Andrews.

Taylor, R. (1995). *A Practical Guide to Ecological Management of the Golf Course.* British and International Greenkeepers Association and Sports Turf Research Institute.

The Scottish Golf Course Wildlife Group (1997). Golf's Natural Heritage. An Introduction to Environmental Stewardship of the Golf Course. The Scottish Golf Course Wildlife Group.

The Scottish Golf Course Wildlife Group (1996). Golf and the Environment in Scotland: Summaries and Future Direction. Unpublished.

The European Golf Association Ecology Unit (1997). *The Committed to Green Handbook for Golf Courses.* Pisces Publications.

Index

The number given is the first page of the relevant paper.

About the Editors

Martin R. Farrally is the director of the World Scientific Congress of Golf Trust. He was the director of the 1990 and 1994 World Scientific Congress of Golf. Mr. Farrally is a senior lecturer in sports science at the University of St. Andrews. The author of two books for the National Coaching Foundation, he also was coeditor of *Science and Golf II*. Mr. Farrally is a member of the British Association of Sport and Exercise Sciences and the British Association of Sports Medicine.

Alastair J. Cochran, for 15 years the technical advisor to the Royal and Ancient Golf Club of St. Andrews, is a part-time consultant on golf. He has been involved in the study of golf science for nearly 40 years. The editor of *Science and Golf I* and *Golf the Scientific Way*, he also was coeditor of *Science and Golf II*. Mr. Cochran served as director of the first comprehensive study of golf, held in the early 1960s, and was cowriter of the book, *The Search for the Perfect Swing*.

Related Books from Human Kinetics

Sports and Fitness Equipment Design

Ellen F. Kreighbaum, PhD, and Mark A. Smith, MS, Editors
1995 • Hardcover • 232 pp • Item BKRE0695
ISBN 0-87322-695-X • $45.00 ($67.50 Canadian)

Presents practical and objective information on designing, evaluating, and selecting equipment, from athletic footwear to rowing machines.

Three-Dimensional Analysis of Human Movement

Paul Allard, PhD, Ian A. F. Stokes, PhD, and Jean-Pierre Blanchi, PhD, Editors
Forewords by Kit Vaughan and Aurelio Cappozzo
1995 • Hardcover • 384 pp • Item BALL0623
ISBN 0-87322-623-2 • $48.00 ($71.95 Canadian)

The first book to explain in a single volume the essential components of three-dimensional analysis of human movement, including methods and technology, concepts and techniques, and application of 3-D analysis.

Precision Woods and Long Iron Shots

Daniel McDonald with Richard A. Goodman
1998 • Paper • 144 pp • Item PMCD0766
ISBN 0-88011-766-4 • $16.95 ($24.95 Canadian)

Fifty-eight long-game situations with 100 photos and 68 illustrations help golfers visualize the required shot and learn how to execute it.

Precision Wedge and Bunker Shots

Jim Fitzgerald with Dave Gould
1998 • Paper • 136 pp • Item PFIT0727
ISBN 0-88011-727-3 • $16.95 ($24.95 Canadian)

Fifty-three real short-game situations and more than 100 photographs and 50 illustrations show how to use creative shotmaking to turn problem shots into pars and routine shots into birdies.

Exercise Guide to Better Golf

Endorsed by the PGA Tour and Senior PGA Tour

Frank W. Jobe, MD; Lewis A. Yocum, MD; Robert E. Mottram, PT, ATC; Marilyn M. Pink, MS, PT
1995 • Paper • 92 pp • Item PJOB0893
ISBN 0-87322-893-6 • $9.95 ($14.95 Canadian)

Shows how to perform the same muscle-strengthening and flexibility exercises top golfers on the PGA and Senior PGA tours use to get in shape and stay on top of their game.

To request more information or to order, U.S. customers call 1-800-747-4457, e-mail us at **humank@hkusa.com**, or visit our Web site at **http://www.humankinetics.com/**. Persons outside the U.S. can contact us via our Web site or use the appropriate telephone number, postal address, or e-mail address shown in the front of this book.

HUMAN KINETICS
The Information Leader in Physical Activity